Guide to Careers in the Health Professions

The Princeton Review

Guide to Careers in the Health Professions

Lynn Borders Caldwell

Random House, Inc.
New York

www.randomhouse.com/princetonreview

The Independent Education Consultants Association recognizes The Princeton Review as a valuable resource for high school and college students applying to college and graduate school.

Princeton Review Publishing, L. L. C.
2315 Broadway
New York, NY 10024
E-mail: comments@review.com

Published in the United States by Random House, Inc. New York, and simultaneously in Canada by Random House of Canada Limited, Toronto.

ISBN 0-375-76158-6

Editor: Julie Mandelbaum
Designer: Greta Englert
Production Coordinator: Scott Harris
Production Editor: Julieanna Lambert

Manufactured in the United States of America on partially recycled paper.

9 8 7 6 5 4 3 2 1

Acknowledgments

Thanks must go first to Larry, the best husband in the whole world! You gave me the time and space to work on this project nearly every weekend and evening. Without you, this never would have come together.

This book definitely would not exist if it were not for my contributors who did such a fabulous job writing their chapters and somehow met my incredibly tight deadlines!

Thanks to Julie at the Princeton Review for spending many, many hours editing various versions of the chapters and offering lots of suggestions for improvement. Thanks also to all the other people at both the Princeton Review and Random House. Although we never spoke, I know you were working hard on this behind the scenes.

Thanks also to all my friends and colleagues in medical publishing. What you have taught me about being a good editor made being an author easier too.

My own authors and reviewers (many of whom have become close friends) have helped me learn so much about health care over the years. Your patient explanations have helped me understand a great deal. Now I have learned what it is like to be an author!

Contributors

Victoria L. Bastecki-Perez, EdD, BS, RDH
Director & Professor
Dental Hygiene
Montgomery County Community College
Blue Bell, Pennsylvania

Susan J. Beck, PhD, CLS(NCA)
Director, Division of Clinical Laboratory Science
Department of Allied Health Sciences
University of North Carolina at Chapel Hill
Chapel Hill, North Carolina

Thomas J. Butler, MS, RRT, RPFT
Director of Clinical Education
Respiratory Care Program
Rockland Community College
Suffern, New York
and
Manager of Respiratory Care
Kessler Rehabilitation Corporation
East Orange, New Jersey

Michael Dryer, PA-C, MPH
Chair
Department of Physician Assistant Studies
Beaver College
Glenside, Pennsylvania

Kathryn S. Durand, RT(R), AS
Director
Inservice Education for Radiology
Lawrence and Memorial Hospital
New London, Connecticut

Nancy Gerber, MS, ATR-BC
Director
Graduate Art Therapy Education
MCP Hahnemann University
Philadelphia, Pennsylvania

Patricia J. Giordano, MS, RT(R)(T)
Assistant Professor/Program Director
Radiation Therapy
Gwynedd-Mercy College
School of Allied Health
Gwynedd Valley, Pennsylvania

Risa Granick, EdD, MPA, PT
Professor and Chair
Department of Rehabiliation Sciences
MCP Hahnemann University
Philadelphia, Pennsylvania

Jeffrey E. Harris, DrPH, MPH, CNS, RD
Associate Professor and Dietetics Program Director
Department of Health
West Chester University
West Chester, Pennsylvania

Andrea Reiley-Helzner, MS, RCIS
Program Director
Cardiovascular Technology
Gwynedd-Mercy College
Gwynedd Valley, Pennsylvania

Jennifer Hornung, MBA, RRA, CPHQ, CCS
Program Director and Assistant Professor
Health Information Management Program
Gwynedd-Mercy College
School of Allied Health
Gwynedd Valley, Pennsylvania

Thomas M. Hunter, BA, ABOC, NCLC
Instructor
Ophthalmic Dispensing
Camden County College
Blackwood, New Jersey

Ky E. Kugler, EdD, ATC
Assistant Athletic Director
Department of Intercollegiate Athletics
California State Polytechnic University, Pomona
Pomona, California

Wilburta Q. (Billie) Lindh, CMA
Program Coordinator
Medical Assisting Department
Highline Community College
Des Moines, Washington

Christine Malaski, MS, OTR/L
Assistant Professor of Occupational Therapy
Occupational Therapy
St. Ambrose University
Davenport, Iowa
Jane M. Verpent, RN, BA
Director of Surgical Technology
University of Medicine & Dentistry School of Health Related Professions
Scotch Plains, New Jersey

Bruce J. Walz, PhD
Associate Professor and Chair
Department of Emergency Health Services
University of Maryland, Baltimore County
Baltimore, Maryland

CONTENTS

Introduction

The Changing World of Health Care

The United States Bureau of Labor Statistics (BLS) has named health services as one of the five fastest-growing industries for 1998–2008.[1] Two of the professions included in this book, medical assistants and physician assistants, are numbers 8 and 10, respectively, in the BLS's list of "The 10 Fastest Growing Occupations, 1998–2008."[2] This continued growth in the health care industry can be attributed primarily to our aging population. Today, more and more members of the baby boom generation are reaching middle age and finding themselves in greater need of health care services. The likely reason why the medical assisting and physician assisting professions are experiencing the greatest growth is that in the eyes of managed care, these are cost-efficient roles. They perform some of the duties of the physician, but are not as highly compensated.

Health care as an industry has experienced quite a few ups and downs in the last decade. Jobs in the health professions were plentiful in the early 1990s. Starting salaries were high, as was job security. This changed for the rehabilitation professions shortly after 1997 when the Balanced Budget Act was signed into law. Some of its goals were to extend the life of the Medicare Trust Fund, reduce Medicare spending, and fight Medicare fraud and abuses.[3] Specifically, beginning on January 1, 1999, Medicare placed a cap on rehabilitation services for each beneficiary. There was one $1500 limit for outpatient physical therapy services (including speech-language pathology services) and a separate $1500 limit for outpatient occupational therapy services. These limits included all outpatient therapy services except for services furnished by hospital outpatient departments.[4] This caused the loss of many jobs in rehabilitation; however, these professions are now beginning to recover for two reasons:

1. In November 1999, Congress passed the Balanced Budget Refinement Act of 1999. This Act secured a two-year suspension of the $1500 caps that began on January 1, 2000. This is expected to put $600 million back into therapy service payments over the next two years.[5]
2. Many health care professionals, especially occupational therapists and physical therapists, are finding and creating new roles for themselves in areas such as community rehabilitation and adult day care centers. They are also looking at ways that they can make themselves more valuable, one of which is increasing the entry-level degree a person must obtain to practice in their field. Respiratory therapists, for example, are not only increasing the requirement for the entry-level degree into their profession, but also learning more advanced level skills so that they will become truly indispensable to the hospitals.

Making Your Decision

What does all of this mean to you? It means that as you consider a career in health care, you should do some careful research regarding the future trends and job opportunities in the career that interests you. Each chapter in this book has been written by an educator currently teaching in his or her profession familiar with the trends in his or her field. In each chapter, there is a section called "Advice for Potential Students." Nearly every educator suggests that you:

- Make an appointment to meet with the director of the program in which you are interested. Ask the director specific questions regarding how many students in that program pass the certification or licensure and how many of its graduating students are getting jobs immediately upon graduation (this information is included in the book for many schools).
- Talk with current professionals in that field and ask them what they like and dislike about their jobs and what they think the future holds.
- Talk with current students at the school(s) in which you are interested to learn about that school's curriculum and to determine if that particular school is right for you.
- Research job opportunities in your geographical area by looking in your local newspaper as well as on the Internet. Opportunities will likely vary in different parts of the country based upon the need for professionals in that specific area. Be reasonably certain that a job will be available to you upon graduation. (There is a section in each chapter called "For Additional Information" that contains organizations, publications, journals, and Internet resources for your reference.)

How This Book Can Help You

The most popular health professions are included in this book. The first part of each chapter includes:

- a description of what a person in that field does
- who they work with
- the type of person that generally enters this profession (but keep in mind that there are no hard-and-fast rules)
- where they work
- the employment outlook
- the current salary range
- descriptions of the educational programs
- information on organizations that accredit the educational programs and offer the certification/licensure examinations
- information on each profession's professional organization

Following this is a list of schools that offer programs in each of these disciplines. We've included contact, program, student and faculty, financial, and employment information, where available.

Once you have decided upon a career that interests you, and after you have done your own research, contact the program director at several schools and request information on that particular program. Read through the material and schedule an appointment to meet with the directors or other faculty members of the programs that are of most interest to you.

Additional Resources

If you are new to health care, you might find it helpful to refer to a medical dictionary such as *Taber's Cyclopedic Medical Dictionary*, (F.A. Davis Company, 1997). A medical dictionary will help you to define terms that are new to you. In addition, be sure to look at the publications listed in the "For Additional Information" section of each chapter. In some cases, the author has listed a publication that is specifically written for potential students who are interested in learning more about that profession.

For additional information regarding changes in health care, I recommend visiting these sites:

The American Medical Association: www.ama-assn.org

The American Medical Association was founded over 150 years ago. It develops and promotes standards in medical practice, research, and education; serves as an advocate for patients and physicians; and provides accurate, timely information on matters important to the health of America.

Health Care Financing Administration: www.hcfa.gov

The Health Care Financing Administration (HCFA) is the federal agency that administers Medicare, Medicaid, and Child Health insurance. Since this organization provides health insurance for over 74 million Americans, its decisions can have a great effect on careers in health care.

Pew Health Professions Commission: www.futurehealth.ucsf.edu/pewcomm.html

The Pew Health Professions Commission was created by The Pew Charitable Trusts in 1989 and closed in January 1999. It was comprised of a national and interdisciplinary group of health care leaders who developed recommendations for changes in health professions education and advocated the development of policies which respond to the nation's health care workforce needs. Its mission was to help policy makers and educators produce health care professionals who meet the changing needs of the American health care system. The Center for the Health Professions at the University of California, San Francisco continues the work of the Pew Health Professions Commission by developing programs that assist schools and professionals in making the necessary accommodations.

Why Choose a Career in Health Care?

People who choose a career in the health professions do so because they have a genuine interest in helping people. Health care professionals should have excellent verbal and written communication skills and an interest in science or social science.

There are many reasons why each of these careers might appeal to you. Perhaps you are looking for a career in which you can earn a respectable starting salary without committing to a four-year education. Maybe you are looking for a career in which you can earn a higher degree and become a leader in that profession. Perhaps you want to do both!

Length of Study

If you are looking for a health career that requires twelve or fewer months of study for entry, you may wish to consider one of the following:

- Dental assistant
- Emergency medical technician-paramedic
- Medical assistant
- Surgical technologist

If you are willing to commit to at least two full-time years of study, you may wish to consider the following careers:

- Cardiovascular technologist
- Clinical laboratory technician
- Dental hygienist
- Dental laboratory technician
- Dietetic technician
- Emergency medical technician-paramedic (if you wish to earn a degree)
- Health information technician
- Occupational therapy assistant
- Ophthalmic dispensing optician
- Physical therapist assistant
- Radiation therapist
- Radiographer
- Registered respiratory therapist

Careers that require four full-time years of study for entry are:

- Athletic trainer
- Clinical laboratory scientist
- Health information administrator
- Occupational therapist
- Physical therapist
- Physician assistant
- Respiratory therapist

The only profession included in this book that currently requires a graduate degree for entry is art therapist; however, beginning in 2002 physical therapists will be required to have a master's degree for entry into the profession, and later, a master's degree will also be required for occupational therapists.

I hope the information we have provided here will start you on your way to an interesting and rewarding career in the health professions. If you would like to send me your comments or suggestions for how this book could be further improved, please write to me in care of my publisher:

Guide to Careers in the Health Professions
c/o Princeton Review Publishing
2315 Broadway, 3rd Floor
New York, NY 10024

About the School Listings

The school listings included in this book were compiled by the staff at The Princeton Review by surveying over 5,000 programs across the country. Programs that returned their surveys are listed with as much information as they chose to provide.

Potential students and program directors should keep in mind the following regarding the school data:

School Name and Address

Programs in the health professions change from time to time. New programs open, and old programs close. Contacting the school itself is always the first step in choosing a program.

Contact Information:

- Program telephone number, fax number, e-mail address, and web address are listed where available to assist you in contacting the school directly.

Program Information:

- Program begins: The month(s) in which a student may enter the program. If multiple months are listed, new students may start the program at more than one time a year.
- Degrees offered/Duration: The degrees that a program offers; some programs offer more than one degree option. Where available, each degree is followed by its duration in months. Durations are given in months rather than years because many programs in the health professions run year-round, with courses that may be completed over the summer months.

Application Information

- Enrollment of program: The total number of students enrolled in the program; compare to the number of applications received for an indication of competitiveness.

Financial Information

- Tuition, resident and non-resident: Tuition is listed here as an annual figure. If a school provided per credit information, annual tuition was calculated based on 15 credit hours per semester, 30 credit hours per year.
- Average cost of books: Schools have estimated the average annual cost of books, figures may include supplies and/or other materials.
- % of students receiving aid: The percentage of students who receive financial aid from the school and/or program.

Employment Profile

- % of students who pass the boards on their first try: Indicates the percentage of graduates who were able to pass the examination for their profession on their first attempt.
- % employed within the first 6 months following graduation: Indicates the percentage of graduates who found employment within six months of graduating from the program.
- Average starting salary: Figures are annual and based on entry-level positions. If schools provided hourly or weekly rates, these were converted to an annual figure based on an 8 hour day, 5 days per week and 50 weeks per year.

Art Therapist

Nancy Gerber, MS, ATR-BC
Director
Graduate Art Therapy Education
MCP Hahnemann University

Job Description

According to the American Art Therapy Association, "Art therapy is a human service profession that uses art media, images, the creative art process, and patient/client responses to the created products as reflections of an individual's development, abilities, personality, interests, concerns, and conflicts. Art therapy practice is based on knowledge of human developmental and psychological theories which are implemented in the full spectrum of models of assessment and treatment including educational, psychodynamic, cognitive, transpersonal and other therapeutic means of reconciling emotional conflicts, fostering self-awareness, developing social skills, managing behavior, solving problems, reducing anxiety, aiding in reality orientation, and increasing self-esteem."[1]

What Do They Do?

Art therapists primarily work with people who are experiencing psychological, emotional, cognitive, or interpersonal difficulties in their lives. Their patients' problems may be the results of developmental, psychiatric, family, medical, community, or legal problems. Art therapists are trained to work with all ages of people, ranging from small children to the elderly, in diverse locations such as schools, hospitals, clinics, nursing homes, and prisons.

The art therapist generally works with these individuals by using the art process to assess and treat their patients' problems. He or she learns to evaluate the types of problems people are having through verbal interviews and art therapy assessments. Once the art therapist understands his or her patients' problems, he or she can work with individual patients, groups or families by providing different art media and techniques that will aid in communication, self-expression, self-control, and ultimately, self-understanding.

The theory behind art therapy is that people often have certain feelings and behaviors that they are unable to characterize in words. This may result in frustration, isolation, depression, destructive behaviors, or other problems that the individual may not understand or be able to communicate. By using the nonverbal language of images, the individual can begin to find a way to communicate, initially through artwork and ultimately through words. The art making process and verbalization about art production act as a bridge between the internal world of the individual and the external world of others.

Type of Person

Art therapists are people who have interest in both art and psychology. Passion for art and a love of people drives them toward this profession. They are usually people who are interested in art, but do not want to make it their sole livelihood. People who enter this field also have an inquisitive nature and want to learn about human nature and behavior. It is important that art therapists be artists themselves, since artists tend to have experienced the creative and curative aspects of their own art forms and often wish to help others do the same. Artists also understand how imagery tells the story of a human life and often know how to help other human beings express their stories in their individualized art language.

With Whom Do They Work?

Art therapists generally work as a part of an interdisciplinary treatment team. The art therapist is trained to work with other professionals and knows that communication with these professionals is essential for the treatment of the patient or client. When art therapists work in a psychiatric facility they serve as part of a team with psychiatrists, nurses, psychologists, social workers, occupational therapists, and recreation therapists. If the art therapist is working in a medical hospital, he or she will often work with doctors, nurses, and child life workers. Some art therapists have their own private practices where they work independently.

Employment

Places of Employment

Art therapists have traditionally worked in the field of mental health or psychiatry. They are often employed in hospitals, residential treatment centers, partial hospitals (day treatment centers where patients go home at night), or outpatient clinics. More recently, art therapists have expanded into other treatment venues such as school systems, nursing homes, mobile therapy, medical hospitals, corporations, community crisis intervention, and prisons. Some art therapists also work in private practice and consulting. The principles of art therapy and the education of the art therapist provide a strong foundation from which the art therapist can adapt into a wide range of treatment settings.

Employment Outlook

Art therapy is a relatively new profession. In the formative years of the profession, jobs were often scarce. Art therapists had to take positions that were often meant for other types of therapists and then gradually introduce art therapy. In recent years, the development of standards and the scope of the profession have created specific job opportunities for art therapists. As a result of the growth and development of the profession, art therapists are now licensed as Master's level counselors in almost all fifty states. Licensure has opened many more employment opportunities for art therapists in the current healthcare environment.

As the profession has matured, areas of specialization have developed, resulting in increased job opportunities. Art therapists have been moving out of traditional mental health fields and have created positions for themselves in medical hospitals, prisons, schools and courtrooms, as well as boardrooms. Employment opportunities for art therapists seem to be growing.

Each art therapist's creativity, motivation, and dedication brings a new job opportunity as each writes grants or develops positions for herself in new settings. Every time an art therapist creates a new position for himself, he has also created the same opportunity for other art therapists.

Salary

Entry level salaries for art therapists vary depending upon the type of agency in which the art therapist works. Typically, starting salaries range from $28,000 to $33,000. In national surveys, the potential for earning up to $50,000 has been demonstrated, though earning ability depends upon the art therapist's chosen career path.[2] Many art therapists can advance to supervisory or administrative positions, which can potentially increase their salaries. Some art therapists supplement their salaries with private practice or private supervision work after they become registered and board certified.

Educational Programs

Length

In order to practice, earn their credentials from the American Art Therapy Association (AATA), and be eligible for licensure, art therapists are required to have a Master's degree. The Master's degree programs generally are two years in length. Many art therapists also pursue doctoral degrees.

Prerequisites

The American Art Therapy Association stipulates prerequisites for admission to approved graduate art therapy programs. These prerequisites include a Bachelor's Degree, 15 credits in studio art, and 12 credits in psychology. The studio art credits should include experiences in different art media. The psychology credits should include an introduction to psychology, developmental psychology, abnormal psychology, and possibly a course in behavioral research. A personal interview and the presentation of an art portfolio are also required for admission.

There are some undergraduate preparatory tracks in art therapy, although these programs do not prepare students to practice as art therapists. These tracks include introductory courses in art therapy and are designed for those students who wish to continue in a graduate art therapy program. These tracks are not necessary for admission to a graduate program; however, taking such courses may help an interested student decide if art therapy is a direction that they want to pursue. Additionally, students who take introductory course work in art therapy often find themselves much better prepared for the graduate work. Contact the AATA for more information on these undergraduate programs.

Curriculum

The curriculum in art therapy generally includes integration of three components: academic study, clinical experience, and supervisory experience. The academic course work includes the study of human behavior and human development, psychopathology and psychotherapy, creativity and the art making process. These courses are integrated with study of the history and theory of art therapy, as well as the study of practical techniques in the application of art therapy for different age groups and diverse populations. Additionally, methods of assessment and diagnosis are studied. The curriculum also covers professional issues, such as the study of ethical and legal issues of art therapy practice and the standards of practice. While students are studying these academic areas, they also perform supervised clinical fieldwork. Additionally, many graduate programs will include some aspect of experiential art making as a part of the curriculum so that the student can engage in a self-exploratory process through their art. This results in greater understanding of their personal reactions to different art making processes as well as the development of empathy for the individuals with whom they will work. Finally, the art therapy graduate student is expected to complete a Master's thesis or equivalent research project.

Accrediting Body

The American Art Therapy Association has an internal approval body called the Educational Programs Approval Board (EPAB). The EPAB evaluates all educational programs in art therapy to assure standards of excellence. The programs that receive approval from the EPAB must adhere to the educational standards that have been established by the American Art Therapy Association. Each program applying for approval or renewal must submit an extensive and comprehensive program self-study document to the EPAB. This approval process ensures the highest quality of art therapy education.

Educational Programs Approval Board
c/o The American Art Therapy Association
1202 Allanson Road
Mundelein, IL 60060-3808
Telephone: 888-290-0878
Web address: www.arttherapy.org

Certification Board

The Art Therapy Credentials Board, Inc. (ATCB) oversees the standards for individuals practicing art therapy. Once a student receives his or her Master's degree, he or she must complete certain requirements to become registered and board certified. To become registered, an art therapist must complete 1000–2000 hours of clinical work while supervised by a registered art therapist (ATR or ATR-BC). One hour of supervision is required for every 10 hours of clinical work. Once an art therapist completes these requirements, he or she can submit an application for registration to the ATCB. The ATCB then examines the application and determines whether the standards for registration have been met. Upon approval, the student receives the ATR credential. He or she is then eligible to sit for the board certification examination, which is a national, standardized examination for art therapists. Once the applicant passes that exam, he or she has earned the ATR-BC credential. Registration and board certification signify to others that an art therapist has completed the requirements to be professionally recognized by the art therapy community and by the licensure boards.

Art Therapy Credentials Board, Inc.
3 Terrace Way, Suite B
Greensboro, NC 27403
Telephone: 877-213-2822
Fax: 336-547-0017
Web address: www.atcb.org
E-mail: info@atcb.org

Advice for Potential Students

There are many ways to learn about the profession of art therapy and to determine which educational program might suit your needs. A few of these are listed below:

- Contact the American Art Therapy Association and ask them to send you an information packet. In this packet you will receive a copy of the association's ethical standards as well as general information about art therapy.

- Study the programs offering Master's degrees in art therapy. Call a few of them and ask them to send you information about their programs. If you are close to one of the schools, ask if you can visit classes and talk to students. Set up an informational interview with the director of the program.
- If you are able to, volunteer in a setting in which you think you might want to work, for example, a hospital or a clinic. If there is an art therapist working in that setting, talk with him or her about the profession and his or her job.
- Attend local or national conferences on art therapy. At these events you will be able to talk with many different art therapists who have different types of jobs. You might also be able to attend a variety of presentations about art therapy.
- If you have not done so already, take the prerequisite courses necessary for admission to a graduate art therapy program. You will learn whether you have the aptitudes and the interest in these areas.

For Additional Information

Organizations

The American Art Therapy Association
1202 Allanson Road
Mundelein, IL 60060-3808
Telephone: 888-290-0878
Web address: www.arttherapy.org

Publications

Books

Landgarten, H.B. *Clinical Art Therapy.* New York: Brunner/Mazel, 1991.

Rubin, J.A. *Art Therapy: An Introduction.* Philadelphia: Brunner/Mazel, 1999.

Wadeson, H. *Art Psychotherapy.* New York: John Wiley & Sons, 1980.

Journals

The Arts in Psychotherapy. Elsevier Science, 655 Avenue of the Americas, New York, NY 10010-5107. www.elsevier.nl

An international journal that presents articles on all of the creative arts therapies including art therapy, dance/movement therapy, music therapy, poetry therapy, and drama therapy.

Art Therapy: Journal of the American Art Therapy Association. American Art Therapy Association, 1202 Allanson Road, Mundelein, IL 60060-3808. www.arttherapy.org.

A national journal that publishes articles specifically related to the progression of art therapy.

Internet Resources

The American Art Therapy Association (AATA): www.arttherapy.org
Art Therapy Credentials Board (ATCB) www.atcb.org
National Coalition of Arts Therapies Associations (NCATA) www.ncata.com

District of Columbia

George Washington University

2129 G Street, NW
Building L
Washington, DC 20052

Contact Information:
Telephone: 202-994-6285
Fax: 202-994-1404
E-mail: kathw@gwis2.circ.gwu.edu
Web: www.gwu.edu

Program Information:
Program begins: September, January
Duration of program: 24 months
Evening or weekend classes are available.

Application Information:
Enrollment of program: 48

Financial Information:
Tuition, resident: $13,755

Illinois

Southern Illinois University—Edwardsville

Box 1764
Department of Art and Design
Edwardsville, IL 62026-1764

Contact Information:
Telephone: 618-650-3183
Fax: 618-650-3106
Web: www.siue.edu

Program Information:
Program begins: August
Degrees offered: Master's, 24 months

Application Information:
Enrollment of program: 20

Financial Information:
Tuition, resident: $2,160
Tuition, non-resident: $6,480
% of students receiving aid: 80

Employment Profile:
% employed within the first 6 months following graduation: 90
Average starting salary: $25,000

University of Illinois at Chicago

929 West Harrison Street MC 036
Chicago, IL 60607-7038

Contact Information:
Telephone: 312-996-5728
Fax: 312-413-2333
Web: www.uic.edu

Program Information:
Program begins: August
Degrees offered: Certificate program; Associate's
Evening or weekend classes are available.

Application Information:
Enrollment of program: 30

Financial Information:
Tuition, resident: $2,620
Tuition, non-resident: $6,039
% of students receiving aid: 50

Employment Profile:
% employed within the first 6 months following graduation: 100

Kentucky

University of Louisville
Expressive Therapies Program
Gardiner Hall 331
Louisville, KY 40292

Contact Information:
Telephone: 502-852-8796
Fax: 502-852-4598
E-mail: carona@gwise.louisville.edu
Web: www.louisville.edu

Program Information:
Duration of program: 16 months

Application Information:
Enrollment of program: 35

Financial Information:
Tuition, resident: $3,546
Tuition, non-resident: $10,066

Massachusetts

Lesley College
Expressive Therapies
29 Everett Street
Cambridge, MA 02138

Contact Information:
Telephone: 617-349-8436
Fax: 617-349-8431
E-mail: jbyers@mail.lesley.edu
Web: www.lesley.edu

Program Information:
Program begins: September, January
Duration of program: 24 months
Evening or weekend classes are available.

Application Information:
Transfer students are accepted.

Financial Information:
Average cost of books: $200

Employment Profile:
% employed within the first 6 months following graduation: 80
Average starting salary: $32,000

Michigan

Wayne State University
163 Community Arts Building
Detroit, MI 48202

Contact Information:
Telephone: 313-577-0490
Fax: 313-577-4091
Web: www.wayne.edu

Program Information:
Program begins: August
Duration of program: 28 months

Financial Information:
Tuition, resident: $2,700

Missouri

St. Louis Institute of Art Psychotherapy
308A North Euclid
St. Louis, MO 63108

Contact Information:
Telephone: 314-367-8550 ext. 1

Program Information:
Program begins: September, January, June
Degrees offered: Post-master's Certificate, 16 months; Post-bachelor's Certificate, 16 months
Evening or weekend classes are available.

Application Information:
Enrollment of program: 8
Transfer students are accepted.

Financial Information:
Tuition, resident: $9,000
Average cost of books: $250

Employment Profile:
% employed within the first 6 months following graduation: 92
Average starting salary: $25,000

New York

College of New Rochelle
29 Castle Place
New Rochelle, NY 10805

Contact Information:
Telephone: 914-654-5280
Fax: 914-654-5593

Program Information:
Program begins: August, January, June
Duration of program: 24 months
Evening or weekend classes are available.

Application Information:
Transfer students are accepted.

Employment Profile:
Average starting salary: $30,000

Long Island University—CW Post Campus
720 Northern Boulevard
Brookville, NY 11548

Contact Information:
Telephone: 516-299-2944
Fax: 516-299-2858

Program Information:
Program begins: September
Duration of program: 24 months
Evening or weekend classes are available.

Application Information:
Enrollment of program: 30
Transfer students are accepted.

Financial Information:
Average cost of books: $500

Employment Profile:
% employed within the first 6 months following graduation: 90
Average starting salary: $30,000

Nazareth College of Rochester
4245 East Avenue
Rochester, NY 14618-3790

Contact Information:
Telephone: 716-389-2815
Fax: 716-586-2452
E-mail: eghorovi@naz.edu
Web: www.naz.edu

Program Information:
Program begins: September, March, June
Degrees offered: Master's, 24 months
Evening or weekend classes are available.

Application Information:
Enrollment of program: 42
Transfer students are accepted.

Financial Information:
Average cost of books: $1,500
% of students receiving aid: 20

Employment Profile:
% employed within the first 6 months following graduation: 75
Average starting salary: $26,000

Pratt Institute
200 Willoughby Avenue, East 3
Brooklyn, NY 11205

Contact Information:
Telephone: 718-636-3428
Fax: 718-636-3597
E-mail: lthompso@pratt.edu
Web: www.pratt.edu/ad/therapy

Program Information:
Program begins: September, January, June
Duration of program: 24 months
Evening or weekend classes are available.

Application Information:
Enrollment of program: 75
Transfer students are accepted.

Financial Information:
% of students receiving aid: 90

Employment Profile:
% employed within the first 6 months following graduation: 95
Average starting salary: $30,000

Oregon

Marylhurst University
PO Box 261
Marylhurst, OR 97036

Contact Information:
Telephone: 503-699-6244

Fax: 503-636-1957
E-mail: cturner@marylhurst.edu
Web: www.marylhurst.edu

Program Information:
Program begins: September
Degrees offered: PhD, 21 months; Post-master's Certificate, 18 months
Evening or weekend classes are available.

Application Information:
Enrollment of program: 40
Transfer students are accepted.

Financial Information:
Average cost of books: $700
% of students receiving aid: 80

Employment Profile:
% of students who pass the boards on their first try: 100
% employed within the first 6 months following graduation: 80

Pennsylvania

Marywood University

Art Department
2300 Adams Avenue
Scranton, PA 18509

Contact Information:
Telephone: 570-348-6278 ext. 2525
Fax: 570-340-6023
E-mail: moon@ac.marywood.edu
Web: www.marywood.edu

Program Information:
Program begins: June
Duration of program: 27 months
Evening or weekend classes are available.

Application Information:
Enrollment of program: 36

Financial Information:
Tuition, resident: $9,600
Average cost of books: $400
% of students receiving aid: 90

Employment Profile:
% employed within the first 6 months following graduation: 100
Average starting salary: $28,000

MCP Hahnemann University

1505 Race Street
10th Floor, HS 905
Philadelphia, PA 19102-1192

Contact Information:
Telephone: 215-762-6928
Fax: 215-762-6933
E-mail: nancy.gerber@drexel.edu
Web: www.mcphu.edu

Program Information:
Program begins: September
Duration of program: 24 months

Application Information:
Enrollment of program: 100
Transfer students are accepted.

Financial Information:
Tuition, resident: $12,000
Average cost of books: $700
% of students receiving aid: 95

Employment Profile:
% employed within the first 6 months following graduation: 99
Average starting salary: $30,000

Vermont

Vermont College of Norwich University

Admissions Office
Northfield, VT 05663

Contact Information:
Telephone: 802-828-8810
Fax: 802-828-8585
E-mail: gagell@norwich.edu
Web: www.norwich.edu/grad/arttherapy

Program Information:
Program begins: September, January, June
Duration of program: 27 months

Financial Information:
Tuition, resident: $15,950

Virginia

Eastern Virginia Medical School

PO Box 1980
Norfolk, VA 23501

Contact Information:
Telephone: 757-446-5895
Fax: 757-446-5918
E-mail: art@picard.evms.edu
Web: www.evms.edu

Program Information:
Program begins: August, January
Duration of program: 24 months

Application Information:
Enrollment of program: 23
Transfer students are accepted.

Athletic Trainer

Ky E. Kugler, EdD, ATC
Assistant Athletic Director
Department of Intercollegiate Athletics
California State Polytechnic University, Pomona

Job Description

What Do They Do?

The Certified Athletic Trainer is a highly educated and skilled professional specializing in healthcare for the physically active. In cooperation with physicians and other healthcare providers, certified athletic trainers function as integral members of the healthcare team in secondary schools, colleges and universities, sports medicine clinics, professional sports programs and other athletic healthcare settings involving the physically active.[1]

The duties and responsibilities for certified athletic trainers vary by employment setting. Primarily, athletic trainers specialize in the prevention, recognition and rehabilitation of injuries incurred by physically active people. Certified athletic trainers administer immediate emergency care under the supervision of a licensed physician. They also use their knowledge of the injuries incurred by physically active individuals and the factors influencing them to develop treatment programs based on medical research and exercise science protocols, exercise, and sports science.[2] Related duties can include clinical education of student athletic trainers, as well as taping, bandaging, wrapping, bracing, and administering other measures to aid the physically active.

Type of Person

Athletic training professionals come from very diverse ethnic and multi-cultural backgrounds, reflecting our country's ethnic and cultural make-up. Athletic trainers generally have an interest in sports, a willingness to care for others, and a strong desire to educate themselves in a variety of healthcare and medical disciplines.

With Whom Do They Work?

Communication among athletes, coaches, physicians and other healthcare providers is a critical component of the day-to-day duties of the certified athletic trainer.

Employment

Places of Employment

At one time, certified athletic trainers were employed primarily in traditional athletic settings such as high schools, universities, colleges, or professional sports teams. The largest employment growth in the past ten years has been within non-traditional venues, mainly in sports medicine clinics and other industrial/corporate employment arenas.

Employment Outlook

Following tremendous growth in the field throughout the 1970s and 1980s, steps were taken in the early 1990s to slow the growth of the profession. At the time, NATA believed that there were too many students graduating relative to the number of jobs available. In addition, the association wanted to reform education to make it more consistent and focus on licensure requirements.

As the profession faces an increasing healthcare responsibility for a changing society and clientele, the future of athletic training will continue to shift from traditional settings towards new clinical and industrial sports medicine areas. If students are willing to relocate, they will probably find it easier to locate employment following graduation. In addition, students will be more marketable if they have also earned a teaching credential or have included teaching preparation in their undergraduate education.

Salary

Salaries vary greatly within the athletic training profession. A graduate assistant intern at a university may earn a salary in the low teens, while salaries for certified athletic trainers who work for professional sport teams and/or private sports medicine practices may be as high as $100,000 per year.

Educational Programs

Length

At minimum, a certified athletic trainer must have a Bachelor's degree, usually in athletic training, health, physical education (kinesiology), or exercise science.

Prerequisites

Prerequisites vary among programs. Many AT programs are part of Kinesiology departments, while others are housed in departments such as Health, Allied Health, Biology, Education, etc.

Curriculum

Athletic trainers study human anatomy, human physiology, biomechanics, exercise physiology, athletic training, nutrition, and psychology/counseling. During the course of their education, students in athletic training programs participate in extensive clinical affiliations with athletic teams and with physically active people. This helps them to become competent in the clinical proficiencies of the profession.[3]

Accrediting Body

NATA sets standards for athletic trainers through its educational programs. Two educational paths exist for the aspiring athletic trainer:

1. Certification through an internship while an undergraduate.
   This route offers limited course work, but students attain a high number of clinical hours.
2. Following an approved curriculum.
   This route offers the student a high number of courses, but a limited number of clinical hours.

Beginning in 2002, only the approved curriculum route will be in place. In other words, only programs that are accredited through the Commission on Accreditation of Allied Health Education Programs (CAAHEP) and the Joint Review Committee-Athletic Training will exist.

In the early 1990s, NATA established the Education Council, which initiated the educational reforms that have been taking place in the profession. The Education Council's mission was to consolidate all entities and sub-committees related to undergraduate education, graduate education, continuing education, and certification. There are twelve competencies (areas of entry-level proficiency) that the Education Council has identified. These are the areas that a student should master in preparation for the entry-level certification exam. They include:

1. Risk Management and Injury Prevention
2. Pathology of Injuries and Illnesses
3. Assessment and Evaluation
4. Acute Care of Injury and Illness
5. Pharmacology
6. Therapeutic Modalities
7. Therapeutic Exercise
8. General Medical Conditions and Disabilities
9. Nutritional Aspects of Injury and Illness
10. Psychosocial Intervention and Referral
11. Health Care Administration
12. Professional Development and Responsibilities [4]

In conjunction with the writing of these new competencies, the Education Council also established a Clinical Education Committee, which wrote clinical proficiencies that correspond with these new competencies. This committee recommended a clinical proficiencies list of clinical teaching objectives and psychomotor skills, clinical education guidelines, and a model for developing clinical educators.[5]

Commission on Accreditation of Allied Health Education Programs
35 East Wacker Drive, Suite 1970
Chicago, IL 60601-2208
Telephone: 312-553-9355
Fax: 312-553-9616
E-mail: caahep@caahep.org
Web address: www.caahep.org

Certification Board

The NATA Board of Certification is an incorporated agency that certifies entry-level athletic trainers and identifies quality healthcare professionals for the public through a system of certification, adjudication, standards of practice, and continuing competency programs.

NATA Board of Certification
1512 South 60th Street
Omaha, NE 68106
Telephone: 402-559-0091
Fax: 402-561-0598
Web address: www.nataboc.org

Advice for Potential Students

Visit a school that offers a NATA accredited program, and arrange for an appointment to discuss your personal situation with the program director and/or dean of the department in which athletic training is housed. Ask pertinent questions related to

- certification exam success of students
- job placement history and potential
- affiliated clinical settings
- types of equipment
- library and other educational resources

Above all, find a program that best suits your individual needs.

For Additional Information

Organizations

National Athletic Trainers' Association
2952 Stemmons Freeway
Dallas, TX 75247-6196
Phone: 214-637-6282
Fax: 214-637-2206
Web address: www.nata.org

Publications

Journals

Journal of Athletic Training. National Athletic Trainers' Association, 2952 Stemmons Freeway, Dallas, TX 75247-6196. www.nata.org

A research journal with a goal to enhance communication among professionals interested in the quality of healthcare for the physically active.

NATA News. National Athletic Trainers' Association, 2952 Stemmons Freeway, Dallas, TX 75247-6196. www.nata.org

A news publication for the NATA membership that highlights people and events.

Internet Resources

National Athletic Trainers' Association: www.nata.org
National Athletic Trainer's Association Education Council: www.cewl.com

Alabama

Troy State University

Eldridge Hall
Troy, AL 36082

Contact Information:

Telephone: 334-670-3722
Fax: 334-670-3870
Web: www.troyst.edu

Program Information:

Program begins: January
Duration of program: 24 months

Application Information:

Enrollment of program: 30
Transfer students are accepted.

Financial Information:

Tuition, resident: $2,660
Tuition, non-resident: $5,320
Average cost of books: $360
% of students receiving aid: 70

Employment Profile:

% of students who pass the boards on their first try: 50
% employed within the first 6 months following graduation: 90
Average starting salary: $28,500

University of Alabama

Department of Health Science
PO Box 8700311
Tuscaloosa, AL 35487-0311

Contact Information:

Telephone: 205-348-8683
Fax: 205-348-4707
E-mail: dleaver@bama.ua.edu
Web: www.ua.edu

Program Information:

Program begins: September
Degrees offered: Bachelor's, 23 months

Application Information:

Enrollment of program: 46
Transfer students are accepted.

Financial Information:

Tuition, resident: $2,684
Tuition, non-resident: $7,216

Employment Profile:

% of students who pass the boards on their first try: 64
% employed within the first 6 months following graduation: 100

California

California State University—Northridge

18111 Nordhoff Street
Northridge, CA 91330-8287

Contact Information:

Telephone: 818-677-3205
Fax: 818-677-3207
E-mail: alice.mclaine@csun.edu
Web: www.csun.edu

Program Information:

Program begins: August
Degrees offered: Bachelor's, 26 months

Financial Information:

Tuition, resident: $1,980
Tuition, non-resident: $7,884

Delaware

University of Delaware

Bob Carpenter Center
Newark, DE 19716

Contact Information:

Telephone: 302-831-2287
Fax: 302-831-8653
E-mail: handling@udel.edu
Web: www.udel.edu

Program Information:

Program begins: September
Degrees offered: Bachelor's, 48 months

Application Information:

Enrollment of program: 32
Transfer students are accepted.

Financial Information:

Tuition, resident: $4,250
Tuition, non-resident: $12,250
Average cost of books: $500

Employment Profile:

% of students who pass the boards on their first try: 75
% employed within the first 6 months following graduation: 100

Florida

Barry University

11300 Northeast 2nd Avenue
Miami Shores, FL 33161-6695

Contact Information:

Telephone: 305-899-3497
Fax: 305-899-3556
E-mail: ccramer@mail.barry.edu
Web: www.barry.edu

Program Information:

Program begins: August, January
Degrees offered: Bachelor's, 48 months; Master's, 24 months
Evening or weekend classes are available.

Application Information:

Enrollment of program: 36
Transfer students are accepted.

Financial Information:

Average cost of books: $400
% of students receiving aid: 78

Employment Profile:

% of students who pass the boards on their first try: 78
% employed within the first 6 months following graduation: 100
Average starting salary: $30,000

Stetson University

421 North Woodland Boulevard Unit 8359
Deland, FL 32720-3770

Contact Information:

Telephone: 904-822-8121
Fax: 904-822-8148
E-mail: sguyer@stetson.edu
Web: www.stetson.edu/departments

Program Information:

Program begins: September
Duration of program: 32 months

Application Information:

Enrollment of program: 17
Transfer students are accepted.

Financial Information:

Average cost of books: $200
% of students receiving aid: 70

Employment Profile:

% employed within the first 6 months following graduation: 100
Average starting salary: $20,000

Georgia

Valdosta State University

Department KSPE
Valdosta, GA 31698

Contact Information:

Telephone: 912-333-7161 ext. 5469
Fax: 912-333-5972
E-mail: mgarber@grits.valdosta.peachnet.edu
Web: www.valdosta.edu

Program Information:

Program begins: September
Degrees offered: Bachelor's, 36 months

Application Information:

Enrollment of program: 32
Transfer students are accepted.

Financial Information:

Tuition, resident: $1,101
Tuition, non-resident: $3,711
Average cost of books: $400
% of students receiving aid: 50

Employment Profile:

% of students who pass the boards on their first try: 65
% employed within the first 6 months following graduation: 95
Average starting salary: $30,000

Idaho

Boise State University

Department of Kinesiology
1910 University Drive
Boise, ID 83725

Contact Information:
Telephone: 208-385-1481
Fax: 208-385-1894
E-mail: jmcches@boisestate.edu
Web: www.idbsu.edu

Program Information:
Program begins: August
Degrees offered: Bachelor's, 36 months

Application Information:
Enrollment of program: 24
Transfer students are accepted.

Financial Information:
Tuition, resident: $2,104
Tuition, non-resident: $7,450
Average cost of books: $300
% of students receiving aid: 30

Employment Profile:
% of students who pass the boards on their first try: 70
% employed within the first 6 months following graduation: 85
Average starting salary: $25,000

Illinois

Southern Illinois University—Carbondale

Department of Physical Education
Carbondale, IL 62901-4310

Contact Information:
Telephone: 618-453-5053
Fax: 618-453-3329
E-mail: sallyatc@siu.edu
Web: www.siue.edu

Program Information:
Program begins: August
Duration of program: 28 months

Application Information:
Enrollment of program: 40
Transfer students are accepted.

Financial Information:
Tuition, resident: $1,146
Tuition, non-resident: $2,292

Employment Profile:
% employed within the first 6 months following graduation: 100
Average starting salary: $27,000

University of Illinois at Urbana-Champaign

Department of Kinesiology, 209 Freer Hall
906 South Goodwin Avenue
Urbana, IL 61801

Contact Information:
Telephone: 217-333-7699
Fax: 217-244-7322
E-mail: g-bell@uiuc.edu
Web: www.kines.uiuc.edu/atcentral

Program Information:
Program begins: August
Duration of program: 45 months

Application Information:
Enrollment of program: 36

Financial Information:
Tuition, resident: $4,588
Tuition, non-resident: $11,404
Average cost of books: $670
% of students receiving aid: 70

Employment Profile:
% of students who pass the boards on their first try: 90
% employed within the first 6 months following graduation: 100
Average starting salary: $25,000

Indiana

Anderson University

1100 East 5th Street
Anderson, IN 46012-1362

Contact Information:
Telephone: 765-641-4491
Fax: 765-641-3841
E-mail: sdrising@anderson.edu
Web: www.anderson.edu

Program Information:
Program begins: August
Duration of program: 27 months

Application Information:
Enrollment of program: 30
Transfer students are accepted.

Financial Information:
Average cost of books: $580
% of students receiving aid: 90

Employment Profile:
% of students who pass the boards on their first try: 85
% employed within the first 6 months following graduation: 100
Average starting salary: $27,000

Indiana State University

Athletic Training Department
Terre Haute, IN 47809

Contact Information:
Telephone: 812-237-8496
Fax: 812-237-4368
E-mail: merrick@indstate.edu
Web: www.indstate.edu

Program Information:
Program begins: August
Duration of program: 9 months

Application Information:
Enrollment of program: 124
Transfer students are accepted.

Financial Information:
Tuition, resident: $1,713
Tuition, non-resident: $4,277

Employment Profile:
% of students who pass the boards on their first try: 70
% employed within the first 6 months following graduation: 100
Average starting salary: $28,000

Indiana University—Bloomington

Sports Medicine Department, Assembly Hall
1001 East 17th Street
Bloomington, IN 47408

Contact Information:
Telephone: 812-855-4509
Fax: 812-855-1810
E-mail: kagrove@indiana.edu
Web: www.indiana.edu

Program Information:
Program begins: September
Degrees offered: Bachelor's, 36 months

Application Information:
Enrollment of program: 54
Transfer students are accepted.

Financial Information:
Tuition, resident: $3,582
Tuition, non-resident: $10,700

Employment Profile:
% of students who pass the boards on their first try: 75
Average starting salary: $25,500

Purdue University

Department of HKLS
1362 Lambert
West Lafayette, IN 47907

Contact Information:
Telephone: 765-494-3167
Fax: 765-496-1239
E-mail: llevere@purdue.edu

Program Information:
Program begins: August
Duration of program: 27 months

Application Information:
Enrollment of program: 34
Transfer students are accepted.

Financial Information:
Tuition, resident: $3,500
Tuition, non-resident: $11,720
Average cost of books: $300

Employment Profile:
% of students who pass the boards on their first try: 74
% employed within the first 6 months following graduation: 99
Average starting salary: $30,000

Iowa

University of Iowa

414 FH
Iowa City, IA 52242

Contact Information:
Telephone: 319-335-9393
Fax: 319-335-9398
E-mail: danny-foster@uiowa.edu
Web: www.uiowa.edu

Program Information:
Program begins: September
Degrees offered: Bachelor's, 30 months; Master's, 18 months

Application Information:
Enrollment of program: 45
Transfer students are accepted.

Financial Information:
Tuition, resident: $2,666
Tuition, non-resident: $9,788
Average cost of books: $1,000
% of students receiving aid: 90

Employment Profile:
% of students who pass the boards on their first try: 86
% employed within the first 6 months following graduation: 100

Maryland

Salisbury State University
1101 Camden Avenue
Salisbury, MD 21801

Contact Information:
Telephone: 410-543-6348
Fax: 410-546-2639
E-mail: jrsciffers@ssu.edu
Web: www.ssu.edu

Program Information:
Program begins: August
Duration of program: 24 months

Application Information:
Enrollment of program: 27
Transfer students are accepted.

Financial Information:
Tuition, resident: $3,842
Tuition, non-resident: $7,594
Average cost of books: $600

Employment Profile:
% of students who pass the boards on their first try: 25
% employed within the first 6 months following graduation: 100

Massachusetts

Boston University
Department of Physical Therapy
635 Commonwealth Avenue
Boston, MA 02215

Contact Information:
Telephone: 617-353-7507
Fax: 617-353-9463
E-mail: sara@bu.edu
Web: www.bu.edu

Program Information:
Program begins: August
Duration of program: 36 months

Application Information:
Enrollment of program: 40
Transfer students are accepted.

Employment Profile:
% of students who pass the boards on their first try: 67

Endicott College
376 Hale Street
Beverly, MA 01915

Contact Information:
Telephone: 978-232-2433
Fax: 978-232-2600
E-mail: dswanton@endicott.edu
Web: www.endicott.edu

Program Information:
Program begins: September
Duration of program: 32 months

Application Information:
Transfer students are accepted.

Financial Information:
Average cost of books: $500
% of students receiving aid: 76

Salem State College
352 Lafayette Street
Salem, MA 01970-5353

Contact Information:
Telephone: 978-542-6583
Fax: 978-548-6554
Web: www.salem.mass.edu

Program Information:
Program begins: September, January
Degrees offered: Bachelor's, 48 months
Evening or weekend classes are available.

Application Information:
Enrollment of program: 21
Transfer students are accepted.

Financial Information:
Tuition, resident: $1,408
Tuition, non-resident: $5,542
Average cost of books: $600
% of students receiving aid: 20

Employment Profile:
% of students who pass the boards on their first try: 8
% employed within the first 6 months following graduation: 50
Average starting salary: $24,000

Michigan

Central Michigan University
Sports Medicine Curriculum
Room 145
Mt. Pleasant, MI 48859

Contact Information:
Telephone: 517-774-6687
Fax: 517-774-1095
E-mail: david.kaiser@cmich.edu
Web: www.cmich.edu

Program Information:
Program begins: August
Duration of program: 36 months

Application Information:
Enrollment of program: 70
Transfer students are accepted.

Financial Information:
Tuition, resident: $3,637
Tuition, non-resident: $8,655

Employment Profile:
% of students who pass the boards on their first try: 80
% employed within the first 6 months following graduation: 100
Average starting salary: $25,000

Eastern Michigan University
318P Porter Building
Ypsilanti, MI 48197

Contact Information:
Telephone: 734-487-0090
E-mail: jodi.schumacher@emich.edu
Web: www.emich.edu

Program Information:
Program begins: August
Degrees offered: Bachelor's, 48 months

Application Information:
Enrollment of program: 40
Transfer students are accepted.

Financial Information:
Tuition, resident: $2,500
Tuition, non-resident: $4,295

Employment Profile:
% of students who pass the boards on their first try: 92

Hope College
PO Box 9000
Holland, MI 49422-9000

Contact Information:
Telephone: 616-395-7708
Fax: 616-395-7175
E-mail: ray@hope.edu
Web: www.hope.edu/academic/kinesiology/athtrain/

Program Information:
Program begins: September
Duration of program: 36 months

Application Information:
Enrollment of program: 20
Transfer students are accepted.

Financial Information:
Average cost of books: $300
% of students receiving aid: 55

Employment Profile:
% of students who pass the boards on their first try: 80
% employed within the first 6 months following graduation: 100
Average starting salary: $26,000

Minnesota

Gustavus Adolphus College
800 West College Avenue
St. Peter, MN 56082

Contact Information:
Telephone: 507-933-7674
Fax: 507-933-8412
E-mail: gdratcr@gac.edu
Web: www.gac.edu

Program Information:
Program begins: September
Degrees offered: Bachelor's, 36 months
Evening or weekend classes are available.

Application Information:
Transfer students are accepted.

Financial Information:
Average cost of books: $200
% of students receiving aid: 60

Employment Profile:
% of students who pass the boards on their first try: 75
% employed within the first 6 months following graduation: 50
Average starting salary: $25,000

Minnesota State University—Mankato
MSU Box 28
123 Highland Center
Mankato, MN 56002-8400

Contact Information:
Telephone: 507-389-2092
Fax: 507-389-5618
E-mail: patrick.sexton@mankato.msu.edu
Web: www.mankato.msus.edu

Program Information:
Program begins: August
Duration of program: 24 months
Evening or weekend classes are available.

Application Information:
Enrollment of program: 32
Transfer students are accepted.

Financial Information:
Tuition, resident: $2,492
Tuition, non-resident: $5,570
Average cost of books: $625

Employment Profile:
% of students who pass the boards on their first try: 85
% employed within the first 6 months following graduation: 100
Average starting salary: $25,000

Missouri

Southwest Missouri State University
Sports Medicine & Athletic Training Curriculum
901 South National Avenue
Springfield, MO 65804

Contact Information:
Telephone: 417-836-8553
Fax: 417-836-8554
E-mail: krt858f@wpgate.smsu.edu
Web: www.smsu.edu/sportsmed

Program Information:
Program begins: August
Duration of program: 32 months

Application Information:
Enrollment of program: 62
Transfer students are accepted.

Financial Information:
Tuition, resident: $2,818
Tuition, non-resident: $5,636

Employment Profile:
% of students who pass the boards on their first try: 80

New Hampshire

Plymouth State College
MSC 22
Plymouth, NH 03264

Contact Information:
Telephone: 603-535-2915
Fax: 603-535-2395
Web: www.plymouth.edu

Program Information:
Program begins: August
Duration of program: 48 months

Application Information:
Enrollment of program: 30
Transfer students are accepted.

Financial Information:
Tuition, resident: $3,830
Tuition, non-resident: $9,140
Average cost of books: $650

Employment Profile:
% employed within the first 6 months following graduation: 100

University of New Hampshire
Department of Kinesiology
145 Main Street
Field House
Durham, NH 03824

Contact Information:
Telephone: 603-862-1831
Fax: 603-862-4198
E-mail: drs@cisunix.unh.edu
Web: www.unh.edu

Program Information:
Program begins: September
Degrees offered: Bachelor's, 48 months

Application Information:
Enrollment of program: 44
Transfer students are accepted.

Financial Information:
Tuition, resident: $6,000
Tuition, non-resident: $15,000
Average cost of books: $400

Employment Profile:
% of students who pass the boards on their first try: 75
% employed within the first 6 months following graduation: 80
Average starting salary: $23,000

New Jersey

Kean University
Department of Physical Education, Recreation & Health
Kean University PO Box 411
Union, NJ 07083

Contact Information:
Telephone: 908-527-2103
Fax: 908-353-7199
E-mail: gbkuatc@fast.net
Web: www.kean.edu

Program Information:
Program begins: September
Degrees offered: Bachelor's, 32 months

Application Information:
Enrollment of program: 20
Transfer students are accepted.

Financial Information:
Tuition, resident: $1,544
Tuition, non-resident: $2,144
Average cost of books: $600

Employment Profile:
% of students who pass the boards on their first try: 65
% employed within the first 6 months following graduation: 50

William Paterson University of New Jersey
300 Pompton Road
Wayne, NJ 07470

Contact Information:
Telephone: 973-720-2267
Fax: 973-720-2034
E-mail: middlemasd@wpunj.edu
Web: www.wpunj.edu

Program Information:
Program begins: August, January
Duration of program: 30 months

Application Information:
Enrollment of program: 40
Transfer students are accepted.

Financial Information:
Tuition, resident: $3,380
Tuition, non-resident: $5,360
Average cost of books: $500

Employment Profile:
% of students who pass the boards on their first try: 65
% employed within the first 6 months following graduation: 85
Average starting salary: $33,000

New Mexico

New Mexico State University

Box 30001
Department 3SMC
Las Cruces, NM 88003-0001

Contact Information:
Telephone: 505-646-5038
Fax: 505-646-4065
E-mail: lputman@nmsu.edu
Web: www.nmsu.edu

Program Information:
Program begins: August
Duration of program: 32 months

Application Information:
Enrollment of program: 36
Transfer students are accepted.

Financial Information:
Tuition, resident: $2,196
Tuition, non-resident: $7,152

New York

Canisius College

2001 Main Street
Buffalo, NY 14208-1098

Contact Information:
Telephone: 716-888-2954
Fax: 716-888-3219
E-mail: koehneke@canisius.edu
Web: www.canisius.edu

Program Information:
Program begins: August
Degrees offered: Bachelor's, 36 months

Application Information:
Enrollment of program: 40
Transfer students are accepted.

Financial Information:
Average cost of books: $800
% of students receiving aid: 100

Employment Profile:
% of students who pass the boards on their first try: 85
% employed within the first 6 months following graduation: 100
Average starting salary: $28,000

Hofstra University

220 Hofstra University
Hempstead, NY 11550

Contact Information:
Telephone: 516-463-6952
Fax: 516-463-6275
E-mail: hprssm@hofstra.edu
Web: www.hofstra.edu

Program Information:
Program begins: September, January, June
Duration of program: 32 months

Application Information:
Transfer students are accepted.

Employment Profile:
% employed within the first 6 months following graduation: 100
Average starting salary: $30,000

Ithaca College

Hill Center
Ithaca, NY 14850

Contact Information:
Telephone: 607-274-3178
Fax: 607-274-1943
E-mail: kscriber@ithaca.edu
Web: www.ithaca.edu

Program Information:
Program begins: August
Duration of program: 48 months

Application Information:
Enrollment of program: 75

Financial Information:
Tuition, resident: $16,130
Average cost of books: $500

Employment Profile:
% of students who pass the boards on their first try: 75
% employed within the first 6 months following graduation: 90

Long Island University—CW Post Campus

720 Northern Boulevard
Brookville, NY 11548

Contact Information:
Telephone: 516-299-2744
Fax: 516-299-2858

Program Information:
Program begins: August, January
Duration of program: 24 months
Evening or weekend classes are available.

Application Information:
Enrollment of program: 30
Transfer students are accepted.

Financial Information:
Average cost of books: $500

Employment Profile:
% employed within the first 6 months following graduation: 70
Average starting salary: $30,000

North Carolina

East Carolina University

ECU-Sports Medicine Division
245 Ward Sports Medicine Building
Greenville, NC 27858

Contact Information:
Telephone: 919-328-4560
Fax: 919-328-0097
E-mail: walshk@mail.ecu.edu
Web: www.ecu.edu

Program Information:
Program begins: September
Duration of program: 36 months

Application Information:
Enrollment of program: 52
Transfer students are accepted.

Financial Information:
Tuition, resident: $1,752
Tuition, non-resident: $8,906

University of North Carolina at Chapel Hill

211 Fetzer CB 8700
UNC-Chapel Hall
Chapel Hill, NC 27599-8700

Contact Information:
Telephone: 919-962-5175
Fax: 919-962-0489
E-mail: gus@email.unc.edu

Program Information:
Program begins: September
Degrees offered: Bachelor's, Master's

Application Information:
Enrollment of program: 30
Transfer students are accepted.

Financial Information:
Tuition, resident: $1,348
Tuition, non-resident: $9,917

Employment Profile:
% of students who pass the boards on their first try: 70
% employed within the first 6 months following graduation: 60
Average starting salary: $27,000

North Dakota

University of North Dakota School of Medicine and Health Science

Division of Sports Medicine
Box 9013
Grand Forks, ND 58202-9013

Contact Information:
Telephone: 701-777-3102
Fax: 701-777-4352
E-mail: jrudd@medicine-nodak.edu
Web: www.med.und.nodak.edu

Program Information:
Program begins: September
Duration of program: 36 months

Application Information:
Enrollment of program: 30
Transfer students are accepted.

Financial Information:
Tuition, resident: $2,956
Tuition, non-resident: $7,098
Average cost of books: $600

Ohio

Marietta College
215 Fifth Street
Marietta, OH 45750

Contact Information:
Telephone: 740-376-4773
Fax: 740-376-4405
E-mail: beckettj@marietta.edu
Web: www.marietta.edu

Program Information:
Program begins: August
Duration of program: 9 months

Application Information:
Enrollment of program: 30
Transfer students are accepted.

Financial Information:
Average cost of books: $500
% of students receiving aid: 91

Miami University
PHS Department Room
7 Withrow Court
Oxford, OH 45056

Contact Information:
Telephone: 513-529-7526
Fax: 513-529-5006
E-mail: troescpj@muohio.edu
Web: www.muohio.edu/sportsmedicine/

Program Information:
Program begins: August
Degrees offered: Bachelor's, 36 months

Application Information:
Enrollment of program: 40
Transfer students are accepted.

Financial Information:
Tuition, resident: $4,810
Tuition, non-resident: $5,157
Average cost of books: $350

Employment Profile:
% of students who pass the boards on their first try: 25
% employed within the first 6 months following graduation: 75
Average starting salary: $25,000

Mount Union College
1972 Clark Avenue
Alliance, OH 44601

Contact Information:
Telephone: 330-823-4882
Fax: 330-823-2399
E-mail: gormandm@muc.edu
Web: www.muc.edu

Program Information:
Program begins: August
Degrees offered: Bachelor's, 48 months

Application Information:
Enrollment of program: 35
Transfer students are accepted.

Financial Information:
Average cost of books: $2,100
% of students receiving aid: 90

Employment Profile:
% of students who pass the boards on their first try: 55
% employed within the first 6 months following graduation: 95
Average starting salary: $23,000

Ohio Northern University
525 South Main Street
Ada, OH 45810

Contact Information:
Telephone: 419-772-2443
Fax: 419-772-2470
E-mail: m-glon@onu.edu
Web: www.onu.edu

Program Information:
Program begins: Program begins quarterly.
Duration of program: 27 months

Application Information:
Enrollment of program: 21
Transfer students are accepted.

Financial Information:
Average cost of books: $1,000

Employment Profile:
% of students who pass the boards on their first try: 17
% employed within the first 6 months following graduation: 80
Additional information: Application fee can be waived if the student visits the campus before December 15.

Pennsylvania

California University of Pennsylvania
250 University Avenue
California, PA 15419

Contact Information:
Telephone: 724-938-4562
Fax: 724-938-4342
E-mail: barnhart@cup.edu
Web: www.cup.edu

Program Information:
Program begins: August
Duration of program: 45 months
Evening or weekend classes are available.

Application Information:
Enrollment of program: 140
Transfer students are accepted.

Financial Information:
Tuition, resident: $1,684
Tuition, non-resident: $4,283
Average cost of books: $600

Employment Profile:
% of students who pass the boards on their first try: 50
% employed within the first 6 months following graduation: 95
Average starting salary: $23,000

Duquesne University
123 Health Sciences Building
Pittsburgh, PA 15282

Contact Information:
Telephone: 412-396-4766
Fax: 412-396-4160
E-mail: sammaron@duq2.cc.duq.edu
Web: www.duq.edu

Program Information:
Program begins: August, January
Duration of program: 32 months

Application Information:
Enrollment of program: 100
Transfer students are accepted.

Financial Information:
Average cost of books: $400

Employment Profile:
% of students who pass the boards on their first try: 70
% employed within the first 6 months following graduation: 100
Average starting salary: $27,000

East Stroudsburg University
200 Prospect Street
East Stroudsburg, PA 18301

Contact Information:
Telephone: 570-422-3065
Fax: 570-422-3306
E-mail: jthatch@esu.edu
Web: www.esu.edu

Program Information:
Program begins: August, January
Degrees offered: Bachelor's, 48 months

Application Information:
Enrollment of program: 40
Transfer students are accepted.

Financial Information:
Tuition, resident: $3,368
Tuition, non-resident: $8,566
Average cost of books: $500
% of students receiving aid: 55

Employment Profile:
% of students who pass the boards on their first try: 52

% employed within the first 6 months following graduation: 75
Average starting salary: $25,000

Temple University
1801 North Broad Street
Philadelphia, PA 19122

Contact Information:
Telephone: 215-204-8836
Fax: 215-204-8705
E-mail: kswanik@unix.temple.edu
Web: www.temple.edu

Program Information:
Program begins: August, January
Duration of program: 48 months

Application Information:
Enrollment of program: 32
Transfer students are accepted.

Financial Information:
Tuition, resident: $6,332
Tuition, non-resident: $11,450
Average cost of books: $800
% of students receiving aid: 42

Waynesburg College
51 West College Street
Waynesburg, PA 15370

Contact Information:
Telephone: 724-852-3295
Fax: 724-852-4122
E-mail: kalberta@waynesburg.edu
Web: www.waynesburg.edu

Program Information:
Program begins: September, January, May
Duration of program: 16 months

Application Information:
Transfer students are accepted.

Financial Information:
Average cost of books: $300

Employment Profile:
% of students who pass the boards on their first try: 40
% employed within the first 6 months following graduation: 70
Average starting salary: $26,000

West Chester University
Department of Sports Medicine
Messikomer Hall, Rosedale Avenue
West Chester, PA 19383

Contact Information:
Telephone: 610-436-2969
Fax: 610-436-2803
E-mail: cjimenez@wcupa.edu
Web: www.wcupa.edu

Program Information:
Program begins: August
Duration of program: 45 months

Application Information:
Enrollment of program: 54

Financial Information:
Tuition, resident: $3,468
Tuition, non-resident: $8,824

South Dakota

South Dakota State University
Department of HPER—PEC 265
Brookings, SD 57007

Contact Information:
Telephone: 605-688-5824
Fax: 605-688-5999
E-mail: james_booher@sdstate.edu
Web: www.sdstate.edu

Program Information:
Program begins: September
Duration of program: 24 months

Application Information:
Enrollment of program: 38
Transfer students are accepted.

Financial Information:
Tuition, resident: $1,207
Tuition, non-resident: $2,310

Employment Profile:
% of students who pass the boards on their first try: 40

Tennessee

David Lipscomb University
3901 Granny White Pike
Nashville, TN 37204-3951

Contact Information:
Telephone: 615-279-5700
Fax: 615-269-1806
E-mail: adams_dl@lipscomb.edu
Web: www.lipscomb.edu

Program Information:
Program begins: January
Duration of program: 28 months

Financial Information:
Tuition, resident: $5,852
Tuition, non-resident: $8,430

Texas

Southwest Texas State University
601 University Drive
San Marcos, TX 78666

Contact Information:
Telephone: 512-245-2938
Fax: 512-245-8678
E-mail: rp03@swt.edu
Web: www.swt.edu

Program Information:
Program begins: August
Duration of program: 48 months

Application Information:
Enrollment of program: 38
Transfer students are accepted.

Financial Information:
Tuition, resident: $1,107
Tuition, non-resident: $3,675
Average cost of books: $250

Employment Profile:
% of students who pass the boards on their first try: 50
% employed within the first 6 months following graduation: 80
Average starting salary: $31,000

Utah

Brigham Young University
1137 SFH
Provo, UT 84602

Contact Information:
Telephone: 801-378-4670
Fax: 801-378-3665
E-mail: gaye_merrill@byu.edu
Web: www.byu.edu

Program Information:
Program begins: September
Duration of program: 32 months

Application Information:
Enrollment of program: 110
Transfer students are accepted.

Financial Information:
Tuition, resident: $2,720
Tuition, non-resident: $4,080
Average cost of books: $1,000

Employment Profile:
% of students who pass the boards on their first try: 63

Vermont

University of Vermont
Sports Therapy/Patrick Gymnasium
Spear Street
Burlington, VT 05405

Contact Information:
Telephone: 802-656-7678
Fax: 802-656-0949
E-mail: kculpo@zoo.uvm.edu
Web: www.uvm.edu

Program Information:
Program begins: August
Duration of program: 36 months

Financial Information:
Tuition, resident: $7,464
Tuition, non-resident: $18,672

West Virginia

Marshall University

College of Education & Human Services
400 Hal Greer Bôulevard
Huntington, WV 25755

Contact Information:
Telephone: 304-696-2412
Fax: 304-696-2928
E-mail: martind@marshall.edu
Web: www.marshall.edu

Program Information:
Program begins: August
Duration of program: 48 months
Evening or weekend classes are available.

Application Information:
Enrollment of program: 20
Transfer students are accepted.

Financial Information:
Tuition, resident: $2,184
Tuition, non-resident: $4,076
Average cost of books: $750
% of students receiving aid: 65

Employment Profile:
% of students who pass the boards on their first try: 70
% employed within the first 6 months following graduation: 80
Average starting salary: $27,500

West Virginia University

PO Box 6116 Coliseum
Morgantown, WV 26506

Contact Information:
Telephone: 304-293-3295 ext. 5148
Fax: 304-293-4641
E-mail: vstilger@wvu.edu
Web: www.wvu.edu

Program Information:
Program begins: August
Duration of program: 36 months

Application Information:
Enrollment of program: 34
Transfer students are accepted.

Financial Information:
Tuition, resident: $2,128
Tuition, non-resident: $6,370
Average cost of books: $500
% of students receiving aid: 50

Employment Profile:
% of students who pass the boards on their first try: 60
% employed within the first 6 months following graduation: 100
Average starting salary: $27,500

Wisconsin

University Wisconsin—LaCrosse-Gundersen Mayo

135 Mitchell Hall
La Crosse, WI 54601

Contact Information:
Telephone: 608-785-8190
Fax: 608-785-8172
E-mail: gibso_mh@mail.uwlax.edu
Web: www.perth.uwlax.edu

Program Information:
Program begins: September, January
Duration of program: 33 months

Application Information:
Enrollment of program: 51
Transfer students are accepted.

Financial Information:
Tuition, resident: $3,239
Tuition, non-resident: $10,103
Average cost of books: $150
% of students receiving aid: 53

Employment Profile:
% of students who pass the boards on their first try: 80
% employed within the first 6 months following graduation: 100
Average starting salary: $28,000

Cardiovascular Technologist

Andrea Reiley-Helzner, MS, RCIS
Program Director
Cardiovascular Technology
Gwynedd-Mercy College
Gwynedd Valley, Pennsylvania

Job Description

What Do They Do?

A CVT is a highly specialized and knowledgeable healthcare professional who is educated and trained to perform diagnostic procedures in order to document the presence and degree of cardiac (heart) or vascular (blood vessel) disease. A CVT can specialize in noninvasive cardiovascular testing, invasive cardiovascular testing, or vascular ultrasound.

The noninvasive technologist usually works one-on-one with the patient. The invasive CVT is part of a team of specialized individuals who work in cardiac catheterization laboratories under the direction of a physician. An invasive CVT's duties include, but are not limited to: assisting the physician during the procedure, monitoring and recording heart blood pressure and ECG tracings, and administering cardiovascular drugs.

Type of Person

CVTs must be highly responsible and organized people who can perform well even during stressful emergency situations. They should be able to work both independently and as part of a team and must possess good written and verbal communication skills. Good physical conditioning is essential since the work often requires walking, standing, lifting, and pushing heavy equipment. Good color and depth perception and the ability to work in the dark are also necessary physical standards.

With Whom Do They Work?

CVTs work with physicians, physician assistants, nurses, radiologic technologists, and nuclear technologists.

Employment

Places of Employment

Invasive CVTs work primarily in hospitals; however, the number of cardiac catheterization laboratories in outpatient diagnostic centers is growing. This has led to new job opportunities for CVTs outside the hospital setting. Noninvasive CVTs may work in hospitals, outpatient diagnostic centers, doctor's offices, and mobile diagnostic units.

Employment Outlook

As people age, they are more likely to develop cardiac and vascular disease. Since our aging population is expanding and Medicare and other third-party payers are requiring that laboratories employ credentialed (registered) cardiovascular technologists, employment opportunities for cardiovascular technologists are increasing.

Salary

Salaries are commensurate with experience and geographic location. The last salary survey was conducted by the Society of Vascular Technology in 1995. The median yearly income of vascular technologists was $38,140 with a range of less than $20,000 to greater than $60,000. [1]

Educational Programs

Length

Programs vary in length. Individuals who have had no education or training beyond the high school level may expect to attend a 24-month program of study. This includes one year of general education and training followed by an additional year of education and training for each area of specialization.

Prerequisites

Minimum requirements are a high school diploma or its equivalent with a strong math and science background.

Curriculum

The usual curriculum incorporates studies in the liberal arts and sciences along with specialization lecture and laboratory courses. Students also participate in clinical educational experiences.

Accrediting Body

The following organization accredits cardiovascular technology educational programs:

Joint Review Committee on Education
in Cardiovascular Technology
3525 Ellicott Mills Drive, Suite N
Ellicott City, MD 21043-44547
Telephone: 410-418-4800
Fax: 410-418-4805
E-mail: JRC@assochq.com

Certification Boards

Following successful completion of an accredited educational program, qualified individuals may choose to sit for the appropriate registry examinations. CVTs who specialize in cardiac ultrasound and vascular ultrasound may choose to be registered through Cardiovascular Credentialing International or the American Registry of Diagnostic Medical Sonographers (ARDMS). CVTs who specialize in invasive cardiovascular testing may register through Cardiovascular Credentialing International.

Cardiovascular Credentialing International
4456 Corporation Lane, Suite 120
Virginia Beach, VA 23462
Telephone: 800-326-0268
Fax: 804-628-3259

American Registry of Diagnostic Medical
Sonographers
600 Jefferson Plaza, Suite 360
Rockville, MD 20852-1150
Telephone: 301-738-8401
Fax: 301-738-0312

Advice for Potential Students

Individuals who are interested in pursuing careers in cardiovascular technology must be goal-oriented and dedicated to study. If you are interested in pursuing cardiovascular technology, be sure to schedule an appointment with the program director at the schools in which you are interested.

For Additional Information

Organizations

Alliance of Cardiovascular Professionals
910 Charles Street
Fredericksburg, VA 22401
Telephone: 540-370-0102
Fax: 540-370-0015
E-mail: SeanMcE@aol.com

Society of Invasive Cardiovascular Professionals
950 West Valley Road, Suite 2800
Wayne, PA 19087
Telephone: 800-237-7285

Society of Vascular Technology
4601 President's Drive, Suite 260
Lanham, MD 20706
Telephone: 301-459-7550

Publications

Cath-Lab Digest, Health Management Publications, Inc.Web address: www.cathlab.com

The professional publication for invasive cardiovascular practitioners. (Cath-Lab is the abbreviation for cardiac catheterization laboratory.)

Internet Resources

Society of Diagnostic Medical Sonographers: www.sdms.org
Alliance of Cardiovascular Professionals: www.acp-online.org
American Society of Echocardiography: www.asecho.org
Society of Invasive Cardiovascular Professionals: www.sicp.com

California

Grossmont College

Invasive/Noninvasive
8800 Grossmont College Drive
El Cajon, CA 92020-1799

Contact Information:
Telephone: 619-644-7302
Fax: 619-644-7961
E-mail: rick_kirby@gcccd.cc.net
Web: www.grossmont.gcccd.cc.ca.us

Program Information:
Program begins: September
Duration of program: 24 months

Application Information:
Enrollment of program: 120
Transfer students are accepted.

Financial Information:
Tuition, resident: $636
Tuition, non-resident: $7,260
Average cost of books: $800

Employment Profile:
% of students who pass the boards on their first try: 90
% employed within the first 6 months following graduation: 60
Average starting salary: $30,000

Florida

Edison Community College

Invasive Track
8099 College Parkway Southwest
Ft. Myers, FL 33906

Contact Information:
Telephone: 941-489-9430
Fax: 941-489-9037
E-mail: jdavis@edison.edu
Web: www.edison.edu

Program Information:
Program begins: February
Duration of program: 22 months
Evening or weekend classes are available.

Application Information:
Enrollment of program: 32
Transfer students are accepted.

Financial Information:
Tuition, resident: $1,660
Tuition, non-resident: $6,179
Average cost of books: $500
% of students receiving aid: 40

Employment Profile:
% of students who pass the boards on their first try: 96
% employed within the first 6 months following graduation: 85
Average starting salary: $30,000

Georgia

Augusta Technical Institute—University Hospital

Georgia Heart Institute, Invasive and Noninvasive Tracts
1350 Walton Way
Augusta, GA 30901-2629

Contact Information:
Telephone: 706-774-5044
Fax: 706-774-8644
E-mail: pthomas@uh.org

Program Information:
Program begins: September, January, June
Duration of program: 24 months

Application Information:
Transfer students are accepted.

Financial Information:
Average cost of books: $1,250
% of students receiving aid: 50

Employment Profile:
% of students who pass the boards on their first try: 100
% employed within the first 6 months following graduation: 100
Average starting salary: $30,000

Maryland

Naval School of Health Sciences—Maryland

8901 Wisconsin Avenue
Bethesda, MD 20889-5611

Contact Information:
Telephone: 301-319-4759
Fax: 301-295-0621
E-mail: ggarretson@nsh10.med.navy.mil
Web: www.nshs.med.navy.mil

Program Information:
Program begins: September
Duration of program: 12 months

Employment Profile:
% employed within the first 6 months following graduation: 100
Additional information: Military program, no tuition fees.

Minnesota

Northwest Technical College—East Grand Forks
2022 Central Avenue Northeast
East Grand Forks, MN 56721

Contact Information:
Telephone: 218-773-3441 ext. 423
Fax: 218-773-4502
E-mail: susan.rick@mail.ntc.mnscu.edu
Web: www.ntc-online.com

Program Information:
Program begins: July
Duration of program: 24 months
Evening or weekend classes are available.

Application Information:
Enrollment of program: 10
Transfer students are accepted.

Financial Information:
Tuition, resident: $5,068
Tuition, non-resident: $10,137
Average cost of books: $1,200
% of students receiving aid: 75

Employment Profile:
% of students who pass the boards on their first try: 86
% employed within the first 6 months following graduation: 100
Average starting salary: $32,000

New Jersey

Morristown Memorial Hospital
Invasive/Noninvasive/Vascular Tracks
100 Madison Avenue
Morristown, NJ 07962-1956

Contact Information:
Telephone: 201-971-5096
Fax: 201-540-0336

Program Information:
Program begins: August
Duration of program: 18 months

Financial Information:
Average cost of books: $500

Employment Profile:
% of students who pass the boards on their first try: 99
% employed within the first 6 months following graduation: 98
Average starting salary: $34,000

New York

Molloy College
Invasive/Noninvasive Tracks
1000 Hempstead Avenue
Rockville Centre, NY 11570

Contact Information:
Telephone: 516-255-2438
Fax: 516-255-3270
E-mail: m_buckley@sfhmmc.org
Web: www.molloy.edu

Program Information:
Program begins: August
Degrees offered: Associate's; Bachelor's
Evening or weekend classes are available.

Application Information:
Transfer students are accepted.

Financial Information:
Tuition, non-resident: $10,600
Average cost of books: $900
% of students receiving aid: 50

Employment Profile:
% of students who pass the boards on their first try: 99
% employed within the first 6 months following graduation: 100
Average starting salary: $49,000

Ohio

Cuyahoga Community College
Noninvasive Track
11000 Pleasant Valley Road
Parma, OH 44130

Contact Information:
Telephone: 216-987-5574
Fax: 216-987-5066
E-mail: ed.stacey@tri-c.cc.oh.us
Web: www.tri-c.cc.us

Program Information:
Program begins: June
Duration of program: 22 months

Financial Information:
Tuition, resident: $4,700
Tuition, non-resident: $12,300

University of Toledo
College of Health and Human Services
Department: Health Professions
Toledo, OH 43606

Contact Information:
Telephone: 419-530-3193
Fax: 419-530-3096
E-mail: swambol@utnet.utoledo.edu
Web: www.utoledo.edu

Program Information:
Program begins: September
Degrees offered: Certificate program, 12 months; Associate's, 24 months
Evening or weekend classes are available.

Application Information:
Enrollment of program: 18
Transfer students are accepted.

Financial Information:
Tuition, resident: $4,000
Average cost of books: $300

Employment Profile:
% of students who pass the boards on their first try: 70
% employed within the first 6 months following graduation: 80
Average starting salary: $30,000

Pennsylvania

Gwynedd-Mercy College
Invasive/Noninvasive Tracks
Sumneytown Pike
Gwynedd Valley, PA 19437

Contact Information:
Telephone: 215-646-7300 ext. 476
Fax: 215-641-5559
E-mail: reiley.a@gmc.edu
Web: www.gmc.edu

Program Information:
Program begins: August
Degrees offered: Associate's, 24 months; Bachelor's, 48 months
Evening or weekend classes are available.

Application Information:
Enrollment of program: 20
Transfer students are accepted.

Financial Information:
Average cost of books: $250
% of students receiving aid: 90

Employment Profile:
% of students who pass the boards on their first try: 90
% employed within the first 6 months following graduation: 100
Average starting salary: $35,000

Lancaster Institute for Health Education
Invasive Track
555 North Duke Street/PO Box 3555
Lancaster, PA 17604-3555

Contact Information:
Telephone: 717-290-5511 ext. 4700
Fax: 717-290-5970
E-mail: wlfisher@lha.org
Web: www.lha.org

Program Information:
Program begins: August, June
Duration of program: 12 months

Financial Information:
Tuition, resident: $5,000

Penn State Geisinger Health System

Invasive Track
100 North Academy Avenue
Danville, PA 17822-2011

Contact Information:

Telephone: 570-271-6638
Fax: 570-271-5962
E-mail: dandreasen@psghs.edu
Web: www.cathlab.com

Program Information:

Program begins: August
Duration of program: 12 months

Financial Information:

Average cost of books: $300

Employment Profile:

% of students who pass the boards on their first try: 95

South Dakota

Southeast Technical Institute

Invasive/Noninvasive/Vascular Tracks
2301 Career Place
Sioux Falls, SD 57107

Contact Information:

Telephone: 605-367-8459
Fax: 605-367-6108
E-mail: townlrar@sti.tec.sd.us
Web: www.sti.tec.sd.us

Program Information:

Program begins: August
Duration of program: 24 months

Employment Profile:

% employed within the first 6 months following graduation: 98
Average starting salary: $30,000

Texas

El Centro College

Invasive & Echocardiology Tracks
Main and Lamar Streets
Dallas, TX 75202-3604

Contact Information:

Telephone: 214-860-2314
Fax: 214-860-2268
E-mail: kam5527@dcccd.edu
Web: www.ecc.deeed.edu

Program Information:

Program begins: September
Duration of program: 22 months

Application Information:

Enrollment of program: 8
Transfer students are accepted.

Financial Information:

Tuition, resident: $1,600
Tuition, non-resident: $3,700
Average cost of books: $500
% of students receiving aid: 90

Employment Profile:

% of students who pass the boards on their first try: 100
% employed within the first 6 months following graduation: 99
Average starting salary: $33,000

Virginia

Sentara Norfolk General Hospital

Invasive/Noninvasive/Vascular Tracks
600 Gresham Drive
Norfolk, VA 23507

Contact Information:

Telephone: 757-628-2827
Fax: 757-668-2905
E-mail: klbutter@sentara.com
Web: www.sentara.com

Program Information:

Program begins: August
Duration of program: 18 months

Application Information:

Enrollment of program: 22

Financial Information:

Average cost of books: $300

Employment Profile:

% of students who pass the boards on their first try: 88
% employed within the first 6 months following graduation: 100
Average starting salary: $27,500

Clinical Laboratory Technician and Scientist

Susan J. Beck, PhD, CLS (NCA)
Director, Division of Clinical Laboratory Science
Department of Allied Health Sciences
University of North Carolina at Chapel

Job Description

What Do They Do?

There are two main levels of employment in clinical laboratory science—the clinical laboratory technician (CLT), also called medical laboratory technician (MLT) and the clinical laboratory scientist (CLS), also called medical technologist (MT).

Clinical laboratory technicians perform routine laboratory tests in blood banking (finding compatible blood for transfusion), clinical chemistry, hematology (evaluating red cells, white cells and platelets for evidence of disease), and microbiology. They often work under the supervision of a clinical laboratory scientist or laboratory director. Examples of a clinical laboratory technician's responsibilities include:

- Detecting the abnormal cells that cause leukemia
- Analyzing cardiac enzyme activity released during a heart attack
- Identifying the type of bacteria causing an infection
- Performing blood typing for transfusions

Clinical laboratory scientists perform both routine and specialized laboratory tests, ensure the quality of the test results, explain the significance of laboratory tests, evaluate new methods, study the effectiveness of laboratory tests, and supervise others who are performing laboratory tests. Examples of a clinical laboratory scientist's responsibilities include:

- Establishing quality assurance procedures for laboratory tests
- Identifying antibodies and finding compatible donors for blood transfusions
- Detecting the DNA sequences that indicate genetic diseases
- Teaching students and new employees
- Consulting with physicians on appropriate laboratory testing protocols

Type of Person

Clinical laboratory practitioners have good communication skills, are organized, take an analytical approach to problems, can handle many assignments at one time, and are dedicated to providing quality laboratory results.

With Whom Do They Work?

Clinical Laboratory practitioners work most often with physicians, nurses, and other laboratory professionals.

Employment

Places of Employment

Clinical laboratory scientists and clinical laboratory technicians are employed as generalists and specialists in a variety of laboratory settings. Generalists work in many sections of the clinical laboratory and are often found in small to medium sized hospitals. In larger institutions, clinical laboratory professionals may specialize in one area. Some specialties include microbiology, hematology, blood banking, chemistry, molecular biology (diagnostic testing based on DNA methods) , histocompatibility (matching patients and donors for organ transplantation) , virology (identifying viruses that cause disease), immunology (identifying antibodies and antigens related to disease), or quality assurance (using statistics to ensure the quality of results). With experience, clinical laboratory scientists may become laboratory managers, administrators and directors. Clinical laboratory professionals may also find employment in research laboratories, pharmaceutical companies, companies that manufacture and market laboratory instruments and supplies, contract research organizations, forensic (crime) laboratories, and veterinary laboratories.

Employment Outlook

The current employment outlook is excellent and most graduates of educational programs find jobs easily. The increased use of automated instruments in most laboratories has replaced many manual laboratory tests, yet automation has not resulted in fewer employment opportunities. Automation has reduced repetitive work and has given laboratory practitioners more time to perform complex tests, solve problems, and improve services. The future employment outlook in any healthcare profession is difficult to predict because changes in financing and regulations can cause rapid changes in the employment situation; however, the important role that laboratory testing and services play in the majority of medical diagnoses suggests a continued need for qualified laboratory practitioners.

Salary

The Medical Laboratory Observer (MLO) conducted a national survey of clinical laboratory practitioners in 1998. The median salary for clinical laboratory technicians (medical laboratory technicians) was $29,414 with a range of $15,500 to $57,000. The median salary for clinical laboratory scientists (medical technologists) was $38,395 with a range of $15,360 to $76,000. In 1997, the MLO salary survey also included laboratory managers who had a median salary of $45,280 (with a range of $17,000 to $85,000) and non-MD laboratory directors who reported a median salary of $62,766 (with a range of $20,400 to $160,000).[1, 2]

Educational Programs

Length

Clinical laboratory technicians complete two-year Associate's degree programs that include general education courses, courses in the major areas of clinical laboratory science and clinical rotations.

Clinical laboratory scientists complete four-year Bachelor's degree programs. Most clinical laboratory science Bachelor's degree programs are described as 3+1, 4+1 or 2+2. The numbers refer to the number of years that students spend in general education courses and in professional (clinical laboratory) courses. In 3+1 and 4+1 programs, students complete 3 or 4 years of prerequisite science courses and other general college requirements and a 1-year clinical rotation. In 2+2 programs, students complete 2 years of general education course and then begin 2 years of professional courses in clinical laboratory science. The first year of the professional curriculum includes lecture and laboratory courses covering all of the major areas of clinical laboratory practice. In the second professional year, students complete rotations in clinical laboratories where they apply their knowledge and skills in practical settings. Master's degree programs are available for practitioners who wish to specialize in a scientific area of laboratory practice, in education, or in laboratory management. Some entry-level Master's degree programs in CLS are available. For additional information on these Master's degree programs, contact the ASCLS.

Prerequisites

Applicants to Associate's degree Clinical Laboratory Technician programs must have a high school diploma and must meet the requirements of the community college offering the Associate's degree program. Students usually apply to Clinical Laboratory Science programs after they have been accepted to a college or university.

Curriculum

Clinical Laboratory Technician students generally complete one year of general education, science and math courses and then progress to professional courses and clinical rotations in chemistry, hematology, microbiology, and blood bank. The curriculum covers the routine testing that is performed in the clinical laboratory.

Clinical Laboratory Science students complete general education courses and prerequisite courses in biology, chemistry, and math before applying to a professional program. The CLS curriculum covers both routine and specialized procedures performed in the clinical laboratory. In addition, the CLS curriculum addresses laboratory management, education, and information systems.

Accrediting Body

The National Accrediting Agency for Clinical Laboratory Sciences (NAACLS) evaluates and accredits CLT/MLT and CLS/MT programs. Students in accredited programs can be assured that the curriculum, faculty, and clinical experiences meet the standards established by the profession. Graduation from an accredited program is often a requirement for certification examinations.

National Accrediting Agency for Clinical Laboratory Sciences
8410 West Bryn Mawr Avenue, Suite 670
Chicago, IL 60631-3415
Telephone: 773-714-8880
Fax: 773-714-8886
E-mail: naaclsinfo@naacls.org
Web address: www.naacls.org

Certification Board

Certification is a process by which an individual's qualifications are recognized by a non-governmental organization or agency. The purpose of certification is to assure the public and employers that individuals are competent to practice in the profession. After completion of an educational program, graduates are eligible to take national certification examinations. There are several agencies that certify laboratory personnel as generalists in the United States. They include the National Credentialing Agency for Laboratory Personnel (NCA), the American Society for Clinical Pathology (ASCP), and the American Medical Technologists (AMT).

Title / Certification	Educational Level
Clinical Laboratory Technician CLT (NCA)	Associate Degree
Clinical Laboratory Scientist CLS (NCA)	Baccalaureate Degree
Medical Laboratory Technician MLT (ASCP)	Associate Degree
Medical Technologist MT (ASCP)	Baccalaureate Degree
Medical Technologist MT (AMT)	Baccalaureate Degree

After acquiring additional experience and expertise, clinical laboratory scientists may seek advanced certification in their area of interest. Although certification is a voluntary process, most employers prefer to hire certified practitioners.

National Credentialing Agency for Laboratory Personnel
PO Box 15945-289
Lenexa, KS 66285
Telephone: 913-438-5110 ext. 647
Fax: 913-541-0156
E-mail: NCA-INFO@applmeapro.com
Web address: www.nca-info.org

ASCP Board of Registry
PO Box 12277
Chicago, IL 60612-0277
Telephone: 800-621-4142, press 4
in Illinois 312-738-1336, ext.1430
Fax: 312-738-5808.
E-mail: bor@ascp.org
Web address: www.ascp.org

American Medical Technologists
710 Higgins Road
Park Ridge, IL 60068-5765
Telephone: 847-823-5169
Fax: 847-823-0458

Licensure

Licensure is granted by individual states. A growing number of states have enacted licensure regulations for laboratory personnel. Listed below is contact information for states that require licensure:

California Department of Health Services: 510-873-6327

Florida Board of Clinical Laboratory Personnel: 850-487-3240

Georgia Department of Human Resources – Office of Regulatory Services: 404-657-5450

Hawaii Department of Health – State Laboratory Division: 808-453-6653

Louisiana Clinical Laboratory Science Department – Northeast Louisiana University: 318-342-1632

Montana Board of Clinical Laboratory Science Practitioners: 406-444-3561

Nevada Bureau of Licensure and Certification: 702-687-4475

North Dakota Department of Health: 701-328-5262

Puerto Rico Department of Public Health: 787-792-6400

Rhode Island Department of Health – Laboratory and Licensure Certifi cation: 401-222-4526

Tennessee Medical Laboratory Board Personnel: 615-532-5126

West Virginia Department of Health and Human Resources – Office of Laboratory Services: 304-558-3530. [3]

Advice for Potential Students

Students interested in clinical laboratory science should learn all they can about the profession by visiting a hospital laboratory, talking with a laboratory practitioner, contacting state professional organizations, and meeting with educational program directors. People who like to solve problems, enjoy science, have a desire to help people, and want to enter a health profession with an Associate's or Baccalaureate degree often find that the clinical laboratory profession is a good match for their talents and interests.

For Additional Information

Organizations

The American Society for Clinical Laboratory Science
7910 Woodmont Avenue, Suite 530
Bethesda, MD 20814
Telephone: 301-657-2768
Fax: 301-657-2909
E-mail: ascls@ascls.org
Web address: www.ascls.org

Publications

Books

Beck, S.J., and LeGrys V.A. *Clinical Laboratory Education.* Dubuque, IA: Kendall/Hunt Publishing Company, 1996.

Karni, K. *Opportunities in Medical Technology* (Clinical Laboratory Science). Lincolnwood, IL: VGM Career Horizons, NTC Publishing Group, 1997.

A book that describes the clinical laboratory profession and career opportunities.

Journals

Advance for Medical Laboratory Professionals. Merion Publications, 2900 Horizon Drive, King of Prussia, PA 19406. www.advanceweb.com

A biweekly magazine that covers current topics in clinical laboratory science.

Clinical Laboratory Science. The American Society for Clinical Laboratory Science, 7910 Woodmont Avenue, Suite 530, Bethesda, MD 20814. www.ascls.org

The official journal of the American Society for Clinical Laboratory Science.

Internet Resources

The American Society for Clinical Laboratory Science: www.ascls.org
Clinical Laboratory Scientists of Alaska: www.mosquitonet.com/~clsa/
California Society for Clinical Laboratory Science: www.access1.net/bshan/
Georgia Society for Clinical Laboratory Science: www.gscls.armstrong.edu
Hawaii Society for Clinical Laboratory Science: www2.hawaii.edu/medtech/HSCLS/hscls.html
Idaho Society for Clinical Laboratory Science: www.constance.com/idscls/
Illinois Clinical Laboratory Science Association: www.ASCLSRegionVI.org/iclsa/index.html
Iowa Association for Clinical Laboratory Science: ourworld.compuserve.com/homepages/Kumor
Kansas Society for Clinical Laboratory Science: www.kumc.edu/ASCLS/kscls/index.html
Louisiana Society for Clinical Laboratory Science: www.gnofn.org/~lscls/
Michigan Society for Clinical Laboratory Science: www.ferris.edu/htmls/academics/course.offerings/clinlabs/mscls/homepage.htm

Missouri Organization for Clinical Laboratory Science: www.ASCLSRegionVI.org/mocls/index.html
Montana Society for Clinical Laboratory Science: www.mtscls.org
Nebraska Society for Clinical Laboratory Science: www.ASCLSRegionVI.org/nscls/index.html
New York Society for Clinical Laboratory Science: www.medtechnet.com/nyscls/
Pennsylvania Society for Clinical Laboratory Science: www.pscls.org
South Carolina Society for Clinical Laboratory Science: www.octech.org/scscls/welcome.htm
Tennessee Society for Clinical Laboratory Science: www.utmem.edu/ASCLS/TSCLS/Home.html
Vermont Society for Clinical Laboratory Science: www.vtmednet.org/vscls/
Virginia Society for Clinical Laboratory Science: vscls.vavalleyweb.com
West Virginia Society for Clinical Laboratory Science: nccvax.northern.wvnet.edu/~wvscls/
Wisconsin Society for Clinical Laboratory Science: wiscls1.uwsp.edu

Clinical Laboratory Technician

Alabama

Wallace State Community College

PO Box 2000
Hanceville, AL 35077-2000

Contact Information:
Telephone: 256-352-8347
Fax: 256-352-8320
E-mail: jhewes@aol.com
Web: www.wscc.cc.al.us

Program Information:
Program begins: August, January
Degrees offered: Associate's, 19 months

Application Information:
Enrollment of program: 34
Transfer students are accepted.

Financial Information:
Tuition, resident: $1,200
Tuition, non-resident: $2,400
% of students receiving aid: 90

Employment Profile:
% of students who pass the boards on their first try: 90
% employed within the first 6 months following graduation: 100
Average starting salary: $23,000

Arkansas

Garland County Community College

101 College Drive
Hot Springs, AR 71913-9174

Contact Information:
Telephone: 501-760-4278
Fax: 501-760-4100
E-mail: jwilborn@admin.gccc.cc.ar.us
Web: www.gccc.cc.ar.us

Program Information:
Program begins: August
Degrees offered: Associate's, 18 months

Application Information:
Enrollment of program: 20
Transfer students are accepted.

Financial Information:
Tuition, resident: $888
Tuition, non-resident: $1,104
% of students receiving aid: 50

Employment Profile:
% of students who pass the boards on their first try: 80
% employed within the first 6 months following graduation: 90
Average starting salary: $21,120

North Arkansas College

1515 Pioneer Drive
Harrison, AR 72601-5599

Contact Information:
Telephone: 870-391-3327
Fax: 870-743-5326
E-mail: bmosley@northark.cc.ar.us
Web: www.northark.cc.ar.us

Program Information:
Program begins: Program begins quarterly.
Degrees offered: Associate's, 24 months

Application Information:
Enrollment of program: 20
Transfer students are accepted.

Employment Profile:
% of students who pass the boards on their first try: 79
% employed within the first 6 months following graduation: 70
Average starting salary: $21,800

Phillips Community College/University of Arkansas

PO Box 785
Helena, AR 72342

Contact Information:
Telephone: 870-338-6474 ext. 1116
Fax: 870-338-7542
E-mail: mlocke@pccua.cc.ar.us
Web: www.pccc.cc.ar.us

Program Information:
Program begins: August
Degrees offered: Associate's, 22 months

Application Information:
Transfer students are accepted.

Financial Information:
Tuition, resident: $456
Tuition, non-resident: $1,020

Employment Profile:
% of students who pass the boards on their first try: 90
% employed within the first 6 months following graduation: 90

South Arkansas Community College

300 South West Avenue
El Dorado, AR 71730

Contact Information:
Telephone: 870-862-8131
Fax: 870-864-7122
E-mail: borden@eagle.saccw.cc.ar.us

Program Information:
Program begins: January
Degrees offered: Associate's, 24 months
Evening or weekend classes are available.

Application Information:
Enrollment of program: 20
Transfer students are accepted.

Financial Information:
Tuition, resident: $1,728
Tuition, non-resident: $3,627
Average cost of books: $700
% of students receiving aid: 60

Employment Profile:
% of students who pass the boards on their first try: 80
% employed within the first 6 months following graduation: 100
Average starting salary: $19,200

Colorado

Arapahoe Community College

2500 West College Drive
PO Box 9002
Littleton, CO 80160-9002

Contact Information:
Telephone: 303-797-5796
Fax: 303-797-5935
E-mail: lcomeaux@arapahoe.edu
Web: www.arapahoe.edu

Program Information:
Program begins: September, January
Degrees offered: Associate's, 24 months
Evening or weekend classes are available.

Application Information:
Transfer students are accepted.

Financial Information:
Tuition, resident: $3,530
Tuition, non-resident: $15,400

Employment Profile:
% of students who pass the boards on their first try: 98
% employed within the first 6 months following graduation: 75
Average starting salary: $23,000

Connecticut

Housatonic Community College

900 Lafayette Boulevard
Bridgeport, CT 06604-4704

Contact Information:
Telephone: 203-332-5106
Fax: 203-332-5123
E-mail: ho_gutowski@commnet.edu
Web: www.hctc.commnet.edu

Program Information:
Program begins: August
Degrees offered: Associate's, 21 months
Evening or weekend classes are available.

Application Information:
Transfer students are accepted.

Financial Information:
Tuition, resident: $1,814
Tuition, non-resident: $5,438

Employment Profile:
% of students who pass the boards on their first try: 100

Manchester Community-Technical College

60 Bidwell Street MS 29
PO Box 1046
Manchester, CT 06045-1046

Contact Information:
Telephone: 860-647-6190
Fax: 860-647-6370
E-mail: ma_digan@commnet.edu
Web: www.commnet.edu

Program Information:
Program begins: September
Degrees offered: Associate's, 23 months

Application Information:
Enrollment of program: 23
Transfer students are accepted.

Financial Information:
Tuition, resident: $1,814
Tuition, non-resident: $5,438

Florida

Brevard Community College

1519 Clearlake Road
Cocoa, FL 32922

Contact Information:
Telephone: 407-632-1111 ext. 64361
Fax: 407-634-3731
E-mail: hulmem@brevard.cc.fl.us
Web: www.brevard.cc.fl.us

Program Information:
Program begins: August
Degrees offered: Associate's, 22 months

Application Information:
Enrollment of program: 10
Transfer students are accepted.

Financial Information:
Tuition, resident: $3,420
Tuition, non-resident: $10,488
Average cost of books: $300
% of students receiving aid: 60

Employment Profile:
% of students who pass the boards on their first try: 80
% employed within the first 6 months following graduation: 100
Average starting salary: $22,000

David G. Erwin Technical Center

2010 East Hillsborough Avenue
Tampa, FL 33610-8299

Contact Information:
Telephone: 813-231-1800 ext. 2426
Fax: 813-231-1820
E-mail: dickson-1-@popmail.firn.edu
Web: www.erwintech.org

Program Information:
Program begins: August, February
Degrees offered: Certificate program, 14 months

Application Information:
Enrollment of program: 18

Financial Information:
Tuition, resident: $1,024
Tuition, non-resident: $6,825

Employment Profile:
% of students who pass the boards on their first try: 100
% employed within the first 6 months following graduation: 50
Average starting salary: $22,000

Lake City Community College

Rte 19 PO Box 1030
Lake City, FL 32025

Contact Information:
Telephone: 904-752-1822 ext. 1157
Fax: 904-758-9959
E-mail: vansiclenc@mail.lakecity.cc.fl.us
Web: www.lakecity.cc.fl.us

Program Information:
Program begins: August
Degrees offered: Associate's, 24 months
Evening or weekend classes are available.

Application Information:
Enrollment of program: 24
Transfer students are accepted.

Financial Information:
Tuition, resident: $1,396
Tuition, non-resident: $4,188
Average cost of books: $500
% of students receiving aid: 68

Employment Profile:
% of students who pass the boards on their first try: 90
% employed within the first 6 months following graduation: 50
Average starting salary: $19,200

Miami-Dade Community College

Medical Center Campus
950 Northwest 20th Street
Miami, FL 33127

Contact Information:
Telephone: 305-237-4434
Fax: 305-237-4278
E-mail: bamole@mdcc.edu
Web: www.mdcc.edu

Program Information:
Program begins: August
Degrees offered: Associate's, 24 months
Evening or weekend classes are available.

Application Information:
Enrollment of program: 60
Transfer students are accepted.

Financial Information:
Tuition, resident: $1,898
Tuition, non-resident: $6,670
% of students receiving aid: 50

Employment Profile:
% of students who pass the boards on their first try: 77
Average starting salary: $24,000

Sheridan Vocational Technical Center

5400 Sheridan Street
Hollywood, FL 33021

Contact Information:
Telephone: 954-985-3280
Fax: 954-985-3229
E-mail: pjd2@aol.com

Program Information:
Program begins: August, February
Degrees offered: Certificate program, 12 months

Application Information:
Enrollment of program: 60
Transfer students are accepted.

Financial Information:
Tuition, resident: $1,800

Tuition, non-resident: $5,633
Average cost of books: $300

Employment Profile:
% of students who pass the boards on their first try: 80
% employed within the first 6 months following graduation: 90
Average starting salary: $24,000

St. Petersburg Junior College
PO Box 13489
St. Petersburg, FL 33733-3489

Contact Information:
Telephone: 727-341-3714
Fax: 727-341-3744
E-mail: polanskyv@spjc.edu
Web: www.spj.edu

Program Information:
Program begins: January
Degrees offered: Associate's, 24 months

Application Information:
Enrollment of program: 18
Transfer students are accepted.

Financial Information:
Tuition, resident: $1,741
Tuition, non-resident: $6,330

Employment Profile:
% of students who pass the boards on their first try: 100
% employed within the first 6 months following graduation: 100
Average starting salary: $21,000

Georgia

Coastal Georgia Community College
3700 Altama Avenue
Brunswick, GA 31523

Contact Information:
Telephone: 912-264-7382
Fax: 912-262-3283
E-mail: nzell@bc9000.bc.peachnet.edu
Web: www.coastal.cc.nc.us

Program Information:
Program begins: August
Degrees offered: Associate's, 21 months

Application Information:
Enrollment of program: 20
Transfer students are accepted.

Financial Information:
Tuition, resident: $1,708
Tuition, non-resident: $5,940
Average cost of books: $300
% of students receiving aid: 60

Employment Profile:
% of students who pass the boards on their first try: 85
% employed within the first 6 months following graduation: 90
Average starting salary: $25,000

Dalton College
213 North College Drive
Dalton, GA 30720

Contact Information:
Telephone: 706-272-4512 ext. 257
Fax: 706-272-2517
E-mail: dshoemaker@carpet.dalton.peachnet.edu
Web: www.dalton.peachnet.edu

Program Information:
Program begins: August
Degrees offered: Associate's, 24 months

Application Information:
Enrollment of program: 29
Transfer students are accepted.

Financial Information:
Tuition, resident: $1,480
Tuition, non-resident: $5,352
% of students receiving aid: 95

Employment Profile:
% employed within the first 6 months following graduation: 98

Darton College
2400 Gillionville Road
Albany, GA 31707

Contact Information:
Telephone: 912-430-6846
Fax: 912-430-6910
E-mail: beamonn@mail.dartnet.peachnet.edu
Web: www.dartnet.peachnet.edu

Program Information:
Program begins: January, April, August
Degrees offered: Associate's, 24 months

Application Information:
Enrollment of program: 12
Transfer students are accepted.

Financial Information:
Tuition, resident: $1,851
Tuition, non-resident: $5,553

DeKalb Technical Institute
495 North Indian Creek Drive
Clarkston, GA 30021-2397

Contact Information:
Telephone: 404-297-9522 ext. 1179
Fax: 404-294-6290
E-mail: sharon@admin2.dekalb.tec.ga.us
Web: www.dekalb.tec.ga.us

Program Information:
Program begins: October
Degrees offered: Certificate program, 15 months; Diploma, 15 months

Application Information:
Enrollment of program: 24
Transfer students are accepted.

Financial Information:
Tuition, resident: $1,665
Tuition, non-resident: $5,805
Average cost of books: $800
% of students receiving aid: 95

Employment Profile:
% of students who pass the boards on their first try: 99
% employed within the first 6 months following graduation: 100
Average starting salary: $21,800

Okefenokee Technical Institute
1701 Carswell Avenue
Waycross, GA 31501

Contact Information:
Telephone: 912-287-6584
Fax: 912-287-4865
E-mail: ambert@waycross.tech.ga.us
Web: www.waycross.tec.ga.us

Program Information:
Program begins: September
Degrees offered: Certificate program, 15 months

Application Information:
Enrollment of program: 16
Transfer students are accepted.

Financial Information:
Tuition, resident: $1,250
Average cost of books: $500
% of students receiving aid: 100

Employment Profile:
% of students who pass the boards on their first try: 85
% employed within the first 6 months following graduation: 100
Average starting salary: $20,000

Thomas Technical Institute
15689 US Highway 19 North
Thomasville, GA 31792

Contact Information:
Telephone: 912-225-4078
Fax: 912-225-5289
E-mail: rmiller@ttin1.thomas.tec.ga.us
Web: www.thomas.tec

Program Information:
Program begins: August
Degrees offered: Associate's, 24 months

Application Information:
Enrollment of program: 15
Transfer students are accepted.

Financial Information:
Tuition, resident: $1,128
Tuition, non-resident: $2,136
Average cost of books: $1,000
% of students receiving aid: 90

Employment Profile:
% of students who pass the boards on their first try: 70
% employed within the first 6 months following graduation: 90
Average starting salary: $22,000

Hawaii

Kapiolani Community College

Health Sciences Department
4303 Diamond Head Road
Honolulu, HI 96816

Contact Information:

Telephone: 808-734-9231
Fax: 808-734-9126
E-mail: marciaa@hawaii.edu
Web: www.kcc.hawaii.edu

Program Information:

Program begins: June
Degrees offered: Associate's, 21 months

Application Information:

Enrollment of program: 25
Transfer students are accepted.

Financial Information:

Tuition, resident: $1,056
Tuition, non-resident: $6,503
Average cost of books: $400
% of students receiving aid: 75

Employment Profile:

% of students who pass the boards on their first try: 98
% employed within the first 6 months following graduation: 50
Average starting salary: $29,000

Illinois

College of Lake County

19351 West Washington Street
Grayslake, IL 60030-1198

Contact Information:

Telephone: 847-543-2312
Fax: 847-223-1357
E-mail: b105555@clc.cc.il.us
Web: www.clc.cc.il.us

Program Information:

Program begins: August
Degrees offered: Associate's, 19 months
Evening or weekend classes are available.

Application Information:

Enrollment of program: 25
Transfer students are accepted.

Financial Information:

Tuition, resident: $3,922
Tuition, non-resident: $17,924

Employment Profile:

% of students who pass the boards on their first try: 83
% employed within the first 6 months following graduation: 79
Average starting salary: $26,000

Elgin Community College

1700 Spartan Drive
Elgin, IL 60123-7193

Contact Information:

Telephone: 847-2147-308
Fax: 847-214-7527
E-mail: wmiller@mail.elgin.cc.il.us
Web: www.elgin.cc.il.us

Program Information:

Program begins: August
Degrees offered: Certificate program, 6 months; Associate's, 21 months
Evening or weekend classes are available.

Application Information:

Enrollment of program: 15
Transfer students are accepted.

Financial Information:

Tuition, resident: $1,800
Tuition, non-resident: $8,600
Average cost of books: $400
% of students receiving aid: 25

Employment Profile:

% of students who pass the boards on their first try: 86
% employed within the first 6 months following graduation: 99
Average starting salary: $27,500

Illinois Central College

Health and Public Services Building
201 Southwest Adams Street
Peoria, IL 61635-0001

Contact Information:

Telephone: 309-999-4661
Fax: 309-673-9626
E-mail: jkinsinger@icc.cc.il.us
Web: www.icc.cc.il.us

Program Information:

Program begins: August
Degrees offered: Associate's, 22 months
Evening or weekend classes are available.

Application Information:

Enrollment of program: 16
Transfer students are accepted.

Financial Information:

Tuition, resident: $1,603
Tuition, non-resident: $7,400
Average cost of books: $600
% of students receiving aid: 75

Employment Profile:

% of students who pass the boards on their first try: 95
% employed within the first 6 months following graduation: 95
Average starting salary: $22,000

Kankakee Community College

River Road
PO Box 888
Kankakee, IL 60901

Contact Information:

Telephone: 815-933-0296
Fax: 815-933-0217
E-mail: nsawalha@kcc.cc.Il.us
Web: www.kcc.cc.il.us

Program Information:

Program begins: August
Degrees offered: Associate's, 18 months

Application Information:

Enrollment of program: 18
Transfer students are accepted.

Financial Information:

Tuition, resident: $1,430
Tuition, non-resident: $2,723

Employment Profile:

% of students who pass the boards on their first try: 100
% employed within the first 6 months following graduation: 100
Average starting salary: $24,000

Lewis & Clark Community College

5800 Godfrey Road
Godfrey, IL 62035-2466

Contact Information:

Telephone: 618-466-3411 ext. 4421
Fax: 618-466-2798
E-mail: lhostetl@lc.cc.il.us
Web: www.lc.cc.il.us

Program Information:

Program begins: August
Degrees offered: Associate's, 22 months

Application Information:

Enrollment of program: 16
Transfer students are accepted.

Financial Information:

Tuition, resident: $1,968
Tuition, non-resident: $5,554

Employment Profile:

% of students who pass the boards on their first try: 95
% employed within the first 6 months following graduation: 25
Average starting salary: $22,080

Oakton Community College

1600 East Golf Road
Des Plaines, IL 60016

Contact Information:

Telephone: 847-635-1889
Fax: 874-635-1764
E-mail: lynne@oakton.edu
Web: www.oakton.edu

Program Information:

Program begins: August
Degrees offered: Certificate program, 6 months; Associate's, 22 months
Evening or weekend classes are available.

Application Information:

Enrollment of program: 20
Transfer students are accepted.

Financial Information:

Tuition, resident: $1,900
Tuition, non-resident: $5,700
Average cost of books: $400
% of students receiving aid: 80

Employment Profile:
% of students who pass the boards on their first try: 100
% employed within the first 6 months following graduation: 100
Average starting salary: $23,000

Sauk Valley Community College

173 Illinois Route 2
Dixon, IL 61021-9110

Contact Information:
Telephone: 815-288-5511
Fax: 815-288-5958
Web: www.succ.edu

Program Information:
Program begins: August
Degrees offered: Associate's, 22 months

Application Information:
Enrollment of program: 12
Transfer students are accepted.

Financial Information:
Tuition, resident: $1,450
Tuition, non-resident: $10,151
Average cost of books: $350
% of students receiving aid: 50

Employment Profile:
% of students who pass the boards on their first try: 100
% employed within the first 6 months following graduation: 99
Average starting salary: $25,000

Southern Illinois Collegiate Common Market

3213 South Park Avenue
Herrin, IL 62948

Contact Information:
Telephone: 618-942-6902
Fax: 618-942-6658
E-mail: pberry@midwest.net

Program Information:
Program begins: October
Degrees offered: Certificate program, 22 months
Evening or weekend classes are available.

Application Information:
Enrollment of program: 24

Financial Information:
Tuition, resident: $1,494
Tuition, non-resident: $4,372

Employment Profile:
% of students who pass the boards on their first try: 82
% employed within the first 6 months following graduation: 100
Average starting salary: $19,000

Indiana

Indiana University Northwest

3400 Broadway
Gary, IN 46408

Contact Information:
Telephone: 219-980-6541
Fax: 219-980-6649
E-mail: jlareau@iunhaw1.iun.indiana.edu
Web: www.iun.indiana.edu

Program Information:
Program begins: June, August
Degrees offered: Certificate program, 12 months; Associate's, 24 months; Bachelor's

Application Information:
Transfer students are accepted.

Financial Information:
Tuition, resident: $2,823
Tuition, non-resident: $7,326

Employment Profile:
% employed within the first 6 months following graduation: 100
Average starting salary: $24,000

Ivy Tech State College—Terre Haute

7999 US Highway 41 South
Terre Haute, IN 47802-4894

Contact Information:
Telephone: 812-299-1121 ext. 266
Fax: 812-299-5723
E-mail: jgambill@earthlink.net
Web: www.ivytech.cc.in.us

Program Information:
Program begins: September
Degrees offered: Associate's, 21 months

Financial Information:
Tuition, resident: $2,647
Tuition, non-resident: $4,867

Ivy Tech State College NC—South Bend

220 Dean Johnson Boulevard
South Bend, IN 46601-3415

Contact Information:
Telephone: 219-289-7001
Fax: 219-236-7165
E-mail: pprimros@ivy.tec.in.us
Web: www.ivytec.in.us

Program Information:
Program begins: August
Degrees offered: Associate's, 22 months

Application Information:
Enrollment of program: 14
Transfer students are accepted.

Financial Information:
Average cost of books: $400
% of students receiving aid: 95

Employment Profile:
% of students who pass the boards on their first try: 100
% employed within the first 6 months following graduation: 90
Average starting salary: $26,000

Iowa

Des Moines Area Community College

2006 Ankeny Boulevard
Ankeny, IA 50021

Contact Information:
Telephone: 515-964-6296
Fax: 515-964-6440
E-mail: kjcampbell@dmacc.cc.ia.us
Web: www.dmacc.cc.ia.us

Program Information:
Program begins: September
Degrees offered: Associate's, 22 months

Application Information:
Enrollment of program: 16
Transfer students are accepted.

Financial Information:
Tuition, resident: $1,939
Tuition, non-resident: $3,878
Average cost of books: $300

Employment Profile:
% of students who pass the boards on their first try: 96
% employed within the first 6 months following graduation: 90
Average starting salary: $21,000

Iowa Central Community College

330 Avenue M
Fort Dodge, IA 50501

Contact Information:
Telephone: 515-576-7201 ext. 2393
Fax: 515-576-7206
E-mail: dedward@duke.icc.cc.ia.us
Web: www.iccc.cc.ia.us

Program Information:
Program begins: September
Degrees offered: Associate's, 23 months

Application Information:
Enrollment of program: 26
Transfer students are accepted.

Financial Information:
Tuition, resident: $2,530
Tuition, non-resident: $3,630
Average cost of books: $400
% of students receiving aid: 50

Employment Profile:
% of students who pass the boards on their first try: 80
% employed within the first 6 months following graduation: 75
Average starting salary: $23,040

Kansas

Seward County Community College

PO Box 1137
Liberal, KS 67901

Contact Information:
Telephone: 316-626-3077

Fax: 316-626-3040
E-mail: scampbel.sccc.cc.ks.us
Web: www.sccc.cc.ks.us

Program Information:
Program begins: June
Degrees offered: Associate's, 24 months
Evening or weekend classes are available.

Application Information:
Enrollment of program: 18
Transfer students are accepted.

Financial Information:
Tuition, resident: $1,400
Tuition, non-resident: $2,100
Average cost of books: $300

Employment Profile:
% of students who pass the boards on their first try: 90
% employed within the first 6 months following graduation: 100
Average starting salary: $22,000

Wichita Area Technical College

324 North Emporia Street
Wichita, KS 67202

Contact Information:
Telephone: 316-973-4370
Fax: 316-973-4332
E-mail: watchhs@feist.com
Web: www.watc.tec.ks.us

Program Information:
Program begins: August
Degrees offered: Associate's, 24 months

Application Information:
Enrollment of program: 11
Transfer students are accepted.

Financial Information:
Tuition, resident: $1,350
Tuition, non-resident: $9,112
Average cost of books: $450
% of students receiving aid: 75

Employment Profile:
% of students who pass the boards on their first try: 90
% employed within the first 6 months following graduation: 100
Average starting salary: $21,000

Kentucky

Eastern Kentucky University

Disney 220
521 Lancaster Avenue
Richmond, KY 404753102

Contact Information:
Telephone: 606-622-3078
Fax: 606-622-1140
E-mail: clshuffo@acs.eku.edu
Web: www.clinicallab.eku.edu

Program Information:
Program begins: August
Degrees offered: Associate's, 22 months

Application Information:
Enrollment of program: 30

Financial Information:
Tuition, resident: $2,060
Tuition, non-resident: $5,660

Henderson Community College

2660 South Green Street
Henderson, KY 42420

Contact Information:
Telephone: 502-830-5318
Fax: 502-830-5355
E-mail: randa.hawa@kctcs.net
Web: www.kctcs.net

Program Information:
Program begins: August
Degrees offered: Associate's, 22 months

Financial Information:
Tuition, resident: $1,100
Tuition, non-resident: $3,300

Kentucky Tech—Madisonville Health Tech Center

750 North Laffoon Street
Madisonville, KY 42431

Contact Information:
Telephone: 502-824-7552
Fax: 270-824-7552
Web: www.madtechcollege.com

Program Information:
Program begins: August
Degrees offered: Associate's, 15 months

Application Information:
Enrollment of program: 30
Transfer students are accepted.

Financial Information:
Tuition, resident: $760
Tuition, non-resident: $1,520
Average cost of books: $500
% of students receiving aid: 40

Employment Profile:
% of students who pass the boards on their first try: 99
% employed within the first 6 months following graduation: 98
Average starting salary: $21,000

Somerset Community College

Monticello Street
Somerset, KY 42501

Contact Information:
Telephone: 606-679-8501
Fax: 606-679-5139
E-mail: nancy.powell@kctcs.net
Web: www.somccuky.edu

Program Information:
Program begins: August, January
Degrees offered: Associate's, 21 months

Application Information:
Transfer students are accepted.

Financial Information:
Tuition, resident: $2,630
Tuition, non-resident: $7,594
Average cost of books: $600
% of students receiving aid: 88

Employment Profile:
% of students who pass the boards on their first try: 81
% employed within the first 6 months following graduation: 55
Average starting salary: $19,000

Louisiana

Southern University at Shreveport—Bossier City

3050 Martin Luther King Jr. Drive
Shreveport, LA 71107

Contact Information:
Telephone: 318-674-3410
Fax: 318-674-3338
E-mail: hjoinerjr@aol.com
Web: www.susbo.edu

Program Information:
Program begins: August
Degrees offered: Associate's, 24 months

Application Information:
Enrollment of program: 45
Transfer students are accepted.

Financial Information:
Tuition, resident: $1,500
Tuition, non-resident: $2,900
Average cost of books: $300
% of students receiving aid: 50

Employment Profile:
% of students who pass the boards on their first try: 90
% employed within the first 6 months following graduation: 100
Average starting salary: $17,600

Maine

Central Maine Technical College

1250 Turner Street
Auburn, ME 04210

Contact Information:
Telephone: 207-755-5420 ext. 405
Fax: 207-755-5491
E-mail: ferran@cmtc.net
Web: www.cmtc.net

Program Information:
Program begins: August
Degrees offered: Associate's, 20 months
Evening or weekend classes are available.

Application Information:
Enrollment of program: 17
Transfer students are accepted.

Financial Information:
Tuition, resident: $4,080
Tuition, non-resident: $8,940
Average cost of books: $800
% of students receiving aid: 75

Employment Profile:
% of students who pass the boards on their first try: 99
% employed within the first 6 months following graduation: 100
Average starting salary: $40,000

Eastern Maine Technical College
354 Hogan Road
Bangor, ME 04401

Contact Information:
Telephone: 207-941-4645
Fax: 207-941-4608
E-mail: admerkel@aol.com
Web: www.emtc.org

Program Information:
Program begins: Program begins quarterly.
Degrees offered: Associate's, 21 months
Evening or weekend classes are available.

Application Information:
Enrollment of program: 6
Transfer students are accepted.

Financial Information:
Tuition, resident: $2,584
Tuition, non-resident: $5,662

Employment Profile:
% of students who pass the boards on their first try: 87
Average starting salary: $24,700

University of Maine—Augusta
46 University Drive
Augusta, ME 04330

Contact Information:
Telephone: 956-544-8925
Fax: 956-544-8910
Web: www.uma.maine.edu

Program Information:
Program begins: August
Degrees offered: Associate's, 21 months

Application Information:
Enrollment of program: 13
Transfer students are accepted.

Financial Information:
Tuition, resident: $3,500
Tuition, non-resident: $8,568
% of students receiving aid: 70

Employment Profile:
% of students who pass the boards on their first try: 100
% employed within the first 6 months following graduation: 70
Average starting salary: $20,000

University of Maine—Presque Isle
181 Main-317 South Hall
Presque Isle, ME 04769

Contact Information:
Telephone: 207-626-1407
Fax: 207-626-1046
E-mail: graves@polaris.umpi.maine.edu
Web: www.bliss.umpi.maine.edu

Program Information:
Program begins: September, January
Degrees offered: Associate's, 20 months

Application Information:
Enrollment of program: 20
Transfer students are accepted.

Financial Information:
Tuition, resident: $2,940
Tuition, non-resident: $7,200

Maryland

Allegany College of Maryland
12401 Willowbrook Road Southeast
Cumberland, MD 21502-2596

Contact Information:
Telephone: 301-784-5521
Fax: 301-784-5521
E-mail: brocks@acc7.ac.cc.md.us
Web: www.ac.cc.md.us

Program Information:
Program begins: September
Degrees offered: Associate's, 17 months

Application Information:
Enrollment of program: 24
Transfer students are accepted.

Financial Information:
Tuition, resident: $1,800
Tuition, non-resident: $5,688

Employment Profile:
% of students who pass the boards on their first try: 95
% employed within the first 6 months following graduation: 90
Average starting salary: $30,000

Essex Community College
7201 Rossville Boulevard
Baltimore, MD 21237-3899

Contact Information:
Telephone: 410-780-6406
Fax: 410-780-6504
E-mail: lsimmons@essex.cc.md.us

Program Information:
Program begins: September
Degrees offered: Associate's, 24 months

Application Information:
Enrollment of program: 60

Financial Information:
Tuition, resident: $5,700
Tuition, non-resident: $15,770

Villa Julie College
1525 Greenspring Valley Road
Stevenson, MD 21153

Contact Information:
Telephone: 410-602-7256
Fax: 410-486-3552
E-mail: fac-grif@mail.vjc.edu
Web: www.vjc.edu

Program Information:
Program begins: September
Degrees offered: Associate's, 17 months
Evening or weekend classes are available.

Application Information:
Enrollment of program: 12
Transfer students are accepted.

Financial Information:
Average cost of books: $800

Employment Profile:
% of students who pass the boards on their first try: 100
% employed within the first 6 months following graduation: 100
Average starting salary: $23,040

Massachusetts

Bristol Community College
777 Elsbree Street
Fall River, MA 02720

Contact Information:
Telephone: 508-678-2811
Fax: 508-676-7146
E-mail: scampos@bristol.mass.educ
Web: www.bristol.mass.edu

Program Information:
Program begins: September
Degrees offered: Associate's, 18 months
Evening or weekend classes are available.

Application Information:
Enrollment of program: 30

Financial Information:
Tuition, resident: $2,070
Tuition, non-resident: $7,206
Average cost of books: $450
% of students receiving aid: 90

Employment Profile:
% of students who pass the boards on their first try: 85
% employed within the first 6 months following graduation: 90
Average starting salary: $28,000

Michigan

Baker College of Owosso
1020 South Washington Street
Owosso, MI 48867

Contact Information:
Telephone: 517-729-3418 ext. 409
Fax: 517-729-3411
E-mail: nelson_d@owosso.baker.edu
Web: www.baker.edu

Program Information:
Program begins: June
Degrees offered: Associate's, 21 months

Application Information:
Enrollment of program: 40
Transfer students are accepted.

Financial Information:
Average cost of books: $1,000
% of students receiving aid: 70

Employment Profile:
% of students who pass the boards on their first try: 93
% employed within the first 6 months following graduation: 80
Average starting salary: $27,000

Kellogg Community College
450 North Avenue
Battle Creek, MI 49017

Contact Information:
Telephone: 616-965-3931 ext. 2316
Fax: 616-965-4133
E-mail: paffk@kellogg.cc.mi.us
Web: www.kellogg.cc.mi.us

Program Information:
Program begins: August, January
Degrees offered: Associate's, 22 months

Application Information:
Transfer students are accepted.

Financial Information:
Tuition, resident: $2,440
Tuition, non-resident: $3,535

Employment Profile:
% employed within the first 6 months following graduation: 75
Average starting salary: $25,000

Minnesota

Fergus Falls Community College
1414 College Way
Fergus Falls, MN 56537

Contact Information:
Telephone: 218-739-7529
Fax: 218-739-7475
E-mail: eunice.macfar@ff.cc.mn.us
Web: www.ff.cc.mn.us

Program Information:
Program begins: September
Degrees offered: Associate's, 18 months

Application Information:
Enrollment of program: 15
Transfer students are accepted.

Financial Information:
Tuition, resident: $2,800
Tuition, non-resident: $5,600
Average cost of books: $500
% of students receiving aid: 70

Employment Profile:
% of students who pass the boards on their first try: 94
% employed within the first 6 months following graduation: 100
Average starting salary: $21,120

Lake Superior College
2101 Trinity Road
Duluth, MN 55811

Contact Information:
Telephone: 218-733-7679
Fax: 218-723-4921
E-mail: j.wallgren@lsc.mnscu.edu
Web: www.mnscu.edu

Program Information:
Program begins: August
Degrees offered: Associate's, 20 months

Application Information:
Enrollment of program: 20
Transfer students are accepted.

Financial Information:
Tuition, resident: $2,544
Tuition, non-resident: $4,956
Average cost of books: $700
% of students receiving aid: 75

Employment Profile:
% of students who pass the boards on their first try: 92
% employed within the first 6 months following graduation: 90
Average starting salary: $22,000

Mayo Clinic/Mayo Foundation
School of Health Related Sciences
200 First Street Southwest
Rochester, MN 55905

Contact Information:
Telephone: 507-284-6008
Fax: 507-284-9758
E-mail: cummings.john@mayo.edu

Program Information:
Program begins: August
Degrees offered: Associate's, 24 months

Application Information:
Enrollment of program: 36

Financial Information:
Tuition, resident: $2,800
Average cost of books: $2,115
% of students receiving aid: 98

Employment Profile:
% of students who pass the boards on their first try: 95
% employed within the first 6 months following graduation: 90
Average starting salary: $42,000

Medical Institute of Minnesota
5503 Green Valley Drive
Bloomington, MN 55437

Contact Information:
Telephone: 612-844-0064
Fax: 612-844-0671
E-mail: info@mim.tec.mn.us
Web: www.mim.tec.mn.us

Program Information:
Program begins: September
Degrees offered: Associate's, 24 months
Evening or weekend classes are available.

North Hennepin Community College
7411 85th Avenue North
Brooklyn Park, MN 55445

Contact Information:
Telephone: 612-863-4674
Fax: 612-863-3089
E-mail: jreinke@nh.cc.mn.us
Web: www.nh.cc.mn.us

Program Information:
Program begins: August
Degrees offered: Associate's, 24 months

Application Information:
Transfer students are accepted.

Financial Information:
Tuition, resident: $2,631
Tuition, non-resident: $5,086

Employment Profile:
% of students who pass the boards on their first try: 95
% employed within the first 6 months following graduation: 100
Average starting salary: $23,300

Northwest Technical College—East Grand Forks
2022 Central Avenue Northeast
East Grand Forks, MN 56721

Contact Information:
Telephone: 218-773-3441
Fax: 218-773-4502
E-mail: sue.kuntz@mail.ntc.mnscu.edu
Web: www.ntc-online.com

Program Information:
Program begins: August
Degrees offered: Associate's, 24 months

Application Information:
Enrollment of program: 16
Transfer students are accepted.

Financial Information:
Tuition, resident: $2,534
Tuition, non-resident: $5,069
Average cost of books: $430
% of students receiving aid: 80

Employment Profile:
% of students who pass the boards on their first try: 100
% employed within the first 6 months following graduation: 100

South Central Technical College
1225 Third Street Southwest
Faribault, MN 55021

Contact Information:
Telephone: 507-334-3965
Fax: 507-332-5888
Web: www.sctc.mnscu.edu

Program Information:
Program begins: August
Degrees offered: Associate's, 22 months

Application Information:
Enrollment of program: 19
Transfer students are accepted.

Financial Information:
Tuition, resident: $2,355
Tuition, non-resident: $4,709

Mississippi

Copiah—Lincoln Community College
PO Box 457
Wesson, MS 39191-0457

Contact Information:
Telephone: 601-643-8391
Fax: 601-643-8214

Program Information:
Program begins: August
Degrees offered: Associate's, 24 months

Application Information:
Enrollment of program: 25
Transfer students are accepted.

Financial Information:
Tuition, resident: $1,500
Tuition, non-resident: $2,950
Average cost of books: $250
% of students receiving aid: 95

Employment Profile:
% of students who pass the boards on their first try: 90
% employed within the first 6 months following graduation: 100
Average starting salary: $20,000

Hinds Community College
Nursing/Allied Health Center
1750 Chadwick Drive
Jackson, MS 39204-3402

Contact Information:
Telephone: 601-371-3515
Fax: 601-371-3529
Web: www.hinds.cc.ms.us

Program Information:
Program begins: August, January
Degrees offered: Associate's, 24 months
Evening or weekend classes are available.

Application Information:
Enrollment of program: 40

Financial Information:
Tuition, resident: $1,530
Tuition, non-resident: $4,839

Meridian Community College
910 Highway 19 North
Meridian, MS 39307

Contact Information:
Telephone: 601-483-8241
Fax: 601-482-3936
E-mail: kpoole@mcc.cc.ms.us
Web: www.mcc.cc.ms.us

Program Information:
Program begins: August, January
Degrees offered: Associate's, 24 months

Application Information:
Enrollment of program: 16
Transfer students are accepted.

Financial Information:
Tuition, resident: $1,440
Tuition, non-resident: $3,000
Average cost of books: $600
% of students receiving aid: 50

Employment Profile:
% of students who pass the boards on their first try: 90
% employed within the first 6 months following graduation: 97
Average starting salary: $20,000

Mississippi Delta Community College
PO Box 668
Moorhead, MS 38761

Contact Information:
Telephone: 662-246-6500
Fax: 662-246-6507
E-mail: jbrocato@mdcc.cc.ms.us
Web: www.mdcc.cc.ms.us

Program Information:
Program begins: August
Degrees offered: Diploma, 24 months; Associate's, 24 months

Application Information:
Enrollment of program: 30
Transfer students are accepted.

Financial Information:
Tuition, resident: $1,150
Tuition, non-resident: $2,430
Average cost of books: $400
% of students receiving aid: 90

Employment Profile:
% of students who pass the boards on their first try: 99
% employed within the first 6 months following graduation: 100
Average starting salary: $21,000

Northeast Mississippi Community College
Cunningham Boulevard
Booneville, MS 38829

Contact Information:
Telephone: 601-720-7388
Fax: 601-728-1165
E-mail: rjones@necc.cc.ms.us
Web: www.necc.cc.ms.us

Program Information:
Program begins: August
Degrees offered: Associate's, 22 months

Application Information:
Enrollment of program: 20
Transfer students are accepted.

Financial Information:
Tuition, resident: $500
Tuition, non-resident: $1,195

Employment Profile:
% of students who pass the boards on their first try: 100
% employed within the first 6 months following graduation: 100
Average starting salary: $27,000

Pearl River Community College—Poplarville
5448 US Highway 49 South
Hattiesburg, MS 39401

Contact Information:
Telephone: 601-554-9123
Fax: 601-554-9148
E-mail: ewallace@prcc.cc.ms.us
Web: www.prcc.ms.us

Program Information:
Program begins: August
Degrees offered: Associate's, 24 months

Application Information:
Enrollment of program: 40
Transfer students are accepted.

Financial Information:
Tuition, resident: $475
Tuition, non-resident: $1,175
Average cost of books: $350
% of students receiving aid: 67

Employment Profile:
% of students who pass the boards on their first try: 75
% employed within the first 6 months following graduation: 90
Average starting salary: $20,160

Missouri

Three Rivers Community College
2080 Three Rivers Boulevard
Poplar Bluff, MO 63901

Contact Information:
Telephone: 573-840-9677
Fax: 573-840-9657

E-mail: deubanks@trcc.cc.mo.us
Web: www.trcc.cc.mo.us

Program Information:
Program begins: August
Degrees offered: Associate's, 22 months

Application Information:
Enrollment of program: 32
Transfer students are accepted.

Financial Information:
Tuition, resident: $1,598
Tuition, non-resident: $2,209
% of students receiving aid: 90

Employment Profile:
% of students who pass the boards on their first try: 90
% employed within the first 6 months following graduation: 100
Average starting salary: $19,200

Nebraska

Mid Plains Community College
601 West State Farm Road
North Platte, NE 69101

Contact Information:
Telephone: 308-532-8980 ext. 254
Fax: 308-532-8590
E-mail: mdsteinb@ziggy.mpcc.cc.ne.us
Web: www.mpcc.cc.ne.us

Program Information:
Program begins: August
Degrees offered: Associate's, 24 months

Application Information:
Enrollment of program: 6
Transfer students are accepted.

Financial Information:
Tuition, resident: $1,720
Tuition, non-resident: $1,806

Employment Profile:
% of students who pass the boards on their first try: 95
% employed within the first 6 months following graduation: 75
Average starting salary: $21,120

Southeast Community College
8800 O Street
Lincoln, NE 68520

Contact Information:
Telephone: 402-437-2760
Fax: 402-437-2404
Web: www.sccm.cc.ne.us

Program Information:
Program begins: August
Degrees offered: Associate's, 24 months
Evening or weekend classes are available.

Application Information:
Enrollment of program: 33
Transfer students are accepted.

Financial Information:
Tuition, resident: $1,836
Tuition, non-resident: $2,161
Average cost of books: $1,586

Employment Profile:
% of students who pass the boards on their first try: 95
% employed within the first 6 months following graduation: 89
Average starting salary: $20,409

New Hampshire

New Hampshire Community Technical College
1 College Drive
Claremont, NH 03743

Contact Information:
Telephone: 605-427-744 ext. 2536
Fax: 603-543-1844
E-mail: agordon@tec.nh.us
Web: www.nhctcs.tec.nh.us

Program Information:
Program begins: July
Degrees offered: Associate's, 20 months
Evening or weekend classes are available.

Application Information:
Transfer students are accepted.

Financial Information:
Tuition, resident: $3,960
Tuition, non-resident: $9,108

Employment Profile:
% of students who pass the boards on their first try: 96
% employed within the first 6 months following graduation: 100
Average starting salary: $21,000

New Jersey

County College of Morris
Rte 10 and Center Grove Road
Randolph, NJ 07869

Contact Information:
Telephone: 973-328-5370
Fax: 973-328-5379
E-mail: ralisauskas@ccm.edu
Web: www.ccm.edu

Program Information:
Program begins: August
Degrees offered: Associate's, 23 months
Evening or weekend classes are available.

Application Information:
Enrollment of program: 20
Transfer students are accepted.

Financial Information:
Tuition, resident: $1,386
Tuition, non-resident: $2,425

Employment Profile:
% of students who pass the boards on their first try: 82
% employed within the first 6 months following graduation: 50
Average starting salary: $23,000

Felician College
262 South Main Street
Lodi, NJ 07644

Contact Information:
Telephone: 201-559-6185 ext. 6025
Fax: 201-559-6188
E-mail: rubinm@inet.felician.edu
Web: www.felician.edu

Program Information:
Program begins: August
Degrees offered: Associate's, 20 months
Evening or weekend classes are available.

Application Information:
Transfer students are accepted.

Financial Information:
Tuition, resident: $14,000
Average cost of books: $600

Employment Profile:
% of students who pass the boards on their first try: 100
Average starting salary: $30,000

Middlesex County College
2600 Woodbridge Avenue
Edison, NJ 08818-3050

Contact Information:
Telephone: 732-906-2581
Web: www.middlesex.cc.nj.us

Program Information:
Program begins: September
Degrees offered: Associate's, 21 months
Evening or weekend classes are available.

Application Information:
Enrollment of program: 20

Financial Information:
Tuition, resident: $2,500
Tuition, non-resident: $5,000

Employment Profile:
% of students who pass the boards on their first try: 98
% employed within the first 6 months following graduation: 95
Average starting salary: $26,000

Ocean County College
Nursing and Allied Health
Ocean County College Drive
Toms River, NJ 08754

Contact Information:
Telephone: 732-255-0395
Fax: 732-255-0418
E-mail: caltagir@csionline.net
Web: www.ocean.cc.nj.us

Program Information:
Program begins: August

Degrees offered: Associate's, 10 months
Evening or weekend classes are available.

Application Information:
Enrollment of program: 6
Transfer students are accepted.

Financial Information:
Tuition, resident: $2,520
Tuition, non-resident: $2,898
Average cost of books: $350
% of students receiving aid: 30

Employment Profile:
% employed within the first 6 months following graduation: 100
Average starting salary: $30,000

University of Medicine & Dentistry of New Jersey

1776 Raritan Road
Scotch Plains, NJ 07076

Contact Information:
Telephone: 207-768-9451
Fax: 207-768-9553
E-mail: keohanem@umdnj.edu
Web: www.umdnj.edu/shrpweb

Program Information:
Program begins: June
Degrees offered: Associate's, 12 months

Application Information:
Enrollment of program: 20
Transfer students are accepted.

Financial Information:
Tuition, resident: $4,656
Tuition, non-resident: $9,313
Average cost of books: $425

Employment Profile:
% of students who pass the boards on their first try: 90
% employed within the first 6 months following graduation: 90
Average starting salary: $28,000

New Mexico

Albuquerque Tech Vocational Institute

525 Buena Vista Southeast
Albuquerque, NM 87106

Contact Information:
Telephone: 505-224-4132
Fax: 505-224-4120
E-mail: monya@tvi.cc.nm.us
Web: www.tvi.cc.nm.us

Program Information:
Program begins: August
Degrees offered: Associate's, 20 months

Application Information:
Enrollment of program: 23
Transfer students are accepted.

Financial Information:
Tuition, resident: $823
Tuition, non-resident: $3,499

Employment Profile:
% of students who pass the boards on their first try: 29
% employed within the first 6 months following graduation: 100
Average starting salary: $24,000

New York

CUNY New York City Technical College

300 Jay Street
Brooklyn, NY 11201

Contact Information:
Telephone: 718-260-5671
Fax: 718-260-5069
E-mail: clavender@msn.com
Web: www.nyctc.cuny.edu

Program Information:
Program begins: January
Degrees offered: Associate's, 24 months

Application Information:
Enrollment of program: 50
Transfer students are accepted.

Financial Information:
Tuition, resident: $3,200
Tuition, non-resident: $6,550
Average cost of books: $550
% of students receiving aid: 50

Employment Profile:
% of students who pass the boards on their first try: 90
% employed within the first 6 months following graduation: 95

Hudson Valley Community College

80 Vandenburgh Avenue
Troy, NY 12180

Contact Information:
Telephone: 518-629-7407
Fax: 518-270-7594
E-mail: olearjoh@hvcc.edu
Web: www.hucc.edu

Program Information:
Program begins: September, February, June
Degrees offered: Associate's, 18 months
Evening or weekend classes are available.

Application Information:
Enrollment of program: 26
Transfer students are accepted.

Financial Information:
Tuition, resident: $2,350
Tuition, non-resident: $6,135
Average cost of books: $600
% of students receiving aid: 90

Employment Profile:
% of students who pass the boards on their first try: 100
% employed within the first 6 months following graduation: 100
Average starting salary: $21,000

SUNY at Farmingdale

Route 110/Gleeson Hal
Room 304
Farmingdale, NY 11735

Contact Information:
Telephone: 516-420-2171
Fax: 516-420-2784
E-mail: escolakm@farmingdale.edu
Web: www.farmingdale,edu

Program Information:
Program begins: September
Degrees offered: Associate's, 24 months

Financial Information:
Tuition, resident: $3,200
Tuition, non-resident: $8,300

Employment Profile:
% of students who pass the boards on their first try: 70
% employed within the first 6 months following graduation: 50
Average starting salary: $33,000

SUNY College of Technology at Alfred

Allied Health Building
Room 204
Alfred, NY 14802

Contact Information:
Telephone: 607-587-3620
Fax: 607-587-3684
E-mail: boltonvl@alfredtech.edu
Web: www.alfred.edu

Program Information:
Program begins: September
Degrees offered: Diploma, 18 months; Associate's, 18 months

Application Information:
Enrollment of program: 25
Transfer students are accepted.

Financial Information:
Tuition, resident: $3,200
Tuition, non-resident: $5,000
Average cost of books: $500
% of students receiving aid: 50

Employment Profile:
% of students who pass the boards on their first try: 100
% employed within the first 6 months following graduation: 100
Average starting salary: $24,000

SUNY College of Technology at Canton

Cornell Drive
Canton, NY 13617

Contact Information:
Telephone: 315-386-7400
Fax: 315-386-7959
E-mail: pellett@canton.edu
Web: www.canton.edu

Program Information:
Program begins: August
Degrees offered: Associate's, 18 months

Application Information:
Transfer students are accepted.

Financial Information:
Tuition, resident: $3,200
Tuition, non-resident: $5,000

North Carolina

Alamance Community College
PO Box 8000
Graham, NC 27253-8000

Contact Information:
Telephone: 336-578-2002 ext. 2317
Fax: 336-578-1987
E-mail: simpsonp@alamance.cc.nc.us
Web: www.alamance.cc.nc.us

Program Information:
Program begins: August
Degrees offered: Associate's, 24 months

Application Information:
Enrollment of program: 35
Transfer students are accepted.

Financial Information:
Tuition, resident: $840
Tuition, non-resident: $6,846
Average cost of books: $300
% of students receiving aid: 70

Employment Profile:
% of students who pass the boards on their first try: 95
% employed within the first 6 months following graduation: 95
Average starting salary: $23,500

Asheville Buncombe Technical Community College
340 Victoria Road
Asheville, NC 28801

Contact Information:
Telephone: 828-254-1921
Fax: 828-251-6355
Web: www.asheville.cc.nc.us

Program Information:
Program begins: September
Degrees offered: Associate's, 21 months

Application Information:
Enrollment of program: 12

Financial Information:
Tuition, resident: $1,123
Tuition, non-resident: $7,129
Average cost of books: $450

Employment Profile:
% employed within the first 6 months following graduation: 100
Average starting salary: $20,000

Beaufort County Community College
PO Box 1069
Washington, NC 27889

Contact Information:
Telephone: 919-946-6194
Fax: 919-946-0271
E-mail: artk@email.beaufort.cc.nc.us
Web: www.beaufort.cc.nc.us

Program Information:
Program begins: September
Degrees offered: Associate's, 22 months
Evening or weekend classes are available.

Application Information:
Enrollment of program: 24
Transfer students are accepted.

Financial Information:
Tuition, resident: $766
Tuition, non-resident: $6,044
% of students receiving aid: 75

Employment Profile:
% employed within the first 6 months following graduation: 90
Average starting salary: $22,000

Central Piedmont Community College
PO Box 35009
Charlotte, NC 28235-5009

Contact Information:
Telephone: 704-330-5028
Fax: 704-330-5930
E-mail: becky_sanders@cpcc.cc.nc.us
Web: www.cpcc.cc.nc.us

Program Information:
Program begins: August
Degrees offered: Associate's, 21 months

Financial Information:
Tuition, resident: $840
Tuition, non-resident: $6,846

Davidson County Community College
PO Box 1287
Lexington, NC 27293-1287

Contact Information:
Telephone: 336-249-8186 ext. 289
Fax: 336-249-9060
E-mail: srohr@davidson.cc.nc.us
Web: www.davidson.cc.nc.us

Program Information:
Program begins: June
Degrees offered: Associate's, 18 months

Application Information:
Enrollment of program: 16
Transfer students are accepted.

Financial Information:
Average cost of books: $500
% of students receiving aid: 60

Employment Profile:
% of students who pass the boards on their first try: 85
% employed within the first 6 months following graduation: 90
Average starting salary: $24,500

Southwestern Community College
447 College Drive
Sylva, NC 28779

Contact Information:
Telephone: 828-586-4091 ext. 312
Fax: 828-586-3129
E-mail: andrea@southwest.cc.nc.us
Web: www.southwest.cc.nc.us

Program Information:
Program begins: August
Degrees offered: Associate's, 22 months

Financial Information:
Tuition, resident: $749
Tuition, non-resident: $4,564
Average cost of books: $400

Employment Profile:
% of students who pass the boards on their first try: 90
% employed within the first 6 months following graduation: 90
Average starting salary: $24,960

Wake Technical Community College
9101 Fayetteville Road
Raleigh, NC 27603

Contact Information:
Telephone: 919-212-3818
Fax: 919-250-4329
E-mail: pbhorton@mail.wake.tec.nc.us
Web: www.wake.tec.nc.us

Program Information:
Program begins: August
Degrees offered: Associate's, 21 months

Application Information:
Enrollment of program: 16
Transfer students are accepted.

Financial Information:
Tuition, resident: $749
Tuition, non-resident: $4,653
Average cost of books: $450
% of students receiving aid: 25

Employment Profile:
% of students who pass the boards on their first try: 100
% employed within the first 6 months following graduation: 100
Average starting salary: $25,333

Western Piedmont Community College
1001 Burkemont Avenue
Morganton, NC 28655-0680

Contact Information:
Telephone: 828-438-6126
Fax: 828-438-6015
E-mail: gjennings@wp.cc.nc.us
Web: www.wp.cc.nc.us

Program Information:
Program begins: August
Degrees offered: Associate's, 21 months

Application Information:
Enrollment of program: 25
Transfer students are accepted.

Financial Information:
Tuition, resident: $749
Tuition, non-resident: $4,772
Average cost of books: $600
% of students receiving aid: 60

Employment Profile:
% of students who pass the boards on their first try: 90
% employed within the first 6 months following graduation: 95
Average starting salary: $24,000

North Dakota

Bismarck State College
1500 Edwards Avenue
Bismarck, ND 58501

Contact Information:
Telephone: 701-224-5469
Fax: 701-224-5550
E-mail: mdurick@gwmail.nodak.edu
Web: www.bsc.nodak.edu

Program Information:
Program begins: August
Degrees offered: Associate's, 22 months
Evening or weekend classes are available.

Application Information:
Enrollment of program: 7
Transfer students are accepted.

Financial Information:
Tuition, resident: $1,890
Tuition, non-resident: $4,540
% of students receiving aid: 80

Employment Profile:
% of students who pass the boards on their first try: 100
% employed within the first 6 months following graduation: 100
Average starting salary: $20,000

Ohio

Clark State Community College
570 East Leffel Lane
Springfield, OH 45505

Contact Information:
Telephone: 937-328-8077
Fax: 937-328-6138
E-mail: horns@clark.cc.oh.us
Web: www.clark.cc.oh.us

Program Information:
Program begins: August
Degrees offered: Associate's, 21 months

Application Information:
Enrollment of program: 10
Transfer students are accepted.

Financial Information:
Tuition, resident: $2,466
Tuition, non-resident: $4,722

Jefferson Community College
4000 Sunset Boulevard
Steubenville, OH 43952

Contact Information:
Telephone: 740-264-5591 ext. 165
Fax: 740-264-1338
E-mail: ssutherlan@jefferson.cc.oh.us
Web: www.jeffersoncc.org

Program Information:
Program begins: June
Degrees offered: Associate's, 24 months

Application Information:
Enrollment of program: 12
Transfer students are accepted.

Financial Information:
Tuition, resident: $2,240
Tuition, non-resident: $2,870
Average cost of books: $500
% of students receiving aid: 47

Employment Profile:
% of students who pass the boards on their first try: 100
% employed within the first 6 months following graduation: 50
Average starting salary: $17,280

Lakeland Community College
7700 Clocktower Drive
Kirtland, OH 44094-5198

Contact Information:
Telephone: 216-953-7257
Fax: 216-975-4733
E-mail: dpfeifer@lakeland.cc.oh.us
Web: www.lakeland.cc.oh.us

Program Information:
Program begins: August
Degrees offered: Associate's, 22 months
Evening or weekend classes are available.

Application Information:
Enrollment of program: 4
Transfer students are accepted.

Financial Information:
Tuition, resident: $2,376
Tuition, non-resident: $2,990

Employment Profile:
% of students who pass the boards on their first try: 100
% employed within the first 6 months following graduation: 100
Average starting salary: $30,000

Marion Technical College
1467 Mount Vernon Avenue
Marion, OH 43302

Contact Information:
Telephone: 740-389-4636
Fax: 740-389-6136
E-mail: jenkinsm@mtc.tec.oh.us
Web: www.mtc.tec.oh.us

Program Information:
Program begins: September
Degrees offered: Associate's, 21 months

Application Information:
Enrollment of program: 18
Transfer students are accepted.

Financial Information:
Tuition, resident: $2,907
Tuition, non-resident: $5,253
Average cost of books: $500
% of students receiving aid: 60

Employment Profile:
% of students who pass the boards on their first try: 80
% employed within the first 6 months following graduation: 100
Average starting salary: $24,000

Shawnee State University
940 Second Street
Portsmouth, OH 45662

Contact Information:
Telephone: 740-355-2388
Fax: 740-355-2354
E-mail: mthoroughman@shawnee edu
Web: www.shawnee.edu

Program Information:
Program begins: August
Degrees offered: Associate's, 21 months
Evening or weekend classes are available.

Application Information:
Enrollment of program: 16
Transfer students are accepted.

Financial Information:
Tuition, resident: $3,968
Tuition, non-resident: $6,868
Average cost of books: $800

Employment Profile:
% of students who pass the boards on their first try: 95
% employed within the first 6 months following graduation: 100

Stark State College of Technology
6200 Frank Avenue Northwest
Canton, OH 44720

Contact Information:
Telephone: 330-494-6170
Fax: 330-966-6586
Web: www.stark.cc.oh.us

Program Information:
Program begins: August
Degrees offered: Associate's, 21 months

Financial Information:
Tuition, resident: $3,818
Tuition, non-resident: $4,933

University of Rio Grande
218 North College Avenue
MSC-F-39
Rio Grande, OH 45674-3131

Contact Information:
Telephone: 505-722-1721
Fax: 505-863-7513
E-mail: rcheadle@rio.edu
Web: www.rio.edu

Program Information:
Program begins: June
Degrees offered: Associate's, 24 months

Application Information:
Enrollment of program: 20
Transfer students are accepted.

Financial Information:
Tuition, resident: $3,437
Tuition, non-resident: $10,172
Average cost of books: $900
% of students receiving aid: 30

Employment Profile:
% of students who pass the boards on their first try: 80
% employed within the first 6 months following graduation: 80
Average starting salary: $19,000

Washington State Community College
710 Colegate Drive
Marietta, OH 45750

Contact Information:
Telephone: 740-374-8716
Fax: 740-373-7496
E-mail: hkincaid@wscc.edu
Web: www.wscc.edu

Program Information:
Program begins: June
Degrees offered: Associate's, 21 months

Application Information:
Enrollment of program: 14
Transfer students are accepted.

Financial Information:
Tuition, resident: $3,495
Tuition, non-resident: $6,990
Average cost of books: $800

Employment Profile:
% employed within the first 6 months following graduation: 85
Average starting salary: $21,120

Youngstown State University
Department of Health Professions
One University Plaza
Youngstown, OH 44555

Contact Information:
Telephone: 330-742-1761
Fax: 330-742-2921
E-mail: medelost@cc.ysu.edu
Web: www.ysu.edu

Program Information:
Program begins: August
Degrees offered: Associate's, 24 months; Bachelor's
Evening or weekend classes are available.

Application Information:
Enrollment of program: 12
Transfer students are accepted.

Financial Information:
Tuition, resident: $3,366
Tuition, non-resident: $4,986

Employment Profile:
% of students who pass the boards on their first try: 85-90
% employed within the first 6 months following graduation: 85

Oklahoma

Northeastern Oklahoma A & M College
Second and First Streets Northeast
Miami, OK 74354

Contact Information:
Telephone: 918-540-6315
Fax: 918-540-6471
E-mail: kharris@neoam.cc.ok.us
Web: www.neo.cc.ok.us.academics

Program Information:
Program begins: September
Degrees offered: Associate's, 18 months

Application Information:
Enrollment of program: 5
Transfer students are accepted.

Financial Information:
Tuition, resident: $1,890
Tuition, non-resident: $4,690
Average cost of books: $340
% of students receiving aid: 75

Employment Profile:
% of students who pass the boards on their first try: 100
% employed within the first 6 months following graduation: 100
Average starting salary: $27,000

Tulsa Community College
909 South Boston Avenue
Tulsa, OK 74119

Contact Information:
Telephone: 918-595-7008
Fax: 918-595-7091
E-mail: kholmes@tulsa.cc.ok.us
Web: www.tulsa.cc.ok.us

Program Information:
Program begins: September
Degrees offered: Associate's, 24 months
Evening or weekend classes are available.

Application Information:
Enrollment of program: 8
Transfer students are accepted.

Financial Information:
Tuition, resident: $1,364
Tuition, non-resident: $4,091
Average cost of books: $600
% of students receiving aid: 80

Employment Profile:
% of students who pass the boards on their first try: 100
% employed within the first 6 months following graduation: 100
Average starting salary: $22,000

Pennsylvania

Community College of Allegheny County
1750 Clairton Road
Route 885
West Mifflin, PA 15122

Contact Information:
Telephone: 412-469-6280
Fax: 412-469-6371
E-mail: jcoughanour@ccac.edu
Web: www.ccac.edu

Program Information:
Program begins: August
Degrees offered: Associate's, 20 months

Application Information:
Enrollment of program: 10
Transfer students are accepted.

Financial Information:
Tuition, resident: $2,448
Tuition, non-resident: $7,344
Average cost of books: $250
% of students receiving aid: 90

Employment Profile:
% of students who pass the boards on their first try: 94
% employed within the first 6 months following graduation: 100
Average starting salary: $26,000

Community College of Beaver County
1 Campus Drive
Monaca, PA 15061

Contact Information:
Telephone: 724-775-8561
Fax: 724-728-7599
E-mail: b.valicenti@ccbc.cc.pa.us
Web: www.ccbc.cc.pa.us

Program Information:
Program begins: September, January
Degrees offered: Associate's, 21 months

Application Information:
Enrollment of program: 20
Transfer students are accepted.

Financial Information:
Tuition, resident: $3,100
Tuition, non-resident: $6,200

Employment Profile:
% of students who pass the boards on their first try: 90
% employed within the first 6 months following graduation: 60
Average starting salary: $22,000

Community College of Philadelphia

1700 Spring Garden Street
Philadelphia, PA 19130

Contact Information:
Telephone: 215-751-8511
Fax: 215-751-8937
E-mail: rkrefetz@ccp.cc.pa.us
Web: www.ccp.cc.pa.us

Program Information:
Program begins: September
Degrees offered: Associate's, 21 months
Evening or weekend classes are available.

Application Information:
Enrollment of program: 30
Transfer students are accepted.

Financial Information:
Tuition, resident: $2,240
Tuition, non-resident: $5,640
Average cost of books: $300

Employment Profile:
% of students who pass the boards on their first try: 85
Average starting salary: $32,000

Harcum College

750 Montgomery Avenue
Bryn Mawr, PA 19010

Contact Information:
Telephone: 610-526-6662
Fax: 610-526-6031
Web: www.harcum edu

Program Information:
Program begins: September
Degrees offered: Associate's, 24 months
Evening or weekend classes are available.

Application Information:
Transfer students are accepted.

Financial Information:
Tuition, resident: $6,500
Tuition, non-resident: $6,962
% of students receiving aid: 90

Employment Profile:
% of students who pass the boards on their first try: 80
% employed within the first 6 months following graduation: 90

Montgomery County Community College

340 DeKalb Pike
Blue Bell, PA 19422-1412

Contact Information:
Telephone: 215-641-6486
Fax: 215-619-7178
E-mail: jflynn@admin.mc3.edu
Web: www.mc3.edu

Program Information:
Program begins: September
Degrees offered: Associate's, 21 months

Application Information:
Enrollment of program: 20
Transfer students are accepted.

Employment Profile:
% of students who pass the boards on their first try: 100
% employed within the first 6 months following graduation: 75
Average starting salary: $25,000

Reading Area Community College

Ten South Second Street
PO Box 1706
Reading, PA 19603

Contact Information:
Telephone: 610-372-4721 ext. 5428
Fax: 610-607-6254
E-mail: sn7974@email.racc.cc.pa.us
Web: www.racc.cc.pa.us

Program Information:
Program begins: August, January
Degrees offered: Associate's, 20 months
Evening or weekend classes are available.

Application Information:
Transfer students are accepted.

Financial Information:
Tuition, resident: $2,436
Tuition, non-resident: $4,872

Employment Profile:
% of students who pass the boards on their first try: 98
% employed within the first 6 months following graduation: 95

Rhode Island

Community College of Rhode Island

1762 Louisquisset Pike
Lincoln, RI 02865

Contact Information:
Telephone: 401-333-7252
Fax: 401-333-7242
E-mail: lmorgan@ccri.cc.ri.us
Web: www.ccri.cc.ri.us

Program Information:
Program begins: May
Degrees offered: Associate's, 18 months

Application Information:
Enrollment of program: 20
Transfer students are accepted.

Financial Information:
Tuition, resident: $1,746
Tuition, non-resident: $2,383
Average cost of books: $250
% of students receiving aid: 100

Employment Profile:
% of students who pass the boards on their first try: 98
% employed within the first 6 months following graduation: 50
Average starting salary: $26,000

South Carolina

Florence-Darlington Technical College

PO Box 100548
Florence, SC 29501-0548

Contact Information:
Telephone: 843-661-8105
Fax: 843-661-8116
E-mail: hanrahank@flo.tec.sc.us
Web: www.flo.tec.sc.us

Program Information:
Program begins: August
Degrees offered: Associate's, 20 months

Application Information:
Enrollment of program: 12
Transfer students are accepted.

Financial Information:
Tuition, resident: $1,650
Tuition, non-resident: $1,875
Average cost of books: $300
% of students receiving aid: 75

Employment Profile:
% of students who pass the boards on their first try: 75
% employed within the first 6 months following graduation: 99

Midlands Technical College

PO Box 2408
Columbia, SC 29202

Contact Information:
Telephone: 803-822-3557
Fax: 803-822-3343
E-mail: brecim@mtc.mid.tec.sc.us
Web: www.mid.tec.sc.us

Program Information:
Program begins: August
Degrees offered: Associate's, 24 months

Application Information:
Enrollment of program: 25

Financial Information:
Tuition, resident: $1,800
Tuition, non-resident: $5,400

Employment Profile:
% of students who pass the boards on their first try: 88
% employed within the first 6 months following graduation: 85
Average starting salary: $24,000

Orangeburg Calhoun Technical College
3250 St. Matthews Road
Orangeburg, SC 29118

Contact Information:
Telephone: 803-535-1349
Fax: 803-535-1388
E-mail: fanningb@org.tec.sc.us
Web: www.octech.org

Program Information:
Program begins: August
Degrees offered: Associate's, 21 months

Application Information:
Enrollment of program: 13
Transfer students are accepted.

Financial Information:
Tuition, resident: $1,656
Tuition, non-resident: $1,908
Average cost of books: $700
% of students receiving aid: 90

Employment Profile:
% of students who pass the boards on their first try: 100
% employed within the first 6 months following graduation: 100
Average starting salary: $25,000

Spartanburg Technical College
PO Drawer 4386
Spartanburg, SC 29305

Contact Information:
Telephone: 864-591-3866
Fax: 864-591-3708
E-mail: dickerson@spt.tec.sc.us
Web: www.spt.tec.sc.us

Program Information:
Program begins: August
Degrees offered: Associate's, 21 months

Application Information:
Enrollment of program: 16
Transfer students are accepted.

Financial Information:
Tuition, resident: $1,950
Tuition, non-resident: $2,445

Employment Profile:
% of students who pass the boards on their first try: 100
% employed within the first 6 months following graduation: 100

Tri-County Technical College
PO Box 587
Pendleton, SC 29670-0587

Contact Information:
Telephone: 864-646-8361 ext. 2175
Fax: 864-646-8256
E-mail: djones@tricty.tricounty.tec.sc.us
Web: www.tricounty.tec.sc.us

Program Information:
Program begins: August
Degrees offered: Associate's, 21 months

Application Information:
Enrollment of program: 34
Transfer students are accepted.

Financial Information:
Tuition, resident: $1,500
Tuition, non-resident: $1,788
Average cost of books: $900
% of students receiving aid: 85

Employment Profile:
% of students who pass the boards on their first try: 85
% employed within the first 6 months following graduation: 90
Average starting salary: $23,000

Trident Technical College
PO Box 118067
Charleston, SC 29423-8067

Contact Information:
Telephone: 803-572-6067
Fax: 803-569-6585
E-mail: zsmitha@trident.tec.sc.us
Web: www.trident.tec.sc.us

Program Information:
Program begins: August
Degrees offered: Associate's, 21 months
Evening or weekend classes are available.

Application Information:
Enrollment of program: 30
Transfer students are accepted.

Financial Information:
Tuition, resident: $1,536
Tuition, non-resident: $2,598
Average cost of books: $500
% of students receiving aid: 60

Employment Profile:
% of students who pass the boards on their first try: 100
% employed within the first 6 months following graduation: 100
Average starting salary: $26,000

York Technical College
452 South Anderson Road
Rock Hill, SC 29730

Contact Information:
Telephone: 803-981-7118
Fax: 803-327-8059
E-mail: westbrook@york.tec.sc.us
Web: www.york.tec.sc.us

Program Information:
Program begins: August
Degrees offered: Associate's, 21 months

Application Information:
Enrollment of program: 32
Transfer students are accepted.

Financial Information:
Tuition, resident: $1,692
Tuition, non-resident: $2,052
Average cost of books: $300
% of students receiving aid: 80

Employment Profile:
% of students who pass the boards on their first try: 85
% employed within the first 6 months following graduation: 100
Average starting salary: $20,800

South Dakota

Lake Area Technical Institute
200 North East 9th Street
Watertown, SD 57201

Contact Information:
Telephone: 605-882-5284 ext. 324
Fax: 605-882-6347
E-mail: mhleyste@lati.tec.sd.us
Web: www.lati.tech.sd.us

Program Information:
Program begins: September
Degrees offered: Associate's, 22 months
Evening or weekend classes are available.

Application Information:
Enrollment of program: 12
Transfer students are accepted.

Financial Information:
Tuition, resident: $2,600
Average cost of books: $1,000

Mitchell Technical Institute
821 North Capital
Mitchell, SD 57301

Contact Information:
Telephone: 605-995-3024
Fax: 605-996-3299
E-mail: feilmeierB@mti.tec.sd.us
Web: www.mti.tec.sd.us

Program Information:
Program begins: August
Degrees offered: Associate's, 20 months

Application Information:
Enrollment of program: 34
Transfer students are accepted.

Financial Information:
Tuition, resident: $6,600
Average cost of books: $400
% of students receiving aid: 75

Employment Profile:
% of students who pass the boards on their first try: 89

% employed within the first 6 months following graduation: 100
Average starting salary: $20,480

Presentation College

1500 North Main Street
Aberdeen, SD 57401

Contact Information:
Telephone: 605-229-8464
Fax: 605-229-8518
E-mail: kervinb@presentation.edu
Web: www.presentation.edu

Program Information:
Program begins: September, January
Degrees offered: Associate's, 19 months

Application Information:
Enrollment of program: 20
Transfer students are accepted.

Financial Information:
Average cost of books: $200
% of students receiving aid: 94

Employment Profile:
% of students who pass the boards on their first try: 70
% employed within the first 6 months following graduation: 90
Average starting salary: $22,000

Tennessee

Cumberland School of Technology

1065 East 10th Street
Cookeville, TN 38501

Contact Information:
Telephone: 931-526-3660
Fax: 931-372-2603
E-mail: cst@multipro.com

Program Information:
Program begins: Program begins quarterly.
Degrees offered: Associate's, 18 months

Application Information:
Enrollment of program: 50
Transfer students are accepted.

Financial Information:
Average cost of books: $750
% of students receiving aid: 80

Employment Profile:
% of students who pass the boards on their first try: 90
% employed within the first 6 months following graduation: 90
Average starting salary: $20,000

Roane State Community College

132 Hayfield Road
Knoxville, TN 37922

Contact Information:
Telephone: 423-539-6906
Fax: 423-539-6907
E-mail: white_bm@l.rscc.cc.tn.us
Web: www.rscc.cc.tn.us

Program Information:
Program begins: April
Degrees offered: Associate's, 24 months

Application Information:
Enrollment of program: 15
Transfer students are accepted.

Financial Information:
Tuition, resident: $1,872
Average cost of books: $300

Employment Profile:
% of students who pass the boards on their first try: 87
% employed within the first 6 months following graduation: 87
Average starting salary: $22,080

Texas

Amarillo College

PO Box 447
Amarillo, TX 79178

Contact Information:
Telephone: 806-354-6059
Fax: 806-354-6076
E-mail: jmbohach@actx.edu
Web: www.actx.edu

Program Information:
Program begins: August
Degrees offered: Associate's, 24 months

Application Information:
Enrollment of program: 16
Transfer students are accepted.

Financial Information:
Tuition, resident: $2,022
Tuition, non-resident: $5,106
Average cost of books: $1,120
% of students receiving aid: 80

Employment Profile:
% of students who pass the boards on their first try: 40
% employed within the first 6 months following graduation: 100
Average starting salary: $22,000

Army Medical Department Center and School

3151 Scott Road
Ft. Sam Houston, TX 78234-6137

Contact Information:
Telephone: 210-221-8708
Fax: 210-221-7679
E-mail: richard.brown2@com.amedd.army.mil
Web: www.cs.amedd.army.mil

Program Information:
Degrees offered: Associate's, 12 months

Application Information:
Enrollment of program: 500

Employment Profile:
% of students who pass the boards on their first try: 50
% employed within the first 6 months following graduation: 100

Austin Community College

1020 Grove Boulevard
Austin, TX 78741

Contact Information:
Telephone: 512-223-6114
Fax: 512-223-6700
E-mail: cragland@austin.cc.tx.us
Web: www.austin.cc.tx.us

Program Information:
Program begins: August
Degrees offered: Associate's, 21 months

Application Information:
Enrollment of program: 16
Transfer students are accepted.

Financial Information:
Tuition, resident: $2,484
Tuition, non-resident: $3,833
Average cost of books: $500

Employment Profile:
% of students who pass the boards on their first try: 95
% employed within the first 6 months following graduation: 75
Average starting salary: $25,000

Central Texas College

US Highway 190 West
PO Box 1800
Killeen, TX 76541-9990

Contact Information:
Telephone: 817-526-1187
Fax: 817-526-1765
E-mail: dpoteet@ctcd.cc.tx.us
Web: www.ctcd.cc.tx.us

Program Information:
Program begins: August
Degrees offered: Associate's, 24 months

Application Information:
Enrollment of program: 50

Financial Information:
Tuition, resident: $720
Tuition, non-resident: $2,200

Del Mar College

101 Baldwin and Ayers Streets
Corpus Christi, TX 78404

Contact Information:
Telephone: 361-698-1107
Fax: 361-698-1598
E-mail: dsamo@delmar.edu
Web: www.delmar.edu

Program Information:
Program begins: September
Degrees offered: Associate's, 21 months

Application Information:
Enrollment of program: 20
Transfer students are accepted.

Financial Information:
Tuition, resident: $1,000
Tuition, non-resident: $1,900
Average cost of books: $300
% of students receiving aid: 50

Employment Profile:
% of students who pass the boards on their first try: 90
Average starting salary: $21,500

Grayson County College
6101 Grayson Drive
Denison, TX 75020

Contact Information:
Telephone: 903-786-4468
Fax: 903-786-8056
E-mail: jacksena@grayson.edu
Web: www.grayson.edu

Program Information:
Program begins: August
Degrees offered: Associate's, 22 months

Application Information:
Enrollment of program: 15
Transfer students are accepted.

Financial Information:
Tuition, resident: $2,201
Tuition, non-resident: $2,627
Average cost of books: $800

Employment Profile:
% of students who pass the boards on their first try: 75
% employed within the first 6 months following graduation: 88
Average starting salary: $22,000

Houston Community College
John B. Coleman Health Science Center
1900 Salem
Houston, TX 77030

Contact Information:
Telephone: 713-718-7637
Fax: 713-718-7401
E-mail: murphy-m@hcco.cc.tx
Web: www.hcco.cc.tx.us

Program Information:
Program begins: September
Degrees offered: Diploma, 24 months; Associate's, 24 months
Evening or weekend classes are available.

Application Information:
Enrollment of program: 17
Transfer students are accepted.

Financial Information:
Tuition, resident: $624
Tuition, non-resident: $1,449

Employment Profile:
% of students who pass the boards on their first try: 84
% employed within the first 6 months following graduation: 88
Average starting salary: $30,000

Laredo Community College
West End Washington Street
Laredo, TX 78040

Contact Information:
Telephone: 210-721-5264
Fax: 956-721-5431
E-mail: dhill@laredo.cc.tx.us
Web: www.laredo.cc.tx.us

Program Information:
Program begins: August
Degrees offered: Associate's, 21 months

Financial Information:
Tuition, resident: $1,303
Tuition, non-resident: $2,454
Average cost of books: $300

Employment Profile:
% of students who pass the boards on their first try: 100
% employed within the first 6 months following graduation: 100
Average starting salary: $32,000

McLennan Community College
1400 College Drive
Waco, TX 76708

Contact Information:
Telephone: 254-299-8417
Fax: 254-299-8435
E-mail: brm@mcc.cc.tx.us
Web: www.mcc.cc.tx.us

Program Information:
Program begins: September
Degrees offered: Associate's, 24 months

Application Information:
Enrollment of program: 32
Transfer students are accepted.

Financial Information:
Tuition, resident: $3,532
Tuition, non-resident: $3,872

Employment Profile:
Average starting salary: $23,040

San Jacinto College Central Campus
8060 Spencer Highway
PO Box 2007
Pasadena, TX 77501-2007

Contact Information:
Telephone: 281-478-2730
Fax: 281-478-2754
E-mail: bstahl@central.sjcd.cc.tx.us

Program Information:
Program begins: August
Degrees offered: Associate's, 23 months

Application Information:
Enrollment of program: 30
Transfer students are accepted.

Financial Information:
Tuition, resident: $1,899
Tuition, non-resident: $2,907
Average cost of books: $450
% of students receiving aid: 50

Employment Profile:
% of students who pass the boards on their first try: 93
% employed within the first 6 months following graduation: 95
Average starting salary: $22,500

St. Philip's College
1801 Martin Luther King Drive
San Antonio, TX 78203-2098

Contact Information:
Telephone: 210-531-3449
Fax: 210-531-3459
E-mail: jreynold@accd.edu
Web: www.accd.edu

Program Information:
Program begins: August, January, June
Degrees offered: Associate's, 24 months
Evening or weekend classes are available.

Application Information:
Enrollment of program: 16
Transfer students are accepted.

Financial Information:
Tuition, resident: $720
Tuition, non-resident: $1,380
Average cost of books: $250

Employment Profile:
% of students who pass the boards on their first try: 69
% employed within the first 6 months following graduation: 75
Average starting salary: $18,000

Temple College
2600 South First Street
Temple, TX 76504

Contact Information:
Telephone: 254-778-4811
Fax: 254-771-4528
Web: www.temple.edu

Program Information:
Program begins: August
Degrees offered: Diploma; Associate's, 24 months

Application Information:
Enrollment of program: 30
Transfer students are accepted.

Financial Information:
Tuition, resident: $1,460
Tuition, non-resident: $1,900
Average cost of books: $500
% of students receiving aid: 95

Employment Profile:
% of students who pass the boards on their first try: 85
% employed within the first 6 months following graduation: 100
Average starting salary: $26,000

University of Texas at Brownsville/ Texas Southmost College
83 Ft. Brown
Brownsville, TX 78520

Contact Information:
Telephone: 740-245-7319
Fax: 740-245-7440
E-mail: sgdavis@utb1.utb.edu

Program Information:
Program begins: August
Degrees offered: Associate's, 21 months

Financial Information:
Tuition, resident: $1,158
Tuition, non-resident: $4,092

Wharton County Junior College
911 Boling Highway
Wharton, TX 77488

Contact Information:
Telephone: 409-532-4560 ext. 6364
Fax: 409-532-6489
E-mail: janiceh@wcjc.cc.tx.us
Web: www.whatcom.ctc.edu

Program Information:
Program begins: August
Degrees offered: Associate's, 24 months

Application Information:
Transfer students are accepted.

Financial Information:
Tuition, resident: $1,053
Tuition, non-resident: $1,794

Utah

Salt Lake Community College
PO Box 30808
Salt Lake City, UT 84130

Contact Information:
Telephone: 801-581-3544
Fax: 801-581-2463
E-mail: karen_brown@medschool.med.utah.edu
Web: www.slcc.edu

Program Information:
Program begins: August
Degrees offered: Associate's, 24 months

Application Information:
Enrollment of program: 4
Transfer students are accepted.

Financial Information:
Tuition, resident: $1,600
Tuition, non-resident: $4,800
Average cost of books: $350
% of students receiving aid: 50

Employment Profile:
% of students who pass the boards on their first try: 95
% employed within the first 6 months following graduation: 100
Average starting salary: $21,700

Virginia

Centra Health Systems of Lynchburg
3300 Rivermont Avenue
Lynchburg, VA 24503

Contact Information:
Telephone: 804-947-4551
Fax: 804-947-4035
E-mail: robin.smith@centrahealth.com
Web: www.centralhealth.com

Program Information:
Program begins: March
Degrees offered: Associate's, 12 months

Financial Information:
Tuition, resident: $1,632
Tuition, non-resident: $5,530

J. Sargeant Reynolds Community College
PO Box 85622
Richmond, VA 23285-5622

Contact Information:
Telephone: 804-371-3253
Fax: 804-371-3311
E-mail: rharris@jsr.cc.va.us
Web: www.jsr.cc.va.us

Program Information:
Program begins: August, January
Degrees offered: Associate's, 21 months
Evening or weekend classes are available.

Application Information:
Enrollment of program: 36
Transfer students are accepted.

Financial Information:
Tuition, resident: $2,136
Tuition, non-resident: $6,948

Employment Profile:
% of students who pass the boards on their first try: 95
% employed within the first 6 months following graduation: 100
Average starting salary: $27,500

Northern Virginia Community College
8333 Little River Turnpike
Annandale, VA 22003

Contact Information:
Telephone: 703-323-2331
Fax: 703-323-4576
Web: www.nv.cc.va.us

Program Information:
Program begins: September
Degrees offered: Associate's, 21 months

Application Information:
Transfer students are accepted.

Financial Information:
Tuition, resident: $2,592
Tuition, non-resident: $6,800

Employment Profile:
% of students who pass the boards on their first try: 95
% employed within the first 6 months following graduation: 90
Average starting salary: $30,000

Wytheville Community College
1000 East Main Street
Wytheville, VA 24382

Contact Information:
Telephone: 540-223-4827
Fax: 540-223-4778
E-mail: wccrafb@wc.cc.va.us
Web: www.wc.cc.va.us

Program Information:
Program begins: August
Degrees offered: Associate's, 21 months

Application Information:
Enrollment of program: 28
Transfer students are accepted.

Financial Information:
Tuition, resident: $2,311
Tuition, non-resident: $7,245
Average cost of books: $780
% of students receiving aid: 70

Employment Profile:
% of students who pass the boards on their first try: 100
% employed within the first 6 months following graduation: 100

Washington

Shoreline Community College
16101 Greenwood Avenue North
Seattle, WA 98133

Contact Information:
Telephone: 206-546-4710
Fax: 206-533-5103
E-mail: lbreiwic@ctc.edu
Web: www.oscar.ctc.edu

Program Information:
Program begins: August
Degrees offered: Associate's, 24 months
Evening or weekend classes are available.

Application Information:
Enrollment of program: 11
Transfer students are accepted.

Financial Information:
Tuition, resident: $2,050
Tuition, non-resident: $8,000
Average cost of books: $500

Employment Profile:
% of students who pass the boards on their first try: 97
% employed within the first 6 months following graduation: 90
Average starting salary: $25,000

West Virginia

Bluefield Regional Medical Center

500 Cherry Street
Bluefield, WV 24701

Contact Information:

Telephone: 304-327-1596
Fax: 304-327-1591
E-mail: cunningham@netlinkcorp.com
Web: www.brmc.org

Program Information:

Program begins: August
Degrees offered: Certificate program, 12 months

Application Information:

Enrollment of program: 6

Financial Information:

Average cost of books: $400

Employment Profile:

% of students who pass the boards on their first try: 80
% employed within the first 6 months following graduation: 100
Average starting salary: $25,000

Fairmont State College

Locust Avenue
Fairmont, WV 26554

Contact Information:

Telephone: 304-367-4284
Fax: 304-367-4268
E-mail: rromesburg@mail.fscwv.edu
Web: www.fscwv.edu

Program Information:

Program begins: August
Degrees offered: Associate's, 22 months
Evening or weekend classes are available.

Application Information:

Enrollment of program: 17
Transfer students are accepted.

Financial Information:

Tuition, resident: $2,040
Tuition, non-resident: $4,840
Average cost of books: $500
% of students receiving aid: 65

Southern West Virginia Community College

Logan Campus
PO Box 2900
Mt Gay, WV 25637

Contact Information:

Telephone: 304-792-7098 ext. 243
Fax: 304-792-7028
E-mail: vernone@southern.wvnet.edu
Web: www.southern.wunet.edu

Program Information:

Program begins: September
Degrees offered: Associate's, 21 months

Application Information:

Enrollment of program: 27
Transfer students are accepted.

Financial Information:

Tuition, resident: $1,210
Tuition, non-resident: $4,754

Employment Profile:

% of students who pass the boards on their first try: 100
% employed within the first 6 months following graduation: 30
Average starting salary: $24,000

West Virginia Northern Community College

15th and Jacob Streets
Wheeling, WV 26003

Contact Information:

Telephone: 304-233-5900 ext. 4409
Fax: 304-233-5837
E-mail: gpickett@northern.wvnet.edu
Web: www.northern.wvnet.edu

Program Information:

Program begins: August
Degrees offered: Associate's, 20 months
Evening or weekend classes are available.

Application Information:

Enrollment of program: 32
Transfer students are accepted.

Financial Information:

Tuition, resident: $1,416
Tuition, non-resident: $3,864
Average cost of books: $400

Employment Profile:

% of students who pass the boards on their first try: 90
% employed within the first 6 months following graduation: 70
Average starting salary: $25,000

Wisconsin

Chippewa Valley Technical College

620 West Clairemont Avenue
Eau Claire, WI 54701

Contact Information:

Telephone: 715-833-6420
Fax: 715-833-6470
E-mail: pgriffin@chippewa.tec.wi.us
Web: www.chippewa.tec.wi.us

Program Information:

Program begins: September
Degrees offered: Associate's, 21 months
Evening or weekend classes are available.

Application Information:

Enrollment of program: 18
Transfer students are accepted.

Financial Information:

Tuition, resident: $2,160
Tuition, non-resident: $16,344
Average cost of books: $600
% of students receiving aid: 40

Employment Profile:

% of students who pass the boards on their first try: 85
% employed within the first 6 months following graduation: 90
Average starting salary: $23,000

Madison Area Technical College

3550 Anderson Street
Madison, WI 53704-2599

Contact Information:

Telephone: 608-246-6510
Fax: 608-246-6013
E-mail: manelson@madison.tec.wi.us
Web: www.madison.tec.wi.us

Program Information:

Program begins: September, January
Degrees offered: Associate's, 18 months

Application Information:

Enrollment of program: 40
Transfer students are accepted.

Financial Information:

Tuition, resident: $3,093
Tuition, non-resident: $10,975
Average cost of books: $1,400

Employment Profile:

% of students who pass the boards on their first try: 100
% employed within the first 6 months following graduation: 80
Average starting salary: $24,000

Milwaukee Area Technical College

700 West State Street
Milwaukee, WI 53233

Contact Information:

Telephone: 414-297-7142
Fax: 414-297-6851
E-mail: schmidtd@milwaukee.tec.wi.us
Web: www.matc.edu

Program Information:

Program begins: January, August
Degrees offered: Associate's, 19 months
Evening or weekend classes are available.

Application Information:

Enrollment of program: 16
Transfer students are accepted.

Financial Information:

Tuition, resident: $1,650
Tuition, non-resident: $11,734
Average cost of books: $350
% of students receiving aid: 24

Employment Profile:

% of students who pass the boards on their first try: 80
% employed within the first 6 months following graduation: 92
Average starting salary: $24,840

Northeast Wisconsin Technical College
2740 West Mason Street
PO Box 19042
Green Bay, WI 54307-9042

Contact Information:
Telephone: 920-498-6374
Fax: 920-498-5560
E-mail: moorepm@nwtc.tec.wi.us
Web: www.nwtc.tec.wi.us

Program Information:
Program begins: August
Degrees offered: Associate's, 21 months
Evening or weekend classes are available.

Application Information:
Enrollment of program: 32
Transfer students are accepted.

Financial Information:
Tuition, resident: $2,209
Tuition, non-resident: $4,418
Average cost of books: $550

Employment Profile:
% of students who pass the boards on their first try: 95
% employed within the first 6 months following graduation: 95

Western Wisconsin Technical College
304 North Sixth Street
PO Box 908
La Crosse, WI 54602-0908

Contact Information:
Telephone: 608-785-9169
Fax: 608-785-9194
E-mail: cipriano@a1.western.tec.wi.us
Web: www.western.tec.wi.us

Program Information:
Program begins: September
Degrees offered: Associate's, 20 months

Application Information:
Enrollment of program: 20
Transfer students are accepted.

Financial Information:
Tuition, resident: $2,543
Tuition, non-resident: $16,717

Employment Profile:
% of students who pass the boards on their first try: 89
% employed within the first 6 months following graduation: 95
Average starting salary: $22,000

Clinical Laboratory Scientist

Alabama

Alabama Reference Laboratories
543 South Hull Street
PO Box 4600
Montgomery, AL 36103-4600

Contact Information:
Telephone: 334-263-5745
Fax: 334-241-0513

Program Information:
Program begins: January, July
Duration of program: 12 months

Application Information:
Enrollment of program: 7

Employment Profile:
% of students who pass the boards on their first try: 94
% employed within the first 6 months following graduation: 100
Average starting salary: $25,000

Auburn University at Montgomery
School of Science
Department of Biology/Box 244023
Montgomery, AL 36124

Contact Information:
Telephone: 334-244-3606
Fax: 334-244-3826
E-mail: barksjm@strudel.aum.edu
Web: www.aum.edu

Program Information:
Program begins: August
Degrees offered: Bachelor's, 36 months

Application Information:
Enrollment of program: 12
Transfer students are accepted.

Financial Information:
Tuition, resident: $2,872
Tuition, non-resident: $8,616

Employment Profile:
% of students who pass the boards on their first try: 90
% employed within the first 6 months following graduation: 100
Average starting salary: $26,000

Tuskegee University
C-255 John A. Andrew Building
Tuskegee, AL 36088

Contact Information:
Telephone: 334-727-8051
Fax: 334-727-8259
Web: www.tusk.edu

Program Information:
Program begins: March
Duration of program: 24 months

Application Information:
Enrollment of program: 3
Transfer students are accepted.

Financial Information:
Average cost of books: $400
% of students receiving aid: 88

Employment Profile:
% of students who pass the boards on their first try: 66
% employed within the first 6 months following graduation: 98

University of Alabama at Birmingham
School of Health Related Professions
1714 9th Avenue South/Room 381
Birmingham, AL 35294-1270

Contact Information:
Telephone: 501-686-5776
Fax: 501-686-6513
E-mail: randolph@uab.edu
Web: www.uab.edu.

Program Information:
Program begins: September

Application Information:
Enrollment of program: 19
Transfer students are accepted.

Employment Profile:
% of students who pass the boards on their first try: 93
% employed within the first 6 months following graduation: 95
Average starting salary: $27,000

University of South Alabama
Department of Clinical Laboratory Sciences
1504 Springhill Avenue Room 2309
Mobile, AL 36604

Contact Information:
Telephone: 787-758-2525
Fax: 787-759-3645
Web: www.usouthal.edu

Program Information:
Program begins: August
Duration of program: 21 months

Application Information:
Enrollment of program: 20
Transfer students are accepted.

Financial Information:
Tuition, resident: $2,478
Tuition, non-resident: $4,783
Average cost of books: $400

Employment Profile:
% of students who pass the boards on their first try: 80
% employed within the first 6 months following graduation: 50
Average starting salary: $26,000

Arizona

Arizona State University

Clinical Lab Science/Department of Microbiology
PO Box 872701
Tempe, AZ 85287-2701

Contact Information:
Telephone: 602-965-7090
Fax: 602-965-0098
E-mail: jem16@asu.edu
Web: www.asu.edu

Program Information:
Program begins: January
Degrees offered: Bachelor's, 16 months

Application Information:
Enrollment of program: 14
Transfer students are accepted.

Financial Information:
Tuition, resident: $1,988
Tuition, non-resident: $8,640
Average cost of books: $500

Employment Profile:
% of students who pass the boards on their first try: 98
% employed within the first 6 months following graduation: 100
Average starting salary: $30,000

University of Arizona

School of Health Professions
1435 North Fremont
Tucson, AZ 85719

Contact Information:
Telephone: 916-734-0231
Fax: 916-734-0320
E-mail: hplotter@u.arizona.edu
Web: www.arizona.edu

Program Information:
Program begins: August
Duration of program: 18 months

Application Information:
Enrollment of program: 30

Financial Information:
Tuition, resident: $2,264
Tuition, non-resident: $9,416
Average cost of books: $300

Employment Profile:
% of students who pass the boards on their first try: 90
% employed within the first 6 months following graduation: 100
Average starting salary: $28,400

Arkansas

Baptist Health

11900 Colonel Glenn Road
Suite 1000
Little Rock, AR 72210-2820

Contact Information:
Telephone: 501-202-7409
Fax: 501-202-7406
Web: www.palmettohealth.org

Program Information:
Program begins: September
Duration of program: 12 months

Application Information:
Enrollment of program: 39

Financial Information:
Average cost of books: $410
% of students receiving aid: 5

Employment Profile:
% of students who pass the boards on their first try: 90
% employed within the first 6 months following graduation: 100
Average starting salary: $27,500

University of Arkansas for Medical Sciences

4301 West Markham Street
Slot 597
Little Rock, AR 72205

Contact Information:
Telephone: 714-456-5037
Fax: 714-456-8272
E-mail: lakemarthaj@exchange.uams.edu
Web: www.uams.edu

Program Information:
Program begins: July
Duration of program: 18 months

Application Information:
Enrollment of program: 52
Transfer students are accepted.

Financial Information:
Tuition, resident: $2,208
Tuition, non-resident: $5,520
Average cost of books: $600

Employment Profile:
% of students who pass the boards on their first try: 90
% employed within the first 6 months following graduation: 90
Average starting salary: $27,000

California

Eisenhower Memorial Hospital

39000 Bob Hope Drive
Rancho Mirage, CA 92270

Contact Information:
Telephone: 760-773-4525
Fax: 760-773-4363
E-mail: jsteiner@emc.org
Web: www.emc.org

Program Information:
Program begins: July, January
Duration of program: 12 months

San Francisco State University

Center for Biomedical Laboratory Science 211
San Francisco, CA 94132

Contact Information:
Telephone: 415-338-2332
Fax: 415-338-7747
E-mail: carola@sfsu.edu
Web: www.sfsu.edu

Program Information:
Program begins: February, July
Duration of program: 15 months

Financial Information:
Tuition, resident: $2,700
Tuition, non-resident: $10,800

Santa Barbara Cottage Hospital

Pueblo at Bath Street
PO Box 689
Santa Barbara, CA 93102

Contact Information:
Telephone: 805-569-7378
Fax: 805-569-8223
Web: www.cottagehealthsystem.org

Program Information:
Program begins: August
Duration of program: 12 months

Financial Information:
Average cost of books: $200
% of students receiving aid: 50

Employment Profile:
% of students who pass the boards on their first try: 100
% employed within the first 6 months following graduation: 100
Average starting salary: $33,000

Colorado

Centura Health/Penrose—St. Francis Health Service

2215 North Cascade Avenue
PO Box 7021
Colorado Springs, CO 80933

Contact Information:
Telephone: 719-776-5221
Fax: 719-776-5584
E-mail: rosebrown@centura.org
Web: www.centura.org

Program Information:
Program begins: August
Degrees offered: Certificate program, 12 months

Application Information:
Enrollment of program: 4

Financial Information:
Average cost of books: $675

Employment Profile:
% of students who pass the boards on their first try: 95

% employed within the first 6 months following graduation: 100
Average starting salary: $34,320

Connecticut

Danbury Hospital
24 Hospital Avenue
Danbury, CT 06810

Contact Information:
Telephone: 203-797-7804
Fax: 203-731-8061
E-mail: rebecca.brewer@danhosp.org
Web: www.danhosp.org

Program Information:
Program begins: July
Degrees offered: Certificate program, 12 months; Post-bachelor's Certificate, 12 months

Application Information:
Enrollment of program: 3

Financial Information:
Average cost of books: $500

Employment Profile:
% of students who pass the boards on their first try: 90
% employed within the first 6 months following graduation: 100
Average starting salary: $35,000

Quinnipiac College
275 Mt. Carmel Avenue
Hamden, CT 06518

Contact Information:
Telephone: 203-281-8609
Fax: 203-281-8706
E-mail: brady@quinnipiac.edu
Web: www.quinnipiac.edu

Program Information:
Program begins: August
Duration of program: 27 months

Application Information:
Enrollment of program: 95

Financial Information:
Average cost of books: $3,860
% of students receiving aid: 85

Employment Profile:
% of students who pass the boards on their first try: 98
% employed within the first 6 months following graduation: 71
Average starting salary: $58,000

University of Hartford
Dana Hall/Room 232
200 Bloomfield Avenue
West Hartford, CT 06117-1599

Contact Information:
Telephone: 205-934-4863
Fax: 205-975-7302
E-mail: bitnet:barrett@hartford.edu
Web: www.hartford.edu

Program Information:
Program begins: August
Duration of program: 12 months
Evening or weekend classes are available.

Application Information:
Transfer students are accepted.

Financial Information:
Tuition, resident: $8,955
Tuition, non-resident: $17,910

Delaware

University of Delaware
050 McKinly Laboratory
Department of Medical Technology
Newark, DE 19716

Contact Information:
Telephone: 302-831-2849
Fax: 302-831-4180
E-mail: aciulla@udel.edu
Web: www.udel.edu

Program Information:
Program begins: July, August
Degrees offered: Bachelor's, 18 months

Application Information:
Enrollment of program: 40
Transfer students are accepted.

Financial Information:
Tuition, resident: $4,380
Tuition, non-resident: $12,750

Employment Profile:
% of students who pass the boards on their first try: 93
% employed within the first 6 months following graduation: 90
Average starting salary: $33,500

Howard University
Division of Allied Health
Sixth & Bryant Streets Northwest, C/AHS
Washington, DC 20059

Contact Information:
Telephone: 202-806-7573
Fax: 202-462-9569
E-mail: hkarnik@fac.howard.edu
Web: www.howard.edu

Program Information:
Program begins: August
Degrees offered: Bachelor's, 18 months

Application Information:
Enrollment of program: 35
Transfer students are accepted.

Financial Information:
Tuition, resident: $4,890
Average cost of books: $150
% of students receiving aid: 65

Employment Profile:
% of students who pass the boards on their first try: 73
% employed within the first 6 months following graduation: 35
Average starting salary: $26,500

Washington Hospital Center
110 Irving Street Northwest
Washington, DC 20010

Contact Information:
Telephone: 202-877-3346
Fax: 202-877-8235
E-mail: amf3@mhg.edu

Program Information:
Program begins: August
Degrees offered: Certificate program, 12 months

Application Information:
Enrollment of program: 12

Financial Information:
Average cost of books: $500

Employment Profile:
% of students who pass the boards on their first try: 90
% employed within the first 6 months following graduation: 100
Average starting salary: $29,000

Florida

Bayfront Medical Center
701 Sixth Street South
St. Petersburg, FL 33701

Contact Information:
Telephone: 727-893-6604
Fax: 727-893-6604
Web: www.baycare.org

Program Information:
Program begins: July
Degrees offered: Certificate program, 12 months; Post-bachelor's Certificate, 12 months

Application Information:
Enrollment of program: 6

Financial Information:
Average cost of books: $450

Employment Profile:
% of students who pass the boards on their first try: 100
% employed within the first 6 months following graduation: 100
Average starting salary: $24,000

Bethune-Cookman College
640 Dr. Mary McLeod Bethune Boulevard
Daytona Beach, FL 32114-3099

Contact Information:
Telephone: 904-255-1401 ext. 422
Fax: 904-253-7726
E-mail: kennedj@cookman.edu
Web: www.cookman.edu

Program Information:
Program begins: August, January
Degrees offered: Certificate program, 36 months; Bachelor's, 12 months; Post master's Certificate, 12 months; Post-bachelor's Certificate, 12 months

Application Information:
Enrollment of program: 10
Transfer students are accepted.

Financial Information:
Average cost of books: $250
% of students receiving aid: 90

Employment Profile:
% of students who pass the boards on their first try: 80
% employed within the first 6 months following graduation: 100

Florida Hospital College of Health Sciences

601 East Rollins Street
Orlando, FL 32803

Contact Information:
Telephone: 407-897-1855
Fax: 407-893-6943
E-mail: pat-rogers@fhmis.net

Program Information:
Program begins: August
Degrees offered: Certificate program; Diploma, 12 months

Application Information:
Enrollment of program: 13

Financial Information:
Average cost of books: $400

Employment Profile:
% employed within the first 6 months following graduation: 100
Average starting salary: $30,000

Shands—Jacksonville

655 West Eighth Street
Jacksonville, FL 32209

Contact Information:
Telephone: 904-549-4660
Fax: 904-549-4629

Program Information:
Program begins: July, January
Degrees offered: Certificate program, 12 months; Post-bachelor's Certificate, 12 months

Application Information:
Enrollment of program: 6

Financial Information:
Average cost of books: $300

Employment Profile:
% of students who pass the boards on their first try: 100
% employed within the first 6 months following graduation: 100
Average starting salary: $30,000

St. Vincent's Medical Center

School of Medical Center
1800 Barrs Street
Jacksonville, FL 32203

Contact Information:
Telephone: 313-343-3508
Fax: 313-343-7842

Program Information:
Program begins: January, July
Degrees offered: Certificate program, 12 months

Application Information:
Enrollment of program: 10

Financial Information:
Average cost of books: $110
% of students receiving aid: 25

Employment Profile:
% of students who pass the boards on their first try: 95
% employed within the first 6 months following graduation: 100
Average starting salary: $30,000

Tampa General Hospital

PO Box 1289
Tampa, FL 33601

Contact Information:
Telephone: 813-251-7246
Fax: 813-253-4073

Program Information:
Program begins: August
Degrees offered: Certificate program, 12 months; Post-bachelor's Certificate, 12 months

Application Information:
Enrollment of program: 5

Financial Information:
Average cost of books: $350

Employment Profile:
% of students who pass the boards on their first try: 100
% employed within the first 6 months following graduation: 100
Average starting salary: $28,000

University of Central Florida

4000 Central Florida Boulevard/B10 306
Orlando, FL 32816-2360

Contact Information:
Telephone: 701-777-2636
Fax: 701-777-3108
E-mail: hitchcod@mail.ucf.edu
Web: www.ucf.edu

Program Information:
Program begins: August
Duration of program: 24 months

Application Information:
Enrollment of program: 25
Transfer students are accepted.

Financial Information:
Tuition, resident: $1,586
Tuition, non-resident: $3,030

Employment Profile:
% employed within the first 6 months following graduation: 100

University of West Florida

Department of Biology
11000 University Parkway
Pensacola, FL 32514-5751

Contact Information:
Telephone: 850-474-2988
Fax: 850-474-2749
E-mail: skrothap@nautilus.uwf.edu
Web: www.uwf.edu

Program Information:
Program begins: September
Duration of program: 15 months

Financial Information:
Tuition, resident: $2,143
Tuition, non-resident: $8,799

Georgia

Armstrong Atlantic State University

11935 Abercorn Street
Savannah, GA 31419-1997

Contact Information:
Telephone: 912-927-5204
Fax: 912-921-5585
E-mail: hardegle@mail.armstrong.edu
Web: www.armstrong.edu

Program Information:
Program begins: August
Degrees offered: Bachelor's, 16 months; Post-bachelor's Certificate, 16 months
Evening or weekend classes are available.

Application Information:
Enrollment of program: 15
Transfer students are accepted.

Financial Information:
Tuition, resident: $2,616
Tuition, non-resident: $8,564
Average cost of books: $500
% of students receiving aid: 80

Employment Profile:
% of students who pass the boards on their first try: 90
% employed within the first 6 months following graduation: 100
Average starting salary: $26,000

Medical College of Georgia

Department of Medical Technology
AL-106
Augusta, GA 30912-0500

Contact Information:
Telephone: 706-721-3046
Fax: 706-721-7631
E-mail: jcrowley@mail.mcg.edu
Web: www.mcg.edu

Program Information:
Program begins: July
Duration of program: 22 months

Application Information:
Enrollment of program: 40
Transfer students are accepted.

Financial Information:
Tuition, resident: $2,700
Tuition, non-resident: $9,940
Average cost of books: $500
% of students receiving aid: 60

Employment Profile:
% of students who pass the boards on their first try: 60
% employed within the first 6 months following graduation: 90
Average starting salary: $24,000

Illinois

Finch University of Health Science/ Chicago Medical School

3333 Green Bay Road
North Chicago, IL 60064

Contact Information:
Telephone: 847-578-3418
Fax: 847-578-8651
E-mail: deroberj@misfinchcms.edu
Web: www.finchcms.edu

Program Information:
Program begins: August
Duration of program: 24 months

Application Information:
Transfer students are accepted.

Employment Profile:
% employed within the first 6 months following graduation: 100
Average starting salary: $28,000

Northern Illinois University

Clinical Laboratory Scientist Program
DeKalb, IL 60115-2854

Contact Information:
Telephone: 815-753-1382
Fax: 815-753-1653
E-mail: dcearlock@niu.edu
Web: www.niu.edu

Program Information:
Program begins: September
Duration of program: 18 months

Application Information:
Enrollment of program: 75
Transfer students are accepted.

Financial Information:
Tuition, resident: $4,347
Tuition, non-resident: $10,619
% of students receiving aid: 70

Employment Profile:
% of students who pass the boards on their first try: 88
% employed within the first 6 months following graduation: 50
Average starting salary: $33,000

Rush University

1653 West Harrison Street
Chicago, IL 60612

Contact Information:
Telephone: 312-942-7251
Fax: 312-942-6464
E-mail: hmiller@rush.edu
Web: www.rushu.rush.edu/modtech

Program Information:
Program begins: January, July
Duration of program: 20 months

Application Information:
Enrollment of program: 40
Transfer students are accepted.

Financial Information:
Tuition, resident: $12,700
Average cost of books: $300
% of students receiving aid: 50

Employment Profile:
% of students who pass the boards on their first try: 90
% employed within the first 6 months following graduation: 100
Average starting salary: $32,000

St. Elizabeth Hospital

211 South Third Street
Belleville, IL 62222

Contact Information:
Telephone: 920-738-2128
Fax: 920-831-8518
E-mail: jbdenaro@comp-type.net

Program Information:
Program begins: July
Duration of program: 12 months

Application Information:
Enrollment of program: 3

Financial Information:
Average cost of books: $300

Employment Profile:
% of students who pass the boards on their first try: 95
% employed within the first 6 months following graduation: 100
Average starting salary: $27,000

St. Francis Medical Center

530 Northeast Glen Oak Avenue
Peoria, IL 61637

Contact Information:
Telephone: 309-624-9021
Fax: 309-624-9150
E-mail: cathy.r.moewe@osfhealthcare.org
Web: www.osfsaintfrancis.org

Program Information:
Program begins: August
Duration of program: 11 months

Financial Information:
Average cost of books: $300

Employment Profile:
% of students who pass the boards on their first try: 98
% employed within the first 6 months following graduation: 90
Average starting salary: $26,000

St. John's Hospital

800 East Carpenter Street
Springfield, IL 62769

Contact Information:
Telephone: 417-885-2880
E-mail: groncanc@st-johns.org
Web: www.stjohns.org

Program Information:
Program begins: May
Duration of program: 12 months

Application Information:
Enrollment of program: 6

Financial Information:
Average cost of books: $450

Employment Profile:
% of students who pass the boards on their first try: 95
% employed within the first 6 months following graduation: 80
Average starting salary: $27,000

Swedish American Hospital

1400 Charles Street
Rockford, IL 61104

Contact Information:
Telephone: 815-489-4268
Fax: 815-966-3967
Web: www.cmrg.com

Program Information:
Program begins: June
Degrees offered: Certificate program, 9 months

Application Information:
Enrollment of program: 6

Financial Information:
Average cost of books: $300

Employment Profile:
% of students who pass the boards on their first try: 96
% employed within the first 6 months following graduation: 100
Average starting salary: $29,000

University of Illinois at Chicago

808 South Wood Street
Room 690 M/C 518
Chicago, IL 60612-7305

Contact Information:
Telephone: 407-823-2968
Fax: 407-823-3095
E-mail: dweaver@uic.edu
Web: www.uic.edu

Program Information:
Program begins: August
Duration of program: 22 months

Application Information:
Enrollment of program: 45
Transfer students are accepted.

Financial Information:
Tuition, resident: $5,402
Tuition, non-resident: $12,300
Average cost of books: $750

Employment Profile:
% of students who pass the boards on their first try: 90
% employed within the first 6 months following graduation: 95
Average starting salary: $28,000

Indiana

Ball Memorial Hospital
2401 University Avenue
Muncie, IN 47303

Contact Information:
Telephone: 765-741-2930
Fax: 765-747-3326
E-mail: replogles@palab.com

Program Information:
Program begins: June
Duration of program: 12 months

Application Information:
Enrollment of program: 6
Transfer students are accepted.

Financial Information:
Tuition, resident: $2,500
Average cost of books: $500
% of students receiving aid: 50

Employment Profile:
% of students who pass the boards on their first try: 90
% employed within the first 6 months following graduation: 100
Average starting salary: $31,000

Good Samaritan Hospital
520 South Seventh Street
Vincennes, IN 47591

Contact Information:
Telephone: 812-885-3367
Fax: 812-885-3135
Web: www.goodsamaritan.com

Program Information:
Program begins: August
Duration of program: 12 months

Employment Profile:
% employed within the first 6 months following graduation: 100

Methodist Hospital—Clarian Health
1701 North Senate Boulevard
PO Box 1367
Indianapolis, IN 46206

Contact Information:
Telephone: 317-929-8280
Fax: 317-929-2102
E-mail: coliver@clarian.com
Web: www.clarian.com

Program Information:
Program begins: June
Degrees offered: Certificate program, 12 months

Application Information:
Enrollment of program: 24

Financial Information:
Average cost of books: $400

Employment Profile:
% of students who pass the boards on their first try: 97
% employed within the first 6 months following graduation: 100

Parkview Memorial Hospital
2200 Randallia
Ft. Wayne, IN 46805

Contact Information:
Telephone: 219-482-5834 ext. 30208
Fax: 219-483-1373
E-mail: fran.williams@parkview.com
Web: www.parkview.com

Program Information:
Program begins: August
Duration of program: 11 months

Application Information:
Enrollment of program: 4
Transfer students are accepted.

Financial Information:
Average cost of books: $325

Employment Profile:
% of students who pass the boards on their first try: 96
% employed within the first 6 months following graduation: 100
Average starting salary: $30,000

St. Francis Hospital and Health Centers
1600 Albany Street
Beech Grove, IN 46107

Contact Information:
Telephone: 317-783-8195
Fax: 317-783-8801
E-mail: d_maxwell@iquest.net
Web: www.stfrancis-indy.org

Program Information:
Program begins: July
Degrees offered: Certificate program, 12 months; Bachelor's, 12 months

Application Information:
Enrollment of program: 8

Financial Information:
Average cost of books: $250

Employment Profile:
% of students who pass the boards on their first try: 100
% employed within the first 6 months following graduation: 100
Average starting salary: $26,000

Iowa

St. Luke's Hospitals
1026 A Avenue Northeast
Cedar Rapids, IA 52402

Contact Information:
Telephone: 219-932-2300 ext. 34199
Fax: 219-933-2136
E-mail: sojkan@crstlukes.com
Web: www.stlukes.cr.org

Program Information:
Program begins: August
Duration of program: 12 months

Application Information:
Enrollment of program: 6

Financial Information:
Average cost of books: $250
% of students receiving aid: 35

Employment Profile:
% of students who pass the boards on their first try: 95
% employed within the first 6 months following graduation: 100
Average starting salary: $30,000

Kansas

Wichita State University
Campus Box 43
Wichita, KS 67260

Contact Information:
Telephone: 316-978-5655
Fax: 316-978-3025
E-mail: conrad@chp.twsu.edu
Web: www.wichita.edu

Program Information:
Program begins: January, June, August
Degrees offered: Bachelor's, 17 months

Application Information:
Enrollment of program: 35
Transfer students are accepted.

Financial Information:
Tuition, resident: $4,906
Tuition, non-resident: $17,114
Average cost of books: $700
% of students receiving aid: 95

Employment Profile:
% of students who pass the boards on their first try: 98

% employed within the first 6 months following graduation: 100
Average starting salary: $32,000

Kentucky

St. Elizabeth Medical Center

One Medical Village Drive
Edgewood, KY 41017

Contact Information:
Telephone: 606-344-2417
Fax: 606-344-5560

Program Information:
Program begins: July
Degrees offered: Certificate program, 12 months

Application Information:
Enrollment of program: 4

Financial Information:
Average cost of books: $350
% of students receiving aid: 20

Employment Profile:
% of students who pass the boards on their first try: 100
% employed within the first 6 months following graduation: 100
Average starting salary: $30,000

Louisiana

Louisiana State University Medical Center—New Orleans

1900 Gravier Street
New Orleans, LA 70112

Contact Information:
Telephone: 504-568-4276
Fax: 504-568-6761
E-mail: llawre@lsumc.edu
Web: www.lsumc.edu

Program Information:
Program begins: May
Degrees offered: Bachelor's, 15 months

Application Information:
Enrollment of program: 37
Transfer students are accepted.

Financial Information:
Tuition, resident: $3,409
Tuition, non-resident: $6,534
Average cost of books: $485

Employment Profile:
% of students who pass the boards on their first try: 94
% employed within the first 6 months following graduation: 100
Average starting salary: $30,500

Overton Brooks VA Medical Center

510 East Stoner Avenue
Shreveport, LA 71101-4295

Contact Information:
Telephone: 318-424-6169
Fax: 318-424-6093
E-mail: beene.mary.e@shreveport.va.gov
Web: www.shreve.net

Program Information:
Program begins: January, July
Duration of program: 12 months

Financial Information:
Average cost of books: $210

Employment Profile:
% of students who pass the boards on their first try: 95
% employed within the first 6 months following graduation: 100
Average starting salary: $27,000

Rapides Regional Medical Center

211 Fourth Street
PO Box 30101
Alexandria, LA 71301

Contact Information:
Telephone: 318-473-3175
Fax: 318-473-3079

Program Information:
Program begins: September
Degrees offered: Certificate program, 12 months

Application Information:
Enrollment of program: 8

Financial Information:
Average cost of books: $350

Employment Profile:
% of students who pass the boards on their first try: 86
% employed within the first 6 months following graduation: 100
Average starting salary: $32,000

St. Patrick Hospital

524 South Ryan Street
PO Box 3401
Lake Charles, LA 70602-3401

Contact Information:
Telephone: 814-452-5365
Fax: 814-456-4784

Program Information:
Program begins: August
Duration of program: 12 months

Application Information:
Enrollment of program: 20

Financial Information:
Average cost of books: $400
% of students receiving aid: 50

Employment Profile:
% employed within the first 6 months following graduation: 100

Maine

Eastern Maine Medical Center

489 State Street
Bangoe, ME 04401

Contact Information:
Telephone: 207-973-7616
Fax: 207-973-7609
E-mail: emlibby@maine.edu
Web: www.emh.org

Program Information:
Program begins: August
Duration of program: 11 months

Application Information:
Transfer students are accepted.

Financial Information:
Average cost of books: $250
% of students receiving aid: 50

Employment Profile:
% of students who pass the boards on their first try: 90
% employed within the first 6 months following graduation: 60
Average starting salary: $28,000

Maryland

Salisbury State University

1101 Camden Avenue
Salisbury, MD 21801

Contact Information:
Telephone: 410-543-6364
Fax: 410-548-9185
E-mail: jwlaird@ssu.edu
Web: www.ssu.edu

Program Information:
Program begins: August, January, June
Duration of program: 24 months

Application Information:
Enrollment of program: 25

Financial Information:
Tuition, resident: $2,972
Tuition, non-resident: $7,366
Average cost of books: $500
% of students receiving aid: 63

Employment Profile:
% of students who pass the boards on their first try: 95
% employed within the first 6 months following graduation: 80
Average starting salary: $30,000

Massachusetts

Berkshire Medical Center

725 North Street
Pittsfield, MA 01201

Contact Information:
Telephone: 413-447-2580
Fax: 413-447-2097
E-mail: lbillings@bhs1.org

Program Information:
Degrees offered: Certificate program, 12 months

Application Information:
Enrollment of program: 8

Financial Information:
Tuition, resident: $1,000

Employment Profile:
% of students who pass the boards on their first try: 90
% employed within the first 6 months following graduation: 100
Average starting salary: $31,000

Fitchburg State College

160 Pearl Street
Fitchburg, MA 01420

Contact Information:
Telephone: 978-665-3080
Fax: 978-665-3578
E-mail: dboisvert@fsc.edu
Web: www.fsc.edu

Program Information:
Program begins: August
Duration of program: 48 months

Application Information:
Enrollment of program: 48
Transfer students are accepted.

Financial Information:
Tuition, resident: $1,210
Tuition, non-resident: $6,450
Average cost of books: $750

Employment Profile:
% of students who pass the boards on their first try: 97
% employed within the first 6 months following graduation: 80
Average starting salary: $29,000

University of Massachusetts—Dartmouth

Department of Medical Lab Science
285 Old Westport Road
North Dartmouth, MA 02747-2300

Contact Information:
Telephone: 217-786-6589
Fax: 217-786-7188
E-mail: dbergeron@umassd.edu
Web: www.umassd.edu

Program Information:
Program begins: September, January
Degrees offered: Bachelor's, 48 months

Application Information:
Transfer students are accepted.

Financial Information:
Tuition, resident: $4,129
Tuition, non-resident: $11,783
Average cost of books: $300
% of students receiving aid: 70

Employment Profile:
% of students who pass the boards on their first try: 95
% employed within the first 6 months following graduation: 95
Average starting salary: $32,000

University of Massachusetts—Lowell

3 Solomon Way Suite 4
Lowell, MA 018545125

Contact Information:
Telephone: 319-335-9545
Fax: 319-335-8348
E-mail: kathleendoyle_uml.edu
Web: www.uml.edu

Program Information:
Program begins: January, July
Duration of program: 36 months

Application Information:
Enrollment of program: 20-30
Transfer students are accepted.

Financial Information:
Tuition, resident: $1,454
Tuition, non-resident: $7,871
Average cost of books: $500

Employment Profile:
% of students who pass the boards on their first try: 85
% employed within the first 6 months following graduation: 88
Average starting salary: $30,000

Michigan

Andrews University

Allied Health Department
Berrien Springs, MI 49104

Contact Information:
Telephone: 616-471-3336
Fax: 616-471-6218
E-mail: cls@andrews.edu
Web: www.andrews.edu

Program Information:
Program begins: August
Duration of program: 11 months

Eastern Michigan University

327 King Hall
Ypsilanti, MI 48197

Contact Information:
Telephone: 313-487-3223
Fax: 313-427-4095
E-mail: ahp_hammerbe@online.emich.edu
Web: www.emich.edu

Program Information:
Program begins: June
Degrees offered: Bachelor's, 36 months

Application Information:
Enrollment of program: 60
Transfer students are accepted.

Financial Information:
Tuition, resident: $2,300
Tuition, non-resident: $6,000
Average cost of books: $500

Employment Profile:
% of students who pass the boards on their first try: 80
% employed within the first 6 months following graduation: 90
Average starting salary: $27,000

Ferris State University

College of Allied Health Sciences
200 Ferris Drive/VFS 303
Big Rapids, MI 49307-2740

Contact Information:
Telephone: 231-591-2283
Fax: 231-591-3788
E-mail: landisj@ferris.edu
Web: www.ferris.edu

Program Information:
Program begins: July
Degrees offered: Bachelor's, 48 months

Application Information:
Enrollment of program: 17
Transfer students are accepted.

Financial Information:
Tuition, resident: $3,808
Tuition, non-resident: $7,850
Average cost of books: $250

Employment Profile:
% of students who pass the boards on their first try: 80
% employed within the first 6 months following graduation: 96
Average starting salary: $31,000

Michigan State University

322 North Kedzie Lab
East Lansing, MI 48824-1031

Contact Information:
Telephone: 517-353-7800
Fax: 517-432-2006
E-mail: estry@.msu.edu
Web: www.msu.edu

Program Information:
Program begins: August
Duration of program: 30 months

Application Information:
Enrollment of program: 26
Transfer students are accepted.

Financial Information:
Tuition, resident: $5,006
Tuition, non-resident: $11,801
Average cost of books: $320

Employment Profile:
% of students who pass the boards on their first try: 85
% employed within the first 6 months following graduation: 80
Average starting salary: $35,000

Spectrum Health
100 Michigan Street Northeast
Grand Rapids, MI 49503

Contact Information:
Telephone: 616-391-1839
Fax: 616-391-1986
E-mail: suzanne.tomlinson@spectrum-health.org
Web: www.spectrum.com

Program Information:
Program begins: June
Duration of program: 11 months

Application Information:
Enrollment of program: 4

Financial Information:
Average cost of books: $200

Employment Profile:
% of students who pass the boards on their first try: 95
% employed within the first 6 months following graduation: 90
Average starting salary: $27,000

Wayne State University
233 Shapero Hall
Detroit, MI 48202

Contact Information:
Telephone: 313-577-5516
Fax: 313-577-5497
Web: www.wayne.edu

Program Information:
Program begins: July
Duration of program: 24 months

Application Information:
Enrollment of program: 30
Transfer students are accepted.

Financial Information:
Tuition, resident: $4,500
Tuition, non-resident: $8,000
Average cost of books: $500

Employment Profile:
% of students who pass the boards on their first try: 85
% employed within the first 6 months following graduation: 90
Average starting salary: $30,000

William Beaumont Hospital
3601 West 13 Mile Road
Royal Oak, MI 48073-6769

Contact Information:
Telephone: 248-551-8023
Fax: 248-551-3694
E-mail: nramirez@beaumont.edu
Web: www.beaumont.edu

Program Information:
Program begins: July
Degrees offered: Certificate program, 11 months

Application Information:
Enrollment of program: 6

Financial Information:
Average cost of books: $300

Employment Profile:
% of students who pass the boards on their first try: 95
% employed within the first 6 months following graduation: 100
Average starting salary: $33,300

Minnesota

College of St. Scholastica
1200 Kenwood Avenue
Duluth, MN 55811

Contact Information:
Telephone: 218-723-6621
Fax: 218-723-6472
E-mail: lbirnbau@css.edu
Web: www.css.edu

Program Information:
Program begins: September
Duration of program: 21 months

Application Information:
Enrollment of program: 6
Transfer students are accepted.

Employment Profile:
% of students who pass the boards on their first try: 98
% employed within the first 6 months following graduation: 95
Average starting salary: $30,000

Hennepin County Medical Center
701 Park Avenue South
Lab 812
Minneapolis, MN 55415

Contact Information:
Telephone: 612-347-3009
Fax: 612-904-4229
E-mail: pat.ellinger@co.hennepin.mn.us
Web: www.co.hennepin.mn.us

Program Information:
Program begins: July
Duration of program: 12 months

Financial Information:
Average cost of books: $200
% of students receiving aid: 50

Employment Profile:
% of students who pass the boards on their first try: 100
% employed within the first 6 months following graduation: 100
Average starting salary: $31,000

University of Minnesota Hospital and Clinic
420 Delaware Street Southeast
Box 609 Mayo
Minneapolis, MN 55455

Contact Information:
Telephone: 410-706-7729
Fax: 410-706-5229
E-mail: karni@tc.umn.edu
Web: www.umn.edu

Program Information:
Program begins: September
Duration of program: 24 months

Application Information:
Enrollment of program: 60
Transfer students are accepted.

Financial Information:
Tuition, resident: $4,100
Tuition, non-resident: $12,000
Average cost of books: $500
% of students receiving aid: 25

Employment Profile:
% of students who pass the boards on their first try: 95
% employed within the first 6 months following graduation: 98
Average starting salary: $33,000

Mississippi

Mississippi Baptist Medical Center
1225 North State Street
PO Box 23668
Jackson, MS 39225-3668

Contact Information:
Telephone: 601-968-3070
Fax: 601-974-6286
Web: www.mbhs.org

Program Information:
Program begins: June
Duration of program: 12 months

Application Information:
Enrollment of program: 6

Employment Profile:
% of students who pass the boards on their first try: 97

North Mississippi Medical Center
830 South Gloster
Tupelo, MS 38801

Contact Information:
Telephone: 601-841-3082
Fax: 601-841-3337
E-mail: lmontgomery@nmhs.net
Web: www.nmhs.net

Program Information:
Program begins: May
Duration of program: 12 months

University of Southern Mississippi
PO Box 5134
Hattiesburg, MS 39406-5134

Contact Information:
Telephone: 334-434-3461
Fax: 334-434-3403
Web: www.dept.usm.edu

Program Information:
Program begins: August
Duration of program: 15 months

Application Information:
Enrollment of program: 106
Transfer students are accepted.

Financial Information:
Tuition, resident: $2,870
Tuition, non-resident: $6,976
Average cost of books: $500
% of students receiving aid: 75

Employment Profile:
% of students who pass the boards on their first try: 95
% employed within the first 6 months following graduation: 97
Average starting salary: $30,000

Missouri

Avila College
11901 Wornall Road
Kansas City, MO 64145

Contact Information:
Telephone: 816-942-8400 ext. 2386
Fax: 816-942-3362
E-mail: hostetlerev@mail.avila.edu
Web: www.avila.edu

Program Information:
Program begins: January, June
Duration of program: 10 months

Application Information:
Enrollment of program: 6
Transfer students are accepted.

Financial Information:
Average cost of books: $200
% of students receiving aid: 100

Employment Profile:
% of students who pass the boards on their first try: 95
% employed within the first 6 months following graduation: 100
Average starting salary: $30,000

Cox Health Systems
3801 South National Avenue
Springfield, MO 65807

Contact Information:
Telephone: 417-269-6633
Fax: 417-269-4600
Web: www.cox.com

Program Information:
Program begins: June
Degrees offered: Certificate program, 24 months

Application Information:
Enrollment of program: 27
Transfer students are accepted.

Financial Information:
Average cost of books: $650
% of students receiving aid: 20

Employment Profile:
% of students who pass the boards on their first try: 100
% employed within the first 6 months following graduation: 100
Average starting salary: $25,000

Jewish Hospital College of Nursing and Allied Health
306 South Kings Highway
St. Louis, MO 63110

Contact Information:
Telephone: 314-454-8486
Fax: 314-454-5239
E-mail: dduberg@bjc.org
Web: www.jhconah.org

Program Information:
Program begins: June
Degrees offered: Certificate program, 12 months; Bachelor's, 39 months

Application Information:
Enrollment of program: 9
Transfer students are accepted.

Financial Information:
Average cost of books: $600
% of students receiving aid: 22

Employment Profile:
% employed within the first 6 months following graduation: 100
Average starting salary: $29,000

North Kansas City Hospital
2800 Clay Edwards Drive
North Kansas City, MO 64116

Contact Information:
Telephone: 816-691-1321
Fax: 816-691-1317
E-mail: cooperje@aol.com

Program Information:
Program begins: June
Degrees offered: Certificate program, 12 months

Application Information:
Transfer students are accepted.

Financial Information:
Average cost of books: $350
% of students receiving aid: 10

Employment Profile:
% of students who pass the boards on their first try: 98
% employed within the first 6 months following graduation: 100
Average starting salary: $30,000

Saint Louis University Health Sciences Center
3437 Caroline Street
St. Louis, MO 631041111

Contact Information:
Telephone: 314-577-8518
Fax: 314-577-8503
E-mail: edwardsp@slu.edu
Web: www.slu.edu

Program Information:
Program begins: July
Duration of program: 36 months

Application Information:
Enrollment of program: 45
Transfer students are accepted.

Financial Information:
Average cost of books: $865
% of students receiving aid: 76

St. John's Mercy Medical Center
615 South New Ballas Road
St. Louis, MO 631418277

Contact Information:
Telephone: 417-625-2135
Fax: 417-659-6429
E-mail: taffta@stlo.smhs.com
Web: www.mercy-fammed.com

Program Information:
Program begins: July
Duration of program: 12 months

Financial Information:
Tuition, resident: $4,600
Average cost of books: $200

St. John's Regional Medical Center
2727 McClelland Boulevard
Joplin, MO 64804-1695

Contact Information:
Telephone: 714-771-8155
Fax: 714-744-8522
E-mail: dlorimer@stj.com
Web: www.stj.com

Program Information:
Program begins: August
Duration of program: 12 months

Application Information:
Transfer students are accepted.

Financial Information:
% of students receiving aid: 50

Employment Profile:
% of students who pass the boards on their first try: 100
% employed within the first 6 months following graduation: 100
Average starting salary: $28,000

Montana

Benefis Health Care—West Campus
500 15th Avenue South
Great Falls, MT 59405

Contact Information:
Telephone: 406-455-2018
Fax: 406-455-2126
Web: www.benefis.org

Program Information:
Program begins: August
Duration of program: 12 months

Nebraska

Nebraska Methodist Hospital
8303 Dodge Street
Omaha, NE 68114

Contact Information:
Telephone: 402-354-4563
Fax: 402-354-4535
E-mail: jrichard@nmhs.org
Web: www.hnmc.edu

Program Information:
Program begins: August
Duration of program: 12 months

Financial Information:
Tuition, resident: $3,054
Tuition, non-resident: $8,313
Average cost of books: $350

Employment Profile:
% of students who pass the boards on their first try: 100
% employed within the first 6 months following graduation: 100
Average starting salary: $28,000

University of Nebraska Medical Center
98315 Nebraska Medical Center
Omaha, NE 68198-3135

Contact Information:
Telephone: 978-934-4520 ext. 4425
Fax: 978-934-3006
E-mail: pmuellen@unmc.edu

Program Information:
Program begins: June
Degrees offered: Bachelor's, 12 months

Application Information:
Enrollment of program: 24
Transfer students are accepted.

Financial Information:
Tuition, resident: $3,050
Tuition, non-resident: $8,312
Average cost of books: $350
% of students receiving aid: 80

Employment Profile:
% of students who pass the boards on their first try: 48
% employed within the first 6 months following graduation: 100
Average starting salary: $27,500

New Hampshire

University of New Hampshire
Hewitt Hall
4 Library Way
Durham, NH 03824

Contact Information:
Telephone: 601-984-6309
Fax: 601-984-6344
E-mail: sgs@cisunix.unh.edu
Web: www.unh.edu

Program Information:
Program begins: August, January, July
Degrees offered: Bachelor's, 39 months

Application Information:
Enrollment of program: 70
Transfer students are accepted.

Financial Information:
Tuition, resident: $5,450
Tuition, non-resident: $14,275
Average cost of books: $800

Employment Profile:
% of students who pass the boards on their first try: 81
% employed within the first 6 months following graduation: 90
Average starting salary: $28,000
Additional information: Out of state

New Jersey

Cooper Hospital—University Medical Center
One Cooper Plaza
Camden, NJ 08103

Contact Information:
Telephone: 856-342-2456
Fax: 856-962-8312
E-mail: hullihen_diana@cooperhealth.edu
Web: www.cooperhealth.org

Program Information:
Program begins: June
Duration of program: 12 months

Financial Information:
Average cost of books: $400
% of students receiving aid: 25

Employment Profile:
% of students who pass the boards on their first try: 50
% employed within the first 6 months following graduation: 90
Average starting salary: $32,000

Jersey Shore Medical Center/ Meridian Health System
1945 Corlies Avenue
Neptune, NJ 07753

Contact Information:
Telephone: 732-776-4140
Fax: 732-776-4592

Program Information:
Program begins: August
Degrees offered: Bachelor's, 11 months; Post-bachelor's Certificate, 11 months

Monmouth Medical Center
300 2nd Avenue
Long Branch, NJ 07740

Contact Information:
Telephone: 732-923-7367
Fax: 732-923-7355
E-mail: jmihok@sbhcs.com

Program Information:
Program begins: September
Degrees offered: Certificate program, 12 months

Application Information:
Enrollment of program: 6
Transfer students are accepted.

Financial Information:
Average cost of books: $550
% of students receiving aid: 20

Employment Profile:
% of students who pass the boards on their first try: 90
% employed within the first 6 months following graduation: 90
Average starting salary: $30,000

University of Medicine & Dentistry of New Jersey
School of Health Related Professions
65 Bergen Street
Newark, NJ 07107-3006

Contact Information:
Telephone: 502-852-5345
Fax: 502-852-4597
E-mail: keohanem@umdnj.edu
Web: www.umdnj.edu

Program Information:
Program begins: August
Duration of program: 15 months

Application Information:
Enrollment of program: 18
Transfer students are accepted.

Financial Information:
Tuition, resident: $6,776
Tuition, non-resident: $10,164
Average cost of books: $425

Employment Profile:
% employed within the first 6 months following graduation: 80
Average starting salary: $36,000

New Mexico

University of New Mexico School of Medicine
Health Sciences & Services Building
Albuquerque, NM 87131-5651

Contact Information:
Telephone: 402-559-7628
Fax: 402-559-9044
E-mail: bfricke@salud.unm.edu
Web: www.unm.edu

Program Information:
Program begins: August, January
Degrees offered: Bachelor's, 18 months; Post-bachelor's Certificate, 18 months

Application Information:
Enrollment of program: 20
Transfer students are accepted.

Financial Information:
Tuition, resident: $2,430
Tuition, non-resident: $9,171
Average cost of books: $175
% of students receiving aid: 50

Employment Profile:
% of students who pass the boards on their first try: 90
% employed within the first 6 months following graduation: 100
Average starting salary: $24,000

New York

Catholic Medical Center of Brooklyn & Queens Inc

Health Professions & Nursing Institution
175-07 Horace Harding Express
Fresh Meadows, NY 11365

Contact Information:
Telephone: 718-357-0500 ext. 110
Fax: 718-357-4575

Program Information:
Program begins: June
Degrees offered: Certificate program, 12 months; Bachelor's, 12 months

Application Information:
Enrollment of program: 16

Financial Information:
Average cost of books: $400
% of students receiving aid: 10

Employment Profile:
% of students who pass the boards on their first try: 88
% employed within the first 6 months following graduation: 100
Average starting salary: $32,000

Daemen College

4380 Main Street
Amherst, NY 14226-3592

Contact Information:
Telephone: 716-839-8425
Fax: 716-834-8516
E-mail: vkotlarz@daemen.edu
Web: www.daemen.edu

Program Information:
Program begins: September, January
Degrees offered: Bachelor's, 12 months

Application Information:
Transfer students are accepted.

Financial Information:
Average cost of books: $450

Employment Profile:
% of students who pass the boards on their first try: 95
% employed within the first 6 months following graduation: 80
Average starting salary: $27,000

Long Island University—CW Post Campus

720 Northern Boulevard
Brookville, NY 11548

Contact Information:
Telephone: 516-299-3039
Fax: 516-299-3106
Web: www.cwpost.liunet.edu

Program Information:
Program begins: August
Duration of program: 18 months

Marist College

Medical Technology Department
290 North Road
Poughkeepsie, NY 12601-1387

Contact Information:
Telephone: 914-575-3000 ext. 2496
Fax: 914-575-3180
E-mail: jzmz@musicb.marist.edu
Web: www.marist.edu

Program Information:
Program begins: July
Duration of program: 35 months

Application Information:
Enrollment of program: 30

Financial Information:
Tuition, resident: $21,792
Average cost of books: $50
% of students receiving aid: 80

Employment Profile:
% of students who pass the boards on their first try: 65
% employed within the first 6 months following graduation: 90
Average starting salary: $33,000

Rochester General Hospital

1425 Portland Avenue
Rochester, NY 14621

Contact Information:
Telephone: 716-338-4274
Fax: 716-338-4128
E-mail: nancy.mitchell@viaheath.org
Web: www.viahealth.org/rgh/medical_technology

Program Information:
Program begins: August
Duration of program: 12 months

Financial Information:
Average cost of books: $350

Employment Profile:
% of students who pass the boards on their first try: 95
% employed within the first 6 months following graduation: 90

St. Vincent's Hospital & Medical Center of New York

153 West 11th Street
New York, NY 10011

Contact Information:
Telephone: 314-569-6855
Fax: 314-569-6866
Web: www.st.vincents.org

Program Information:
Program begins: June
Degrees offered: Certificate program, 12 months

Application Information:
Enrollment of program: 8
Transfer students are accepted.

Financial Information:
Average cost of books: $450

Employment Profile:
% of students who pass the boards on their first try: 72
% employed within the first 6 months following graduation: 75
Average starting salary: $36,000

SUNY at Buffalo

26 Cary Hall
3435 Main Street
Buffalo, NY 14214-3005

Contact Information:
Telephone: 716-829-3630
Fax: 716-829-3601
E-mail: klick@acsu.buffalo.edu
Web: www.wings.buffalo.edu

Program Information:
Program begins: July
Duration of program: 16 months

Financial Information:
Tuition, resident: $3,400
Tuition, non-resident: $8,300

Employment Profile:
Average starting salary: $30,000

SUNY Health Science Center at Stony Brook

School of Health Technical and Management
Stony Brook, NY 11794-8205

Contact Information:
Telephone: 315-464-4608
Fax: 315-464-4609
E-mail: dfirestone@epo.hsc.edu
Web: www.hsc.sunysb.edu

Program Information:
Program begins: June
Duration of program: 20 months

Application Information:
Enrollment of program: 43
Transfer students are accepted.

Financial Information:
Tuition, resident: $8,742
Tuition, non-resident: $13,592

Employment Profile:
% of students who pass the boards on their first try: 92
% employed within the first 6 months following graduation: 100
Average starting salary: $35,000

SUNY Health Science Center at Syracuse
750 East Adams Street
Syracuse, NY 13210

Contact Information:
Telephone: 516-444-3221
Fax: 516-444-7621
E-mail: markh@vax.cs.hscsyr.edu
Web: www.hscsyr.edu

Program Information:
Program begins: July
Duration of program: 21 months

Application Information:
Transfer students are accepted.

Financial Information:
Tuition, resident: $5,100
Tuition, non-resident: $12,450
Average cost of books: $875

Employment Profile:
% of students who pass the boards on their first try: 95
% employed within the first 6 months following graduation: 90

Woman's Christian Association Hospital
Box 840
207 Foote Avenue
Jamestown, NY 14701-7077

Contact Information:
Telephone: 716-664-8484
Fax: 716-664-8306

Program Information:
Program begins: August
Degrees offered: Certificate program, 11 months

Application Information:
Enrollment of program: 10
Transfer students are accepted.

Financial Information:
Average cost of books: $400
% of students receiving aid: 80

Employment Profile:
% of students who pass the boards on their first try: 90
% employed within the first 6 months following graduation: 80
Average starting salary: $26,000

North Carolina

Carolinas College of Health Sciences
PO Box 32861
Charlotte, NC 28232

Contact Information:
Telephone: 704-355-4275
Fax: 704-355-5967
E-mail: banderson@carolinas.org
Web: www.carolinas.org

Program Information:
Program begins: July
Duration of program: 12 months

Application Information:
Enrollment of program: 10

Financial Information:
Average cost of books: $500

Employment Profile:
% of students who pass the boards on their first try: 98
% employed within the first 6 months following graduation: 100
Average starting salary: $28,000

East Carolina University
Department Clinical Lab Science
School of Allied Health Sciences
Greenville, NC 27858

Contact Information:
Telephone: 919-328-4417
Fax: 919-328-4470
E-mail: smithsu@mail.ecu.edu
Web: www.ecu.edu

Program Information:
Program begins: September
Degrees offered: Master's

Application Information:
Enrollment of program: 22
Transfer students are accepted.

Financial Information:
Tuition, resident: $1,830
Tuition, non-resident: $9,000

Employment Profile:
% of students who pass the boards on their first try: 90
% employed within the first 6 months following graduation: 90

Moses H. Cone Memorial Hospital
1200 North Elm Street
Greensboro, NC 27401

Contact Information:
Telephone: 336-832-7485
Fax: 336-832-8270
E-mail: theresa.o'laughlin@mosescone.com

Program Information:
Program begins: July
Degrees offered: Certificate program, 12 months

Application Information:
Enrollment of program: 12
Transfer students are accepted.

Financial Information:
Average cost of books: $500
% of students receiving aid: 30

Employment Profile:
% of students who pass the boards on their first try: 100
% employed within the first 6 months following graduation: 100
Average starting salary: $27,800

University of North Carolina at Chapel Hill
Allied Health Sciences, CB 7145
Medical School Wing East
Chapel Hill, NC 27599-7145

Contact Information:
Telephone: 702-895-0977
Fax: 702-895-3872
E-mail: sbeck@css.unc.edu
Web: www.alliedhealth.unc.edu

Program Information:
Program begins: August, February
Duration of program: 16 months

Financial Information:
Tuition, resident: $2,262
Tuition, non-resident: $11,430

Western Carolina University
129 Moore Building
Cullowhee, NC 28723

Contact Information:
Telephone: 828-227-3512
Fax: 828-227-7071
E-mail: southern@wcu.edu
Web: www.wcu.wsu

Program Information:
Program begins: September
Duration of program: 18 months

Application Information:
Enrollment of program: 35
Transfer students are accepted.

Financial Information:
Tuition, resident: $1,839
Tuition, non-resident: $8,993
Average cost of books: $200
% of students receiving aid: 50

Employment Profile:
% of students who pass the boards on their first try: 90
% employed within the first 6 months following graduation: 100
Average starting salary: $27,000

North Dakota

Trinity Medical Center
One Burdick Expressway
Minot, ND 58701

Contact Information:
Telephone: 701-857-5210
Fax: 701-857-5485
Web: www.trinitymedicalcenter.com

Program Information:
Program begins: June
Duration of program: 12 months

Application Information:
Enrollment of program: 6
Transfer students are accepted.

Financial Information:
Average cost of books: $250
% of students receiving aid: 66

Employment Profile:
% of students who pass the boards on their first try: 100
% employed within the first 6 months following graduation: 100
Average starting salary: $24,000

Ohio

Bowling Green State University

504 Life Science Building
Bowling Green, OH 43403

Contact Information:
Telephone: 419-372-8109
Fax: 419-372-0332
E-mail: rharr@bgnet.bgsu.edu
Web: www.bgsu.edu

Program Information:
Program begins: July
Duration of program: 14 months

Application Information:
Enrollment of program: 15
Transfer students are accepted.

Financial Information:
Tuition, resident: $6,482
Tuition, non-resident: $14,003

Children's Hospital Medical Center of Akron

One Perkins Square
Akron, OH 44308

Contact Information:
Telephone: 330-379-8720
Web: www.akronchildrens.org

Program Information:
Program begins: July
Duration of program: 12 months

Ohio State University

1583 Perry Street
Columbus, OH 43210

Contact Information:
Telephone: 614-292-7303
Fax: 614-292-0210
E-mail: rudmann.l@osu.edu
Web: www.amp.ohio-state.edu

Program Information:
Program begins: May
Duration of program: 22 months

Application Information:
Enrollment of program: 39
Transfer students are accepted.

Financial Information:
Tuition, resident: $4,137
Tuition, non-resident: $12,087
Average cost of books: $800
% of students receiving aid: 50

Employment Profile:
% of students who pass the boards on their first try: 79
% employed within the first 6 months following graduation: 100
Average starting salary: $29,000

Southwest General Health Center

18697 East Bagley Road
Middleburg Hts, OH 44130

Contact Information:
Telephone: 440-816-8859
Fax: 440-816-8690

Program Information:
Program begins: August
Duration of program: 12 months

Trinity Medical Center East

380 Summit Avenue
Steubenville, OH 43952

Contact Information:
Telephone: 740-264-8185
Fax: 740-264-8649
E-mail: schend@1st.net

Program Information:
Program begins: July
Degrees offered: Certificate program, 12 months

Application Information:
Enrollment of program: 8

Financial Information:
Average cost of books: $225
% of students receiving aid: 50

Employment Profile:
% of students who pass the boards on their first try: 95
% employed within the first 6 months following graduation: 85
Average starting salary: $37,500

University of Cincinnati

202 Goodman Avenue, Room 371
PO Box 670394
Cincinnati, OH 452670374

Contact Information:
Telephone: 919-966-3011
Fax: 919-966-8384
E-mail: graetel@email.uc.edu
Web: www.uc.edu

Program Information:
Program begins: July
Degrees offered: Certificate program, 12 months; Bachelor's, 12 months; Post-bachelor's Certificate, 12 months

Application Information:
Enrollment of program: 15
Transfer students are accepted.

Financial Information:
Tuition, resident: $5,532
Tuition, non-resident: $13,952
Average cost of books: $250

Employment Profile:
% of students who pass the boards on their first try: 85
% employed within the first 6 months following graduation: 100
Average starting salary: $30,000

Wright State University

Department of Biological Sciences
235 Biological Sciences Building
Dayton, OH 45435

Contact Information:
Fax: 937-775-3320
Web: www.wright.edu

Program Information:
Program begins: September
Duration of program: 12 months

Application Information:
Enrollment of program: 8
Transfer students are accepted.

Financial Information:
Tuition, resident: $5,240
Tuition, non-resident: $10,480
Average cost of books: $450

Employment Profile:
% of students who pass the boards on their first try: 100
% employed within the first 6 months following graduation: 100
Average starting salary: $27,000

Oklahoma

St. Francis Hospital

6161 South Yale Avenue
Tulsa, OK 74136

Contact Information:
Telephone: 918-494-6342
Fax: 918-494-1399
E-mail: tdfoster@saintfrancis.com
Web: www.saintfrancis.com

Program Information:
Program begins: September, February
Duration of program: 12 months

Application Information:
Enrollment of program: 6

Financial Information:
Average cost of books: $310
% of students receiving aid: 50

Employment Profile:
% of students who pass the boards on their first try: 95
% employed within the first 6 months following graduation: 83
Average starting salary: $27,000

Valley View Regional Hospital
430 North Monte Vista
Ada, OK 74820

Contact Information:
Telephone: 405-421-1550
Fax: 405-421-1525
E-mail: cweens@vvrh.com
Web: www.vvrh.com

Program Information:
Program begins: September
Degrees offered: Certificate program, 12 months

Application Information:
Enrollment of program: 4-6

Financial Information:
Average cost of books: $350

Employment Profile:
% of students who pass the boards on their first try: 95
% employed within the first 6 months following graduation: 100
Average starting salary: $29,000

Oregon

Oregon Health Sciences University
3181 Southwest Sam Jackson Park Road
Portland, OR 97201

Contact Information:
Telephone: 503-494-8698
Fax: 503-494-2730
E-mail: ewellm@ohsu.edu
Web: www.ohsu.edu/alliedhealth

Program Information:
Program begins: July
Duration of program: 15 months

Financial Information:
Tuition, resident: $8,300
Tuition, non-resident: $14,446

Employment Profile:
% of students who pass the boards on their first try: 100
Average starting salary: $34,000

Pennsylvania

Abington Memorial Hospital
1200 Old York Road
Abington, PA 19001

Contact Information:
Telephone: 215-481-2362
Fax: 215-481-4481

Program Information:
Program begins: June
Degrees offered: Certificate program, 12 months

Application Information:
Enrollment of program: 4

Financial Information:
Average cost of books: $450

Employment Profile:
% of students who pass the boards on their first try: 100
% employed within the first 6 months following graduation: 100
Average starting salary: $32,000

Allegheny University Hospitals Elkins Park
60 East Township Line Road
Elkins Park, PA 19027

Contact Information:
Telephone: 215-663-6101
Fax: 215-663-8842

Program Information:
Program begins: August
Duration of program: 12 months

Application Information:
Transfer students are accepted.

Financial Information:
Tuition, resident: $8,000
Average cost of books: $400

Employment Profile:
% of students who pass the boards on their first try: 80
% employed within the first 6 months following graduation: 100
Average starting salary: $36,000

Altoona Hospital
620 Howard Avenue
Altoona, PA 16601-4899

Contact Information:
Telephone: 814-946-2835
Fax: 814-946-5279
Web: www.altoonahospital.org

Program Information:
Program begins: July
Duration of program: 12 months

Financial Information:
Average cost of books: $480
% of students receiving aid: 60

Employment Profile:
% of students who pass the boards on their first try: 100
% employed within the first 6 months following graduation: 70
Average starting salary: $29,000

Conemaugh Valley Memorial Hospital
1086 Franklin Street
Johnstown, PA 15905-4398

Contact Information:
Telephone: 814-534-9831
Fax: 814-534-3253
Web: www.conemaugh.org

Program Information:
Program begins: August
Duration of program: 12 months

Application Information:
Enrollment of program: 7

Financial Information:
Average cost of books: $400

Employment Profile:
% of students who pass the boards on their first try: 100
% employed within the first 6 months following graduation: 100
Average starting salary: $30,000

Lancaster Institute for Health Education
Lancaster General Hospital
143 East Lemon Street
Lancaster, PA 17602

Contact Information:
Telephone: 717-290-5511 ext. 7335
Fax: 717-290-5970
Web: www.lha.org

Program Information:
Program begins: July
Degrees offered: Certificate program, 12 months

Application Information:
Enrollment of program: 6

Financial Information:
Average cost of books: $300
% of students receiving aid: 50

Employment Profile:
% of students who pass the boards on their first try: 100
% employed within the first 6 months following graduation: 100
Average starting salary: $29,000

Reading Hospital and Medical Center
PO Box 16052
Reading, PA 19612-6052

Contact Information:
Telephone: 610-988-5951
Fax: 610-988-5185
E-mail: strauss@readinghospital.org
Web: www.readinghospital.org

Program Information:
Program begins: July
Duration of program: 11 months

St. Vincent Health Center
232 West 25th Street
Erie, PA 16544

Contact Information:
Telephone: 212-604-8385
Fax: 212-604-8426
E-mail: sjohnson@svhs.org
Web: www.svhs.org

Program Information:
Program begins: September
Duration of program: 12 months

Financial Information:
Average cost of books: $540

Susquehanna Health System Williamsport Hospital
777 Rural Avenue
Williamsport, PA 17701

Contact Information:
Telephone: 570-321-2326
Fax: 570-321-2489

Program Information:
Program begins: August
Duration of program: 12 months

Financial Information:
Average cost of books: $350

Employment Profile:
% of students who pass the boards on their first try: 97
% employed within the first 6 months following graduation: 100
Average starting salary: $27,000

Thomas Jefferson University
130 South Ninth Street
Edison Building
Philadelphia, PA 19107

Contact Information:
Telephone: 215-503-8187
Fax: 215-503-2189
E-mail: calderl@jeflin.tju.edu
Web: www.jeffline.tju.edu

Program Information:
Program begins: August
Duration of program: 24 months

Wyoming Valley Health Care System—Hospital
575 North River Street
Wilkes-Barre, PA 18764

Contact Information:
Telephone: 717-552-1404
Fax: 717-552-1415

Program Information:
Program begins: August
Duration of program: 12 months

York Hospital
1001 South George Street
York, PA 17405

Contact Information:
Telephone: 717-851-2458
Fax: 717-851-2934
E-mail: bkile@yorkhospital.edu
Web: www.yorkhospital.edu

Program Information:
Program begins: July
Duration of program: 12 months

Application Information:
Enrollment of program: 6

Financial Information:
Average cost of books: $350

Employment Profile:
% of students who pass the boards on their first try: 95
% employed within the first 6 months following graduation: 99
Average starting salary: $30,000

Puerto Rico

Catholic University of Puerto Rico
2250 Las Americas Avenue
Suite 588
Ponce, PR 007170777

Contact Information:
Telephone: 787-841-1585 ext. 1585
Fax: 787-841-2000
E-mail: tecmed@pucpr.edu
Web: www.pucpr.edu

Program Information:
Program begins: July
Degrees offered: Certificate program, 12 months

Application Information:
Enrollment of program: 19
Transfer students are accepted.

Financial Information:
Tuition, resident: $5,750
Average cost of books: $350
% of students receiving aid: 90

Employment Profile:
% of students who pass the boards on their first try: 85
% employed within the first 6 months following graduation: 85

Inter-American University—Metro Campus
Sein Street - Road 1
San Juan, PR 00926

Contact Information:
Telephone: 787-767-5081
Fax: 787-250-8736
Web: www.metro.inter.edu

Program Information:
Program begins: August
Duration of program: 12 months

Application Information:
Enrollment of program: 25
Transfer students are accepted.

Inter-American University—San German
Call Box 5100
San German, PR 00753-3906

Contact Information:
Telephone: 787-834-6070
Fax: 787-892-6350
Web: www.sg.inter.edu

Program Information:
Program begins: July
Duration of program: 12 months

Application Information:
Enrollment of program: 40

Financial Information:
Tuition, resident: $4,500
Average cost of books: $250
% of students receiving aid: 90

Employment Profile:
% employed within the first 6 months following graduation: 67

University of the Sacred Heart
PO Box 12383
San Juan, PR 00914-0383

Contact Information:
Telephone: 787-728-1515 ext. 4297
Fax: 787-727-7880
E-mail: tmedica@sagrado.edu
Web: www.sagrado.edu

Program Information:
Program begins: August, February
Degrees offered: Certificate program, 12 months; Bachelor's, 60 months

Application Information:
Enrollment of program: 48
Transfer students are accepted.

Financial Information:
Average cost of books: $400

Employment Profile:
% of students who pass the boards on their first try: 50
% employed within the first 6 months following graduation: 70
Average starting salary: $14,000

South Carolina

Baptist Medical Center at Columbia
Taylor at Marion Streets
Columbia, SC 29220

Contact Information:
Telephone: 803-296-5014

Program Information:
Program begins: August
Duration of program: 12 months

Application Information:
Enrollment of program: 40

Employment Profile:
% employed within the first 6 months following graduation: 90

McLeod Regional Medical Center

555 East Cheves Street
PO Box 100551
Florence, SC 29501-0551

Contact Information:
Telephone: 843-777-2497
Fax: 843-777-2071
E-mail: vanderson@mcleodhealth.org
Web: www.ahec.net

Program Information:
Program begins: August
Degrees offered: Certificate program, 12 months

Application Information:
Enrollment of program: 3

Financial Information:
Average cost of books: $550

Employment Profile:
% of students who pass the boards on their first try: 100
% employed within the first 6 months following graduation: 100
Average starting salary: $26,000

South Dakota

Rapid City Regional Hospital

353 Fairmont Boulevard
Rapid City, SD 57701

Contact Information:
Telephone: 605-341-8092
Fax: 605-399-2205
E-mail: pkieffer@rcrh.org
Web: www.rcrh.org

Program Information:
Program begins: August
Duration of program: 12 months

Application Information:
Transfer students are accepted.

Financial Information:
Average cost of books: $500
% of students receiving aid: 50

Employment Profile:
% of students who pass the boards on their first try: 100
% employed within the first 6 months following graduation: 100
Average starting salary: $27,000

Sioux Valley Hospital

1100 South Euclid Avenue
Sioux Falls, SD 57117-5039

Contact Information:
Telephone: 605-333-7104
Fax: 605-333-1532
E-mail: barnettm@siouxvalley.org

Program Information:
Program begins: July
Duration of program: 12 months

Financial Information:
Average cost of books: $450

Employment Profile:
% employed within the first 6 months following graduation: 100

Tennessee

Austin Peay State University

PO Box 4718
Clarksville, TN 37044

Contact Information:
Telephone: 931-221-7781
Fax: 931-221-6323
E-mail: thompsonj@apsu.edu
Web: www.apsu.edu/medtech

Program Information:
Program begins: July
Degrees offered: Certificate program, 13 months; Bachelor's, 48 months

Application Information:
Enrollment of program: 8-16
Transfer students are accepted.

Financial Information:
Tuition, resident: $3,217
Tuition, non-resident: $9,693
Average cost of books: $500
% of students receiving aid: 75

Employment Profile:
% of students who pass the boards on their first try: 80
% employed within the first 6 months following graduation: 95

University of Tennessee Medical Center at Knoxville

1924 Alcoa Highway Southwest
Knoxville, TN 37920

Contact Information:
Telephone: 601-266-4908
Fax: 601-266-4913
E-mail: gmaner@mc.utmck.edu
Web: www.utmck.edu

Program Information:
Program begins: June, January
Degrees offered: Bachelor's; Post master's Certificate, 12 months; Post-bachelor's Certificate, 12 months

Application Information:
Enrollment of program: 14
Transfer students are accepted.

Financial Information:
Tuition, resident: $3,630
Tuition, non-resident: $10,134
Average cost of books: $300
% of students receiving aid: 50

Employment Profile:
% of students who pass the boards on their first try: 100
% employed within the first 6 months following graduation: 100
Average starting salary: $32,000

Vanderbilt University Medical Center

4605D The Vanderbilt Clinic
1165 21st Avenue South
Nashville, TN 37232-5310

Contact Information:
Telephone: 615-322-6940
Fax: 615-343-8420
E-mail: maralie.exton@mcmail.vanderbilt.edu
Web: www.mc.vanderbilt.edu

Program Information:
Program begins: June
Degrees offered: Certificate program, 12 months

Application Information:
Enrollment of program: 8

Financial Information:
Average cost of books: $400
% of students receiving aid: 25

Employment Profile:
% of students who pass the boards on their first try: 100
% employed within the first 6 months following graduation: 100
Average starting salary: $27,000

Texas

Hillcrest Baptist Medical Center

3000 Herring Avenue
Waco, TX 76708

Contact Information:
Telephone: 254-202-8653
Fax: 254-202-7922
E-mail: apetree@hillcrest.net
Web: www.hillcrest.net

Program Information:
Program begins: July
Degrees offered: Certificate program, 12 months

Financial Information:
Average cost of books: $400

Employment Profile:
% of students who pass the boards on their first try: 100
% employed within the first 6 months following graduation: 98
Average starting salary: $25,580

Scott & White Memorial Hospital and Clinic

2401 South 3rd Street
Temple, TX 76508

Contact Information:
Telephone: 254-724-5177
Fax: 254-724-8396
E-mail: jengelkirk@swmail.sw.org
Web: www.sw.org

Program Information:
Program begins: August
Degrees offered: Certificate program, 12 months

Application Information:
Enrollment of program: 8
Transfer students are accepted.

Financial Information:
Average cost of books: $400

Employment Profile:
% of students who pass the boards on their first try: 100
% employed within the first 6 months following graduation: 100
Average starting salary: $27,000

Southwest Texas State University

601 University Drive
San Marcos, TX 78666-4616

Contact Information:
Telephone: 512-245-3500
Fax: 512-245-7860
E-mail: df03@.swt.edu
Web: www.swt.edu

Program Information:
Program begins: July
Duration of program: 24 months

Application Information:
Enrollment of program: 80
Transfer students are accepted.

Financial Information:
Tuition, resident: $3,240
Tuition, non-resident: $10,482
Average cost of books: $800
% of students receiving aid: 75

Employment Profile:
% employed within the first 6 months following graduation: 90
Average starting salary: $28,000

Tarleton State University

1625 West Myrtle Street
Ft. Worth, TX 76104

Contact Information:
Telephone: 817-926-1101
Fax: 817-922-8103
E-mail: cls@tarleton.edu
Web: www.tarleton.edu

Program Information:
Program begins: August
Duration of program: 13 months

Application Information:
Enrollment of program: 32
Transfer students are accepted.

Financial Information:
Tuition, resident: $3,000
Tuition, non-resident: $10,000
Average cost of books: $500
% of students receiving aid: 50

Employment Profile:
% of students who pass the boards on their first try: 100
% employed within the first 6 months following graduation: 80
Average starting salary: $30,000

Texas A & M University—Corpus Christi

College of Science and Technology
6300 Ocean Drive
Corpus Christi, TX 78412

Contact Information:
Telephone: 361-825-2473
Fax: 361-825-2742
E-mail: cthomp@falcon.tamucc.edu
Web: www.tamucc.edu

Program Information:
Program begins: August
Degrees offered: Bachelor's, 48 months; Post-bachelor's Certificate, 12 months

Application Information:
Enrollment of program: 18
Transfer students are accepted.

Financial Information:
Tuition, resident: $1,800
Tuition, non-resident: $12,000
Average cost of books: $650
% of students receiving aid: 50

Employment Profile:
% of students who pass the boards on their first try: 90
% employed within the first 6 months following graduation: 100

Texas Tech University Health Science Center

School of Allied Health
3601 4th Street
Lubbock, TX 79430

Contact Information:
Telephone: 806-743-3252
Fax: 806-743-3249
E-mail: alhlrs@ttuhsc.edu
Web: www.ttuhsc.edu

Program Information:
Program begins: August
Duration of program: 21 months

Application Information:
Transfer students are accepted.

Financial Information:
Tuition, resident: $3,200
Tuition, non-resident: $9,104

Employment Profile:
% employed within the first 6 months following graduation: 90

United Regional Health Care Systems

1600 Eighth Street
Wichita Falls, TX 76301

Contact Information:
Telephone: 940-764-8123
Fax: 940-764-8994

Program Information:
Program begins: August
Duration of program: 12 months

Application Information:
Enrollment of program: 25

Financial Information:
Tuition, resident: $2,000
Average cost of books: $400

Employment Profile:
% of students who pass the boards on their first try: 80
% employed within the first 6 months following graduation: 80
Average starting salary: $24,000

University of Texas—Pan American

1201 West University Drive
Edinburg, TX 78539

Contact Information:
Telephone: 423-544-9087
Fax: 423-544-6866
E-mail: kchandler@panam.edu
Web: www.panam.edu

Program Information:
Program begins: August
Degrees offered: Bachelor's, 15 months

Application Information:
Enrollment of program: 15

Financial Information:
Tuition, resident: $2,650
Tuition, non-resident: $12,494

Employment Profile:
% employed within the first 6 months following graduation: 100
Average starting salary: $29,000

University of Texas at El Paso

1101 North Campbell Room 610
El Paso, TX 79902

Contact Information:
Telephone: 956-318-5269
Fax: 956-318-5253
E-mail: gharwell@utep.edu
Web: www.utep.edu

Program Information:
Program begins: June

Application Information:
Enrollment of program: 17
Transfer students are accepted.

Financial Information:
Tuition, resident: $2,380
Tuition, non-resident: $9,940
Average cost of books: $425
% of students receiving aid: 80

Employment Profile:
% of students who pass the boards on their first try: 89
% employed within the first 6 months following graduation: 95
Average starting salary: $30,000

University of Texas at Tyler

3900 University Boulevard
Tyler, TX 75701

Contact Information:
Telephone: 915-747-8233
Fax: 915-747-7207
E-mail: jkoukl@mail.uttyl.edu
Web: www.uttuler.edu

Program Information:
Program begins: August
Duration of program: 12 months

Application Information:
Enrollment of program: 12
Transfer students are accepted.

Financial Information:
Tuition, resident: $2,788
Tuition, non-resident: $11,562
Average cost of books: $400

Employment Profile:
% of students who pass the boards on their first try: 96
% employed within the first 6 months following graduation: 100
Average starting salary: $28,000

University of Texas Health Science Center at San Antonio

7703 Floyd Curl Drive
San Antonio, TX 78284-7772

Contact Information:
Telephone: 903-566-7009
Fax: 903-566-7189
E-mail: mckenzie@uthscsa.edu
Web: www.uthsca.edu

Program Information:
Program begins: July
Duration of program: 39 months

Application Information:
Enrollment of program: 65
Transfer students are accepted.

Financial Information:
Tuition, resident: $1,360
Tuition, non-resident: $8,432
Average cost of books: $500

Employment Profile:
% of students who pass the boards on their first try: 95
% employed within the first 6 months following graduation: 100
Average starting salary: $26,000

University of Texas MD Anderson Cancer Center

1515 Holcombe Boulevard
Houston, TX 77030

Contact Information:
Telephone: 210-567-8860
Fax: 210-567-8875
E-mail: kmcclure@mdacc.tmc.edu
Web: www.mdanderson.org

Program Information:
Program begins: August
Duration of program: 12 months

Application Information:
Transfer students are accepted.

Financial Information:
% of students receiving aid: 25

Employment Profile:
% of students who pass the boards on their first try: 100
% employed within the first 6 months following graduation: 90
Average starting salary: $30,000

University of Texas Medical Branch

School of Allied Health Sciences
301 University Boulevard
Galveston, TX 77555-1028

Contact Information:
Telephone: 713-745-1688
Fax: 713-745-3337
E-mail: vfreeman@utmb.edu
Web: www.utmb.edu

Program Information:
Program begins: September
Duration of program: 24 months
Evening or weekend classes are available.

Application Information:
Enrollment of program: 50
Transfer students are accepted.

Financial Information:
Tuition, resident: $1,200
Tuition, non-resident: $9,225

Employment Profile:
% of students who pass the boards on their first try: 89
% employed within the first 6 months following graduation: 100
Average starting salary: $32,000

University of Texas Southwestern Medical Center—Dallas

5323 Harry Hines Boulevard
Dallas, TX 75235-8878

Contact Information:
Telephone: 409-772-3056
Fax: 409-747-1610
E-mail: llittl@mednet.swmed.edu
Web: www.swmed.edu

Program Information:
Program begins: June, January
Duration of program: 12 months

Application Information:
Enrollment of program: 11
Transfer students are accepted.

Financial Information:
Tuition, resident: $1,976
Tuition, non-resident: $13,038
Average cost of books: $385
% of students receiving aid: 50

Employment Profile:
% of students who pass the boards on their first try: 85
% employed within the first 6 months following graduation: 50
Average starting salary: $27,000

Wadley Regional Medical Center

1000 Pine Street
Texarkana, TX 75501

Contact Information:
Telephone: 903-798-7140
Fax: 903-798-7196
E-mail: jnantze@wadleyrmc.com
Web: www.wadleyrmc.com

Program Information:
Program begins: August
Degrees offered: Certificate program, 12 months

Application Information:
Enrollment of program: 4

Financial Information:
Average cost of books: $350
% of students receiving aid: 100

Employment Profile:
% of students who pass the boards on their first try: 75
% employed within the first 6 months following graduation: 100

Utah

Brigham Young University

761 WIDB
Provo, UT 84602

Contact Information:
Telephone: 801-378-8757
Fax: 801-378-9197
E-mail: shauna_andersen@byu.edu
Web: www.byu.edu

Program Information:
Program begins: May
Duration of program: 12 months

Application Information:
Enrollment of program: 65

Financial Information:
Tuition, resident: $2,720
Tuition, non-resident: $4,080
Average cost of books: $1,000
% of students receiving aid: 10

Employment Profile:
% of students who pass the boards on their first try: 97
% employed within the first 6 months following graduation: 100
Average starting salary: $28,000

University of Utah Health Sciences Center

Department of Pathology
50 North Medical Drive
Salt Lake City, UT 84132

Contact Information:
Telephone: 801-585-6989
Fax: 801-585-2463
E-mail: lschoeff@hsc.utah.edu

Program Information:
Program begins: August
Duration of program: 20 months

Financial Information:
Tuition, resident: $1,200
Tuition, non-resident: $3,600

Weber State University
3905 University Circle
Ogden, UT 84408-3905

Contact Information:
Telephone: 801-626-7080
Fax: 801-626-7683
E-mail: ysimonian@weber.edu
Web: www.weber.edu

Program Information:
Program begins: August
Degrees offered: Master's, 36 months
Evening or weekend classes are available.

Application Information:
Enrollment of program: 16
Transfer students are accepted.

Financial Information:
Tuition, resident: $1,935
Tuition, non-resident: $5,730
Average cost of books: $700
% of students receiving aid: 60

Employment Profile:
% of students who pass the boards on their first try: 98
% employed within the first 6 months following graduation: 100
Average starting salary: $32,000

Vermont

University of Vermont
302 Rowell Building
Burlington, VT 05405

Contact Information:
Telephone: 802-656-3811
Fax: 802-656-2191
E-mail: ahuot@cosmos.uvm.edu
Web: www.uvm.edu

Program Information:
Program begins: June
Degrees offered: Bachelor's, 48 months; Master's; Post-bachelor's Certificate, 24 months

Application Information:
Enrollment of program: 75
Transfer students are accepted.

Financial Information:
Tuition, resident: $7,464
Tuition, non-resident: $18,672
Average cost of books: $628

Virginia

Augusta Medical Center
PO Box 1000
Fishersville, VA 22939

Contact Information:
Telephone: 540-332-4539
Fax: 540-332-4543
E-mail: bbekken@cfw.com
Web: www.augustamed.com

Program Information:
Program begins: July
Duration of program: 12 months

Financial Information:
Average cost of books: $375

Employment Profile:
% of students who pass the boards on their first try: 100
% employed within the first 6 months following graduation: 100
Average starting salary: $26,000

Carilion Health System/Carilion Roanoke Memorial Hospital
Belleview at Jefferson Street
Roanoke, VA 24014

Contact Information:
Telephone: 540-981-8032
Fax: 540-982-3473
E-mail: jhiler@carilion.com
Web: www.canilion.com

Program Information:
Program begins: August
Duration of program: 12 months

Application Information:
Enrollment of program: 8

Financial Information:
Tuition, resident: $3,500
Tuition, non-resident: $4,000
% of students receiving aid: 25

Employment Profile:
% of students who pass the boards on their first try: 92
% employed within the first 6 months following graduation: 100
Average starting salary: $25,500

Fairfax Hospital
3300 Gallows Road
Falls Church, VA 22046

Contact Information:
Telephone: 703-698-2891
Fax: 703-698-2407
E-mail: amy.shoemaker@inova.com

Program Information:
Program begins: August
Degrees offered: Diploma, 12 months

Application Information:
Enrollment of program: 7

Financial Information:
Average cost of books: $500
% of students receiving aid: 14

Employment Profile:
% of students who pass the boards on their first try: 100
% employed within the first 6 months following graduation: 100
Average starting salary: $31,096

Norfolk State University
700 Park Avenue
Norfolk, VA 23504

Contact Information:
Telephone: 757-823-2366
Fax: 757-823-2909
E-mail: mkfuller@nsu.edu
Web: www.nsu.edu

Program Information:
Program begins: September, January
Duration of program: 18 months

Application Information:
Enrollment of program: 22

Financial Information:
Tuition, resident: $1,350
Tuition, non-resident: $6,900

Old Dominion University
School of Medical Sciences
Spring Hall/209
Norfolk, VA 23529

Contact Information:
Telephone: 757-683-3588
Fax: 757-683-5028
E-mail: fcoleman@odu.edu
Web: www.odu.edu

Program Information:
Program begins: July
Duration of program: 22 months
Evening or weekend classes are available.

Application Information:
Enrollment of program: 30

Financial Information:
Tuition, resident: $4,795
Tuition, non-resident: $12,425
Average cost of books: $450

Employment Profile:
% of students who pass the boards on their first try: 80
% employed within the first 6 months following graduation: 90
Average starting salary: $28,500

Virginia Commonwealth University/Med College of VA Campus
PO Box 980583
MCV Campus
Richmond, VA 23298-0583

Contact Information:
Telephone: 804-828-9469

Fax: 804-828-1911
E-mail: bjlindse@hsc.vcu.edu
Web: www.medschool.vcu.edu

Program Information:
Program begins: August
Degrees offered: Bachelor's; Master's; PhD

Application Information:
Enrollment of program: 60
Transfer students are accepted.

Financial Information:
Tuition, resident: $3,575
Tuition, non-resident: $13,029
Average cost of books: $650

Employment Profile:
% of students who pass the boards on their first try: 92
% employed within the first 6 months following graduation: 100
Average starting salary: $29,500

Washington

Central Washington University

Center for Medical Technology
1120 West Spruce
Yakima, WA 98902

Contact Information:
Telephone: 509-248-7784
Fax: 509-454-6117
E-mail: steenc@cluster.cwu.edu
Web: www.cwu.edu

Program Information:
Program begins: August
Duration of program: 12 months

Application Information:
Enrollment of program: 8
Transfer students are accepted.

Financial Information:
Tuition, resident: $3,652
Tuition, non-resident: $12,984
% of students receiving aid: 60

Employment Profile:
% of students who pass the boards on their first try: 98
% employed within the first 6 months following graduation: 90
Average starting salary: $36,000

Sacred Heart Medical Center

101 West Eighth Avenue
Spokane, WA 99220-2555

Contact Information:
Telephone: 509-474-3339
Fax: 509-474-2052
E-mail: hambyc@shmc.org
Web: www.shmc.org

Program Information:
Program begins: July
Duration of program: 12 months

Application Information:
Enrollment of program: 8

Financial Information:
Average cost of books: $500

Employment Profile:
% of students who pass the boards on their first try: 100
% employed within the first 6 months following graduation: 100
Average starting salary: $33,000

University of Washington

School of Medicine
Department of Laboratory Medicine
Box 357110
Seattle, WA 98195-7110

Contact Information:
Telephone: 206-598-2135
Fax: 206-598-6189
E-mail: lampe@uwashington.edu
Web: www.washington.edu

Program Information:
Program begins: July
Duration of program: 21 months

Application Information:
Enrollment of program: 47
Transfer students are accepted.

Financial Information:
Tuition, resident: $1,213
Tuition, non-resident: $4,010
Average cost of books: $750

Employment Profile:
% employed within the first 6 months following graduation: 90
Average starting salary: $33,000

West Virginia

West Liberty State College

Department of Medical Technology
West Liberty, WV 26074

Contact Information:
Telephone: 304-336-8177
Fax: 304-336-8266
E-mail: wagnerw@wlsc.wvnet.edu
Web: www.wlsc.wvnet.edu

Program Information:
Program begins: August
Duration of program: 24 months

Application Information:
Enrollment of program: 25
Transfer students are accepted.

Financial Information:
Tuition, resident: $2,320
Tuition, non-resident: $5,760

Employment Profile:
% of students who pass the boards on their first try: 80
% employed within the first 6 months following graduation: 80
Average starting salary: $25,000

West Virginia University

2163 East Health Sciences Center North
PO Box 9211
Morgantown, WV 26506-9211

Contact Information:
Telephone: 304-293-2069
Fax: 304-293-6249
E-mail: jholter@wvu.edu
Web: www.hsc.wvu.edu

Program Information:
Program begins: May
Degrees offered: Bachelor's, 21 months

Application Information:
Enrollment of program: 60
Transfer students are accepted.

Financial Information:
Tuition, resident: $2,884
Tuition, non-resident: $8,984
Average cost of books: $400
% of students receiving aid: 90

Employment Profile:
% of students who pass the boards on their first try: 95
% employed within the first 6 months following graduation: 90
Average starting salary: $30,000

Wisconsin

Clement J. Zablocki VA Medical Center

5000 West National Avenue
Milwaukee, WI 53295

Contact Information:
Telephone: 414-384-2000 ext. 1332
Fax: 414-382-5319
E-mail: mark.maticek@mfo.va.gov

Program Information:
Program begins: July
Degrees offered: Certificate program, 9 months

Application Information:
Enrollment of program: 10
Transfer students are accepted.

Financial Information:
Average cost of books: $250

Employment Profile:
% of students who pass the boards on their first try: 95
% employed within the first 6 months following graduation: 100
Average starting salary: $32,000

Sacred Heart Hospital

900 West Clairemont Avenue
Eau Claire, WI 54701

Contact Information:
Telephone: 715-839-3973
Fax: 715-833-4941
Web: www.shh.org

Program Information:
Program begins: February, August
Duration of program: 9 months

Application Information:
Enrollment of program: 2

Financial Information:
Average cost of books: $100

Employment Profile:
% of students who pass the boards on their first try: 100
% employed within the first 6 months following graduation: 100
Average starting salary: $31,000

St. Elizabeth Hospital
1506 South Oneida Street
Appleton, WI 54915

Contact Information:
Telephone: 618-233-3428
Fax: 618-234-8713
E-mail: clandin@affinityhealth.org

Program Information:
Program begins: August
Duration of program: 9 months

Application Information:
Enrollment of program: 6

Financial Information:
Average cost of books: $100

Employment Profile:
% of students who pass the boards on their first try: 100
% employed within the first 6 months following graduation: 80

St. Joseph's Hospital
611 Saint Joseph Avenue
Marshfield, WI 54449

Contact Information:
Telephone: 319-369-7309
Fax: 319-369-8095
E-mail: ultowss@mfldclin.edu
Web: www.marshmed.org/lab

Program Information:
Program begins: September
Duration of program: 12 months

Application Information:
Enrollment of program: 12

Financial Information:
Average cost of books: $275

Employment Profile:
% of students who pass the boards on their first try: 100
% employed within the first 6 months following graduation: 100
Average starting salary: $29,000

University of Wisconsin—Madison
1300 University Avenue/6175 MSC
Madison, WI 53706

Contact Information:
Telephone: 608-262-2085
Fax: 608-262-9520
E-mail: ehrmeyer@facstaff.wisc.edu
Web: www.medsch.wisc.edu

Program Information:
Program begins: September
Duration of program: 18 months

Application Information:
Enrollment of program: 100
Transfer students are accepted.

Financial Information:
Tuition, resident: $3,242
Tuition, non-resident: $10,981
Average cost of books: $660
% of students receiving aid: 30

Employment Profile:
% of students who pass the boards on their first try: 97
% employed within the first 6 months following graduation: 100
Average starting salary: $32,000

Wausau Hospital
333 Pine Ridge Boulevard
Wausau, WI 54401

Contact Information:
Telephone: 715-847-2136 ext. 53210
Fax: 715-847-2930
E-mail: susanj@waushosp.org
Web: www.wausauhospital.com

Program Information:
Program begins: May
Duration of program: 9 months

Application Information:
Enrollment of program: 5
Transfer students are accepted.

Financial Information:
Average cost of books: $250

Employment Profile:
% of students who pass the boards on their first try: 95
% employed within the first 6 months following graduation: 100
Average starting salary: $27,000

Dental Hygienist, Dental Assistant, Dental Laboratory Technician

Victoria Bastecki-Perez, RDH, BS, EdD
Program Director and Professor
Dental Hygiene
Montgomery County Community College
Blue Bell, Pennsylvania

Job Description

What Do They Do?

Once dental hygienists have graduated from an accredited dental hygiene program and become licensed, they can seek employment in traditional and nontraditional dental hygiene settings. They can take on the roles of administrator/manager, change agent (one who takes a leadership role in managing the process of change), clinician, client advocate, educator/oral health promoter, or researcher. In a clinical setting, dental hygienists are primary care providers who collaborate with dentists and other members of the healthcare team to provide comprehensive dental hygiene care to clients. These patient care services include, but are not limited to:

- Dental prophylaxis (teeth cleaning)
- Non-surgical periodontal therapy
- Soft and hard tissue examinations
- Apply preventive agents such as fluoride and pit and fissure sealants
- Expose, develop, mount, and review radiographs (x-rays)
- Provide oral and overall health instructions

The ability to perform dental hygiene services legally varies from state to state and is dictated by each state's dental practice act.

Type of Person

Dental hygienists tend to:

- Possess good interpersonal skills
- Have effective verbal and written communication skills
- Have the ability to integrate and apply knowledge from general education, basic science, dental and dental hygiene science courses in order to provide comprehensive dental hygiene care to clients
- Possess manual dexterity
- Have a commitment to life-long learning

With Whom Do They Work?

Dental hygienists work most frequently with a diverse client population, general and specialty dentists, dental assistants, practice managers, and various members of the medical community.

Employment

Places of Employment

Examples of some of the settings in which dental hygienists may work include:

- General dental practices (sole, partnerships, or group)
- Specialty dental practices (pediatric, periodontics, orthodontics, geriatrics, and others)
- Hospitals
- Nursing homes
- Public health centers and community agencies
- Educational institutions
- Research facilities
- Corporations
- Armed forces
- Lobbyist organizations, working for legislative change
- Correctional facilities
- Oral healthcare industries
- Professional organizations

In some instances, places of employment are contingent upon completion of additional education and/or obtainment of professional experiences, as well as other factors.

Employment Outlook

Dental hygiene is ranked 8th in the list of "Top 25 Hot Programs" in *Community College Week*.[1] It was also ranked first in the highest starting salary category. A career in dental hygiene offers employment variety, creativity, flexibility, credibility, and personal satisfaction.

Salary

Dental hygiene salary and benefits packages vary according to geographic location, job responsibilities, practice setting, professional experience, and educational background. In comparison to similar healthcare professionals, dental hygienists can expect comparable salaries and benefit opportunities.

Educational Programs

Length

Dental hygiene educational programs must be at least two years in length and must be offered at a post-secondary educational institution. Two-year entry-level programs culminate in the attainment of a certificate, an Associate in Arts (AA), Associate in Science (AS), an Associate in Applied Arts (AAA) or an Associate in Applied Sciences (AAS) degree. A four-year dental hygiene degree, specific to the field, awards a Bachelor of Science Dental Hygiene degree (BSDH). Some students may also choose to pursue a Bachelor of Science (BS) or Bachelor of Arts (BA) degree in a field other than dental hygiene. The terminal degree in dental hygiene is a Master's degree; dental hygienists who wish to obtain a doctoral degree (PhD or EdD) may do so outside of the profession. An advanced degree affords the dental hygienists a vast array of alternative career opportunities.

Prerequisites

Admission prerequisites differ according to specific college or university requirements. Interested parties should take high school and/or college level courses in chemistry, biological sciences (human anatomy, physiology, and histology), social sciences (sociology and psychology) and humanities (English composition and communications). In addition, cardiopulmonary resuscitation (CPR) certification is required at most institutions prior to matriculation. Contacting individual dental hygiene programs to obtain exact admission policies and procedures is strongly recommended.

Curriculum

Each dental hygiene program has a specific curriculum to meet the needs of its students, reflect professional practices, and meet accreditation standards. However, each entry-level dental hygiene program is required by the accrediting body to offer courses in general education, basic sciences, and dental and dental hygiene sciences. In addition to didactic classes, dental hygiene programs offer laboratory, preclinical and clinical courses so that students may integrate and apply their knowledge to client care using a multidisciplinary approach.

Accrediting Body

The Commission on Dental Accreditation of the American Dental Association is the accrediting body for dental hygiene programs. The CODA ADA is responsible for evaluating dental hygiene programs to decide whether or not they meet established standards.

Commission on Dental Accreditation
American Dental Association
211 East Chicago Avenue
Chicago, IL 60611
Telephone: 312-440-4653
Web address: www.ada.org

Licensure

In order to obtain state licensure to practice dental hygiene, applicants must meet specified requirements such as successfully completing national and/or regional examinations. These tests may be written or computer-based, or they may consist of client simulations.

For information regarding the National Board Dental Hygiene Examination, contact:

Joint Commission on National Dental Examinations
211 East Chicago Avenue, Suite 1846
Chicago, IL 60611
Telephone: 312-440-2678
Web address: www.ada.org

For information regarding regional board examinations, contact your region's testing agency as indicated below:

Colorado, Illinois, Iowa, Kansas, Minnesota, Missouri, Nebraska, North Dakota, South Dakota, Wisconsin, and Wyoming:

Central Regional Dental Testing Services, Inc.
1725 Gage Boulevard
Topeka, KS 66604
Phone: 913-273-5015

Connecticut, District of Columbia, Illinois, Maine, Maryland, Massachusetts, Michigan, New Hampshire, New Jersey, New York, Ohio, Pennsylvania, Rhode Island, Vermont, and West Virginia:

Northeast Regional Board of Dental Examiners, Inc.
8484 Georgia Avenue, Suite 900
Silver Spring, MD 20910
Phone: 301-563-3300
Web site: www.nerb.org

Arkansas, Georgia, Kentucky, Illinois, Ohio, Tennessee, and Virginia:

Approved by the Dental State Boards of Southern Regional Testing Agency, Inc.
303 34th Street, Suite 7
Virginia Beach, VA 23451
Phone: 804-428-1003
Web site: www.srta.org

Alaska, Arizona, Idaho, Montana, New Mexico, Oklahoma, Oregon, Texas, Utah, and Washington:

Western Regional Examining Board
2400 West Dunlap, #155
Phoenix, AZ 85021
Phone: 602-944-3315
Web site: www.wreb.org

Alabama, California, Delaware, Florida, Hawaii, Indiana, Louisiana, Mississippi, Nevada, North Carolina, Puerto Rico, South Carolina, and the Virgin Islands administer their own clinical examinations.

Advice for Potential Students

Contact the school you are interested in and make an appointment with the program director or designee. During that appointment, inquire about national, state, and regional examination successes for the institution, request an opportunity to observe a clinic session, and talk with a current student, ask about fees and expenses (instruments, uniforms, etc.) specific to dental hygiene students, job placement rates, request dental hygiene admission policies/procedures, and address other issues that concern you.

Other Dental Auxiliary Careers

Dental assisting and dental laboratory technician careers offer individuals other opportunities to pursue auxiliary employment in dentistry.

Dental Assistant

Dental assistants can perform general duties or specialized functions such as chairside assisting or office administration, or with formal education, they may also become Extended Function Dental Assistants (EFDAs). Responsibilities delegated to a dental assistant are contingent upon the regulations of the dental practice act for each state. A certification examination is available for individuals who meet specified criteria. Contacting your state's board of dentistry for information regarding dental assisting duties, educational requirements (if applicable), licensure (if applicable), laws and regulations is highly recommended.

The American Dental Assistants Association is the professional organization of dental assistants.

American Dental Assistants Association
203 North LaSalle, Suite 1320
Chicago, IL 60601-1225
Telephone: 312-541-1550
Web address: members.aol.com/adaa1/index.html

Dental Laboratory Technician

Dental laboratory technicians perform written, prescribed tasks specified by a dentist. These duties include fabricating corrective devices and replacements for natural teeth. Candidates should have good manual dexterity, artistic ability, and attention for detail. Dental laboratory technicians are typically employed by dental laboratories, the military, or are self-employed. Education can be obtained through apprenticeships, commercial schools, or nonprofit schools. The ADA has approved some two-year and four-year educational programs that meet established standards. A certification examination is available for individuals who meet specified criteria. For additional information, contact:

The National Association of Dental Laboratories
8201 Greensboro Drive, Suite 300
McLean VA 22102
Phone: 703-610-9035
Web site: www.nadl.org

For Additional Information

Organizations

American Association of Dental Schools
1625 Massachusetts Avenue, NW
Washington, DC 20036-2212
Telephone: 202-667-9438
Web address: www.aads.jhu.edu

American Dental Association
211 East Chicago Avenue
Chicago, IL 60611
Telephone: 312-440-2718
Web address: www.ada.org

American Dental Hygienists' Association
444 North Michigan Avenue, Suite 3400
Chicago, IL 60611-3902
Telephone: 312-440-8900
Web address: www.adha.org

Publications

Books

Dental Hygiene: Word of Mouth—Careers in the Dental Profession. Chicago: American Dental Association, 1998.

Torres, H.O. & Erlich, A. *Modern Dental Assisting, 2nd edition.* Philadelphia: WB Saunders Company, 1980.

Wilkins, EM. *Clinical Practice of the Dental Hygienists, 8th edition.* Philadelphia: Lippincott Williams & Wilkins, 1999.

Darby, M.L. & Walsh, N.M. Dental Hygiene *Theory and Practice. Philadelphia*: WB Saunders Company, 1994.

Dental Hygiene Brochure. Blue Bell, PA: Montgomery County Community College, 1997. www.mc3.edu

Journals

Access. American Dental Hygienists' Association, 444 North Michigan Avenue, Suite 3400, Chicago, IL 60611. www.adha.org

A four-color magazine that focuses on health and practice news, professional issues, and legislative developments. It provides late-breaking news on issues that are important to dental hygienists—managed care, multiple practice settings, infection control, genetic engineering, women's health, product news, new technology, and periodontal trends.

The Journal of Practical Hygiene. Montage Media Corporation, 1000 Wyckoff Avenue, Mahwah, NJ 07430. www.montagemedia.com.

Provides step-by-step information in an easy-to-read format.

The Journal of the American Dental Association. American Dental Association, 211 E Chicago Avenue, Chicago, IL 60611. www.ada.org/adapco/jada/j-menu.html.

Peer-reviewed source for information on dentistry and dental science.

Journal of Dental Technology. National Association of Dental Laboratories, 8201 Greensboro Drive, Suite 300, McLean VA 22102. www.nadl.org/jdt.

Peer-reviewed publication for dental technology professionals.

RDH. PennWell Corporation, 1421 South Sheridan Road, Tulsa, OK 74112. www.pennwell.com.

Includes general interest articles on topics such as clinical management and continuing education.

The Dental Assistant Journal. American Dental Assistants Association, 203 North LaSalle, Suite 1320, Chicago, IL 60601-1225. members.aol.com/adaa1.index.html.

The official publication of the American Dental Assistants Association.

Internet Resources

Alaska State Dental Hygiene Association: www.alaska.net/~asdha
American Association of Dental Schools: www.aads.jhu.edu
American Dental Assistants Association: members.aol.com/ada1/index.html
American Dental Association: www.ada.org
American Dental Hygienists' Association: www.adha.org
Arizona State Dental Hygiene Association: www.asdha.org
California State Dental Hygiene Association: www.cdha.org
Georgia State Dental Hygiene Association: www.gdha.org
International Federation of Dental Hygienists: www.ifdh.org
Maine State Dental Hygiene Association: www.home.maine.rr.com/medha
Minnesota State Dental Hygiene Association: www.mindspring.com/~askmdha/hygiene
National Association of Dental Laboratories: www.nadl.org
National Center for Dental Hygiene Research-DHNet: jeffline.tju.edu/DHNet
National Dental Hygienists' Association: www.ndha.org

North Carolina State Dental Hygiene Association: www.angelfire.com/nc/NCDHA
Pennsylvania Dental Hygienists' Association: www.pct.edu/pdha
Texas State Dental Hygiene Association: members.aol.com/tpatrdh/private/tdha/default.htm
Vermont State Dental Hygiene Association: www.vdha.org
Virginia State Dental Hygiene Association: www.rdh-vdha.org
West Virginia State Dental Hygiene Association: angus.hsc.wvu.edu/wvdha.html

Dental Hygienist

Alaska

University of Alaska Anchorage

3211 Providence Drive
AHS 124
Anchorage, AK 99508-8371

Contact Information:
Telephone: 203-576-4138
Fax: 203-576-4220
E-mail: afsel@uaa.alaska.edu
Web: www.uaa.alaska.edu

Program Information:
Program begins: August
Duration of program: 9 months

Application Information:
Enrollment of program: 12

Financial Information:
Tuition, resident: $7,154
Tuition, non-resident: $11,765
Average cost of books: $245

Employment Profile:
% of students who pass the boards on their first try: 100
% employed within the first 6 months following graduation: 100

Arizona

Northern Arizona University

Box 15065
Flagstaff, AZ 86011-5065

Contact Information:
Telephone: 520-523-6195
Fax: 520-523-4315
E-mail: evelyn.hobbs@nau.edu
Web: www.nau.edu

Program Information:
Program begins: August
Degrees offered: Bachelor's, 27 months
Evening or weekend classes are available.

Application Information:
Enrollment of program: 75
Transfer students are accepted.

Financial Information:
Tuition, resident: $2,314
Average cost of books: $300
% of students receiving aid: 75

Employment Profile:
% of students who pass the boards on their first try: 99
% employed within the first 6 months following graduation: 100
Average starting salary: $52,000

Arkansas

University of Arkansas & VA Medical Center

4301 West Markham Street
Little Rock, AR 72205

Contact Information:
Telephone: 513-745-5635
Fax: 513-792-8623

Program Information:
Program begins: August
Duration of program: 19 months

Application Information:
Enrollment of program: 60

Financial Information:
Tuition, resident: $1,050
Tuition, non-resident: $1,284

Employment Profile:
% of students who pass the boards on their first try: 99
% employed within the first 6 months following graduation: 100
Average starting salary: $40,000

California

Cabrillo College

6500 Soquel Drive
Aptos, CA 95003

Contact Information:
Telephone: 408-479-6472
Fax: 408-479-5054
E-mail: bapaige@cabrillo.cc.ca.us
Web: www.cabrillo.cc.ca.us

Program Information:
Program begins: August
Duration of program: 24 months

Application Information:
Enrollment of program: 44

Financial Information:
Tuition, resident: $563
Tuition, non-resident: $4,693

Employment Profile:
% of students who pass the boards on their first try: 89
% employed within the first 6 months following graduation: 100
Average starting salary: $60,000

Cerritos College

11110 East Alondra Boulevard
Norwalk, CA 90650

Contact Information:
Telephone: 562-860-2451 ext. 2557
Fax: 562-467-5077
E-mail: izive@cerritos.edu
Web: www.cerritos.edu

Program Information:
Program begins: August
Duration of program: 20 months

Application Information:
Enrollment of program: 48

Financial Information:
Tuition, resident: $570
Average cost of books: $1,200
% of students receiving aid: 80

Employment Profile:
% of students who pass the boards on their first try: 95
% employed within the first 6 months following graduation: 90
Average starting salary: $67,250

Chabot College

25555 Hesperian Boulevard
Hayward, CA 94545

Contact Information:
Telephone: 510-723-6906
Fax: 510-723-7089
Web: www.cerritos.edu

Program Information:
Program begins: August
Duration of program: 2 months

Financial Information:
Tuition, resident: $780
Tuition, non-resident: $7,320
Average cost of books: $1,000
% of students receiving aid: 39

Employment Profile:
% of students who pass the boards on their first try: 44
% employed within the first 6 months following graduation: 100

Cypress College

9200 Valley View Street
Cypress, CA 90630

Contact Information:
Telephone: 562-826-2710
Fax: 562-421-0988
E-mail: rydalch@ptconnect.infi.net
Web: www.cypress.cc.ca.us

Program Information:
Program begins: August
Duration of program: 18 months

Application Information:
Enrollment of program: 36

Financial Information:
Tuition, resident: $377
Tuition, non-resident: $2,166
Average cost of books: $2,000
% of students receiving aid: 40

Employment Profile:
% of students who pass the boards on their first try: 85
% employed within the first 6 months following graduation: 100

Loma Linda University

School of Dentistry
Loma Linda, CA 92350

Contact Information:
Telephone: 909-558-4631
Fax: 909-558-0313
E-mail: ksimpson@sd.llu.edu
Web: www.llu.edu

Program Information:
Program begins: September
Degrees offered: Bachelor's, 22 months

Application Information:
Enrollment of program: 80

Financial Information:
Average cost of books: $350

Employment Profile:
% of students who pass the boards on their first try: 95
% employed within the first 6 months following graduation: 95

Sacramento City College

3835 Freeport Boulevard
Sacramento, CA 95822

Contact Information:
Telephone: 916-558-2650
Fax: 916-558-2392
E-mail: dunnem@scc.Losr10s.cc.ca.us
Web: www.scc.losrios.cc.ca.us

Program Information:
Program begins: August
Duration of program: 20 months

Application Information:
Enrollment of program: 48

Financial Information:
Tuition, resident: $517
Tuition, non-resident: $4,969

Employment Profile:
% of students who pass the boards on their first try: 80
% employed within the first 6 months following graduation: 100

San Joaquin Valley College—Visalia Campus

8400 West Mineral King
Visalia, CA 93291

Contact Information:
Telephone: 209-651-1617
Fax: 209-651-3645
Web: www.sjvc.com

Program Information:
Program begins: June
Duration of program: 15 months

Application Information:
Enrollment of program: 60

Employment Profile:
% of students who pass the boards on their first try: 99
% employed within the first 6 months following graduation: 90

University of California—San Francisco

Division of Dental Hygiene
Box 0754
San Francisco, CA 94143

Contact Information:
Telephone: 907-786-6926
Fax: 907-786-6937
E-mail: dperry@itsa.ucsf.edu
Web: www.ucsf.edu

Program Information:
Program begins: September
Degrees offered: Bachelor's, 18 months

Application Information:
Enrollment of program: 36

Financial Information:
Tuition, resident: $4,184
Tuition, non-resident: $8,394
Average cost of books: $200
% of students receiving aid: 75

Employment Profile:
% of students who pass the boards on their first try: 80
% employed within the first 6 months following graduation: 100

West Los Angeles College

4800 Freshman Drive
Culver City, CA 90230

Contact Information:
Telephone: 310-287-4342
Fax: 310-287-4461
E-mail: lemboru@laccd.cc.ca.us
Web: www.wlac.cc.ca.us

Program Information:
Program begins: August
Duration of program: 18 months

Application Information:
Enrollment of program: 49

Financial Information:
Tuition, resident: $390
Tuition, non-resident: $4,230
Average cost of books: $500
% of students receiving aid: 50

Employment Profile:
% of students who pass the boards on their first try: 80
% employed within the first 6 months following graduation: 100
Average starting salary: $50,000

Colorado

Community College of Denver

Building 753
960 Xanthia Street
Denver, CO 80230

Contact Information:
Telephone: 303-365-7771
Fax: 303-365-8330
Web: www.ccd.rightchoice.org

Program Information:
Program begins: August
Duration of program: 18 months

Financial Information:
Tuition, resident: $2,168
Tuition, non-resident: $8,900
Average cost of books: $1,100
% of students receiving aid: 61

Employment Profile:
% employed within the first 6 months following graduation: 75
Average starting salary: $60,000

Pueblo Community College

900 West Orman Avenue
Pueblo, CO 81004

Contact Information:
Telephone: 719-549-3286
Fax: 719-549-3136
E-mail: learned@pcc.ccoes.edu
Web: www.pcc.cccpes.edu

Program Information:
Program begins: September
Duration of program: 20 months

Application Information:
Enrollment of program: 30
Transfer students are accepted.

Financial Information:
Tuition, resident: $3,804
Tuition, non-resident: $20,721

University of Colorado Health Science Center

School of Dentistry
4200 East Ninth Ave Campus Box C284
Denver, CO 80262

Contact Information:
Telephone: 415-476-9884

Fax: 415-476-0858
E-mail: gail.cross-poline@uchsc.edu
Web: www.uchsc.edu

Program Information:
Program begins: September
Duration of program: 23 months

Financial Information:
Tuition, resident: $4,364
Tuition, non-resident: $14,956

Connecticut

Tunxis Community Technical College

271 Scott Swamp Road
Farmington, CT 06032-3187

Contact Information:
Telephone: 860-679-9667
Fax: 860-676-8906
E-mail: tx_benciveng@mail.commnet.edu
Web: www.tunxies.cc.ct.us

Program Information:
Program begins: September
Duration of program: 24 months

Application Information:
Enrollment of program: 64
Transfer students are accepted.

Financial Information:
Tuition, resident: $2,000
Tuition, non-resident: $5,400
Average cost of books: $1,500
% of students receiving aid: 90

Employment Profile:
% of students who pass the boards on their first try: 93
% employed within the first 6 months following graduation: 100
Average starting salary: $46,000

District of Columbia

Howard University

600 West Street, NW
Washington, DC 20059

Contact Information:
Telephone: 202-806-0079
Fax: 202-806-0354
E-mail: mfrazier-kelley@fac.howard.edu
Web: www.howard.edu

Program Information:
Program begins: August
Degrees offered: Certificate program, 18 months

Application Information:
Enrollment of program: 36
Transfer students are accepted.

Financial Information:
% of students receiving aid: 90

Employment Profile:
% of students who pass the boards on their first try: 100
% employed within the first 6 months following graduation: 80

Florida

Brevard Community College

1519 Clearlake Road
Cocoa, FL 32922

Contact Information:
Telephone: 407-632-1111 ext. 64010
Fax: 407-634-3731
E-mail: raulersonj@brevard.cc.fl.us
Web: www.brevard.cc.fl.us

Program Information:
Program begins: August
Degrees offered: Associate's, 24 months

Application Information:
Enrollment of program: 24
Transfer students are accepted.

Financial Information:
Tuition, resident: $1,716
Average cost of books: $300

Employment Profile:
% of students who pass the boards on their first try: 95
% employed within the first 6 months following graduation: 100
Average starting salary: $35,000

Broward Community College

3501 Southwest Davie Road
Ft. Lauderdale, FL 33314

Contact Information:
Telephone: 954-475-6563
Fax: 954-473-9037
E-mail: llong@broward.cc.fl.us
Web: www.broward.cc.fl.us

Program Information:
Program begins: August
Duration of program: 12 months

Application Information:
Enrollment of program: 16
Transfer students are accepted.

Financial Information:
Tuition, resident: $4,072
Tuition, non-resident: $7,944
Average cost of books: $1,000

Employment Profile:
% of students who pass the boards on their first try: 100
% employed within the first 6 months following graduation: 80
Average starting salary: $45,000

Daytona Beach Community College

1200 West International Speedway Boulevard
PO Box 2811
Daytona Beach, FL 32114

Contact Information:
Telephone: 904-255-8131 ext. 3746
Fax: 904-254-4491
E-mail: pryorm@dbcc.cc.fl.us
Web: www.dbcc.cc.fl.us

Program Information:
Program begins: August
Degrees offered: Associate's, 18 months

Application Information:
Enrollment of program: 15
Transfer students are accepted.

Financial Information:
Tuition, resident: $4,067
Tuition, non-resident: $15,098
Average cost of books: $520
% of students receiving aid: 45

Employment Profile:
% of students who pass the boards on their first try: 95
% employed within the first 6 months following graduation: 100
Average starting salary: $44,000

Edison Community College

8099 College Parkway Southwest
Ft. Meyers, FL 33919

Contact Information:
Telephone: 941-489-9107
Fax: 941-489-9037
E-mail: gwelling@edison.edu
Web: www.edison.edu

Program Information:
Program begins: August
Degrees offered: Associate's, 18 months

Application Information:
Enrollment of program: 48
Transfer students are accepted.

Financial Information:
Tuition, resident: $1,684
Tuition, non-resident: $6,265

Employment Profile:
% of students who pass the boards on their first try: 100
% employed within the first 6 months following graduation: 95
Average starting salary: $30,000

Florida Community College—Jacksonville

4501 Capper Road
Jacksonville, FL 32218

Contact Information:
Telephone: 904-466-6575
Fax: 904-766-6654
E-mail: hkerr@fccj.org
Web: www.fccj.org

Program Information:
Program begins: June
Duration of program: 21 months

Application Information:
Enrollment of program: 45
Transfer students are accepted.

Financial Information:
Tuition, resident: $3,651
Tuition, non-resident: $13,851
Average cost of books: $1,430

Employment Profile:
% of students who pass the boards on their first try: 98
% employed within the first 6 months following graduation: 93
Average starting salary: $24,000

Gulf Coast Community College
5230 West US Highway 98
Panama City, FL 32114

Contact Information:
Telephone: 850-872-3827
Fax: 850-747-3241
E-mail: gdaugherry@ccmail.gc.cc.fl.us
Web: www.gc.cc.fl.us

Program Information:
Program begins: August
Duration of program: 24 months

Application Information:
Enrollment of program: 28
Transfer students are accepted.

Financial Information:
Tuition, resident: $1,924
Tuition, non-resident: $7,696

Employment Profile:
% employed within the first 6 months following graduation: 80
Average starting salary: $27,000

Miami-Dade Community College
Medical Center Campus
950 Northwest 20th Street
Miami, FL 33127

Contact Information:
Telephone: 305-237-4029
Fax: 305-237-4278
E-mail: kasss@mdcc.edu
Web: www.mdcc.edu

Program Information:
Program begins: August
Degrees offered: Associate's, 19 months

Application Information:
Enrollment of program: 95

Financial Information:
Tuition, resident: $1,396
Tuition, non-resident: $4,359

Palm Beach Community College
4200 South Congress Avenue
Lake Worth, FL 33461

Contact Information:
Telephone: 561-439-8098
Fax: 561-439-8314
E-mail: zinser@pbcc.cc.fl.us
Web: www.pbcc.cc.fl.us

Program Information:
Program begins: August
Duration of program: 19 months

Financial Information:
Tuition, resident: $1,700
Tuition, non-resident: $3,600

Pensacola Junior College
5555 West Highway 98
Pensacola, FL 32507

Contact Information:
Telephone: 904-484-2244
Fax: 904-484-2365
E-mail: lfazio@pjc.cc.fl.us
Web: www.pjc.cc.fl.us

Program Information:
Program begins: August
Duration of program: 24 months

Application Information:
Enrollment of program: 100

Financial Information:
Tuition, resident: $3,000
Tuition, non-resident: $14,825
Average cost of books: $600

Employment Profile:
% of students who pass the boards on their first try: 100
% employed within the first 6 months following graduation: 70

St. Petersburg Junior College
PO Box 13489
St. Petersburg, FL 33733

Contact Information:
Telephone: 727-341-3671
Fax: 727-341-3744
E-mail: grzesikowskit@spjc.edu
Web: www.spj.edu

Program Information:
Program begins: May
Degrees offered: Associate's, 24 months

Application Information:
Enrollment of program: 69

Financial Information:
Tuition, resident: $1,421
Tuition, non-resident: $5,164
Average cost of books: $500

Employment Profile:
% of students who pass the boards on their first try: 85
% employed within the first 6 months following graduation: 100
Average starting salary: $45,000

Valencia Community College
1800 South Kirkman Road
Orlando, FL 32811

Contact Information:
Telephone: 407-299-5000
Fax: 407-293-8839
Web: www.valencia.cc.fl.us

Program Information:
Program begins: May
Duration of program: 19 months

Application Information:
Enrollment of program: 48
Transfer students are accepted.

Financial Information:
Tuition, resident: $4,162
Average cost of books: $3,400
% of students receiving aid: 20

Employment Profile:
% of students who pass the boards on their first try: 95
% employed within the first 6 months following graduation: 100

Georgia

Armstrong Atlantic State University
11935 Abercorn Street
Savannah, GA 31419-1997

Contact Information:
Telephone: 912-927-5308
Fax: 912-921-7466
E-mail: tanenbba@mail.armstrong.edu
Web: www.armstrong.edu

Program Information:
Program begins: August
Duration of program: 21 months

Financial Information:
Tuition, resident: $2,098
Tuition, non-resident: $7,522

Clayton College and State University
5900 North Lee Street
Morrow, GA 30260

Contact Information:
Telephone: 770-961-3596
Fax: 770-961-3639
E-mail: loisposs@mail.clayton.edu
Web: www.clayton.edu

Program Information:
Program begins: October
Duration of program: 17 months

Application Information:
Transfer students are accepted.

Financial Information:
Tuition, resident: $3,284
Tuition, non-resident: $9,232

Columbus Technical Institute

928 Manchester Expressway
Columbus, GA 31904-6572

Contact Information:
Telephone: 706-649-1979
Fax: 706-649-1980
E-mail: kkaufman@mail.columbus.tec.ga.us
Web: www.columbus.tec.ga.us

Program Information:
Program begins: August
Duration of program: 21 months

Application Information:
Enrollment of program: 24
Transfer students are accepted.

Financial Information:
Tuition, resident: $1,008
Tuition, non-resident: $2,016
Average cost of books: $1,600
% of students receiving aid: 20

Employment Profile:
% of students who pass the boards on their first try: 100
% employed within the first 6 months following graduation: 100
Average starting salary: $32,000

Darton College

2400 Gillionville Road
Albany, GA 31707

Contact Information:
Telephone: 912-430-6840
Fax: 912-430-6910
E-mail: smarshal@dmail.dartnet.peachnet.edu
Web: www.dartnet.peachnet.edu

Program Information:
Program begins: August
Duration of program: 24 months

Financial Information:
Tuition, resident: $1,700
Tuition, non-resident: $5,980

Georgia Perimeter College

2101 Womack Road
Dunwoody, GA 30338

Contact Information:
Telephone: 770-551-3096
Fax: 770-604-3797
E-mail: rkarelit@gpc.peachnet.edu
Web: www.gpc.peachnet.edu

Program Information:
Program begins: August
Duration of program: 22 months

Application Information:
Transfer students are accepted.

Financial Information:
Tuition, resident: $1,592
Tuition, non-resident: $5,232
Average cost of books: $800

Employment Profile:
% of students who pass the boards on their first try: 95
% employed within the first 6 months following graduation: 100
Average starting salary: $30,000

Lanier Technical Institute

2990 Landrum Education Drive
Oakwood, GA 30566

Contact Information:
Telephone: 770-531-6368
Fax: 770-531-6306
E-mail: hmapp@admin1.lanier.tec.ga.us
Web: www.lanier.tec.ga.us

Program Information:
Program begins: August
Duration of program: 21 months

Application Information:
Enrollment of program: 28

Financial Information:
Tuition, resident: $2,720
Tuition, non-resident: $4,640
Average cost of books: $750
% of students receiving aid: 60

Employment Profile:
% of students who pass the boards on their first try: 100
% employed within the first 6 months following graduation: 100

Macon State College

100 College Station Drive
Macon, GA 31206

Contact Information:
Telephone: 912-471-2738
Fax: 912-757-6656
E-mail: sbailey@cennet.mc.peachnet.edu

Program Information:
Program begins: August
Duration of program: 21 months

Financial Information:
Tuition, resident: $1,644
Tuition, non-resident: $5,876

Medical College of Georgia

1120 15th Street
Augusta, GA 30912

Contact Information:
Telephone: 706-721-2938
Fax: 706-721-8857
E-mail: gwinkley@mail.mcg.edu
Web: www.mcg.edu/sah/hygiene

Program Information:
Program begins: August
Duration of program: 21 months

Application Information:
Enrollment of program: 56

Financial Information:
Tuition, resident: $2,541
Tuition, non-resident: $8,478
Average cost of books: $394

Employment Profile:
% of students who pass the boards on their first try: 100
% employed within the first 6 months following graduation: 84
Average starting salary: $45,000

Illinois

Illinois Central College

201 Southwest Adams Street
East Peoria, IL 61635

Contact Information:
Telephone: 309-999-4662
Fax: 309-673-9626
Web: www.icc.cc.il.us

Program Information:
Program begins: August
Duration of program: 18 months

Application Information:
Enrollment of program: 48

Financial Information:
Tuition, resident: $3,251
Tuition, non-resident: $12,020
Average cost of books: $1,500
% of students receiving aid: 30

Employment Profile:
% of students who pass the boards on their first try: 92
% employed within the first 6 months following graduation: 90

Kennedy-King College—University of Illinois

6800 South Wentworth Avenue
Chicago, IL 60621

Contact Information:
Telephone: 773-602-5229
Fax: 312-996-1022
E-mail: sbeaver@WC.edu

Program Information:
Program begins: June
Duration of program: 24 months

Employment Profile:
% employed within the first 6 months following graduation: 100

Lake Land College

5001 Lake Land Boulevard
Mattoon, IL 61938-9366

Contact Information:
Telephone: 217-234-5203
Fax: 217-234-5357
E-mail: mjorstad@lakeland.cc.il.us
Web: www.lakeland.cc.il.us

Program Information:
Program begins: August
Degrees offered: Associate's, 21 months
Evening or weekend classes are available.

Application Information:
Enrollment of program: 56
Transfer students are accepted.

Financial Information:
Tuition, resident: $4,575
Tuition, non-resident: $9,980
Average cost of books: $200
% of students receiving aid: 50

Employment Profile:
% employed within the first 6 months following graduation: 88
Average starting salary: $40,000

Lewis & Clark Community College

5800 Godfrey Road
Godfrey, IL 62035

Contact Information:
Telephone: 618-466-3411
Fax: 618-467-2394
E-mail: msingley@lc.cc.il.us
Web: www.lc.cc.il.us

Program Information:
Program begins: August
Duration of program: 30 months

Application Information:
Enrollment of program: 48
Transfer students are accepted.

Financial Information:
Tuition, resident: $2,500
Tuition, non-resident: $5,000
Average cost of books: $2,000
% of students receiving aid: 75

Employment Profile:
% of students who pass the boards on their first try: 98
% employed within the first 6 months following graduation: 100
Average starting salary: $40,000

Prairie State College

202 South Halsted
Chicago Heights, IL 60411

Contact Information:
Telephone: 708-709-3714
Fax: 708-709-3777
E-mail: bgorbitz@prairie.cc.il.us
Web: www.prairie.cc.il.us

Program Information:
Program begins: June
Degrees offered: Certificate program, 24 months

Application Information:
Enrollment of program: 32

Financial Information:
Tuition, resident: $3,801
Tuition, non-resident: $5,380
Average cost of books: $300
% of students receiving aid: 23

Employment Profile:
% of students who pass the boards on their first try: 90
% employed within the first 6 months following graduation: 100
Average starting salary: $40,000

Southern Illinois University—Carbondale

College of Applied Sciences and Arts
Mail Code 6615
Carbondale, IL 62901

Contact Information:
Telephone: 618-453-7213
Fax: 618-453-7020
E-mail: maurizio@siu.edu
Web: www.siue.edu

Program Information:
Program begins: August
Duration of program: 32 months

Application Information:
Enrollment of program: 108
Transfer students are accepted.

Financial Information:
Tuition, resident: $6,010
Tuition, non-resident: $14,330
Average cost of books: $600

Employment Profile:
% of students who pass the boards on their first try: 92
% employed within the first 6 months following graduation: 98

William Rainey Harper College

1200 West Algonquin Road
Palatine, IL 60067

Contact Information:
Telephone: 847-925-6474
Fax: 847-925-6047
E-mail: pbelmont@harper.cc.il.us
Web: www.harper.cc.il.us

Program Information:
Program begins: August
Degrees offered: Associate's, 27 months

Application Information:
Enrollment of program: 72

Financial Information:
Tuition, resident: $7,000
Tuition, non-resident: $17,700
Average cost of books: $2,100
% of students receiving aid: 10

Employment Profile:
% of students who pass the boards on their first try: 100
% employed within the first 6 months following graduation: 90
Average starting salary: $46,000

Indiana

Indiana University—Purdue University Fort Wayne

2102 Coliseum Boulevard East
Fort Wayne, IN 46805

Contact Information:
Telephone: 219-481-6837
Fax: 219-481-5767
E-mail: foley@ipfw.edu
Web: www.ipfw.edu

Program Information:
Program begins: August
Duration of program: 16 months

Application Information:
Enrollment of program: 48
Transfer students are accepted.

Financial Information:
Tuition, resident: $3,500
Tuition, non-resident: $8,100
Average cost of books: $600
% of students receiving aid: 30

Employment Profile:
% of students who pass the boards on their first try: 95
% employed within the first 6 months following graduation: 100
Average starting salary: $36,000

Indiana University—South Bend

1700 Mishawaka Avenue
South Bend, IN 46634

Contact Information:
Telephone: 219-237-4154
Fax: 219-237-4854
E-mail: nyokom@iusb.edu

Program Information:
Program begins: August
Duration of program: 16 months

Application Information:
Enrollment of program: 30
Transfer students are accepted.

Financial Information:
Tuition, resident: $2,798
Tuition, non-resident: $3,653
Average cost of books: $1,500
% of students receiving aid: 50

Employment Profile:
% of students who pass the boards on their first try: 90
% employed within the first 6 months following graduation: 80
Average starting salary: $36,000

Indiana University Northwest

3223 Broadway
Gary, IN 46409

Contact Information:
Telephone: 219-980-6734
Fax: 219-981-4249

E-mail: jrobins@iunhaw1.iun.indiana.edu
Web: www.iun.indiana.edu

Program Information:
Program begins: August
Duration of program: 18 months

Application Information:
Enrollment of program: 48

Financial Information:
Tuition, resident: $62,440
Tuition, non-resident: $16,409

Employment Profile:
% of students who pass the boards on their first try: 90
% employed within the first 6 months following graduation: 80
Average starting salary: $44,000

Indiana University School of Dentistry
1121 West Michigan Street
Indianapolis, IN 46202-5186

Contact Information:
Telephone: 317-274-7801
Fax: 317-274-2419
E-mail: e.oldsen@iusd.iupui.edu
Web: www.iusd.iu.pui.edu

Program Information:
Program begins: August
Degrees offered: Associate's, 20 months; Bachelor's, 48 months

Application Information:
Enrollment of program: 100

Financial Information:
Tuition, resident: $3,800
Tuition, non-resident: $11,000
Average cost of books: $600
% of students receiving aid: 60

Employment Profile:
% of students who pass the boards on their first try: 95
% employed within the first 6 months following graduation: 100
Average starting salary: $30,000

University of Southern Indiana
8600 University Boulevard
Evansville, IN 47712

Contact Information:
Telephone: 812-464-1707
Fax: 812-465-7092
E-mail: dcarl.ucs@usi.edu
Web: www.usi.edu

Program Information:
Program begins: January, July
Duration of program: 16 months

Application Information:
Enrollment of program: 52
Transfer students are accepted.

Financial Information:
Tuition, resident: $2,880
Tuition, non-resident: $7,029

Employment Profile:
% of students who pass the boards on their first try: 100
% employed within the first 6 months following graduation: 90
Average starting salary: $34,000

Iowa

Hawkeye Community College
1501 East Orange Road
PO Box 8015
Waterloo, IA 50704

Contact Information:
Telephone: 319-296-2320 ext. 1352
Fax: 319-296-2874
E-mail: sturner@hawkeye.cc.ia.us
Web: www.hawkeye.cc.ia.us

Program Information:
Program begins: August
Degrees offered: Associate's, 21 months

Application Information:
Enrollment of program: 22
Transfer students are accepted.

Financial Information:
Tuition, resident: $2,886
Tuition, non-resident: $5,772
Average cost of books: $1,500
% of students receiving aid: 90

Employment Profile:
% of students who pass the boards on their first try: 90
% employed within the first 6 months following graduation: 95

Iowa Western Community College
2700 College Road
PO Box 4C
Council Bluffs, IA 51502-3004

Contact Information:
Telephone: 712-325-3736
Fax: 712-325-3736
E-mail: jhillis@iwcc.cc.ia.us
Web: www.iwcc.cc.ia.us

Program Information:
Program begins: August, January
Duration of program: 22 months

Application Information:
Enrollment of program: 18
Transfer students are accepted.

Financial Information:
Tuition, resident: $2,700
Tuition, non-resident: $3,798
Average cost of books: $1,100
% of students receiving aid: 90

Kansas

Johnson County Community College
12345 College Boulevard
Overland Park, KS 66210-1299

Contact Information:
Telephone: 913-469-2582
Fax: 913-469-2518
E-mail: mlog@jccc.net
Web: www.jccc.net

Program Information:
Program begins: August
Duration of program: 24 months

Application Information:
Enrollment of program: 53

Financial Information:
Tuition, resident: $1,840
Tuition, non-resident: $4,880
Average cost of books: $3,105
% of students receiving aid: 20

Employment Profile:
% of students who pass the boards on their first try: 90
% employed within the first 6 months following graduation: 90
Average starting salary: $47,000

Wichita State University
1845 North Fairmount
Wichita, KS 67260-0144

Contact Information:
Telephone: 316-978-3614
Fax: 316-978-3025
E-mail: maseman@chp.twsu.edu
Web: www.wichita.edu

Program Information:
Program begins: August
Duration of program: 19 months

Application Information:
Enrollment of program: 60
Transfer students are accepted.

Financial Information:
Tuition, resident: $1,986
Tuition, non-resident: $7,000

Employment Profile:
% of students who pass the boards on their first try: 90
% employed within the first 6 months following graduation: 90
Average starting salary: $30,000

Kentucky

Lexington Community College
Cooper Drive, Oswald Building
Lexington, KY 40506

Contact Information:
Telephone: 606-257-4872 ext. 4091
Fax: 606-257-2992

E-mail: lcchis00@pop.uky.edu
Web: www.uky.edu

Program Information:
Program begins: August
Duration of program: 24 months

Application Information:
Enrollment of program: 47
Transfer students are accepted.

Financial Information:
Tuition, resident: $978
Tuition, non-resident: $2,598
Average cost of books: $600
% of students receiving aid: 50

Employment Profile:
% of students who pass the boards on their first try: 98
% employed within the first 6 months following graduation: 100

Western Kentucky University

Academic Complex
Room 207
Bowling Green, KY 42101

Contact Information:
Telephone: 502-745-2427
Fax: 502-745-6869
E-mail: douglas.schutte@wku.edu
Web: www.wku.edu/dept/academic

Program Information:
Program begins: August
Degrees offered: Associate's, 17 months; Bachelor's, 33 months

Application Information:
Enrollment of program: 48
Transfer students are accepted.

Financial Information:
Tuition, resident: $2,390
Tuition, non-resident: $6,430
Average cost of books: $450
% of students receiving aid: 50

Employment Profile:
% of students who pass the boards on their first try: 92
% employed within the first 6 months following graduation: 100
Average starting salary: $32,000

Louisiana

Louisiana State University

1100 Florida Avenue
New Orleans, LA 70119

Contact Information:
Telephone: 504-619-8530
Fax: 504-619-8676
E-mail: cmason@/susd./sumc.edu

Program Information:
Program begins: August
Duration of program: 18 months

Financial Information:
Tuition, resident: $1,800
Tuition, non-resident: $3,100

Northeast Louisiana University

700 University Avenue
Monroe, LA 71209

Contact Information:
Telephone: 318-342-1619
Fax: 318-342-1687
E-mail: aljarrell@alpha.nlu.edu

Program Information:
Program begins: August
Duration of program: 24 months
Evening or weekend classes are available.

Application Information:
Enrollment of program: 48
Transfer students are accepted.

Financial Information:
Tuition, resident: $11,320
Tuition, non-resident: $18,388
Average cost of books: $300

Employment Profile:
% of students who pass the boards on their first try: 96
% employed within the first 6 months following graduation: 90
Average starting salary: $53,800

Maine

University of Maine—Bangor

Lincoln Hall
29 Texas Avenue
Bangor, ME 04401-4324

Contact Information:
Telephone: 502-852-1278
E-mail: acurtis@maine.edu
Web: www.maine.uma.edu

Program Information:
Program begins: August
Duration of program: 27 months
Evening or weekend classes are available.

Application Information:
Enrollment of program: 70
Transfer students are accepted.

Financial Information:
Average cost of books: $500
% of students receiving aid: 90

Employment Profile:
% of students who pass the boards on their first try: 90
% employed within the first 6 months following graduation: 100

Massachusetts

Bristol Community College

777 Elsbree Street
Fall River, MA 02720

Contact Information:
Telephone: 508-678-2811 ext. 2143
Fax: 508-675-2318
E-mail: bfastoso@bristol.mass.edu
Web: www.bristol.mass.edu

Program Information:
Program begins: September
Duration of program: 7 months

Application Information:
Enrollment of program: 41
Transfer students are accepted.

Financial Information:
Average cost of books: $250

Employment Profile:
% of students who pass the boards on their first try: 97
Average starting salary: $40,000

Forsyth School

140 The Fenway
Boston, MA 02115

Contact Information:
Telephone: 617-262-5200
Fax: 617-262-4021
E-mail: lhanlon@forsyth.org
Web: www.forsyth.org

Program Information:
Program begins: September
Duration of program: 48 months

Application Information:
Enrollment of program: 165
Transfer students are accepted.

Financial Information:
Tuition, resident: $14,449
Tuition, non-resident: $14,447
Average cost of books: $500
% of students receiving aid: 25

Employment Profile:
% of students who pass the boards on their first try: 95
% employed within the first 6 months following graduation: 75
Average starting salary: $45,000

Mt. Ida College

777 Dedham Street
Newton Centre, MA 02159

Contact Information:
Telephone: 617-928-4528
Fax: 617-928-4760
E-mail: csacchetti@mountida.edu
Web: www.mountida.edu

Program Information:
Program begins: September
Degrees offered: Associate's, 18 months

Application Information:
Enrollment of program: 23
Transfer students are accepted.

Financial Information:
Average cost of books: $600

Springfield Technical Community College

One Armory Square
Springfield, MA 01105

Contact Information:
Telephone: 413-755-4934
Fax: 413-733-0688
E-mail: dryan@stcc.mass.edu
Web: www.stcc.mass.edu

Program Information:
Program begins: September, January
Degrees offered: Associate's, 24 months

Application Information:
Enrollment of program: 36
Transfer students are accepted.

Financial Information:
Tuition, resident: $2,955
Tuition, non-resident: $10,681
Average cost of books: $500
% of students receiving aid: 90

Employment Profile:
% of students who pass the boards on their first try: 100
% employed within the first 6 months following graduation: 100
Average starting salary: $47,500

Michigan

Baker College of Port Huron

3403 Lapeer Road
Port Huron, MI 48060

Contact Information:
Telephone: 810-985-7000
Fax: 810-985-7066
E-mail: duff_s@porthuron.baker.edu
Web: www.baker.edu

Program Information:
Program begins: September, January, March
Degrees offered: Associate's, 27 months

Application Information:
Enrollment of program: 60
Transfer students are accepted.

Financial Information:
Average cost of books: $1,300
% of students receiving aid: 95

Employment Profile:
% of students who pass the boards on their first try: 95
% employed within the first 6 months following graduation: 90
Average starting salary: $44,000

Charles Stewart Mott Community College

1401 East Court Street
Flint, MI 48503

Contact Information:
Telephone: 810-762-0328
Fax: 810-232-8874
E-mail: csmith@email.mcc.edu
Web: www.mcc.edu

Program Information:
Program begins: July
Duration of program: 24 months

Application Information:
Enrollment of program: 37
Transfer students are accepted.

Financial Information:
Tuition, resident: $2,712
Tuition, non-resident: $3,912
Average cost of books: $700
% of students receiving aid: 80

Employment Profile:
% of students who pass the boards on their first try: 80
% employed within the first 6 months following graduation: 90
Average starting salary: $36,000

Delta College

F-56 Allied Health Building
University Center, MI 48710

Contact Information:
Telephone: 517-686-9383
Fax: 517-667-2218
E-mail: v|przygo@alpha.delta.edu
Web: www.delta.edu

Program Information:
Program begins: August
Degrees offered: Associate's, 18 months

Application Information:
Enrollment of program: 36
Transfer students are accepted.

Financial Information:
Tuition, resident: $2,240
Tuition, non-resident: $4,000
Average cost of books: $500
% of students receiving aid: 61

Employment Profile:
% of students who pass the boards on their first try: 95
% employed within the first 6 months following graduation: 100
Average starting salary: $28,000

Ferris State University

College of Allied Health Sciences
200 Ferris Drive
Big Rapids, MI 49307-2740

Contact Information:
Telephone: 231-591-2272
Fax: 231-591-3788
E-mail: stolberm@ferris.edu
Web: www.ferris.edu

Program Information:
Program begins: September
Duration of program: 21 months

Application Information:
Enrollment of program: 120
Transfer students are accepted.

Financial Information:
Tuition, resident: $4,178
Tuition, non-resident: $6,266
Average cost of books: $3,330

Grand Rapids Community College

143 Bostwick Street Northeast
Grand Rapids, MI 49503

Contact Information:
Telephone: 616-234-4239
Fax: 616-234-4234
Web: www.grcc.cc.mi.us

Program Information:
Program begins: September
Duration of program: 22 months

Application Information:
Enrollment of program: 32

Financial Information:
Tuition, resident: $4,845
Tuition, non-resident: $7,140

Employment Profile:
% employed within the first 6 months following graduation: 100
Average starting salary: $30,000

Kellogg Community College

450 North Avenue
Battle Creek, MI 49016

Contact Information:
Telephone: 616-965-3931 ext. 2300
Fax: 616-965-4144
E-mail: kellogg.cc.mi.us
Web: www.kellogg.cc.mi.us

Program Information:
Program begins: August
Duration of program: 24 months

Application Information:
Enrollment of program: 40
Transfer students are accepted.

Employment Profile:
% of students who pass the boards on their first try: 90
% employed within the first 6 months following graduation: 100
Average starting salary: $40,000

Oakland Community College—Waterford

7350 Cooley Lake Road
Waterford, MI 48327

Contact Information:
Telephone: 248-360-3025
Fax: 248-360-6263
E-mail: mmboguck@occ.cc.mi.us
Web: www.occ.cc.mi.us

Program Information:
Program begins: August
Degrees offered: Diploma, 18 months

Application Information:
Enrollment of program: 30
Transfer students are accepted.

Financial Information:
Tuition, resident: $2,865
Tuition, non-resident: $5,511
Average cost of books: $900
% of students receiving aid: 32

Employment Profile:
% of students who pass the boards on their first try: 96
% employed within the first 6 months following graduation: 100
Average starting salary: $50,000

University of Michigan
1011 North University
Ann Arbor, MI 48109

Contact Information:
Telephone: 908-889-2419
Fax: 908-889-2477
E-mail: wendyek@umich.edu

Program Information:
Program begins: August
Duration of program: 44 months

Application Information:
Enrollment of program: 100
Transfer students are accepted.

Financial Information:
Tuition, resident: $7,074
Tuition, non-resident: $21,086
Average cost of books: $800

Employment Profile:
% of students who pass the boards on their first try: 90
% employed within the first 6 months following graduation: 80
Average starting salary: $40,000

Wayne County Community College
8551 Greenfield
Room 316
Detroit, MI 48228

Contact Information:
Telephone: 313-943-4055
Fax: 313-943-4025
E-mail: drfloss@flash.net
Web: www.wccc.edu

Program Information:
Program begins: September
Duration of program: 24 months
Evening or weekend classes are available.

Application Information:
Enrollment of program: 48
Transfer students are accepted.

Financial Information:
Tuition, resident: $14,700
Tuition, non-resident: $17,000
% of students receiving aid: 29

Employment Profile:
% of students who pass the boards on their first try: 100
% employed within the first 6 months following graduation: 100

Minnesota

Century Community and Technical College
3300 Century Avenue North
White Bear Lake, MN 55110

Contact Information:
Telephone: 612-779-3983
Fax: 612-779-5779
Web: www.century.cc.mn.us

Program Information:
Program begins: August
Degrees offered: Associate's, 18 months
Evening or weekend classes are available.

Application Information:
Enrollment of program: 12
Transfer students are accepted.

Financial Information:
Tuition, resident: $2,632
Tuition, non-resident: $7,498

Employment Profile:
% of students who pass the boards on their first try: 90
% employed within the first 6 months following graduation: 100
Average starting salary: $56,000

Lake Superior College
2101 Trinity Road
Duluth, MN 55811

Contact Information:
Telephone: 218-733-5938
Fax: 218-723-4921
Web: www.lsc.cc.mn.us

Program Information:
Program begins: September
Duration of program: 18 months

Application Information:
Enrollment of program: 40
Transfer students are accepted.

Financial Information:
Tuition, resident: $1,747
Tuition, non-resident: $3,495
Average cost of books: $700
% of students receiving aid: 70

Employment Profile:
% of students who pass the boards on their first try: 99
% employed within the first 6 months following graduation: 100
Average starting salary: $17,000

Minnesota State University—Mankato
3 Morris Hall
Mankato, MN 56001

Contact Information:
Telephone: 507-389-1313
Fax: 507-389-5850
E-mail: william.johnson_1@mankato.msus.edu
Web: www.mankato.msus.edu

Program Information:
Program begins: August
Duration of program: 20 months

Application Information:
Enrollment of program: 48

Financial Information:
Tuition, resident: $2,363
Tuition, non-resident: $4,513

Employment Profile:
% of students who pass the boards on their first try: 100
% employed within the first 6 months following graduation: 85

Normandale Community College
9700 France Avenue South
Bloomington, MN 55431

Contact Information:
Telephone: 612-832-6522
Fax: 612-832-6571
E-mail: g.chovanec@nr.cc.mn.us
Web: www.nr.cc.mn.us

Program Information:
Program begins: August
Degrees offered: Diploma, 24 months; Associate's, 9 months

Application Information:
Enrollment of program: 32

Financial Information:
Tuition, resident: $3,460
Tuition, non-resident: $6,480
Average cost of books: $1,100
% of students receiving aid: 30

Employment Profile:
% of students who pass the boards on their first try: 67
% employed within the first 6 months following graduation: 100
Average starting salary: $50,000

Northwest Technical College—Moorhead
Allied Dental Careers Department
1900 28th Avenue South
Moorhead, MN 56560-4809

Contact Information:
Telephone: 218-299-6560
Fax: 218-236-0342
E-mail: ste566@mail.ntc.mnscu.edu
Web: www.ntc-online.com

Program Information:
Program begins: August
Degrees offered: Diploma, 20 months; Associate's, 20 months
Evening or weekend classes are available.

Application Information:
Enrollment of program: 36
Transfer students are accepted.

Financial Information:
Tuition, resident: $5,184
Tuition, non-resident: $9,842

Employment Profile:
% of students who pass the boards on their first try: 66
% employed within the first 6 months following graduation: 100
Average starting salary: $33,000

Rochester Community and Technical College
851 30th Avenue Southeast
Rochester, MN 55904

Contact Information:
Telephone: 507-280-3114
Fax: 507-280-3180
E-mail: anne.niccolai@roch.edu
Web: www.roch.edu

Program Information:
Program begins: September
Duration of program: 24 months

Application Information:
Enrollment of program: 32
Transfer students are accepted.

Financial Information:
Tuition, resident: $5,600
Tuition, non-resident: $11,200
Average cost of books: $800
% of students receiving aid: 50

Employment Profile:
% of students who pass the boards on their first try: 94
% employed within the first 6 months following graduation: 100
Average starting salary: $34,000

University of Minnesota—Twin Cities
9-436 Moos Tower
Minneapolis, MN 55455

Contact Information:
Telephone: 734-763-3392
Fax: 734-763-5503
E-mail: newel001@tc.umn.edu
Web: www.umn.edu/dental

Program Information:
Program begins: September
Duration of program: 27 months

Application Information:
Enrollment of program: 108
Transfer students are accepted.

Financial Information:
Tuition, resident: $11,000
Tuition, non-resident: $32,832
Average cost of books: $400

Employment Profile:
% of students who pass the boards on their first try: 98
% employed within the first 6 months following graduation: 100
Average starting salary: $45,000

Mississippi

Pearl River Community College—Poplarville
5448 US Highway 49 South
Hattiesburg, MS 39401

Contact Information:
Telephone: 601-554-9109
Fax: 601-554-9148
E-mail: slhill@prcc.cc.ms.us
Web: www.prcc.ms.us

Program Information:
Program begins: August
Duration of program: 20 months

Application Information:
Enrollment of program: 32
Transfer students are accepted.

Financial Information:
Tuition, resident: $1,350
Tuition, non-resident: $1,700
Average cost of books: $600
% of students receiving aid: 75

Employment Profile:
% of students who pass the boards on their first try: 100
% employed within the first 6 months following graduation: 100
Average starting salary: $34,000

Missouri

Missouri Southern State College
3950 East Newman and Duquesne Roads
Joplin, MO 64801-1595

Contact Information:
Telephone: 417-625-9379
Fax: 417-625-3078
E-mail: burns-fa@marc.mssced

Program Information:
Program begins: September
Duration of program: 22 months

Application Information:
Enrollment of program: 30
Transfer students are accepted.

Financial Information:
Tuition, resident: $2,160
Tuition, non-resident: $4,320
Average cost of books: $500
% of students receiving aid: 80

Employment Profile:
% of students who pass the boards on their first try: 91
% employed within the first 6 months following graduation: 100
Average starting salary: $37,000

University of Missouri—Kansas City
650 East 25th Street
Kansas City, MO 64108

Contact Information:
Telephone: 601-984-6310
Fax: 601-984-6344
E-mail: overmanp@umkc.edu
Web: www.umkc.edu/dentistry/acadarog/denthyg.html

Program Information:
Program begins: September
Degrees offered: Bachelor's

Application Information:
Enrollment of program: 60
Transfer students are accepted.

Financial Information:
Tuition, resident: $5,000
Tuition, non-resident: $14,000
Average cost of books: $600
% of students receiving aid: 60

Employment Profile:
% of students who pass the boards on their first try: 95
% employed within the first 6 months following graduation: 95
Average starting salary: $35,000

Nebraska

Central Community College
PO Box 1024
Hastings, NE 68902-1024

Contact Information:
Telephone: 402-461-2470
Fax: 402-460-2138
E-mail: wcloet@cccneb.edu
Web: www.cccneb.edu

Program Information:
Program begins: August
Duration of program: 24 months

Application Information:
Transfer students are accepted.

Financial Information:
Tuition, resident: $1,747
Tuition, non-resident: $2,374
Average cost of books: $1,500

Employment Profile:
Average starting salary: $45,000

New Jersey

Bergen Community College
400 Paramus Road
Paramus, NJ 076521595

Contact Information:
Telephone: 201-447-7944 ext. 7939
Fax: 201-612-8225
Web: www.bergen.cc.nj.us

Program Information:
Program begins: September
Duration of program: 23 months

Application Information:
Transfer students are accepted.

Financial Information:
Tuition, resident: $2,006
Average cost of books: $400

Employment Profile:
% of students who pass the boards on their first try: 85
% employed within the first 6 months following graduation: 75
Average starting salary: $36,000

Camden County College
PO Box 200
College Drive
Blackwood, NJ 08012

Contact Information:
Telephone: 856-227-7200
Fax: 856-374-5048
Web: www.camdencc.edu

Program Information:
Program begins: September
Degrees offered: Associate's, 24 months

Application Information:
Enrollment of program: 22

Financial Information:
Tuition, resident: $2,537
Tuition, non-resident: $2,709
Average cost of books: $350
% of students receiving aid: 30

Employment Profile:
% of students who pass the boards on their first try: 95
% employed within the first 6 months following graduation: 100
Average starting salary: $44,000

Middlesex County College
2600 Woodbridge Avenue
Edison, NJ 08818

Contact Information:
Telephone: 732-906-2580
Fax: 732-906-2366
Web: www.middlesex.cc.nj.us

Program Information:
Program begins: September
Duration of program: 15 months
Evening or weekend classes are available.

Application Information:
Enrollment of program: 50
Transfer students are accepted.

Financial Information:
Tuition, resident: $2,340
Tuition, non-resident: $5,993
Average cost of books: $1,000

Employment Profile:
% of students who pass the boards on their first try: 80
% employed within the first 6 months following graduation: 90
Average starting salary: $27,500

University of Medicine & Dentistry of New Jersey
1776 Raritan Road
Scotch Plains, NJ 07076

Contact Information:
Telephone: 410-706-7773
Fax: 410-706-0349
E-mail: breen@umdnj.edu
Web: www.umdnj.edu/shrpweb/programs

Program Information:
Program begins: January
Degrees offered: Certificate program; Bachelor's, 24 months; PhD
Evening or weekend classes are available.

Application Information:
Enrollment of program: 44
Transfer students are accepted.

Financial Information:
Tuition, resident: $2,200
Tuition, non-resident: $4,400
Average cost of books: $400
% of students receiving aid: 50

Employment Profile:
% of students who pass the boards on their first try: 98
% employed within the first 6 months following graduation: 100
Average starting salary: $45,000

New Mexico

University of New Mexico
2320 Tucker Northeast
Albuquerque, NM 87131-1391

Contact Information:
Telephone: 203-931-6025
Fax: 203-931-6083
E-mail: dlogothetis@salvd.unm.edu
Web: www.unm.edu

Program Information:
Program begins: August
Duration of program: 25 months

Application Information:
Enrollment of program: 48

Financial Information:
Tuition, resident: $2,164
Tuition, non-resident: $8,174
Average cost of books: $300
% of students receiving aid: 60

Employment Profile:
% of students who pass the boards on their first try: 100
% employed within the first 6 months following graduation: 100

New York

Broome Community College
PO Box 1017
Binghamton, NY 13902

Contact Information:
Telephone: 607-778-5149
Fax: 607-778-5467
E-mail: walsh_d@mail.sunybroome.edu
Web: www.sunybroome.edu

Program Information:
Program begins: August
Duration of program: 15 months

Application Information:
Enrollment of program: 72
Transfer students are accepted.

Financial Information:
Tuition, resident: $2,268
Tuition, non-resident: $4,536
Average cost of books: $600
% of students receiving aid: 75

Employment Profile:
% of students who pass the boards on their first try: 95
% employed within the first 6 months following graduation: 75
Average starting salary: $30,000

Erie Community College—North Campus
6205 Main Street
Williamsville, NY 14221-7095

Contact Information:
Telephone: 716-851-1390
Fax: 716-851-1429
E-mail: sowinski@ecc.edu
Web: www.ecc.edu

Program Information:
Program begins: September
Duration of program: 24 months
Evening or weekend classes are available.

Application Information:
Enrollment of program: 140
Transfer students are accepted.

Financial Information:
Tuition, resident: $2,475
Tuition, non-resident: $4,950
Average cost of books: $500
% of students receiving aid: 85

Employment Profile:
% of students who pass the boards on their first try: 95
% employed within the first 6 months following graduation: 60
Average starting salary: $30,000

Hostos Community College of CUNY
475 Grand Concourse
Bronx, NY 10451

Contact Information:
Telephone: 718-518-4235
Fax: 718-518-4294
E-mail: sejho@mail.hostos.cuny.edu
Web: www.hostos.cuny.edu

Program Information:
Program begins: September
Duration of program: 26 months

Application Information:
Enrollment of program: 80
Transfer students are accepted.

Financial Information:
Tuition, resident: $2,500
Tuition, non-resident: $3,076
Average cost of books: $475

Employment Profile:
% of students who pass the boards on their first try: 93
% employed within the first 6 months following graduation: 85
Average starting salary: $27,000

Hudson Valley Community College
80 Vandenburgh Avenue
Troy, NY 12180

Contact Information:
Telephone: 518-629-7442
Fax: 518-629-8111
E-mail: daviscat@hvcc.com

Program Information:
Program begins: January
Duration of program: 10 months

Application Information:
Enrollment of program: 99
Transfer students are accepted.

Financial Information:
Tuition, resident: $2,534
Tuition, non-resident: $6,059
Average cost of books: $500
% of students receiving aid: 98

Employment Profile:
% of students who pass the boards on their first try: 98
% employed within the first 6 months following graduation: 98
Average starting salary: $20,000

Monroe Community College
1000 East Henrietta Road
Rochester, NY 14623-5780

Contact Information:
Telephone: 716-292-2761
E-mail: dlawrence@monroecc.edu
Web: www.monroecc.edu

Program Information:
Program begins: September
Degrees offered: Diploma, 24 months

Application Information:
Enrollment of program: 86
Transfer students are accepted.

Financial Information:
Tuition, resident: $2,500
Tuition, non-resident: $5,000
Average cost of books: $350

Employment Profile:
% of students who pass the boards on their first try: 95
Average starting salary: $35,000

New York University
345 East 24th Street
New York, NY 10010

Contact Information:
Telephone: 212-998-9390
Fax: 212-995-4593
E-mail: cmw@isa.nyu.edu
Web: www.nyu.edu

Program Information:
Program begins: September, January
Degrees offered: Associate's; Bachelor's
Evening or weekend classes are available.

Application Information:
Enrollment of program: 120
Transfer students are accepted.

Financial Information:
Average cost of books: $1,000
% of students receiving aid: 80

Employment Profile:
% of students who pass the boards on their first try: 85
% employed within the first 6 months following graduation: 100
Average starting salary: $47,500

SUNY at Farmingdale
Route 110
Farmingdale, NY 11735

Contact Information:
Telephone: 516-420-2060
Fax: 516-420-2582
E-mail: friedmjm@bnyfarva.cc.farmingdale.edu
Web: www.farmingdale.edu

Program Information:
Program begins: August
Duration of program: 21 months

Application Information:
Enrollment of program: 100
Transfer students are accepted.

Financial Information:
Tuition, resident: $3,400
Tuition, non-resident: $8,300

Employment Profile:
% of students who pass the boards on their first try: 94
% employed within the first 6 months following graduation: 100
Average starting salary: $50,000

North Carolina

Central Piedmont Community College
1201 Elizabeth Avenue
Kings Drive
Charlotte, NC 28204

Contact Information:
Telephone: 704-330-6431
Fax: 704-330-6533
Web: www.cpcc.cc.nc.us

Program Information:
Program begins: August
Duration of program: 21 months

Application Information:
Enrollment of program: 60
Transfer students are accepted.

Financial Information:
Tuition, resident: $840
Tuition, non-resident: $6,846
Average cost of books: $2,000
% of students receiving aid: 25

Employment Profile:
% of students who pass the boards on their first try: 90
% employed within the first 6 months following graduation: 100

Coastal Carolina Community College
444 Western Boulevard
Jacksonville, NC 28540

Contact Information:
Telephone: 910-938-6270
Fax: 910-455-4989
E-mail: brancheb.coastal.cc.nc.us
Web: www.coastal.cc.nc.us

Program Information:
Program begins: August
Degrees offered: Associate's, 23 months

Application Information:
Enrollment of program: 48
Transfer students are accepted.

Financial Information:
Tuition, resident: $291
Tuition, non-resident: $2,293
Average cost of books: $1,500
% of students receiving aid: 33

Employment Profile:
% of students who pass the boards on their first try: 100
% employed within the first 6 months following graduation: 100
Average starting salary: $36,000

Fayetteville Technical Community College
2201 Hull Road
PO Box 35236
Fayetteville, NC 28303

Contact Information:
Telephone: 910-678-8532
Fax: 910-678-8500
E-mail: mumfordr@ftccmail.faytech.cc.nc.us
Web: www.fayech.cc.nc.us

Program Information:
Program begins: August
Duration of program: 27 months

Application Information:
Enrollment of program: 56
Transfer students are accepted.

Financial Information:
Tuition, resident: $880
Tuition, non-resident: $7,172
Average cost of books: $500
% of students receiving aid: 50

Employment Profile:
% of students who pass the boards on their first try: 85
% employed within the first 6 months following graduation: 100
Average starting salary: $38,900

Guilford Technical Community College
PO Box 309
Jamestown, NC 27282

Contact Information:
Telephone: 336-334-4822 ext. 2452
Fax: 336-841-4350
E-mail: smithl@gtcc.cc.nc.us
Web: www.tech.net.gtcc.cc.nc.us

Program Information:
Program begins: June
Duration of program: 22 months

Application Information:
Enrollment of program: 66

Financial Information:
Tuition, resident: $2,167
Tuition, non-resident: $6,785
Average cost of books: $500
% of students receiving aid: 33

Employment Profile:
% of students who pass the boards on their first try: 95
% employed within the first 6 months following graduation: 100
Average starting salary: $44,000

University of North Carolina at Chapel Hill
Allied Dental Education Programs
367 Old Dental Building/CB 7450
Chapel Hill, NC 27599-7450

Contact Information:
Telephone: 505-272-4513
Fax: 505-272-5584
E-mail: joyce_jensano@dentistry.unc.edu
Web: www.dent.unc.edu

Program Information:
Program begins: August
Duration of program: 18 months

Financial Information:
Tuition, resident: $2,772
Tuition, non-resident: $11,538

Wayne Community College
Caller Box 8002
Goldsboro, NC 27530

Contact Information:
Telephone: 919-735-5152 ext. 364
Fax: 919-736-3204
E-mail: anna@wcc.wayne.cc.nc.us
Web: www.wayne.cc.nc.us

Program Information:
Program begins: September
Duration of program: 20 months

Application Information:
Enrollment of program: 24
Transfer students are accepted.

Financial Information:
Tuition, resident: $2,052
Tuition, non-resident: $12,062
Average cost of books: $900
% of students receiving aid: 30

Employment Profile:
% of students who pass the boards on their first try: 100
% employed within the first 6 months following graduation: 100
Average starting salary: $43,000

Ohio

Cuyahoga Community College
2900 Community College Avenue
Cleveland, OH 44115

Contact Information:
Telephone: 216-987-4494
Fax: 216-987-4386
E-mail: mary-lou.gerosky@tri-c.cc.oh.us
Web: www.tri-c.cc.us

Program Information:
Program begins: September
Duration of program: 21 months

Application Information:
Enrollment of program: 47
Transfer students are accepted.

Financial Information:
Tuition, resident: $4,500
Tuition, non-resident: $5,950
Average cost of books: $500
% of students receiving aid: 80

Employment Profile:
% of students who pass the boards on their first try: 91
% employed within the first 6 months following graduation: 100
Average starting salary: $44,000

Lakeland Community College
7700 Clocktower Drive
Kirtland, OH 44094-5198

Contact Information:
Telephone: 440-953-7190
Fax: 440-975-4733
E-mail: cpatters@lakeland.cc.oh.us
Web: www.lakeland.cc.oh.us

Program Information:
Program begins: August
Duration of program: 18 months

Application Information:
Enrollment of program: 40

Financial Information:
Tuition, resident: $2,877
Tuition, non-resident: $7,531
Average cost of books: $1,000
% of students receiving aid: 75

Employment Profile:
% of students who pass the boards on their first try: 100
% employed within the first 6 months following graduation: 80
Average starting salary: $42,000

Lorain County Community College
1005 North Abbe Road
Elyria, OH 44035-1691

Contact Information:
Telephone: 440-365-5222 ext. 7196
Fax: 440-366-4116
E-mail: dprice@loraincc.edu
Web: www.lorain.ccc.edu

Program Information:
Program begins: August
Duration of program: 21 months
Evening or weekend classes are available.

Application Information:
Enrollment of program: 15
Transfer students are accepted.

Financial Information:
Tuition, resident: $1,750

Ohio State University
305 West 12th Avenue
Columbus, OH 43210

Contact Information:
Telephone: 614-292-2228
Fax: 614-292-8013
E-mail: devore.2@osu.edu
Web: www.dent.ohio-state.edu

Program Information:
Program begins: September
Duration of program: 36 months

Application Information:
Enrollment of program: 100
Transfer students are accepted.

Financial Information:
Tuition, resident: $4,110
Tuition, non-resident: $12,060
Average cost of books: $415
% of students receiving aid: 69

Employment Profile:
% of students who pass the boards on their first try: 97
% employed within the first 6 months following graduation: 88

Sinclair Community College
444 West Third Street
Dayton, OH 45402

Contact Information:
Telephone: 937-512-2779
Fax: 937-512-5192
E-mail: pedwards@sinclair.edu
Web: www.sinclair.edu

Program Information:
Program begins: June
Duration of program: 21 months

Financial Information:
Tuition, resident: $3,565
Tuition, non-resident: $5,450

Stark State College of Technology
6200 Frank Avenue Northwest
Canton, OH 44720-7299

Contact Information:
Telephone: 330-966-5458 ext. 307
Fax: 330-966-6586
E-mail: mrude@stark.cc.oh.us
Web: www.stark.cc.oh.us

Program Information:
Program begins: June
Duration of program: 22 months

Application Information:
Enrollment of program: 37

Financial Information:
Tuition, resident: $3,160
Tuition, non-resident: $4,225

University of Cincinnati
Raymond Walters College
9555 Plainfield Road
Cincinnati, OH 45236

Contact Information:
Telephone: 501-686-5733
Fax: 501-686-8519
E-mail: carroldkeucrwcu.rwc.uc.edu
Web: www.rwc.uc.edu

Program Information:
Program begins: September
Duration of program: 20 months

Application Information:
Enrollment of program: 40

Financial Information:
Tuition, resident: $3,471
Tuition, non-resident: $16,842
Average cost of books: $300
% of students receiving aid: 90

Employment Profile:
% of students who pass the boards on their first try: 95
% employed within the first 6 months following graduation: 100
Average starting salary: $36,000

Oklahoma

Rose State College
6420 Southeast 15th Street
Midwest City, OK 73110

Contact Information:
Telephone: 405-733-7336
Fax: 405-736-0338
Web: www.rose.cc.ok.us

Program Information:
Program begins: August
Duration of program: 18 months

Application Information:
Enrollment of program: 12
Transfer students are accepted.

Financial Information:
Tuition, resident: $1,209
Tuition, non-resident: $3,069
Average cost of books: $1,225
% of students receiving aid: 90

Employment Profile:
% of students who pass the boards on their first try: 100
% employed within the first 6 months following graduation: 100
Average starting salary: $45,000

Tulsa Community College
909 South Boston Avenue
Room MP 458
Tulsa, OK 74119-2094

Contact Information:
Telephone: 918-595-7023
Fax: 918-595-7091
E-mail: cmatthi@tulsa.cc.ok.us
Web: www.tulsa.cc.us

Program Information:
Program begins: September
Duration of program: 16 months

Application Information:
Enrollment of program: 28
Transfer students are accepted.

Financial Information:
Tuition, resident: $1,679
Tuition, non-resident: $4,229

University of Oklahoma Health Sciences Center
PO Box 26901
Oklahoma City, OK 73190

Contact Information:
Telephone: 405-271-4435
Fax: 405-271-3423
E-mail: pat-nunn@ouhsc.edu
Web: www.ouhs.edu

Program Information:
Program begins: August
Degrees offered: Bachelor's, 21 months

Application Information:
Enrollment of program: 48
Transfer students are accepted.

Financial Information:
Tuition, resident: $8,901
Tuition, non-resident: $17,645
Average cost of books: $474
% of students receiving aid: 60

Employment Profile:
% of students who pass the boards on their first try: 96
% employed within the first 6 months following graduation: 100
Average starting salary: $47,000

Oregon

Mt. Hood Community College
26000 Southeast Stark Street
Gresham, OR 97030

Contact Information:
Telephone: 503-491-7691
Fax: 503-491-6005
E-mail: tongt@mhcc.cc.or.us
Web: www.mhcc.cc.or.us

Program Information:
Program begins: September
Degrees offered: Diploma, 20 months

Application Information:
Enrollment of program: 16
Transfer students are accepted.

Financial Information:
Tuition, resident: $1,620
Tuition, non-resident: $6,996
Average cost of books: $535
% of students receiving aid: 35

Employment Profile:
% of students who pass the boards on their first try: 100
% employed within the first 6 months following graduation: 100
Average starting salary: $50,000

Oregon Institute of Technology
3201 Campus Drive
Klamath Falls, OR 97601

Contact Information:
Telephone: 541-885-1352
Fax: 541-885-1849
E-mail: copej@oit.edu
Web: www.oit.edu

Program Information:
Program begins: September
Duration of program: 27 months

Application Information:
Enrollment of program: 60
Transfer students are accepted.

Financial Information:
Tuition, resident: $1,103
Tuition, non-resident: $3,611
Average cost of books: $855
% of students receiving aid: 90

Employment Profile:
% of students who pass the boards on their first try: 40

Portland Community College
PO Box 19000
Portland, OR 97219-0990

Contact Information:
Telephone: 503-977-4235
Fax: 503-977-8300
E-mail: ajackson@pcc.edu
Web: www.pcc.edu

Program Information:
Program begins: September
Degrees offered: Diploma, 18 months

Application Information:
Enrollment of program: 36
Transfer students are accepted.

Financial Information:
Tuition, resident: $1,596
Tuition, non-resident: $4,788
Average cost of books: $800

Employment Profile:
% of students who pass the boards on their first try: 90
% employed within the first 6 months following graduation: 100
Average starting salary: $40,000

Pennsylvania

Community College of Philadelphia
1700 Spring Garden Street
Philadelphia, PA 19130

Contact Information:
Telephone: 215-751-8927
Fax: 215-751-8937
Web: www.ccp.cc.pa.us

Program Information:
Program begins: July
Degrees offered: Associate's, 24 months
Evening or weekend classes are available.

Application Information:
Enrollment of program: 30
Transfer students are accepted.

Financial Information:
Tuition, resident: $3,600
Tuition, non-resident: $9,800
Average cost of books: $960
% of students receiving aid: 37

Employment Profile:
% of students who pass the boards on their first try: 95
% employed within the first 6 months following graduation: 92
Average starting salary: $52,000

Manor Junior College
700 Fox Chase Road
Jenkintown, PA 19046-3399

Contact Information:
Telephone: 215-885-2360 ext. 284
Fax: 215-576-6564
Web: www.manor.edu

Program Information:
Program begins: July
Degrees offered: Associate's, 24 months
Evening or weekend classes are available.

Application Information:
Enrollment of program: 28

Financial Information:
Average cost of books: $1,000

Employment Profile:
% of students who pass the boards on their first try: 100
% employed within the first 6 months following graduation: 100
Average starting salary: $46,000

Montgomery County Community College
340 DeKalb Pike
Blue Bell, PA 19422-0796

Contact Information:
Telephone: 215-641-6483
Fax: 215-619-7171
E-mail: vbasteck@mc3.edu
Web: www.mc3.edu

Program Information:
Program begins: August
Duration of program: 16 months

Application Information:
Transfer students are accepted.

Financial Information:
Tuition, resident: $5,250
Tuition, non-resident: $15,120
% of students receiving aid: 95

Employment Profile:
% employed within the first 6 months following graduation: 100

Pennsylvania College of Technology
One College Avenue
Williamsport, PA 17701

Contact Information:
Telephone: 717-320-8007
Fax: 717-321-5556
E-mail: mcosgrove@pct.edu
Web: www.pct.edu

Program Information:
Program begins: August
Duration of program: 22 months

Financial Information:
Tuition, resident: $7,800

University of Pittsburgh
B-23 Salk Hall
Pittsburgh, PA 15261

Contact Information:
Telephone: 412-648-8432
Fax: 412-383-8737
E-mail: riccelli+@pitt.edu
Web: www.univ-relations.pitt.edu

Program Information:
Program begins: September
Duration of program: 22 months

Application Information:
Enrollment of program: 83
Transfer students are accepted.

Financial Information:
Tuition, resident: $3,059
Tuition, non-resident: $6,717
Average cost of books: $850

Employment Profile:
% of students who pass the boards on their first try: 89
% employed within the first 6 months following graduation: 100
Average starting salary: $32,000

Westmoreland County Community College
Armbrust Road
Youngwood, PA 15697-1895

Contact Information:
Telephone: 412-925-4163
Fax: 412-925-5808
E-mail: rinchua@astro.westmoreland.cc.pa.us
Web: www.westmoreland.cc.pa.us

Program Information:
Program begins: August
Degrees offered: Associate's, 21 months
Evening or weekend classes are available.

Application Information:
Enrollment of program: 48
Transfer students are accepted.

Financial Information:
Tuition, resident: $2,208
Tuition, non-resident: $4,416

Average cost of books: $800
% of students receiving aid: 80

Employment Profile:

% of students who pass the boards on their first try: 93
% employed within the first 6 months following graduation: 100
Average starting salary: $30,000

Puerto Rico

University of Puerto Rico

GPO Box 5067
San Juan, PR 00936

Contact Information:

Telephone: 787-758-2525 ext. 1161
Fax: 787-758-3061
E-mail: blancarodriguez@cpr.rcm.upr.edu
Web: www.cprsweb.rcm.upr.edu

Program Information:

Program begins: August
Degrees offered: Associate's, 15 months

Application Information:

Enrollment of program: 15
Transfer students are accepted.

Financial Information:

Tuition, resident: $3,562
Average cost of books: $620
% of students receiving aid: 95

Employment Profile:

% employed within the first 6 months following graduation: 50
Average starting salary: $13,000

South Carolina

Florence-Darlington Technical College

PO Box 100548
Florence, SC 29501-0548

Contact Information:

Telephone: 843-661-8023
Fax: 843-661-8306
E-mail: hewittm@flo.tec.sc.us
Web: www.flo.tec.sc.us

Program Information:

Program begins: August
Degrees offered: Associate's, 22 months

Application Information:

Enrollment of program: 18
Transfer students are accepted.

Financial Information:

Tuition, resident: $2,063
Tuition, non-resident: $4,605
Average cost of books: $1,500
% of students receiving aid: 60

Employment Profile:

% of students who pass the boards on their first try: 90
% employed within the first 6 months following graduation: 100
Average starting salary: $34,000

Horry-Georgetown Technical College

PO Box 261966
2050 Highway 501 East
Conway, SC 29528-6066

Contact Information:

Telephone: 843-349-5331
Fax: 843-347-4207
E-mail: derouen@hor.tec.sc.us
Web: www.hor.tec.sc.us

Program Information:

Program begins: August
Duration of program: 24 months

Application Information:

Enrollment of program: 30
Transfer students are accepted.

Financial Information:

Tuition, resident: $1,120
Tuition, non-resident: $4,212
Average cost of books: $400
% of students receiving aid: 90

Trident Technical College

PO Box 118067
Charleston, SC 29423-8067

Contact Information:

Telephone: 843-574-6439
Fax: 843-574-6585
E-mail: zpankersenb@trident.tec.sc.us
Web: www.trident.tec.sc.us

Program Information:

Program begins: January
Duration of program: 21 months

Financial Information:

Tuition, resident: $550
Tuition, non-resident: $1,633

South Dakota

University of South Dakota

East Hall
414 East Clark Street
Vermillion, SD 57069

Contact Information:

Telephone: 605-677-5379
Fax: 605-677-5638
E-mail: abrunick@usd.edu
Web: www.usd.edu

Program Information:

Program begins: May
Duration of program: 28 months

Application Information:

Enrollment of program: 63
Transfer students are accepted.

Financial Information:

Tuition, resident: $5,063
Tuition, non-resident: $6,973
Average cost of books: $300

Employment Profile:

% of students who pass the boards on their first try: 97
% employed within the first 6 months following graduation: 85
Average starting salary: $36,000

Tennessee

East Tennessee State University

PO Box 70690
Johnson City, TN 37614-0690

Contact Information:

Telephone: 423-439-4497
Fax: 423-439-5238
E-mail: nunley@etsu-tn.edu
Web: www.etsu.edu

Program Information:

Program begins: August
Degrees offered: Diploma, 19 months

Application Information:

Enrollment of program: 49
Transfer students are accepted.

Financial Information:

Tuition, resident: $3,129
Tuition, non-resident: $9,633
Average cost of books: $500
% of students receiving aid: 60

Employment Profile:

% of students who pass the boards on their first try: 98
% employed within the first 6 months following graduation: 98
Average starting salary: $31,250

Texas

Amarillo College

PO Box 447
Amarillo, TX 79178

Contact Information:

Telephone: 806-354-6056
Fax: 806-354-6076
E-mail: csnorton@actx.edu
Web: www.actx.edu

Program Information:

Program begins: September
Degrees offered: Associate's, 26 months

Application Information:

Transfer students are accepted.

Financial Information:

Tuition, resident: $1,100
Tuition, non-resident: $2,743
Average cost of books: $650
% of students receiving aid: 72

Employment Profile:

% of students who pass the boards on their first try: 94

% employed within the first 6 months following graduation: 100

Baylor College of Dentistry

The Texas A & M University System
PO Box 660677
Dallas, TX 75266-0677

Contact Information:
Telephone: 214-828-8341
Fax: 214-828-8196
E-mail: jdewald@tambcd.edu
Web: www.tambcd.edu

Program Information:
Program begins: August
Duration of program: 21 months

Financial Information:
Tuition, resident: $2,500
Tuition, non-resident: $17,400

Blinn College

PO Box 6030
Bryan, TX 778456030

Contact Information:
Telephone: 409-821-0283
Fax: 409-821-0289
E-mail: ssemler@acmail.blinncol.edu
Web: www.blinncol.edu

Program Information:
Program begins: September
Duration of program: 24 months

Application Information:
Enrollment of program: 24
Transfer students are accepted.

Financial Information:
Tuition, resident: $585
Tuition, non-resident: $1,665
Average cost of books: $500
% of students receiving aid: 30

Employment Profile:
% of students who pass the boards on their first try: 100
% employed within the first 6 months following graduation: 100
Average starting salary: $50,000

Collin County Community College District

2200 West University Drive
McKinney, TX 75069

Contact Information:
Telephone: 972-548-6535
Fax: 972-548-6536
E-mail: jfletcher@pmail.ccccd.edu
Web: www.cccd.edu

Program Information:
Program begins: August
Duration of program: 24 months

Application Information:
Enrollment of program: 32
Transfer students are accepted.

Financial Information:
Tuition, resident: $936
Tuition, non-resident: $2,000
Average cost of books: $1,200

Employment Profile:
% of students who pass the boards on their first try: 100
% employed within the first 6 months following graduation: 100
Average starting salary: $44,000

Del Mar College

101 Baldwin and Ayers Streets
Corpus Christi, TX 78404

Contact Information:
Telephone: 361-698-1358
Fax: 361-698-1175
Web: www.delmar.edu

Program Information:
Program begins: August
Degrees offered: Associate's, 18 months

Application Information:
Enrollment of program: 18
Transfer students are accepted.

Financial Information:
Tuition, resident: $768
Tuition, non-resident: $1,650
Average cost of books: $375
% of students receiving aid: 50

Employment Profile:
% of students who pass the boards on their first try: 89
% employed within the first 6 months following graduation: 100
Average starting salary: $35,000

Lamar University Institute of Technology—Beaumont

PO Box 10061
Beaumont, TX 77710

Contact Information:
Telephone: 409-880-8858
Fax: 409-880-8955
E-mail: reynardbj@hal.edu
Web: www.theinstitute.lamar.edu

Program Information:
Program begins: July
Duration of program: 24 months

Application Information:
Enrollment of program: 43
Transfer students are accepted.

Financial Information:
Tuition, resident: $2,400

Employment Profile:
% employed within the first 6 months following graduation: 96

Midwestern State University

3410 Taft Boulevard
Wichita Falls, TX 76308-2099

Contact Information:
Telephone: 940-397-4764
Fax: 940-397-4513
E-mail: dental.hygiene@nexus.mwsu.edu
Web: www.mwsu.edu

Program Information:
Program begins: August
Duration of program: 18 months

Financial Information:
Tuition, resident: $2,300
Tuition, non-resident: $9,000

Tarrant County College—Northeast

828 Harwood Road
Hurst, TX 76054

Contact Information:
Telephone: 817-515-6640
Fax: 817-515-6700
E-mail: bshear@tcjc.cc.tx.us
Web: www.tccd.net

Program Information:
Program begins: August
Duration of program: 21 months

Application Information:
Enrollment of program: 24
Transfer students are accepted.

Financial Information:
Tuition, resident: $1,064
Tuition, non-resident: $5,498
Average cost of books: $2,000
% of students receiving aid: 75

Employment Profile:
% of students who pass the boards on their first try: 95
Average starting salary: $52,000

Texas Woman's University

Box 425796
TWU Station
Denton, TX 76204

Contact Information:
Telephone: 940-898-2870
Fax: 940-898-2869
E-mail: cbeatty@twu.edu
Web: www.twu.edu.hs

Program Information:
Program begins: June
Duration of program: 48 months
Evening or weekend classes are available.

Application Information:
Enrollment of program: 78
Transfer students are accepted.

Financial Information:
Tuition, resident: $7,812
Tuition, non-resident: $34,596
Average cost of books: $3,198
% of students receiving aid: 56

Employment Profile:
% of students who pass the boards on their first try: 95
% employed within the first 6 months following graduation: 95
Average starting salary: $50,000

University of Texas Health Science Center at San Antonio

7703 Floyd Curl Drive
San Antonio, TX 78284-6244

Contact Information:
Telephone: 210-567-8820
Fax: 210-567-8843
E-mail: wallacej@uthscsa.edu
Web: www.uthsca.edu

Program Information:
Program begins: August
Degrees offered: Certificate program, 22 months; Bachelor's, 12 months; Master's, 24 months
Evening or weekend classes are available.

Application Information:
Enrollment of program: 80
Transfer students are accepted.

Financial Information:
Tuition, resident: $1,056
Tuition, non-resident: $8,052
Average cost of books: $1,000
% of students receiving aid: 95

Employment Profile:
% of students who pass the boards on their first try: 94
% employed within the first 6 months following graduation: 100
Average starting salary: $40,000

Wharton County Junior College

911 Boling Highway
Wharton, TX 77488

Contact Information:
Telephone: 409-532-6398
Fax: 409-532-6489
Web: www.whatcom.ctc.edu

Program Information:
Program begins: September
Duration of program: 24 months

Application Information:
Enrollment of program: 52
Transfer students are accepted.

Financial Information:
Tuition, resident: $1,283
Tuition, non-resident: $2,138

Employment Profile:
% employed within the first 6 months following graduation: 100

Utah

Weber State University

3920 University Circle
Ogden, UT 84408-3920

Contact Information:
Telephone: 801-626-6130
Fax: 801-626-7304
E-mail: stoevs@weber.edu
Web: www.weber.edu

Program Information:
Program begins: August
Duration of program: 18 months

Application Information:
Enrollment of program: 30
Transfer students are accepted.

Financial Information:
Tuition, resident: $2,042
Tuition, non-resident: $6,058
Average cost of books: $1,000
% of students receiving aid: 75

Employment Profile:
% of students who pass the boards on their first try: 98
% employed within the first 6 months following graduation: 90

Vermont

University of Vermont

Rowell Building
Room 002
Burlington, VT 05405

Contact Information:
Telephone: 802-656-2587
Fax: 802-656-8440
E-mail: chill@cosmos.uvm.edu
Web: www.uvm.edu

Program Information:
Program begins: August
Degrees offered: Associate's, 18 months

Application Information:
Enrollment of program: 43
Transfer students are accepted.

Financial Information:
Tuition, resident: $7,464
Tuition, non-resident: $18,672
Average cost of books: $250
% of students receiving aid: 55

Employment Profile:
% of students who pass the boards on their first try: 90
% employed within the first 6 months following graduation: 100
Average starting salary: $34,000

Virginia

Old Dominion University

Old Dominion University
School of Dental Hygiene
Norfolk, VA 23529-0499

Contact Information:
Telephone: 757-683-3338
Fax: 757-683-5239
E-mail: dshuman@odu.edu
Web: www.odu.edu

Program Information:
Program begins: August
Duration of program: 34 months
Evening or weekend classes are available.

Application Information:
Enrollment of program: 97
Transfer students are accepted.

Financial Information:
Average cost of books: $500
% of students receiving aid: 98

Employment Profile:
% of students who pass the boards on their first try: 97
% employed within the first 6 months following graduation: 100
Average starting salary: $46,000

Virginia Commonwealth University, Medical College of VA Campus

School of Dentistry
Box 980566
Richmond, VA 232980566

Contact Information:
Telephone: 804-828-9096
Fax: 804-828-4913
E-mail: jscharer@vcu.edu
Web: www.views.vcuedu/dentistry

Program Information:
Program begins: August
Duration of program: 20 months

Application Information:
Transfer students are accepted.

Financial Information:
Tuition, resident: $3,587
Tuition, non-resident: $13,041

Employment Profile:
% of students who pass the boards on their first try: 100
% employed within the first 6 months following graduation: 95
Average starting salary: $67,250

Wytheville Community College

1000 East Main Street
Wytheville, VA 24382

Contact Information:
Telephone: 540-223-4832
Fax: 540-223-4778
Web: www.wc.cc.va.us

Program Information:
Program begins: September
Duration of program: 21 months

Application Information:
Transfer students are accepted.

Financial Information:
Tuition, resident: $2,280
Tuition, non-resident: $7,332

Washington

Lake Washington Technical College

11605 132nd Avenue Northeast
Kirkland, WA 98034

Contact Information:

Telephone: 425-739-8332
Fax: 425-739-8298
E-mail: sandy.dow@lwtc.ete.edu
Web: www.lwtc.ctc.edu

Program Information:

Program begins: September
Degrees offered: Diploma, 21 months

Application Information:

Enrollment of program: 24

Financial Information:

Average cost of books: $800
% of students receiving aid: 50

Employment Profile:

% of students who pass the boards on their first try: 80
% employed within the first 6 months following graduation: 100
Average starting salary: $50,000

Pierce College

9401 Farwest Drive Southwest
Lakewood, WA 98498-1999

Contact Information:

Telephone: 253-964-6661
Fax: 253-964-6313
E-mail: sgolight@pierce.ctc.edu
Web: www.pierce.ctc.edu

Program Information:

Program begins: September
Duration of program: 21 months

Application Information:

Transfer students are accepted.

Financial Information:

Tuition, resident: $1,828
Tuition, non-resident: $5,511
Average cost of books: $1,200
% of students receiving aid: 70

Employment Profile:

% employed within the first 6 months following graduation: 85
Average starting salary: $48,000

Shoreline Community College

16101 Greenwood Avenue North
North Seattle, WA 98133

Contact Information:

Telephone: 206-546-4709
Fax: 206-546-5830
E-mail: brenshaw@ctc.edu
Web: www.shoreline.ctc.edu

Program Information:

Program begins: May
Duration of program: 20 months

Application Information:

Transfer students are accepted.

Financial Information:

Tuition, resident: $1,932
Tuition, non-resident: $7,632

Yakima Valley Community College

PO Box 22520
Yakima, WA 989072520

Contact Information:

Telephone: 509-574-4918
Fax: 509-574-6875
E-mail: phakala@yvcc.wa.us
Web: www.yvcc.cc.wa.us

Program Information:

Program begins: June
Duration of program: 24 months

Application Information:

Enrollment of program: 36

Financial Information:

Tuition, resident: $3,318
Tuition, non-resident: $6,300
Average cost of books: $1,300
% of students receiving aid: 50

Employment Profile:

% of students who pass the boards on their first try: 88
% employed within the first 6 months following graduation: 100
Average starting salary: $56,000

West Virginia

West Liberty State College

PO Box 295
West Liberty, WV 26074

Contact Information:

Telephone: 304-336-8030
Fax: 304-336-8905
E-mail: frumcl@wlsc.wvnet.edu
Web: www.wlsc.wvnet.edu

Program Information:

Program begins: August
Degrees offered: Associate's, 18 months; Bachelor's, 48 months

Financial Information:

Tuition, resident: $2,120
Tuition, non-resident: $5,560

Wisconsin

Madison Area Technical College

3550 Anderson Street
Madison, WI 53704

Contact Information:

Telephone: 608-258-2470
Fax: 608-258-2480
E-mail: egoetsch@madison.tec.wi.us
Web: www.madison.tec.wi.us

Program Information:

Program begins: September
Duration of program: 18 months

Application Information:

Enrollment of program: 36
Transfer students are accepted.

Financial Information:

Tuition, resident: $1,802
Tuition, non-resident: $10,200
Average cost of books: $600
% of students receiving aid: 15

Employment Profile:

% of students who pass the boards on their first try: 85
% employed within the first 6 months following graduation: 80
Average starting salary: $39,000

Marquette University

604 North 16th Street
Milwaukee, WI 53233

Contact Information:

Telephone: 414-288-7153
Fax: 414-288-3126
E-mail: halulak@vmscsd.mu.edu
Web: www.marquette.edu

Program Information:

Program begins: August
Duration of program: 36 months

Application Information:

Enrollment of program: 114
Transfer students are accepted.

Financial Information:

Tuition, resident: $15,160

Employment Profile:

% of students who pass the boards on their first try: 97
% employed within the first 6 months following graduation: 90
Average starting salary: $50,000

Northeast Wisconsin Technical College

2740 West Mason Street
PO Box 19042
Green Bay, WI 54307-9042

Contact Information:

Telephone: 920-498-5451
Fax: 920-498-5673
E-mail: hardydl@nwtc.tec.wi.us
Web: www.nwtc.tec.wi.us

Program Information:

Program begins: August
Duration of program: 12 months

Application Information:

Enrollment of program: 47
Transfer students are accepted.

Financial Information:

Tuition, resident: $2,114
Tuition, non-resident: $14,547
Average cost of books: $800

Employment Profile:
% of students who pass the boards on their first try: 100
% employed within the first 6 months following graduation: 100
Average starting salary: $20,000

Wyoming

Laramie County Community College
1400 East College Drive
Cheyenne, WY 82007

Contact Information:
Telephone: 307-778-1387
Fax: 307-778-1395
E-mail: lsnell@mail.lee.whecn.edu
Web: www.lee.whecn.edu

Program Information:
Program begins: August
Duration of program: 20 months

Application Information:
Enrollment of program: 18

Financial Information:
Tuition, resident: $894
Tuition, non-resident: $2,682
Average cost of books: $500
% of students receiving aid: 67

Employment Profile:
% of students who pass the boards on their first try: 92
% employed within the first 6 months following graduation: 75

Sheridan College
3059 Coffeen Avenue
Sheridan, WY 82801

Contact Information:
Telephone: 307-674-6446 ext. 6177
Fax: 307-673-1641
E-mail: csharuga@radar.sc.whecn.edu
Web: www.sc.whecn.edu

Program Information:
Program begins: August
Duration of program: 18 months

Application Information:
Enrollment of program: 48

Financial Information:
Tuition, resident: $1,182
Tuition, non-resident: $2,970
Average cost of books: $500

Employment Profile:
% of students who pass the boards on their first try: 100
% employed within the first 6 months following graduation: 100
Average starting salary: $40,000

Dental Assistant

Alabama

James Faulkner State Community College
1900 Highway 31 South
Bay Minette, AL 36507-2619

Contact Information:
Telephone: 334-580-2110
Fax: 334-580-2253
E-mail: bhardin@faulkner.cc.al.us
Web: www.faulkner.cc.al.us

Program Information:
Program begins: August
Degrees offered: Certificate program, 12 months; Associate's, 18 months

Application Information:
Enrollment of program: 20
Transfer students are accepted.

Financial Information:
Tuition, resident: $2,247
Tuition, non-resident: $4,497
Average cost of books: $350
% of students receiving aid: 35

Employment Profile:
% of students who pass the boards on their first try: 98
% employed within the first 6 months following graduation: 99
Average starting salary: $17,000

Wallace State Community College
PO Box 2000
Hanceville, AL 35077-2000

Contact Information:
Telephone: 205-352-2090
Fax: 205-352-8380
E-mail: dallen419@earthlink.net
Web: www.wscc.cc.al.us

Program Information:
Program begins: August
Degrees offered: Certificate program, 12 months; Associate's, 18 months

Application Information:
Enrollment of program: 16
Transfer students are accepted.

Financial Information:
Tuition, resident: $2,266
Tuition, non-resident: $4,532
Average cost of books: $350
% of students receiving aid: 50

Employment Profile:
% employed within the first 6 months following graduation: 90
Average starting salary: $14,500

Alaska

University of Alaska Anchorage
3211 Providence Drive
AHS 124
Anchorage, AK 99508-8371

Contact Information:
Telephone: 205-934-7016
E-mail: cjz@uaa.alaska.edu
Web: www.uaa.alaska.edu

Program Information:
Program begins: August
Duration of program: 9 months

Application Information:
Enrollment of program: 16

Financial Information:
Tuition, resident: $3,520
Tuition, non-resident: $7,560
Average cost of books: $300
% of students receiving aid: 75

Employment Profile:
% of students who pass the boards on their first try: 85
% employed within the first 6 months following graduation: 87
Average starting salary: $25,000

Arizona

Phoenix College
1202 West Thomas Road
Phoenix, AZ 85013

Contact Information:
Telephone: 602-285-7327
Fax: 602-285-7330
E-mail: wilburn.janet@a1.pc.maricopa.edu
Web: www.pc.maricopa.edu

Program Information:
Program begins: August
Duration of program: 9 months

Application Information:
Transfer students are accepted.

Financial Information:
Tuition, resident: $1,424
Tuition, non-resident: $6,237
Average cost of books: $400
% of students receiving aid: 50

Employment Profile:
% of students who pass the boards on their first try: 95
% employed within the first 6 months following graduation: 100
Average starting salary: $27,000

Pima Community College
2202 West Anklam Road
HRP 220
Tucson, AZ 85709

Contact Information:
Telephone: 520-206-6916

Fax: 520-206-6632
Web: www.pima.edu

Program Information:
Program begins: August
Duration of program: 9 months

Application Information:
Enrollment of program: 25
Transfer students are accepted.

Financial Information:
Tuition, resident: $942
Tuition, non-resident: $6,310
Average cost of books: $200
% of students receiving aid: 45

Employment Profile:
% of students who pass the boards on their first try: 98
% employed within the first 6 months following graduation: 95
Average starting salary: $17,000

Arkansas

Cotton Boll Technical Institute

Box 36
Burdette, AR 72321

Contact Information:
Telephone: 870-763-1486
Fax: 870-763-1496
Web: www.arknet.edu

Program Information:
Program begins: August
Degrees offered: Certificate program, 11 months

Application Information:
Enrollment of program: 18

Financial Information:
Average cost of books: $400
% of students receiving aid: 35

Employment Profile:
% of students who pass the boards on their first try: 50
% employed within the first 6 months following graduation: 75

Pulaski Technical College

3000 West Scenic Drive
North Little Rock, AR 72118-3399

Contact Information:
Telephone: 501-812-2236
Fax: 501-812-2316
E-mail: ddavis@mail.ptc.tec.ar.us
Web: www.ptc.tec.ar.us

Program Information:
Program begins: August
Duration of program: 9 months

Financial Information:
Tuition, resident: $1,260
Tuition, non-resident: $2,400

Employment Profile:
% employed within the first 6 months following graduation: 95
Average starting salary: $17,000

California

Cerritos College

11110 East Alondra Boulevard
Norwalk, CA 90650

Contact Information:
Telephone: 562-860-2451 ext. 2561
Fax: 562-467-5077
Web: www.cerritos.edu

Program Information:
Program begins: August
Duration of program: 11 months

Application Information:
Enrollment of program: 32
Transfer students are accepted.

Financial Information:
Tuition, resident: $1,117
Tuition, non-resident: $4,349

Employment Profile:
% employed within the first 6 months following graduation: 85
Average starting salary: $20,000

Chaffey Community College

5885 Haven Avenue
Rancho Cucamonga, CA 91737-3002

Contact Information:
Telephone: 909-941-2189
Fax: 909-941-2783
Web: www.chaffey.cc.ca.us

Program Information:
Program begins: August
Degrees offered: Certificate program, 9 months; Diploma, 24 months
Evening or weekend classes are available.

Application Information:
Enrollment of program: 60
Transfer students are accepted.

Financial Information:
Tuition, resident: $954
Tuition, non-resident: $3,821
Average cost of books: $95
% of students receiving aid: 35

Employment Profile:
% of students who pass the boards on their first try: 93
% employed within the first 6 months following graduation: 95
Average starting salary: $19,000

Citrus College

1000 West Foothill
Glendora, CA 91741

Contact Information:
Telephone: 626-914-8727
E-mail: cdimit@citrus.cc.ca.us
Web: www.fls.net/citrus.htm

Program Information:
Program begins: August, October, January
Duration of program: 9 months

Financial Information:
Tuition, resident: $1,000

City College of San Francisco

50 Phelan Avenue
San Francisco, CA 94112

Contact Information:
Telephone: 415-239-3919
Fax: 415-239-3719
E-mail: anelson@ccsf.org
Web: www.ccsf.cc.ca.us

Program Information:
Program begins: September
Duration of program: 10 months

Application Information:
Enrollment of program: 31
Transfer students are accepted.

Financial Information:
Tuition, resident: $435
Tuition, non-resident: $4,790
Average cost of books: $100
% of students receiving aid: 76

Employment Profile:
% of students who pass the boards on their first try: 79
% employed within the first 6 months following graduation: 90
Average starting salary: $27,000

College of Alameda

555 Atlantic Avenue
Alameda, CA 94501

Contact Information:
Telephone: 910-938-6276
Fax: 910-455-7027
Web: www.peralta.cc.ca.us

Program Information:
Program begins: August
Duration of program: 9 months

Application Information:
Enrollment of program: 15
Transfer students are accepted.

Financial Information:
Tuition, resident: $527
Tuition, non-resident: $5,436
Average cost of books: $365
% of students receiving aid: 25

Employment Profile:
% employed within the first 6 months following graduation: 25
Average starting salary: $24,000

College of Marin

835 College Avenue
Kentfield, CA 94904

Contact Information:
Telephone: 510-748-2262
Fax: 510-769-6019
E-mail: barbara.cancilla@marin.cc.ca.us
Web: www.marin.cc.ca.us

Program Information:
Program begins: August
Duration of program: 10 months

Application Information:
Transfer students are accepted.

Financial Information:
Tuition, resident: $658
Tuition, non-resident: $5,082
Average cost of books: $400
% of students receiving aid: 40

Employment Profile:
% of students who pass the boards on their first try: 85
% employed within the first 6 months following graduation: 100
Average starting salary: $26,000

College of San Mateo

1700 West Hillsdale Boulevard
San Mateo, CA 94402-3795

Contact Information:
Telephone: 415-485-9327
Fax: 415-485-0135
Web: www.smcccd.cc.ca.us

Program Information:
Program begins: August
Duration of program: 9 months

Financial Information:
Tuition, resident: $2,200

Employment Profile:
% of students who pass the boards on their first try: 90
% employed within the first 6 months following graduation: 90
Average starting salary: $32,000

Cypress College

9200 Valley View Street
Cypress, CA 90630

Contact Information:
Telephone: 714-484-7297
Web: www.cypress.cc.ca.us

Program Information:
Program begins: August
Duration of program: 8 months

Application Information:
Enrollment of program: 32
Transfer students are accepted.

Financial Information:
Tuition, resident: $1,279
Tuition, non-resident: $4,149
Average cost of books: $650
% of students receiving aid: 70

Employment Profile:
% of students who pass the boards on their first try: 85
% employed within the first 6 months following graduation: 100
Average starting salary: $26,000

East Los Angeles Occupational Center

2100 Marengo Street
Los Angeles, CA 90033

Contact Information:
Telephone: 323-223-1283 ext. 151
Fax: 323-223-6365

Program Information:
Program begins: September
Degrees offered: Certificate program

Application Information:
Enrollment of program: 25

Financial Information:
Average cost of books: $200

Employment Profile:
% of students who pass the boards on their first try: 80
% employed within the first 6 months following graduation: 95
Average starting salary: $29,000

Foothill College

12345 El Monte Road
Los Altos Hills, CA 94022

Contact Information:
Telephone: 650-949-7351
Fax: 650-949-7375
Web: www.foothill.fhda.edu

Program Information:
Program begins: August
Duration of program: 10 months

Application Information:
Enrollment of program: 30
Transfer students are accepted.

Financial Information:
Tuition, resident: $600
Tuition, non-resident: $4,800
Average cost of books: $300
% of students receiving aid: 80

Employment Profile:
% of students who pass the boards on their first try: 90
% employed within the first 6 months following graduation: 90
Average starting salary: $32,000

Hacienda LaPuente Adult Education

15540 East Fairgrove Avenue
La Puente, CA 91744

Contact Information:
Telephone: 626-855-3136
Fax: 626-855-3160

Program Information:
Duration of program: 12 months
Evening or weekend classes are available.

Monterey Peninsula College

980 Fremont Avenue
Monterey, CA 93940

Contact Information:
Telephone: 831-646-4137
Fax: 831-645-1353
E-mail: patricia_lewis@mpc.cc.ca.us
Web: www.pmc.edu

Program Information:
Program begins: October, March
Duration of program: 10 months
Evening or weekend classes are available.

Application Information:
Enrollment of program: 30

Financial Information:
Tuition, resident: $405
Tuition, non-resident: $4,053

Palomar Community College

1140 West Mission Road
San Marcos, CA 92069

Contact Information:
Telephone: 760-744-1150 ext. 2573
Fax: 760-744-8123
E-mail: jlandmesser@palomar.edu
Web: www.palomar.edu

Program Information:
Program begins: August
Duration of program: 10 months

Application Information:
Enrollment of program: 45
Transfer students are accepted.

Financial Information:
Tuition, resident: $656
Tuition, non-resident: $6,060
Average cost of books: $250
% of students receiving aid: 10

Employment Profile:
% of students who pass the boards on their first try: 97
% employed within the first 6 months following graduation: 100
Average starting salary: $27,000

Pasadena City College

1570 East Colorado Boulevard R-505
Pasadena, CA 91106

Contact Information:
Telephone: 626-585-7542
Fax: 626-585-7966
E-mail: ligagliardi@paccd.cc.ca.us
Web: www.paccd.cc.ca.us

Program Information:
Program begins: August
Duration of program: 9 months

Application Information:
Enrollment of program: 30

Financial Information:
Tuition, resident: $403
Tuition, non-resident: $4,030
Average cost of books: $500

Employment Profile:
% of students who pass the boards on their first try: 90
% employed within the first 6 months following graduation: 100
Average starting salary: $10,000

Sacramento City College
3835 Freeport Boulevard
Sacramento, CA 95822

Contact Information:
Telephone: 916-558-2650
Fax: 916-538-2392
E-mail: dunnem@scc.losrios.cc.ca.us
Web: www.scc.losrios.cc.ca.us

Program Information:
Program begins: September, January
Degrees offered: Certificate program, 11 months
Evening or weekend classes are available.

Application Information:
Enrollment of program: 30
Transfer students are accepted.

Financial Information:
Tuition, resident: $351
Tuition, non-resident: $3,375
Average cost of books: $300
% of students receiving aid: 50

Employment Profile:
% of students who pass the boards on their first try: 85
% employed within the first 6 months following graduation: 83
Average starting salary: $23,000

San Diego Mesa College
7250 Mesa College Drive
San Diego, CA 92111-2697

Contact Information:
Telephone: 619-627-2697
Fax: 619-627-2677
E-mail: mfickess@intergate.sdccd.cc.ca.us
Web: www.sdmesa.sdccd.cc.ca.us

Program Information:
Program begins: August
Duration of program: 10 months

Application Information:
Enrollment of program: 21

Financial Information:
Tuition, resident: $286
Tuition, non-resident: $2,420

Employment Profile:
% of students who pass the boards on their first try: 75
% employed within the first 6 months following graduation: 80
Average starting salary: $20,000

Santa Rosa Junior College
1501 Mendocino Avenue
Santa Rosa, CA 95401

Contact Information:
Telephone: 707-527-4447
Fax: 707-527-4426
E-mail: dbird@floyd.santarosa.edu

Program Information:
Program begins: August
Duration of program: 11 months

Application Information:
Enrollment of program: 24

Financial Information:
Tuition, resident: $975
Tuition, non-resident: $5,317
Average cost of books: $600

Employment Profile:
% of students who pass the boards on their first try: 100
% employed within the first 6 months following graduation: 98
Average starting salary: $32,000

Colorado

Emily Griffith Opportunity School
1250 Welton Street
Denver, CO 80204

Contact Information:
Telephone: 303-575-4737
Fax: 303-575-4840
Web: www.egos-school.com

Program Information:
Program begins: August
Duration of program: 10 months

Application Information:
Enrollment of program: 10
Transfer students are accepted.

Financial Information:
Tuition, resident: $2,115
Tuition, non-resident: $6,735
Average cost of books: $460
% of students receiving aid: 80

Employment Profile:
% of students who pass the boards on their first try: 85
% employed within the first 6 months following graduation: 100
Average starting salary: $20,000

Front Range Community College—Westminster
3645 West 112th Avenue
Westminster, CO 80030

Contact Information:
Telephone: 970-226-2500 ext. 8221
Fax: 970-825-6819
E-mail: fr_jan@cccs.ccccs.edu
Web: www.frontrange.rightchoice.org

Program Information:
Program begins: August
Degrees offered: Certificate program, 10 months
Evening or weekend classes are available.

Application Information:
Enrollment of program: 25
Transfer students are accepted.

Financial Information:
Tuition, resident: $2,773
Tuition, non-resident: $11,284
Average cost of books: $600
% of students receiving aid: 90

Employment Profile:
% of students who pass the boards on their first try: 90
% employed within the first 6 months following graduation: 100
Average starting salary: $27,000

Pikes Peak Community College
11195 Highway 83
Colorado Springs, CO 80921-3602

Contact Information:
Telephone: 719-538-5404
Fax: 719-538-5439
E-mail: anne.maestas@ppcc.cccoes.edu
Web: www.ppcc.cccoes.edu

Program Information:
Program begins: August, September
Degrees offered: Certificate program, 10 months

Application Information:
Enrollment of program: 30
Transfer students are accepted.

Financial Information:
Tuition, resident: $4,565
Tuition, non-resident: $15,340
Average cost of books: $300

Employment Profile:
% of students who pass the boards on their first try: 98
% employed within the first 6 months following graduation: 100
Average starting salary: $25,000

Pueblo Community College
900 West Orman Avenue
TE Room 137
Pueblo, CO 81004

Contact Information:
Telephone: 719-549-3286
Fax: 719-549-3136
E-mail: Learned@pcc.cccoes.edl
Web: www.pcc.cccoes.edu

Program Information:
Program begins: September
Duration of program: 20 months

Application Information:
Enrollment of program: 30
Transfer students are accepted.

Financial Information:
Tuition, resident: $3,804
Tuition, non-resident: $20,721

Connecticut

A I Prince Regional Vocational Technical School
500 Bookfield Street
Hartford, CT 06106

Contact Information:
Telephone: 860-951-7122 ext. 323
Fax: 860-951-1529

Program Information:
Program begins: August
Degrees offered: Certificate program, 10 months

Application Information:
Enrollment of program: 18

Financial Information:
Tuition, resident: $800
Tuition, non-resident: $5,600
Average cost of books: $200
% of students receiving aid: 20

Employment Profile:
% of students who pass the boards on their first try: 40
% employed within the first 6 months following graduation: 100
Average starting salary: $28,000

Briarwood College
2279 Mt. Vernon Road
Southington, CT 06489

Contact Information:
Telephone: 860-628-4751 ext. 69
Fax: 860-628-6444
Web: www.briarwood.edu

Program Information:
Program begins: September
Duration of program: 9 months
Evening or weekend classes are available.

Application Information:
Enrollment of program: 10
Transfer students are accepted.

Financial Information:
Tuition, resident: $13,021
Tuition, non-resident: $10,725
Average cost of books: $357
% of students receiving aid: 60

Employment Profile:
% of students who pass the boards on their first try: 50
% employed within the first 6 months following graduation: 100
Average starting salary: $24,000

Eli Whitney Regional Vocational Technical School
71 Jones Road
Hamden, CT 06514

Contact Information:
Telephone: 203-397-4031 ext. 344
Fax: 203-397-4129

Program Information:
Program begins: August
Duration of program: 9 months

Financial Information:
Tuition, resident: $1,025
Tuition, non-resident: $8,700

Tunxis Community Technical College
271 Scott Swamp Road
Farmington, CT 06032-3187

Contact Information:
Telephone: 203-679-9636
Fax: 203-676-8906
E-mail: tx_seaver@comnet.edu
Web: www.tunxis.commnet.edu

Program Information:
Program begins: August
Duration of program: 10 months
Evening or weekend classes are available.

Application Information:
Enrollment of program: 32

Financial Information:
Tuition, resident: $1,488
Tuition, non-resident: $4,464
Average cost of books: $800
% of students receiving aid: 60

Employment Profile:
% of students who pass the boards on their first try: 88
% employed within the first 6 months following graduation: 100
Average starting salary: $27,000

Florida

Brevard Community College
1519 Clearlake Road
Cocoa, FL 32922

Contact Information:
Telephone: 407-632-1111 ext. 64180
Fax: 407-634-3731
E-mail: kahlerh@brevard.cc.ll.us
Web: www.brevard.cc.fl.us

Program Information:
Duration of program: 12 months
Evening or weekend classes are available.

Application Information:
Enrollment of program: 44
Transfer students are accepted.

Financial Information:
Tuition, resident: $1,946
Tuition, non-resident: $5,250
Average cost of books: $450

Employment Profile:
% of students who pass the boards on their first try: 95
% employed within the first 6 months following graduation: 90
Average starting salary: $22,000

Broward Community College
3501 Southwest Davie Road
Ft. Lauderdale, FL 33314

Contact Information:
Telephone: 954-475-6904
Fax: 954-473-9037
E-mail: jmoskowi@broward.cc.fl.us
Web: www.broward.cc.fl.us

Program Information:
Program begins: August
Degrees offered: Certificate program, 10 months

Application Information:
Enrollment of program: 34
Transfer students are accepted.

Financial Information:
Tuition, resident: $1,931
Tuition, non-resident: $3,862
Average cost of books: $250

Employment Profile:
% of students who pass the boards on their first try: 96
% employed within the first 6 months following graduation: 80
Average starting salary: $22,000

Charlotte Vocational Technical Center
18300 Toledo Blade Boulevard
Port Charlotte, FL 33948-3399

Contact Information:
Telephone: 941-255-2500
Fax: 941-255-7509
E-mail: ann_o'flaherty@ccps.k12.fl.us
Web: www.ccps.k12.fl.us

Program Information:
Program begins: August
Duration of program: 11 months

Application Information:
Enrollment of program: 28
Transfer students are accepted.

Employment Profile:
% of students who pass the boards on their first try: 78
Average starting salary: $16,000

Daytona Beach Community College
1200 West International Speedway Boulevard
PO Box 2811
Daytona Beach, FL 32114

Contact Information:
Telephone: 904-225-8131 ext. 2082
Fax: 904 255-4491
E-mail: pryorm@dbcc.cc.fl.us
Web: www.dbcc.cc.fl.us

Program Information:
Program begins: August
Degrees offered: Certificate program, 10.5 months

Application Information:
Enrollment of program: 24
Transfer students are accepted.

Financial Information:
Tuition, resident: $1,844
Tuition, non-resident: $8,416
Average cost of books: $375
% of students receiving aid: 50

Employment Profile:
% of students who pass the boards on their first try: 93
% employed within the first 6 months following graduation: 100
Average starting salary: $17,500

Gulf Coast Community College

5230 West US Highway 98
Panama City, FL 32401

Contact Information:
Telephone: 904-872-3829
Fax: 904-447-3246
E-mail: gdaugherty@ccmail.gc.cc.fl.us
Web: www.gc.cc.fl.us

Program Information:
Program begins: August
Duration of program: 10 months
Evening or weekend classes are available.

Application Information:
Enrollment of program: 16

Financial Information:
Tuition, resident: $1,200
Tuition, non-resident: $4,800

Employment Profile:
% of students who pass the boards on their first try: 95
% employed within the first 6 months following graduation: 100
Average starting salary: $17,000

J. Walker Vocational Technical Center

3702 Estey Avenue
Naples, FL 33942-4498

Contact Information:
Telephone: 941-643-0919 ext. 6642
Fax: 941-643-7462

Program Information:
Program begins: September, January
Degrees offered: Certificate program, 12 months

Application Information:
Enrollment of program: 16

Financial Information:
Average cost of books: $120
% of students receiving aid: 50

Employment Profile:
% of students who pass the boards on their first try: 99
% employed within the first 6 months following graduation: 100
Average starting salary: $18,000

Manatee Technical Institute

5603 34th Street West
Bradenton, FL 34210

Contact Information:
Telephone: 914-751-7900 ext. 1128
Fax: 941-751-7927
Web: www.mcsb.org

Program Information:
Program begins: August
Duration of program: 11 months
Evening or weekend classes are available.

Application Information:
Enrollment of program: 28
Transfer students are accepted.

Financial Information:
Average cost of books: $280
% of students receiving aid: 65

Employment Profile:
% of students who pass the boards on their first try: 83
% employed within the first 6 months following graduation: 89
Average starting salary: $18,000

Orlando Technical Education Centers

301 West Amelia Street
Orlando, FL 32801

Contact Information:
Telephone: 407-246-7060 ext. 4835
Fax: 407-246-3372
E-mail: meansd@ocps.k12.fl.us
Web: www.ocps.k12.fl.us

Program Information:
Program begins: August
Duration of program: 10 months
Evening or weekend classes are available.

Application Information:
Enrollment of program: 25
Transfer students are accepted.

Financial Information:
Tuition, resident: $2,900
Average cost of books: $275
% of students receiving aid: 75

Employment Profile:
% of students who pass the boards on their first try: 100
% employed within the first 6 months following graduation: 95
Average starting salary: $20,000

Palm Beach Community College

4200 South Congress Avenue
Lake Worth, FL 33461

Contact Information:
Telephone: 561-439-8095
Fax: 561-439-8314
E-mail: hansons@pbcc.cc.fl.us
Web: www.pbcc.cc.fl.us

Program Information:
Program begins: August, January
Duration of program: 9 months

Financial Information:
Tuition, resident: $3,600
Tuition, non-resident: $11,000

Pensacola Junior College

5555 West Highway 98
Pensacola, FL 32507

Contact Information:
Telephone: 904-484-2246
Fax: 904-484-2365
E-mail: bharris@pjc.cc.fl.us
Web: www.pjc.cc.fl.us

Program Information:
Program begins: September
Degrees offered: Certificate program, 10 months

Application Information:
Enrollment of program: 30
Transfer students are accepted.

Financial Information:
Tuition, resident: $605
Tuition, non-resident: $1,099

Employment Profile:
% of students who pass the boards on their first try: 75
Average starting salary: $18,000

Pinellas Technical Education Center—St. Petersburg

901 34th Street South
St. Petersburg, FL 33711

Contact Information:
Telephone: 727-893-2500 ext. 1073
Fax: 813-893-2776
E-mail: bthomasz@ptecsp.pinellas.k12.fl.us
Web: www.pinellas.k12.fl.us

Program Information:
Duration of program: 12 months

Application Information:
Enrollment of program: 15
Transfer students are accepted.

Financial Information:
Tuition, resident: $1,722
Tuition, non-resident: $3,444
% of students receiving aid: 85

Employment Profile:
% of students who pass the boards on their first try: 90
% employed within the first 6 months following graduation: 100
Average starting salary: $19,000

R. Morgan Vocational Technical Institute
18180 Southwest 122nd Avenue
Miami, FL 33177

Contact Information:
Telephone: 305-253-9920
Fax: 305-253-3023

Program Information:
Duration of program: 12 months

Application Information:
Enrollment of program: 60

Financial Information:
Tuition, resident: $1,464
Average cost of books: $412
% of students receiving aid: 70

Employment Profile:
% employed within the first 6 months following graduation: 100
Average starting salary: $19,000

Traviss Technical Center
3225 Winter Lake Road
Lakeland, FL 33803

Contact Information:
Telephone: 941-499-2700 ext. 286
Fax: 941-413-2067
E-mail: cbelcher@traviss.pcsb.k12.fl.us
Web: www.pcsb.k12.fl.us

Program Information:
Program begins: August
Degrees offered: Certificate program, 10 months

Application Information:
Enrollment of program: 15
Transfer students are accepted.

Financial Information:
Average cost of books: $543
% of students receiving aid: 45

Employment Profile:
% of students who pass the boards on their first try: 90
% employed within the first 6 months following graduation: 90
Average starting salary: $18,000

Georgia

Gwinnett Technical Institute
5150 Sugarloaf Parkway
Box 1505
Lawrenceville, GA 30246-1505

Contact Information:
Telephone: 770-962-7580 ext. 175
Fax: 770-962-7985
E-mail: wturner@gwinnett.tec.ga.us
Web: www.gwinnett.tech.org

Program Information:
Program begins: August
Duration of program: 18 months

Application Information:
Enrollment of program: 20
Transfer students are accepted.

Financial Information:
Tuition, resident: $2,034
Tuition, non-resident: $3,690
Average cost of books: $325
% of students receiving aid: 85

Employment Profile:
% of students who pass the boards on their first try: 90
% employed within the first 6 months following graduation: 100
Average starting salary: $20,000

Lanier Technical Institute
PO Box 58
Oakwood, GA 30566

Contact Information:
Telephone: 770-531-6370
Fax: 770-531-6426
E-mail: skirk@admin1.lanier.tec.ga.us
Web: www.lanier.tec.ga.us

Program Information:
Program begins: August, January, June
Degrees offered: Diploma, 12 months

Application Information:
Enrollment of program: 12
Transfer students are accepted.

Financial Information:
Tuition, resident: $1,192
Tuition, non-resident: $2,384
Average cost of books: $535
% of students receiving aid: 100

Employment Profile:
% of students who pass the boards on their first try: 90
% employed within the first 6 months following graduation: 100
Average starting salary: $19,760

Idaho

Boise State University
College of Applied Technology
1910 University Drive
Boise, ID 83725

Contact Information:
Telephone: 208-426-1541
Fax: 208-426-3155
Web: www.idbsu.edu

Program Information:
Program begins: August
Duration of program: 9 months

Application Information:
Enrollment of program: 23

Financial Information:
Tuition, resident: $2,200
Tuition, non-resident: $10,000
Average cost of books: $300
% of students receiving aid: 70

Employment Profile:
% of students who pass the boards on their first try: 75
% employed within the first 6 months following graduation: 95
Average starting salary: $16,000

Illinois

Illinois Central College
201 Southwest Adams Street
East Peoria, IL 61635-0001

Contact Information:
Telephone: 309-999-4600
Fax: 309-673-9626
Web: www.icc.cc.il.us

Program Information:
Program begins: August
Duration of program: 12 months

Application Information:
Enrollment of program: 48
Transfer students are accepted.

Financial Information:
Tuition, resident: $3,251
Tuition, non-resident: $12,020
Average cost of books: $1,500
% of students receiving aid: 30

Employment Profile:
% of students who pass the boards on their first try: 92
% employed within the first 6 months following graduation: 78
Average starting salary: $30,000

Illinois Valley Community College
815 North Orlando Avenue
Oglesby, IL 61348-9692

Contact Information:
Telephone: 815-224-2720 ext. 359
Fax: 815-224-3033
E-mail: pearson@ivcc.edu
Web: www.ivcc.edu

Program Information:
Program begins: June
Duration of program: 9 months

Application Information:
Enrollment of program: 13
Transfer students are accepted.

Financial Information:
Tuition, resident: $1,728
Tuition, non-resident: $3,821

John A. Logan College
Rural Route 2
Carterville, IL 62918

Contact Information:
Telephone: 618-985-3741
Fax: 618-985-4654
E-mail: kathygibson@jal.cc.il.us
Web: www.jal.cc.il.us

Program Information:
Program begins: August
Degrees offered: Certificate program, 12 months

Application Information:
Enrollment of program: 25
Transfer students are accepted.

Financial Information:
Tuition, resident: $1,655
Tuition, non-resident: $4,965
Average cost of books: $300
% of students receiving aid: 50

Employment Profile:
% of students who pass the boards on their first try: 85
% employed within the first 6 months following graduation: 100
Average starting salary: $16,000

Kaskaskia College

27210 College Road
Centralia, IL 62801

Contact Information:
Telephone: 618-532-1981
Fax: 618-532-1990
Web: www.kc.cc.il.us

Program Information:
Duration of program: 9 months

Application Information:
Enrollment of program: 8
Transfer students are accepted.

Financial Information:
Tuition, resident: $2,300
Average cost of books: $150
% of students receiving aid: 20

Employment Profile:
% employed within the first 6 months following graduation: 98
Average starting salary: $17,000

Lewis & Clark Community College

5800 Godfrey Road
Godfrey, IL 62035

Contact Information:
Telephone: 618-466-3411 ext. 4411
Fax: 618-466-2798
E-mail: cperofox@lc.cc.il.us
Web: www.lc.cc.il.us

Program Information:
Program begins: August
Duration of program: 9 months

Application Information:
Enrollment of program: 24

Financial Information:
Tuition, resident: $2,014
Tuition, non-resident: $6,925
Average cost of books: $500

Employment Profile:
% of students who pass the boards on their first try: 99
% employed within the first 6 months following graduation: 100
Average starting salary: $16,000

Indiana

Indiana University—Purdue University Fort Wayne

2101 Coliseum Boulevard East
Fort Wayne, IN 46805

Contact Information:
Telephone: 219-481-6837
Fax: 219-481-6083
E-mail: kracher@ipfw.edu
Web: www.ipfw.edu

Program Information:
Program begins: August
Degrees offered: Certificate program, 10 months

Application Information:
Enrollment of program: 24
Transfer students are accepted.

Financial Information:
Tuition, resident: $4,500
Tuition, non-resident: $9,500
Average cost of books: $800
% of students receiving aid: 90

Employment Profile:
% of students who pass the boards on their first try: 90
% employed within the first 6 months following graduation: 100
Average starting salary: $24,000

Indiana University—South Bend

1700 Mishawaka Avenue
South Bend, IN 46634

Contact Information:
Telephone: 219-374154
Web: www.indiana.edu

Program Information:
Program begins: August
Duration of program: 10 months

Financial Information:
Tuition, resident: $4,900

Indiana University School of Dentistry

1121 West Michigan Street
Indianapolis, IN 46202-5186

Contact Information:
Telephone: 317-274-4407
Fax: 317-274-2419
E-mail: pspence@iusd.iupui.edu
Web: www.iusd.iupui.edu

Program Information:
Program begins: August
Duration of program: 10 months

Application Information:
Enrollment of program: 14

Financial Information:
Tuition, resident: $3,661
Tuition, non-resident: $11,392
Average cost of books: $600

Employment Profile:
% of students who pass the boards on their first try: 90
% employed within the first 6 months following graduation: 95
Average starting salary: $23,000

Ivy Tech State College—Lafayette

3208 Ross Road
PO Box 6299
Lafayette, IN 47903

Contact Information:
Telephone: 765-772-9205
Fax: 765-772-9248
Web: www.ivy.tec.in.us

Program Information:
Program begins: August
Duration of program: 12 months

Application Information:
Enrollment of program: 30

Financial Information:
Tuition, resident: $2,581
Tuition, non-resident: $5,187

University of Southern Indiana

8600 University Boulevard
Evansville, IN 47712

Contact Information:
Telephone: 812-464-1778
Fax: 812-465-7092
E-mail: lmatheso@usI.edu
Web: www.usi.edu

Program Information:
Program begins: August
Duration of program: 11 months

Application Information:
Enrollment of program: 14
Transfer students are accepted.

Financial Information:
Tuition, resident: $4,244
Tuition, non-resident: $10,400
Average cost of books: $800
% of students receiving aid: 30

Employment Profile:
% of students who pass the boards on their first try: 85
% employed within the first 6 months following graduation: 100
Average starting salary: $15,000

Iowa

Iowa Western Community College

2700 College Road
PO Box 4C
Council Bluffs, IA 51502

Contact Information:
Telephone: 712-325-3351
Fax: 712-325-3736
E-mail: jmiller@iwcc.cc.ia.us
Web: www.iwcc.cc.ia.us

Program Information:
Program begins: August
Duration of program: 11 months

Application Information:
Enrollment of program: 16
Transfer students are accepted.

Financial Information:
Tuition, resident: $3,149
Tuition, non-resident: $4,159
Average cost of books: $250
% of students receiving aid: 20

Employment Profile:
% of students who pass the boards on their first try: 95
% employed within the first 6 months following graduation: 100
Average starting salary: $20,000

Northeast Iowa Community College

10250 Sundown Road
Peosta, IA 52068

Contact Information:
Telephone: 800-728-7367 ext. 227
Fax: 319-556-5058
E-mail: kluesneg@nicc.cc.ia.us
Web: www.nicc.ia.us

Program Information:
Program begins: August
Degrees offered: Diploma, 11 months
Evening or weekend classes are available.

Application Information:
Enrollment of program: 25
Transfer students are accepted.

Financial Information:
Tuition, resident: $2,709
Tuition, non-resident: $3,792
Average cost of books: $600
% of students receiving aid: 50

Employment Profile:
% of students who pass the boards on their first try: 80
% employed within the first 6 months following graduation: 95
Average starting salary: $16,000

Scott Community College

500 Belmont Road
Bettendorf, IA 52722-5649

Contact Information:
Telephone: 319-441-4260
Fax: 319-441-4204
Web: www.bridge.eiccd.cc.ia.us

Program Information:
Program begins: August
Duration of program: 9 months

Financial Information:
Tuition, resident: $1,107
Tuition, non-resident: $1,161
Average cost of books: $400

Employment Profile:
% of students who pass the boards on their first try: 90
% employed within the first 6 months following graduation: 90
Average starting salary: $18,000

Kansas

Flint Hills Technical School

3301 West 18th Avenue
Emporia, KS 66801

Contact Information:
Telephone: 316-343-2300 ext. 214
Fax: 316-343-7252
E-mail: mjones@fhtc.kansas.net
Web: www.fhtc.kansas.net

Program Information:
Program begins: August
Duration of program: 9 months

Application Information:
Enrollment of program: 20

Employment Profile:
% employed within the first 6 months following graduation: 89
Average starting salary: $14,237

Salina Area Technical School

2562 Scanlan Avenue
Salina, KS 67401

Contact Information:
Telephone: 913-827-0134
Fax: 913-825-2904

Program Information:
Program begins: August
Duration of program: 9 months

Application Information:
Enrollment of program: 11

Financial Information:
Tuition, resident: $1,216
Average cost of books: $254
% of students receiving aid: 90

Employment Profile:
Average starting salary: $14,000

Wichita Area Technical College

324 North Emporia
Wichita, KS 67202

Contact Information:
Telephone: 316-973-4370 ext. 4368
Fax: 316-973-4332
E-mail: watchhs.feist.com
Web: www.watc.tec.ks.us

Program Information:
Program begins: August
Duration of program: 9 months

Application Information:
Enrollment of program: 16
Transfer students are accepted.

Financial Information:
Tuition, resident: $1,110
Tuition, non-resident: $6,660
Average cost of books: $300
% of students receiving aid: 50

Employment Profile:
% of students who pass the boards on their first try: 90
% employed within the first 6 months following graduation: 100
Average starting salary: $17,000

Kentucky

Central Kentucky Technical College

308 Vocational -Technical Road
Lexington, KY 40511-1020

Contact Information:
Telephone: 606-246-2400 ext. 234
Fax: 606-246-2504
E-mail: sandra.mullins@kctcs.net
Web: www.kctcs.net

Program Information:
Program begins: September
Degrees offered: Diploma, 12 months

Application Information:
Enrollment of program: 20
Transfer students are accepted.

Financial Information:
Tuition, resident: $1,805
Average cost of books: $1,500
% of students receiving aid: 50

Employment Profile:
% of students who pass the boards on their first try: 75
% employed within the first 6 months following graduation: 100
Average starting salary: $19,000

West Kentucky Technical College

5200 Blandville Road
PO Box 7408
Paducah, KY 42002-7408

Contact Information:
Telephone: 270-554-4991
Fax: 270-554-9754
Web: www.wkytech.com

Program Information:
Program begins: August, January
Duration of program: 11 months

Application Information:
Enrollment of program: 13
Transfer students are accepted.

Financial Information:
Tuition, resident: $680
Tuition, non-resident: $1,360
Average cost of books: $520
% of students receiving aid: 80

Employment Profile:
% of students who pass the boards on their first try: 100
% employed within the first 6 months following graduation: 100
Average starting salary: $17,000

Massachusetts

Charles H. McCann Technical School

70 Hodges Cross Road
North Adams, MA 01247

Contact Information:
Telephone: 413-663-5383
Fax: 413-664-9424
Web: www.berkshire.net/mccanntech/index.html

Program Information:
Program begins: August
Duration of program: 9 months

Financial Information:
Tuition, resident: $500
Tuition, non-resident: $9,151

Middlesex Community College—Lowell

33 Kearney Square
Lowell, MA 01852

Contact Information:
Telephone: 508-656-3200 ext. 3053
Fax: 508-656-3078
E-mail: bloyp@middlesex.cc.ma.us
Web: www.middlesex.cc.ma.us

Program Information:
Program begins: September
Degrees offered: Certificate program, 9 months; Associate's

Application Information:
Enrollment of program: 20
Transfer students are accepted.

Financial Information:
Tuition, resident: $3,290
Tuition, non-resident: $3,614
Average cost of books: $400
% of students receiving aid: 35

Employment Profile:
% of students who pass the boards on their first try: 90
% employed within the first 6 months following graduation: 100
Average starting salary: $25,000

Mt. Ida College

777 Dedham Street
Newton Centre, MA 02159

Contact Information:
Telephone: 617-928-4562
Fax: 617-928-4760
Web: www.mountida.edu

Program Information:
Program begins: September
Degrees offered: Certificate program, 8 months; Associate's, 16 months
Evening or weekend classes are available.

Application Information:
Enrollment of program: 10
Transfer students are accepted.

Financial Information:
Average cost of books: $300

Employment Profile:
% of students who pass the boards on their first try: 50
% employed within the first 6 months following graduation: 100
Average starting salary: $28,000

Northern Essex Community College

45 Franklin Street
Lawrence, MA 01841

Contact Information:
Telephone: 978-738-7427
Fax: 978-738-7450
E-mail: khamidiani@necc.mass.edu
Web: www.necc.mass.edu

Program Information:
Program begins: September
Duration of program: 9 months

Application Information:
Enrollment of program: 19
Transfer students are accepted.

Financial Information:
Tuition, resident: $2,400
Tuition, non-resident: $3,000
Average cost of books: $300
% of students receiving aid: 100

Employment Profile:
% of students who pass the boards on their first try: 75
% employed within the first 6 months following graduation: 100
Average starting salary: $26,000

Southeastern Technical Institute

250 Foundry Street
South Easton, MA 02375

Contact Information:
Telephone: 508-238-1860
Fax: 508-238-7266

Program Information:
Program begins: September
Duration of program: 9 months

Application Information:
Enrollment of program: 22
Transfer students are accepted.

Financial Information:
Tuition, resident: $1,000
Tuition, non-resident: $2,307
Average cost of books: $500
% of students receiving aid: 45

Employment Profile:
% of students who pass the boards on their first try: 95
% employed within the first 6 months following graduation: 75
Average starting salary: $29,000

Springfield Technical Community College

One Armory Square
PO Box 9000
Springfield, MA 01105

Contact Information:
Telephone: 413-755-4861
Fax: 413-733-0688
E-mail: giquinto@stcc.mass.edu
Web: www.stcc.mass.edu

Program Information:
Program begins: September
Degrees offered: Certificate program, 12 months
Evening or weekend classes are available.

Application Information:
Enrollment of program: 20
Transfer students are accepted.

Financial Information:
Tuition, resident: $5,175
Tuition, non-resident: $9,175
Average cost of books: $1,200
% of students receiving aid: 80

Employment Profile:
% of students who pass the boards on their first try: 100
% employed within the first 6 months following graduation: 100
Average starting salary: $25,000

Michigan

Charles Stewart Mott Community College

1401 East Court Street
Flint, MI 48503

Contact Information:
Telephone: 810-762-0328
Fax: 810-232-8874
E-mail: csmith@mcc.edu
Web: www.mcc.edu

Program Information:
Program begins: September
Duration of program: 10 months

Application Information:
Enrollment of program: 16
Transfer students are accepted.

Financial Information:
Tuition, resident: $4,100
Tuition, non-resident: $6,000
Average cost of books: $700
% of students receiving aid: 90

Employment Profile:
% of students who pass the boards on their first try: 75
% employed within the first 6 months following graduation: 100
Average starting salary: $24,000

Delta College
F-56 Allied Health Building
University Center, MI 48710

Contact Information:
Telephone: 517-686-9428
Web: www.delta.edu

Program Information:
Program begins: August, January, June
Degrees offered: Certificate program, 12 months; Associate's, 15 months

Application Information:
Enrollment of program: 20
Transfer students are accepted.

Financial Information:
Tuition, resident: $2,520
Tuition, non-resident: $3,150
Average cost of books: $225
% of students receiving aid: 50

Employment Profile:
% of students who pass the boards on their first try: 80
% employed within the first 6 months following graduation: 100
Average starting salary: $19,000

Grand Rapids Community College
143 Bostwick Street Northeast
Grand Rapids, MI 49503

Contact Information:
Telephone: 616-234-4225
Fax: 616-234-4234
E-mail: mcampo@post.grcc.cc.mi.us
Web: www.grcc.cc.mi.us

Program Information:
Program begins: August
Duration of program: 10 months

Application Information:
Enrollment of program: 32
Transfer students are accepted.

Financial Information:
Tuition, resident: $4,875
Tuition, non-resident: $7,140

Employment Profile:
% employed within the first 6 months following graduation: 90
Average starting salary: $36,000

Lake Michigan College
2755 East Napier Avenue
Benton Harbor, MI 49022

Contact Information:
Telephone: 616-927-8100
Fax: 616-927-6585
E-mail: burch@raptor.lmc.cc.mi.us
Web: www.lmc.cc.mi.us

Program Information:
Program begins: August
Degrees offered: Certificate program, 12 months; Associate's, 24 months
Evening or weekend classes are available.

Application Information:
Enrollment of program: 15
Transfer students are accepted.

Financial Information:
Tuition, resident: $3,187
Tuition, non-resident: $3,622
Average cost of books: $439
% of students receiving aid: 18

Employment Profile:
% of students who pass the boards on their first try: 95
% employed within the first 6 months following graduation: 100

Lansing Community College
PO Box 40010
Lansing, MI 48901-7210

Contact Information:
Telephone: 517-483-1457
Fax: 517-483-9925
E-mail: bbrown3@lansing.cc.mi.us
Web: www.lansing.cc.mi.us

Program Information:
Program begins: August
Duration of program: 10 months

Financial Information:
Tuition, resident: $1,600
Tuition, non-resident: $2,600

Employment Profile:
% of students who pass the boards on their first try: 90
% employed within the first 6 months following graduation: 100

Washtenaw Community College
4800 East Huron River Drive
Ann Arbor, MI 48106

Contact Information:
Telephone: 313-973-3332
Fax: 313-973-5414
E-mail: blf@wccnet.org
Web: www.wccnet.org

Program Information:
Program begins: September
Duration of program: 12 months

Application Information:
Enrollment of program: 21
Transfer students are accepted.

Financial Information:
Tuition, resident: $2,400
Tuition, non-resident: $3,160
Average cost of books: $200
% of students receiving aid: 20

Employment Profile:
% of students who pass the boards on their first try: 95
% employed within the first 6 months following graduation: 100
Average starting salary: $31,000

Wayne County Community College
8551 Greenfield
Room 310
Detroit, MI 48228

Contact Information:
Telephone: 313-943-4055
Fax: 313-943-4025
E-mail: drfloss@flash.net
Web: www.wccc.edu

Program Information:
Program begins: August
Duration of program: 12 months
Evening or weekend classes are available.

Application Information:
Enrollment of program: 15

Financial Information:
Tuition, resident: $1,890
Tuition, non-resident: $2,450
% of students receiving aid: 40

Employment Profile:
% employed within the first 6 months following graduation: 100

Minnesota

Central Lakes College
501 West College Drive
Brainerd, MN 56401

Contact Information:
Telephone: 218-825-8106
Fax: 218-821-8220
E-mail: lschoenl@gwmail.clc.mnscu.edu
Web: www.clc.mnscu.edu

Program Information:
Program begins: September
Duration of program: 11 months

Financial Information:
Tuition, resident: $3,392
Tuition, non-resident: $6,484

Century Community and Technical College
3300 Century Avenue North
White Bear Lake, MN 55110

Contact Information:
Telephone: 612-773-1771
Fax: 612-779-5779
Web: www.century.cc.mn.us

Program Information:
Program begins: September
Duration of program: 12 months
Evening or weekend classes are available.

Application Information:
Enrollment of program: 12
Transfer students are accepted.

Financial Information:
Tuition, resident: $3,283
Tuition, non-resident: $6,196

Employment Profile:
% of students who pass the boards on their first try: 90
% employed within the first 6 months following graduation: 100
Average starting salary: $52,000

Dakota County Technical College

1300 145th Street East
Rosemont, MN 55068

Contact Information:
Telephone: 612-423-8483
Fax: 651-423-8775
E-mail: diana.sullivan@dctc.mnsu.edu
Web: www.dctc.mnscu.edu

Program Information:
Program begins: August
Duration of program: 16 months

Application Information:
Enrollment of program: 45
Transfer students are accepted.

Financial Information:
Tuition, resident: $2,950
Tuition, non-resident: $5,900
Average cost of books: $600

Employment Profile:
% of students who pass the boards on their first try: 98
% employed within the first 6 months following graduation: 100
Average starting salary: $24,000

Duluth Business University—MN School of Business

412 West Superior Street
Duluth, MN 55802

Contact Information:
Telephone: 218-722-3361 ext. 27
Fax: 218-722-8376
Web: www.dbumn.com

Program Information:
Program begins: April, October
Duration of program: 15 months

Financial Information:
Tuition, resident: $13,916

Minneapolis Community and Technical College

1501 Hennepin Avenue South
Room 403B
Minneapolis, MN 55403

Contact Information:
Telephone: 612-359-1491
Fax: 612-359-1357
E-mail: laphamka@mail.mctc.mnscu.edu
Web: www.mctc.mnscu.edu

Program Information:
Program begins: August
Duration of program: 12 months
Evening or weekend classes are available.

Application Information:
Enrollment of program: 14
Transfer students are accepted.

Financial Information:
Tuition, resident: $3,219
Tuition, non-resident: $6,089
Average cost of books: $140

Employment Profile:
% of students who pass the boards on their first try: 77
% employed within the first 6 months following graduation: 100
Average starting salary: $24,000

Minnesota School of Business—Brooklyn Center

5910 Shingle Creek Parkway
Brooklyn Center, MN 55430

Contact Information:
Telephone: 612-566-7777
Fax: 612-566-7030
E-mail: kolson@bc.mnschoolbiz.com
Web: www.mnschoolbiz.com

Program Information:
Program begins: August
Degrees offered: Diploma, 12 months
Evening or weekend classes are available.

Minnesota West Community and Technical College

1011 First Street West
Canby, MN 56220

Contact Information:
Telephone: 507-223-7252
Fax: 507-223-5291
E-mail: danp@cb.mnwest.mnscu.edu
Web: www.stcc.tec.mn.us

Program Information:
Program begins: June
Duration of program: 11 months

Application Information:
Enrollment of program: 22
Transfer students are accepted.

Financial Information:
Tuition, resident: $2,720
Tuition, non-resident: $5,800
Average cost of books: $425
% of students receiving aid: 75

Employment Profile:
% of students who pass the boards on their first try: 75
% employed within the first 6 months following graduation: 90
Average starting salary: $20,000

South Central Technical College

1920 Lee Boulevard
North Mankato, MN 56002-1920

Contact Information:
Telephone: 507-389-5846
Fax: 507-389-5850
E-mail: karon.metz@mankato.msus.edu
Web: www.mankato.ms-us.edu

Program Information:
Program begins: August
Duration of program: 12 months

Application Information:
Enrollment of program: 27
Transfer students are accepted.

Financial Information:
Tuition, resident: $3,982
Tuition, non-resident: $6,589
% of students receiving aid: 86

Employment Profile:
% of students who pass the boards on their first try: 93
% employed within the first 6 months following graduation: 100
Average starting salary: $25,000

Missouri

East Central College

Box 529
1964 Prairie Dell Road
Union, MO 63084

Contact Information:
Telephone: 314-583-5195 ext. 2495
Fax: 314-583-6637
E-mail: scottbj@ecmail.ecc.cc.mo.us
Web: www.embark.com

Program Information:
Program begins: August
Duration of program: 12 months

Application Information:
Enrollment of program: 23
Transfer students are accepted.

Financial Information:
Tuition, resident: $2,025
Tuition, non-resident: $2,475
Average cost of books: $220
% of students receiving aid: 70

Employment Profile:
% of students who pass the boards on their first try: 70
% employed within the first 6 months following graduation: 77
Average starting salary: $17,000

Nichols Career Center
609 Union Street
Jefferson City, MO 65101

Contact Information:
Telephone: 573-659-3112
Fax: 503-659-3154

Program Information:
Program begins: August
Duration of program: 9 months

Application Information:
Enrollment of program: 16
Transfer students are accepted.

Financial Information:
% of students receiving aid: 95

Employment Profile:
% of students who pass the boards on their first try: 90
% employed within the first 6 months following graduation: 90
Average starting salary: $26,000

Ozarks Technical Community College
PO Box 5958
Springfield, MO 65801

Contact Information:
Telephone: 417-895-7124
Fax: 417-895-7057
Web: www.otc.cc.mo.us

Program Information:
Program begins: August
Duration of program: 9 months

Application Information:
Enrollment of program: 20

Employment Profile:
% of students who pass the boards on their first try: 80
% employed within the first 6 months following graduation: 100
Average starting salary: $17,000

Montana

Montana State University College of Technology—Great Falls
Box 610
2100 16th Avenue South
Great Falls, MT 59405

Contact Information:
Telephone: 406-771-4351
Fax: 406-771-4317
E-mail: abuer@msugf.edu
Web: www.msucotgf.montana.edu

Program Information:
Program begins: August
Duration of program: 12 months

Application Information:
Enrollment of program: 18
Transfer students are accepted.

Financial Information:
Tuition, resident: $2,944
Tuition, non-resident: $7,332
Average cost of books: $650

Salish Kootenai College
Box 117
Pablo, MT 59855

Contact Information:
Telephone: 406-675-4800 ext. 323
Fax: 406-675-4801
E-mail: donna_kotyk@skc.edu
Web: www.skcweb.skc.edu

Program Information:
Program begins: August
Duration of program: 20 months

Application Information:
Transfer students are accepted.

Financial Information:
Tuition, resident: $3,676
Tuition, non-resident: $5,116

Nebraska

Central Community College
PO Box 1024
Hastings, NE 68902-1024

Contact Information:
Telephone: 402-461-2467
Fax: 402-460-2138
E-mail: mcecil@cccneb.edu
Web: www.cccneb.edu

Program Information:
Program begins: August
Degrees offered: Diploma, 11 months
Evening or weekend classes are available.

Application Information:
Enrollment of program: 30
Transfer students are accepted.

Financial Information:
Tuition, resident: $1,764
Tuition, non-resident: $2,646
Average cost of books: $350

Employment Profile:
% employed within the first 6 months following graduation: 95

Metropolitan Community College
PO Box 3777
Omaha, NE 68103-0777

Contact Information:
Telephone: 402-738-4510
Fax: 402-738-4005
Web: www.mccneb.edu

Program Information:
Program begins: August
Degrees offered: Certificate program, 12 months

Application Information:
Enrollment of program: 26
Transfer students are accepted.

Financial Information:
Tuition, resident: $2,020
Tuition, non-resident: $2,713
Average cost of books: $300
% of students receiving aid: 50

Employment Profile:
% of students who pass the boards on their first try: 90
% employed within the first 6 months following graduation: 95
Average starting salary: $20,000

Mid Plains Community College
1101 Halligan Drive
North Platte, NE 69101

Contact Information:
Telephone: 308-532-8740
Fax: 308-532-8494
E-mail: rmwhite@ziggy.mpcc.cc.ne.us
Web: www.mpcca.cc.ne.us

Program Information:
Program begins: October, April
Duration of program: 11 months

Application Information:
Enrollment of program: 11
Transfer students are accepted.

Financial Information:
Tuition, resident: $1,350
Tuition, non-resident: $1,553
Average cost of books: $300
% of students receiving aid: 70

Employment Profile:
% of students who pass the boards on their first try: 66
% employed within the first 6 months following graduation: 100
Average starting salary: $15,500

Omaha College of Health Careers
225 North 80th Street
Omaha, NE 68114-3617

Contact Information:
Telephone: 402-392-1300
E-mail: ochc1@tadl.com

Program Information:
Program begins: October, April
Duration of program: 8 months

Application Information:
Enrollment of program: 5
Transfer students are accepted.

Financial Information:
Tuition, resident: $6,772
Average cost of books: $350
% of students receiving aid: 90

Employment Profile:
% employed within the first 6 months following graduation: 90
Average starting salary: $16,723

New Jersey

Cumberland County Technical Education Center
601 Bridgeton Avenue
Bridgeton, NJ 08302

Contact Information:
Telephone: 856-451-9000 ext. 346
Fax: 856-451-8487
E-mail: jzirkle@cumberland.tec.nj.us

Program Information:
Program begins: September
Degrees offered: Certificate program
Evening or weekend classes are available.

Application Information:
Enrollment of program: 15

Financial Information:
Tuition, resident: $1,550
Average cost of books: $300
% of students receiving aid: 40

Employment Profile:
% of students who pass the boards on their first try: 90
% employed within the first 6 months following graduation: 100
Average starting salary: $21,000

Dental Studies Institute
7 Spielman Road
Fairfield, NJ 07004

Contact Information:
Telephone: 973-808-1666

Program Information:
Program begins: September, January, May
Duration of program: 8 months
Evening or weekend classes are available.

Application Information:
Enrollment of program: 60
Transfer students are accepted.

Financial Information:
Tuition, resident: $5,500
Average cost of books: $425
% of students receiving aid: 75

Employment Profile:
Average starting salary: $23,000

Mercer County Technical Schools
Health Careers Center
1070 Klockner Road
Hamilton, NJ 08619

Contact Information:
Telephone: 609-587-7640
Fax: 609-587-3304

Program Information:
Program begins: August
Degrees offered: Diploma, 12 months

Application Information:
Enrollment of program: 20

Financial Information:
Tuition, resident: $1,320
Tuition, non-resident: $5,200
Average cost of books: $383
% of students receiving aid: 25

Employment Profile:
% of students who pass the boards on their first try: 100
% employed within the first 6 months following graduation: 100
Average starting salary: $25,000

Technical Institute of Camden County
343 Berlin - Cross Keys Road
Sicklerville, NJ 08081-9709

Contact Information:
Telephone: 856-767-7000
Fax: 856-767-6625
E-mail: smichaleski@ccts.edu

Program Information:
Program begins: September
Degrees offered: Diploma, 10 months
Evening or weekend classes are available.

Application Information:
Enrollment of program: 24
Transfer students are accepted.

Financial Information:
Tuition, resident: $1,120
Tuition, non-resident: $1,436
Average cost of books: $400
% of students receiving aid: 20

Employment Profile:
% of students who pass the boards on their first try: 95
% employed within the first 6 months following graduation: 100
Average starting salary: $25,000

University of Medicine & Dentistry of New Jersey
1776 Raritan Road
Scotch Plains, NJ 07076

Contact Information:
Telephone: 207-581-6056
Fax: 207-581-6075
E-mail: breen@umdnj.edu
Web: www.umdnj.edu/shrpweb/programs

Program Information:
Program begins: January
Degrees offered: DiplomaAssociate's; Bachelor's, 24 months; Master's; PhD

Application Information:
Enrollment of program: 20
Transfer students are accepted.

Financial Information:
Tuition, resident: $2,448
Tuition, non-resident: $9,792
Average cost of books: $250
% of students receiving aid: 75

Employment Profile:
% of students who pass the boards on their first try: 90
% employed within the first 6 months following graduation: 100
Average starting salary: $20,000

New York

Monroe Community College
1000 East Henrietta Road
Rochester, NY 14623-5780

Contact Information:
Telephone: 716-282-2761
E-mail: dlawrence@monroecc.edu
Web: www.monroecc.edu

Program Information:
Program begins: September
Degrees offered: Certificate program, 10 months

Application Information:
Enrollment of program: 130

Financial Information:
Tuition, resident: $2,500
Tuition, non-resident: $5,000
Average cost of books: $150

Employment Profile:
% of students who pass the boards on their first try: 90
% employed within the first 6 months following graduation: 100
Average starting salary: $24,000

New York University
345 East 24th Street
New York, NY 10010

Contact Information:
Telephone: 212-998-9777
Fax: 212-995-4841
E-mail: jlcl@is2.nyu.edu
Web: www.nyu.edu

Program Information:
Program begins: September, March
Duration of program: 11 months
Evening or weekend classes are available.

North Carolina

Cape Fear Community College
411 North Front Street
Wilmington, NC 28401-3993

Contact Information:
Telephone: 910-251-6943
Fax: 910-251-6945
E-mail: zzbahn@washburn.edu
Web: www.cfcc.net

Program Information:
Program begins: August
Degrees offered: Diploma, 20 months

Application Information:
Enrollment of program: 18
Transfer students are accepted.

Financial Information:
Tuition, resident: $1,017
Tuition, non-resident: $6,451
Average cost of books: $500
% of students receiving aid: 20

Employment Profile:
% of students who pass the boards on their first try: 94
% employed within the first 6 months following graduation: 100
Average starting salary: $16,000

Central Piedmont Community College
1201 Elizabeth Avenue
Kings Drive
Charlotte, NC 28204

Contact Information:
Telephone: 704-330-5951
Fax: 704-330-6533
E-mail: jane_lavin@cpcc.nc.us
Web: www.cpcc.cc.nc.us

Program Information:
Duration of program: 12 months

Application Information:
Enrollment of program: 36
Transfer students are accepted.

Financial Information:
Tuition, resident: $2,224
Tuition, non-resident: $7,522
Average cost of books: $800
% of students receiving aid: 17

Employment Profile:
% of students who pass the boards on their first try: 90
% employed within the first 6 months following graduation: 100
Average starting salary: $28,000

Coastal Carolina Community College
444 Western Boulevard
Jacksonville, NC 28546

Contact Information:
Telephone: 212-305-3017
Fax: 212-305-7134
E-mail: bealle@coastal.cc.nc.us
Web: www.coastal.cc.nc.us

Program Information:
Program begins: August
Degrees offered: Diploma, 12 months

Application Information:
Enrollment of program: 28
Transfer students are accepted.

Financial Information:
Tuition, resident: $760
Tuition, non-resident: $6,270
Average cost of books: $350
% of students receiving aid: 25

Employment Profile:
% of students who pass the boards on their first try: 96
% employed within the first 6 months following graduation: 80
Average starting salary: $17,000

Fayetteville Technical Community College
2201 Hull Road
PO Box 35236
Fayetteville, NC 28303

Contact Information:
Telephone: 910-678-8280
Fax: 910-678-8500
E-mail: dmcgrath@post.faytech.cc.nc.us
Web: www.fayech.cc.nc.us

Program Information:
Program begins: September
Duration of program: 11 months

Application Information:
Enrollment of program: 30

Financial Information:
Tuition, resident: $742
Tuition, non-resident: $6,020
Average cost of books: $350
% of students receiving aid: 67

Employment Profile:
% of students who pass the boards on their first try: 80
% employed within the first 6 months following graduation: 95
Average starting salary: $18,000

Guilford Technical Community College
PO Box 309
Jamestown, NC 27282

Contact Information:
Telephone: 336-334-4822 ext. 2212
Fax: 336-841-4350
E-mail: sniderl@gtcc.cc.nc.us
Web: www.gtcc.cc.nc.us

Program Information:
Program begins: August
Degrees offered: Diploma, 11 months

Application Information:
Enrollment of program: 36
Transfer students are accepted.

Financial Information:
Tuition, resident: $1,020
Tuition, non-resident: $6,454
Average cost of books: $620
% of students receiving aid: 33

Employment Profile:
% of students who pass the boards on their first try: 95
% employed within the first 6 months following graduation: 100
Average starting salary: $11,000

University of North Carolina at Chapel Hill
367 Old Dental Building
CB 7450
Chapel Hill, NC 27599-7450

Contact Information:
Telephone: 908-889-2419
Fax: 908-889-2477
E-mail: mary_george@dentistry.unc.edu
Web: www.dent.unc.edu

Program Information:
Program begins: August
Duration of program: 10 months

Wilkes Community College
PO Box 120
Wilkesboro, NC 28697-0120

Contact Information:
Telephone: 336-838-6253
Fax: 336-838-6255
E-mail: billingd@wilkes.cc.nc.us
Web: www.wilkes.cc.nc.us

Program Information:
Program begins: September
Duration of program: 12 months

Application Information:
Enrollment of program: 15

Financial Information:
Tuition, resident: $990
Tuition, non-resident: $6,281
Average cost of books: $700
% of students receiving aid: 50

Employment Profile:
% of students who pass the boards on their first try: 100
% employed within the first 6 months following graduation: 100
Average starting salary: $19,000

Ohio

Cuyahoga Community College
2900 Community College Avenue
Cleveland, OH 44115

Contact Information:
Telephone: 216-987-4494
Fax: 216-987-4386
E-mail: mary-lou.gerosky@tri-c.cc.oh.us
Web: www.tri-c.cc.us

Program Information:
Program begins: August
Duration of program: 9 months

Application Information:
Enrollment of program: 7

Financial Information:
Tuition, resident: $1,845
Tuition, non-resident: $2,445
Average cost of books: $400
% of students receiving aid: 80

Employment Profile:
% employed within the first 6 months following graduation: 100
Average starting salary: $18,000

Jefferson Community College
4000 Sunset Boulevard
Steubenville, OH 43952

Contact Information:
Telephone: 614-264-5591 ext. 164
Fax: 614-264-1335
E-mail: drobinson@jeferson.cc.oh.us
Web: www.jefferson.cc.org

Program Information:
Program begins: August
Degrees offered: Certificate program, 10 months; Associate's, 20 months

Application Information:
Enrollment of program: 16

Financial Information:
Tuition, resident: $2,419
Tuition, non-resident: $2,624
Average cost of books: $500
% of students receiving aid: 90

Employment Profile:
% of students who pass the boards on their first try: 85
% employed within the first 6 months following graduation: 90
Average starting salary: $26,000

Youngstown Public School
Choffin Career Center
200 East Wood Street
Youngstown, OH 44503

Contact Information:
Telephone: 330-744-8749
Fax: 330-744-8749

Program Information:
Program begins: August
Duration of program: 9 months

Application Information:
Transfer students are accepted.

Financial Information:
Average cost of books: $560

Employment Profile:
% of students who pass the boards on their first try: 95
% employed within the first 6 months following graduation: 85
Average starting salary: $18,000

Oklahoma

Metro Technical Health Careers Center
1720 Springlake Drive
Oklahoma City, OK 73111

Contact Information:
Telephone: 405-424-8324 ext. 4613
Fax: 405-424-9403
Web: www.metrotech.org

Program Information:
Program begins: September
Duration of program: 10 months
Evening or weekend classes are available.

Application Information:
Enrollment of program: 13
Transfer students are accepted.

Financial Information:
Tuition, resident: $1,050
Average cost of books: $250
% of students receiving aid: 60

Employment Profile:
% employed within the first 6 months following graduation: 85
Average starting salary: $15,000

Rose State College
6420 Southeast 15th Street
Midwest City, OK 73110

Contact Information:
Telephone: 405-733-7336
Fax: 405-736-0338
Web: www.rose.cc.ok.us

Program Information:
Program begins: September
Duration of program: 10 months

Application Information:
Enrollment of program: 12
Transfer students are accepted.

Financial Information:
Tuition, resident: $1,365
Tuition, non-resident: $3,469
Average cost of books: $1,225
% of students receiving aid: 85

Employment Profile:
% of students who pass the boards on their first try: 92
% employed within the first 6 months following graduation: 100
Average starting salary: $20,000

Oregon

Blue Mountain Community College
2411 Northwest Carden
Pendleton, OR 97801

Contact Information:
Telephone: 541-278-5876
Fax: 541-276-6119
E-mail: cpatton@bmcc.cc.or.us
Web: www.bmcc.cc.or.us

Program Information:
Program begins: September
Degrees offered: Certificate program, 9 months

Application Information:
Enrollment of program: 17
Transfer students are accepted.

Financial Information:
Tuition, resident: $1,575
Average cost of books: $200
% of students receiving aid: 90

Employment Profile:
% of students who pass the boards on their first try: 92
% employed within the first 6 months following graduation: 80
Average starting salary: $18,000

Chemeketa Community College
4000 Lancaster Drive Northeast
Salem, OR 97305

Contact Information:
Telephone: 503-399-5265
Fax: 503-399-5496
E-mail: lorene@chemeketa.edu
Web: www.chemeketa.edu

Program Information:
Program begins: September
Degrees offered: Certificate program, 9 months

Application Information:
Enrollment of program: 30
Transfer students are accepted.

Financial Information:
Tuition, resident: $1,872
Tuition, non-resident: $6,500
Average cost of books: $400
% of students receiving aid: 70

Employment Profile:
% of students who pass the boards on their first try: 91
% employed within the first 6 months following graduation: 95
Average starting salary: $22,000

Linn-Benton Community College
6500 Southwest Pacific Boulevard
Albany, OR 97321

Contact Information:
Telephone: 541-917-4496
Fax: 541-917-4508
E-mail: billets@gw.lbcc.cc.or.us
Web: www.lbcc.cc.or.us

Program Information:
Duration of program: 11 months

Application Information:
Enrollment of program: 25
Transfer students are accepted.

Financial Information:
Tuition, resident: $2,065
Tuition, non-resident: $7,139
Average cost of books: $300
% of students receiving aid: 10

Employment Profile:
% of students who pass the boards on their first try: 100
% employed within the first 6 months following graduation: 100
Average starting salary: $24,000

Portland Community College
PO Box 19000
Portland, OR 97219-0990

Contact Information:
Telephone: 503-977-4235
Fax: 503-977-4869
E-mail: ajackson@pcc.edu
Web: www.pcc.edu

Program Information:
Program begins: September
Degrees offered: Certificate program, 9 months

Application Information:
Enrollment of program: 50
Transfer students are accepted.

Financial Information:
Tuition, resident: $1,620
Tuition, non-resident: $5,850
Average cost of books: $400

Employment Profile:
% of students who pass the boards on their first try: 80
% employed within the first 6 months following graduation: 95
Average starting salary: $22,000

Pennsylvania

Community College of Philadelphia
1700 Spring Garden Street
Philadelphia, PA 19130

Contact Information:
Telephone: 215-751-8927
Fax: 215-751-8937
E-mail: rwertheimer@ccp.cc.pa.us
Web: www.ccp.cc.pa.us

Program Information:
Program begins: July
Degrees offered: Certificate program, 10 months

Application Information:
Enrollment of program: 36
Transfer students are accepted.

Financial Information:
Tuition, resident: $3,486
Tuition, non-resident: $9,702
Average cost of books: $840
% of students receiving aid: 63

Employment Profile:
% of students who pass the boards on their first try: 90
Average starting salary: $25,000

Harcum College
750 Montgomery Avenue
Bryn Mawr, PA 19010

Contact Information:
Telephone: 610-526-6109
Fax: 610-526-6182
E-mail: dossiec@harcum.edu
Web: www.harcum.edu

Program Information:
Program begins: August
Duration of program: 10 months
Evening or weekend classes are available.

Application Information:
Enrollment of program: 20
Transfer students are accepted.

Financial Information:
Tuition, resident: $8,808
Tuition, non-resident: $14,020

Employment Profile:
% employed within the first 6 months following graduation: 100
Average starting salary: $26,000

Harrisburg Area Community College
One HACC Drive
Harrisburg, PA 17110-2999

Contact Information:
Telephone: 717-780-2396
Fax: 717-780-2551
E-mail: danickey@hacc.edu
Web: www.hacc.edu

Program Information:
Program begins: August
Duration of program: 10 months

Financial Information:
Tuition, resident: $2,500
Tuition, non-resident: $4,883
Average cost of books: $350
% of students receiving aid: 50

Employment Profile:
% of students who pass the boards on their first try: 45
% employed within the first 6 months following graduation: 100
Average starting salary: $16,000

Manor Junior College
700 Fox Chase Road
Jenkintown, PA 19046-3399

Contact Information:
Telephone: 215-885-2360 ext. 288
Fax: 215-885-6084
Web: www.manor.edu

Program Information:
Program begins: September
Degrees offered: Associate's, 18 months

Application Information:
Enrollment of program: 17
Transfer students are accepted.

Financial Information:
Tuition, resident: $9,760
Tuition, non-resident: $13,860
Average cost of books: $180

Employment Profile:
% employed within the first 6 months following graduation: 100
Average starting salary: $22,500

Median School of Allied Health Careers
125 Seventh Street
Pittsburgh, PA 15222-3400

Contact Information:
Telephone: 412-391-0422
Fax: 412-232-4348

Program Information:
Program begins: August
Duration of program: 9 months

Financial Information:
Tuition, resident: $5,400
Average cost of books: $500

Employment Profile:
% of students who pass the boards on their first try: 99
% employed within the first 6 months following graduation: 90
Average starting salary: $18,000

Westmoreland County Community College
400 Armbrust Road
Youngwood, PA 15697-1895

Contact Information:
Telephone: 724-925-4163
Fax: 724-925-5808
E-mail: rinchua@astro.westmoreland.cc.pa.us
Web: www.westmoreland.cc.pa.us

Program Information:
Program begins: August
Degrees offered: Diploma, 12 months
Evening or weekend classes are available.

Application Information:
Enrollment of program: 12
Transfer students are accepted.

Financial Information:
Tuition, resident: $1,932
Tuition, non-resident: $3,864
Average cost of books: $620
% of students receiving aid: 25

Employment Profile:
% of students who pass the boards on their first try: 70
% employed within the first 6 months following graduation: 100

Puerto Rico

University of Puerto Rico
GPO Box 5067
San Juan, PR 00936

Contact Information:
Telephone: 787-758-2525 ext. 1157
Fax: 787-751-3061
E-mail: angelaja@cpts.tcm.upr.edu
Web: www.cprsweb.rcm.upr.edu

Program Information:
Program begins: August
Degrees offered: Diploma, 13 months

Application Information:
Enrollment of program: 25
Transfer students are accepted.

Financial Information:
Tuition, resident: $2,796
Average cost of books: $350
% of students receiving aid: 100

Employment Profile:
% of students who pass the boards on their first try: 98
% employed within the first 6 months following graduation: 100

South Carolina

Florence-Darlington Technical College
PO Box 100548
Florence, SC 29501-0548

Contact Information:
Telephone: 843-661-8023
Fax: 843-661-8306
E-mail: hewittm@flo.tec.sc.us
Web: www.flo.tec.sc.us

Program Information:
Program begins: August
Degrees offered: Diploma, 12 months

Application Information:
Enrollment of program: 18
Transfer students are accepted.

Financial Information:
Tuition, resident: $2,063
Tuition, non-resident: $4,605
Average cost of books: $950
% of students receiving aid: 50

Employment Profile:
% of students who pass the boards on their first try: 80
% employed within the first 6 months following graduation: 90
Average starting salary: $25,000

York Technical College
452 South Anderson Road
Rock Hill, SC 29730

Contact Information:
Telephone: 803-327-8039
Fax: 803-327-8059
E-mail: dsmith@york.tec.sc.us
Web: www.york.tec.sc.us

Program Information:
Program begins: August
Degrees offered: Diploma, 12 months
Evening or weekend classes are available.

Application Information:
Enrollment of program: 20

Financial Information:
Tuition, resident: $1,168
Tuition, non-resident: $1,728
Average cost of books: $1,010

Employment Profile:
% of students who pass the boards on their first try: 80
% employed within the first 6 months following graduation: 100
Average starting salary: $18,000

South Dakota

Lake Area Technical Institute
230 11th Street Northeast
Watertown, SD 57201

Contact Information:
Telephone: 605-882-5284 ext. 214
Fax: 605-882-6299
E-mail: bradberr@lati.tech.sd.us
Web: www.lati.tech.sd.us

Program Information:
Program begins: August
Degrees offered: Diploma, 11 months

Application Information:
Enrollment of program: 30
Transfer students are accepted.

Financial Information:
Average cost of books: $374
% of students receiving aid: 90

Employment Profile:
% of students who pass the boards on their first try: 80
% employed within the first 6 months following graduation: 83
Average starting salary: $17,360

Tennessee

East Tennessee State University
1000 West East Street
Elizabethton, TN 37643

Contact Information:
Telephone: 423-547-4911
Fax: 423-547-4921
Web: www.etsu.tn.us

Program Information:
Program begins: August
Duration of program: 12 months

Financial Information:
Tuition, resident: $2,892
Tuition, non-resident: $9,396

Volunteer State Community College
Nashville Pike
Gallatin, TN 37066

Contact Information:
Telephone: 615-741-3215
Web: www.vscc.tn.us

Program Information:
Program begins: August
Duration of program: 12 months

Application Information:
Enrollment of program: 24

Financial Information:
Tuition, resident: $1,500
Tuition, non-resident: $2,346

Employment Profile:
% of students who pass the boards on their first try: 500
% employed within the first 6 months following graduation: 100
Average starting salary: $24,000

Texas

Del Mar College
101 Baldwin and Ayers Streets
Corpus Christi, TX 78404

Contact Information:
Telephone: 361-698-1358
Fax: 361-698-1175
E-mail: bblanke@delmar.edu
Web: www.delmar.edu

Program Information:
Program begins: September, January, April
Duration of program: 12 months

Application Information:
Enrollment of program: 22

Financial Information:
Tuition, resident: $965
Tuition, non-resident: $2,165
Average cost of books: $220
% of students receiving aid: 50

Employment Profile:
% of students who pass the boards on their first try: 73
% employed within the first 6 months following graduation: 75
Average starting salary: $10,000

Grayson County College
6101 Grayson Drive
Denison, TX 75020-8299

Contact Information:
Telephone: 903-786-4468
Fax: 903-786-8056
E-mail: perkinsp@grayson.edu
Web: www.grayson.edu

Program Information:
Program begins: August
Duration of program: 11 months

Application Information:
Enrollment of program: 14
Transfer students are accepted.

Financial Information:
Tuition, resident: $1,302
Tuition, non-resident: $3,066
Average cost of books: $450
% of students receiving aid: 85

Employment Profile:
% of students who pass the boards on their first try: 95

% employed within the first 6 months following graduation: 85
Average starting salary: $21,000

Houston Community College
1900 Galen Drive
Houston, TX 77030

Contact Information:
Telephone: 713-718-7350
Fax: 713-718-7401
E-mail: perez_ros@hccs.cc.tx.hs
Web: www.hcc.cc.tx.us

Program Information:
Program begins: August
Duration of program: 12 months

Financial Information:
Tuition, resident: $1,176
Tuition, non-resident: $1,974

San Antonio College
1300 San Pedro Avenue
NTC 125
San Antonio, TX 78212

Contact Information:
Telephone: 210-785-6041
Fax: 210-733-2429
E-mail: slovato@accdvm.accd.edu
Web: www.accd.edu

Program Information:
Duration of program: 12 months

Application Information:
Enrollment of program: 26
Transfer students are accepted.

Financial Information:
Tuition, resident: $1,800
Tuition, non-resident: $2,100
Average cost of books: $188
% of students receiving aid: 35

Employment Profile:
% of students who pass the boards on their first try: 90
% employed within the first 6 months following graduation: 96
Average starting salary: $17,000

Texas State Technical College
3801 Campus Drive
Waco, TX 76705

Contact Information:
Telephone: 254-867-4864
Fax: 254-867-2239
E-mail: destes@tstc.edu
Web: www.tstc.edu

Program Information:
Duration of program: 12 months

Application Information:
Enrollment of program: 170

Financial Information:
Tuition, resident: $2,752
Tuition, non-resident: $4,000
Average cost of books: $600
% of students receiving aid: 80

Employment Profile:
% employed within the first 6 months following graduation: 90
Average starting salary: $16,000

Utah

American Institute of Medical—Dental Technology
1675 North Freedom Boulevard
Building 5A
Provo, UT 84604

Contact Information:
Telephone: 435-652-0900
Fax: 435-652-1079
Web: www.americaninstitute.net

Program Information:
Duration of program: 8 months

Application Information:
Enrollment of program: 40

Financial Information:
Average cost of books: $258
% of students receiving aid: 50

Employment Profile:
% employed within the first 6 months following graduation: 90

Vermont

Essex Technical Center
3 Educational Drive
Essex Junction, VT 05452

Contact Information:
Telephone: 802-879-4832
Fax: 802-879-5593
Web: www.ejhs.k12.vt.us

Program Information:
Program begins: Program begins quarterly.
Duration of program: 9 months

Application Information:
Enrollment of program: 25
Transfer students are accepted.

Financial Information:
Average cost of books: $90
% of students receiving aid: 50

Employment Profile:
% of students who pass the boards on their first try: 85
% employed within the first 6 months following graduation: 95
Average starting salary: $16,000

Virginia

J. Sargeant Reynolds Community College
PO Box 85622
Richmond, VA 23285-5622

Contact Information:
Telephone: 804-786-5298
Web: www.jsr.cc.va.us

Program Information:
Program begins: August, January
Duration of program: 9 months
Evening or weekend classes are available.

Financial Information:
Tuition, resident: $1,640
Tuition, non-resident: $6,748

Wytheville Community College
1000 East Main Street
Wytheville, VA 24382

Contact Information:
Telephone: 540-223-4832
Fax: 540-223-4778
Web: www.wc.cc.va.us

Program Information:
Program begins: August
Duration of program: 21 months

Application Information:
Transfer students are accepted.

Financial Information:
Tuition, resident: $2,280
Tuition, non-resident: $7,332

Washington

Bates Technical College
1101 South Yakima Avenue
Tacoma, WA 98405

Contact Information:
Telephone: 206-596-1563
Web: www.bates.edu

Program Information:
Program begins: August
Degrees offered: Certificate program, 11 months

Application Information:
Enrollment of program: 45

Financial Information:
Tuition, resident: $2,331
Average cost of books: $315

Employment Profile:
% employed within the first 6 months following graduation: 80
Average starting salary: $24,000

Bellingham Technical College
3028 Lindbergh Avenue
Bellingham, WA 98225

Contact Information:
Telephone: 360-738-3105 ext. 408
Fax: 360-676-3798
E-mail: jshuler@belltc.etc.edu
Web: www.belltc.ctc.edu

Program Information:
Program begins: September, March
Degrees offered: Certificate program, 11 months

Application Information:
Enrollment of program: 40
Transfer students are accepted.

Financial Information:
Tuition, resident: $1,998
Tuition, non-resident: $9,969
Average cost of books: $704
% of students receiving aid: 55

Employment Profile:
% of students who pass the boards on their first try: 75
% employed within the first 6 months following graduation: 80
Average starting salary: $16,778

Highline Community College

PO Box 98000
Des Moines, WA 98198-9800

Contact Information:
Telephone: 206-878-3710
Web: www.highline.ctc.edu

Program Information:
Program begins: September
Degrees offered: Certificate program

Application Information:
Enrollment of program: 20

Financial Information:
Tuition, resident: $1,700
Tuition, non-resident: $6,500
Average cost of books: $240

Employment Profile:
% of students who pass the boards on their first try: 100
% employed within the first 6 months following graduation: 100
Average starting salary: $30,500

Lake Washington Technical College

11605 132nd Avenue Northeast
Kirkland, WA 98034

Contact Information:
Telephone: 425-739-8377
Fax: 425-739-8292
Web: www.lwtc.ctc.edu

Program Information:
Program begins: March, September
Duration of program: 11 months

Application Information:
Enrollment of program: 60

Financial Information:
Average cost of books: $400

Employment Profile:
% of students who pass the boards on their first try: 90
% employed within the first 6 months following graduation: 85
Average starting salary: $28,000

Renton Technical College

3000 Northeast Fourth Street
Renton, WA 98056

Contact Information:
Telephone: 425-235-2352 ext. 5560
Fax: 425-235-7832
E-mail: kleviton@ctc.ctc.edu
Web: www.rentontc.ctc.edu

Program Information:
Program begins: September
Duration of program: 9 months

Financial Information:
Tuition, resident: $1,900

South Puget Sound Community College

2011 Mottman Road Southwest
Olympia, WA 98502

Contact Information:
Telephone: 360-754-7711 ext. 295
Fax: 360-664-0780
E-mail: martin_joan/spuget@ctc.edu

Program Information:
Program begins: September
Degrees offered: Certificate program, 11 months; Diploma, 15 months

Application Information:
Enrollment of program: 32
Transfer students are accepted.

Financial Information:
Average cost of books: $250
% of students receiving aid: 30

Employment Profile:
% of students who pass the boards on their first try: 95
% employed within the first 6 months following graduation: 98
Average starting salary: $16,000

Wisconsin

Gateway Technical College

3520 30th Avenue
Kenosha, WI 53144-1690

Contact Information:
Telephone: 414-656-6900 ext. 8964
Fax: 414-656-8966
E-mail: lopiccoloa@gateway.tec.wi.us
Web: www.gateway.tec.wi.us

Program Information:
Program begins: August, January
Duration of program: 10 months

Application Information:
Enrollment of program: 14

Financial Information:
Tuition, resident: $1,903
Tuition, non-resident: $11,565
Average cost of books: $90
% of students receiving aid: 67

Employment Profile:
% employed within the first 6 months following graduation: 100

Lakeshore Technical College

1290 North Avenue
Cleveland, WI 53015

Contact Information:
Telephone: 920-693-1186
Fax: 920-693-8955
E-mail: pacar@ltc.tec.wi.us
Web: www.gotoltc.com

Program Information:
Program begins: September, March
Duration of program: 10 months

Application Information:
Enrollment of program: 24
Transfer students are accepted.

Financial Information:
Tuition, resident: $1,951
Tuition, non-resident: $13,457
Average cost of books: $500
% of students receiving aid: 90

Employment Profile:
% of students who pass the boards on their first try: 100
% employed within the first 6 months following graduation: 100
Average starting salary: $18,000

Madison Area Technical College

3550 Anderson Street
Room 320A
Madison, WI 53704

Contact Information:
Telephone: 608-246-6685
Fax: 608-246-6013
E-mail: nbingham@madison.tec.wi.us
Web: www.madison.tec.wi.us

Program Information:
Program begins: August
Duration of program: 9 months

Application Information:
Enrollment of program: 20
Transfer students are accepted.

Financial Information:
Tuition, resident: $1,643
Tuition, non-resident: $9,300
Average cost of books: $150
% of students receiving aid: 35

Employment Profile:
Average starting salary: $21,000

Western Wisconsin Technical College

304 North 6th Street
La Crosse, WI 46012

Contact Information:
Telephone: 608-785-9137
Fax: 608-785-9194
E-mail: fergusonc@email.western.tec.wi.us
Web: www.western.tec.wi.us

Program Information:
Program begins: August
Duration of program: 10 months

Application Information:
Enrollment of program: 24
Transfer students are accepted.

Financial Information:
Tuition, resident: $2,447
Tuition, non-resident: $16,117
Average cost of books: $1,066

Employment Profile:
% employed within the first 6 months following graduation: 100
Average starting salary: $17,000

Wyoming

Sheridan College

3059 Coffeen Avenue
Whitney Building
Sheridan, WY 82801

Contact Information:
Telephone: 307-674-6446 ext. 6185
Web: www.sc.whecn.edu

Program Information:
Program begins: August
Duration of program: 11 months

Application Information:
Enrollment of program: 10
Transfer students are accepted.

Financial Information:
Tuition, resident: $1,746
Tuition, non-resident: $4,494
Average cost of books: $950
% of students receiving aid: 67

Employment Profile:
% of students who pass the boards on their first try: 95
Average starting salary: $18,000

Dental Laboratory Technician

Alabama

Wallace State Community College

PO Box 2000
Hanceville, AL 35077-2000

Contact Information:
Telephone: 205-352-8380
Fax: 205-352-8382
E-mail: dalleb419@earthlink.net
Web: www.wscc.cc.al.us

Program Information:
Program begins: August
Degrees offered: Associate's, 22 months

Application Information:
Enrollment of program: 43
Transfer students are accepted.

Financial Information:
Tuition, resident: $2,728
Tuition, non-resident: $5,456
Average cost of books: $375
% of students receiving aid: 40

Employment Profile:
% of students who pass the boards on their first try: 90
% employed within the first 6 months following graduation: 100
Average starting salary: $22,000

Arizona

Pima Community College

2202 West Anklam Road
HRP 220
Tucson, AZ 85709-0080

Contact Information:
Telephone: 520-206-6916
E-mail: matwell@westpima.edu
Web: www.pima.edu

Program Information:
Program begins: August
Degrees offered: Associate's, 18 months

Application Information:
Enrollment of program: 16

Financial Information:
Tuition, resident: $724
Tuition, non-resident: $4,596
Average cost of books: $120
% of students receiving aid: 70

Employment Profile:
% of students who pass the boards on their first try: 95
% employed within the first 6 months following graduation: 100

California

Los Angeles City College

855 North Vermont Avenue
Los Angeles, CA 90029

Contact Information:
Telephone: 323-953-4259
Fax: 323-953-4294
Web: www.lacc.cc.ca.us

Program Information:
Program begins: August, January
Duration of program: 18 months
Evening or weekend classes are available.

Application Information:
Enrollment of program: 321

Financial Information:
Tuition, resident: $970
Tuition, non-resident: $3,619

Pasadena City College

1570 East Colorado Boulevard R505
Pasadena, CA 91106

Contact Information:
Telephone: 626-585-7884
Fax: 626-585-7912
E-mail: ambobich@ppaccd.cc.ca.us
Web: www.paccd.cc.ca.us

Program Information:
Program begins: August
Degrees offered: Diploma

Application Information:
Enrollment of program: 52
Transfer students are accepted.

Financial Information:
Tuition, resident: $1,000
Tuition, non-resident: $1,700
Average cost of books: $200
% of students receiving aid: 30

Employment Profile:
% of students who pass the boards on their first try: 98
% employed within the first 6 months following graduation: 100

Florida

McFatter Technical Center

6500 Nova Drive
Davie, FL 33317

Contact Information:
Telephone: 954-370-8324
Fax: 954-382-6520

Program Information:
Program begins: August
Duration of program: 18 months

Application Information:
Enrollment of program: 25
Transfer students are accepted.

Financial Information:
Tuition, resident: $2,500
Tuition, non-resident: $10,000
Average cost of books: $310
% of students receiving aid: 33

Employment Profile:
% employed within the first 6 months following graduation: 95
Average starting salary: $15,000

Georgia

Atlanta Technical Institute
1560 Metropolitan Parkway Southwest
Atlanta, GA 30310

Contact Information:
Telephone: 404-756-3724
Fax: 404-758-8522

Program Information:
Program begins: Program begins quarterly.
Degrees offered: Certificate program, 12 months; Diploma, 15 months

Application Information:
Enrollment of program: 36
Transfer students are accepted.

Financial Information:
Tuition, resident: $1,772
Tuition, non-resident: $2,876
Average cost of books: $200
% of students receiving aid: 80

Employment Profile:
% employed within the first 6 months following graduation: 96
Average starting salary: $20,800

Gwinnett Technical Institute
5150 Sugarloaf Parkway
Box 1505
Lawrenceville, GA 30246-1505

Contact Information:
Telephone: 770-962-7580 ext. 175
Fax: 770-962-7985
E-mail: wturner@gwinnett.tec.ga.us
Web: www.gwinnett.tech.org

Program Information:
Program begins: September
Duration of program: 18 months

Application Information:
Enrollment of program: 20
Transfer students are accepted.

Financial Information:
Tuition, resident: $2,034
Tuition, non-resident: $3,690
Average cost of books: $325
% of students receiving aid: 85

Employment Profile:
% of students who pass the boards on their first try: 90
% employed within the first 6 months following graduation: 100
Average starting salary: $20,000

Idaho

Idaho State University
Dental Lab Technical Box 8380
Pocatello, ID 83209-8380

Contact Information:
Telephone: 208-236-3141
Fax: 208-236-3975
E-mail: georgary@isu.edu
Web: www.isu.edu

Program Information:
Program begins: August
Duration of program: 26 months

Financial Information:
Tuition, resident: $4,424
Tuition, non-resident: $19,854

Employment Profile:
% of students who pass the boards on their first try: 100
% employed within the first 6 months following graduation: 100
Average starting salary: $18,500

Illinois

Triton College
2000 North Fifth Avenue
River Grove, IL 60171

Contact Information:
Telephone: 708-456-0300 ext. 3422
E-mail: cburchet@triton.cc.il.us

Program Information:
Program begins: Program begins quarterly.
Duration of program: 21 months

Application Information:
Enrollment of program: 43
Transfer students are accepted.

Financial Information:
Tuition, resident: $2,140
Tuition, non-resident: $4,759
Average cost of books: $85
% of students receiving aid: 20

Employment Profile:
% employed within the first 6 months following graduation: 100

Indiana

Indiana University—Purdue University Fort Wayne
2101 Coliseum Boulevard East
Fort Wayne, IN 46805

Contact Information:
Telephone: 219-481-6837
Fax: 219-481-5767
Web: www.iuinfo-indiana.edu

Program Information:
Program begins: August
Degrees offered: Diploma, 18 months; Associate's, 18 months

Application Information:
Enrollment of program: 22
Transfer students are accepted.

Financial Information:
Tuition, resident: $3,500
Tuition, non-resident: $8,500
Average cost of books: $400
% of students receiving aid: 75

Employment Profile:
% of students who pass the boards on their first try: 95
% employed within the first 6 months following graduation: 90
Average starting salary: $18,500

Iowa

Kirkwood Community College
6301 Kirkwood Boulevard Southwest
PO Box 2068
Cedar Rapids, IA 52406-9973

Contact Information:
Telephone: 319-398-5400
Fax: 319-398-1293
E-mail: bmitche@kirkwood.cc.ia.us
Web: www.kirkwood.cc.ia.us

Program Information:
Program begins: August
Duration of program: 24 months

Application Information:
Enrollment of program: 12
Transfer students are accepted.

Financial Information:
Tuition, resident: $2,558
Tuition, non-resident: $5,115
% of students receiving aid: 80

Employment Profile:
% employed within the first 6 months following graduation: 80
Average starting salary: $17,000

Kentucky

Lexington Community College
University of Kentucky
Cooper Drive
Oswald Building
Lexington, KY 40506-0235

Contact Information:
Telephone: 606-257-4872 ext. 4098
E-mail: gzoll@pop.uky.edu
Web: www.uky.edu

Program Information:
Program begins: August
Duration of program: 16 months

Application Information:
Enrollment of program: 30
Transfer students are accepted.

Financial Information:
Tuition, resident: $1,956
Tuition, non-resident: $5,196

Louisiana

Louisiana State University
1100 Florida Avenue
New Orleans, LA 70119

Contact Information:
Telephone: 504-619-8684
Fax: 504-619-8740
Web: www.lsu.edu

Program Information:
Program begins: August
Degrees offered: Diploma, 24 months; Bachelor's, 36 months

Application Information:
Enrollment of program: 25

Financial Information:
Tuition, resident: $3,215
Tuition, non-resident: $5,015
Average cost of books: $250
% of students receiving aid: 90

Employment Profile:
% of students who pass the boards on their first try: 95
% employed within the first 6 months following graduation: 100
Average starting salary: $20,000

Massachusetts

Middlesex Community College—Lowell
33 Kearney Square
Lowell, MA 01852

Contact Information:
Telephone: 508-656-3056
Fax: 508-656-3078

Program Information:
Program begins: September
Duration of program: 18 months

Application Information:
Transfer students are accepted.

Financial Information:
Tuition, resident: $2,870
Tuition, non-resident: $3,235
Average cost of books: $150

Employment Profile:
% of students who pass the boards on their first try: 100
% employed within the first 6 months following graduation: 100
Average starting salary: $24,000

New York

CUNY New York City Technical College
300 Jay Street - P201
Brooklyn, NY 11201

Contact Information:
Telephone: 718-260-5137
Fax: 718-260-5995
Web: www.nyctc.cuny.edu

Program Information:
Program begins: September
Duration of program: 20 months

Application Information:
Enrollment of program: 155

Financial Information:
Tuition, resident: $1,650
Tuition, non-resident: $3,300
Average cost of books: $250
% of students receiving aid: 75

Employment Profile:
% employed within the first 6 months following graduation: 80
Average starting salary: $16,000

Erie Community College—South Campus
4041 Southwestern Boulevard
Orchard Park, NY 14127-2199

Contact Information:
Telephone: 716-851-1759
Fax: 716-851-1629
E-mail: herman@sstaff.sunyerie.edu
Web: www.sunyerie.edu

Program Information:
Program begins: September
Duration of program: 24 months

Application Information:
Enrollment of program: 38
Transfer students are accepted.

Financial Information:
Tuition, resident: $2,500
Tuition, non-resident: $5,000
Average cost of books: $65
% of students receiving aid: 60

Employment Profile:
% of students who pass the boards on their first try: 100
% employed within the first 6 months following graduation: 65

North Carolina

Durham Technical Community College
1637 Lawson Street
Durham, NC 27703

Contact Information:
Telephone: 919-686-3737
Web: www.dtcc.cc.nc.us

Program Information:
Program begins: August
Duration of program: 21 months

Application Information:
Enrollment of program: 22
Transfer students are accepted.

Financial Information:
Tuition, resident: $1,053
Tuition, non-resident: $6,132
Average cost of books: $300
% of students receiving aid: 60

Employment Profile:
% employed within the first 6 months following graduation: 86
Average starting salary: $16,000

Ohio

Columbus State Community College
550 East Spring Street
Columbus, OH 43215

Contact Information:
Telephone: 614-287-2547
Fax: 614-287-5198
E-mail: cnarcros@cscc.edu
Web: www.cscc.edu

Program Information:
Program begins: September
Duration of program: 21 months

Application Information:
Enrollment of program: 29
Transfer students are accepted.

Financial Information:
Tuition, resident: $3,188
Tuition, non-resident: $6,692
Average cost of books: $100

Employment Profile:
% of students who pass the boards on their first try: 90
% employed within the first 6 months following graduation: 92
Average starting salary: $20,000

Oregon

Portland Community College
PO Box 19000
Portland, OR 97219-0990

Contact Information:
Telephone: 503-977-4235
Fax: 503-977-8300
E-mail: ajackson@pcc.edu
Web: www.pcc.edu

Program Information:
Program begins: September
Degrees offered: Associate's, 18 months

Application Information:
Enrollment of program: 30
Transfer students are accepted.

Financial Information:
Tuition, resident: $1,476
Tuition, non-resident: $5,330
Average cost of books: $700

Employment Profile:
% of students who pass the boards on their first try: 90
% employed within the first 6 months following graduation: 100
Average starting salary: $20,000

Tennessee

East Tennessee State University

1000 West Feat Street
Elizabethton, TN 37643

Contact Information:
Telephone: 423-547-4911
Fax: 423-547-4921
Web: www.etsu.tn.us

Program Information:
Program begins: August
Duration of program: 18 months

Financial Information:
Tuition, resident: $2,892
Tuition, non-resident: $9,396

Texas

University of Texas Health Science Center at San Antonio

7703 Floyd Curl Drive
San Antonio, TX 78284-7902

Contact Information:
Telephone: 210-567-3056
Fax: 210-567-3061
E-mail: davisrd@uthscsa.edu
Web: www.uthsca.edu

Program Information:
Program begins: August
Duration of program: 24 months

Application Information:
Enrollment of program: 24
Transfer students are accepted.

Financial Information:
Tuition, resident: $2,700
Tuition, non-resident: $17,500
Average cost of books: $500
% of students receiving aid: 50

Employment Profile:
% of students who pass the boards on their first try: 100
% employed within the first 6 months following graduation: 100
Average starting salary: $20,000

Virginia

J. Sargeant Reynolds Community College

PO Box 85622
Richmond, VA 23285-5622

Contact Information:
Telephone: 804-786-6931
Fax: 804-786-5298
E-mail: ewolfe@jsr.cc.va.us
Web: www.jsr.cc.va.us

Program Information:
Program begins: August
Degrees offered: Associate's, 21 months
Evening or weekend classes are available.

Application Information:
Enrollment of program: 30
Transfer students are accepted.

Financial Information:
Tuition, resident: $1,477
Tuition, non-resident: $6,074
Average cost of books: $300
% of students receiving aid: 75

Employment Profile:
% of students who pass the boards on their first try: 90
% employed within the first 6 months following graduation: 100

Washington

Bates Technical College

1101 South Yakima Avenue
Tacoma, WA 98405

Contact Information:
Telephone: 206-596-1577
Fax: 206-596-1540
E-mail: rmarosti@ctc.ctc.edu
Web: www.bates.ctc.edu

Program Information:
Program begins: September
Degrees offered: Diploma, 22 months; Associate's

Application Information:
Enrollment of program: 36
Transfer students are accepted.

Financial Information:
Average cost of books: $195

Employment Profile:
% of students who pass the boards on their first try: 100
% employed within the first 6 months following graduation: 100
Average starting salary: $20,000

Dietitian/ Nutritionist

Jeffrey E. Harris, DrPH, MPH, CNS, RD
Associate Professor and Dietetics Program Director
Department of Health
West Chester University
West Chester, Pennsylvania

Job Description

What Do They Do?

Dietetics is the science or art of applying the principles of food and nutrition to health. Dietitians help people make smart food choices to keep them healthy, advise doctors and nurses regarding nutrition, teach people about the importance of good nutrition and healthful food choices, plan nutritional programs for large groups of people, manage food service businesses, and supervise people who prepare and serve food. Dietitians may work in groups as team leaders or in their own businesses. In order to practice, dietitians must earn at least a Bachelor's degree, complete an internship and pass a credentialing examination in order to earn the "registered dietitian" or "RD" credential.[1]

How do the professions of dietitian and nutritionist relate to one another? In the United States, anyone who gives nutrition advice may call him or herself a nutritionist. However, the term best applies to dietitians or to individuals who have received academic training in nutrition beyond a Bachelor's degree (a Master's or Doctorate). Those in the latter category have not necessarily become dietitians in the manner specified in the previous paragraph. They have received a high quality education in nutrition, but have not completed an internship or the credentialing examination to become a registered dietitian. So all dietitians can be considered to be nutritionists, but not all nutritionists are dietitians.

The term "nutritionist" refers to professionals who have rigorous training in nutrition and give credible advice about nutrition. Since dietitians have this rigorous training and, among other tasks, give nutritional advice, they are considered to be nutritionists. Thus, the term "dietitian" may be used synonymously with the term "nutritionist." Most nutritionists are dietitians. However, only dietitians can receive third party payment from insurance companies. They may work as clinical or administrative dietitians in hospitals. Most nutrition jobs require that the person be a registered dietitian.

Type of Person

Dietitians enjoy working with people and have a strong interest in food and nutrition. They have an interest in the sciences and applying them to solve nutrition-related problems, the motivations and initiative to work independently, the ability to identify and solve problems. In addition, dietitians need to demonstrate good judgment and an understanding of human nature.

With Whom Do They Work?

Dietitians work with physicians and health care professionals such as respiratory therapists, nurses, occupational therapists, physical therapists, health educators, psychologists, social workers, exercise physiologists, food service professionals, community health educators, coaches, and chefs.

Employment

Places of Employment

A dietitian can practice in many areas:

- A clinical dietitian works in hospitals or other healthcare facilities.
- An administrative dietitian manages food service systems in healthcare, education, business, and industry.
- A community dietitian plans and implements programs for improved health and prevention of disease.

Dietitians may also work in education and research at colleges, universities, medical centers, and research laboratories. Other employment opportunities include working as a consultant in private practice; writing articles for newspapers, magazines, or books; or reporting on nutrition and health for radio or television.

Many work environments, particularly those in medical and health care settings, require that an individual be credentialed as a registered dietitian (RD). Specific roles that dietitians play include:

- Educating patients about nutrition and administering medical nutrition therapy as part of a health care team at hospitals or other health care facilities.
- Managing food service operations at hospitals or other health care facilities as well as schools, day-care centers, and correctional facilities.
- Educating clients of sports nutrition or corporate wellness programs about the connection between food, fitness, and health.
- Working in communications, consumer affairs, public relations, marketing, or product development for food and nutrition-related businesses and industries.
- Providing services to food service or restaurant managers, food vendors, and distributors.
- Teaching physicians, nurses, dietetics students, and others about the science of foods and nutrition.
- Researching clinical nutrition questions or finding alternative food or nutrition recommendations for food and pharmaceutical companies, universities, and hospitals.[2]

Employment Outlook

According to the U.S. Bureau of Labor Statistics, the need for dietitians is expected to grow through the year 2005 due to increased emphasis on disease prevention, a growing and aging population, and public interest in nutrition. Employment in hospitals is expected to show little change because of anticipated slow growth and reduced lengths of hospital stays. Faster growth, however, is anticipated in nursing homes, residential care facilities, and physician clinics.[3]

Salary

According to ADA's 1997 Membership Database, among entry-level registered dietitians employed full-time five years or less in their primary position, 45 percent earned between $25,000–35,000 a year and 32 percent earned between $35,000–$45,000. As with any profession, salaries and fees vary by region of the country, employment settings, scope of responsibility, and supply of RDs. Salaries increase with years of experience and many RDs, particularly those in private practice, business, and consulting, earn incomes above $50,000.[4]

Educational Programs

Length

Dietetics education programs are accredited by the Commission on Accreditation/Approval for Dietetics Education (CAADE), the ADA's accrediting agency for educational programs. Students must graduate from an accredited dietetics education academic program in order to become a registered dietitian. Educational programs in dietetics are generally four-year Bachelor's degree programs. Upon completion of a Bachelor's degree, students must complete 900 hours of supervised practice (dietetic internship) over 6 to 12 months at a CAADE-accredited site. Some educational programs are called "coordinated programs" because they have the supervised practice built into their programs.[5] Following the successful completion of the supervised practice, students can take the registration examination to become registered dietitians.

Students who have already earned a non-dietetics Bachelor's degree may be able to earn a Bachelor's degree in dietetics by having their college transcripts evaluated by the director of a CAADE-accredited dietetics program. The director will evaluate the student's previous academic preparation and identify the courses that would need to be completed at that school to meet the academic requirements for dietetics registration. Completion of these academic requirements will normally take a minimum of three years. These students may also complete their academic requirements in Master's or Doctoral programs. These programs usually take a minimum of 2–3 years for completion. No matter which route they take, students must also complete a 6 to 12 month CAADE accredited supervised practice following or during their academic preparation.[6]

Prerequisites

Applicants to dietetic education programs must have a high school diploma.

Curriculum

Dietitians study a variety of subjects including sociology, biochemistry, physiology, microbiology, anatomy, chemistry, business, economics, computer science, culinary arts, food and nutrition sciences, and food service systems management. Following or during their didactic education, students must complete a 6 to 12 month supervised practice in which they get practical experience in food service, community nutrition, and clinical nutrition. They must then successfully complete the Commission on Dietetics Registration examination. Once they pass this examination, they can use the credential Registered Dietitian or RD.[7]

Accrediting Body

The Commission on Accreditation/Approval for Dietetics Education (CAADE) of the ADA is the organization that evaluates educational programs and supervised practices to make sure that they are teaching the necessary skills and knowledge to adequately prepare dietitians.

Commission on Accreditation/Approval for
Dietetics Education (CAADE)
The American Dietetic Association
Education and Accreditation Team
216 West Jackson Boulevard
Chicago, IL 60606-6995
Telephone: 800-877-1600, ext. 5400
Fax: 312-899-4817
E-mail: education@eatright.org

Certification Board

The Commission on Dietetic Registration is the credentialing agency for the American Dietetic Association. It is responsible for creating and administering the registration examination that all graduating students must pass in order to be deemed registered dietitians.

The Commission on Dietetic Registration
216 West Jackson Boulevard
Chicago, IL 60606-6995
Telephone: 312-899-0040 ext. 5500
Fax: 312-899-4772
E-mail: CDR@eatright.org

Advice for Potential Students

Ask someone at the school you are considering to send you information about the program and curriculum. Visit the school and make an appointment to meet with the program director. You may want to ask the director about the program's job placement rates and where its graduates work. Inquire as to what percentage of its students obtain placement in supervised practices. Go to a university library and find a copy of the *Journal of the American Dietetic Association* and look in the job opportunities section to see the number and kind of jobs available. In addition, it might be helpful to interview a dietitian in your community and ask if you could observe him or her while working.

For Additional Information

Organizations

American Dietetic Association Networks Team
216 West Jackson Boulevard, Suite 800
Chicago, IL 60606-6995
Telephone: 800-877-1600, ext. 4897
Fax: 312-899-0008
E-mail: network@eatright.org

Publications

The American Dietetic Association: What is Dietetics? (The American Dietetic Association, 1999) www.eatright.org

The American Dietetic Association: Becoming A Registered Dietitian (The American Dietetic Association, 1999) www.eatright.org

Internet Resources

The American Dietetic Association: www.eatright.org
Nutritionjobs.com: www.nutritionjobs.com
Dietetics Online: www.dietetics.com
Ask the Dietitian: www.dietitian.com
State Dietetic Associations: www.eatright.org/states.html

Alabama

Wallace State Community College

PO Box 2000
Hanceville, AL 35077-2000

Contact Information:
Telephone: 256-352-8318
Fax: 256-352-8320
Web: www.wscc.cc.al.us

Program Information:
Program begins: August
Duration of program: 16 months

Application Information:
Enrollment of program: 24
Transfer students are accepted.

Financial Information:
Tuition, resident: $2,200
Tuition, non-resident: $4,400
Average cost of books: $500
% of students receiving aid: 75

Employment Profile:
% of students who pass the boards on their first try: 60
% employed within the first 6 months following graduation: 80
Average starting salary: $31,200

University of Montevallo

Family and Consumer Sciences
Station 6385
Montevallo, AL 35115-6000

Contact Information:
Telephone: 313-763-6170
E-mail: andrews@montavallo.edu

Program Information:
Degrees offered: Bachelor's

Application Information:
Enrollment of program: 40
Transfer students are accepted.

Financial Information:
Average cost of books: $200
% of students receiving aid: 85

Employment Profile:
% of students who pass the boards on their first try: 100
Average starting salary: $25,000

Arizona

Arizona State University

Family Resources & Human Development
PO Box 872502
Tempe, AZ 85287-2502

Contact Information:
Telephone: 480-965-7034
Fax: 480-965-6978
E-mail: rose.martin@asu.edu
Web: www.asu.edu

Program Information:
Duration of program: 24 months

Application Information:
Enrollment of program: 23

Financial Information:
Tuition, resident: $2,188
Tuition, non-resident: $9,340

Employment Profile:
% of students who pass the boards on their first try: 94
Additional information:
Offers both a dietitc program and internship.

Northern Arizona University

Food and Nutrition Science
NAU Box 15095
Flagstaff, AZ 86011-5095

Contact Information:
Telephone: 480-963-7731
Fax: 480-965-6978
E-mail: linda.vaughan@asu.edu
Web: www.nau.edu

Program Information:
Program begins: August
Degrees offered: Bachelor's, 48 months; Master's, 24 months
Evening or weekend classes are available.

Application Information:
Transfer students are accepted.

Financial Information:
Tuition, resident: $2,188
Tuition, non-resident: $9,340
Average cost of books: $500

Employment Profile:
% of students who pass the boards on their first try: 97
% employed within the first 6 months following graduation: 90
Average starting salary: $32,000

Arkansas

Harding University

Family and Consumer Sciences
900 East Center Avenue Box 12233
Searcy, AR 72149-0001

Contact Information:
Telephone: 501-279-4472
Fax: 501—279-4098
Web: www.harding.edu

Program Information:
Degrees offered: Bachelor's

University of Arkansas

Human Environmental Sciences
118 HOEC
Fayetteville, AR 72701

Contact Information:
Telephone: 214-648-1520
Fax: 214-648-1514
E-mail: mfitch@comp.uart.edu
Web: www.uark.edu

Program Information:
Degrees offered: Bachelor's, 48 months

California

California State Polytechnic University

Food Nutrition & Consumer Sciences
3801 West Temple Avenue
Pomona, CA 91768-2557

Contact Information:
Telephone: 909-869-2163
Fax: 909-869-5078
E-mail: kcaldwellfre@csupomona

Program Information:
Program begins: September
Duration of program: 9 months

Application Information:
Enrollment of program: 19

Financial Information:
Tuition, resident: $1,000
Average cost of books: $200
% of students receiving aid: 20

Employment Profile:
% of students who pass the boards on their first try: 92

% employed within the first 6 months following graduation: 20
Average starting salary: $30,000

California State University—Los Angeles

Health & Nutritional Sciences
5151 State University Drive
Los Angeles, CA 90032-8172

Contact Information:
Telephone: 323-343-5439
Fax: 323-343-5016
Web: www.calstatela.edu

Program Information:
Program begins: September
Degrees offered: Bachelor's, 48 months; Master's, 24 months
Evening or weekend classes are available.

Application Information:
Enrollment of program: 50
Transfer students are accepted.

Financial Information:
Tuition, resident: $2,400
Tuition, non-resident: $1,100
Average cost of books: $500

Employment Profile:
% of students who pass the boards on their first try: 90
% employed within the first 6 months following graduation: 95
Average starting salary: $34,000

California State University—Northridge

Family Environmental Sciences
18111 Nordhoff Street
Northridge, CA 91330-8308

Contact Information:
Telephone: 818-677-3051
Fax: 818-677-4778
E-mail: christine.smith@cson.edu
Web: www.csun.edu

Program Information:
Duration of program: 42 months
Evening or weekend classes are available.

Application Information:
Enrollment of program: 200
Transfer students are accepted.

Financial Information:
Tuition, resident: $3,969
Tuition, non-resident: $7,749

Employment Profile:
% of students who pass the boards on their first try: 98

California State University—San Bernardino

Health Science & Human Ecology
5500 University Parkway
San Bernardino, CA 92407-2318

Contact Information:
Telephone: 909-880-5340
Fax: 909-880-7037
E-mail: dchen@csusb.edu

Program Information:
Program begins: September
Degrees offered: Bachelor's, 48 months

Application Information:
Enrollment of program: 70
Transfer students are accepted.

Financial Information:
Tuition, resident: $1,500
Tuition, non-resident: $5,166
Average cost of books: $384
% of students receiving aid: 80

Loma Linda University

School of Public Health Nutrition Department
Nichol Hall
Room 1102
Loma Linda, CA 92350

Contact Information:
Telephone: 909-558-4598
Fax: 909-558-4095
E-mail: ehaddad@sph.llu.edu
Web: www.llu.edu

Program Information:
Duration of program: 30 months

Application Information:
Enrollment of program: 40
Transfer students are accepted.

Financial Information:
Average cost of books: $500

Employment Profile:
% of students who pass the boards on their first try: 95
% employed within the first 6 months following graduation: 100
Average starting salary: $30,000

Napa State Hospital

2100 Napa Vallejo Highway
Napa, CA 94558-6293

Contact Information:
Telephone: 707-253-5428
Fax: 707-254-2422

Program Information:
Program begins: August
Duration of program: 11 months

Application Information:
Enrollment of program: 4

Employment Profile:
% of students who pass the boards on their first try: 98
% employed within the first 6 months following graduation: 95

Patton State Hospital

3102 East Highland Avenue
Patton, CA 92369

Contact Information:
Telephone: 909-425-7297
Fax: 909-425-7069
E-mail: dotomar@dmhpsh/state.ca.us

Program Information:
Program begins: August
Duration of program: 10 months

Financial Information:
Average cost of books: $500

Employment Profile:
% of students who pass the boards on their first try: 95
% employed within the first 6 months following graduation: 100

Pepperdine University

Natural Science Division
Malibu, CA 90263

Contact Information:
Telephone: 310-456-4339
Fax: 310-456-4339
E-mail: jpalacio@pepperdine.edu
Web: www.pepperdine.edu

Program Information:
Program begins: January, August
Degrees offered: Bachelor's, 48 months

Application Information:
Enrollment of program: 35
Transfer students are accepted.

Financial Information:
% of students receiving aid: 50

Employment Profile:
% of students who pass the boards on their first try: 100

Porterville Development Center

PO Box 2000
Porterville, CA 93258-2000

Contact Information:
Telephone: 559-782-2753
Fax: 559-782-2756
E-mail: aoblintern@ocsnet.net

Program Information:
Program begins: August
Duration of program: 9 months

Application Information:
Enrollment of program: 6

Financial Information:
Average cost of books: $200

Employment Profile:
% of students who pass the boards on their first try: 97
% employed within the first 6 months following graduation: 70
Average starting salary: $35,000

San Jose State University

Nutrition & Food Science
One Washington Square
San Jose, CA 95192-0058

Contact Information:
Telephone: 408-924-3109
Fax: 408-924-3114
E-mail: ksucher@email.sjsu.edu
Web: www.sjsu.edu

Program Information:
Program begins: August, January
Duration of program: 48 months

Application Information:
Enrollment of program: 200
Transfer students are accepted.

Employment Profile:
% of students who pass the boards on their first try: 95
% employed within the first 6 months following graduation: 90
Average starting salary: $40,000

University of California—Berkeley
Department of Nutritional Sciences
119 Morgan Hall
Berkeley, CA 94720

Contact Information:
Telephone: 330-972-6046
Fax: 330-972-4934
E-mail: hudson@natura.berkeley.edu
Web: www.cnr.berkeley.edu

Program Information:
Duration of program: 48 months

Application Information:
Enrollment of program: 41
Transfer students are accepted.

Financial Information:
Average cost of books: $822

Colorado

University of Northern Colorado
Community Health & Nutrition
Gunter 2280
Greeley, CO 80639

Contact Information:
Telephone: 904-620-2840
Fax: 904-620-2848
E-mail: jerskine@hhs.unco.edu
Web: www.hhs.unco.edu/diet.htm

Program Information:
Duration of program: 48 months

Application Information:
Enrollment of program: 80
Transfer students are accepted.

Financial Information:
Tuition, resident: $1,967
Tuition, non-resident: $8,997
% of students receiving aid: 50

Florida

Florida International University
Dietetics & Nutrition
University Park HB 208
Miami, FL 33199

Contact Information:
Telephone: 305-348-2878
Fax: 305-348-1996
E-mail: ciccazzo@fiu.edu
Web: www.fiu.edu

Program Information:
Degrees offered: Bachelor's, 18 months

Application Information:
Enrollment of program: 140
Transfer students are accepted.

Financial Information:
Tuition, resident: $16,248
Tuition, non-resident: $18,248
Average cost of books: $905
% of students receiving aid: 75

Employment Profile:
% of students who pass the boards on their first try: 100
% employed within the first 6 months following graduation: 90
Average starting salary: $28,000

Florida State University
Nutrition Food & Movement Sciences
400 Sandels Building
Tallahassee, FL 323061493

Contact Information:
Telephone: 850-644-1828
Fax: 850-645-5000
E-mail: utate@mailer.fsu.edu
Web: www.fsu.edu

Program Information:
Program begins: September
Duration of program: 2 months

Application Information:
Enrollment of program: 45
Transfer students are accepted.

Financial Information:
Average cost of books: $300

Employment Profile:
% of students who pass the boards on their first try: 100
% employed within the first 6 months following graduation: 100
Average starting salary: $28,000

Sarasota Memorial Hospital
Food & Nutrition Services
1700 South Tamiami Trail
Sarasota, FL 34239-3555

Contact Information:
Telephone: 941-917-1080
Fax: 941-917-6196

Program Information:
Program begins: September
Duration of program: 7 months

Application Information:
Enrollment of program: 5

Financial Information:
Average cost of books: $200

Employment Profile:
% of students who pass the boards on their first try: 97
% employed within the first 6 months following graduation: 100
Average starting salary: $28,000

University of Florida
Food Science & Human Nutrition
359 FSB
Gainesville, FL 32611

Contact Information:
Telephone: 415-476-1461
E-mail: psm@gnu..ufl.edu
Web: www.ufl.edu

Program Information:
Program begins: August, January, June
Degrees offered: Bachelor's, 48 months; Master's, 24 months; PhD

Application Information:
Enrollment of program: 200
Transfer students are accepted.

Financial Information:
Tuition, resident: $2,130
Tuition, non-resident: $9,120
Average cost of books: $600

Employment Profile:
% of students who pass the boards on their first try: 85
Average starting salary: $28,000

Additional information:
Offers both a dietitc program and internship.

University of North Florida
College of Health
4567 St. Johns Bluff Road South
Jacksonville, FL 32224-2645

Contact Information:
Telephone: 505-277-6434
E-mail: jrodrigu@unf.edu
Web: www.unf.edu

Program Information:
Duration of program: 48 months
Evening or weekend classes are available.

Application Information:
Enrollment of program: 50
Transfer students are accepted.

Employment Profile:
% of students who pass the boards on their first try: 100
Average starting salary: $27,500

Georgia

Georgia Southern University
Family & Consumer Sciences
Box 8034
Statesboro, GA 30460

Contact Information:
Telephone: 912-681-5345
Fax: 912-681-0276
E-mail: fbrown@gasou.edu
Web: www.gasou.edu

Program Information:
Program begins: August
Degrees offered: Bachelor's, 48 months

Application Information:
Enrollment of program: 90
Transfer students are accepted.

Financial Information:
Tuition, resident: $2,400
Tuition, non-resident: $6,000
Average cost of books: $500

Employment Profile:
% of students who pass the boards on their first try: 83
% employed within the first 6 months following graduation: 70
Average starting salary: $24,000

Georgia State University
Department Nutrition
University Plaza PO Box 873
Atlanta, GA 30303-3083

Contact Information:
Telephone: 404-651-1102
Fax: 404-651-1235
E-mail: dbaxter@gsu.edu
Web: www.gsu.edu

Program Information:
Program begins: September
Duration of program: 24 months

Application Information:
Enrollment of program: 60
Transfer students are accepted.

Financial Information:
Tuition, resident: $3,498
Tuition, non-resident: $12,555
Average cost of books: $400
% of students receiving aid: 50

Employment Profile:
% of students who pass the boards on their first try: 95
% employed within the first 6 months following graduation: 100
Average starting salary: $29,000

Life University
Department of Nutrition
1269 Barclay Circle
Marietta, GA 30060-2903

Contact Information:
Telephone: 770-426-2736
Fax: 770-426-2698
E-mail: tbrigman@life.edu
Web: www.life.edu

Application Information:
Enrollment of program: 100
Transfer students are accepted.

Southern Regional Medical Center
11 Upper Riverdale Road Southwest
Riverdale, GA 30274-2600

Contact Information:
Telephone: 770-991-8053
Fax: 770-991-8690
E-mail: crocker_stephanie@promina.org
Web: www.srmc.org

Program Information:
Program begins: August
Degrees offered: Certificate Program, 9 months

Application Information:
Enrollment of program: 12

Financial Information:
Average cost of books: $100

Employment Profile:
% of students who pass the boards on their first try: 90
% employed within the first 6 months following graduation: 100
Average starting salary: $29,000

Hawaii

University of Hawaii at Manoa
Food Science & Human Nutrition
Miller Hall 12
2515 Campus Road
Honolulu, HI 96822-2218

Contact Information:
Telephone: 405-974-5787
Fax: 405-974-3850
E-mail: shovic@hawaii.edu
Web: www.hawaii.edu/dietetics

Program Information:
Program begins: August
Degrees offered: Bachelor's, 48 months

Application Information:
Enrollment of program: 125
Transfer students are accepted.

Financial Information:
Tuition, resident: $1,500
Tuition, non-resident: $4,700

Employment Profile:
% of students who pass the boards on their first try: 98
% employed within the first 6 months following graduation: 100
Average starting salary: $30,000

Illinois

Loyola University of Chicago
Department of Food & Nutrition
6525 North Sheridan Road
Chicago, IL 60626-5311

Contact Information:
Telephone: 773-508-8299
Fax: 773-508-8296
E-mail: tcarlyl@wpo.it.luc.edu
Web: www.luc.edu

Program Information:
Degrees offered: Bachelor's, 48 months; Post-bachelor's Certificate, 32 months
Evening or weekend classes are available.

Application Information:
Enrollment of program: 95
Transfer students are accepted.

Financial Information:
Tuition, resident: $8,875

Employment Profile:
% of students who pass the boards on their first try: 85

Northern Illinois University
Family Consumer and Nutrition Sciences
DeKalb, IL 60115-2854

Contact Information:
Telephone: 815-753-6386
Fax: 815-753-1321
E-mail: lrobins@niu.edu
Web: www.niu.edu

Program Information:
Program begins: August, January
Duration of program: 16 months

Application Information:
Enrollment of program: 18
Transfer students are accepted.

Financial Information:
Tuition, resident: $2,784
Tuition, non-resident: $6,904
Average cost of books: $250
% of students receiving aid: 100

Employment Profile:
% of students who pass the boards on their first try: 93

Southern Illinois University—Carbondale
Animal Science Food & Nutrition/MC 4317
Carbondale, IL 62901-4317

Contact Information:
Telephone: 618-453-7512
Fax: 618-453-7517
E-mail: saraland@siu.edu
Web: www.siue.edu

Program Information:
Program begins: August, January, June
Duration of program: 48 months

Application Information:
Enrollment of program: 75

Employment Profile:
% of students who pass the boards on their first try: 93

St. John's Hospital
800 East Carpenter Street
Springfield, IL 62769

Contact Information:
Telephone: 217-544-6464 ext. 44818
Fax: 212-757-6871
E-mail: slopinsk@st-johns.org
Web: www.st-johns.org

Program Information:
Program begins: August
Degrees offered: Post-bachelor's Certificate, 11 months

Application Information:
Enrollment of program: 6

Financial Information:
Average cost of books: $50
% of students receiving aid: 34

Employment Profile:
% of students who pass the boards on their first try: 90
% employed within the first 6 months following graduation: 100
Average starting salary: $28,000

Indiana

Ball State University
Family and Consumer Sciences
150 Applied Technology Building
Muncie, IN 47306

Contact Information:
Telephone: 765-285-5940
Fax: 765-285-2314
E-mail: mkurtz@bsu.edu
Web: www.bsu.edu

Program Information:
Program begins: January, June
Duration of program: 7 months
Evening or weekend classes are available.

Indiana State University
Family and Consumer Sciences
Terre Haute, IN 47809

Contact Information:
Telephone: 812-237-3309
Fax: 812-237-3304
Web: www.indstate.edu

Program Information:
Duration of program: 24 months
Evening or weekend classes are available.

Application Information:
Enrollment of program: 24
Transfer students are accepted.

Financial Information:
% of students receiving aid: 10

Employment Profile:
% of students who pass the boards on their first try: 95
Average starting salary: $22,500

Marian College
Dietetics Nursing & Nutritional Sciences
3200 Cold Springs Road
Indianapolis, IN 46222-1997

Contact Information:
Telephone: 317-955-6346
Fax: 317-955-6448
E-mail: raosborn@marian.edu
Web: www.marian.edu

Program Information:
Duration of program: 48 months
Evening or weekend classes are available.

Application Information:
Enrollment of program: 30
Transfer students are accepted.

Financial Information:
Tuition, resident: $14,012
Average cost of books: $1,000
% of students receiving aid: 75

Employment Profile:
% of students who pass the boards on their first try: 95
% employed within the first 6 months following graduation: 100
Average starting salary: $24,000

Purdue University
Department of Foods and Nutrition
1264 Stone Hall
West Lafayette, IN 47907-1264

Contact Information:
Telephone: 765-494-8238
Fax: 765-494-0674
E-mail: woodo@cfs.purdue.edu
Web: www.cfs.purdue.edu/fdsnutr

Program Information:
Degrees offered: Bachelor's, 48 months

Application Information:
Enrollment of program: 200
Transfer students are accepted.

Financial Information:
Tuition, resident: $11,000
Tuition, non-resident: $20,000

Employment Profile:
% of students who pass the boards on their first try: 100
% employed within the first 6 months following graduation: 100
Average starting salary: $28,000

Iowa

University of Northern Iowa
Design Family & Consumer Sciences
235 Latham Hall
Cedar Falls, IA 50614-0332

Contact Information:
Telephone: 970-351-1706
Fax: 970-351-1489
E-mail: hattie.middleton@uni.edu
Web: www.uni.edu

Application Information:
Enrollment of program: 51
Transfer students are accepted.

Financial Information:
Tuition, resident: $1,393
Tuition, non-resident: $3,773
Average cost of books: $729
% of students receiving aid: 61

Employment Profile:
% of students who pass the boards on their first try: 92
% employed within the first 6 months following graduation: 90

Kansas

Kansas State University
Hotel Restaurant Institution Management & Dietetics
Justin Hall 103
Manhattan, KS 66506-1404

Contact Information:
Telephone: 785-532-2216
Fax: 785-532-5522
E-mail: canter@ksu.edu
Web: www.ksu.edu/humec/hrimd/hr_diet.htm

Program Information:
Program begins: August, January
Duration of program: 8 months

Application Information:
Enrollment of program: 135
Transfer students are accepted.

Financial Information:
Tuition, resident: $2,100
Tuition, non-resident: $8,550
Average cost of books: $600
% of students receiving aid: 75

Employment Profile:
% of students who pass the boards on their first try: 83
% employed within the first 6 months following graduation: 100
Average starting salary: $32,000

University of Kansas Medical Center
Department of Dietetics & Nutrition
3901 Rainbow Boulevard
Kansas City, KS 66160-7250

Contact Information:
Telephone: 808-956-3847
Fax: 808-956-7096

E-mail: rbarkley@kumc.edu
Web: www.kumc.edu

Program Information:
Program begins: June
Duration of program: 24 months

Application Information:
Transfer students are accepted.

Financial Information:
Tuition, resident: $103
Tuition, non-resident: $338

Kentucky

University of Kentucky

Nutrition and Food Science
204 Funkhouser
Lexington, KY 40506-0054

Contact Information:
Telephone: 713-743-4120
Fax: 713-743-4033
E-mail: vabl@pop.uky.edu
Web: www.uky.edu

Program Information:
Program begins: January
Duration of program: 6 months

Application Information:
Enrollment of program: 8
Transfer students are accepted.

Financial Information:
Tuition, resident: $2,976
Tuition, non-resident: $8,256
Average cost of books: $75
% of students receiving aid: 50

Employment Profile:
% of students who pass the boards on their first try: 100
% employed within the first 6 months following graduation: 94
Average starting salary: $28,000

Western Kentucky University

Consumer & Family Science
Academy Complex 302F
One Big Red Way
Bowling Green, KY 42101-3576

Contact Information:
Telephone: 270-745-4352
Fax: 270-745-3999
E-mail: danita.kelley@wku.edu

Program Information:
Evening or weekend classes are available.

Application Information:
Enrollment of program: 55
Transfer students are accepted.

Financial Information:
Tuition, resident: $1,195
Tuition, non-resident: $3,215

Louisiana

Louisiana State University and A & M College

School of Human Ecology
125 Human Ecology Building
Baton Rouge, LA 70803-4301

Contact Information:
Telephone: 504-388-1537
E-mail: ecross@univl.sncc.lsu.edu

Program Information:
Duration of program: 8 months

Application Information:
Enrollment of program: 6

Financial Information:
Tuition, resident: $2,836
Tuition, non-resident: $7,036

Employment Profile:
% of students who pass the boards on their first try: 100
% employed within the first 6 months following graduation: 100

Louisiana Technical University

School of Human Ecology
PO Box 3167
Ruston, LA 71272

Contact Information:
Telephone: 318-257-3043
Fax: 318-257-4014
E-mail: erickson@hec.latech.edu
Web: www.latech.edu

Program Information:
Program begins: June
Duration of program: 12 months
Evening or weekend classes are available.

Application Information:
Enrollment of program: 20

Financial Information:
Tuition, resident: $3,944
Tuition, non-resident: $9,364
Average cost of books: $330
% of students receiving aid: 58

Employment Profile:
% of students who pass the boards on their first try: 89
% employed within the first 6 months following graduation: 95
Average starting salary: $28,000

McNeese State University

PO Box 92820
Lake Charles, LA 706092820

Contact Information:
Telephone: 318-475-5970
Fax: 318-475-5681
E-mail: dholl205@aol.com
Web: www.mcneese.edu

Program Information:
Program begins: August
Duration of program: 9 months

Application Information:
Enrollment of program: 8

Financial Information:
Tuition, resident: $2,760
Tuition, non-resident: $8,310
Average cost of books: $300
% of students receiving aid: 50

Employment Profile:
% of students who pass the boards on their first try: 97
% employed within the first 6 months following graduation: 100
Average starting salary: $27,000

Southern University and A & M College

PO Box 11342
Baton Rouge, LA 70813-1342

Contact Information:
Telephone: 504-771-4660
Fax: 225-771-4660
E-mail: bmcgee@subr.edu
Web: www.subr.edu

Program Information:
Program begins: August
Evening or weekend classes are available.

Financial Information:
Tuition, resident: $2,761
Tuition, non-resident: $1,104

University of Southwestern Louisiana

School of Human Resources
PO Box 40399
Lafayette, LA 70504-0399

Contact Information:
Telephone: 601-924-9769
E-mail: rmfo931@usl.edu
Web: www.usl.edu

Program Information:
Duration of program: 10 months

Application Information:
Enrollment of program: 175
Transfer students are accepted.

Financial Information:
Tuition, resident: $600
Tuition, non-resident: $800
Average cost of books: $150

Employment Profile:
% of students who pass the boards on their first try: 100
% employed within the first 6 months following graduation: 90
Average starting salary: $30,000

Maryland

National Institutes of Health

Clinic Center Nutrition Department
Building Room BIS-234/10 Center Drive MSC 1078
Bethesda, MD 20892-1078

Contact Information:
Telephone: 301-496-3311
Fax: 301-496-0622
E-mail: dord@nih.gov
Web: www.cc.nih.gov/nutr

Program Information:
Duration of program: 45 months

Sodexho Marriott Services
10500 Little Pataxent Parkway
Suite 620
Columbia, MD 21044

Contact Information:
Telephone: 410-715-1206 ext. 30
Fax: 410-715-1694
E-mail: jldmard@aol.com
Web: www.sodehomarriott.com

Program Information:
Program begins: September
Duration of program: 9 months

Application Information:
Enrollment of program: 10

Financial Information:
Average cost of books: $150

Employment Profile:
% of students who pass the boards on their first try: 95
% employed within the first 6 months following graduation: 100
Average starting salary: $30,000

University of Maryland at College Park
Nutrition & Food Science
College Park, MD 20742-7521

Contact Information:
Telephone: 217-244-2884
E-mail: sc49@umail.umd.edu
Web: www.agnr.umd.edu/users/nfsc/cover.htm

Program Information:
Degrees offered: Bachelor's, 48 months

Financial Information:
Tuition, resident: $4,050
Tuition, non-resident: $10,938

Massachusetts

Boston University
Sargent College
Graduate Nutrition Division
635 Commonwealth Avenue
Boston, MA 02215-1605

Contact Information:
Telephone: 617-353-7470
Fax: 617-353-7567
E-mail: charland@bu.edu
Web: www.bu.edu

Program Information:
Program begins: September
Degrees offered: Master's, 24 months

Application Information:
Enrollment of program: 26

Financial Information:
% of students receiving aid: 75

Framingham State College
Family and Consumer Sciences
100 State Street
Framingham, MA 01701-9101

Contact Information:
Telephone: 508-626-4759
Fax: 508-626-4003
E-mail: pluoto@frc.mass.edu
Web: www.framingham

Program Information:
Degrees offered: Bachelor's, 48 months

Application Information:
Enrollment of program: 142
Transfer students are accepted.

Employment Profile:
% of students who pass the boards on their first try: 92
Average starting salary: $25,000

Simmons College
Department of Nutrition
300 The Fenway
Boston, MA 02115

Contact Information:
Telephone: 617-521-2711
Fax: 617-521-3137
E-mail: herbald@simmons.edu
Web: www.simmons.edu/programs/gshg/gpn/htm

Program Information:
Evening or weekend classes are available.

Application Information:
Enrollment of program: 30
Transfer students are accepted.

Michigan

Andrews University
Department of Nutrition
Berrien Springs, MI 49104-0210

Contact Information:
Telephone: 616-471-3370
Fax: 616-471-3485
E-mail: wcraig@andrews.edu
Web: www.andrews.edu

Program Information:
Program begins: August
Degrees offered: Bachelor's, 44 months; Master's, 24 months
Evening or weekend classes are available.

Application Information:
Enrollment of program: 30
Transfer students are accepted.

Financial Information:
Average cost of books: $400

Employment Profile:
% of students who pass the boards on their first try: 95
% employed within the first 6 months following graduation: 95
Average starting salary: $30,000

Madonna University
Biological and Health Sciences
36600 Schoolcraft Road
Livonia, MI 48150-1173

Contact Information:
Telephone: 734-432-5534
Fax: 734-432-5393
E-mail: schmitz@smtp.munet.edu
Web: www.munet.edu

Program Information:
Degrees offered: Bachelor's, 48 months
Evening or weekend classes are available.

Application Information:
Enrollment of program: 50
Transfer students are accepted.

Financial Information:
% of students receiving aid: 75

Employment Profile:
% of students who pass the boards on their first try: 100

Michigan State University
Food Science & Human Nutrition
236 G. Malcolm Trout
East Lansing, MI 48824-1030

Contact Information:
Telephone: 517-355-6483
Fax: 517-353-1676
E-mail: shcash@pilot.msu.edu
Web: www.msu.edu

Program Information:
Degrees offered: Bachelor's, 48 months

Application Information:
Enrollment of program: 300

Wayne State University
Nutrition & Food Science
3009 Science Hall
Detroit, MI 48202

Contact Information:
Telephone: 313-577-2500
Fax: 313-577-8616
E-mail: treinha@lifesci.wayne.edu
Web: www.wayne.edu

Program Information:
Program begins: September

Degrees offered: Certificate Program; Bachelor's; Master's; PhD
Evening or weekend classes are available.

Application Information:
Enrollment of program: 16
Transfer students are accepted.

Financial Information:
Tuition, resident: $4,000
Tuition, non-resident: $6,400
Average cost of books: $375
% of students receiving aid: 60

Employment Profile:
% of students who pass the boards on their first try: 95
% employed within the first 6 months following graduation: 100
Average starting salary: $32,000
Additional information: Offers both a dietitc program and internship.

Western Michigan University
Family and Consumer Sciences
3024 Kohrman Hall
Kalamazoo, MI 49008

Contact Information:
Telephone: 616-387-3729
Web: www.wmich.edu

Program Information:
Evening or weekend classes are available.

Application Information:
Enrollment of program: 125
Transfer students are accepted.

Financial Information:
Average cost of books: $200

Employment Profile:
% of students who pass the boards on their first try: 98
Average starting salary: $32,500

Minnesota

College of St. Benedict
St. John's University/ Nutrition Department
37 South College Avenue
St. Joseph, MN 56374-2099

Contact Information:
Telephone: 320-363-5057
Fax: 320-363-5582
E-mail: aolson@csbsju.edu
Web: www.csbsju.edu

Program Information:
Duration of program: 32 months

Application Information:
Enrollment of program: 13

Financial Information:
% of students receiving aid: 91

Employment Profile:
% of students who pass the boards on their first try: 90
% employed within the first 6 months following graduation: 60

College of St. Catherine
Family Consumer & Nutrition Science
2004 Randolph Avenue
St. Paul, MN 55105-1750

Contact Information:
Telephone: 651-690-6204
Fax: 651-690-6024
E-mail: peode@stkate.edu
Web: www.stkate.edu

Program Information:
Degrees offered: Bachelor's
Evening or weekend classes are available.

Application Information:
Enrollment of program: 50
Transfer students are accepted.

Employment Profile:
% of students who pass the boards on their first try: 95

Concordia College—Moorhead
Family & Nutrition Sciences
Moorhead, MN 56562

Contact Information:
Telephone: 218-299-3748
Fax: 218-299-4308
E-mail: blarson@cord.edu
Web: www.cord.edu

Program Information:
Program begins: September
Duration of program: 48 months

Application Information:
Enrollment of program: 60

University of Minnesota
269 Food Science & Nutrition
1334 Eckles Avenue
St. Paul, MN 55108-6099

Contact Information:
Telephone: 908-889-2488
E-mail: mhanson@che2.umn.edu
Web: www.umn.edu

Program Information:
Program begins: September
Degrees offered: Diploma, 36 months; Bachelor's, 36 months

Application Information:
Enrollment of program: 20
Transfer students are accepted.

Financial Information:
Tuition, resident: $2,520
Tuition, non-resident: $4,950
Average cost of books: $100

Employment Profile:
% of students who pass the boards on their first try: 98
% employed within the first 6 months following graduation: 100
Average starting salary: $30,000

Mississippi

University of Mississippi
Family and Consumer Sciences
Meek Hall
University, MS 38677

Contact Information:
Telephone: 901-678-2301
E-mail: kknight@olemiss.edu
Web: www.olemiss.edu

Program Information:
Program begins: August

Application Information:
Enrollment of program: 50

Missouri

Central Missouri State University
Human Environmental Sciences
Grinstead 235
Warrensburg, MO 64093

Contact Information:
Telephone: 660-543-4217
Fax: 660-543-8295
E-mail: drake@cmsui.cmsu.edu
Web: www.cmsu.edu

Program Information:
Degrees offered: Bachelor's, 48 months
Evening or weekend classes are available.

Application Information:
Enrollment of program: 200
Transfer students are accepted.

Employment Profile:
% of students who pass the boards on their first try: 95
% employed within the first 6 months following graduation: 95
Average starting salary: $30,000

Southeast Missouri State University
Human Environmental Studies
Cape Girardeau, MO 63701-4799

Contact Information:
Telephone: 573-651-2994
Fax: 573-651-2949
E-mail: mnelms@semovm.semo.edu
Web: www.semo.edu

Program Information:
Program begins: August, January
Degrees offered: Bachelor's, 36 months
Evening or weekend classes are available.

Application Information:
Enrollment of program: 50
Transfer students are accepted.

Employment Profile:
% of students who pass the boards on their first try: 93

Montana

Montana State University
Health and Human Development
201 Romney
Bozeman, MT 59717

Contact Information:
Telephone: 406-994-6338
Fax: 406-994-6314
E-mail: pharris@montana.edu
Web: www.montana.edu

Program Information:
Duration of program: 12 months

Application Information:
Enrollment of program: 80
Transfer students are accepted.

Financial Information:
Tuition, resident: $2,677
Tuition, non-resident: $7,776
Average cost of books: $600

Employment Profile:
% of students who pass the boards on their first try: 98

Nebraska

University of Nebraska—Kearney
Family & Consumer Science
Otto Olsen Building Room 205C
Kearney, NE 68849-2130

Contact Information:
Telephone: 313-936-5199
E-mail: daviss@unk.edu
Web: www.unk.edu

Program Information:
Program begins: August
Duration of program: 48 months
Evening or weekend classes are available.

Application Information:
Enrollment of program: 35
Transfer students are accepted.

Financial Information:
Tuition, resident: $6,700
Tuition, non-resident: $12,550

University of Nebraska—Lincoln
Nutrition Science & Dietetics
202 Ruth Leverton Hall
Lincoln, NE 68583-0806

Contact Information:
Telephone: 612-624-9278
Fax: 612-625-5272
E-mail: lyoung3@unl.edu
Web: www.unl.edu

Application Information:
Enrollment of program: 125

Financial Information:
Tuition, resident: $2,968
Tuition, non-resident: $6,951
Average cost of books: $620
% of students receiving aid: 60

New York

Cornell University
Division of Nutritional Sciences
3MS MVR Hall
Ithaca, NY 14853-4401

Contact Information:
Telephone: 607-255-1354
Fax: 607-255-0178
E-mail: ak53@cornell.edu
Web: www.nutrition.cornell.edul

Program Information:
Program begins: August
Duration of program: 48 months

Application Information:
Enrollment of program: 30
Transfer students are accepted.

Financial Information:
Tuition, resident: $10,330
Tuition, non-resident: $19,830
Average cost of books: $575
% of students receiving aid: 69

Employment Profile:
% of students who pass the boards on their first try: 100

CUNY Brooklyn College
Department of Health and Nutrition Sciences
2900 Bedford Avenue
Brooklyn, NY 11210-2889

Contact Information:
Telephone: 718-951-5909
Fax: 718-951-4670
Web: www.academic.brooklyn.cuny.edu

Program Information:
Program begins: September
Evening or weekend classes are available.

Application Information:
Enrollment of program: 250
Transfer students are accepted.

Employment Profile:
% of students who pass the boards on their first try: 93

CUNY Herbert H. Lehman College
Department of Health Services
Bedford Park Boulevard West
Bronx, NY 10468-1589

Contact Information:
Telephone: 718-960-8084
Fax: 718-960-8908
E-mail: aboyar@lehman.cuny.edu
Web: www.lehman.cuny.edu

Application Information:
Transfer students are accepted.
Additional information:
Offers both a dietetic program and internship.

CUNY Queens College
Family Nutrition and Exercise Sciences
65-30 Kissena Boulevard
Flushing, NY 11367-1597

Contact Information:
Telephone: 718-997-4150
Fax: 718-997-4163
E-mail: mcm$heco@qc1.qc.edu
Web: www.qc.edu

Program Information:
Program begins: September, February
Degrees offered: Bachelor's, 48 months
Evening or weekend classes are available.

Application Information:
Enrollment of program: 300
Transfer students are accepted.

Employment Profile:
Average starting salary: $35,000
Additional information: Offers both a dietitc program and internship.

Long Island University—CW Post Campus
Department of Nutrition
Brookville, NY 11548

Contact Information:
Telephone: 516-299-3046
Fax: 516-299-3106
E-mail: rouderetotam.liu.edu
Web: www.liu.edu

Program Information:
Evening or weekend classes are available.

Employment Profile:
Average starting salary: $33,000

Marymount College
Department of Human Ecology
Marian Hall
Tarrytown, NY 10591

Contact Information:
Telephone: 914-332-6559
E-mail: gezo@mmc.marymt.edu
Web: www.marymt.edu

Program Information:
Degrees offered: Bachelor's, 32 months
Evening or weekend classes are available.

Application Information:
Enrollment of program: 13
Transfer students are accepted.

Financial Information:
Tuition, resident: $14,125
Average cost of books: $600

Employment Profile:
% of students who pass the boards on their first try: 80

New York University
Nutrition and Food Studies
35 West 4th Street, 10th Floor
New York, NY 10012-1120

Contact Information:
Telephone: 212-998-5580
Fax: 212-995-4194
E-mail: nutrition@nyu.edu
Web: www.nyu.edu

Program Information:
Degrees offered: Bachelor's
Evening or weekend classes are available.

Application Information:
Enrollment of program: 85
Transfer students are accepted.

Financial Information:
Tuition, resident: $20,000
Average cost of books: $600
% of students receiving aid: 67

Employment Profile:
% of students who pass the boards on their first try: 90
Average starting salary: $34,000

Russell Sage College
Division of Health & Rehab Sciences
Program in Physical Therapy
Troy, NY 12180

Contact Information:
Telephone: 518-244-2266
Fax: 518-244-4524
Web: www.sage.edu

Program Information:
Program begins: September
Degrees offered: Bachelor's; Master's
Evening or weekend classes are available.

Application Information:
Enrollment of program: 45
Transfer students are accepted.

Financial Information:
Average cost of books: $650
% of students receiving aid: 90

Employment Profile:
% employed within the first 6 months following graduation: 100
Average starting salary: $37,500
Additional information:
BS and MS programs are combined.

SUNY at Stonybrook
Department of Family Medicine
Health Sciences Center Level 4
Stonybrook, NY 11794-8461

Contact Information:
Telephone: 516-444-8246
Fax: 516-444-7552
E-mail: jconnoll@fammed.som.sunysb.edu
Web: www.sunysb.edu

Program Information:
Program begins: September

Financial Information:
Average cost of books: $200

Employment Profile:
% of students who pass the boards on their first try: 88
% employed within the first 6 months following graduation: 80

SUNY College at Buffalo
Nutrition Hospitality & Fashion
1300 Elmwood Avenue
Buffalo, NY 14222-1095

Contact Information:
Telephone: 716-878-4333
Fax: 718-878-5834
E-mail: raot@buffalostate.edu
Web: www.buffalostate.edu

Program Information:
Degrees offered: Bachelor's, 48 months

Application Information:
Enrollment of program: 95
Transfer students are accepted.

Financial Information:
Tuition, resident: $6,800
Average cost of books: $700
% of students receiving aid: 50

Employment Profile:
% of students who pass the boards on their first try: 90
% employed within the first 6 months following graduation: 100

SUNY College at Oneonta
Department of Human Ecology
Oneonta, NY 13820-4015

Contact Information:
Telephone: 607-436-2705
Fax: 607-436-2051
E-mail: haessicj@oneonta.edu
Web: www.oneonta.edu

Program Information:
Program begins: August, January
Degrees offered: Bachelor's, 36 months
Evening or weekend classes are available.

Application Information:
Enrollment of program: 150
Transfer students are accepted.

Financial Information:
Tuition, resident: $3,400
Tuition, non-resident: $8,300
% of students receiving aid: 62

Employment Profile:
% of students who pass the boards on their first try: 90

SUNY College at Plattsburgh
101 Broad Street
Hawkins Hall
Plattsburgh, NY 12901-2681

Contact Information:
Telephone: 518-564-4222
Fax: 518-564-3100
E-mail: jean.coates@plattsburgh.edu

Program Information:
Evening or weekend classes are available.

Application Information:
Transfer students are accepted.

Syracuse University
Nutrition & Foodservice Management
034 Slocum Hall
Syracuse, NY 13244-1250

Contact Information:
Telephone: 315-443-2386
Web: www.syracuse.edu

Program Information:
Program begins: August, May
Degrees offered: Bachelor's, 48 months

Application Information:
Enrollment of program: 20

Financial Information:
Average cost of books: $960
% of students receiving aid: 80

Employment Profile:
% of students who pass the boards on their first try: 88
Average starting salary: $30,000
Additional information:
Offers both a dietitc program and internship.

North Carolina

East Carolina University
Nutrition and Hospitality Management
Greenville, NC 27858-4353

Contact Information:
Telephone: 252-328-1352
Fax: 252-328-4276
E-mail: escottstumps@mail.ecu.edu
Web: www.ecu.edu

Program Information:
Program begins: August
Degrees offered: Post-bachelor's Certificate

Application Information:
Enrollment of program: 22
Transfer students are accepted.

Financial Information:
Tuition, resident: $2,000
Tuition, non-resident: $4,000
Average cost of books: $150

Employment Profile:
% of students who pass the boards on their first try: 90
% employed within the first 6 months following graduation: 90
Average starting salary: $29,000

North Carolina Central University
Department of Human Sciences
PO Box 19615
Durham, NC 27707-0099

Contact Information:
Telephone: 919-530-7439
Fax: 919-530-7983
Web: www.nccu.edu

Program Information:
Program begins: August
Duration of program: 10 months

Financial Information:
Tuition, resident: $2,500
Tuition, non-resident: $9,000
Average cost of books: $500
% of students receiving aid: 60

Employment Profile:
% of students who pass the boards on their first try: 87
% employed within the first 6 months following graduation: 100

Ohio

Bluffton College
Family & Consumer Sciences
280 West College Avenue Box 896
Bluffton, OH 45817-1196

Contact Information:
Telephone: 419-358-3233
Fax: 419-358-3323
E-mail: solteszk@bluffton.edu
Web: www.bluffton.edu

Program Information:
Program begins: August
Duration of program: 48 months

Application Information:
Enrollment of program: 45
Transfer students are accepted.

Employment Profile:
% of students who pass the boards on their first try: 99

Bowling Green State University
Family and Consumer Sciences
206 Johnston Hall
Bowling Green, OH 43403-0254

Contact Information:
Telephone: 419-372-7859
Fax: 419-372-7854
E-mail: ykim@bgnet.bgsu.edu
Web: www.bgsu.edu

Program Information:
Duration of program: 48 months
Evening or weekend classes are available.

Cleveland Veterans Affairs Medical Center
10701 East Boulevard
Cleveland, OH 44106-1702

Contact Information:
Telephone: 216-421-3028
Fax: 216-421-3014
E-mail: anne.raguso@med.va.gov
Web: www.cwru.edu

Program Information:
Program begins: August
Degrees offered: Master's, 16 months

Application Information:
Enrollment of program: 10

Financial Information:
Tuition, resident: $20,800
Average cost of books: $250
% of students receiving aid: 90

Employment Profile:
% of students who pass the boards on their first try: 100
% employed within the first 6 months following graduation: 100
Average starting salary: $40,000

Kent State University
Family & Consumer Studies
Nixon Hall/Nutrition & Dietetics
Kent, OH 44242

Contact Information:
Telephone: 330-672-2197 ext. 2248
Fax: 330-672-2194
E-mail: klowry@kent.edu
Web: www.kent.edu

Program Information:
Degrees offered: Bachelor's, 48 months
Evening or weekend classes are available.

Application Information:
Enrollment of program: 120
Transfer students are accepted.

Employment Profile:
% of students who pass the boards on their first try: 95

Miami University
Physical Education Health & Sports Studies
150 Phillips Hall
Oxford, OH 45056

Contact Information:
Telephone: 513-529-5036
Fax: 513-529-5036
E-mail: rudgesj@muohio.edu
Web: www.muohio.edu

Program Information:
Degrees offered: Bachelor's, 48 months

Application Information:
Enrollment of program: 120
Transfer students are accepted.

Financial Information:
Tuition, resident: $2,741
Tuition, non-resident: $5,091
Average cost of books: $668

Employment Profile:
% of students who pass the boards on their first try: 98
% employed within the first 6 months following graduation: 80
Average starting salary: $27,000

Ohio State University
School of Allied Medical Professions
1583 Perry Street
Columbus, OH 43210-1234

Contact Information:
Telephone: 614-292-0635
Fax: 614-292-0210
E-mail: schiller.1@osu.edu
Web: www.amp.ohio-state.edu

Program Information:
Program begins: September
Duration of program: 36 months

Application Information:
Enrollment of program: 60
Transfer students are accepted.

Financial Information:
Average cost of books: $800

Employment Profile:
% of students who pass the boards on their first try: 100
% employed within the first 6 months following graduation: 100
Average starting salary: $32,000

Ohio University
Human and Consumer Sciences
101 A. Tupper Hall
Athens, OH 45701-2979

Contact Information:
Telephone: 740-593-2874
Fax: 740-593-0289
E-mail: hagerman@ohio.edu
Web: www.cats.ohiou.edu

Program Information:
Program begins: September, June
Degrees offered: Bachelor's
Evening or weekend classes are available.

Application Information:
Transfer students are accepted.

Financial Information:
Tuition, resident: $6,040
Tuition, non-resident: $12,708

Employment Profile:
% of students who pass the boards on their first try: 100

University of Akron
School of Family and Consumer Science
215 Schrank Hall South
Akron, OH 44325-6103

Contact Information:
Telephone: 301-405-4532
Fax: 301-314-9327
E-mail: sue@uakron.edu
Web: www.uakron.edu

Program Information:
Program begins: September
Degrees offered: Certificate Program, 32 months; Bachelor's, 32 months

Application Information:
Enrollment of program: 50
Transfer students are accepted.

Financial Information:
Tuition, resident: $3,800
Tuition, non-resident: $6,595
Average cost of books: $500
% of students receiving aid: 50

Employment Profile:
% of students who pass the boards on their first try: 100
Additional information: Offers both a dietitc program and internship.

University of Cincinnati
Dietetics and Nutrition Education French Building
PO Box 670394/364
Cincinnati, OH 45267-0394

Contact Information:
Telephone: 501-575-4305
Fax: 501-575-7171
E-mail: ritasmith@uc.edu
Web: www.oz.uc.edu/chcp

Program Information:
Duration of program: 48 months

Application Information:
Enrollment of program: 110
Transfer students are accepted.

Financial Information:
Tuition, resident: $3,320
Tuition, non-resident: $8,586
Average cost of books: $600

Employment Profile:
% of students who pass the boards on their first try: 100

Youngstown State University
One University Plaza
Youngstown, OH 44555-0001

Contact Information:
Telephone: 330-742-1822
Fax: 330-742-1824
E-mail: jhassel@cc.ysu.edu
Web: www.ysu.edu

Program Information:
Program begins: August
Degrees offered: Bachelor's, 49 months
Evening or weekend classes are available.

Application Information:
Enrollment of program: 24
Transfer students are accepted.

Financial Information:
Tuition, resident: $3,800
Tuition, non-resident: $6,800
Average cost of books: $300
% of students receiving aid: 75

Employment Profile:
% of students who pass the boards on their first try: 90
% employed within the first 6 months following graduation: 80
Average starting salary: $28,000

Oklahoma

Langston University
Department of Home Ecology
302 Jones Hall
Langston, OK 73050

Contact Information:
Telephone: 405-466-3337
Fax: 405-466-3364
E-mail: ssangiah@lunet.edu
Web: www.lunet.edu

Program Information:
Program begins: September
Degrees offered: Bachelor's, 36 months

Application Information:
Transfer students are accepted.

Financial Information:
Tuition, resident: $2,000
Tuition, non-resident: $4,190
Average cost of books: $800

Employment Profile:
% of students who pass the boards on their first try: 70
% employed within the first 6 months following graduation: 80
Average starting salary: $30,000

University of Central Oklahoma
College of Education
Human Environmental Sciences
Edmond, OK 73034

Contact Information:
Telephone: 602-621-1449
E-mail: vknotts@ucok.edu
Web: www.educ.ucok.edu

Program Information:
Program begins: July, January
Duration of program: 12 months
Evening or weekend classes are available.

Application Information:
Enrollment of program: 18

Financial Information:
Tuition, resident: $2,604
Tuition, non-resident: $4,784
Average cost of books: $500
% of students receiving aid: 90

Employment Profile:
% of students who pass the boards on their first try: 99
% employed within the first 6 months following graduation: 100
Average starting salary: $32,000

University of Oklahoma Health Sciences Center
Department of Nutritional Sciences
PO Box 26910 CHB
Oklahoma City, OK 73190

Contact Information:
Telephone: 319-273-6007
Fax: 319-273-7096
E-mail: marinell-guild@ ouhsc.edu
Web: www.ouhsc.edu

Program Information:
Program begins: September
Duration of program: 24 months

Application Information:
Enrollment of program: 32

Employment Profile:
% of students who pass the boards on their first try: 95
% employed within the first 6 months following graduation: 100
Average starting salary: $30,000

Oregon

Oregon State University
Nutrition and Food Management
14B Milam Hall
Corvallis, OR 97331-5103

Contact Information:
Telephone: 541-737-0960
Fax: 541-737-6914
E-mail: cluskeym@orst.edu
Web: www.nfm.orst.edu

Program Information:
Program begins: September
Duration of program: 48 months

Application Information:
Enrollment of program: 130

Pennsylvania

Edinboro University of Pennsylvania
Biology and Health Services
Edinboro, PA 16444

Contact Information:
Telephone: 814-732-2447
Fax: 814-732-2422
E-mail: lanz@edinboro.edu
Web: www.edinboro.edu

Program Information:
Degrees offered: Bachelor's, 32 months
Evening or weekend classes are available.

Application Information:
Enrollment of program: 30
Transfer students are accepted.

Financial Information:
Tuition, resident: $3,468
Tuition, non-resident: $5,202
Average cost of books: $450

Employment Profile:
% of students who pass the boards on their first try: 95
% employed within the first 6 months following graduation: 100
Average starting salary: $30,000

Indiana University of Pennsylvania
Department of Food & Nutrition
10 Ackerman Hall
Indiana, PA 15705-1087

Contact Information:
Telephone: 724-357-4440
Fax: 724-357-7582
E-mail: jsteiner@grove.iup.edu
Web: www.hhs.iup.edu

Program Information:
Program begins: August
Evening or weekend classes are available.

Application Information:
Enrollment of program: 150

Mansfield University
203C Elliott Hall
Department of Health Sciences
Mansfield, PA 16933

Contact Information:
Telephone: 570-662-4628
Fax: 570-662-4111
E-mail: kwright@mnsfld.edu
Web: www.mnsfld.edu

Program Information:
Program begins: August, January
Degrees offered: Bachelor's, 48 months
Evening or weekend classes are available.

Application Information:
Enrollment of program: 38
Transfer students are accepted.

Financial Information:
Tuition, resident: $3,468
Tuition, non-resident: $8,824
Average cost of books: $750
% of students receiving aid: 80

Employment Profile:
% of students who pass the boards on their first try: 93
% employed within the first 6 months following graduation: 80
Average starting salary: $24,000

Marywood University
Department of Nutrition and Dietetics
2300 Adams Avenue
Scranton, PA 18509-1598

Contact Information:
Telephone: 570-348-6277
Fax: 570-340-6029
E-mail: nutrition@ac.marywood.edu
Web: www.marywood.edu

Program Information:
Program begins: July
Degrees offered: Bachelor's, 36 months; Master's
Evening or weekend classes are available.

Application Information:
Transfer students are accepted.

Employment Profile:
% of students who pass the boards on their first try: 91

Messiah College
Department of Natural Sciences
Grantham, PA 17027

Contact Information:
Telephone: 717-766-2511 ext. 2430
Fax: 717-691-6046
E-mail: mmihok@messiah.edu
Web: www.messiah.edu

Program Information:
Program begins: August
Degrees offered: Bachelor's, 36 months

Application Information:
Enrollment of program: 50
Transfer students are accepted.

Employment Profile:
% of students who pass the boards on their first try: 100
% employed within the first 6 months following graduation: 100

Seton Hill College
College Drive
Greensburg, PA 15601

Contact Information:
Telephone: 724-830-1045
Fax: 724-830-4611
E-mail: sandrick@setonhill.edu
Web: www.setonhill.edu

Program Information:
Program begins: August
Degrees offered: Certificate Program; Post-bachelor's Certificate, 48 months
Evening or weekend classes are available.

Application Information:
Enrollment of program: 12
Transfer students are accepted.

Financial Information:
Average cost of books: $250
% of students receiving aid: 100

Employment Profile:
% of students who pass the boards on their first try: 86
% employed within the first 6 months following graduation: 100
Average starting salary: $28,000
Additional information:
Offers both a dietitc program and internship.

West Chester University
Department of Health
#302 Sturtzebecker Health Sciences Center
West Chester, PA 19383

Contact Information:
Telephone: 610-436-2655
Fax: 610-436-2860
E-mail: jharris@wcupa.edu
Web: www.wcupa.edu

Program Information:
Degrees offered: Bachelor's, 48 months

Application Information:
Enrollment of program: 80
Transfer students are accepted.

Financial Information:
Tuition, resident: $3,468
Tuition, non-resident: $8,824
Average cost of books: $400
% of students receiving aid: 60

Employment Profile:
% of students who pass the boards on their first try: 70
% employed within the first 6 months following graduation: 99
Average starting salary: $30,000

Rhode Island

University of Rhode Island
Food Science & Nutrition
110 Ranger Hall
Kingston, RI 02881-0804

Contact Information:
Telephone: 809-763-6599
E-mail: cathy@uri.edu
Web: www.uri.edu

Program Information:
Program begins: September, January
Degrees offered: Bachelor's, 48 months; Master's, 24 months; PhD, 36 months

Application Information:
Transfer students are accepted.

Financial Information:
Tuition, resident: $3,372
Tuition, non-resident: $11,592
Average cost of books: $700

Employment Profile:
% of students who pass the boards on their first try: 90

South Carolina

Clemson University
Department of Food Science
223 Poole, Agricultural Center
Clemson, SC 29634-0371

Contact Information:
Telephone: 864-656-5690
Web: www.clemson.edu/foodscience

Program Information:
Degrees offered: Bachelor's, 48 months; Master's, 24 months; PhD, 48 months

Application Information:
Enrollment of program: 60
Transfer students are accepted.

Financial Information:
Average cost of books: $600

Employment Profile:
% of students who pass the boards on their first try: 100
% employed within the first 6 months following graduation: 100

Medical University of South Carolina

PO Box 250602
96 Jonathon Lucas
Charleston, SC 29425

Contact Information:
Telephone: 843-792-1454
Fax: 843-792-6486
E-mail: milkerjr/2musc.edu

Program Information:
Program begins: August
Duration of program: 10 months

Application Information:
Enrollment of program: 6

Financial Information:
Tuition, resident: $175
Tuition, non-resident: $225
Average cost of books: $75

Employment Profile:
% of students who pass the boards on their first try: 100
% employed within the first 6 months following graduation: 75
Average starting salary: $28,000

Winthrop University

Department of Human Nutrition
Rock Hill, SC 29733

Contact Information:
Telephone: 803-323-4520
Fax: 803-323-2254
E-mail: wolmanp@winthrop.edu
Web: www.winthrop.edu/nutrition

Program Information:
Program begins: August, January, May
Degrees offered: Bachelor's, 48 months; Master's, 24 months; Post-bachelor's Certificate
Evening or weekend classes are available.

Application Information:
Enrollment of program: 70
Transfer students are accepted.

Financial Information:
Tuition, resident: $3,800
Tuition, non-resident: $7,840
Average cost of books: $800
% of students receiving aid: 24

Employment Profile:
% of students who pass the boards on their first try: 92
% employed within the first 6 months following graduation: 99
Average starting salary: $30,000

South Dakota

South Dakota State University

Family and Consumer Sciences
PO Box 2275A
Brookings, SD 57007-0497

Contact Information:
Telephone: 605-688-5161 ext. 4045
Fax: 605-688-5603
E-mail: kendra_kattelmann@sdstate.edu
Web: www.sdstate.edu

Program Information:
Program begins: September, January
Degrees offered: Bachelor's, 48 months; Master's, 24 months

Application Information:
Enrollment of program: 60
Transfer students are accepted.

Financial Information:
Tuition, resident: $1,850
Tuition, non-resident: $5,400
Average cost of books: $700
% of students receiving aid: 85

Employment Profile:
% of students who pass the boards on their first try: 90
% employed within the first 6 months following graduation: 100
Average starting salary: $25,000

University of South Dakota

School of Medicine
414 East Clark Street
Vermillion, SD 57069-2390

Contact Information:
Telephone: 401-874-5869
E-mail: gjohanns@usd.edu
Web: www.usd.edu

Program Information:
Program begins: August
Duration of program: 10 months

Application Information:
Enrollment of program: 4
Transfer students are accepted.

Financial Information:
Tuition, resident: $443
Tuition, non-resident: $1,306
% of students receiving aid: 10

Employment Profile:
% of students who pass the boards on their first try: 94
% employed within the first 6 months following graduation: 95
Average starting salary: $23,000

Tennessee

Carson-Newman College

PO Box 71881
Jefferson City, TN 37760-7001

Contact Information:
Telephone: 423-471-3295
Fax: 423-471-3502
E-mail: coffey@cncacc.edu
Web: www.cn.edu

Program Information:
Program begins: August, January
Duration of program: 48 months
Evening or weekend classes are available.

Application Information:
Enrollment of program: 12
Transfer students are accepted.

Financial Information:
Average cost of books: $300
% of students receiving aid: 85

David Lipscomb University

Family & Consumer Sciences
3901 Granny White Pike
Nashville, TN 37204-3951

Contact Information:
Telephone: 615-279-5767
Fax: 615-269-1808
E-mail: nancy.huntdlipscomb.edu
Web: www.lipscomb.edu

Program Information:
Program begins: September
Degrees offered: Bachelor's, 40 months

Application Information:
Enrollment of program: 40
Transfer students are accepted.

Financial Information:
Average cost of books: $300

Employment Profile:
% of students who pass the boards on their first try: 85
% employed within the first 6 months following graduation: 80
Average starting salary: $30,000

East Tennessee State University

Applied Human Sciences
PO Box 70671
Johnson City, TN 37614-0671

Contact Information:
Telephone: 423-439-7532
Fax: 423-439-7539
E-mail: verhegge@etsu.edu
Web: www.etsu.edu

Program Information:
Degrees offered: Bachelor's, 48 months; Master's, 24 months

Application Information:
Enrollment of program: 65
Transfer students are accepted.

Financial Information:
Tuition, resident: $1,906
Average cost of books: $500

Employment Profile:
% of students who pass the boards on their first try: 90
% employed within the first 6 months following graduation: 80
Average starting salary: $20,000
Additional information:
Offers both a dietitc program and internship.

Middle Tennessee State University

Department of Human Sciences
PO Box 86
Murfreesboro, TN 37133-0086

Contact Information:
Telephone: 615-898-2091
Fax: 615-898-5130
E-mail: dewalker@mtsu.edu
Web: www.mtsu.edu

Program Information:
Evening or weekend classes are available.

Application Information:
Enrollment of program: 110
Transfer students are accepted.

National HealthCare Corporation

PO Box 1398
Murfreesboro, TN 37133-1398

Contact Information:
Telephone: 615-890-2020
Fax: 615-890-0123

Program Information:
Program begins: August
Duration of program: 10 months

Application Information:
Enrollment of program: 10

Financial Information:
Tuition, resident: $400
Tuition, non-resident: $1,000
% of students receiving aid: 60

Employment Profile:
% of students who pass the boards on their first try: 98
% employed within the first 6 months following graduation: 90
Average starting salary: $28,000

Tennessee State University

Family Consumer Sciences
PO Box 9598
3500 John A. Merritt Boulevard
Nashville, TN 37209-1561

Contact Information:
Telephone: 615-963-5619
Fax: 615-963-5033
E-mail: godwin@acad.tristate.edu
Web: www.tristate.edu

Application Information:
Enrollment of program: 20
Transfer students are accepted.

Financial Information:
Average cost of books: $400
% of students receiving aid: 90

Employment Profile:
% of students who pass the boards on their first try: 100
% employed within the first 6 months following graduation: 80
Average starting salary: $28,000

Tennessee Technological University

School of Home Economics
Box 5035
Cookeville, TN 38505

Contact Information:
Telephone: 615-372-3376
Fax: 931-372-3376
Web: www.tntech.edu

Program Information:
Program begins: August
Duration of program: 10 months
Evening or weekend classes are available.

Application Information:
Enrollment of program: 45
Transfer students are accepted.

Financial Information:
Tuition, resident: $953
Tuition, non-resident: $3,366
Average cost of books: $600
% of students receiving aid: 60

Employment Profile:
% of students who pass the boards on their first try: 100
% employed within the first 6 months following graduation: 100
Average starting salary: $26,000

University of Tennessee—Chattanooga

Department of Human Ecology
202 Hunter Hall
Chattanooga, TN 37403

Contact Information:
Telephone: 318-482-5724
E-mail: patricia-garrett@utc.edu
Web: www.utc.edu

Program Information:
Degrees offered: Bachelor's, 48 months
Evening or weekend classes are available.

Application Information:
Enrollment of program: 45
Transfer students are accepted.

Financial Information:
Tuition, resident: $2,660
Tuition, non-resident: $7,920
Average cost of books: $600
% of students receiving aid: 65

Employment Profile:
% of students who pass the boards on their first try: 85

Texas

Abilene Christian University

Family & Consumer Sciences
ACU Box 28155
Abilene, TX 79699

Contact Information:
Telephone: 915-674-2089
Fax: 915-674-2086
E-mail: joness@acu.edu
Web: www.acu.edu

Program Information:
Degrees offered: Bachelor's, 48 months
Evening or weekend classes are available.

Application Information:
Enrollment of program: 25

Baylor University

Family and Consumer Sciences
BU Box 97346
Waco, TX 76798-7346

Contact Information:
Telephone: 254-710-6258
Fax: 254-710-3629
E-mail: luann_soliah@baylor.edu
Web: www.baylor.edu

Program Information:
Program begins: August, January
Degrees offered: Bachelor's, 48 months

Application Information:
Enrollment of program: 53
Transfer students are accepted.

Financial Information:
Average cost of books: $550
% of students receiving aid: 50

Employment Profile:
% of students who pass the boards on their first try: 90
Average starting salary: $28,000

Baylor University Medical Center

3500 Gaston Avenue
Dallas, TX 75246-2045

Contact Information:
Telephone: 214-820-4019
Fax: 214-820-2263
Web: www.baylorhealth.com

Program Information:
Duration of program: 10 months

Employment Profile:
% of students who pass the boards on their first try: 100

Presbyterian Hospital of Dallas

8200 Walnut Hill Lane
Dallas, TX 75231-4402

Contact Information:
Telephone: 214-345-7558

Financial Information:
Average cost of books: $510

Employment Profile:
% of students who pass the boards on their first try: 94
% employed within the first 6 months following graduation: 100
Average starting salary: $25,000

Sam Houston State University

Food Science & Nutrition
Huntsville, TX 77341

Contact Information:
Telephone: 409-294-1242
Fax: 409-294-4204
E-mail: hec_zak@shsu.edu
Web: www.shsu.edu

Program Information:
Degrees offered: Bachelor's, 48 months

Application Information:
Enrollment of program: 35
Transfer students are accepted.

Financial Information:
Tuition, resident: $2,068
Tuition, non-resident: $7,252
Average cost of books: $600
% of students receiving aid: 20

Employment Profile:
% of students who pass the boards on their first try: 100
% employed within the first 6 months following graduation: 100
Average starting salary: $29,000

Southwest Texas State University

Family & Consumer Sciences
601 University Drive
San Marcos, TX 78666-4616

Contact Information:
Telephone: 512-245-2482
Fax: 512-245-3829
Web: www.swt.edu

Program Information:
Program begins: September

Application Information:
Enrollment of program: 8

Financial Information:
Average cost of books: $250

Employment Profile:
% of students who pass the boards on their first try: 100
% employed within the first 6 months following graduation: 95
Average starting salary: $32,000

Stephen F. Austin State University

Department of Human Sciences
SFA Station 13014
Nacogdoches, TX 75962-3014

Contact Information:
Telephone: 409-468-2060
Fax: 409-468-2140
E-mail: sweems@sfasu.edu
Web: www.sfasu.edu

Program Information:
Degrees offered: Bachelor's, 48 months; Master's, 24 months
Evening or weekend classes are available.

Application Information:
Enrollment of program: 70
Transfer students are accepted.

Financial Information:
% of students receiving aid: 70

Employment Profile:
% of students who pass the boards on their first try: 90
% employed within the first 6 months following graduation: 99
Average starting salary: $28,000

Tarleton State University

Department of Human Sciences
Mailstop TO380
Stephenville, TX 76402

Contact Information:
Telephone: 254-968-9196
Fax: 254-968-9728
E-mail: arichmond@tarleton.edu
Web: www.tarleton.edu

Program Information:
Program begins: August
Degrees offered: Bachelor's, 48 months
Evening or weekend classes are available.

Application Information:
Enrollment of program: 15
Transfer students are accepted.

Financial Information:
Tuition, resident: $1,953
Tuition, non-resident: $2,268
Average cost of books: $700
% of students receiving aid: 75

Employment Profile:
% of students who pass the boards on their first try: 80
% employed within the first 6 months following graduation: 99
Average starting salary: $28,000

Texas A & M University

Department of Animal Science
Human Nutrition Section
College Station, TX 77843-2471

Contact Information:
Telephone: 409-845-2142
Fax: 409-862-2378
E-mail: kkubena@tamu.edu
Web: www.tamu.edu

Application Information:
Enrollment of program: 200
Transfer students are accepted.

Financial Information:
Tuition, resident: $5,016
Tuition, non-resident: $32,868

Employment Profile:
% of students who pass the boards on their first try: 97

Texas A & M University—Kingsville

Department of Human Sciences
Campus Box 168
Kingsville, TX 78363

Contact Information:
Telephone: 361-593-2212
Fax: 361-593-2230
E-mail: l-appelt@tamuk.edu
Web: www.tamuk.edu/aghs

Application Information:
Enrollment of program: 50

Texas Christian University

Department of Nutrition & Dietetics
Box 298600
Ft. Worth, TX 76129

Contact Information:
Telephone: 817-257-7309
Fax: 817-257-5849
E-mail: a.vanbeber@tcu.edu
Web: www.nut.tcu.edu/nutl

Program Information:
Program begins: August
Duration of program: 24 months

Application Information:
Enrollment of program: 24
Transfer students are accepted.

Employment Profile:
% of students who pass the boards on their first try: 91
% employed within the first 6 months following graduation: 75
Average starting salary: $25,000

Texas Woman's University

Nutrition & Food Sciences
TWU Station 425888
Denton, TX 76204-5888

Contact Information:
Telephone: 940-898-2636
Fax: 940-898-2634
Web: www.twu.edu/hs/nfs

Program Information:
Degrees offered: Bachelor's, 48 months; Master's, 30 months; PhD, 40 months
Evening or weekend classes are available.

Application Information:
Enrollment of program: 130
Transfer students are accepted.

Financial Information:
Average cost of books: $500
% of students receiving aid: 50

Employment Profile:
% of students who pass the boards on their first try: 97
% employed within the first 6 months following graduation: 90
Average starting salary: $25,000

University of Houston
Human Development and Consumer Science
4800 Calhoun Road
Houston, TX 772046861

Contact Information:
Telephone: 513-558-4542
E-mail: scoscro@bayou.uh.edu
Web: www.tech.uh.edu

Program Information:
Program begins: August, January
Evening or weekend classes are available.

University of Texas—Pan American
College of Health & Human Services
1201 West University Drive
Edinburg, TX 78539-2909

Contact Information:
Telephone: 423-755-4550
Fax: 423-755-4479
E-mail: ebriones@panam.edu
Web: www.panam.edu

Program Information:
Program begins: September
Degrees offered: Bachelor's, 48 months

Application Information:
Enrollment of program: 15
Transfer students are accepted.

Financial Information:
Tuition, resident: $4,132
Tuition, non-resident: $17,864
Average cost of books: $900
% of students receiving aid: 74

Employment Profile:
% of students who pass the boards on their first try: 70
% employed within the first 6 months following graduation: 100
Average starting salary: $29,500

University of Texas Southwestern Medical Center—Dallas
Department of Clinical Nutrition
5323 Harry Hines Boulevard
Dallas, TX 75235-8877

Contact Information:
Telephone: 713-500-9347
E-mail: clindiet@email.swmed.edu
Web: www.swmed.edu

Program Information:
Program begins: May
Degrees offered: Bachelor's, 21 months

Application Information:
Enrollment of program: 27
Transfer students are accepted.

Financial Information:
Tuition, resident: $1,140
Tuition, non-resident: $7,620
Average cost of books: $1,180

Employment Profile:
% of students who pass the boards on their first try: 98
% employed within the first 6 months following graduation: 80

University of the Incarnate Word
4301 Broadway Street
San Antonio, TX 78209-6318

Contact Information:
Telephone: 210-829-3167
Fax: 210-829-3153
E-mail: morse@universe.uiwtx.edu
Web: www.uiw.edu

Program Information:
Duration of program: 48 months
Evening or weekend classes are available.

Utah

Brigham Young University
Food Science and Nutrition
S-221 ESC
Provo, UT 846021041

Contact Information:
Telephone: 801-378-3912
Fax: 801-378-8714
E-mail: nora-nyland@byu.edu
Web: www.byu.edu

Program Information:
Program begins: August
Duration of program: 24 months

Application Information:
Enrollment of program: 40
Transfer students are accepted.

Financial Information:
Tuition, resident: $2,830
Tuition, non-resident: $4,250
Average cost of books: $600

Employment Profile:
% of students who pass the boards on their first try: 100

Vermont

University of Vermont
Department of Nutrition and Food Sciences
Terrill Hall
Burlington, VT 05405

Contact Information:
Telephone: 802-656-0539
E-mail: jross@zoo.uvm.edu
Web: www.uvm.edu

Program Information:
Program begins: August, January
Degrees offered: Bachelor's, 48 months; Master's, 24 months
Evening or weekend classes are available.

Application Information:
Enrollment of program: 160
Transfer students are accepted.

Financial Information:
Tuition, resident: $7,464
Tuition, non-resident: $18,672
Average cost of books: $628
% of students receiving aid: 55

Employment Profile:
% of students who pass the boards on their first try: 99

Virginia

James Madison University
Department of Health Sciences MSC 1202
Moody Hall 213A
Harrisonburg, VA 22807

Contact Information:
Telephone: 540-568-6362
Fax: 540-568-8166
E-mail: brevarpb@jmu.edu
Web: www.jmu.edu

Program Information:
Program begins: August, January
Duration of program: 48 months

Application Information:
Enrollment of program: 100
Transfer students are accepted.

Virginia Commonwealth University/ Medical College of VA Campus
PO Box 980294
Richmond, VA 23298-0294

Contact Information:
Telephone: 804-828-9108
Fax: 804-828-9108
E-mail: aerobbin@hsu.vcu.edu
Web: www.views.vcu.edu/dietetic

Program Information:
Program begins: August, January
Duration of program: 11 months

Financial Information:
Tuition, resident: $1,200

Employment Profile:
% of students who pass the boards on their first try: 100
% employed within the first 6 months following graduation: 100

Virginia State University
Department of Human Ecology
PO Box 9211
Petersburg, VA 23806

Contact Information:
Telephone: 804-524-5502

Fax: 804-524-5561
E-mail: gyoung@vsu.edu
Web: www.vsu.edu

Program Information:
Degrees offered: Certificate Program, 7 months; Bachelor's, 48 months
Evening or weekend classes are available.

Application Information:
Enrollment of program: 8

Financial Information:
Average cost of books: $150

Employment Profile:
% of students who pass the boards on their first try: 81
% employed within the first 6 months following graduation: 95
Average starting salary: $28,000
Additional information:
Offers both a dietitc program and internship.

Washington

University of Washington
305 Raitt Hall
Box 353410
Seattle, WA 981953410

Contact Information:
Telephone: 206-616-7362
Fax: 206-685-1696
E-mail: bbruemme@u.washington.edu
Web: www.washington.edu

Program Information:
Program begins: September
Degrees offered: Master's, 25 months; PhD, 48 months

Application Information:
Enrollment of program: 45
Transfer students are accepted.

Financial Information:
Tuition, resident: $7,232
Tuition, non-resident: $17,960
Average cost of books: $900
% of students receiving aid: 40

Employment Profile:
% of students who pass the boards on their first try: 100
% employed within the first 6 months following graduation: 100
Average starting salary: $40,000
Additional information:
Offers both a dietitc program and internship.

Washington State University
Food Science & Human Nutrition
Pullman, WA 99164-6376

Contact Information:
Telephone: 509-335-8448
Fax: 509-358-7505
E-mail: msandall@mail.wsu.edu
Web: www.wsu.edu

Program Information:
Program begins: June
Duration of program: 6 months

Application Information:
Enrollment of program: 6

Financial Information:
Tuition, resident: $2,774
Tuition, non-resident: $6,958
Average cost of books: $140

Employment Profile:
% of students who pass the boards on their first try: 75
% employed within the first 6 months following graduation: 75
Average starting salary: $26,000

Wisconsin

Mt. Mary College
Department of Dietetics
2900 North Menomonee River Parkway
Milwaukee, WI 532224545

Contact Information:
Telephone: 414-256-1216 ext. 359
Fax: 414-256-1224
Web: www.mtmary.edu

Application Information:
Enrollment of program: 65

University of Wisconsin—Madison
Department of Nutritional Sciences
1415 Linden Drive
Madison, WI 53706-1571

Contact Information:
Telephone: 608-262-5847
Fax: 608-262-5860
E-mail: karls@nutrisci.wisc.edu
Web: www.wisc.edu

Program Information:
Degrees offered: Bachelor's, 48 months

Application Information:
Enrollment of program: 12
Transfer students are accepted.

Financial Information:
Tuition, resident: $3,730
Tuition, non-resident: $13,050
Average cost of books: $620

Employment Profile:
% of students who pass the boards on their first try: 98
% employed within the first 6 months following graduation: 95
Average starting salary: $35,000
Additional information: Offers both a dietitc program and internship.

University of Wisconsin—Stevens Point
Health Promotion & Human Development
Stevens Point, WI 54481

Contact Information:
Telephone: 715-346-4087
Fax: 715-346-3751
E-mail: jchithar@uwsp.edu
Web: www.guwsp.edu

Program Information:
Degrees offered: Bachelor's; Master's

Application Information:
Enrollment of program: 100
Transfer students are accepted.

Financial Information:
Average cost of books: $100

University of Wisconsin—Stout
College of Human Development Dietetics
Menomonie, WI 54751

Contact Information:
Telephone: 715-232-2216
Fax: 715-232-2317
E-mail: seabornc@uwstout.edu
Web: www.uwstout.edu

Program Information:
Program begins: September, January, May
Degrees offered: Bachelor's, 30 months
Evening or weekend classes are available.

Application Information:
Enrollment of program: 140
Transfer students are accepted.

Financial Information:
Tuition, resident: $1,629
Tuition, non-resident: $5,061
% of students receiving aid: 75

Employment Profile:
% of students who pass the boards on their first try: 90
% employed within the first 6 months following graduation: 100
Average starting salary: $28,000

Viterbo College
Nutrition and Dietetics Department
815 South 9th Street
La Crosse, WI 54601-4797

Contact Information:
Telephone: 608-796-3660
Fax: 608-796-3050
E-mail: klewis@viterbo.edu
Web: www.viterbo.edu/academic/gr/dietintern

Program Information:
Duration of program: 11 months

Application Information:
Enrollment of program: 10

Financial Information:
Average cost of books: $150

Employment Profile:
% of students who pass the boards on their first try: 89
% employed within the first 6 months following graduation: 20
Average starting salary: $28,000

Dietetic Technician

Jeffrey E. Harris, DrPH, MPH, CNS, RD
Associate Professor and Dietetics Program Director
Department of Health
West Chester University
West Chester, Pennsylvania

Job Description

What Do They Do?

A DT is a trained food and nutrition professional who can help provide cost-effective patient care. DTs promote health through proper nutrition by providing personalized services to meet the patient's needs, and ensure balanced diets through the provision of wholesome, quality food. They work under the direction of dietitians to provide food service administration and nutrition services in healthcare and other facilities. They are responsible for:

- taking diet histories from patients
- screening patients for nutritional status
- developing menus and standard recipes
- calculating special diets
- maintaining standards of safety and sanitation
- teaching nutrition

Additional duties of DTs may include:

- supervising food production
- planning nutritional programs based on evaluations of patients' dietary histories
- counseling individuals and families about food selection, preparation, and menu planning[1]

Type of Person

DTs must be able to understand and use standard recipes and menus. In addition, they need mathematical skills to measure ingredients accurately and to modify recipes. They need to have knowledge of basic nutrition and of state and local health regulations. DTs must have the physical coordination and endurance necessary to operate kitchen machinery and to stand and walk for long periods. Heavy lifting may also be required. DTs should enjoy working with people and should have a strong interest in food and nutrition. In addition, DTs should possess good judgment, an understanding of human nature, the motivation and initiative to work independently, and the ability to identify and solve problems.

With Whom Do They Work?

DTs work under the supervision of dietitians. They also work with physicians and other health professionals (respiratory therapists, physical therapists, and nurses) as well as social workers, psychologists, and food service directors.

Employment

Places of Employment

DTs work independently or in teams with registered dietitians in a variety of employment settings, including healthcare, business and industry, public health, food service, and research. A DT may do any of the following:

- Administer medical nutrition therapy as a part of the healthcare team at hospitals, clinics, nursing homes, retirement centers, hospices, home healthcare programs, and research facilities.
- Manage employees, purchase items, and prepare food and budgets within food service operations at schools, day-care centers, correctional facilities, restaurants, healthcare facilities, corporations, and hospitals.
- Work for the special supplemental food program for Women, Infants, and Children (WIC), public health agencies, and Meals on Wheels.
- Educate clients about the connections among food, fitness, and health at health clubs, weight management clinics, and community wellness centers.
- Develop menus, oversee food service sanitation and food safety, prepare food abeling information and perform nutrient analysis for food companies, contract food management companies, or food vending and distributing operations.

Employment Outlook

The job market for registered DTs is similar to that for dietitians and nutritionists. According to the U.S. Bureau of Labor Statistics, employment of dietitians and nutritionists is expected to grow about as fast as the average for all occupations through the year 2005 because of increased emphasis on disease prevention, a growing and aging population, and increased public interest in nutrition. Employment in hospitals is expected to show little change. There will be an increase in the number of jobs in nursing homes, residential care facilities, and physician clinics.[2]

Salary

The most recent salary data was collected in 1997. According to the ADA's 1997 Membership Database, among entry-level registered DTs employed full-time five years or less in their primary position, 63 percent reported incomes between $20,001 and $30,000, and 15 percent earned between $30,001 and $40,000. Salary level varies by region, employment setting, geographical location, scope of responsibility, and supply of registered DTs (DTRs).[3]

Educational Programs

Length

DT educational programs generally include completion of at least a two-year Associate's degree at a regionally accredited college or university as well as 450 hours of supervised practice experience in various community programs, healthcare, and food service facilities. Students should choose programs that are accredited by the Commission on Accreditation/Approval for Dietetics Education of the American Dietetic Association (ADA).

Following completion of the degree and the supervised practice, the student must pass a national examination to become a registered DT.

Prerequisites

Applicants to DT programs must have a high school diploma.

Curriculum

The Associate's degree course work for DTs includes a variety of classes in food and nutrition sciences, food service systems management, and a range of general science courses. A 450-hour supervised practice experience is integrated with the classroom education. Some DT programs are offered in a distance learning format.

Accrediting Body

The accrediting body is the organization that evaluates the educational programs to make sure they are teaching the necessary skills and have the appropriate resources available for students. The organization that offers accreditation for DT programs is:

Commission on Accreditation/Approval for
Dietetics Education (CAADE)
The American Dietetic Association
Education and Accreditation Team
216 West Jackson Boulevard
Chicago, IL 60606-6995
Telephone: 800-877-1600, ext. 5400
Fax: 312-899-4817
E-mail: education@eatright.org

Certification Board

The Commission on Dietetic Registration (CDR) is the credentialing agency for The American Dietetic Association. The purpose of the Commission is to protect the nutritional health and welfare of the public by establishing and enforcing certification and recertification standards for the dietetics profession. Credentials to practice in the profession are issued to individuals who meet its standards. The contact information for the CDR is:

The Commission on Dietetic Registration
216 West Jackson Boulevard
Chicago, IL 60606-6995
Telephone: 312-899-0040, ext. 5500
Fax: 312-899-4772
E-mail: cdr@eatright.org

Advice for Potential Students

Ask someone at the school you are considering to send you information about its program and curriculum. Visit the school and make an appointment to meet with the program director. You may want to ask the director about the school's job placement rates and where its graduates work. To find out what the job opportunities are in your area, go to a college or university library and find a copy of the *Journal of the American Dietetic Association* and look in the job opportunities section to see the number and types of jobs available. Look in your local newspaper to see how many job openings there are for DTs.

For Additional Information

Organizations

American Dietetic Association Networks Team
216 West Jackson Boulevard, Suite 800
Chicago, IL 60606-6995
Telephone: 800-877-1600, ext. 4897
Fax: 312-899-0008
E-mail: network@eatright.org

Publications

The American Dietetic Association. *What is Dietetics?* Chicago: The American Dietetic Association, 1999.

Arena, Judy & Walters, Penny. "Do You Know What A Dietetic Technician Can Do? A Focus on Clinical Technicians and Their Expanded Roles and Responsibilities." *Journal of the American Dietetic Association*, Chicago, 1997.

Internet Resources

The American Dietetic Association: www.eatright.org
Nutritionjobs.com: www.nutritionjobs.com
State Dietetic Associations: www.eatright.org/states.html

Arkansas

Black River Technical College

PO Box 468
Pocahontas, AR 72455

Contact Information:
Telephone: 870-892-4566 ext. 261
Fax: 870-892-3546
E-mail: angelac@brtc.brtc.tec.ar.us
Web: www.brtc.tec.ar.us

Program Information:
Program begins: August, January
Degrees offered: Certificate program, 9 months; Associate's, 18 months
Evening or weekend classes are available.

Application Information:
Enrollment of program: 24
Transfer students are accepted.

Financial Information:
Average cost of books: $300
% of students receiving aid: 75

Employment Profile:
% of students who pass the boards on their first try: 75
% employed within the first 6 months following graduation: 100
Average starting salary: $21,000

California

Chaffey Community College

Food Service Management
5885 Haven Avenue
Rancho Cucamonga, CA 91737-3002

Contact Information:
Telephone: 909-941-2711

Fax: 909-466-2831
E-mail: dsuzannej@mailexcite.com
Web: www.chaffey.cc.ca.us

Program Information:
Program begins: August
Degrees offered: Associate's, 9 months
Evening or weekend classes are available.

Application Information:
Enrollment of program: 350
Transfer students are accepted.

Financial Information:
Average cost of books: $500

Employment Profile:
% employed within the first 6 months following graduation: 98
Average starting salary: $27,000

Loma Linda University

Nutrition and Dietetics
School of Allied Health Professions
Loma Linda, CA 92350

Contact Information:
Telephone: 909-824-4593
Fax: 909-824-4291
E-mail: ghodgkin@ccmail.llu.edu
Web: www.llu.edu

Financial Information:
Average cost of books: $500
% of students receiving aid: 100

Employment Profile:
% of students who pass the boards on their first try: 70
% employed within the first 6 months following graduation: 100
Average starting salary: $19,000

Long Beach City College

Family and Consumer Studies Division
Liberal Arts Campus
4901 East Carson Street
Long Beach, CA 90808-1706

Contact Information:
Telephone: 562-938-4550
Fax: 562-938-4118
E-mail: lhuy@lbcc.cc.ca.us
Web: www.lbcc.cc.ca.us

Program Information:
Program begins: January, June, August
Degrees offered: Certificate program, 24 months; Diploma, 24 months
Evening or weekend classes are available.

Application Information:
Enrollment of program: 106
Transfer students are accepted.

Financial Information:
Average cost of books: $150
% of students receiving aid: 80

Employment Profile:
% of students who pass the boards on their first try: 80
% employed within the first 6 months following graduation: 90
Average starting salary: $27,500

Los Angeles City College

Family and Consumer Studies
855 North Vermont Avenue
Los Angeles, CA 90029-3590

Contact Information:
Telephone: 323-953-4259
Fax: 323-953-4294
Web: www.lacc.cc.ca.us

Program Information:
Program begins: August, January
Degrees offered: Associate's, 16 months
Evening or weekend classes are available.

Application Information:
Enrollment of program: 50
Transfer students are accepted.

Financial Information:
Tuition, resident: $432
Tuition, non-resident: $4,896

Employment Profile:
% employed within the first 6 months following graduation: 100

San Bernardino Valley College

Family and Consumer Science
701 South Mount Vernon
San Bernardino, CA 92410-2748

Contact Information:
Telephone: 909-888-6511 ext. 1503

Program Information:
Program begins: August
Duration of program: 24 months
Evening or weekend classes are available.

Application Information:
Enrollment of program: 25

Colorado

Front Range Community College—Westminster

3645 West 112th Avenue
Westminster, CO 80031

Contact Information:
Telephone: 303-404-5260 ext. 5260
Fax: 303-404-2178
E-mail: looanngie@aol.com
Web: www.frontrange.rightchoice.org

Program Information:
Duration of program: 24 months
Evening or weekend classes are available.

Application Information:
Enrollment of program: 28
Transfer students are accepted.

Financial Information:
Tuition, resident: $2,160
Tuition, non-resident: $10,080
Average cost of books: $550
% of students receiving aid: 60

Employment Profile:
% of students who pass the boards on their first try: 85
% employed within the first 6 months following graduation: 80
Average starting salary: $21,000

Florida

Palm Beach Community College

4200 South Congress Avenue
Mail Station 32
Lake Worth, FL 33461-4796

Contact Information:
Telephone: 561-439-8126
Fax: 561-439-8314
E-mail: froehlit@pbcc.cc.fl.us
Web: www.pbcc.cc.fl.us

Program Information:
Duration of program: 24 months

Application Information:
Transfer students are accepted.

Financial Information:
Tuition, resident: $1,330
Tuition, non-resident: $4,953

Employment Profile:
% of students who pass the boards on their first try: 95
% employed within the first 6 months following graduation: 70

Maine

Southern Maine Technical College

Fort Road
South Portland, ME 04106

Contact Information:
Telephone: 207-767-9606
Fax: 207-767-2731
E-mail: lgabriel@smtc.net
Web: www.smtc.net

Program Information:
Program begins: August, January
Degrees offered: Associate's, 24 months

Application Information:
Enrollment of program: 29
Transfer students are accepted.

Financial Information:
Tuition, resident: $2,040
Tuition, non-resident: $4,500
Average cost of books: $350
% of students receiving aid: 70

Employment Profile:
% of students who pass the boards on their first try: 85
% employed within the first 6 months following graduation: 85
Average starting salary: $24,000

Massachusetts

North Shore Community College

One Ferncroft Road
PO Box 3343
Danvers, MA 01923

Contact Information:
Telephone: 978-762-4000 ext. 263
Fax: 978-762-4038
Web: www.nscc.cc.ma.us

Program Information:
Evening or weekend classes are available.

Application Information:
Enrollment of program: 24
Transfer students are accepted.

Financial Information:
Tuition, resident: $2,130

Employment Profile:
% employed within the first 6 months following graduation: 80
Average starting salary: $24,000

New Hampshire

University of New Hampshire

Thompson School of Applied Sciences
Cole Hall
Durham, NH 03824

Contact Information:
Telephone: 603-862-1050
Fax: 603-862-2915
E-mail: njohnson@cisunix.unh.edu
Web: www.unh.edu

Program Information:
Program begins: September
Duration of program: 24 months

Financial Information:
Tuition, resident: $6,555
Tuition, non-resident: $15,275

New Jersey

Middlesex County College

2600 Woodbridge Avenue
PO Box 3050
Edison, NJ 08818-3050

Contact Information:
Telephone: 732-906-2538
Fax: 732-906-7745
E-mail: jychenrd@aol.com
Web: www.middlesex.cc.nj.us

Program Information:
Program begins: September, January, May
Duration of program: 24 months
Evening or weekend classes are available.

Application Information:
Enrollment of program: 50
Transfer students are accepted.

Financial Information:
Tuition, resident: $2,810
Tuition, non-resident: $5,620
Average cost of books: $1,000

Employment Profile:
% of students who pass the boards on their first try: 80
% employed within the first 6 months following graduation: 90
Average starting salary: $27,500

University of Medicine & Dentistry of New Jersey

School of Health Related Professions
65 Bergen Street
Newark, NJ 07107-3001

Contact Information:
Telephone: 973-972-6245
Fax: 973-972-7028
E-mail: maillet@umdnj.edu

Program Information:
Program begins: September
Degrees offered: Bachelor's, 27 months
Evening or weekend classes are available.

Application Information:
Transfer students are accepted.

Financial Information:
Tuition, resident: $4,620
Tuition, non-resident: $6,930

New York

Erie Community College—North Campus

6205 Main Street
Williamsville, NY 14221-7095

Contact Information:
Telephone: 716-851-1598
Fax: 716-851-1629
E-mail: garfoot@nstaff.sunyerie.edu
Web: www.ecc.edu

Program Information:
Program begins: September
Degrees offered: Associate's, 18 months

Financial Information:
Tuition, resident: $2,475
Tuition, non-resident: $4,950

Suffolk County Community College

Eastern Campus
121 Speonk-Riverhead Road
Riverhead, NY 11901-3499

Contact Information:
Telephone: 516-548-2590
Fax: 516-548-2617
E-mail: newman@sunysuffolk.edu
Web: www.sunysuffolk.edu

Program Information:
Evening or weekend classes are available.

Application Information:
Enrollment of program: 35
Transfer students are accepted.

Financial Information:
Average cost of books: $100

Employment Profile:
% of students who pass the boards on their first try: 90
% employed within the first 6 months following graduation: 100
Average starting salary: $30,000

Westchester Community College

75 Grasslands Road
Valhalla, NY 10595-1636

Contact Information:
Telephone: 914-785-6750
Fax: 914-785-6423
E-mail: juliana-snyder@sunywcc.edu
Web: www.wcc.co.westchester.ny.us

Program Information:
Program begins: September
Duration of program: 24 months
Evening or weekend classes are available.

Application Information:
Enrollment of program: 50
Transfer students are accepted.

Financial Information:
Tuition, resident: $2,940
Tuition, non-resident: $7,350
Average cost of books: $200

Employment Profile:
% of students who pass the boards on their first try: 80
% employed within the first 6 months following graduation: 100
Average starting salary: $27,750

Ohio

Columbus State Community College

550 East Spring Street
PO Box 1609
Columbus, OH 43216-1609

Contact Information:
Telephone: 614-287-2580
Fax: 614-287-5973
E-mail: lconway@cscc.edu
Web: www.cscc.edu

Program Information:
Duration of program: 20 months
Evening or weekend classes are available.

Application Information:
Enrollment of program: 50
Transfer students are accepted.

Financial Information:
Tuition, resident: $1,830
Tuition, non-resident: $4,020
% of students receiving aid: 52

Employment Profile:
% of students who pass the boards on their first try: 80
Average starting salary: $22,500

Cuyahoga Community College

2900 Community College Avenue
Cleveland, OH 44115-3196

Contact Information:
Telephone: 216-987-4497
Fax: 216-987-4386
E-mail: barbara.mikuszewski@tri-c.cc.oh.us
Web: www.tri-c.cc.us

Program Information:
Program begins: August

Application Information:
Enrollment of program: 25
Transfer students are accepted.

Financial Information:
Average cost of books: $500

Employment Profile:
% of students who pass the boards on their first try: 82
% employed within the first 6 months following graduation: 50
Average starting salary: $22,500

Lima Technical College

4240 Campus Drive
Lima, OH 458043576

Contact Information:
Telephone: 419-995-8328 ext. 328
Fax: 419-995-8818
E-mail: gilroym@ltc.tec.oh.us
Web: www.itc.tec.oh.us

Program Information:
Program begins: September, May
Duration of program: 24 months
Evening or weekend classes are available.

Application Information:
Enrollment of program: 12
Transfer students are accepted.

Financial Information:
Tuition, resident: $1,965
Tuition, non-resident: $3,930
Average cost of books: $400
% of students receiving aid: 80

Employment Profile:
% of students who pass the boards on their first try: 97
% employed within the first 6 months following graduation: 80
Average starting salary: $20,000

Muskingum Area Technical College

Health Pubic Services and General Studies
1555 Newark Road
Zanesville, OH 43701

Contact Information:
Telephone: 740-588-1219 ext. 219
Fax: 740-454-0035
Web: www.matc.tec.oh.us

Program Information:
Program begins: September
Degrees offered: Associate's, 22 months

Application Information:
Enrollment of program: 20
Transfer students are accepted.

Employment Profile:
% of students who pass the boards on their first try: 100
% employed within the first 6 months following graduation: 65
Average starting salary: $19,000

Owens Community College

PO Box 10,000
Oregon Road
Toledo, OH 43699-1947

Contact Information:
Telephone: 419-661-7214
Fax: 419-661-7251
E-mail: tmadaras@owens.cc.oh.us
Web: www.owens.cc.oh.us

Program Information:
Program begins: August
Duration of program: 24 months

Application Information:
Enrollment of program: 20
Transfer students are accepted.

Financial Information:
Tuition, resident: $2,370
Tuition, non-resident: $4,440

Sinclair Community College

444 West Third Street
Dayton, OH 45402-1460

Contact Information:
Telephone: 937-512-2756
Fax: 937-512-3092
E-mail: bdykes@Sinclair.edu
Web: www.sinclair.edu

Program Information:
Duration of program: 24 months
Evening or weekend classes are available.

Application Information:
Enrollment of program: 47
Transfer students are accepted.

Financial Information:
Tuition, resident: $1,116
Tuition, non-resident: $1,764
Average cost of books: $600
% of students receiving aid: 20

Employment Profile:
% of students who pass the boards on their first try: 95
% employed within the first 6 months following graduation: 100
Average starting salary: $23,000

Oklahoma

Oklahoma State University—Okmulgee

1801 East 4th Street
Okmulgee, OK 74447-3901

Contact Information:
Telephone: 918-293-5004
Fax: 918-293-4628
E-mail: amiller@osu.okmulgee.edu
Web: www.osu-okmulgee.edu

Application Information:
Enrollment of program: 30
Transfer students are accepted.

Financial Information:
Tuition, resident: $1,875

Tennessee

Shelby State Community College

PO Box 40568
Memphis, TN 38174-0568

Contact Information:
Telephone: 901-544-5051
Fax: 901-544-5057
E-mail: tharriss@cc.cc.tn.us

Program Information:
Program begins: September
Duration of program: 22 months
Evening or weekend classes are available.

Application Information:
Enrollment of program: 45
Transfer students are accepted.

Financial Information:
Tuition, resident: $1,728
Tuition, non-resident: $6,612
Average cost of books: $200

Employment Profile:
% of students who pass the boards on their first try: 8
% employed within the first 6 months following graduation: 95
Average starting salary: $20,000

Texas

St. Philip's College

1801 Martin Luther King Jr. Drive
San Antonio, TX 78203-2098

Contact Information:
Telephone: 210-531-3315
Fax: 210-531-3351
E-mail: mkunz@accd.edu
Web: www.accd.edu

Program Information:
Duration of program: 24 months
Evening or weekend classes are available.

Application Information:
Enrollment of program: 37
Transfer students are accepted.

Financial Information:
Tuition, resident: $1,100
Tuition, non-resident: $3,000
Average cost of books: $250
% of students receiving aid: 50

Employment Profile:
% of students who pass the boards on their first try: 60
% employed within the first 6 months following graduation: 80
Average starting salary: $18,500

Virginia

Northern Virginia Community College

Bus Division HRI/DIT
8333 Little River Turnpike
Annandale, VA 22003-3796

Contact Information:
Telephone: 703-323-3458
Fax: 703-323-3509
E-mail: jsass@nv.cc.va.us
Web: www.nv.cc.va.us

Program Information:
Program begins: August, January
Degrees offered: Certificate program, 9 months; Associate's, 18 months

Application Information:
Enrollment of program: 110
Transfer students are accepted.

Financial Information:
Tuition, non-resident: $4,500
Average cost of books: $400

Employment Profile:
% of students who pass the boards on their first try: 93
% employed within the first 6 months following graduation: 90
Average starting salary: $20,000

Washington

Spokane Community College

North 1810 Greene Street
MS 2090
Spokane, WA 99207-5399

Contact Information:
Telephone: 509-533-7314
Fax: 509-533-8621
Web: www.scc.spokane.cc.wa.us

Program Information:
Program begins: September

Wisconsin

Madison Area Technical College

3550 Anderson Street
Madison, WI 53704-2599

Contact Information:
Telephone: 608-246-6319
Fax: 608-246-6880
Web: www.madison.tec.wi.us

Application Information:
Enrollment of program: 20
Transfer students are accepted.

Financial Information:
Average cost of books: $1,500

Employment Profile:
% of students who pass the boards on their first try: 87
% employed within the first 6 months following graduation: 80
Average starting salary: $22,000

Emergency Medical Technician-Paramedic

Bruce J. Walz, PhD
Associate Professor and Chair
Department of Emergency Health Services
University of Maryland, Baltimore County

Job Description

What Do They Do?

EMT-Ps provide basic and advanced life support to victims of acute medical or trauma (injury) conditions outside of hospitals. They are trained to work with all age groups and in all settings including the home, work, roadways, and recreational areas. EMT-Ps assess patients, provide immediate care to stabilize the patient, and transport patients to medical facilities. In most cases, they operate ambulances as a means to respond to the scene and transport the patient. (Some EMT-Ps work as support personnel on chase vehicles or fire engines so do not provide care via ambulances.)

EMT-P's roles and responsibilities include:

- Preparation of self and service for emergency response
- Appropriate response to an incident scene
- Scene assessment
- Patient assessment and triage
- Recognition and management of injuries and illnesses
- Appropriate transport of patient to a medical facility
- Patient transfer
- Incident documentation
- Community involvement and promotion of citizen involvement in emergency medical services
- Support of routine health maintenance (simple health matters for which most people would visit their family physicians)
- Conduct primary illness and injury prevention initiatives
- Engage in personal professional development

EMT-Ps work under the license of a medical director and receive direction from a physician as needed.

Type of Person

EMT-Ps are action-oriented and like to be busy. EMT-Ps are often linear thinkers and are good at following set procedures; however, they also possess the ability to find creative solutions to difficult or unusual situations.

With Whom Do They Work?

EMT-Ps work with a variety of public safety and medical professionals. Most often, they work with basic level EMTs and firefighters. At the hospital, they interact directly with nurses and emergency physicians.

Employment

Places of Employment

EMT-Ps can work in fire departments, rescue squads, police departments, private services, and hospitals as well as for government agencies and in the military. In some communities, EMT-Ps are not paid employees but rather volunteer as members of a community fire department or rescue squad.

Employment Outlook

Overall, the demand for EMT-Ps remains strong. As suburban areas grow, a decline in volunteer providers will lead to increased need for career EMT-Ps. However, in established urban municipal services it is not unusual to have hundreds of applicants for 15–20 positions. Frequent turnover in commercial services provides opportunity for entry-level positions. EMT-Ps with Associate's or Bachelor's degrees are more likely to hold supervisory and management positions.

Salary

The average national salary for EMT-Ps is $31,290. Salary varies by region from a low of $28,146 to a high of $45,287. Most EMT-Ps are paid hourly and are shift-workers.[1]

Educational Programs

Length

EMT-P programs vary in length depending on the educational institution. Certification programs average 1,000 to 1,300 hours in length. College-based programs, through which a student may earn a degree, are two to four years in length. EMT-P students must either already be certified as an EMT-Basic or they must become certified while enrolled in an EMT-P program. EMT-P students take courses on topics such as human development, pathophysiology, pharmacology, illness and injury prevention, legal and ethical issues, communications, ambulance operations, and crime scene awareness.

Prerequisites

Prerequisites often include a high school diploma, certification as an EMT-Basic, a criminal background check, and the physical ability to perform the job requirements. Candidates should be proficient in mathematics, reading, and writing.

Curriculum

EMT-P educational programs follow a National Standard Curriculum established by the United States Department of Transportation. The curriculum includes classroom instruction, skill labs, clinical rotations, and a field internship.

Major divisions of the curriculum include:

- Pre- or co-requisites courses that need to be taken before (pre) or during (co) the paramedic course (an EMT-Basic course or an anatomy and physiology course, for example)
- Preparatory courses that cover topics such as human development, illness and injury prevention, paramedic roles and responsibilities, legal and ethical issues, pharmacology, etc.
- An airway management and ventilation course
- A patient assessment course that includes history taking, physical examination, patient assessment and documentation

- Medical management courses that explain how to manage specific events such as heart attack, stroke, allergic reactions, or birth
- Trauma management courses that explain how to handle victims of spinal cord injury or cause shock
- Special considerations courses that teach EMT-Ps what they need to keep in mind when treating a child or victim of abuse, for example
- Assessment-based management
- EMS operations—how the EMS system works from the initial phone call to 911 through care and transport to the hospital, if appropriate

Accrediting Body

The accrediting body is the organization that evaluates the educational programs to make sure they are teaching according to the National Standard Curriculum and have the appropriate resources available for students. The organization that offers accreditation for EMT-P education is:

Joint Review Committee on Educational Programs for the EMT-P
7108-C South Alton Way, Suite 150
Englewood, CO 80112-2106
Telephone: 303-694-6191
E-mail: coa@ast.org

Not all EMT-P education programs are required to be nationally accredited. However, some employers will only hire graduates of nationally accredited programs. Students who attend accredited programs also know that the program meets recognized national standards. In addition, if a student transfers from a non-accredited EMT-P program to an accredited program, he or she may not receive academic credit for courses completed in the non-accredited program.

Certification Board

EMT-Ps are certified or licensed by the state in which they function. Many states accept registration by a national testing board. National registration is provided by:

National Registry of EMTs
6610 Busch Boulevard
PO Box 29233
Columbus, OH 43229-0233
Telephone: 614-888-4484
Web address: www.nremt.org

Advice for Potential Students

EMT-Ps function in a variety of settings. Students should review the job description and requirements of potential employers. EMT-P is also a physically demanding job, so students should consider participating in a physical training program that employs both strength and endurance training. Students looking to advance in their careers should consider college degree programs.

For Additional Information

Organizations

National Association of Emergency Medical Technicians
408 Monroe Street
Clinton, MS 39056
Telephone: 800-34-NAEMT
E-mail: naemtg@aol.com

International Association of EMTs and Paramedics
159 Burgin Parkway
Quincy, MA 02169
Telephone: 617-376-0220
E-mail: info@iaep.org
Web address: www.iaep.org

Publications

EMT-Paramedic National Standard Curriculum, 1998. National Highway Traffic Safety Administration, U.S. Department of Transportation. Available only online at www.nhtsa.dot.gov/people/injury/ems

Journal of Emergency Medical Services (JEMS). JEMS Communications, PO Box 2789, Carlsbad, CA 92018.

Monthly trade magazine. Traditionally publishes annual salary survey and EMS system statistics.

Internet Resources

American Ambulance Association: www.the-aaa.org
Commission on the Accreditation of Allied Health Education Programs: www.caahep.org
International Association of EMTs and Paramedics: www.iaep.org
National Association of Female Paramedics: www.nafp.webjump.com
National Association of EMS Educators: www.naemse.org
National Association of EMS Physicians: www.naemsp.org
National Flight Paramedics Association: www.nfpa.rotor.com
National Highway Traffic Safety Administration: www.nhtsa.dot.gov/people/injury/ems
National Registry of EMTs: www.nremt.org
Journal of Emergency Medical Services: www.jems.com

Alabama

Lurleen B. Wallace Junior College

PO Box 1418
Andalusia, AL 36420

Contact Information:
Telephone: 334-222-6591 ext. 2210
Fax: 334-222-0136
E-mail: lwryland@yahoo.com

Program Information:
Program begins: August
Duration of program: 9 months

Application Information:
Enrollment of program: 50
Transfer students are accepted.

Financial Information:
Tuition, resident: $1,350
Tuition, non-resident: $2,700
Average cost of books: $300
% of students receiving aid: 70

Employment Profile:
% of students who pass the boards on their first try: 80
% employed within the first 6 months following graduation: 100
Average starting salary: $18,000

California

Daniel Freeman Memorial Hospital

333 North Prairie Avenue
Inglewood, CA 90301

Contact Information:
Telephone: 310-674-7050 ext. 3580
Fax: 310-680-8640
E-mail: rbains@mednet.ucla.edu
Web: www.cpc.mednet.ucla.edu

Program Information:
Program begins: August, January
Duration of program: 7 months
Evening or weekend classes are available.

Financial Information:
Tuition, resident: $3,500
Tuition, non-resident: $4,500

Colorado

Colorado Association of Paramedical Education, Inc.

9191 Grant Street
Thornton, CO 80229

Contact Information:
Telephone: 614-227-2510
Fax: 614-227-5144
Web: www.capemedicsl.com

Program Information:
Program begins: September
Duration of program: 10 months

Application Information:
Enrollment of program: 32
Transfer students are accepted.

Financial Information:
Tuition, resident: $2,650
Average cost of books: $400
% of students receiving aid: 45

Employment Profile:
% of students who pass the boards on their first try: 100

Parkview Medical Center/Pueblo Community College

400 West 16th Street
Pueblo, CO 81003

Contact Information:
Telephone: 719-549-3482
Fax: 719-549-3260
E-mail: terrybitterlich@pcc.cccoes.edu
Web: www.pcc.cccoes.edu

Program Information:
Program begins: September
Duration of program: 13 months
Evening or weekend classes are available.

Application Information:
Enrollment of program: 20
Transfer students are accepted.

Financial Information:
Tuition, resident: $3,100
Tuition, non-resident: $9,000
Average cost of books: $500
% of students receiving aid: 50

Employment Profile:
% of students who pass the boards on their first try: 96
% employed within the first 6 months following graduation: 80
Average starting salary: $24,000

Swedish Medical Center

HealthONE EMS
300 East Hampden Ave #100
Englewood, CO 80110

Contact Information:
Telephone: 303-788-6302
Fax: 303-788-7656
Web: www.healthone-emsandtrauma.com

Program Information:
Program begins: August
Duration of program: 6 months

Application Information:
Transfer students are accepted.

Financial Information:
Average cost of books: $350

Employment Profile:
% of students who pass the boards on their first try: 99

Connecticut

Capital Community Technical College

61 Woodland Street
Hartford, CT 06105-2354

Contact Information:
Telephone: 860-520-7872
Fax: 860-520-7906
E-mail: devito@commnet.eudu
Web: www.cctc.commnet.edu

Program Information:
Program begins: August, January
Duration of program: 11 months
Evening or weekend classes are available.

Financial Information:
Tuition, resident: $1,814
Tuition, non-resident: $5,440

Florida

Broward Community College

3501 Southwest Davie Road
Building 8
Ft. Lauderdale, FL 33314

Contact Information:
Telephone: 954-475-6776
Fax: 954-473-9037
E-mail: ejordan@broward.cc.fl.us
Web: www.broward.cc.fl.us

Program Information:
Program begins: January, May, August
Degrees offered: Certificate program; Associate's
Evening or weekend classes are available.

Application Information:
Enrollment of program: 500
Transfer students are accepted.

Financial Information:
Tuition, resident: $1,314
Tuition, non-resident: $4,305

Employment Profile:
% of students who pass the boards on their first try: 80

Edison Community College

8099 College Parkway Southwest
PO Box 60210
Ft. Myers, FL 33906-6210

Contact Information:
Telephone: 941-489-9108
Fax: 941-489-9331
E-mail: kdickers@edison.edu
Web: www.edison.edu

Program Information:
Program begins: August
Duration of program: 12 months
Evening or weekend classes are available.

Financial Information:
Tuition, resident: $1,945
Tuition, non-resident: $7,182

Employment Profile:
% of students who pass the boards on their first try: 90

Florida Community College—Jacksonville

North Campus
4501 Capper Road
Jacksonville, FL 32218

Contact Information:
Telephone: 904-766-6513
Fax: 904-766-6654
E-mail: mfisher@fccj.org
Web: www.fccj.org

Program Information:
Program begins: August
Duration of program: 12 months
Evening or weekend classes are available.

Application Information:
Enrollment of program: 40

Financial Information:
Tuition, resident: $1,755
Tuition, non-resident: $7,022
Average cost of books: $350
% of students receiving aid: 20

Employment Profile:
% of students who pass the boards on their first try: 85
% employed within the first 6 months following graduation: 60
Average starting salary: $19,000

Miami-Dade Community College

Medical Center Campus
950 Northwest 20th Street
Miami, FL 33127

Contact Information:
Telephone: 305-237-4337
Fax: 305-237-4278
E-mail: myoder@mdcc.edu
Web: www.mdcc.edu

Program Information:
Program begins: August
Duration of program: 12 months
Evening or weekend classes are available.

Financial Information:
Tuition, resident: $1,567
Tuition, non-resident: $5,510

Employment Profile:
% of students who pass the boards on their first try: 80

Pasco-Hernando Community College

10230 Ridge Road
New Port Richey, FL 34654-5199

Contact Information:
Telephone: 727-816-3285
Fax: 727-916-3309
E-mail: toni_vineyard@pasco-hernandocc.com
Web: www.pasco-hernandocc.com

Program Information:
Program begins: August
Duration of program: 11 months
Evening or weekend classes are available.

Application Information:
Enrollment of program: 30
Transfer students are accepted.

Financial Information:
Tuition, resident: $1,885
Tuition, non-resident: $7,052
Average cost of books: $250
% of students receiving aid: 10

Employment Profile:
% of students who pass the boards on their first try: 96
% employed within the first 6 months following graduation: 95
Average starting salary: $25,000

Pensacola Junior College

Warrington Campus
5555 West Highway 98
Pensacola, FL 32507-1097

Contact Information:
Telephone: 904-484-2225
Fax: 904-484-2390
Web: www.pjc.cc.fl.us

Program Information:
Program begins: August
Duration of program: 16 months

Application Information:
Enrollment of program: 6
Transfer students are accepted.

Financial Information:
Tuition, resident: $1,809
Tuition, non-resident: $6,489

Seminole Community College

100 Weldon Boulevard
Sanford, FL 32773-6199

Contact Information:
Telephone: 407-328-2197
Fax: 407-328-2189
E-mail: holbornr@mail.seminole.cc.fl.us
Web: www.seminole.cc.fl.us

Program Information:
Program begins: June
Duration of program: 12 months

Application Information:
Enrollment of program: 60

Financial Information:
Tuition, resident: $1,493
Tuition, non-resident: $5,553
Average cost of books: $300
% of students receiving aid: 30

Employment Profile:
% of students who pass the boards on their first try: 99
Average starting salary: $29,000

Tallahassee Community College

444 Appleyard Drive
Tallahassee, FL 32304

Contact Information:
Telephone: 850-922-8156
Fax: 850-921-5722
E-mail: dunmyerb@mail.tallahassee.cc.fl.us
Web: www.tallahassee.cc.fl.us

Program Information:
Program begins: August, January
Degrees offered: Certificate program, 11 months; Associate's, 24 months
Evening or weekend classes are available.

Application Information:
Enrollment of program: 47
Transfer students are accepted.

Financial Information:
Tuition, resident: $1,380
Tuition, non-resident: $5,110
Average cost of books: $350
% of students receiving aid: 20

Employment Profile:
% of students who pass the boards on their first try: 90
% employed within the first 6 months following graduation: 100
Average starting salary: $23,000

Valencia Community College

PO Box 3028
Orlando, FL 32802-9961

Contact Information:
Telephone: 407-299-5000 ext. 1546
Fax: 407-293-8839
E-mail: rtaylor@gwmail.valencia.cc.fl.us
Web: www.valencia.cc.fl.us

Program Information:
Program begins: August
Degrees offered: Associate's, 24 months
Evening or weekend classes are available.

Application Information:
Enrollment of program: 50
Transfer students are accepted.

Financial Information:
Tuition, resident: $1,679
Tuition, non-resident: $5,540
Average cost of books: $400
% of students receiving aid: 25

Employment Profile:
% of students who pass the boards on their first try: 96
% employed within the first 6 months following graduation: 97
Average starting salary: $29,000

Illinois

Trinity Medical Center

555 6th Street
Suite 404
Moline, IL 61265-1216

Contact Information:
Telephone: 309-757-2500
Fax: 309-757-2912
E-mail: chambersj@trinityqc.com

Program Information:
Program begins: Program begins quarterly.
Duration of program: 12 months
Evening or weekend classes are available.

Application Information:
Enrollment of program: 13
Transfer students are accepted.

Financial Information:
Tuition, resident: $2,200
Average cost of books: $150
% of students receiving aid: 45

Employment Profile:
% of students who pass the boards on their first try: 98
% employed within the first 6 months following graduation: 85
Average starting salary: $25,000

Indiana

St. Francis Hospital and Health Centers

1600 Albany Street
Beech Grove, IN 46107

Contact Information:
Telephone: 317-782-6480
Fax: 317-783-8438
E-mail: bsparksemsedu@hotmail.com
Web: www.stfrancis-indy.org

Program Information:
Program begins: August
Duration of program: 13 months

Application Information:
Enrollment of program: 20

Employment Profile:
% of students who pass the boards on their first try: 90
% employed within the first 6 months following graduation: 100

Iowa

Mercy Medical Center—Des Moines

928 Sixth Avenue
Des Moines, IA 50309-1234

Contact Information:
Telephone: 515-247-4097
Fax: 515-643-6705
Web: www.mercy.desmoines.org

Program Information:
Program begins: August
Duration of program: 9 months
Evening or weekend classes are available.

Application Information:
Enrollment of program: 28

Financial Information:
Average cost of books: $257

Employment Profile:
% of students who pass the boards on their first try: 85
% employed within the first 6 months following graduation: 90

Kansas

Johnson County Community College

12345 College Boulevard
Overland Park, KS 66210-1299

Contact Information:
Telephone: 913-469-3841
Fax: 913-469-2315
E-mail: dkurogi@jccc.net
Web: www.jccc.net

Program Information:
Program begins: August
Degrees offered: Certificate program, 12 months; Diploma, 24 months
Evening or weekend classes are available.

Application Information:
Enrollment of program: 26
Transfer students are accepted.

Financial Information:
Tuition, resident: $2,162
Tuition, non-resident: $5,734
Average cost of books: $400
% of students receiving aid: 20

Employment Profile:
% of students who pass the boards on their first try: 85
% employed within the first 6 months following graduation: 98
Average starting salary: $30,000

Maryland

University of Maryland Baltimore County

Emergency Health Services Department
1000 Hilltop Circle
Baltimore, MD 21250

Contact Information:
Telephone: 513-558-8093
Fax: 513-558-5791
E-mail: polk@umbc.edu
Web: www.umbc.edu

Program Information:
Program begins: September
Duration of program: 16 months

Application Information:
Enrollment of program: 55
Transfer students are accepted.

Financial Information:
Tuition, resident: $4,846
Tuition, non-resident: $9,254

Employment Profile:
% of students who pass the boards on their first try: 93
% employed within the first 6 months following graduation: 50
Average starting salary: $28,000

Michigan

Lansing Community College

3400-HHPS
PO Box 40010
Lansing, MI 48901-7210

Contact Information:
Telephone: 517-483-5274
Fax: 517-483-1508
E-mail: tcooper@lansing.cc.mi.us
Web: www.lansing.cc.mi.us

Program Information:
Program begins: August
Degrees offered: Certificate program, 10 months; Associate's, 10 months

Application Information:
Enrollment of program: 36
Transfer students are accepted.

Financial Information:
Tuition, resident: $1,504
Tuition, non-resident: $2,432
Average cost of books: $350
% of students receiving aid: 40

Employment Profile:
% of students who pass the boards on their first try: 80
% employed within the first 6 months following graduation: 90
Average starting salary: $18,000

Minnesota

Northwest Technical College—East Grand Forks

2022 Central Avenue Northeast
East Grand Forks, MN 56721

Contact Information:
Telephone: 218-773-4634 ext. 420
Fax: 218-773-4502
E-mail: sponsler@mail.ntc.mnscu.edu
Web: www.ntc-online.com

Program Information:
Program begins: August
Duration of program: 21 months

Application Information:
Enrollment of program: 45
Transfer students are accepted.

Financial Information:
Tuition, resident: $5,069
Tuition, non-resident: $10,138
Average cost of books: $1,000
% of students receiving aid: 95

Employment Profile:
% of students who pass the boards on their first try: 90
% employed within the first 6 months following graduation: 75
Average starting salary: $28,000

Mississippi

Southwest Mississippi Community College

SMCC
College Drive
Summit, MS 39666

Contact Information:
Telephone: 601-276-3734
Fax: 601-276-3867
E-mail: ssemt@smcc.cc.ms.us
Web: www.smcc.cc.ms.us

Program Information:
Program begins: August
Degrees offered: Certificate program, 12 months; Diploma, 24 months

Application Information:
Enrollment of program: 15
Transfer students are accepted.

Financial Information:
Average cost of books: $200
% of students receiving aid: 60

Employment Profile:
% of students who pass the boards on their first try: 60
% employed within the first 6 months following graduation: 100
Average starting salary: $25,000

University of Mississippi Medical Center

2500 North State Street
Jackson, MS 39216

Contact Information:
Telephone: 410-455-3223
Fax: 410-455-3045

Program Information:
Program begins: June
Degrees offered: Certificate program, 13 months
Evening or weekend classes are available.

Application Information:
Enrollment of program: 35
Transfer students are accepted.

Financial Information:
Tuition, resident: $733
Tuition, non-resident: $866
Average cost of books: $500
% of students receiving aid: 70

Employment Profile:
% of students who pass the boards on their first try: 98
% employed within the first 6 months following graduation: 100
Average starting salary: $26,500

Missouri

IHM Health Studies Center

2500 Abbott Place
St. Louis, MO 63143

Contact Information:
Telephone: 314-768-1234
Fax: 314-768-1595
E-mail: ihm@abbottems.org
Web: www.abbott-ihm.org

Program Information:
Program begins: January
Degrees offered: Certificate program, 18 months
Evening or weekend classes are available.

Application Information:
Enrollment of program: 54
Transfer students are accepted.

Financial Information:
Tuition, resident: $3,070
Average cost of books: $454
% of students receiving aid: 80

Employment Profile:
% of students who pass the boards on their first try: 55
% employed within the first 6 months following graduation: 100
Average starting salary: $20,800

Nebraska

Creighton University

EMS Education
2514 Cuming Street
Omaha, NE 68131

Contact Information:
Telephone: 412-578-3200
Fax: 412-578-3241
E-mail: cuemse@creighton.edu

Program Information:
Program begins: August
Duration of program: 11 months
Evening or weekend classes are available.

New Hampshire

New England EMS Institute

Elliot Hospital
One Elliot Way
Manchester, NH 03103

Contact Information:
Telephone: 603-663-2641
Fax: 603-663-2110
E-mail: bgleason@optima.org

Program Information:
Program begins: September, January
Duration of program: 11 months
Evening or weekend classes are available.

Application Information:
Enrollment of program: 25
Transfer students are accepted.

Financial Information:
Average cost of books: $260
% of students receiving aid: 10

Employment Profile:
% of students who pass the boards on their first try: 88
% employed within the first 6 months following graduation: 80
Average starting salary: $25,500

New Hampshire Technical Institute

11 Institute Drive
Concord, NH 033017412

Contact Information:
Telephone: 603-271-7164
Fax: 603-271-7182
E-mail: chartn@tec.nh.us

Program Information:
Program begins: August
Degrees offered: Associate's, 21 months

Application Information:
Enrollment of program: 64
Transfer students are accepted.

Financial Information:
Tuition, resident: $2,756
Tuition, non-resident: $6,344
Average cost of books: $300
% of students receiving aid: 80

Employment Profile:
% of students who pass the boards on their first try: 100
% employed within the first 6 months following graduation: 100
Average starting salary: $50,000

North Carolina

Western Carolina University

Cullowhee, NC 28723

Contact Information:
Telephone: 828-227-7113
Fax: 828-227-7071
E-mail: mhubble@wcuvax1.wcu.edu
Web: www.wcu.wsu

Program Information:
Program begins: September
Degrees offered: Bachelor's, 45 months
Evening or weekend classes are available.

Application Information:
Enrollment of program: 30
Transfer students are accepted.

Financial Information:
Tuition, resident: $1,944
Tuition, non-resident: $9,214
% of students receiving aid: 30

Employment Profile:
% of students who pass the boards on their first try: 70
% employed within the first 6 months following graduation: 100
Average starting salary: $28,000

Ohio

Akron General Medical Center

400 Wabash Avenue
Akron, OH 44307

Contact Information:
Telephone: 330-384-6655
Fax: 330-253-8293
E-mail: smartin@agmc.org
Web: www.agmc.org

Program Information:
Program begins: September
Duration of program: 10 months
Evening or weekend classes are available.

Application Information:
Enrollment of program: 35

Financial Information:
Tuition, resident: $2,100
% of students receiving aid: 15

Employment Profile:
% of students who pass the boards on their first try: 94
% employed within the first 6 months following graduation: 95
Average starting salary: $30,000

Parma Community General Hospital

7300 State Road
Parma, OH 44134

Contact Information:
Telephone: 440-886-7323
Fax: 440-886-1295

Program Information:
Program begins: September, January
Duration of program: 11 months

Financial Information:
% of students receiving aid: 20

Employment Profile:
% of students who pass the boards on their first try: 90
Average starting salary: $35,000

University of Cincinnati

231 Bethesda Avenue
Cincinnati, OH 45267-0769

Contact Information:
Telephone: 256-551-4416
Fax: 256-551-4553
Web: www.uc.edu

Program Information:
Program begins: September
Duration of program: 10 months
Evening or weekend classes are available.

Application Information:
Transfer students are accepted.

Financial Information:
Tuition, resident: $3,900
Tuition, non-resident: $9,000
Average cost of books: $300
% of students receiving aid: 90

Employment Profile:
% of students who pass the boards on their first try: 95
% employed within the first 6 months following graduation: 100
Average starting salary: $52,000

Youngstown State University

One University Plaza
Youngstown, OH 44555-3327

Contact Information:
Telephone: 330- 742-3327
Fax: 330-742-2921
E-mail: rwbenner@cc.ysu.edu
Web: www.ysu.edu

Program Information:
Program begins: September
Duration of program: 11 months

Application Information:
Enrollment of program: 25

Financial Information:
Tuition, resident: $5,072
Tuition, non-resident: $9,750
Average cost of books: $200
% of students receiving aid: 75

Employment Profile:
% of students who pass the boards on their first try: 90
% employed within the first 6 months following graduation: 90
Average starting salary: $35,000

South Carolina

Greenville Technical College

PO Box 5616
Station B
Greenville, SC 29606

Contact Information:
Telephone: 864-250-8490
Fax: 864-250-8218
E-mail: fishermaf@qvltec.edu
Web: www.greenvilletech.com

Program Information:
Program begins: August
Duration of program: 21 months

Application Information:
Enrollment of program: 27
Transfer students are accepted.

Financial Information:
Tuition, resident: $1,500
Tuition, non-resident: $1,620
Average cost of books: $250
% of students receiving aid: 40

Employment Profile:
% of students who pass the boards on their first try: 62
% employed within the first 6 months following graduation: 60
Average starting salary: $24,000

Tennessee

Jackson State Community College

2046 North Parkway Street
Jackson, TN 38301-3797

Contact Information:
Telephone: 901-424-3520 ext. 296
Fax: 901-425-9551
E-mail: tcoley@jscc.cc.tn.us
Web: www.jscc.cc.tn.us

Program Information:
Program begins: September
Duration of program: 12 months

Application Information:
Enrollment of program: 35

Financial Information:
Tuition, resident: $1,333
Tuition, non-resident: $4,990

Employment Profile:
% of students who pass the boards on their first try: 97
% employed within the first 6 months following graduation: 100

Volunteer State Community College

EMS Education Program
1480 Nashville Pike
Gallatin, TN 37066

Contact Information:
Telephone: 615-230-3346
Fax: 615-230-3344
E-mail: rcollier@vscc.cc.tn.us
Web: www.vscc.tn.us

Program Information:
Program begins: August
Duration of program: 15 months

Application Information:
Enrollment of program: 16

Financial Information:
Tuition, resident: $1,945
Tuition, non-resident: $4,500
Average cost of books: $400
% of students receiving aid: 30

Employment Profile:
% of students who pass the boards on their first try: 77
% employed within the first 6 months following graduation: 100
Average starting salary: $28,000

Texas

Tarrant County College—Northeast

828 Harwood Road
Hurst, TX 76054-3299

Contact Information:
Telephone: 817-515-6448
Fax: 817-515-6700
E-mail: jmcdonald@tccd.net
Web: www.tccd.net

Program Information:
Program begins: January, August, September
Degrees offered: Associate's, 24 months
Evening or weekend classes are available.

Application Information:
Enrollment of program: 48
Transfer students are accepted.

Financial Information:
Tuition, resident: $800
Tuition, non-resident: $1,700
Average cost of books: $150
% of students receiving aid: 10

Employment Profile:
% of students who pass the boards on their first try: 98
% employed within the first 6 months following graduation: 80
Average starting salary: $20,000

University of Texas Southwestern Medical Center—Dallas

5323 Harry Hines Boulevard
Dallas, TX 75235-8890

Contact Information:
Telephone: 210-567-7860
Fax: 210-567-7887
E-mail: dcason@mednet.swmed.edu
Web: www.swmed.edu

Program Information:
Program begins: August, February
Duration of program: 6 months

Financial Information:
Tuition, resident: $1,200
Tuition, non-resident: $1,800

Employment Profile:
% of students who pass the boards on their first try: 100
% employed within the first 6 months following graduation: 100

Utah

Weber State University

3902 University Circle
Ogden, UT 84408-3902

Contact Information:
Telephone: 801-626-6521
Fax: 801-626-6610
E-mail: vquick@weber.edu
Web: www.weber.edu

Program Information:
Program begins: September, January
Duration of program: 12 months

Application Information:
Enrollment of program: 55
Transfer students are accepted.

Financial Information:
Tuition, resident: $2,488
Tuition, non-resident: $7,367
Average cost of books: $400
% of students receiving aid: 20

Employment Profile:
% of students who pass the boards on their first try: 90
% employed within the first 6 months following graduation: 98
Average starting salary: $24,000

Washington

Tacoma Community College

6501 South 19th Street
Tacoma, WA 98466

Contact Information:
Telephone: 206-566-5220
Fax: 206-566-5273
E-mail: gcurry@tcc.tacoma.ctc.edu
Web: www.tacoma.ctc.edu

Program Information:
Program begins: September
Duration of program: 9 months

Financial Information:
Tuition, resident: $1,400
Tuition, non-resident: $5,500

Employment Profile:
% of students who pass the boards on their first try: 95
% employed within the first 6 months following graduation: 100
Average starting salary: $33,000

Health Information Management Professional

Jennifer Hornung, MBA, RHIA, CPHQ, CCS
Program Director and Assistant Professor
Health Information Management Program
Gwynedd-Mercy College
School of Allied Health
Gwynedd Valley, Pennsylvania

Job Description

What Do They Do?

HIM professionals work in many organizations that provide healthcare services to the public. They also work in industries that support healthcare such as publishing, computer hardware and software companies, and the pharmaceutical industry. HIM professionals collect, maintain, and analyze the information generated from patient care activities.

Type of Person

HIM professionals tend to be detail-oriented individuals who are interested in many or all aspects of healthcare. They enjoy science, math, reading, business, and working with computers. HIM professionals also enjoy working with other healthcare professionals in teams. Because of the breadth of knowledge and skills that HIM professionals possess, they are frequently asked to serve as project managers for organization-wide endeavors such as preparation for accrediting agency surveys and implementation of computer-based patient records.

With Whom Do They Work?

HIM professionals work with physicians, nurses, respiratory therapists, healthcare administrators, dietitians, cardiovascular technicians, radiation therapists, medical technologists, occupational therapists, social workers, and many other healthcare professionals. Health information management professionals help provide these members of the healthcare team with the information they need to treat patients and improve quality of care.

Employment

Places of Employment

HIM professionals work in acute care facilities (hospitals), insurance companies, long-term care facilities (nursing homes), behavioral health facilities, consulting firms, computer companies, outpatient facilities, home healthcare, state and federal government, pharmaceutical companies, medical practices, and medical billing companies.

Employment Outlook

The HIM profession has been cited by the Bureau of Labor Statistics as one of the fastest growing occupations in the United States.[1] Few people know of the profession, which has resulted in a shortage of qualified personnel. The current trends in healthcare have demonstrated a growing need to use health information to improve organizational functioning and reimbursement; therefore, the employment outlook for the profession appears to be strong.

Salary

The salary levels of HIM professionals vary with education. Generally, salary levels increase with education. The majority of HIM professionals with Associate's degrees earn annual salaries of $20,000 to $29,000; those with Bachelor's degrees earn annual salaries of $30,000 to $39,000. According to the American Health Information Management Association (AHIMA), over half of the new graduates with Bachelor's degrees earn a starting salary of $30,000 to $50,000 per year, while Associate's degree graduates have starting salaries of $20,000 to $30,000 per year.[2]

Educational Programs

The health information management profession supports the provision of patient care and the use of patient information in a wide range of settings. There are a variety of job functions that an HIM professional may undertake after completion of academic work at the Associate or Baccalaureate degree level. Completion of an Associate's degree in Health Information Technology (HIT) provides eligibility to take the Registered Health Information Technician (RHIT) examination while the graduate of a Bachelor's degree, or post-baccalaureate certificate in Health Information Administration (HIA), is eligible for the Registered Health Information Administrator (RHIA) examination.

Both types of health information management professionals require a similar knowledge base and work in similar jobs; however, Bachelor's degree programs include research methodology, advanced statistics, more management science, and a greater breadth of the liberal arts and sciences. This allows HIA graduates to pursue advanced degrees and work in organizations that prefer a Bachelor's degree. While HIA graduates may perform technical job functions, they usually strive for management opportunities.

Length

Associate's degree HIM programs vary based upon institutional requirements. The most common type of Associate's degree program requires two years of full-time study. In Bachelor's degree programs, the length varies based on the type of program and institutional requirements. Some Bachelor's programs require four years full time; others require two or fewer full-time years of study following the completion of an Associate's degree. The most common Baccalaureate degree requires two full-time years of general education courses followed by two additional full-time years of study in the major.

Prerequisites

In both Associate's and Bachelor's degree programs, the prerequisites vary based upon the institution; however, grades in computer science, business, science, math, and English may be used to evaluate applicants.

Curriculum

In Associate's degree programs, the HIM core curriculum includes general education requirements (as determined by the college), biomedical sciences (including anatomy and physiology, medical terminology, pharmacology, and medical science), information technology, health data content and structure, healthcare delivery systems, organization and supervision, healthcare statistics and data literacy, and clinical quality assessment. Additionally, students study performance improvement, clinical classification systems, reimbursement methodologies, and law and ethics.

The Bachelor's degree HIM core curriculum includes many of the same courses as an Associate's degree but adds studies in healthcare delivery systems, organization and management, quantitative methods and research, healthcare information requirements and standards, health information systems, healthcare data content and structure, clinical quality assessment and performance improvement, biomedical research support, and health information services management.

Accrediting Bodies

Commission on Accreditation of Allied Health Education Programs (CAAHEP)
515 North State Street, Suite 7530
Chicago, IL 60610-4377
Telephone: 312-464-4623

The American Health Information Management Association (AHIMA) Council on Education
Commission on Accreditation of Allied Health Education Programs
919 North Michigan Avenue, Suite 1400
Chicago, IL 60611-1683
Telephone: 312-787-2672

Certification Board

After completion of the Associate's degree in an accredited Health Information Technology Program, the graduate is eligible to take AHIMA's national credentialing examination to become a Registered Health Information Technician (RHIT). After completion of the Baccalaureate degree in an accredited Health Information Administration Program, the graduate is eligible to take the national credentialing exam to become a Registered Health Information Administrator (RHIA).

American Health Information Management Association
919 North Michigan Avenue, Suite 1400
Chicago, IL 60611-1683
Telephone: 312-787-2672
Web address: www.ahima.org

Advice for Potential Students

Call the school you are thinking of attending and make an appointment with the program director to discuss the program. You may also contact a local hospital and ask to visit the Health Information Management Department. Ask the Health Information Management professional(s) you meet about job opportunities. Look in the local newspaper to determine the job openings for HIM in your area. Visit the AHIMA web site or call AHIMA to gather further information about the profession.

For Additional Information

Organizations

American Health Information Management Association
919 North Michigan Avenue, Suite 1400
Chicago, IL 60611-1683
Telephone: 312-787-2672
Web address: www.ahima.org

Publications

Health Information Management: Management of a Strategic Resource. Abdelhak, Mervat. Philadelphia: W.B. Saunders Company, 1996.

The first of two standard textbooks required in many HIM programs. This text gives a good description of key areas of the HIM profession.

Health Information Management. American Health Information Management Association: Berwyn, Illinois: Physicians' Record Company, 1994.

The second major text in HIM required by many educational programs. It contains basic information regarding many aspects of the HIM profession.

Internet Resources

American Health Information Management Association: www.ahima.org

Health Information Administrator

Arkansas

Arkansas Technical University

Wilson 105
Russellville, AR 72801

Contact Information:
Telephone: 501-968-0441
Fax: 501-964-0504
E-mail: plmh@atuvm.atu.edu
Web: www.atu.edu

Program Information:
Program begins: August
Duration of program: 37 months

Application Information:
Enrollment of program: 75
Transfer students are accepted.

Financial Information:
Tuition, resident: $2,016
Tuition, non-resident: $4,082

Employment Profile:
% of students who pass the boards on their first try: 93
% employed within the first 6 months following graduation: 95
Average starting salary: $22,000

California

Loma Linda University

1905 Nichol Hall
Loma Linda, CA 92350

Contact Information:
Telephone: 909-558-4976
Fax: 909-558-0404

E-mail: mdavidian@sahp.llu.edu
Web: www.llu.edu

Program Information:
Program begins: September, January, April
Duration of program: 21 months

Colorado

Regis University
3333 Regis Boulevard
Denver, CO 80221-1099

Contact Information:
Telephone: 303-458-4157
Fax: 303-964-5533
E-mail: dbwoods@regis.edu
Web: www.regis.edu

Program Information:
Program begins: September
Degrees offered: Bachelor's, 24 months; Post-bachelor's Certificate, 24 months
Evening or weekend classes are available.

Application Information:
Transfer students are accepted.

Financial Information:
Average cost of books: $600
% of students receiving aid: 80

Employment Profile:
% of students who pass the boards on their first try: 100
% employed within the first 6 months following graduation: 85

Florida

Florida International University
3000 Northeast 151 Street
ACI-Room 394C
Miami, FL 33181-3000

Contact Information:
Telephone: 305-919-5631
Fax: 305-919-5507
E-mail: martinez@fiu.edu
Web: www.fiu.edu

Program Information:
Program begins: August
Degrees offered: Bachelor's, 24 months
Evening or weekend classes are available.

Application Information:
Enrollment of program: 100
Transfer students are accepted.

Financial Information:
Tuition, resident: $2,474
Tuition, non-resident: $10,461

Employment Profile:
% employed within the first 6 months following graduation: 95
Average starting salary: $35,000

Georgia

Clark Atlanta University
James P. Brawley Drive at Fair Street Southwest
Atlanta, GA 30314

Contact Information:
Telephone: 404-880-8115
Fax: 404-880-6165
Web: www.cau.edu

Program Information:
Program begins: August, January, May
Duration of program: 36 months

Application Information:
Enrollment of program: 16
Transfer students are accepted.

Financial Information:
Tuition, resident: $8,300
Average cost of books: $500
% of students receiving aid: 90

Employment Profile:
% of students who pass the boards on their first try: 50
% employed within the first 6 months following graduation: 60
Average starting salary: $26,000

Medical College of Georgia
AL-130
Augusta, GA 30912-0400

Contact Information:
Telephone: 706-721-3436
Fax: 706-721-6067
E-mail: cacampbe@mail.mcg.edu
Web: www.mcg.edu

Program Information:
Program begins: August, January
Duration of program: 18 months

Application Information:
Enrollment of program: 30
Transfer students are accepted.

Financial Information:
Tuition, resident: $3,282
Tuition, non-resident: $10,212
Average cost of books: $900
% of students receiving aid: 60

Employment Profile:
% of students who pass the boards on their first try: 100
% employed within the first 6 months following graduation: 80
Average starting salary: $30,000

Illinois

Chicago State University
9501 South King Drive
Business and Health Sciences/BHS-Room 610
Chicago, IL 60628-1598

Contact Information:
Telephone: 773-995-2593
Fax: 773-995-4484
E-mail: l-thomas@email.com
Web: www.csu.edu

Program Information:
Program begins: September, January
Duration of program: 48 months

Application Information:
Enrollment of program: 120
Transfer students are accepted.

Financial Information:
Tuition, resident: $3,151
Tuition, non-resident: $7,735

Illinois State University
5220 Health Sciences
Normal, IL 617905220

Contact Information:
Telephone: 309-438-8329 ext. 8809
Fax: 309-438-2450
E-mail: fwaterst@ilstu.edu
Web: www.cast.ilstu.edu

Program Information:
Program begins: August
Duration of program: 24 months

Application Information:
Enrollment of program: 60
Transfer students are accepted.

Financial Information:
Tuition, resident: $4,080
Tuition, non-resident: $11,160
Average cost of books: $500
% of students receiving aid: 50

Employment Profile:
% of students who pass the boards on their first try: 85
% employed within the first 6 months following graduation: 50
Average starting salary: $28,000

University of Illinois at Chicago
1919 West Taylor
Room 811, M/C 520
Chicago, IL 60612

Contact Information:
Telephone: 312-996-3530
Fax: 312-413-0205
E-mail: patena@uic.edu
Web: www.uic.edu

Program Information:
Program begins: August
Degrees offered: Bachelor's, 24 months; Master's

Application Information:
Enrollment of program: 30
Transfer students are accepted.

Financial Information:
Tuition, resident: $3,138
Tuition, non-resident: $9,414
Average cost of books: $1,000

Employment Profile:
% of students who pass the boards on their first try: 90

Kansas

University of Kansas Medical Center
3901 Rainbow Boulevard
KU Hospital G-124
Kansas City, KS 66160-7607

Contact Information:
Telephone: 913-588-2423
Fax: 913-588-2428
E-mail: dkellogg@kumc.edu
Web: www.kume/sah/him

Program Information:
Program begins: August
Duration of program: 12 months

Application Information:
Enrollment of program: 71
Transfer students are accepted.

Financial Information:
Tuition, resident: $3,030
Tuition, non-resident: $12,604
Average cost of books: $1,000
% of students receiving aid: 33

Employment Profile:
% of students who pass the boards on their first try: 100
% employed within the first 6 months following graduation: 90
Average starting salary: $34,000

Kentucky

Eastern Kentucky University
521 Lancaster Avenue
Richmond, KY 40475-3102

Contact Information:
Telephone: 606-622-1915
Fax: 606-622-2013
E-mail: hrshinds@acs.eku.edu
Web: www.healthinfo.eku.edu

Program Information:
Program begins: August
Duration of program: 36 months

Financial Information:
Tuition, resident: $2,390
Tuition, non-resident: $6,430

Louisiana

Louisiana Technical University
PO Box 3171
Ruston, LA 71272

Contact Information:
Telephone: 318-257-2854
Fax: 318-257-4896
E-mail: kennedy@him.latech.edu
Web: www.latech.edu

Program Information:
Program begins: September
Duration of program: 39 months
Evening or weekend classes are available.

Financial Information:
Tuition, resident: $2,379
Tuition, non-resident: $7,624

Michigan

Ferris State University
College of Allied Health Sciences
200 Ferris Drive/VFS 402
Big Rapids, MI 49307-2740

Contact Information:
Telephone: 231-591-2313
Fax: 231-591-3788
Web: www.ferris.edu

Program Information:
Program begins: August
Degrees offered: Bachelor's, 36 months
Evening or weekend classes are available.

Application Information:
Enrollment of program: 80
Transfer students are accepted.

Financial Information:
Tuition, resident: $3,630
Tuition, non-resident: $7,364
Average cost of books: $500
% of students receiving aid: 88

Employment Profile:
% of students who pass the boards on their first try: 92
% employed within the first 6 months following graduation: 100
Average starting salary: $28,500

Minnesota

College of St. Scholastica
1200 Kenwood Avenue
Duluth, MN 55811

Contact Information:
Telephone: 218-723-6011
Fax: 218-733-2239
E-mail: klatour@css.edu
Web: www.css.edu

Program Information:
Duration of program: 24 months

Application Information:
Enrollment of program: 40
Transfer students are accepted.

Financial Information:
Tuition, resident: $15,420
Average cost of books: $300

Employment Profile:
% of students who pass the boards on their first try: 98
% employed within the first 6 months following graduation: 75
Average starting salary: $32,000

Missouri

Stephens College
Campus Box 2083
Columbia, MO 65215

Contact Information:
Telephone: 573-876-7283
Fax: 573-876-7248
E-mail: joanr@wc.stephens.edu
Web: www.stephens.edu

Program Information:
Program begins: August

Application Information:
Transfer students are accepted.

Financial Information:
Average cost of books: $500

Employment Profile:
% of students who pass the boards on their first try: 95
% employed within the first 6 months following graduation: 100

New York

SUNY Institute of Technology—Utica-Rome
PO Box 3050
Utica, NY 13504-3050

Contact Information:
Telephone: 315-792-7391
Fax: 315-792-7138
E-mail: fdls1@sunyit.edu
Web: www.sunyit.edu

Program Information:
Program begins: August
Degrees offered: Bachelor's, 18 months
Evening or weekend classes are available.

Application Information:
Transfer students are accepted.

Financial Information:
Tuition, resident: $3,400
Tuition, non-resident: $4,150

North Carolina

East Carolina University
School of Allied Health Sciences
Greenville, NC 27858

Contact Information:
Telephone: 252-328-4426
Fax: 252-328-4470
E-mail: laymane@mail.ecu.edu
Web: www.ecu.edu

Program Information:
Program begins: January, April, September
Duration of program: 18 months

Application Information:
Enrollment of program: 35

Financial Information:
Tuition, resident: $1,200
Tuition, non-resident: $5,000
Average cost of books: $300

Employment Profile:
% of students who pass the boards on their first try: 90
% employed within the first 6 months following graduation: 39

Ohio

Ohio State University
1583 Perry Street
Columbus, OH 43210

Contact Information:
Telephone: 614-292-0567
Fax: 614-292-0210
E-mail: brodnik.2@osu.edu
Web: www.amp.ohio-state.edu

Program Information:
Program begins: September
Degrees offered: Bachelor's
Evening or weekend classes are available.

Application Information:
Enrollment of program: 50
Transfer students are accepted.

Financial Information:
Tuition, resident: $3,468
Tuition, non-resident: $10,335
Average cost of books: $350
% of students receiving aid: 35

Employment Profile:
% of students who pass the boards on their first try: 100
% employed within the first 6 months following graduation: 100
Average starting salary: $36,000

Oklahoma

Southwestern Oklahoma State University
100 Campus Drive
Weatherford, OK 73096

Contact Information:
Telephone: 580-774-3287
Fax: 580-774-3795
E-mail: pricham@swosu.edu
Web: www.swosu.edu

Program Information:
Program begins: June
Duration of program: 24 months

Application Information:
Enrollment of program: 15
Transfer students are accepted.

Financial Information:
Tuition, resident: $1,913
Tuition, non-resident: $4,685
Average cost of books: $400
% of students receiving aid: 50

Employment Profile:
% of students who pass the boards on their first try: 100
% employed within the first 6 months following graduation: 75
Average starting salary: $27,500

Pennsylvania

Duquesne University
Chairman, Department of Health Management Systems
429 Fisher Hall
Pittsburgh, PA 15282-0001

Contact Information:
Telephone: 412-396-4772
Fax: 412-396-5554
Web: www.duq.edu

Program Information:
Program begins: September
Duration of program: 24 months
Evening or weekend classes are available.

Application Information:
Enrollment of program: 130
Transfer students are accepted.

Gwynedd-Mercy College
1325 Sumneytown Pike
PO Box 901
Gwynedd Valley, PA 19437

Contact Information:
Telephone: 215-646-7300
Fax: 215-641-5559
E-mail: hornung.j@gmc.edu
Web: www.gmc.edu

Program Information:
Program begins: August
Degrees offered: Bachelor's, 24 months
Evening or weekend classes are available.

Application Information:
Enrollment of program: 15
Transfer students are accepted.

Employment Profile:
% employed within the first 6 months following graduation: 100

University of Pittsburgh
6051 Forbes Tower
Pittsburgh, PA 15260

Contact Information:
Telephone: 412-647-1190
Fax: 412-647-1199
E-mail: madelhak+@pitt.edu
Web: www.him.upmc.edu

Program Information:
Program begins: August
Degrees offered: Bachelor's, 18 months; Master's, 16 months; PhD, 36 months
Evening or weekend classes are available.

Application Information:
Enrollment of program: 100
Transfer students are accepted.

Financial Information:
Tuition, resident: $7,872
Tuition, non-resident: $17,168

Employment Profile:
% of students who pass the boards on their first try: 95
% employed within the first 6 months following graduation: 90
Average starting salary: $45,000

South Dakota

Dakota State University
CB Kennedy Center #151
Madison, SD 57042-1799

Contact Information:
Telephone: 605-256-5137
Fax: 605-256-5060
E-mail: bennettd@pluto.dsu.edu
Web: www.dsu.edu

Program Information:
Program begins: September
Duration of program: 48 months

Application Information:
Enrollment of program: 21

Financial Information:
Tuition, resident: $3,301
Tuition, non-resident: $7,000
Average cost of books: $600

Employment Profile:
% of students who pass the boards on their first try: 100
Average starting salary: $25,000

Tennessee

University of Tennessee—Memphis
Department of Health Information Management
822 Beale Building, Room 321
Memphis, TN 38163
Telephone: 901-448-6304
Fax: 901-448-7545

Contact Information:
Telephone: 901-448-6486
Fax: 901-448-7545
Web: www.utmem.edu

Program Information:
Program begins: September
Duration of program: 12 months

Financial Information:
Tuition, resident: $2,484
Tuition, non-resident: $7,783

Texas

Southwest Texas State University
220 HSC
San Marcos, TX 78666

Contact Information:
Telephone: 512-245-8242
Fax: 512-245-8258
E-mail: sb2@swt.edu
Web: www.health.swt.edu

Program Information:
Program begins: August
Duration of program: 22 months

Application Information:
Enrollment of program: 50

Financial Information:
Tuition, resident: $3,000
Tuition, non-resident: $10,000

Texas Southern University
3100 Cleburne Street
Houston, TX 77004

Contact Information:
Telephone: 713-313-7265
Fax: 713-313-1094
E-mail: fannyhawkins@hotmail.com

Program Information:
Program begins: August
Duration of program: 16 months

Application Information:
Enrollment of program: 47
Transfer students are accepted.

Financial Information:
Tuition, resident: $1,988
Tuition, non-resident: $3,540
Average cost of books: $250
% of students receiving aid: 75

Employment Profile:
% employed within the first 6 months following graduation: 90
Average starting salary: $31,000

University of Texas Medical Branch
School of Allied Health Sciences
301 University Boulevard
Galveston, TX 77555-1028

Contact Information:
Telephone: 409-772-3051
Fax: 409-772-9574
E-mail: dglemire@utmb.edu
Web: www.utmb.edu

Program Information:
Program begins: September
Duration of program: 27 months
Evening or weekend classes are available.

Application Information:
Enrollment of program: 18
Transfer students are accepted.

Financial Information:
Tuition, resident: $1,212
Tuition, non-resident: $5,500
Average cost of books: $200
% of students receiving aid: 73

Employment Profile:
% of students who pass the boards on their first try: 100
% employed within the first 6 months following graduation: 70
Average starting salary: $32,000

Washington

University of Washington
1107 Northeast 45th, Suite 400
Seattle, WA 98105

Contact Information:
Telephone: 206-543-8810
Fax: 206-543-9345
E-mail: gcmurphy@u.washington.edu
Web: www.washington.edu

Program Information:
Program begins: September
Duration of program: 9 months
Evening or weekend classes are available.

Application Information:
Transfer students are accepted.

Employment Profile:
% of students who pass the boards on their first try: 100
% employed within the first 6 months following graduation: 85
Average starting salary: $37,000

Wisconsin

University of Wisconsin—Milwaukee
PO Box 413
Milwaukee, WI 53201

Contact Information:
Telephone: 414-229-3862
Fax: 414-229-3962
E-mail: madson@uwm.edu
Web: www.uwm.edu

Program Information:
Program begins: August
Duration of program: 24 months

Application Information:
Enrollment of program: 13
Transfer students are accepted.

Financial Information:
Tuition, resident: $3,328
Tuition, non-resident: $10,790
Average cost of books: $250

Employment Profile:
% of students who pass the boards on their first try: 98
% employed within the first 6 months following graduation: 50
Average starting salary: $30,000

Health Information Technologist

Alabama

Bishop State Community College
1365 Martin Luther King Jr. Avenue
Mobile, AL 36603

Contact Information:
Telephone: 334-405-4451
Fax: 334-405-4427
E-mail: asharp@bscc.cc.al.us
Web: www.bscc.cc.al.us

Program Information:
Program begins: September
Duration of program: 21 months

Application Information:
Enrollment of program: 20
Transfer students are accepted.

Financial Information:
Tuition, resident: $2,880
Tuition, non-resident: $5,760
Average cost of books: $50

Employment Profile:
% employed within the first 6 months following graduation: 30
Average starting salary: $23,000

Wallace State Community College
Beville Health Education Building
PO Box 2000
Hanceville, AL 35077-9080

Contact Information:
Telephone: 256-352-8327
Fax: 256-352-8320
Web: www.wscc.cc.al.us

Program Information:
Program begins: August
Duration of program: 21 months

Financial Information:
Tuition, resident: $1,932
Tuition, non-resident: $3,864

Arizona

Phoenix College
1202 West Thomas Road
Phoenix, AZ 85013

Contact Information:
Telephone: 602-285-7149
Fax: 602-285-7770
E-mail: petterson@pc.maricopa.edu
Web: www.pc.maricopa.edu

Program Information:
Program begins: August, May
Duration of program: 18 months

Application Information:
Transfer students are accepted.

Financial Information:
Tuition, resident: $1,292
Tuition, non-resident: $5,950

Arkansas

Garland County Community College

101 College Drive
Hot Springs, AR 71913-9174

Contact Information:
Telephone: 501-760-4293
Fax: 501-760-4183
E-mail: swallace@admin.cc.ar.us
Web: www.gccc.cc.ar.us

Program Information:
Program begins: Program begins quarterly.
Duration of program: 21 months
Evening or weekend classes are available.

Application Information:
Enrollment of program: 10
Transfer students are accepted.

Financial Information:
Tuition, resident: $888
Tuition, non-resident: $1,104

Employment Profile:
% of students who pass the boards on their first try: 88
Average starting salary: $17,000

University of Arkansas for Medical Sciences

4301 West Markham Street
Slot 733
Little Rock, AR 72205

Contact Information:
Telephone: 907-747-6653
Fax: 907-747-3552
E-mail: trawickkathyc@exchange.uams
Web: www.uams.edu

Program Information:
Program begins: August, January
Degrees offered: Master's, 20 months
Evening or weekend classes are available.

Application Information:
Enrollment of program: 25
Transfer students are accepted.

Financial Information:
Tuition, resident: $2,568
Tuition, non-resident: $6,408
Average cost of books: $51
% of students receiving aid: 75

Employment Profile:
% of students who pass the boards on their first try: 75
% employed within the first 6 months following graduation: 95
Average starting salary: $25,000

California

Charles R. Drew University of Medicine & Science

1731 East 120th Street
Los Angeles, CA 90059

Contact Information:
Telephone: 323-563-4821
Fax: 323-563-4963
E-mail: etvernon@cdrewu.edu
Web: www.cdrewu.edu

Program Information:
Program begins: August
Duration of program: 6 months
Evening or weekend classes are available.

Application Information:
Enrollment of program: 20
Transfer students are accepted.

Financial Information:
Tuition, resident: $11,085
Average cost of books: $300
% of students receiving aid: 90

City College of San Francisco

John Adams Campus
1860 Hayes Street
San Francisco, CA 94117

Contact Information:
Telephone: 415-561-1818
Fax: 415-561-1861
E-mail: mconde@ccsf.cc.ca.us
Web: www.ccsf.cc.ca.us

Program Information:
Program begins: August
Duration of program: 24 months
Evening or weekend classes are available.

Application Information:
Enrollment of program: 105
Transfer students are accepted.

Financial Information:
Average cost of books: $50
% of students receiving aid: 5

Employment Profile:
% of students who pass the boards on their first try: 70
% employed within the first 6 months following graduation: 90
Average starting salary: $30,000

Cosumnes River College

8401 Center Parkway
Sacramento, CA 95823-5799

Contact Information:
Telephone: 916-688-7452
Fax: 916-688-7443
E-mail: hotzed@crc.losrios.cc.ca.us
Web: www.crc.losrios.cc.ca.us

Program Information:
Program begins: August
Duration of program: 24 months
Evening or weekend classes are available.

Cypress College

9200 Valley View Street
Cypress, CA 90630

Contact Information:
Telephone: 714-484-7283
Fax: 714-527-2175
E-mail: majidr@noccd.cc.ca.us
Web: www.cypress.cc.ca.us

Program Information:
Program begins: August
Degrees offered: Certificate program, 24 months; Associate's, 24 months
Evening or weekend classes are available.

Application Information:
Enrollment of program: 100
Transfer students are accepted.

Financial Information:
Tuition, resident: $330
Tuition, non-resident: $4,020
Average cost of books: $500

Employment Profile:
% of students who pass the boards on their first try: 94
% employed within the first 6 months following graduation: 95
Average starting salary: $27,000

San Diego Mesa College

7250 Mesa College Drive
San Diego, CA 92111

Contact Information:
Telephone: 858-627-2606
Fax: 858-627-5668

Program Information:
Program begins: August
Duration of program: 24 months

Application Information:
Enrollment of program: 50
Transfer students are accepted.

Financial Information:
Tuition, resident: $247
Tuition, non-resident: $2,090
Average cost of books: $500
% of students receiving aid: 20

Employment Profile:
% of students who pass the boards on their first try: 75
% employed within the first 6 months following graduation: 90
Average starting salary: $24,000

Florida

St. Petersburg Junior College

PO Box 13489
St. Petersburg, FL 33733

Contact Information:
Telephone: 813-341-3623
Fax: 813-341-3744
E-mail: spjc.edu
Web: www.spj.edu

Program Information:
Program begins: January, May, September
Duration of program: 22 months
Evening or weekend classes are available.

Application Information:
Enrollment of program: 40
Transfer students are accepted.

Financial Information:
Tuition, resident: $48
Tuition, non-resident: $178
Average cost of books: $1,000

Employment Profile:
% of students who pass the boards on their first try: 93
% employed within the first 6 months following graduation: 85
Average starting salary: $18,000

Georgia

Darton College

2400 Gillionville Road
Albany, GA 31707

Contact Information:
Telephone: 912-430-6894
Fax: 912-430-6910
E-mail: shinglrb@maildartnet.peachnet.edu
Web: www.dartnet.peachnet.edu

Program Information:
Program begins: August
Degrees offered: Associate's, 22 months

Application Information:
Enrollment of program: 15
Transfer students are accepted.

Financial Information:
Tuition, resident: $1,440
Tuition, non-resident: $3,944
Average cost of books: $400

Employment Profile:
% of students who pass the boards on their first try: 90
% employed within the first 6 months following graduation: 100
Average starting salary: $20,000

Idaho

Idaho State University

Campus Box 8380
Pocatello, ID 83209-8380

Contact Information:
Telephone: 208-236-4169
Fax: 208-236-3975
E-mail: grifsuza@isu.edu
Web: www.isu.edu

Program Information:
Program begins: January, August
Degrees offered: Certificate program, 9 months; Associate's, 22 months

Application Information:
Enrollment of program: 20
Transfer students are accepted.

Financial Information:
Tuition, resident: $2,180
Tuition, non-resident: $8,420
Average cost of books: $800
% of students receiving aid: 90

Employment Profile:
% of students who pass the boards on their first try: 100
% employed within the first 6 months following graduation: 90
Average starting salary: $21,000

Illinois

Belleville Area College

2500 Carlyle Avenue
Belleville, IL 62221

Contact Information:
Telephone: 618-235-2700
Fax: 618-235-1578
E-mail: holderwc@smpt.bacnet.edu
Web: www.bacnet.edu

Program Information:
Program begins: August
Duration of program: 22 months

Application Information:
Enrollment of program: 20
Transfer students are accepted.

Financial Information:
Tuition, resident: $1,490
Tuition, non-resident: $3,752
Average cost of books: $500
% of students receiving aid: 50

Employment Profile:
% of students who pass the boards on their first try: 93
% employed within the first 6 months following graduation: 100
Average starting salary: $21,000

College of Lake County

19351 West Washington Street
Grayslake, IL 60030-1198

Contact Information:
Telephone: 847-543-2338
Fax: 847-223-1357
E-mail: danastasio@clc.cc.il.us
Web: www.clc.cc.il.us

Program Information:
Program begins: August
Degrees offered: Associate's, 18 months
Evening or weekend classes are available.

Application Information:
Enrollment of program: 20
Transfer students are accepted.

Financial Information:
Tuition, resident: $1,632
Tuition, non-resident: $6,336
Average cost of books: $400

Employment Profile:
% of students who pass the boards on their first try: 90
% employed within the first 6 months following graduation: 95
Average starting salary: $22,000

Southern Illinois Collegiate Common Market

3213 South Park Avenue
Herrin, IL 62948

Contact Information:
Telephone: 618-942-6902
Fax: 618-942-6658
E-mail: sullivan@midwest.net
Web: www.siccm.com

Program Information:
Program begins: August
Duration of program: 18 months

Financial Information:
Tuition, resident: $2,112
Tuition, non-resident: $8,719

Iowa

Northeast Iowa Community College

Box 400
Calmar, IA 52132

Contact Information:
Telephone: 319-562-3263
Web: www.micc.cc.ia.us

Program Information:
Program begins: August
Degrees offered: Associate's, 24 months

Application Information:
Enrollment of program: 25
Transfer students are accepted.

Financial Information:
Tuition, resident: $1,134
Tuition, non-resident: $1,588
Average cost of books: $800

Employment Profile:
% employed within the first 6 months following graduation: 100

Kansas

Hutchinson Community College and Area Vocational School
1300 North Plum
Hutchinson, KS 67501

Contact Information:
Telephone: 316-665-4955
Fax: 316-665-4924
E-mail: hortonl@hutchcc.edu
Web: www.hutchcc.edu

Program Information:
Program begins: September
Duration of program: 22 months
Evening or weekend classes are available.

Application Information:
Transfer students are accepted.

Financial Information:
Tuition, resident: $2,880
Tuition, non-resident: $6,272
Average cost of books: $400

Employment Profile:
% of students who pass the boards on their first try: 90
% employed within the first 6 months following graduation: 91
Average starting salary: $20,800

Washburn University of Topeka
1700 College Avenue Southwest
Topeka, KS 66621

Contact Information:
Telephone: 785-231-1010 ext. 1397
Fax: 785-231-1027
E-mail: zzship@washburn.edu
Web: www.washburn.edu

Program Information:
Program begins: August
Duration of program: 24 months
Evening or weekend classes are available.

Application Information:
Transfer students are accepted.

Financial Information:
Tuition, resident: $3,813
Tuition, non-resident: $7,831

Kentucky

Kentucky College of Business
3950 Dixie Highway
Louisville, KY 40216

Contact Information:
Telephone: 502-447-7634
Fax: 502-447-7665
E-mail: neichter@entreky.net

Program Information:
Program begins: September
Degrees offered: Diploma, 9 months
Evening or weekend classes are available.

Application Information:
Enrollment of program: 24
Transfer students are accepted.

Financial Information:
% of students receiving aid: 80

Employment Profile:
% of students who pass the boards on their first try: 75
% employed within the first 6 months following graduation: 90

Western Kentucky University
South Campus 2355 Nashville Road
Bowling Green, KY 42101

Contact Information:
Telephone: 270-780-2567
Fax: 270-780-2560
E-mail: karen.sansom@wku.edu
Web: www.wku.edu

Program Information:
Program begins: August
Duration of program: 21 months

Application Information:
Transfer students are accepted.

Financial Information:
Tuition, resident: $2,390
Tuition, non-resident: $6,430

Massachusetts

Laboure College
2120 Dorchester Avenue
Boston, MA 02124

Contact Information:
Telephone: 617-296-8300
Fax: 617-296-7947
Web: www.labourecollege.org

Program Information:
Program begins: August
Degrees offered: Certificate program, 9 months; Diploma, 24 months
Evening or weekend classes are available.

Application Information:
Enrollment of program: 40
Transfer students are accepted.

Financial Information:
Tuition, resident: $5,000
Tuition, non-resident: $6,000
Average cost of books: $200
% of students receiving aid: 75

Employment Profile:
% of students who pass the boards on their first try: 75
% employed within the first 6 months following graduation: 100
Average starting salary: $30,000

Michigan

Baker College
1050 West Bristol Road
Flint, MI 48507

Contact Information:
Telephone: 810-766-4147
Fax: 810-766-4049
E-mail: savag_am@acadfl.baker.edu
Web: www.baker.edu

Program Information:
Program begins: August
Duration of program: 48 months

Application Information:
Enrollment of program: 50
Transfer students are accepted.

Financial Information:
Average cost of books: $1,000
% of students receiving aid: 80

Employment Profile:
% of students who pass the boards on their first try: 84
% employed within the first 6 months following graduation: 100
Average starting salary: $22,000
Additional information: Open enrollment.

Ferris State University
College of Allied Health Sciences
200 Ferris Drive/VFS 402
Big Rapids, MI 49307-2740

Contact Information:
Telephone: 231-591-2313
Fax: 231-591-3788
E-mail: ellen_j_haneline@ferris.edu
Web: www.ferris.edu

Program Information:
Program begins: August
Duration of program: 18 months
Evening or weekend classes are available.

Application Information:
Enrollment of program: 56
Transfer students are accepted.

Financial Information:
Tuition, resident: $3,630
Tuition, non-resident: $7,364

Employment Profile:
% of students who pass the boards on their first try: 86
% employed within the first 6 months following graduation: 96
Average starting salary: $23,000

Henry Ford Community College
22586 Ann Arbor Trail
Dearborn Heights, MI 48127

Contact Information:
Telephone: 313-317-6590
Fax: 313-317-6569
Web: www.hfcc.net

Program Information:
Program begins: August
Degrees offered: Associate's, 24 months
Evening or weekend classes are available.

Application Information:
Transfer students are accepted.

Financial Information:
Tuition, resident: $1,710
Tuition, non-resident: $2,490
Average cost of books: $400
% of students receiving aid: 60

Employment Profile:
% of students who pass the boards on their first try: 98
% employed within the first 6 months following graduation: 100
Average starting salary: $25,000

Schoolcraft College

1751 Radcliff Street
Garden City, MI 48135

Contact Information:
Telephone: 734-462-4770 ext. 6025
Fax: 734-462-4775
E-mail: prubio@schoolcraft.cc.mi.us
Web: www.schoolcraft.cc.mi.us

Program Information:
Program begins: August
Degrees offered: Associate's, 24 months
Evening or weekend classes are available.

Application Information:
Enrollment of program: 40
Transfer students are accepted.

Financial Information:
Tuition, resident: $2,142
Tuition, non-resident: $3,078
Average cost of books: $600

Employment Profile:
% of students who pass the boards on their first try: 100
% employed within the first 6 months following graduation: 90
Average starting salary: $26,000

Minnesota

Northwest Technical College—Moorhead

2022 Central Avenue Northeast
East Grand Forks, MN 56721

Contact Information:
Telephone: 218-773-3441
Fax: 218-773-4502
E-mail: mary.juenemann@mail.ntc.mnscu.edu
Web: www.ntc-online.com

Program Information:
Program begins: September
Duration of program: 24 months
Evening or weekend classes are available.

Financial Information:
Tuition, resident: $4,375
Tuition, non-resident: $8,749

Rasmussen Colleges

12450 Wayzata Boulevard
Suite 226
Minnetonka, MN 55305

Contact Information:
Telephone: 320-251-5600
Fax: 320-257-3702
E-mail: ellena@rasmussen.edu
Web: www.rasmussen.edu

Program Information:
Program begins: September
Duration of program: 18 months
Evening or weekend classes are available.

Application Information:
Enrollment of program: 124
Transfer students are accepted.

Financial Information:
Tuition, resident: $11,600
Average cost of books: $1,050
% of students receiving aid: 66

Employment Profile:
% of students who pass the boards on their first try: 71
% employed within the first 6 months following graduation: 80

Ridgewater College—Willmar Campus

2101 15th Avenue Northwest
PO Box 1097
Willmar, MN 56201

Contact Information:
Telephone: 320-231-2949
Fax: 320-231-7690
E-mail: muppena@ridgewater.mnscu.edu
Web: www.ridgewater.mnscu.edu

Program Information:
Program begins: September, April
Duration of program: 21 months

Application Information:
Enrollment of program: 20
Transfer students are accepted.

Financial Information:
Tuition, resident: $2,870
Tuition, non-resident: $5,420
Average cost of books: $600

Employment Profile:
% of students who pass the boards on their first try: 100
% employed within the first 6 months following graduation: 100

Mississippi

Hinds Community College

1750 Chadwick Drive
Jackson, MS 39204

Contact Information:
Telephone: 601-372-6507 ext. 3514
Fax: 601-371-3703
E-mail: jae1950@aol.com
Web: www.hinds.cc.ms.us

Program Information:
Program begins: August
Degrees offered: Associate's, 24 months

Application Information:
Enrollment of program: 30
Transfer students are accepted.

Financial Information:
Tuition, resident: $1,120
Tuition, non-resident: $3,576
Average cost of books: $500
% of students receiving aid: 40

Employment Profile:
% of students who pass the boards on their first try: 90
% employed within the first 6 months following graduation: 100
Average starting salary: $21,000

Missouri

Penn Valley Community College

3201 Southwest Trafficway
Kansas City, MO 64111

Contact Information:
Telephone: 816-759-4245
Fax: 816-759-4553
Web: www.kcmetro.cc.mo.us/pennvalley

Program Information:
Program begins: September, October
Duration of program: 24 months

Financial Information:
Tuition, resident: $1,575
Tuition, non-resident: $2,647

Montana

Salish Kootenai College

PO Box 117
Pablo, MT 59855

Contact Information:
Telephone: 406-675-4800 ext. 373
Fax: 406-675-4801
E-mail: roberta_yankovich@skc.edu
Web: www.skc.edu

Program Information:
Program begins: August
Duration of program: 18 months

Application Information:
Enrollment of program: 25
Transfer students are accepted.

Financial Information:
Tuition, resident: $4,430
Tuition, non-resident: $10,960
Average cost of books: $600
% of students receiving aid: 95

Employment Profile:
% of students who pass the boards on their first try: 70
Average starting salary: $20,000

New Jersey

Burlington County College

County Route 530
Pemberton, NJ 08068-1599

Contact Information:
Telephone: 609-894-9311 ext. 7339
Fax: 609-726-1781
E-mail: vnguyen@bcc.edu
Web: www.bcc.edu

Program Information:
Program begins: August, January, May
Degrees offered: Associate's, 21 months
Evening or weekend classes are available.

Application Information:
Enrollment of program: 30
Transfer students are accepted.

Employment Profile:
% of students who pass the boards on their first try: 86
% employed within the first 6 months following graduation: 75
Average starting salary: $29,000

New York

Adirondack Community College

634 Bay Road
Queensbury, NY 12804-1498

Contact Information:
Telephone: 518-743-2300 ext. 414
Fax: 518-745-1433
Web: www.sunyacc.edu

Program Information:
Program begins: August, January
Duration of program: 9 months

Financial Information:
Tuition, resident: $2,050

Mohawk Valley Community College

1101 Sherman Drive
Utica, NY 13501

Contact Information:
Telephone: 315-792-5513
Fax: 315-792-5666
E-mail: sbice@linux.mvcc.edu
Web: www.mvcc.edu

Program Information:
Program begins: August
Duration of program: 19 months
Evening or weekend classes are available.

Financial Information:
Tuition, resident: $2,500
Tuition, non-resident: $3,750

Molloy College

1000 Hempstead Avenue
PO Box 5002
Rockville Centre, NY 11571-5002

Contact Information:
Telephone: 516-678-5000
Fax: 516-256-2252
E-mail: jbackerman@molloy.edu
Web: www.molloy.edu

Program Information:
Program begins: September
Degrees offered: Associate's, 24 months
Evening or weekend classes are available.

Application Information:
Enrollment of program: 20
Transfer students are accepted.

Financial Information:
Average cost of books: $350
% of students receiving aid: 70

Employment Profile:
% of students who pass the boards on their first try: 90
% employed within the first 6 months following graduation: 98
Average starting salary: $28,000

North Carolina

Catawba Valley Community College

2550 Highway 70 Southeast
Hickory, NC 28602

Contact Information:
Telephone: 704-327-7000
Fax: 704-327-7276
E-mail: dcook@crcc.ec.nc.us
Web: www.cvcc.cc.nc.us

Program Information:
Program begins: September
Degrees offered: Certificate program, 8 months

Application Information:
Enrollment of program: 30
Transfer students are accepted.

Financial Information:
Tuition, resident: $188
Tuition, non-resident: $1,475
Average cost of books: $500
% of students receiving aid: 30

Employment Profile:
% of students who pass the boards on their first try: 95
% employed within the first 6 months following graduation: 99
Average starting salary: $20,000

Southeastern Regional Allied Health Consortium

PO Box 30
Supply, NC 28462

Contact Information:
Telephone: 910-754-6900
Fax: 910-754-7805
Web: www.brunswick.cc.nc.us

Program Information:
Program begins: August
Degrees offered: Associate's, 21 months

Application Information:
Transfer students are accepted.

Financial Information:
Tuition, resident: $705
Tuition, non-resident: $5,424

Southwestern Community College

447 College Drive
Sylva, NC 28779

Contact Information:
Telephone: 828-586-4091
Fax: 828-586-3129
E-mail: pwells@southwestern.cc.nc.us
Web: www.southwest.cc.nc.us

Program Information:
Program begins: September
Duration of program: 21 months
Evening or weekend classes are available.

Application Information:
Enrollment of program: 25
Transfer students are accepted.

Financial Information:
Tuition, resident: $384
Tuition, non-resident: $2,375
Average cost of books: $500
% of students receiving aid: 30

Employment Profile:
% of students who pass the boards on their first try: 100
% employed within the first 6 months following graduation: 100
Average starting salary: $25,000

North Dakota

United Tribes Technical College

3315 University Drive
Bismarck, ND 58504

Contact Information:
Telephone: 701-255-3285 ext. 245
Fax: 701-255-1844
E-mail: ndkbaxter@hotmail.com
Web: www.unitedtribes.tec.dd.us

Program Information:
Program begins: September
Degrees offered: Associate's, 18 months

Application Information:
Enrollment of program: 17
Transfer students are accepted.

Employment Profile:
% employed within the first 6 months following graduation: 13
Average starting salary: $20,000

Ohio

Bowling Green State University

One University Drive
Huron, OH 44839

Contact Information:
Telephone: 419-433-5560
Fax: 419-433-9696
E-mail: monaj@bgnet.bgsu.edu
Web: www.bgsu.edu

Program Information:
Program begins: September, January
Duration of program: 18 months
Evening or weekend classes are available.

Application Information:
Enrollment of program: 18

Financial Information:
Tuition, resident: $3,166
Tuition, non-resident: $4,848

Employment Profile:
% employed within the first 6 months following graduation: 80
Average starting salary: $21,300

Columbus State Community College

550 East Spring Street
Columbus, OH 43215

Contact Information:
Telephone: 614-287-2541
Fax: 614-287-5144
E-mail: lcerrato@cscc.edu
Web: www.cscc.edu

Program Information:
Program begins: August
Duration of program: 18 months
Evening or weekend classes are available.

Application Information:
Transfer students are accepted.

Financial Information:
Tuition, resident: $2,928
Tuition, non-resident: $6,432
Average cost of books: $300
% of students receiving aid: 58

Employment Profile:
% of students who pass the boards on their first try: 90
% employed within the first 6 months following graduation: 95
Average starting salary: $27,000

Cuyahoga Community College

700 Carnegie Avenue
Cleveland, OH 44115

Contact Information:
Telephone: 216-987-4456
Fax: 216-987-4386
E-mail: nancy.donahue@tri-c.cc.oh.us
Web: www.tri-c.cc.us

Program Information:
Program begins: August
Degrees offered: Associate's, 24 months
Evening or weekend classes are available.

Application Information:
Enrollment of program: 20
Transfer students are accepted.

Financial Information:
Tuition, resident: $2,300
Tuition, non-resident: $3,000
Average cost of books: $500
% of students receiving aid: 50

Employment Profile:
% of students who pass the boards on their first try: 100
% employed within the first 6 months following graduation: 100
Average starting salary: $22,000

Sinclair Community College

444 West Third Street
Dayton, OH 45402

Contact Information:
Telephone: 937-512-2973
Fax: 937-512-2239
Web: www.sinclair.edu

Program Information:
Program begins: September
Duration of program: 22 months
Evening or weekend classes are available.

Financial Information:
Tuition, resident: $3,038
Tuition, non-resident: $4,998

Oklahoma

Rose State College

6420 Southeast 15th Street
Midwest City, OK 73110

Contact Information:
Telephone: 405-733-7578
Fax: 405-736-0338
E-mail: cbrooks@ms.rose.cc.ok.us
Web: www.rose.cc.ok.us

Program Information:
Program begins: September
Duration of program: 21 months

Application Information:
Enrollment of program: 12
Transfer students are accepted.

Financial Information:
Tuition, resident: $1,287
Tuition, non-resident: $3,267
Average cost of books: $450
% of students receiving aid: 85

Employment Profile:
% of students who pass the boards on their first try: 92
% employed within the first 6 months following graduation: 75
Average starting salary: $20,000

Oregon

Central Oregon Community College

Northwest College Way
Bend, OR 97701

Contact Information:
Telephone: 541-383-7736
Fax: 541-383-7535
E-mail: gahern@cocc.edu
Web: www.cocc.edu

Program Information:
Program begins: September
Duration of program: 9 months

Application Information:
Transfer students are accepted.

Financial Information:
Tuition, resident: $1,674

Employment Profile:
% of students who pass the boards on their first try: 97
% employed within the first 6 months following graduation: 90

Pennsylvania

Community College of Allegheny County

808 Ridge Avenue
Pittsburgh, PA 15212-6097

Contact Information:
Telephone: 412-237-2614
Fax: 412-237-4521
E-mail: javoli@ccac.edu
Web: www.ccac.edu

Program Information:
Program begins: August
Duration of program: 18 months
Evening or weekend classes are available.

Application Information:
Transfer students are accepted.

Financial Information:
Tuition, resident: $2,040
Tuition, non-resident: $6,120

Gwynedd-Mercy College
Sumneytown Pike
Gwynedd Valley, PA 19437

Contact Information:
Telephone: 215-646-7300
E-mail: hornung.j.@gmc.edu
Web: www.gmc.edu

Program Information:
Program begins: August
Degrees offered: Associate's, 24 months
Evening or weekend classes are available.

Application Information:
Enrollment of program: 20

Employment Profile:
% employed within the first 6 months following graduation: 100

South Hills School of Business & Technology
480 Waupelani Drive
State College, PA 16801

Contact Information:
Telephone: 814-234-7755
Fax: 814-234-0926
Web: www.southhills.edu

Program Information:
Program begins: August
Duration of program: 20 months

Puerto Rico

Universidad Adventista de las Antillas
PO Box 118
Mayaguez, PR 00681-0118

Contact Information:
Telephone: 501-686-8613
Fax: 501-686-8519
E-mail: zsantiago@hotmail.com
Web: www.uaa.edu

Program Information:
Program begins: January
Duration of program: 26 months

Application Information:
Enrollment of program: 37
Transfer students are accepted.

Financial Information:
Tuition, resident: $2,050
Tuition, non-resident: $3,122
Average cost of books: $1,500

Employment Profile:
% employed within the first 6 months following graduation: 95
Average starting salary: $19,000

South Carolina

Florence-Darlington Technical College
PO Box 100548
Florence, SC 29501-0548

Contact Information:
Telephone: 843-661-8146
Fax: 843-661-8333
E-mail: bennettl@flo.tec.sc.us
Web: www.flo.tec.sc.us

Program Information:
Program begins: August
Degrees offered: Diploma, 24 months
Evening or weekend classes are available.

Application Information:
Enrollment of program: 20
Transfer students are accepted.

Financial Information:
Tuition, resident: $550
Tuition, non-resident: $625
Average cost of books: $150
% of students receiving aid: 75

Employment Profile:
% of students who pass the boards on their first try: 77
% employed within the first 6 months following graduation: 100
Average starting salary: $26,000

Midlands Technical College
PO Box 2408
Columbia, SC 29202

Contact Information:
Telephone: 803-822-3072
Fax: 803-822-3619
E-mail: hickline@mtc.mid.tec.sc.us
Web: www.mid.tec.sc.us

Program Information:
Program begins: September
Degrees offered: Associate's, 24 months
Evening or weekend classes are available.

Application Information:
Enrollment of program: 18
Transfer students are accepted.

Financial Information:
Tuition, resident: $1,620
Tuition, non-resident: $3,240
Average cost of books: $600
% of students receiving aid: 45

Employment Profile:
% of students who pass the boards on their first try: 100
% employed within the first 6 months following graduation: 100
Average starting salary: $25,000

South Dakota

Dakota State University
CB Kennedy Center #151
Madison, SD 57042

Contact Information:
Telephone: 605-256-5137
Fax: 605-256-5060
E-mail: bennett@pluto.dsu.edu
Web: www.dsu.edu

Program Information:
Program begins: August
Duration of program: 24 months

Application Information:
Enrollment of program: 20

Financial Information:
Tuition, resident: $3,301
Tuition, non-resident: $7,000
Average cost of books: $600

Employment Profile:
% of students who pass the boards on their first try: 70
Average starting salary: $19,667

Tennessee

Volunteer State Community College
1480 Nashville Pike
Gallatin, TN 37066-3188

Contact Information:
Telephone: 615-452-8600
Fax: 615-230-3251
E-mail: lknobeloch@uscc.cc.tn.us
Web: www.vscc.tn.us

Program Information:
Program begins: September
Duration of program: 11 months
Evening or weekend classes are available.

Application Information:
Transfer students are accepted.

Financial Information:
Tuition, resident: $1,130
Tuition, non-resident: $3,380
Average cost of books: $500
% of students receiving aid: 90

Employment Profile:
% of students who pass the boards on their first try: 90
% employed within the first 6 months following graduation: 100
Average starting salary: $27,000

Texas

Houston Community College
John B. Coleman Building
1900 Galen Drive
Houston, TX 77021

Contact Information:
Telephone: 713-718-7347
Fax: 713-718-7401
E-mail: tyson_c@hccs.cc.tx.us
Web: www.hcc.cc.tx.us

Program Information:
Program begins: August
Duration of program: 24 months
Evening or weekend classes are available.

Financial Information:
Tuition, resident: $1,080
Tuition, non-resident: $1,500

Lee College
511 South Whiting Street
Baytown, TX 77520-0818

Contact Information:
Telephone: 281-425-6569
Fax: 281-425-6520
E-mail: mivey@lee.edu

Program Information:
Program begins: August
Duration of program: 24 months
Evening or weekend classes are available.

Financial Information:
Tuition, resident: $677
Tuition, non-resident: $1,709

South Plains College
1302 Main Street
Lubbock, TX 79401

Contact Information:
Telephone: 806-747-0576 ext. 4644
Fax: 806-765-2775
E-mail: bgreen@spc.cc.tx.us
Web: www.spc.cc.tx.us

Program Information:
Program begins: September

Application Information:
Enrollment of program: 30
Transfer students are accepted.

Financial Information:
Tuition, resident: $1,918
Tuition, non-resident: $2,581

Employment Profile:
% of students who pass the boards on their first try: 85
% employed within the first 6 months following graduation: 90
Average starting salary: $18,000

Tarrant County College—Northeast
828 Harwood Road
Hurst, TX 76054

Contact Information:
Telephone: 817-575-6544
Fax: 817-515-6700
E-mail: dmcdon@tcjc.cc.tx.us
Web: www.tccd.net

Program Information:
Program begins: August, January
Duration of program: 21 months

Application Information:
Enrollment of program: 24
Transfer students are accepted.

Financial Information:
Tuition, resident: $1,754
Tuition, non-resident: $5,330
Average cost of books: $450

Employment Profile:
% of students who pass the boards on their first try: 100
% employed within the first 6 months following graduation: 100
Average starting salary: $22,500

Texas State Technical College
2424 Boxwood
Harlingen, TX 78551-3697

Contact Information:
Telephone: 956-364-4767
Fax: 956-364-5155
E-mail: gholmes@harlingen.tstc.edu
Web: www.harl.tstc.edu

Program Information:
Program begins: September
Degrees offered: Associate's, 16 months

Application Information:
Enrollment of program: 42
Transfer students are accepted.

Financial Information:
Tuition, resident: $1,256
Tuition, non-resident: $4,424
Average cost of books: $900
% of students receiving aid: 85

Employment Profile:
% of students who pass the boards on their first try: 86
% employed within the first 6 months following graduation: 82
Average starting salary: $24,000

Wharton County Junior College
911 Boling Highway
Wharton, TX 77488

Contact Information:
Telephone: 409-532-6363
Fax: 409-532-6489
E-mail: maryk@wcjc.cc.tx.us
Web: www.whatcom.ctc.edu

Program Information:
Program begins: August
Degrees offered: Associate's, 18 months

Application Information:
Enrollment of program: 25

Financial Information:
Tuition, resident: $1,938
Tuition, non-resident: $5,882
Average cost of books: $1,200
% of students receiving aid: 50

Employment Profile:
% of students who pass the boards on their first try: 80
% employed within the first 6 months following graduation: 45
Average starting salary: $16,640

Washington

Shoreline Community College
16101 Greenwood Avenue North
Seattle, WA 98133

Contact Information:
Telephone: 206-543-4757
Fax: 206-533-5103
E-mail: dwilde@ctc.edu
Web: www.elmo.shore.ctc.edu/hciprograms

Program Information:
Program begins: August
Duration of program: 18 months

Financial Information:
Tuition, resident: $3,150
Tuition, non-resident: $11,904

Spokane Community College
North 1810 Greene Street/MS 2090
Spokane, WA 99217

Contact Information:
Telephone: 509-536-8032
Fax: 509-533-8621
E-mail: gterry@scc.spokane.cc.wa.us
Web: www.scc.spokane.cc.wa.us

Program Information:
Program begins: September
Degrees offered: Diploma, 12 months

Application Information:
Enrollment of program: 30
Transfer students are accepted.

Financial Information:
Tuition, resident: $1,452
Tuition, non-resident: $5,727
Average cost of books: $750
% of students receiving aid: 70

Employment Profile:
% of students who pass the boards on their first try: 88
% employed within the first 6 months following graduation: 80
Average starting salary: $23,000

West Virginia

Fairmont State College
Locust Avenue
Fairmont, WV 26554

Contact Information:
Telephone: 304-367-4764
Fax: 304-367-4268
E-mail: mhervath@mail.fsc.us.edu

Program Information:
Program begins: August
Duration of program: 18 months

Application Information:
Enrollment of program: 30
Transfer students are accepted.

Financial Information:
Tuition, resident: $2,106
Tuition, non-resident: $8,996
Average cost of books: $200

Marshall University
Huntington, WV 25755

Contact Information:
Telephone: 304-696-3048
Fax: 304-696-2396
E-mail: smithjanemarshall.edu
Web: www.marshall.edu

Program Information:
Program begins: June
Duration of program: 21 months
Evening or weekend classes are available.

Application Information:
Enrollment of program: 25
Transfer students are accepted.

Financial Information:
Tuition, resident: $1,174
Tuition, non-resident: $3,147
Average cost of books: $500
% of students receiving aid: 50

Employment Profile:
% of students who pass the boards on their first try: 85
% employed within the first 6 months following graduation: 75
Average starting salary: $20,000

Wisconsin

Chippewa Valley Technical College
620 West Clairemont Avenue
Eau Claire, WI 54701

Contact Information:
Telephone: 715-833-6423
Fax: 715-833-6470
E-mail: chippewa.tech.wi.us
Web: www.chippewa.tec.wi.us

Program Information:
Program begins: August
Degrees offered: Certificate program, 12 months; Associate's, 20 months
Evening or weekend classes are available.

Application Information:
Enrollment of program: 12
Transfer students are accepted.

Financial Information:
Tuition, resident: $2,114
Tuition, non-resident: $16,660
Average cost of books: $300
% of students receiving aid: 80

Employment Profile:
% of students who pass the boards on their first try: 90
Average starting salary: $20,000

Northeast Wisconsin Technical College
2740 West Mason Street
PO Box 19042
Green Bay, WI 54307-9042

Contact Information:
Telephone: 920-498-5577
Fax: 920-498-5673
Web: www.nwtc.tec.wi.us

Program Information:
Program begins: August
Duration of program: 23 months

Financial Information:
Tuition, resident: $2,060
Tuition, non-resident: $16,234

Western Wisconsin Technical College
304 North Sixth Street
Box C-908
La Crosse, WI 54602-0908

Contact Information:
Telephone: 608-785-9549
Fax: 608-785-9497
E-mail: brownt@email.western.tec.wi.us
Web: www.western.tec.wi.us

Program Information:
Program begins: August, January
Degrees offered: Associate's, 21 months
Evening or weekend classes are available.

Application Information:
Enrollment of program: 10

Financial Information:
Tuition, resident: $3,460
Tuition, non-resident: $15,870

Medical Assistant

Wilburta (Billie) Q. Lindh, CMA
Program Coordinator
Medical Assisting Department
Highline Community College
Des Moines, Washington

Job Description

What Do They Do?

Medical assistants perform a multitude of administrative and clinical duties that vary with the type and size of medical practice and its geographic location. The competencies required to practice medical assisting as a profession were first outlined by the AAMA in 1979 then updated in 1984 and 1990. In 1997, in coordination with the National Board of Medical Examiners, educators, and practicing CMAs, the AAMA developed the Medical Assistant Role Delineation Chart.[1] Following are some of the administrative duties that may be performed by practicing medical assistants:

- Perform basic clerical functions
- Schedule, coordinate, and monitor inpatient and outpatient appointments
- Process insurance claims and monitor third-party reimbursement
- Perform medical transcription
- Apply bookkeeping principles and process payroll
- Manage renewals of business and professional insurance policies

Medical assistants may also perform any or all of the following clinical tasks:

- Apply principles of aseptic technique and infection control
- Collect and process specimens
- Perform diagnostic tests
- Obtain patient history and vital signs
- Prepare and maintain examination and treatment areas
- Prepare patients for examinations, procedures, and treatments
- Prepare and administer medications and immunizations
- Recognize and respond to emergencies

General or transdisciplinary tasks may include:

- Project a professional manner and image
- Recognize and respect cultural diversity
- Use effective and correct verbal and written communications
- Use medical terminology appropriately
- Maintain confidentiality
- Practice within the scope of education, training, and personal capabilities
- Document accurately
- Use appropriate guidelines when releasing information
- Follow federal, state, and local legal guidelines
- Maintain and dispose of regulated substances in compliance with government guidelines
- Comply with established risk management and safety procedures

The medical assistant can become highly specialized with additional education and training. For example, some medical assistants are employed in podiatrists' offices, where they make castings of feet, expose and develop x-rays, and assist podiatrists in surgery. Others may be ophthalmic medical assistants. In this setting, they administer diagnostic tests, measure and record vision, and test the function of the eyes and eye muscles. They may also teach patients to use eye dressings, protective shields, and safety glasses and to insert, remove, and care for contact lenses. Medical assistants may also work as optician's assistants. These professionals prepare patients for examinations and assist them in eyewear selection. Another role for medical assistants is that of a chiropractic assistant, whose duties may include participating in the treatment and examination of patients' muscular and skeletal problems.

Type of Person

Medical assistants are professionals who work closely with the public and other healthcare professionals. They should enjoy helping people, demonstrate initiative and responsibility, manage their time effectively, and work as a part of the healthcare team. Medical assistants should also be able to put their patients at ease, explain a physician's instructions, and be courteous at all times. They must respect the confidential nature of the medical profession and should never discuss any private information outside of the office environment or with individuals not directly involved in a patient's care.

Clinical duties require a reasonable level of manual dexterity, and both auditory and visual acuity. The medical assistant may be required to lift weight of 25–30 pounds. Medical assistants should wear footwear that fits well and provides support since they rarely sit during working hours.

With Whom Do They Work?

Medical assistants work with a variety of healthcare practitioners as either administrative or clinical personnel (though many cover both areas). Opportunities to work in general medicine, family practice, internal medicine, pediatrics, geriatrics, ophthalmology, podiatry, and chiropractics exist.

Employment

Places of Employment

Medical assistants are employed primarily in outpatient settings working directly under the supervision of physicians. According to the AAMA, medical assistants held about 225,000 jobs in 1996. Seven in ten jobs were in physicians' offices, and over one in 10 were in offices of other health practitioners. The rest were in hospitals, nursing homes, and other healthcare facilities.

Employment Outlook

Today, the 60+ age group is retiring and a greater number of employment opportunities are available in healthcare. As the industry expands due to technological advances and an increased number of medical facilities, the demand for trained professionals to perform a multitude of tasks will grow. As a result, medical assisting will continue to be one of the fastest growing occupations.

Salary

The earnings of medical assistants vary widely, depending on education and training, experience, skill level, and geographic location. According to the 1997 Staff Salary Survey published by the Health Care Group,[2] average hourly wages for medical assistants with less than two years of experience ranged from $8.07 to $10.90 in 1996. Average hourly wages for medical assistants with more than five years of experience ranged from $10.38 to $13.46. Wages were higher in the Northeast and the West, and lower in the Midwest and South.

Many assistants work forty hours per week while others work part-time. These hours may be during the day, evening, or weekend. Medical assistants are usually given six or seven paid holidays a year, as well as annual paid vacations. Often they receive health and life insurance, a retirement plan, sick leave, and uniform and education allowances.

Educational Programs

Length

Programs may be either two years in length (resulting in an Associate's degree), or one year in length (resulting in either a certificate or diploma).

Prerequisites

A high school diploma or its equivalent is required for enrollment in most vocational schools, community and junior colleges, and private schools. To be eligible for professional liability insurance, students must be 18 years of age or older.

Curriculum

The curriculum for entry-level competencies includes anatomy and physiology, medical terminology, medical law and ethics, psychology, communications (oral and written), and administrative and clinical procedures. An externship that provides opportunity for the student to apply theory learned in the classroom to the practical setting in healthcare is mandatory.

Accrediting Body

The AAMA works in collaboration with the Commission on Accreditation of Allied Health Education Programs (CAAHEP) to accredit medical assistant programs in both public and private post-secondary institutions.

American Association of Medical Assistants
20 North Wacker Drive, Suite 1575
Chicago, IL 60606-2903
Telephone: 312-899-1500
Fax: 312-899-1259
Web address: www.aama-ntl.org

Through the Accrediting Bureau of Health Education Schools (ABHES) the American Medical Technologists (AMT) accredits programs preparing individuals for entry into the medical assisting profession in private post-secondary institutions.

Accrediting Bureau of Health Education Schools
803 West Broad Street, Suite 730
Falls Church, VA 22046
Telephone: 703-533-2082
Web address: www.abhes.org

Certification Board

The Certified Medical Assistant (CMA) credential is awarded by the AAMA to students successfully passing the certification examination. CMAs must be re-certified every five years by participating in continuing education or by retaking the certification examination.

American Association of Medical Assistants
20 North Wacker Drive, Suite 1575
Chicago, IL 60606-2903
Telephone: 312-899-1500
Fax: 312-899-1259
Web address: www.aama-ntl.org

The Registered Medical Assistant (RMA) credential is awarded to students who successfully certify through ABHES accredited schools and AMT. Re-certification is necessary to maintain the credential.

Registered Medical Assistants of American Medical Technologists
710 Higgins Road
Park Ridge, IL 60068-5765
Telephone: 847-823-516
Fax: 847-823-0450
E-mail: amtmail@aol.com
Web address: www.amt1.com

Advice for Potential Students

Call a medical office and ask if you can shadow a medical assistant for several hours or a day. This will help you decide if this is a career that best fits your personality and professional goals. Visit schools that are accredited and discuss prerequisites, curriculum, and employment opportunities with the program director. Read the local newspaper and employment publications to determine the job market and entry level salary. Go to the World Wide Web and search for information about medical assisting.

For Additional Information

Organizations

American Association of Medical Assistants
20 North Wacker Drive, Suite 1575
Chicago, IL 60606-2903
Telephone: 312-899-1500
Fax: 312-899-1259
Web address: www.aama-ntl.org

Accrediting Bureau of Health Education Schools
803 West Broad Street, Suite 730
Falls Church, VA 22046

Registered Medical Assistants of American Medical Technologists
710 Higgins Road
Park Ridge, IL 60068-5765
Telephone: 847-823-5169
Fax: 847-823-0450
E-mail: amtmail@aol.com
Web address: www.amt1.com

Joint Commission on Allied Health Personnel in Ophthalmology
2025 Woodlane Drive
St Paul, MN 55125-2995
Phone: 888-284-3937
Fax: 651-731-0410
E-mail: jcahpo@jcahpo.org
Web address: www.jcahpo.org

American Society of Podiatric Medical Assistants
2124 South Austin Boulevard
Cicero, IL 60650
Telephone: 888-882-7762
E-mail: info@aspma.org
Web address: www.aspma.org

Publications

Books

The Encyclopedia of Careers and Vocational Guidance, 10th ed. Chicago: J.G. Ferguson Publishing Company, 1997.

Lindh, Pooler, Tamparo, Cerrato. *Delmar's Comprehensive Medical Assistant.* Albany: Delmar Publishers, 1998.

Journals

Professional Medical Assistant. The American Association of Medical Assistants, 20 North Wacker Drive, Suite 1575, Chicago IL 60606-2903. www.aama-ntl.org.

This bimonthly publication contains current information regarding healthcare issues and news, continued education articles, educator's forum containing appropriate articles related to education, AAMA Calendar of Events, and the AAMA directory containing names and addresses of the AAMA Board of Trustees, state presidents, and executive officers.

Internet Resources

Accrediting Bureau of Health Education Schools: www.abhes.org
American Association of Medical Assistants: www.aama-ntl.org
American Medical Technologists: www.amt1.com
American Society of Podiatric Medical Assistants: www2.jobtrack.com/help_manuals/outlook/ocos164.html
Association of Technical Personnel in Ophthalmology: www.atpo.com
Joint Commission on Allied Health Personnel in Ophthalmology: www.atpo.com

Alabama

George C. Wallace State Community College

Napier Field Road
Route 6 Box 62
Dothan, AL 36303

Contact Information:
Telephone: 334-983-3521 ext. 207
Fax: 334-983-3600
Web: www.wallace.edu

Program Information:
Program begins: August, January
Duration of program: 24 months

Application Information:
Enrollment of program: 100
Transfer students are accepted.

Financial Information:
Tuition, resident: $3,940
Tuition, non-resident: $7,590
Average cost of books: $500
% of students receiving aid: 68

Employment Profile:
% of students who pass the boards on their first try: 96
% employed within the first 6 months following graduation: 94
Average starting salary: $16,000

South College

122 Commerce Street
Montgomery, AL 36104

Contact Information:
Telephone: 334-263-1013
Fax: 334-262-7326

Program Information:
Program begins: August, January
Duration of program: 24 months
Evening or weekend classes are available.

Application Information:
Enrollment of program: 45

Financial Information:
Tuition, resident: $7,185

Employment Profile:
% employed within the first 6 months following graduation: 95

Alaska

University of Alaska Anchorage

3211 Providence Drive
Anchorage, AK 99508

Contact Information:
Telephone: 907-786-6932
Fax: 907-786-6938
E-mail: afrjw@uaa.alaska.edu
Web: www.uaa.alaska.edu

Program Information:
Program begins: Program begins quarterly.
Duration of program: 15 months
Evening or weekend classes are available.

Financial Information:
Tuition, resident: $3,075
Tuition, non-resident: $6,630

Arizona

Long Technical College

13450 North Black Canyon Highway #104
Phoenix, AZ 85029

Contact Information:
Telephone: 602-548-1955
Fax: 602-548-1956
E-mail: ltcphx2@dancris.com
Web: www.longtechnicalcollege.com

Program Information:
Degrees offered: Diploma, 8 months; Associate's, 18 months
Evening or weekend classes are available.

Application Information:
Enrollment of program: 53
Transfer students are accepted.

Financial Information:
Average cost of books: $210
% of students receiving aid: 94

Employment Profile:
% employed within the first 6 months following graduation: 92
Average starting salary: $16,640

California

Bryman College

A Corinthian School
814 Mission Street
San Francisco, CA 94103

Contact Information:
Telephone: 415-777-2500
Fax: 415-495-3457
Web: www.cci.edu

Program Information:
Program begins: Program begins quarterly.
Duration of program: 8 months
Evening or weekend classes are available.

Application Information:
Enrollment of program: 246
Transfer students are accepted.

Financial Information:
% of students receiving aid: 89

Employment Profile:
% employed within the first 6 months following graduation: 56
Average starting salary: $22,000

Center of Employment Training—Santa Ana

120 West Fifth Street
Suite 120
Santa Ana, CA 92701

Contact Information:
Telephone: 714-568-1755
Fax: 714-568-1331
E-mail: sacet@pacbell.net
Web: www.best.com

Financial Information:
% of students receiving aid: 19

Employment Profile:
Average starting salary: $17,000

City College of San Francisco

1860 Hayes Street
San Francisco, CA 94117

Contact Information:
Telephone: 415-561-1826
Fax: 415-561-1861
Web: www.ccsf.cc.ca.us

Program Information:
Program begins: August, January
Duration of program: 24 months
Evening or weekend classes are available.

Application Information:
Enrollment of program: 60
Transfer students are accepted.

Financial Information:
Tuition, resident: $330
Tuition, non-resident: $3,900
Average cost of books: $500
% of students receiving aid: 50

Employment Profile:
% employed within the first 6 months following graduation: 50
Average starting salary: $24,000

San Diego Mesa College

7250 Mesa College Drive, F204
San Diego, CA 92111

Contact Information:
Telephone: 619-627-2945
Fax: 619-627-2741
E-mail: talmukhj@intergate.sdmes.cc.ca.sdmesa.us
Web: www.intergate.sdmesa.sdccd.cc.ca.us/medical

Program Information:
Program begins: Program begins monthly.
Duration of program: 12 months
Evening or weekend classes are available.

Application Information:
Transfer students are accepted.

Financial Information:
Tuition, resident: $442
Tuition, non-resident: $3,400
Average cost of books: $400
% of students receiving aid: 33

Employment Profile:
% of students who pass the boards on their first try: 100
% employed within the first 6 months following graduation: 80
Average starting salary: $17,000

Southern California Regional Occupational Center

2300 Crenshaw Boulevard
Torrance, CA 90501

Contact Information:
Telephone: 310-224-4262
Fax: 310-782-1589
Web: www.sroc.com

Program Information:
Program begins: May, August
Duration of program: 11 months
Evening or weekend classes are available.

West Valley Community College District

14000 Fruitvale Avenue
Saratoga, CA 95070

Contact Information:
Telephone: 408-741-2498
Fax: 408-741-2145
E-mail: faraneh_javan@wvmccd.cc.ca.us
Web: www.westvalley.edu/careers/healthcareprogram

Program Information:
Program begins: Program begins quarterly.
Duration of program: 11 months
Evening or weekend classes are available.

Application Information:
Enrollment of program: 120

Employment Profile:
% employed within the first 6 months following graduation: 85
Average starting salary: $22,000

Colorado

Arapahoe Community College

2500 West College Drive
PO Box 9002
Littleton, CO 80160-9002

Contact Information:
Telephone: 303-797-5898
Fax: 303-797-5935
E-mail: lmcbride@arapahoe.edu
Web: www.arapahoe.edu

Program Information:
Program begins: August
Degrees offered: Certificate program; Associate's
Evening or weekend classes are available.

Financial Information:
Tuition, resident: $2,000
Tuition, non-resident: $9,000
Average cost of books: $350
% of students receiving aid: 38

Employment Profile:
% of students who pass the boards on their first try: 100
% employed within the first 6 months following graduation: 100
Average starting salary: $20,000

Emily Griffith Opportunity School

1250 Welton Street
Denver, CO 80204

Contact Information:
Telephone: 303-575-4737
Fax: 303-575-4840
Web: www.egos-school.com

Program Information:
Program begins: September, January
Duration of program: 9 months
Evening or weekend classes are available.

Application Information:
Enrollment of program: 22
Transfer students are accepted.

Financial Information:
Tuition, resident: $1,760
Tuition, non-resident: $4,585
Average cost of books: $400
% of students receiving aid: 90

Employment Profile:
% of students who pass the boards on their first try: 80
% employed within the first 6 months following graduation: 60
Average starting salary: $21,000

Front Range Community College—Westminster

2255 North Main
Suite 118
Longmont, CO 80501

Contact Information:
Telephone: 303-516-8916
Fax: 303-516-8998
E-mail: fr_sandie@cccs.cccoes.edu
Web: www.frcc.cc.co.us

Program Information:
Program begins: September, January
Degrees offered: Certificate program, 10 months

Application Information:
Enrollment of program: 16
Transfer students are accepted.

Financial Information:
Tuition, resident: $3,020
Tuition, non-resident: $12,681
Average cost of books: $508
% of students receiving aid: 20

Employment Profile:
% of students who pass the boards on their first try: 96
% employed within the first 6 months following graduation: 100
Average starting salary: $24,648

Connecticut

Capital Community Technical College

61 Woodland Street
Hartford, CT 06105

Contact Information:
Telephone: 860-520-7901
Fax: 860-520-7906
E-mail: cmcmahon@communit.edu
Web: www.cctc.commnet.edu

Program Information:
Program begins: September, January
Degrees offered: Certificate program, 9 months; Associate's, 24 months
Evening or weekend classes are available.

Application Information:
Enrollment of program: 90
Transfer students are accepted.

Financial Information:
Tuition, resident: $1,560
Tuition, non-resident: $4,680
Average cost of books: $200
% of students receiving aid: 60

Employment Profile:
% of students who pass the boards on their first try: 65
% employed within the first 6 months following graduation: 80
Average starting salary: $20,800

Huntington Institute

193 Broadway
Norwich, CT 06360

Contact Information:
Telephone: 860-866-0507
Fax: 860-889-9733

Program Information:
Program begins: Program begins quarterly.
Degrees offered: Diploma, 12 months

Application Information:
Transfer students are accepted.

Financial Information:
Average cost of books: $850
% of students receiving aid: 20

Employment Profile:
% employed within the first 6 months following graduation: 100
Average starting salary: $21,000

Northwestern Connecticut Community College

Park Place East
Winsted, CT 06098

Contact Information:
Telephone: 860-738-6308
Fax: 860-738-6439
E-mail: nw_berger@commnet.edu

Program Information:
Program begins: Program begins quarterly.
Duration of program: 16 months
Evening or weekend classes are available.

Financial Information:
Tuition, resident: $1,814

Porter and Chester Institute—Watertown

320 Sylvan Lake Road
Watertown, CT 06779

Contact Information:
Telephone: 860-274-9294
Fax: 860-274-3075
Web: www.porterchester.com

Program Information:
Program begins: October
Duration of program: 15 months
Evening or weekend classes are available.

Application Information:
Enrollment of program: 28
Transfer students are accepted.

Financial Information:
Average cost of books: $740

Employment Profile:
% of students who pass the boards on their first try: 88
Average starting salary: $23,000

Quinebaug Valley Community Technical College

742 Upper Maple Street
Danielson, CT 06239

Contact Information:
Telephone: 860-774-1130 ext. 427
Fax: 860-774-7768
E-mail: qv_goretti@commenet.edu
Web: www.commnet.edu/quctc/home

Program Information:
Program begins: September, January, June
Duration of program: 18 months
Evening or weekend classes are available.

Application Information:
Transfer students are accepted.

Financial Information:
Tuition, resident: $1,520
Tuition, non-resident: $4,440

Employment Profile:
% of students who pass the boards on their first try: 100
% employed within the first 6 months following graduation: 80
Average starting salary: $20,000

Florida

Brevard Community College

1519 Clearlake Road
Cocoa, FL 32922

Contact Information:
Telephone: 407-632-1111 ext. 64360
Fax: 407-634-3731
E-mail: hayesk@brevard.cc.fl.us
Web: www.brevard.cc.fl.us

Program Information:
Program begins: September
Duration of program: 12 months

Application Information:
Transfer students are accepted.

Financial Information:
Tuition, resident: $1,638
Tuition, non-resident: $5,265
% of students receiving aid: 30

Employment Profile:
% of students who pass the boards on their first try: 98
% employed within the first 6 months following graduation: 98
Average starting salary: $21,000

David G. Erwin Technical Center
2010 East Hillsborough Avenue
Tampa, FL 33610-8299

Contact Information:
Telephone: 813-231-1800 ext. 2444
Fax: 813-231-1820
E-mail: ewaldbart@aol.com
Web: www.erwintech.org

Program Information:
Program begins: August, December, April
Duration of program: 14 months

Application Information:
Enrollment of program: 25
Transfer students are accepted.

Financial Information:
Tuition, resident: $1,782
Tuition, non-resident: $8,920
Average cost of books: $330

Florida Career Institute
4222 South Florida Avenue
Lakeland, FL 33813

Contact Information:
Telephone: 406-756-3918
Fax: 406-756-3815
Web: www.floridacareerinstitute.com

Program Information:
Degrees offered: Diploma, 8 months
Evening or weekend classes are available.

Application Information:
Enrollment of program: 80
Transfer students are accepted.

Financial Information:
Average cost of books: $500
% of students receiving aid: 98

Employment Profile:
% of students who pass the boards on their first try: 80
% employed within the first 6 months following graduation: 90
Average starting salary: $18,000

Florida Metro University System—Tampa College—Pinellas Campus
2471 McMullen Booth Road
Suite 200
Clearwater, FL 33759

Contact Information:
Telephone: 941-646-1400
Fax: 941-646-5236
E-mail: dklieger@ptecsp.pinellas.k12.fl.us

Program Information:
Program begins: January
Duration of program: 13 months

Application Information:
Transfer students are accepted.

Financial Information:
Tuition, resident: $1,820
Tuition, non-resident: $8,450

Employment Profile:
% employed within the first 6 months following graduation: 90
Average starting salary: $20,000

New England Institute of Technology at Palm Beach
1126 53rd Court
West Palm Beach, FL 33407

Contact Information:
Telephone: 561-842-8324
Fax: 561-842-9503
Web: www.newenglandtech.com

Program Information:
Program begins: Program begins quarterly.
Degrees offered: Diploma, 18 months
Evening or weekend classes are available.

Application Information:
Enrollment of program: 63

Financial Information:
Average cost of books: $500

Employment Profile:
% employed within the first 6 months following graduation: 50
Average starting salary: $18,700

North Technical Education Center
7071 Garden Road
Riviera Beach, FL 33404

Contact Information:
Telephone: 561-881-4614
Fax: 561-882-1908

Program Information:
Program begins: Program begins quarterly.
Duration of program: 13 months

Financial Information:
Tuition, resident: $2,000
Tuition, non-resident: $4,300

Pinellas Technical Education Center—St. Petersburg
901 34th Street South
St. Petersburg, FL 33711

Contact Information:
Telephone: 727-893-2500
Fax: 727-893-2776
E-mail: dklieger@ptechp.pinellas.k12.fl.us
Web: www.pinellas.k12.fl.us

Program Information:
Duration of program: 13 months
Evening or weekend classes are available.

Application Information:
Transfer students are accepted.

Financial Information:
Tuition, resident: $1,820
Tuition, non-resident: $8,450

Employment Profile:
% employed within the first 6 months following graduation: 90
Average starting salary: $20,000

Sarasota County Technical Institute
4748 Beneva Road
Sarasota, FL 34233

Contact Information:
Telephone: 941-924-1365 ext. 382
Fax: 941-361-6886

Program Information:
Program begins: December, April, August
Degrees offered: Certificate program

Application Information:
Transfer students are accepted.

Financial Information:
Tuition, resident: $2,542
Tuition, non-resident: $9,420
Average cost of books: $642

Employment Profile:
% of students who pass the boards on their first try: 100
% employed within the first 6 months following graduation: 99
Average starting salary: $20,000

Winter Park Technical
901 Webster Avenue
Winter Park, FL 32789

Contact Information:
Telephone: 407-622-2900 ext. 2228
Fax: 407-975-2435
E-mail: stasias@ocps.k12.fl.us
Web: www.wpt.ocps.k12.fl.us

Program Information:
Program begins: August
Duration of program: 13 months

Application Information:
Enrollment of program: 36
Transfer students are accepted.

Financial Information:
Tuition, resident: $1,750
Tuition, non-resident: $8,500
Average cost of books: $120

Employment Profile:
% of students who pass the boards on their first try: 95
% employed within the first 6 months following graduation: 75
Average starting salary: $17,000

Georgia

Atlanta Technical Institute

1560 Metropolitan Parkway Southwest
Atlanta, GA 30310

Contact Information:
Telephone: 404-756-3779
Fax: 404-758-8522

Program Information:
Program begins: Program begins quarterly.
Degrees offered: Diploma, 15 months

Application Information:
Enrollment of program: 88
Transfer students are accepted.

Financial Information:
Average cost of books: $350

Employment Profile:
% of students who pass the boards on their first try: 60
% employed within the first 6 months following graduation: 85
Average starting salary: $18,000

Chattahoochee Technical Institute

980 South Cobb Drive
Marietta, GA 30060

Contact Information:
Telephone: 770-528-4590
Fax: 770-528-4580
E-mail: jadair@chat-tec.com
Web: www.chat-tec.com

Program Information:
Program begins: October
Duration of program: 12 months

Application Information:
Enrollment of program: 12
Transfer students are accepted.

Financial Information:
Average cost of books: $400

Employment Profile:
% employed within the first 6 months following graduation: 95
Average starting salary: $18,500

Columbus Technical Institute

928 Manchester Expressway
Columbus, GA 31904-6572

Contact Information:
Telephone: 706-649-1499
Fax: 706-649-1549
E-mail: ethompso@mail.columbus.tec.ga.us
Web: www.columbus.tec.ga.us

Program Information:
Program begins: January, August
Degrees offered: Diploma, 15 months

Application Information:
Enrollment of program: 55
Transfer students are accepted.

Financial Information:
Tuition, resident: $1,008
Average cost of books: $650
% of students receiving aid: 90

Employment Profile:
% of students who pass the boards on their first try: 90
% employed within the first 6 months following graduation: 100
Average starting salary: $16,500

Dalton College

213 North College Drive
Dalton, GA 30720

Contact Information:
Telephone: 706-272-4559
Fax: 706-272-4563
Web: www.daltonstate.edu

Program Information:
Duration of program: 24 months

Application Information:
Enrollment of program: 60
Transfer students are accepted.

Financial Information:
Tuition, resident: $370
Tuition, non-resident: $968
% of students receiving aid: 70

Employment Profile:
% of students who pass the boards on their first try: 98
% employed within the first 6 months following graduation: 80
Average starting salary: $19,000

Lanier Technical Institute

2990 Landrum Education Drive
Oakwood, GA 30566

Contact Information:
Telephone: 770-531-6374
Fax: 770-531-6306
E-mail: lscarb@lanier.tec.ga.us
Web: www.lanier.tec.ga.us

Program Information:
Program begins: October, April
Degrees offered: Diploma, 15 months

Application Information:
Enrollment of program: 35
Transfer students are accepted.

Financial Information:
Tuition, resident: $1,378
Tuition, non-resident: $2,755
Average cost of books: $900
% of students receiving aid: 100

Employment Profile:
% of students who pass the boards on their first try: 75
% employed within the first 6 months following graduation: 100
Average starting salary: $22,500

Ogeechee Technical Institute

One Joe Kennedy Boulevard
Statesboro, GA 30458

Contact Information:
Telephone: 912-486-7616
Fax: 912-871-1162
E-mail: mturner@ogeechee.tec.ga.us
Web: www.ogeechee.tec.ga.us

Program Information:
Program begins: September, April
Degrees offered: Diploma, 15 months
Evening or weekend classes are available.

Application Information:
Enrollment of program: 27
Transfer students are accepted.

Financial Information:
Tuition, resident: $1,008
Average cost of books: $750
% of students receiving aid: 35

Employment Profile:
% of students who pass the boards on their first try: 74
% employed within the first 6 months following graduation: 88
Average starting salary: $13,000
Additional information: All students receive a Hope Grant to cover tuition plus a $100 book voucher. (Hope is a lottery funded grant for technical education.)

Swainsboro Technical Institute

346 Kite Road
Swainsboro, GA 30401

Contact Information:
Telephone: 912-289-2243 ext. 32
Fax: 912-289-2214
E-mail: gfulcher@admin1.swainsboro.tec.ga.us
Web: www.swainsboro.tec.ga.us

Program Information:
Duration of program: 15 months
Evening or weekend classes are available.

Application Information:
Enrollment of program: 60

Financial Information:
Tuition, resident: $1,156
Tuition, non-resident: $2,312
Additional information: Open enrollment.

Thomas Technical Institute

15689 US Highway 19 North
Thomasville, GA 31792

Contact Information:
Telephone: 912-225-5081
Fax: 912-225-5289
E-mail: ghatcher@ttin1.thomas.tec.ga.us
Web: www.thomas-tech.com

Program Information:
Program begins: October
Degrees offered: Diploma, 12 months
Evening or weekend classes are available.

Application Information:
Enrollment of program: 20
Transfer students are accepted.

Financial Information:
Tuition, resident: $1,134
Tuition, non-resident: $2,268
Average cost of books: $1,215
% of students receiving aid: 95

Employment Profile:
% of students who pass the boards on their first try: 75
% employed within the first 6 months following graduation: 100
Average starting salary: $16,250

Valdosta Technical Institute
4089 Val Technical Road
PO Box 928
Valdosta, GA 31603-0928

Contact Information:
Telephone: 912-333-2100
Fax: 912-333-2129
E-mail: cbruce@admin1.valdosta.tec.ga.us
Web: www.valdosta.tec.ga.us

Program Information:
Program begins: Program begins quarterly.
Duration of program: 15 months
Evening or weekend classes are available.

Financial Information:
Tuition, resident: $1,216
Tuition, non-resident: $2,024

Hawaii

Kapiolani Community College
Health Sciences Department
4303 Diamond Head Road
Honolulu, HI 96816

Contact Information:
Telephone: 808-734-9349
Fax: 808-734-9126
E-mail: jyoung@leahi.kcc.hawaii.edu
Web: www.kcc.hawaii.edu

Program Information:
Program begins: September
Degrees offered: Certificate program, 13 months

Application Information:
Enrollment of program: 81
Transfer students are accepted.

Financial Information:
Tuition, resident: $546
Tuition, non-resident: $2,934
Average cost of books: $200
% of students receiving aid: 50

Employment Profile:
% of students who pass the boards on their first try: 90
% employed within the first 6 months following graduation: 90
Average starting salary: $28,000

Idaho

College of Southern Idaho
PO Box 1238
Twin Falls, ID 83303-1238

Contact Information:
Telephone: 208-733-9554
Fax: 208-736-4743
E-mail: pglenn@aspen1.csi.cc.id.us
Web: www.csi.cc.id.us

Program Information:
Program begins: August
Duration of program: 10 months
Evening or weekend classes are available.

Application Information:
Enrollment of program: 16
Transfer students are accepted.

Financial Information:
Tuition, resident: $1,100
Average cost of books: $500
% of students receiving aid: 90

Employment Profile:
% of students who pass the boards on their first try: 100
% employed within the first 6 months following graduation: 90
Average starting salary: $20,000

Idaho State University
Campus Box 8310
Pocatello, ID 83209-8310

Contact Information:
Telephone: 208-236-4317
Fax: 208-236-3975
E-mail: birdnorm@isu.edu
Web: www.isu.edu

Program Information:
Program begins: August
Degrees offered: Associate's, 24 months
Evening or weekend classes are available.

Application Information:
Enrollment of program: 40

Financial Information:
Tuition, resident: $1,063
Tuition, non-resident: $7,798

Employment Profile:
% of students who pass the boards on their first try: 98
% employed within the first 6 months following graduation: 95
Average starting salary: $17,000

Illinois

Midstate College
411 West Northmoor Road
Peoria, IL 61614

Contact Information:
Telephone: 309-692-4092
Fax: 309-692-3893
E-mail: jbell_midstate@yahoo.com
Web: www.midstate.edu

Program Information:
Program begins: Program begins quarterly.
Degrees offered: Diploma, 12 months; Associate's, 18 months
Evening or weekend classes are available.

Application Information:
Enrollment of program: 30
Transfer students are accepted.

Financial Information:
Average cost of books: $125
% of students receiving aid: 99

Employment Profile:
% employed within the first 6 months following graduation: 91
Average starting salary: $16,500

Northwestern Business College
Southwest Campus
8020 West 87th Street
Hickory Hills, IL 60457

Contact Information:
Telephone: 773-481-3756
Fax: 773-481-2995
E-mail: cmg1117@aol.com
Web: www.northwesternbc.edu

Program Information:
Program begins: Program begins quarterly.
Duration of program: 18 months
Evening or weekend classes are available.

Application Information:
Enrollment of program: 84
Transfer students are accepted.

Financial Information:
Average cost of books: $1,000
% of students receiving aid: 75

Employment Profile:
% employed within the first 6 months following graduation: 85

Rockford Business College
730 North Church
Rockford, IL 61103

Contact Information:
Telephone: 815-965-8616
Fax: 815-965-0360
Web: www.rbcsuccess.com

Program Information:
Program begins: Program begins quarterly.
Duration of program: 12 months
Evening or weekend classes are available.

Application Information:
Enrollment of program: 100
Transfer students are accepted.

Financial Information:
Tuition, resident: $8,330

Tuition, non-resident: $5,850
% of students receiving aid: 76

Employment Profile:
% employed within the first 6 months following graduation: 90
Average starting salary: $20,000

Indiana

Clarian Health Partners, Inc.
Methodist Hospital
PO Box 1367
Indianapolis, IN 46202

Contact Information:
Telephone: 317-929-3906
Fax: 317-929-2445
E-mail: ubackner@clarian.com
Web: www.clarian.com

Program Information:
Program begins: January
Degrees offered: Certificate program, 11 months

Application Information:
Enrollment of program: 15
Transfer students are accepted.

Financial Information:
Average cost of books: $450
% of students receiving aid: 90

Employment Profile:
% of students who pass the boards on their first try: 93
% employed within the first 6 months following graduation: 100
Average starting salary: $19,000

International Business College—Ft. Wayne
3811 Old Illinois Road
Ft. Wayne, IN 46804-1298

Contact Information:
Telephone: 219-459-4500
Fax: 219-436-1896

Program Information:
Program begins: September, January
Duration of program: 12 months

Application Information:
Enrollment of program: 50
Transfer students are accepted.

Financial Information:
Average cost of books: $1,100
% of students receiving aid: 83

Employment Profile:
% of students who pass the boards on their first try: 57
% employed within the first 6 months following graduation: 69
Average starting salary: $16,680

International Business College—Indianapolis
7205 Shadeland Station
Indianapolis, IN 46256

Contact Information:
Telephone: 317-841-6400
Fax: 317-841-6419

Program Information:
Program begins: Program begins quarterly.
Duration of program: 10 months

Application Information:
Enrollment of program: 29
Transfer students are accepted.

Employment Profile:
% employed within the first 6 months following graduation: 75
Average starting salary: $18,800

Ivy Tech State College—Anderson
104 West 53rd Street
Anderson, IN 46013

Contact Information:
Telephone: 317-643-7133
Fax: 317-643-3294
E-mail: nschulz@ivy.tec.in.us
Web: www.ivy.tec.in.us

Program Information:
Duration of program: 24 months
Evening or weekend classes are available.

Financial Information:
Tuition, resident: $2,500
Tuition, non-resident: $4,500

Ivy Tech State College—Columbus
4475 Central Avenue
Columbus, IN 47203

Contact Information:
Telephone: 812-372-9925 ext. 135
Fax: 812-372-0311
E-mail: lherron@ivy.tec.in.us
Web: www.ivy.tec.in.us

Program Information:
Program begins: August, January, May
Duration of program: 12 months
Evening or weekend classes are available.

Application Information:
Enrollment of program: 45
Transfer students are accepted.

Financial Information:
% of students receiving aid: 85

Employment Profile:
% employed within the first 6 months following graduation: 29
Average starting salary: $18,000

Ivy Tech State College—Kokomo
1815 East Morgan Street
Kokomo, IN 46901

Contact Information:
Telephone: 765-459-0561 ext. 383
Fax: 765-454-5111
E-mail: pslusher@ivy.tec.in.us
Web: www.ivy.tec.in.us

Program Information:
Program begins: August
Duration of program: 18 months
Evening or weekend classes are available.

Application Information:
Enrollment of program: 150
Transfer students are accepted.

Financial Information:
Tuition, resident: $2,976
Tuition, non-resident: $8,928

Ivy Tech State College—Lafayette
3101 South Creasy Lane
PO Box 6299
Lafayette, IN 47903

Contact Information:
Telephone: 765-772-9206
Fax: 765-772-9248
E-mail: cabel@ivy.tec.in.us
Web: www.laf.ivy.tec.in.us

Program Information:
Duration of program: 24 months
Evening or weekend classes are available.

Application Information:
Enrollment of program: 48
Transfer students are accepted.

Financial Information:
Tuition, resident: $3,098
Tuition, non-resident: $5,697

Ivy Tech State College—Terre Haute
7999 US Highway 41 South
Terre Haute, IN 47802-4898

Contact Information:
Telephone: 812-299-1121 ext. 291
Fax: 812-299-5723
E-mail: bhofmann@ivy.tec.in.us
Web: www.ivy.tec.in.us

Program Information:
Program begins: August, January, May
Degrees offered: Certificate program, 12 months; Associate's, 18 months
Evening or weekend classes are available.

Application Information:
Enrollment of program: 80
Transfer students are accepted.

Financial Information:
Tuition, resident: $3,098
Tuition, non-resident: $5,698

Employment Profile:
% of students who pass the boards on their first try: 100
% employed within the first 6 months following graduation: 100
Average starting salary: $20,000

Ivy Tech State College NE—Ft. Wayne

3800 North Anthony Boulevard
Ft. Wayne, IN 46805

Contact Information:
Telephone: 219-480-4273
Fax: 219-480-4149
E-mail: aahill@ivy.tec.in.us

Program Information:
Duration of program: 18 months
Evening or weekend classes are available.

Financial Information:
Tuition, resident: $2,001
Tuition, non-resident: $3,680

Ivy Tech State College SC—Sellersburg

8204 Highway 311
Sellersburg, IN 47172

Contact Information:
Telephone: 812-246-3301 ext. 4218
Fax: 812-246-9905
E-mail: drawles@ivy.tec.in.us
Web: www.ivy.tec.in.us

Program Information:
Program begins: January, May, August
Degrees offered: Certificate program, 12 months
Evening or weekend classes are available.

Application Information:
Enrollment of program: 150
Transfer students are accepted.

Financial Information:
Tuition, resident: $2,418
Tuition, non-resident: $4,401
Average cost of books: $1,847
% of students receiving aid: 80

Employment Profile:
% of students who pass the boards on their first try: 98
% employed within the first 6 months following graduation: 88
Average starting salary: $17,750

Michiana College

1030 East Jefferson Boulevard
South Bend, IN 46617

Contact Information:
Telephone: 219-436-2738
Fax: 219-436-2958

Program Information:
Program begins: August, January, May
Duration of program: 24 months
Evening or weekend classes are available.

Application Information:
Enrollment of program: 70
Transfer students are accepted.

Financial Information:
Average cost of books: $100
% of students receiving aid: 90

Employment Profile:
% employed within the first 6 months following graduation: 80
Average starting salary: $15,500

Iowa

American Institute of Commerce

1801 East Kimberly Road
Davenport, IA 52807

Contact Information:
Telephone: 319-355-3500

Program Information:
Duration of program: 15 months
Evening or weekend classes are available.

Iowa Central Community College

330 Avenue M
Ft. Dodge, IA 50501

Contact Information:
Telephone: 515-576-7201 ext. 2308
Fax: 515-576-5656
E-mail: kolesar@duke.iccc.cc.ia.us
Web: www.iccc.cc.ia.us

Program Information:
Program begins: September
Degrees offered: Diploma, 11 months

Application Information:
Enrollment of program: 20
Transfer students are accepted.

Financial Information:
Tuition, resident: $3,412
Tuition, non-resident: $3,812
Average cost of books: $500
% of students receiving aid: 54

Employment Profile:
% of students who pass the boards on their first try: 98
% employed within the first 6 months following graduation: 98
Average starting salary: $16,640

Kirkwood Community College

6301 Kirkwood Boulevard Southwest
PO Box 2068
Cedar Rapids, IA 52406-9973

Contact Information:
Telephone: 319-398-5564
Fax: 319-398-1293
Web: www.kirkwood.cc.ia.us

Program Information:
Program begins: August
Duration of program: 12 months

Application Information:
Enrollment of program: 90
Transfer students are accepted.

Financial Information:
Tuition, resident: $2,600
Tuition, non-resident: $5,200
Average cost of books: $750
% of students receiving aid: 80

Employment Profile:
% of students who pass the boards on their first try: 90
% employed within the first 6 months following graduation: 80
Average starting salary: $18,000

Kentucky

Central Kentucky Technical College

308 Vocational-Technical Road
Lexington, KY 40511

Contact Information:
Telephone: 606-246-2400 ext. 254
Fax: 606-246-2417
E-mail: rebecca simms@ktcc.state.ky.us
Web: www.ktcc.state.ky.us

Program Information:
Program begins: Program begins quarterly.
Duration of program: 24 months

Application Information:
Enrollment of program: 20
Transfer students are accepted.

Financial Information:
Tuition, resident: $600
Tuition, non-resident: $1,200

Employment Profile:
% of students who pass the boards on their first try: 100
Average starting salary: $22,000

Eastern Kentucky University

Disney 225
Richmond, KY 40475-3135

Contact Information:
Telephone: 606-622-1028
Fax: 606-622-1140
E-mail: mtsnewso@acs.eku.edu

Program Information:
Program begins: September, November, February, April, June
Duration of program: 24 months

Financial Information:
Tuition, resident: $2,190
Tuition, non-resident: $6,030

Fugazzi College

407 Marquis Avenue
Lexington, KY 40502

Contact Information:
Telephone: 606-266-0401

Fax: 606-268-2118
E-mail: falrey@edu.corp.edu

Program Information:
Program begins: March, September
Duration of program: 24 months

Kentucky College of Business—Danville
115 East Lexington Avenue
Danville, KY 40422

Contact Information:
Telephone: 606-236-6991
Fax: 606-236-1063

Program Information:
Program begins: Program begins quarterly.
Degrees offered: Associate's, 24 months
Evening or weekend classes are available.

Application Information:
Enrollment of program: 62
Transfer students are accepted.

Financial Information:
Average cost of books: $800
% of students receiving aid: 80

Employment Profile:
% of students who pass the boards on their first try: 98
% employed within the first 6 months following graduation: 98
Average starting salary: $16,560

West Kentucky Technical College
5200 Blandville Road
PO Box 7408
Paducah, KY 42002-7408

Contact Information:
Telephone: 502-554-4991 ext. 277
Fax: 502-554-2695
Web: www.wkytech.com

Program Information:
Program begins: September
Duration of program: 11 months

Application Information:
Enrollment of program: 7

Financial Information:
Tuition, resident: $1,360
Tuition, non-resident: $2,720
Average cost of books: $500
% of students receiving aid: 75

Employment Profile:
% of students who pass the boards on their first try: 75
% employed within the first 6 months following graduation: 100
Average starting salary: $29,000

Maine

Kennebec Valley Technical College
450 North Avenue
Fairfield, ME 04937-1367

Contact Information:
Telephone: 207-453-5005
Fax: 207-453-5011
Web: www.kvtc.net

Program Information:
Program begins: August
Duration of program: 18 months
Evening or weekend classes are available.

Application Information:
Enrollment of program: 40
Transfer students are accepted.

Financial Information:
Tuition, resident: $1,856
Tuition, non-resident: $4,086
% of students receiving aid: 90

Employment Profile:
% of students who pass the boards on their first try: 100
% employed within the first 6 months following graduation: 100
Average starting salary: $20,000

Maryland

Medix School
700 York Road
Towson, MD 21204

Contact Information:
Telephone: 410-337-5155
Fax: 410-337-5104

Program Information:
Program begins: Program begins quarterly.
Duration of program: 9 months
Evening or weekend classes are available.

Application Information:
Transfer students are accepted.

Financial Information:
Tuition, resident: $7,490

Massachusetts

Southeastern Technical Institute
250 Foundry Street
South Easton, MA 02375

Contact Information:
Telephone: 508-238-1860 ext. 337
Fax: 508-238-7266

Program Information:
Program begins: September
Degrees offered: Diploma, 10 months
Evening or weekend classes are available.

Application Information:
Enrollment of program: 25
Transfer students are accepted.

Financial Information:
Tuition, resident: $1,000
Tuition, non-resident: $2,300
Average cost of books: $400
% of students receiving aid: 25

Employment Profile:
% of students who pass the boards on their first try: 75
% employed within the first 6 months following graduation: 90
Average starting salary: $20,000

Springfield Technical Community College
One Armory Square
PO Box 9000
Springfield, MA 01105

Contact Information:
Telephone: 413-755-4876 ext. 3541
Fax: 413-733-0688
Web: www.stcc.mass.edu

Program Information:
Program begins: September
Degrees offered: Associate's, 24 months
Evening or weekend classes are available.

Application Information:
Enrollment of program: 85
Transfer students are accepted.

Financial Information:
Tuition, resident: $1,156
Tuition, non-resident: $6,936
Average cost of books: $450
% of students receiving aid: 90

Employment Profile:
% of students who pass the boards on their first try: 88
% employed within the first 6 months following graduation: 95
Average starting salary: $20,000

Michigan

Alpena Community College
666 Johnson Street
Alpena, MI 49707

Contact Information:
Telephone: 517-356-9021 ext. 226
Fax: 517-356-0980
Web: www.alpena.cc.mi.us

Program Information:
Program begins: Program begins monthly.
Duration of program: 24 months
Evening or weekend classes are available.

Application Information:
Enrollment of program: 50
Transfer students are accepted.

Financial Information:
Tuition, resident: $2,055
Tuition, non-resident: $2,950

Employment Profile:
% of students who pass the boards on their first try: 100

% employed within the first 6 months following graduation: 100
Average starting salary: $30,000

Baker College—Flint

G 1050 West Bristol Road
Flint, MI 48507

Contact Information:

Telephone: 810-766-4133
Fax: 810-766-4049
E-mail: benedi_m@acadfl.baker.edu
Web: www.baker.edu

Program Information:

Duration of program: 24 months
Evening or weekend classes are available.

Application Information:

Enrollment of program: 75
Transfer students are accepted.

Financial Information:

Average cost of books: $1,000
% of students receiving aid: 80

Employment Profile:

% of students who pass the boards on their first try: 99
% employed within the first 6 months following graduation: 99
Average starting salary: $17,000

Baker College of Cadillac

9600 East 13th Street
Cadillac, MI 49601

Contact Information:

Telephone: 616-775-6503
Fax: 616-775-8505
E-mail: muste_w@cadillac.baker.edu
Web: www.baker.edu

Program Information:

Program begins: August
Duration of program: 24 months
Evening or weekend classes are available.

Application Information:

Enrollment of program: 340

Financial Information:

Tuition, resident: $6,240
Average cost of books: $900
% of students receiving aid: 80

Employment Profile:

% of students who pass the boards on their first try: 100
Average starting salary: $15,500

Baker College of Jackson

2800 Springport Road
Jackson, MI 49202

Contact Information:

Telephone: 517-789-6123
Fax: 517-789-7331
E-mail: alyea_l@jackson.baker.edu
Web: www.baker.edu

Program Information:

Program begins: September, January, March
Degrees offered: Associate's, 18 months

Application Information:

Enrollment of program: 67
Transfer students are accepted.

Financial Information:

Average cost of books: $700
% of students receiving aid: 85

Employment Profile:

% of students who pass the boards on their first try: 100
% employed within the first 6 months following graduation: 100
Average starting salary: $16,640

Baker College of Owosso

1020 South Washington Street
Owosso, MI 48867

Contact Information:

Telephone: 517-7293417
Fax: 517-729-3411
E-mail: poag-k@owosso.baker.edu
Web: www.baker.edu

Program Information:

Program begins: September, January, April
Degrees offered: Associate's, 24 months
Evening or weekend classes are available.

Application Information:

Enrollment of program: 32
Transfer students are accepted.

Financial Information:

Average cost of books: $889
% of students receiving aid: 70

Employment Profile:

% of students who pass the boards on their first try: 89
% employed within the first 6 months following graduation: 86
Average starting salary: $18,000

Baker College of Port Huron

3403 Lapeer Road
Port Huron, MI 48060

Contact Information:

Telephone: 810-985-7000
Fax: 810-985-7066
E-mail: kaltz_j@porthuron.baker.edu
Web: www.baker.edu

Program Information:

Program begins: September, January
Duration of program: 18 months
Evening or weekend classes are available.

Great Lakes College—Saginaw

310 South Washington Avenue
Saginaw, MI 48607

Contact Information:

Telephone: 517-686-1572
Fax: 517-686-2380
E-mail: bheckard@davenport.edu
Web: www.davenport.edu

Program Information:

Program begins: Program begins quarterly.
Duration of program: 24 months
Evening or weekend classes are available.

Application Information:

Transfer students are accepted.

Financial Information:

Tuition, resident: $2,148

Employment Profile:

% of students who pass the boards on their first try: 99

Jackson Community College

2111 Emmons Road
Jackson, MI 49201

Contact Information:

Telephone: 517-796-8557
Fax: 517-796-8633
E-mail: jean_dennerll@jackson.cc.mi.us

Program Information:

Program begins: August, January
Duration of program: 24 months
Evening or weekend classes are available.

Application Information:

Transfer students are accepted.

Financial Information:

Tuition, resident: $1,800
Tuition, non-resident: $2,160

Employment Profile:

% of students who pass the boards on their first try: 100
% employed within the first 6 months following graduation: 90
Average starting salary: $18,000

Lansing Community College

3400 Human Health & Public Service Career
PO Box 40010
Lansing, MI 48901-7210

Contact Information:

Telephone: 517-483-1431
Fax: 517-483-1508
Web: www.lansing.cc.mi.us

Program Information:

Program begins: January, May, September
Duration of program: 12 months
Evening or weekend classes are available.

Application Information:

Enrollment of program: 16
Transfer students are accepted.

Financial Information:

Tuition, resident: $2,620
Tuition, non-resident: $3,722

Employment Profile:

% employed within the first 6 months following graduation: 90
Average starting salary: $16,000

Macomb Community College

Business Health & Human Service
44575 Garfield Road
Clinton Township, MI 48038-1139

Contact Information:
Telephone: 810-286-2097
Fax: 810-286-2098
Web: www.macomb.cc.mi.us

Program Information:
Program begins: September
Duration of program: 10 months
Evening or weekend classes are available.

Application Information:
Enrollment of program: 82

Financial Information:
Tuition, resident: $1,944
Tuition, non-resident: $2,952

Employment Profile:
% of students who pass the boards on their first try: 70
% employed within the first 6 months following graduation: 80
Average starting salary: $18,720

Northwestern Michigan College

1701 East Front Street
Traverse City, MI 49686

Contact Information:
Telephone: 231-922-1263
Fax: 231-922-8960
E-mail: dkeelan@nmc.edu
Web: www.nmc.edu

Program Information:
Program begins: August
Duration of program: 18 months
Evening or weekend classes are available.

Application Information:
Enrollment of program: 40
Transfer students are accepted.

Financial Information:
Tuition, resident: $1,889
Tuition, non-resident: $3,123
Average cost of books: $500
% of students receiving aid: 33

Employment Profile:
% of students who pass the boards on their first try: 100
% employed within the first 6 months following graduation: 100
Average starting salary: $18,000

Oakland Community College—Waterford

7350 Cooley Lake Road
Waterford, MI 48327

Contact Information:
Telephone: 248-360-3094
Fax: 248-360-3203
E-mail: kakittle@occ.cc.mi.us
Web: www.occ.cc.mi.us

Program Information:
Program begins: May, August, January
Evening or weekend classes are available.

Application Information:
Enrollment of program: 60
Transfer students are accepted.

Financial Information:
Tuition, resident: $1,932
Tuition, non-resident: $3,276
Average cost of books: $500
% of students receiving aid: 30

Employment Profile:
% of students who pass the boards on their first try: 99
% employed within the first 6 months following graduation: 85
Average starting salary: $28,000

Schoolcraft College

1751 Radcliff Street
Garden City, MI 48135

Contact Information:
Telephone: 734-462-4770
Fax: 734-462-4775
E-mail: prubio@schoolcraft.cc.mi.us

Program Information:
Program begins: September, January
Duration of program: 12 months
Evening or weekend classes are available.

Application Information:
Enrollment of program: 35
Transfer students are accepted.

Financial Information:
Tuition, resident: $2,193
Tuition, non-resident: $3,225
Average cost of books: $500

Employment Profile:
% employed within the first 6 months following graduation: 80
Average starting salary: $21,000

Minnesota

Dakota County Technical College

1300 145th Street East
Rosemount, MN 55068-2999

Contact Information:
Telephone: 612-423-8355 ext. 355
Fax: 612-423-8775
E-mail: dianne.tempel@dctc.mnscu.edu
Web: www.dctc.mnscu.edu

Program Information:
Program begins: Program begins quarterly.
Duration of program: 12 months

Application Information:
Enrollment of program: 30
Transfer students are accepted.

Financial Information:
Tuition, resident: $1,522
Average cost of books: $450
% of students receiving aid: 80

Employment Profile:
% of students who pass the boards on their first try: 93
% employed within the first 6 months following graduation: 95
Average starting salary: $22,000

Globe College of Business

Oakdale Center
7166 Tenth Street North
Oakdale, MN 55128

Contact Information:
Telephone: 651-730-5100
Fax: 651-730-5151
E-mail: admissions@globecollege.com
Web: www.globecollege.com

Program Information:
Program begins: August
Duration of program: 14 months
Evening or weekend classes are available.

Application Information:
Enrollment of program: 55
Transfer students are accepted.

Financial Information:
Average cost of books: $1,500
% of students receiving aid: 95

Employment Profile:
% employed within the first 6 months following graduation: 90
Average starting salary: $20,000

Lakeland Medical Dental Academy

1402 West Lake Street
Minneapolis, MN 55408

Contact Information:
Telephone: 612-827-5656
Fax: 612-821-9566
Web: www.lakelandacademy.com

Program Information:
Program begins: Program begins quarterly.
Degrees offered: Certificate program, 12 months; Associate's, 18 months
Evening or weekend classes are available.

Application Information:
Enrollment of program: 80
Transfer students are accepted.

Financial Information:
% of students receiving aid: 95

Employment Profile:
% of students who pass the boards on their first try: 50
% employed within the first 6 months following graduation: 98
Average starting salary: $21,000

Medical Institute of Minnesota
5503 Green Valley Drive
Bloomington, MN 55437

Contact Information:
Telephone: 612-844-0064
Fax: 612-844-0671
Web: www.mim.tec.mn.us

Program Information:
Program begins: Program begins quarterly.
Degrees offered: Diploma, 18 months
Evening or weekend classes are available.

Application Information:
Enrollment of program: 52
Transfer students are accepted.

Financial Information:
Average cost of books: $600

Employment Profile:
% of students who pass the boards on their first try: 75
% employed within the first 6 months following graduation: 100
Average starting salary: $24,500

Ridgewater College—Willmar Campus
2101 15th Avenue Northwest
PO Box 1097
Willmar, MN 56201

Contact Information:
Telephone: 320-231-2947
Fax: 320-231-7677
Web: www.ridgewater.mnscu.edu

Program Information:
Program begins: August
Duration of program: 14 months

Application Information:
Enrollment of program: 27
Transfer students are accepted.

Financial Information:
Tuition, resident: $4,239
Tuition, non-resident: $7,290
Average cost of books: $1,100

Employment Profile:
% of students who pass the boards on their first try: 83
% employed within the first 6 months following graduation: 100

Mississippi

Hinds Community College
3805 Highway 80 East
Pearl, MS 39208

Contact Information:
Telephone: 601-936-5582
Fax: 601-936-5569
E-mail: cmking@hinds.cc.ms.us
Web: www.hinds.cc.ms.us

Program Information:
Program begins: August, January
Duration of program: 18 months

Application Information:
Enrollment of program: 10
Transfer students are accepted.

Financial Information:
Tuition, resident: $1,020
Tuition, non-resident: $3,226
Average cost of books: $500
% of students receiving aid: 30

Employment Profile:
% of students who pass the boards on their first try: 96
% employed within the first 6 months following graduation: 90
Average starting salary: $20,500

Montana

Montana State University College of Technology—Great Falls
2100 16th Avenue South
PO Box 6010
Great Falls, MT 59405

Contact Information:
Telephone: 406-771-4383
Fax: 406-771-4317
E-mail: dnewton@msugf.edu
Web: www.msucotgf.montana.edu

Program Information:
Program begins: January
Duration of program: 18 months
Evening or weekend classes are available.

Application Information:
Enrollment of program: 10
Transfer students are accepted.

Financial Information:
Tuition, resident: $1,516
Tuition, non-resident: $3,160

Employment Profile:
% of students who pass the boards on their first try: 95
% employed within the first 6 months following graduation: 80

Nebraska

Omaha College of Health Careers
225 North 80th Street
Omaha, NE 68114-3617

Contact Information:
Telephone: 402-392-1300
Fax: 402-392-2828
E-mail: ochel@aol.com

Program Information:
Program begins: August, January
Duration of program: 8 months
Evening or weekend classes are available.

Application Information:
Enrollment of program: 300
Transfer students are accepted.

Financial Information:
Average cost of books: $700
% of students receiving aid: 95

Employment Profile:
% of students who pass the boards on their first try: 70
% employed within the first 6 months following graduation: 90
Average starting salary: $18,500

Southeast Community College
8800 O Street
Lincoln, NE 68520

Contact Information:
Telephone: 402-437-2756
Web: www.sccm.cc.ne.us

Program Information:
Program begins: September
Duration of program: 12 months
Evening or weekend classes are available.

Application Information:
Enrollment of program: 50
Transfer students are accepted.

Financial Information:
Tuition, resident: $2,390
Tuition, non-resident: $2,795

Employment Profile:
% employed within the first 6 months following graduation: 98
Average starting salary: $17,000

Nevada

Heritage College
3305 Spring Mountain Road
Suite 7
Las Vegas, NV 89102

Contact Information:
Telephone: 702-368-2338
Fax: 702-368-3853
E-mail: melindag.com@aol
Web: www.heritage-college.com/heritage

Program Information:
Program begins: Program begins quarterly.
Duration of program: 9 months
Evening or weekend classes are available.

Application Information:
Enrollment of program: 84
Transfer students are accepted.

Financial Information:
Tuition, resident: $7,795
% of students receiving aid: 85

Employment Profile:
% of students who pass the boards on their first try: 84
% employed within the first 6 months following graduation: 90
Average starting salary: $19,000

New Hampshire

New Hampshire Community Technical College

1066 Front Street
Manchester, NH 03102

Contact Information:
Telephone: 603-668-6706 ext. 231
Fax: 603-668-5354
E-mail: cfeldhousen@tec.nh.us
Web: www.mancstra.tec.nh.us

Program Information:
Program begins: Program begins quarterly.
Duration of program: 10 months
Evening or weekend classes are available.

Application Information:
Enrollment of program: 50
Transfer students are accepted.

Financial Information:
Tuition, resident: $3,300
Tuition, non-resident: $7,590
Average cost of books: $400
% of students receiving aid: 67

Employment Profile:
% of students who pass the boards on their first try: 100
% employed within the first 6 months following graduation: 95
Average starting salary: $20,000

New Jersey

Burlington County Institute of Technology

10 Hawkins Road
Medford, NJ 08055

Contact Information:
Telephone: 609-654-0200
Fax: 609-654-2698
E-mail: mlwebber@marrick.com
Web: www.bcit.tec.nj.us

Program Information:
Program begins: July
Duration of program: 9 months

Financial Information:
Tuition, resident: $1,990
Tuition, non-resident: $2,985

Hudson County Community College

870 Bergen Avenue
Room 211
Jersey City, NJ 07305

Contact Information:
Telephone: 201-239-6007
Fax: 201-418-7800
E-mail: jabender@aol
Web: www.hucc.edu

Program Information:
Program begins: September, January
Duration of program: 24 months
Evening or weekend classes are available.

Application Information:
Enrollment of program: 157

Financial Information:
Tuition, resident: $3,128
Tuition, non-resident: $5,313

Employment Profile:
% of students who pass the boards on their first try: 80
% employed within the first 6 months following graduation: 95
Average starting salary: $22,000
Additional information: Open enrollment.

Mercer County Technical Schools

1070 Klockner Road
Trenton, NJ 08619

Contact Information:
Telephone: 609-587-7640
Fax: 609-587-3304

Program Information:
Duration of program: 12 months

Application Information:
Enrollment of program: 16
Transfer students are accepted.

Financial Information:
Tuition, resident: $2,500
Tuition, non-resident: $5,000
Average cost of books: $400
% of students receiving aid: 25

Employment Profile:
% employed within the first 6 months following graduation: 100
Average starting salary: $23,500

Technical Institute of Camden County

Cross Keys Road
PO Box 566
Sicklerville, NJ 08081

Contact Information:
Telephone: 609-767-7000 ext. 5539
Fax: 609-767-6625
Web: www.ccts.tcc.nj.us

Program Information:
Program begins: Program begins every 6 weeks
Duration of program: 10 months

Financial Information:
Tuition, resident: $1,220
Tuition, non-resident: $1,486
Average cost of books: $300
% of students receiving aid: 20

Employment Profile:
% of students who pass the boards on their first try: 80
% employed within the first 6 months following graduation: 90
Average starting salary: $24,000

Warren County Community College

475 Route 57 West
Washington, NJ 07882

Contact Information:
Telephone: 908-689-2430
Fax: 908-689-8032

Program Information:
Program begins: August
Duration of program: 6 months

Application Information:
Enrollment of program: 28
Transfer students are accepted.

Financial Information:
Average cost of books: $650
% of students receiving aid: 50

Employment Profile:
% of students who pass the boards on their first try: 90
% employed within the first 6 months following graduation: 90
Average starting salary: $22,000

New York

ASA Institute of Business & Computer Technical Inc.

151 Lawrence Street
Brooklyn, NY 11201

Contact Information:
Telephone: 718-522-9073 ext. 149
Fax: 718-834-0835
E-mail: rozcol@asa-lawrence.com
Web: www.asa-lawrence.com

Program Information:
Program begins: February, July, October
Degrees offered: Certificate program, 15 months; Diploma, 18 months
Evening or weekend classes are available.

Application Information:
Enrollment of program: 351

Financial Information:
Tuition, resident: $7,502
Average cost of books: $200
% of students receiving aid: 83

Employment Profile:
% of students who pass the boards on their first try: 60
% employed within the first 6 months following graduation: 94
Average starting salary: $18,200

Bryant & Stratton Business Institute

1259 Central Avenue
Albany, NY 12205

Contact Information:
Telephone: 716-884-9120
Fax: 716-884-0091
E-mail: djcarpenter@bryantstratton.edu
Web: www.bryantstratton.edu

Program Information:
Program begins: January, May, September
Degrees offered: Associate's, 16 months
Evening or weekend classes are available.

Application Information:
Enrollment of program: 30
Transfer students are accepted.

Financial Information:
Average cost of books: $300
% of students receiving aid: 90

Employment Profile:
% of students who pass the boards on their first try: 81
% employed within the first 6 months following graduation: 91
Average starting salary: $26,400

Bryant & Stratton Business Institute
953 James Street
Syracuse, NY 13203

Contact Information:
Telephone: 716-292-5627
Fax: 716-292-6015
Web: www.bryantstratton.edu

Program Information:
Program begins: September, January
Degrees offered: Associate's, 16 months
Evening or weekend classes are available.

Application Information:
Enrollment of program: 45
Transfer students are accepted.

Financial Information:
Tuition, resident: $12,744
Average cost of books: $700
% of students receiving aid: 90

Employment Profile:
% of students who pass the boards on their first try: 64
% employed within the first 6 months following graduation: 85
Average starting salary: $16,850

Bryant & Stratton Business Institute
465 Main Street Suite 400
Buffalo, NY 14203

Contact Information:
Telephone: 315-472-6603 ext. 239
Fax: 315-474-4383
Web: www.bryantstratton.edu

Program Information:
Program begins: Program begins quarterly.
Duration of program: 18 months
Evening or weekend classes are available.

Application Information:
Enrollment of program: 60

Financial Information:
Tuition, resident: $7,025

Employment Profile:
% of students who pass the boards on their first try: 88
% employed within the first 6 months following graduation: 55
Average starting salary: $18,000

Suffolk Community College
Crooked Hill Road
Brentwood, NY 11717

Contact Information:
Telephone: 516-851-6340
Fax: 516-851-6339
Web: www.sunysuffolk.edu

Program Information:
Program begins: Program begins quarterly.
Degrees offered: Diploma, 24 months

Application Information:
Enrollment of program: 30
Transfer students are accepted.

Financial Information:
Tuition, resident: $2,180
Tuition, non-resident: $4,360
% of students receiving aid: 50

Employment Profile:
% of students who pass the boards on their first try: 85
Average starting salary: $23,000

Wood-Tobe Coburn School
8 East 40th Street
New York, NY 10016

Contact Information:
Telephone: 212-686-9040
Fax: 212-686-9171
Web: www.bradfordschools.com

Program Information:
Program begins: September
Degrees offered: Diploma, 10 months

Application Information:
Enrollment of program: 51
Transfer students are accepted.

Financial Information:
Average cost of books: $700
% of students receiving aid: 98

Employment Profile:
% employed within the first 6 months following graduation: 82
Average starting salary: $20,712

North Carolina

Carteret Community College
3505 Arendell Street
Morehead City, NC 28557

Contact Information:
Telephone: 252-247-6000 ext. 168
Fax: 252-247-2514
E-mail: jbh@carteret.cc.nc.us
Web: www.carteret.cc.nc.us

Program Information:
Program begins: August
Duration of program: 12 months

Application Information:
Enrollment of program: 20
Transfer students are accepted.

Financial Information:
Tuition, resident: $660
Tuition, non-resident: $6,845
Average cost of books: $700
% of students receiving aid: 90

Employment Profile:
% of students who pass the boards on their first try: 90
% employed within the first 6 months following graduation: 75
Average starting salary: $16,000

Forsyth Technical Community College
2100 Silas Creek Parkway
Winston-Salem, NC 27103

Contact Information:
Telephone: 910-723-0371 ext. 7362
Fax: 910-725-0669
E-mail: ldurham@forsyth.tec.nc.us
Web: www.forsyth.tec.nc.us

Program Information:
Program begins: August
Degrees offered: Associate's, 21 months

Application Information:
Enrollment of program: 20
Transfer students are accepted.

Financial Information:
Tuition, resident: $909
Tuition, non-resident: $5,771
Average cost of books: $550
% of students receiving aid: 70

Employment Profile:
% of students who pass the boards on their first try: 100
% employed within the first 6 months following graduation: 90
Average starting salary: $22,500

James Sprunt Community College
JSCC PO Box 398
Highway11 South
Kenansville, NC 28349

Contact Information:
Telephone: 910-296-2565
Fax: 910-291-6032
E-mail: agrady@jscc.cc.nc.us

Program Information:
Duration of program: 24 months
Evening or weekend classes are available.

Application Information:
Enrollment of program: 45
Transfer students are accepted.

Financial Information:
Tuition, resident: $415
Tuition, non-resident: $1,735
Average cost of books: $450
% of students receiving aid: 90

Employment Profile:
% of students who pass the boards on their first try: 95
% employed within the first 6 months following graduation: 100
Average starting salary: $18,000

King's College
322 Lamar Avenue
Charlotte, NC 28204

Contact Information:
Telephone: 704-372-0266
Fax: 704-348-2029
E-mail: cenglish@cs.com
Web: www.kings.edu

Program Information:
Program begins: September, January, April
Duration of program: 10 months

Lenoir Community College
PO Box 188
Highway 70 East Bypass
Kinston, NC 28502-0188

Contact Information:
Telephone: 252-527-6223 ext. 815
Fax: 252-527-2712
E-mail: injohnso@eastnet.educ.ecu.edu
Web: www.lenoir.cc.nc.us

Program Information:
Program begins: August
Degrees offered: Associate's, 21 months
Evening or weekend classes are available.

Application Information:
Enrollment of program: 33
Transfer students are accepted.

Financial Information:
Tuition, resident: $1,380
Tuition, non-resident: $8,768
Average cost of books: $900
% of students receiving aid: 75

Employment Profile:
% of students who pass the boards on their first try: 100
% employed within the first 6 months following graduation: 100
Average starting salary: $20,500

Martin Community College
1161 Kehukee Park Road
Williamston, NC 27892

Contact Information:
Telephone: 919-792-1521
Fax: 919-792-4425

Program Information:
Program begins: September
Degrees offered: Diploma, 12 months; Associate's, 24 months

Application Information:
Enrollment of program: 25
Transfer students are accepted.

Financial Information:
Tuition, resident: $664
Tuition, non-resident: $5,188
Average cost of books: $750
% of students receiving aid: 50

Employment Profile:
% of students who pass the boards on their first try: 100
% employed within the first 6 months following graduation: 90
Average starting salary: $18,000

Mitchell Community College
219 North Academy Street
Mooresville, NC 28115

Contact Information:
Telephone: 704-663-1923
Fax: 704-663-5239
E-mail: mmarks@mitchell.cc.nc.usbluenet.net

Program Information:
Program begins: Program begins quarterly.
Duration of program: 12 months

Application Information:
Enrollment of program: 35
Transfer students are accepted.

Financial Information:
Tuition, resident: $1,500
Tuition, non-resident: $6,450
Average cost of books: $450
% of students receiving aid: 85

Employment Profile:
% employed within the first 6 months following graduation: 75
Average starting salary: $1,900

Pitt Community College
PO Drawer 7007
Highway 11 South
Greenville, NC 27835-7007

Contact Information:
Telephone: 919-321-4284
Fax: 919-321-4451
E-mail: mhemby@pcc.pitt.cc.nc.us
Web: www.pitt.cc.nc.us

Program Information:
Program begins: August
Duration of program: 24 months

Application Information:
Enrollment of program: 45
Transfer students are accepted.

Financial Information:
Tuition, resident: $1,000
Tuition, non-resident: $7,600
Average cost of books: $500

Employment Profile:
% of students who pass the boards on their first try: 85
% employed within the first 6 months following graduation: 75
Average starting salary: $15,500

South Piedmont Community College
PO Box 126
Polkton, NC 28135

Contact Information:
Telephone: 704-272-7635
Fax: 704-272-8904

Program Information:
Program begins: August, January, May
Duration of program: 12 months

Application Information:
Enrollment of program: 20
Transfer students are accepted.

Financial Information:
Tuition, resident: $581
Tuition, non-resident: $4,585
Average cost of books: $250
% of students receiving aid: 90

Employment Profile:
% of students who pass the boards on their first try: 98
% employed within the first 6 months following graduation: 90
Average starting salary: $18,000

Wake Technical Community College
9101 Fayetteville Road
Raleigh, NC 27603-5676

Contact Information:
Telephone: 919-231-4500
Fax: 919-250-4329
Web: www.wake.tec.nc.us

Program Information:
Program begins: August
Degrees offered: Diploma, 12 months

Application Information:
Enrollment of program: 25
Transfer students are accepted.

Financial Information:
Tuition, resident: $964
Tuition, non-resident: $6,111
Average cost of books: $250
% of students receiving aid: 50

Employment Profile:
% of students who pass the boards on their first try: 100
% employed within the first 6 months following graduation: 100
Average starting salary: $10,000

Ohio

Ashland County—West Holmes Career Center

1783 State Route 60
Ashland, OH 44805

Contact Information:
Telephone: 419-289-3313 ext. 239
Fax: 419-289-3729
E-mail: cja@bright.net

Program Information:
Program begins: August
Duration of program: 9 months
Evening or weekend classes are available.

Application Information:
Enrollment of program: 14
Transfer students are accepted.

Financial Information:
Tuition, resident: $3,975
Average cost of books: $350
% of students receiving aid: 55

Employment Profile:
% of students who pass the boards on their first try: 92
% employed within the first 6 months following graduation: 85
Average starting salary: $19,500

Belmont Technical College

120 Fox-Shannon Place
St. Clairsville, OH 43950

Contact Information:
Telephone: 614-695-9500
Fax: 614-695-2247
E-mail: dfolmar@belmont.cc.oh.us

Program Information:
Program begins: September
Duration of program: 18 months

Application Information:
Enrollment of program: 40
Transfer students are accepted.

Financial Information:
Tuition, resident: $1,689
Tuition, non-resident: $2,520

Employment Profile:
% employed within the first 6 months following graduation: 95

EHOVE Career Center

316 West Mason Road
Milan, OH 44846

Contact Information:
Telephone: 419-499-4663 ext. 319
Fax: 419-499-5391

Program Information:
Program begins: September
Duration of program: 10 months
Evening or weekend classes are available.

Hocking College

3301 Hocking Parkway
Nelsonville, OH 45764-9704

Contact Information:
Telephone: 614-753-3591
Fax: 614-753-5105
E-mail: west_k@nelie.hocking.cc.oh.us
Web: www.hocking.edu

Program Information:
Program begins: September
Degrees offered: Associate's, 18 months
Evening or weekend classes are available.

Application Information:
Enrollment of program: 40
Transfer students are accepted.

Financial Information:
Tuition, resident: $2,265
Tuition, non-resident: $4,530
Average cost of books: $400
% of students receiving aid: 80

Employment Profile:
% of students who pass the boards on their first try: 90
% employed within the first 6 months following graduation: 90
Average starting salary: $20,000

Jefferson Community College

4000 Sunset Boulevard
Steubenville, OH 43952

Contact Information:
Telephone: 740-264-5591 ext. 159
Fax: 740-264-1338
E-mail: rsflohr@usa.net
Web: www.jefferson.cc.org

Program Information:
Program begins: September
Degrees offered: Certificate program, 12 months; Associate's, 18 months

Application Information:
Enrollment of program: 25
Transfer students are accepted.

Financial Information:
Tuition, resident: $2,700
Tuition, non-resident: $2,900

Employment Profile:
% of students who pass the boards on their first try: 90
% employed within the first 6 months following graduation: 100
Average starting salary: $16,000

Medina County Career Center

1101 West Liberty Street
Medina, OH 44256-9969

Contact Information:
Telephone: 330-725-8461
Fax: 330-725-3842
Web: www.mccc-jusd.org

Program Information:
Program begins: September, January
Degrees offered: Certificate program, 9 months

Application Information:
Enrollment of program: 24

Financial Information:
Tuition, resident: $3,800

Miami-Jacobs College

400 East Second Street
PO Box 1433
Dayton, OH 45401

Contact Information:
Telephone: 937-461-5174 ext. 163
E-mail: christinedosland@miamijacobs.edu
Web: www.miamijacobs.edu

Program Information:
Program begins: August
Duration of program: 18 months
Evening or weekend classes are available.

Financial Information:
Tuition, resident: $5,510

Northwestern College

1441 North Cable Road
Lima, OH 45805

Contact Information:
Telephone: 419-227-3141
Fax: 419-229-6926
Web: www.nc.edu

Program Information:
Duration of program: 18 months

Application Information:
Enrollment of program: 34
Transfer students are accepted.

Financial Information:
Average cost of books: $300
% of students receiving aid: 77

Employment Profile:
% employed within the first 6 months following graduation: 68
Average starting salary: $16,000

Ohio Institute of Photography and Technology

Division of Allied Health
2029 Edgefield Road
Dayton, OH 45439

Contact Information:
Telephone: 513-294-6155
Fax: 513-294-2259

Program Information:
Program begins: Program begins quarterly.
Duration of program: 14 months
Evening or weekend classes are available.

RETS Technical Center
555 East Alex - Bell Road
Centerville, OH 45459

Contact Information:
Telephone: 937-433-3410
Fax: 937-435-6516
E-mail: rets@erinet.com
Web: www.retstechcenter.com

Program Information:
Program begins: September
Duration of program: 15 months
Evening or weekend classes are available.

Application Information:
Enrollment of program: 97
Transfer students are accepted.

Financial Information:
Average cost of books: $800

Employment Profile:
% employed within the first 6 months following graduation: 80
Average starting salary: $22,500

Sinclair Community College
444 West Third Street
Dayton, OH 45402

Contact Information:
Telephone: 937-512-2973
Fax: 937-512-2239
E-mail: jbarr@sinclair.edu
Web: www.sinclair.edu

Program Information:
Program begins: September
Duration of program: 21 months

Financial Information:
Tuition, resident: $1,457
Tuition, non-resident: $2,303

Stautzenberger College
5355 Southwyck Boulevard
Toledo, OH 43614

Contact Information:
Telephone: 419-866-0261
Fax: 419-867-9821
E-mail: morlockdlm@juno.com
Web: www.stautzen.com

Program Information:
Duration of program: 12 months
Evening or weekend classes are available.

Application Information:
Enrollment of program: 75
Transfer students are accepted.

University of Toledo
College of Health and Human Services
2801 West Bancroft Street
Toledo, OH 43606

Contact Information:
Telephone: 419-530-3149
Fax: 419-530-3096
Web: www.utodedo.edu

Program Information:
Program begins: August
Duration of program: 18 months
Evening or weekend classes are available.

Application Information:
Enrollment of program: 125

Financial Information:
Tuition, resident: $4,128
Tuition, non-resident: $9,720

Employment Profile:
% of students who pass the boards on their first try: 90
% employed within the first 6 months following graduation: 90
Average starting salary: $20,000

Youngstown State University
Department of Health Professions
One University Plaza
Youngstown, OH 44555

Contact Information:
Telephone: 330-742-1760
Fax: 330-742-2921
Web: www.ysu.edu

Program Information:
Program begins: September
Duration of program: 24 months
Evening or weekend classes are available.

Application Information:
Enrollment of program: 60
Transfer students are accepted.

Financial Information:
Tuition, resident: $3,498
Tuition, non-resident: $4,455
Average cost of books: $300

Employment Profile:
% of students who pass the boards on their first try: 95
% employed within the first 6 months following graduation: 90
Average starting salary: $15,000

Oklahoma

Francis Tuttle Vocational Technical Center
12777 North Rockwell Avenue
Oklahoma City, OK 73142-2789

Contact Information:
Telephone: 405-717-4142
Fax: 405-717-4789
E-mail: dwiggins@francistuttle.com
Web: www.francistuttle.com

Program Information:
Duration of program: 12 months
Evening or weekend classes are available.

Application Information:
Enrollment of program: 20
Transfer students are accepted.

Financial Information:
Average cost of books: $550
% of students receiving aid: 99

Employment Profile:
% of students who pass the boards on their first try: 75
% employed within the first 6 months following graduation: 95
Average starting salary: $18,000

Metro Area Vocational—Technical School
1720 Springlake Drive
Oklahoma City, OK 73111

Contact Information:
Telephone: 405-605-4644
Fax: 405-424-9403
Web: www.metrotech.org

Program Information:
Program begins: Program begins quarterly.
Duration of program: 12 months

Application Information:
Enrollment of program: 15

Financial Information:
Tuition, resident: $1,350
Tuition, non-resident: $2,050
Average cost of books: $350
% of students receiving aid: 60

Employment Profile:
% of students who pass the boards on their first try: 80
% employed within the first 6 months following graduation: 95
Average starting salary: $17,000

Oregon

Clackamas Community College
19600 South Mololla Avenue
Oregon City, OR 97045

Contact Information:
Telephone: 503-657-6958
Fax: 503-655-5153
E-mail: internet.margb@clackamas.cc.or.us

Program Information:
Program begins: Program begins quarterly
Duration of program: 9 months
Evening or weekend classes are available.

Application Information:
Enrollment of program: 22

Financial Information:
Tuition, resident: $1,470
Average cost of books: $640
% of students receiving aid: 66

Employment Profile:
% of students who pass the boards on their first try: 79

% employed within the first 6 months following graduation: 80
Average starting salary: $16,000

ConCorde Career Institute
1827 Northeast 44th Avenue
Portland, OR 97213

Contact Information:
Telephone: 503-281-4181
Fax: 503-281-6739
E-mail: pstoddard@concordecareercolleges.com
Web: www.concordecareercolleges.com

Program Information:
Program begins: Program begins quarterly.
Duration of program: 10 months

Application Information:
Transfer students are accepted.

Financial Information:
Tuition, resident: $6,739

Employment Profile:
% employed within the first 6 months following graduation: 72

Lane Community College
4000 East 30th Avenue
Eugene, OR 97405

Contact Information:
Telephone: 541-747-4501 ext. 2632
Fax: 541-744-4151
E-mail: garibayj@lanecc.edu
Web: www.lanecc.edu

Program Information:
Program begins: Program begins quarterly.
Duration of program: 10 months

Application Information:
Enrollment of program: 30
Transfer students are accepted.

Financial Information:
Tuition, resident: $1,944
Tuition, non-resident: $4,176
Average cost of books: $450
% of students receiving aid: 30

Employment Profile:
% of students who pass the boards on their first try: 100
% employed within the first 6 months following graduation: 75
Average starting salary: $20,000

Linn-Benton Community College
6500 Southwest Pacific Boulevard
Albany, OR 97321-3755

Contact Information:
Telephone: 541-917-4288
Fax: 541-917-4294
E-mail: kruegep@gw.lbcc.cc.or.us
Web: www.lbcc.cc.or.us

Program Information:
Program begins: Program begins quarterly.
Duration of program: 18 months
Evening or weekend classes are available.

Application Information:
Enrollment of program: 45
Transfer students are accepted.

Financial Information:
Tuition, resident: $1,575
Tuition, non-resident: $5,490
Average cost of books: $1,000
% of students receiving aid: 75

Employment Profile:
% of students who pass the boards on their first try: 100
% employed within the first 6 months following graduation: 90
Average starting salary: $21,000

Mt. Hood Community College
26000 Southeast Stark Street
Gresham, OR 97030

Contact Information:
Telephone: 503-491-7136
Fax: 503-491-7618
E-mail: bouldens@mhcc.cc.or.us
Web: www.mhcc.cc.or.us

Program Information:
Program begins: September, January
Duration of program: 24 months
Evening or weekend classes are available.

Application Information:
Enrollment of program: 15

Financial Information:
Tuition, resident: $1,665
Tuition, non-resident: $5,959

Pennsylvania

Berks Technical Institute
2205 Ridgewood Road
Wyomissing, PA 19609

Contact Information:
Telephone: 610-372-1722
Fax: 610-376-4684
Web: www.berkstech.com

Program Information:
Program begins: September
Duration of program: 8 months
Evening or weekend classes are available.

Application Information:
Enrollment of program: 66

Financial Information:
Tuition, resident: $8,129
Average cost of books: $400
% of students receiving aid: 75

Employment Profile:
% of students who pass the boards on their first try: 70
% employed within the first 6 months following graduation: 70
Average starting salary: $19,000

Butler County Community College
PO Box 1203
Butler, PA 16003-1203

Contact Information:
Telephone: 724-287-8711 ext. 373
Fax: 724-285-6047
Web: www.bc3.cc.pa.us

Program Information:
Program begins: April
Duration of program: 24 months
Evening or weekend classes are available.

Financial Information:
Tuition, resident: $3,762
Average cost of books: $1,000

Employment Profile:
% of students who pass the boards on their first try: 98
% employed within the first 6 months following graduation: 100
Average starting salary: $14,000

Central Pennsylvania College
Campus on College Hill
Summerdale, PA 17093

Contact Information:
Telephone: 717-728-2216
Fax: 717-732-5254
E-mail: crystalwilson@centralpenn.edu
Web: www.centralpenn.edu

Program Information:
Program begins: Program begins quarterly.
Degrees offered: Associate's, 21 months

Application Information:
Enrollment of program: 50
Transfer students are accepted.

Financial Information:
Average cost of books: $100
% of students receiving aid: 90

Employment Profile:
% of students who pass the boards on their first try: 96
% employed within the first 6 months following graduation: 100
Average starting salary: $18,000

Community College of Philadelphia
1700 Spring Garden Street
Philadelphia, PA 19130

Contact Information:
Telephone: 215-751-8947
Fax: 215-751-8937
Web: www.ccp.cc.pa.us

Program Information:
Program begins: January, May, September
Duration of program: 18 months

Application Information:
Enrollment of program: 36

Financial Information:
Tuition, resident: $2,400

Employment Profile:
% of students who pass the boards on their first try: 100

Delaware County Community College
Route 252 and Media Line Road
Media, PA 19063

Contact Information:
Telephone: 610-359-5274
Fax: 610-359-7350
E-mail: medmiston@decc.net.dcccc.edu
Web: www.dccc.edu

Program Information:
Program begins: August
Duration of program: 18 months
Evening or weekend classes are available.

Application Information:
Enrollment of program: 150
Transfer students are accepted.

Financial Information:
Tuition, resident: $4,000
Tuition, non-resident: $8,000

ICM School of Business and Medical Careers
10 Wood Street
Pittsburgh, PA 15222

Contact Information:
Telephone: 412-261-2647 ext. 253
Fax: 412-261-6491
E-mail: lgslack@netscape.net
Web: www.icmschool.com

Program Information:
Program begins: September
Duration of program: 18 months
Evening or weekend classes are available.

Laurel Business Institute
11-15 Penn Street
Uniontown, PA 15401

Contact Information:
Telephone: 724-439-4900
Fax: 724-439-3607
Web: www.laurelbusiness.net

Program Information:
Program begins: Program begins quarterly.
Duration of program: 18 months
Evening or weekend classes are available.

Application Information:
Transfer students are accepted.

Lehigh Carbon Community College
4525 Education Park Drive
Schnecksville, PA 18078-2598

Contact Information:
Telephone: 610-799-1516
Fax: 610-799-1527
E-mail: jk9@lex.lccc.edu
Web: www.lccc.edu

Program Information:
Program begins: August, January
Duration of program: 16 months
Evening or weekend classes are available.

Application Information:
Transfer students are accepted.

Financial Information:
Tuition, resident: $4,800
Tuition, non-resident: $9,600
Average cost of books: $250
% of students receiving aid: 50

Employment Profile:
% of students who pass the boards on their first try: 90
% employed within the first 6 months following graduation: 90
Average starting salary: $18,000

Mt. Aloysius College
7373 Admiral Peary Highway
Cresson, PA 16630-1999

Contact Information:
Telephone: 814-886-6322
Fax: 814-886-2978
E-mail: ckowaiczyk@mtaloy.edu
Web: www.mtaloy.edu

Program Information:
Program begins: Program begins quarterly.
Duration of program: 24 months
Evening or weekend classes are available.

Application Information:
Enrollment of program: 24
Transfer students are accepted.

Employment Profile:
% employed within the first 6 months following graduation: 98

Sawyer School
717 Liberty Avenue
Pittsburgh, PA 15222

Contact Information:
Telephone: 412-261-5701 ext. 580
Fax: 412-281-7269
E-mail: info@sawyer.edu
Web: www.sawyer.edu

Program Information:
Program begins: January, March, May, July, September, November
Degrees offered: Associate's, 16 months
Evening or weekend classes are available.

Application Information:
Enrollment of program: 30
Transfer students are accepted.

Financial Information:
Average cost of books: $1,900
% of students receiving aid: 90

Employment Profile:
% of students who pass the boards on their first try: 75
% employed within the first 6 months following graduation: 100
Average starting salary: $16,650

Thompson Learning Corporation
3440 Market Street, Second Floor
Philadelphia, PA 19104

Contact Information:
Telephone: 215-387-1530
Fax: 215-387-0106
E-mail: cdawson@thompsoninstitute.org
Web: www.thompsoninstitute.org

Program Information:
Program begins: August
Duration of program: 8 months
Evening or weekend classes are available.

South Carolina

Greenville Technical College
PO Box 5616
Greenville, SC 29606-5616

Contact Information:
Telephone: 864-250-8600
Fax: 864-250-8236
Web: www.greenvilletech.com

Program Information:
Program begins: August
Duration of program: 16 months
Evening or weekend classes are available.

Orangeburg Calhoun Technical College
3250 St. Matthews Road
Orangeburg, SC 29118

Contact Information:
Telephone: 803-535-1346
Fax: 803-535-1350
E-mail: cheeks@org.tec.sc.us
Web: www.octech.org

Program Information:
Program begins: August
Degrees offered: Diploma, 12 months

Application Information:
Enrollment of program: 25
Transfer students are accepted.

Financial Information:
Tuition, resident: $1,656
Tuition, non-resident: $1,908
Average cost of books: $750
% of students receiving aid: 90

Employment Profile:
% of students who pass the boards on their first try: 65
% employed within the first 6 months following graduation: 90
Average starting salary: $16,200

Spartanburg Technical College
PO Box 4386
Spartanburg, SC 29305-4386

Contact Information:
Telephone: 864-591-3864
Fax: 864-591-3708
E-mail: buchanand@spt.tec.sc.us
Web: www.spt.tec.sc.us

Program Information:
Program begins: Program begins quarterly.
Duration of program: 12 months

Financial Information:
Tuition, resident: $650
Tuition, non-resident: $815

Trident Technical College
PO Box 118067
Charleston, SC 29423-8067

Contact Information:
Telephone: 843-574-6103
Fax: 843-574-6585
E-mail: zpwhited@trident.tec.sc.us
Web: www.trident.tec.sc.us

Program Information:
Program begins: Program begins quarterly.
Duration of program: 12 months
Evening or weekend classes are available.

Application Information:
Transfer students are accepted.

Financial Information:
Tuition, resident: $1,758
Tuition, non-resident: $4,965

Employment Profile:
% of students who pass the boards on their first try: 85
% employed within the first 6 months following graduation: 40
Average starting salary: $19,000

South Dakota

Lake Area Technical Institute
230 North East 11th Street
Watertown, SD 57201

Contact Information:
Telephone: 605-882-5284
Fax: 605-882-6299
E-mail: latiinfo@lati.tec.sd.us
Web: www.lati.tech.sd.us

Program Information:
Program begins: August
Degrees offered: Diploma, 18 months; Associate's, 18 months
Evening or weekend classes are available.

Application Information:
Enrollment of program: 55

Financial Information:
Tuition, resident: $2,700
Tuition, non-resident: $3,325

Mitchell Technical Institute
821 North Capital
Mitchell, SD 57301

Contact Information:
Telephone: 605-995-3024
Fax: 605-996-3299
E-mail: hoffmanc@mti.tec.sd.us

Program Information:
Program begins: October, April
Duration of program: 18 months

Application Information:
Enrollment of program: 40

Tennessee

West Tennessee Business College
1186 Highway 45 Bypass
Jackson, TN 38301

Contact Information:
Telephone: 901-668-7240 ext. 29
Fax: 901-668-3824
E-mail: wtbc@aeneas.net
Web: www.wtbc.com

Program Information:
Program begins: Program begins quarterly.
Duration of program: 15 months
Evening or weekend classes are available.

Application Information:
Enrollment of program: 88
Transfer students are accepted.

Financial Information:
Tuition, resident: $8,575
% of students receiving aid: 95

Employment Profile:
% employed within the first 6 months following graduation: 66
Average starting salary: $14,500

Texas

Bradford School
4669 Southwest Freeway #300
Houston, TX 77027

Contact Information:
Telephone: 713-629-1500 ext. 207
Fax: 713-629-0059

Program Information:
Degrees offered: Certificate program, 10 months; Diploma, 10 months

Application Information:
Enrollment of program: 200

Financial Information:
Tuition, resident: $11,000
Average cost of books: $400
% of students receiving aid: 90

Employment Profile:
% of students who pass the boards on their first try: 90
% employed within the first 6 months following graduation: 95
Average starting salary: $17,000

El Centro College
Main and Lamar Streets
Dallas, TX 75202

Contact Information:
Telephone: 214-860-2328
Fax: 214-860-2268
E-mail: pgm5704@dcccd.edu

Program Information:
Program begins: January, February, March, April, May, June
Duration of program: 12 months
Evening or weekend classes are available.

Application Information:
Enrollment of program: 15

Financial Information:
Tuition, resident: $950
Tuition, non-resident: $1,900
Average cost of books: $400
% of students receiving aid: 80

Employment Profile:
% employed within the first 6 months following graduation: 85
Average starting salary: $22,000

El Paso Community College
PO Box 20500
El Paso, TX 79998

Contact Information:
Telephone: 915-831-4139
Fax: 915-831-4021
Web: www.epcc.edu

Program Information:
Program begins: August, January
Duration of program: 12 months
Evening or weekend classes are available.

Application Information:
Enrollment of program: 11
Transfer students are accepted.

Financial Information:
Tuition, resident: $1,495
Tuition, non-resident: $4,535

Mountain View College
4849 West Illinois Avenue
Dallas, TX 75211

Contact Information:
Telephone: 214-860-8721
Fax: 214-860-8592

E-mail: pgm3704@dcccd.edu
Web: www.dcccd.edu

Program Information:
Program begins: August
Duration of program: 12 months
Evening or weekend classes are available.

Application Information:
Enrollment of program: 44
Transfer students are accepted.

Financial Information:
Tuition, resident: $950
Tuition, non-resident: $1,900
Average cost of books: $450
% of students receiving aid: 90

Employment Profile:
% employed within the first 6 months following graduation: 90
Average starting salary: $22,000

San Antonio College
1300 San Pedro Avenue
San Antonio, TX 78212

Contact Information:
Telephone: 210-785-6041
E-mail: jmccann@accdvm.edu
Web: www.accd.edu

Program Information:
Program begins: September, April
Duration of program: 13 months
Evening or weekend classes are available.

Application Information:
Enrollment of program: 231

Financial Information:
Tuition, resident: $1,400
Tuition, non-resident: $2,000

Utah

American Institute of Medical-Dental Technology
1675 North Freedom Boulevard
Building 5A
Provo, UT 84604

Contact Information:
Telephone: 801-377-2900
Fax: 801-375-3077
E-mail: aimdt@aol.com
Web: www.americaninstitute.net

Program Information:
Program begins: September, March
Duration of program: 8 months
Evening or weekend classes are available.

Application Information:
Enrollment of program: 60

Financial Information:
Average cost of books: $718
% of students receiving aid: 50

Employment Profile:
% employed within the first 6 months following graduation: 90

Mountain West College
3098 Highland Drive
Salt Lake City, UT 84106

Contact Information:
Telephone: 801-485-0221
Fax: 801-485-0057

Program Information:
Duration of program: 18 months
Evening or weekend classes are available.

Application Information:
Enrollment of program: 85

Salt Lake Community College
4600 South Redwood Road
PO Box 30808
Salt Lake City, UT 84130

Contact Information:
Telephone: 801-957-4090
Fax: 801-957-4612
Web: www.slcc.edu

Program Information:
Program begins: January, May, August
Degrees offered: Certificate program
Evening or weekend classes are available.

Application Information:
Enrollment of program: 40
Transfer students are accepted.

Financial Information:
Tuition, resident: $1,800
Tuition, non-resident: $2,500
Average cost of books: $350
% of students receiving aid: 80

Employment Profile:
% of students who pass the boards on their first try: 87
% employed within the first 6 months following graduation: 70
Average starting salary: $22,000

Utah Career College
1144 West 3300 S
Salt Lake City, UT 84119

Contact Information:
Telephone: 801-975-7000
Fax: 801-975-7872
E-mail: shughes@utahcollege.com
Web: www.utahcollege.com

Program Information:
Program begins: Program begins quarterly.
Duration of program: 15 months
Evening or weekend classes are available.

Application Information:
Enrollment of program: 55
Transfer students are accepted.

Employment Profile:
% of students who pass the boards on their first try: 85
% employed within the first 6 months following graduation: 75
Average starting salary: $18,000

Virginia

Bryant & Stratton College—Richmond
8141 Hull Street Road
Richmond, VA 23235-6411

Contact Information:
Telephone: 804-745-2444
Fax: 804-745-6884
Web: www.bryantstratton.edu

Program Information:
Program begins: August
Duration of program: 24 months
Evening or weekend classes are available.

Application Information:
Enrollment of program: 86
Transfer students are accepted.

Financial Information:
Average cost of books: $160
% of students receiving aid: 97

Employment Profile:
% of students who pass the boards on their first try: 67
% employed within the first 6 months following graduation: 65
Average starting salary: $20,000

Dominion College
5373 Fallowater Lane
Suite B
Roanoke, VA 24017

Contact Information:
Telephone: 540-776-8321
Fax: 540-776-9240
E-mail: domcol@gte.net

Program Information:
Program begins: Program begins quarterly.
Duration of program: 18 months
Evening or weekend classes are available.

Employment Profile:
% of students who pass the boards on their first try: 95
% employed within the first 6 months following graduation: 60

Medical Careers Institute
11790 Jefferson Avenue
Newport News, VA 23606

Contact Information:
Telephone: 757-873-2423
Fax: 757-873-2472
E-mail: legatz@ecpi.edu
Web: www.mcimedicalcareers.com

Program Information:
Duration of program: 10 months
Evening or weekend classes are available.

Application Information:
Transfer students are accepted.

Miller-Motte Business College
1912 Memorial Avenue
Lynchburg, VA 24501

Contact Information:
Telephone: 910-392-4660
Fax: 910-799-6224

Program Information:
Program begins: August, January
Duration of program: 15 months
Evening or weekend classes are available.

Application Information:
Enrollment of program: 105

Financial Information:
Average cost of books: $2,400
% of students receiving aid: 90

Employment Profile:
% employed within the first 6 months following graduation: 80
Average starting salary: $22,000

National Business College of Bluefield
100 Logan Street
PO Box 629
Bluefield, VA 24153

Contact Information:
Telephone: 540-326-3621
Fax: 540-322-5731

Program Information:
Program begins: Program begins quarterly.
Duration of program: 24 months
Evening or weekend classes are available.

National Business College of Harrisonburg
51-B Burgess Road
Harrisonburg, VA 22801

Contact Information:
Telephone: 540-432-0943
Fax: 540-432-1133

Program Information:
Program begins: Program begins quarterly.
Degrees offered: Associate's, 24 months
Evening or weekend classes are available.

Application Information:
Enrollment of program: 30
Transfer students are accepted.

Financial Information:
Average cost of books: $640
% of students receiving aid: 98

Employment Profile:
% of students who pass the boards on their first try: 67
% employed within the first 6 months following graduation: 98
Average starting salary: $19,000

National Business College of Lynchburg
104 Candlewood Court
PO Box 629
Lynchburg, VA 24502

Contact Information:
Telephone: 804-239-3500
Fax: 804-239-3948

Program Information:
Program begins: Program begins quarterly.
Duration of program: 24 months
Evening or weekend classes are available.

Tidewater Community College
1700 College Crescent
Virginia Beach, VA 23456

Contact Information:
Telephone: 757-822-7252
Fax: 757-427-1338
E-mail: tcmcnak@tc.cc.va.us
Web: www.tc.cc.va.us/campuses/vabeach.htm

Program Information:
Degrees offered: Certificate program, 12 months

Application Information:
Transfer students are accepted.

Financial Information:
Tuition, resident: $1,925
Tuition, non-resident: $7,672

Employment Profile:
% of students who pass the boards on their first try: 100
% employed within the first 6 months following graduation: 100
Average starting salary: $16,000

Washington

Eton Technical Institute
209 East Casino Road
Everett, WA 98028

Contact Information:
Telephone: 425-353-4888
Fax: 425-353-1739
Web: www.etontech.com

Program Information:
Duration of program: 10 months
Evening or weekend classes are available.

Application Information:
Enrollment of program: 82

Financial Information:
Tuition, non-resident: $8,428

Highline Community College
PO Box 98000
Des Moines, WA 98198-9800

Contact Information:
Telephone: 206-878-3710 ext. 3494
Fax: 206-870-3780
E-mail: blindh@hcc.ctc.edu
Web: www.highline.ctc.edu

Program Information:
Program begins: September
Duration of program: 18 months

Application Information:
Enrollment of program: 25
Transfer students are accepted.

Financial Information:
Tuition, resident: $1,458
Tuition, non-resident: $5,730
Average cost of books: $250
% of students receiving aid: 40

Employment Profile:
% of students who pass the boards on their first try: 90
% employed within the first 6 months following graduation: 70
Average starting salary: $20,000

Lake Washington Technical College
11605 132nd Avenue Northeast
Kirkland, WA 98034-8506

Contact Information:
Telephone: 425-739-8361
Fax: 425-739-8293
E-mail: valerie.nye@lwtc.ctc.edu
Web: www.lwtc.ctc.edu

Program Information:
Program begins: August, January
Degrees offered: Certificate program, 11 months

Application Information:
Enrollment of program: 60
Transfer students are accepted.

Financial Information:
Average cost of books: $800

Employment Profile:
% employed within the first 6 months following graduation: 90
Average starting salary: $22,880

North Seattle Community College
9600 College Way North
Seattle, WA 98103

Contact Information:
Telephone: 206-528-4561
Fax: 206-527-3715
E-mail: dbedford@sccd.ctc.edu
Web: www.nsccux.sccd.ctc.edu

Program Information:
Program begins: September
Degrees offered: Certificate program, 12 months; Associate's, 21 months

Application Information:
Enrollment of program: 30
Transfer students are accepted.

Financial Information:
Tuition, resident: $1,936
Tuition, non-resident: $7,636
Average cost of books: $300
% of students receiving aid: 80

Employment Profile:
% of students who pass the boards on their first try: 99
% employed within the first 6 months following graduation: 95
Average starting salary: $24,000

Whatcom Community College
237 West Kellogg Road
Bellingham, WA 98226

Contact Information:
Telephone: 360-676-2170 ext. 3306
Fax: 360-752-6767
E-mail: bdahl@whatcom.ctc.edu
Web: www.whatcom.ctc.edu

Program Information:
Program begins: January, February, April, May, July, August
Duration of program: 12 months

Application Information:
Enrollment of program: 24
Transfer students are accepted.

Financial Information:
Tuition, resident: $500
Tuition, non-resident: $1,920
% of students receiving aid: 85

Employment Profile:
% employed within the first 6 months following graduation: 29
Average starting salary: $17,920

West Virginia

Huntington Jr. College of Business
900 Fifth Avenue
Huntington, WV 25701

Contact Information:
Telephone: 304-697-7550
Fax: 304-697-7554

Program Information:
Program begins: September
Duration of program: 18 months

Wisconsin

Blackhawk Technical College
6004 Prairie Road
PO Box 53547
Janesville, WI 53547

Contact Information:
Telephone: 608-757-7608
E-mail: srichard@blackhawk.tec.wi.us
Web: www.blackhawk.tec.wi.us

Program Information:
Program begins: August, January
Duration of program: 9 months

Application Information:
Enrollment of program: 64

Financial Information:
Tuition, resident: $2,007
Tuition, non-resident: $13,696

Concordia University Wisconsin
12800 North Lake Shore Drive
Mequon, WI 53097

Contact Information:
Telephone: 414-243-4362
Fax: 414-243-4438
E-mail: roseann.slota@cuw.edu
Web: www.cuw.edu

Program Information:
Program begins: August
Duration of program: 9 months

Application Information:
Enrollment of program: 25
Transfer students are accepted.

Financial Information:
Average cost of books: $300
% of students receiving aid: 80

Employment Profile:
% of students who pass the boards on their first try: 100
% employed within the first 6 months following graduation: 100
Average starting salary: $20,000

Gateway Technical College
1001 South Main Street
Racine, WI 53403

Contact Information:
Telephone: 262-631-7307
Fax: 262-631-5459
E-mail: raithandreucci@gateway.tec.wi.us
Web: www.gateway.tec.wi.us

Program Information:
Program begins: August, January, June
Duration of program: 10 months

Financial Information:
Tuition, resident: $1,380
Tuition, non-resident: $9,880

Gateway Technical College—Elkhorn
400 County Road H
Elkhorn, WI 53121

Contact Information:
Telephone: 414-741-6802
Fax: 414-741-6148
E-mail: steppc@gateway.tec.wi.us
Web: www.gateway.tec.wi.us

Program Information:
Program begins: August
Degrees offered: Diploma, 10 months
Evening or weekend classes are available.

Application Information:
Enrollment of program: 15
Transfer students are accepted.

Financial Information:
Tuition, resident: $2,618
Tuition, non-resident: $12,608
Average cost of books: $400
% of students receiving aid: 15

Employment Profile:
% of students who pass the boards on their first try: 85
% employed within the first 6 months following graduation: 95
Average starting salary: $22,500

Lakeshore Technical College
1290 North Avenue
Cleveland, WI 53015

Contact Information:
Telephone: 920-693-8213
Fax: 920-693-8955
E-mail: linar@ltc.tec.wi.us
Web: www.ltc.tec.wi.us

Program Information:
Program begins: Program begins quarterly.
Degrees offered: Diploma, 10 months
Evening or weekend classes are available.

Application Information:
Enrollment of program: 26

Financial Information:
Tuition, resident: $3,200
% of students receiving aid: 80

Employment Profile:
% of students who pass the boards on their first try: 95
% employed within the first 6 months following graduation: 98
Average starting salary: $17,000

Madison Area Technical College
3550 Anderson Street
Madison, WI 53791-9674

Contact Information:
Telephone: 608-246-6110
Fax: 608-246-6013
E-mail: sbuboltz@madison.tec.wi.us
Web: www.madison.tec.wi.us

Program Information:
Program begins: August, January
Duration of program: 9 months

Application Information:
Enrollment of program: 65
Transfer students are accepted.

Financial Information:
Average cost of books: $500
% of students receiving aid: 17

Employment Profile:
% of students who pass the boards on their first try: 90
% employed within the first 6 months following graduation: 100
Average starting salary: $18,000

Mid-State Technical College
933 Michigan Avenue
Stevens Point, WI 54481

Contact Information:
Telephone: 715-389-7024
Fax: 715-389-2864
E-mail: blato@mid_state.tec.wi.us
Web: www.midstate.tec.wi.us

Program Information:
Program begins: September, January
Duration of program: 9 months
Evening or weekend classes are available.

Application Information:
Enrollment of program: 36
Transfer students are accepted.

Financial Information:
Tuition, resident: $1,300
Tuition, non-resident: $2,500
Average cost of books: $600
% of students receiving aid: 80

Employment Profile:
% of students who pass the boards on their first try: 98
% employed within the first 6 months following graduation: 88
Average starting salary: $17,000

Waukesha County Technical College
800 Main Street
Pewaukee, WI 53072

Contact Information:
Telephone: 414-691-5563
Fax: 414-691-5451
E-mail: kbraaten@waukesha.tec.wi.us
Web: www.waukesha.tec.wi.us

Program Information:
Program begins: August, January
Degrees offered: Diploma, 9 months
Evening or weekend classes are available.

Application Information:
Enrollment of program: 60
Transfer students are accepted.

Financial Information:
Tuition, resident: $2,200
Tuition, non-resident: $11,000

Employment Profile:
% of students who pass the boards on their first try: 99
% employed within the first 6 months following graduation: 100
Average starting salary: $18,000

Occupational Therapist/ Occupational Therapy Assistant

Christine Malaski, MS, OTR/L
Assistant Professor of Occupational Therapy
Occupational Therapy
St. Ambrose University
Davenport, Iowa

Job Description

What Do They Do?

Occupational therapists and occupational therapy assistants work in a large variety of settings including hospitals, schools, nursing homes, community mental health centers, even private industry. They work with individuals of all ages with a variety of diagnoses.

For example, they may work with any of the following types of patients:

- children diagnosed with cerebral palsy, developmental delays, or attention deficit hyperactivity disorder
- adults diagnosed with traumatic brain injury, stroke, or spinal cord injury
- individuals diagnosed with major depression, personality disorder, schizophrenia, and substance abuse disorders

In addition, some occupational therapists analyze job sites and work environments for large companies to help reduce the number of work-related injuries.

Regardless of the employment location, OTs complete assessments of patient's functional strengths and limitations, develop an appropriate plan for care, carry out the treatment plan, and perform ongoing evaluation of the patient's progress to determine if improvement is being made and if the treatment needs modification.

The primary goal of the OT is to help the client become as independent as possible; therefore, the OT must choose purposeful activities for his or her client that are relevant and meaningful to that individual. Activities are designed to promote feelings of mastery and competence. Occupational therapists may encounter any of the following types of assignments:

- A child who has difficulty writing in school. The OT may work with the child to help him best grasp his writing utensil and position his desk in a way that will help him improve his handwriting skills.
- An adult who has had a cerebrovascular accident or stroke. The OT may work with the patient to strengthen and improve the range of motion in the upper extremities. The OT may teach this person new methods to complete daily tasks such as dressing with one hand.
- An adult in a mental health setting. The OT may help this patient develop new coping skills to deal with life stressors as well as address how his or her diagnosis has affected his or her abilities to complete daily living skills such as bathing, getting dressed, or cooking meals.

Therapists may use adaptive equipment such as a buttonhook to assist individuals with limited arm movement or hand function to be able to button their shirts independently using a single hand. An occupational therapist may also use computers and other forms of assistive technology to enable patients to communicate as well as control their environments after they have experienced functional limitations due to an event such as a head or spinal cord injury. Therapists may even use crafts as a method to improve hand function and increase patients' self-esteem.

Occupational therapy assistants support occupational therapists. They must be supervised by a registered occupational therapist according to state and federal regulations. The American Occupational Therapy Association has established a clear role delineation between the occupational therapist and occupational therapy assistant. In addition, AOTA also specified the roles and responsibilities that may be assigned to occupational therapy aides who perform under supervision of the occupational therapist or the occupational therapy assistant.[1]

Many hospitals, schools, and healthcare facilities use OT aides to assist occupational therapists and occupational therapy assistants in delivering OT services. Some states have regulations indicating how OT aides can be used during therapy with patients. The federal government also has regulations in place with regard to the use of OT aides as they relate to insurance programs administrated by the Health Care Finance Administration (HCFA). Medicare and Medicaid guidelines specify whether aides can be used and in what capacity aides are to perform within therapy sessions as well as what level of supervision is to be provided by the occupational therapist or occupational therapy assistant. OT aides generally have a high school diploma or equivalent (GED) and are trained on the job. Some examples of tasks that an OT aide may perform include transporting patients from their rooms to the clinic, photocopying information for therapists, and possibly ordering clinic supplies. The level at which OT aides become involved in patient care varies from state to state.

The roles and responsibilities of occupational therapists and physical therapists are clearly defined by the American Occupational Therapy Association and the American Physical Therapy Association; however, many individuals are often confused about the differences between these two professions. OTs and PTs may work collaboratively to address similar issues or areas of dysfunction or they may address very different areas of function. For example, in working with a patient who has been diagnosed with a cerebrovascular accident or stroke, the OT may evaluate upper extremity function including range of motion and the client's ability to complete functional daily activities such as dressing and feeding. The OT may also evaluate the patient's cognitive and perceptual skills. OTs and PTs may work together to address the client's balance and trunk control. The PT, on the other hand, may address the patient's lower extremity function, focusing on bed mobility, gait (walking), and transfer ability; however, some physical therapists may also address functional limitations of the upper extremity within the treatment session. OTs and PTs must work collaboratively at all times for the benefit of the patient; specific responsibilities between the professionals may vary depending on the setting. One significant difference between the two professions is the fact that PTs typically do not use purposeful activities, such as crafts, and do not typically work with clients diagnosed with mental illness unless the client has a secondary physical limitation such as a fracture or heart condition that may warrant a physical therapy referral. OTs consistently use purposeful activity since it is considered the foundation of the profession of occupational therapy.

Type of Person

According to the American Occupational Therapy Association, there are seven core values and attitudes of occupational therapists: altruism, equality, freedom, justice, dignity, truth, and prudence.[2] These values and attitudes are at the heart of the profession:

Altruism is demonstrated by unselfish concern and understanding of the client's needs. Equality is important as occupational therapy professionals will work with clients with a variety of different diagnoses, values, beliefs, and cultural and religious backgrounds. The OT needs to provide treatment in an equitable manner by understanding and being respectful of individual differences. Freedom is important to the profession of occupational therapy as the profession focuses on independence. Occupational therapists work toward maximizing functional independence in clients; therefore, clients need to have the freedom to make choices regarding treatment. Freedom is also demonstrated by the occupational therapist through a supportive rather than a strict or controlling attitude. Justice is valued by the profession as all practitioners are held to the laws that govern their practice. OTs also need to be very mindful of the rights of the client. By providing dignity to clients, OTs are able to address each client in an individual and unique manner. They demonstrate the value of dignity to their clients by being respectful and empathetic.

Truth is displayed through the OT's honest, professionally competent, accurate, and accountable behavior. Finally, prudence is demonstrated by the OT's ability to use sound judgment in providing patient care and using discretion in making clinical decisions.[3]

People considering entering occupational therapy should examine their own values and determine their own personal thoughts in regard to these concepts. OTs tend to be caring, flexible, nonjudgmental individuals who demonstrate good problem solving skills and creativity in the provision of therapy services.

With Whom Do They Work?

Occupational therapy professionals typically work as a collaborative member of the rehabilitation team. The environment in which an occupational therapist is employed will determine the team members with whom the therapist will work. Therapists may work with physicians, psychiatrists, psychologists, physical therapists, recreational therapists, speech-language pathologists, nurses, social workers, addiction counselors, nursing and rehabilitation aides, and educators.

Employment

Places of Employment

Occupational therapists may work in a variety of practice settings, including:

- hospital settings in acute care, physical rehabilitation, pain management programs, neonatal intensive care units, outpatient rehabilitation, cardiac rehabilitation, and skilled nursing units
- inpatient, partial hospitalization, outpatient, and community mental health settings
- school systems
- early intervention programs
- home healthcare agencies
- nursing homes
- industrial rehabilitation and work hardening settings
- orthopedic and hand therapy clinics

Employment Outlook

According to the 1998–1999 Bureau of Labor Statistics Occupational Outlook Handbook, the job outlook for occupational therapists and occupational therapy assistants should continue to be favorable. Employment opportunities are anticipated to grow much faster than average, meaning that employment is projected to increase at the rate of 36 percent or more during the ten-year period from 1996–2006.[4] As the "Baby Boomers" age and medical technology continues to advance and extend the lives of individuals with serious injury, the demand for healthcare services, including occupational therapy, will continue to increase. The development of OT educational programs and availability of OT positions has flourished during the last decade. An exception occurred recently when the federal government placed a rather low maximum reimbursement amount on rehabilitation services. As a result, hospitals and nursing homes decreased or eliminated many OT and OTA positions. Recently, however, that reimbursement level was increased so at least some of those positions may exist once again. In addition, therapists have responded to these changes by looking for and even creating positions in emerging markets in the areas of prevention and wellness, assisted living facilities, adult day care centers, and other various community treatment centers.

Salary

According to the Bureau of Labor Statistics, in 1996 occupational therapists earned a median annual salary of $40,560.[5] The American Occupational Therapy Association's statistics suggest that occupational therapy assistants can anticipate earning a mean annual salary of $27,442 for full-time employment. Occupational therapy aides can anticipate earning an annual salary of $13,520 to $15,600.[6] Therapists and assistants who have completed specialized training or who have earned advanced practitioner status may earn an even higher salary.

Educational Programs

Length

Currently, individuals earn a Bachelor's degree to become an occupational therapist and an Associate's degree to become an occupational therapy assistant. Typically, Bachelor's degree programs are four to five years in length, which includes six months of required clinical fieldwork. Upon completion of a Bachelor's degree in occupational therapy, therapists may pursue a post-professional degree at the Master's and/or Doctoral level in occupational therapy. Individuals who complete Bachelor's degrees in fields other than occupational therapy can enter the profession with an entry level Master's degree.

Although the present level of education to become an occupational therapist is a Bachelor's degree, according to the Accreditation Council for Occupational Therapy Education (ACOTE), institutions of higher education have until January 1, 2007, to initiate post-baccalaureate degree programs in occupational therapy education.[7] After this date, those who wish to enter the profession of occupational therapy must possess a Master's degree in occupational therapy.

Individuals interested in pursuing the position of occupational therapy assistant can complete this course of study through a variety of technical, vocational, and community colleges. The occupational therapy assistant program is two years in length including clinical fieldwork.

There are no formal educational programs for occupational therapy aides. They are trained on the job. According to the guidelines established by the American Occupational Therapy Association, OT aides must demonstrate general competency, and this competency must be assessed in a consistent and ongoing manner based on facility, state, and federal regulations.[8]

Prerequisites

Individuals who wish to apply to occupational therapy and occupational therapy assistant programs must have a high school diploma or equivalent. In addition, many programs require potential students to observe an occupational therapist or occupational therapy assistant and document these experiences as a part of the application process. Since each program's prerequisites will vary, it is important to inquire about them at each school to which you are interested in applying.

Curriculum

The curriculum for occupational therapy and occupational therapy assistant programs differs from program to program, although each school is required to meet specific standards as outlined by the Accreditation Council for Occupational Therapy Education (ACOTE). Students can anticipate taking courses in anatomy & physiology, kinesiology (the study of movement), history of the profession, and occupational therapy theory and practice. Depending on the type of program, a student may complete a research project focused on a specific area of occupational therapy. Both occupational therapy and occupational therapy assistant programs require clinical education called fieldwork.

Accrediting Body

The accrediting body for OT and OTA programs is the Accreditation Council for Occupational Therapy Education. This organization evaluates the educational programs to assure that they are teaching the necessary skills and have appropriate and available resources for occupational therapy students. There are two main purposes for accreditation: to ensure the quality of the institution and the education it offers, and to help facilitate improvement and further development of the institutions and/or programs.[9] In addition to ACOTE, state agencies, as well as other accrediting agencies such as the North Central Association of Colleges and Universities, may accredit colleges and universities.

Accreditation Council for Occupational Therapy Education (ACOTE)
c/o American Occupational Therapy Association
4720 Montgomery Lane
Bethesda, MD 20824
Telephone: 301-652-6611
Fax: 301-652-7711
E-mail: accred@aota.org
Web address: www.aota.org

Certification Board

The National Board for Certification in Occupational Therapy, Inc. (NBCOT) is responsible for development and administration of the national certification examination. OT and OTA students can take this examination after completion of all academic and clinical course work. The examination is offered two times a year, in March and September, at various locations throughout the United States. All students must pass the appropriate examination to use the credentials Occupational Therapist Registered (OTR) or Certified Occupational Therapy Assistant (COTA). In addition to the initial assessment of a therapist's competency, NBCOT supports continuing competency through ongoing contact with therapists.

National Board for Certification in Occupational Therapy, Inc.
800 South Frederick Avenue, Suite 200
Gaithersburg, MD 20877-4150
Telephone: 301-990-7979
Fax: 301-869-8492
Web address: www.nbcot.org

Advice for Potential Students

If you are considering a career in occupational therapy, first spend time observing an occupational therapist or occupational therapy assistant in different settings. You may wish to use the book *Occupational Therapy as a Career: An Introduction to the Field and a Structured Method for Observation* to guide you through this observation experience. Visit the institution in which you are interested and meet with a faculty member and a current student in the occupational therapy program. Ask the student about the program, including what he or she believes are the program's strengths and weaknesses. Ask the program director questions regarding the philosophy of the program, accreditation status, costs, prerequisite courses, amount of clinical experienced available during academic education, class size, number of students accepted on an annual basis, as well as any other admissions requirements. Ask how many students graduated within the last year as well as the job placement and certification exam pass rate. Look in the local newspaper and talk with local professionals to determine the availability of occupational therapy positions in your area. Call the AOTA to determine what the job outlook is for the year in which you expect to graduate.

For Additional Information

Organizations

American Occupational Therapy Association
4720 Montgomery Lane
Bethesda, MD 20824
Telephone: 301-652-2682
Fax: 301-652-7711
Web address: www.aota.org
E-mail: praota@aota.org

Publications

Books

Anderson, L. & Malaski, C.K. *Occupational Therapy as a Career: An Introduction to the Field and a Structured Method for Observation.* Philadelphia: F.A. Davis Company, 1999.

Mattingly, C. & Fleming, M. *Clinical Reasoning: Forms of Inquiry in a Therapeutic Practice.* Philadelphia: F.A. Davis Company, 1993.

Niestadt, M.E. & Crepeau, E.B. *Willard and Spackman's Occupational Therapy, 9th ed.* Philadelphia: Lippincott Williams & Wilkins, 1998.

Journals

Advance for Occupational Therapy Practitioners. Merion Publications, 2900 Horizon Drive, King of Prussia, PA. www.advanceweb.com

A national biweekly publication that reports on advances in research, reimbursement, and political and clinical news in the profession.

American Journal of Occupational Therapy, American Occupational Therapy Association, 4720 Montgomery Lane, Bethesda, MD 20824. www.aota.org/nonmembers/area7/links/link3.html

Explores the latest research, practice theory and concepts, and healthcare issues in occupational therapy.

Journal of Occupational Therapy Students, American Occupational Therapy Association, 4720 Montgomery Lane, Bethesda, MD 20824. www.aota.org/nonmembers/area7/links/link4.html

Reports of student research, educational activities, and issues online.

Occupational Therapy Practice, American Occupational Therapy Association, 4720 Montgomery Lane, Bethesda, MD 20824. www.aota.org/nonmembers/area7/links/link1b.html

The clinical and professional magazine of the Association. It provides news and information on all aspects of practice and encourages a dialogue on professional concerns and views.

Occupational Therapy Journal of Research. The American Occupational Therapy Foundation, 4720 Montgomery Lane, PO Box 31220, Bethesda, MD 20824-1220. www.aotf.org/html/otjr.html

Original manuscripts pertaining to the impact of activity on the individual, particularly as such activity is applied in a health-related context to prevent disability and to maintain or restore optimal human function or performance.

Internet Resources

Advance for Occupational Therapists: www.advanceweb.com/ot/ot.html
American Occupational Therapy Association: www.aota.org
American Occupational Therapy Foundation: www.aotf.org
America's Health Care Source: www.call24online.com
Canadian Association of Occupational Therapists: www.caot.ca
Arizona Occupational Therapy Association: www.arizota.com
Florida Occupational Therapy Association: www.flota.org
Georgia Occupational Therapy Association: www.gaota.com
Health Care Recruitment Online: www.healthcareers-online.com/Welcome.htm
Indiana Occupational Therapy Association: www.inota.org
Iowa Occupational Therapy Association: www.iowaot.org
Kentucky Occupational Therapy Association: www.aproctor.com/kota
Maryland Occupational Therapy Association: www.mdota.org
Minnesota Occupational Therapy Association: www.functionfirst.org
National Board for Certification in Occupational Therapy, Inc.: www.nbcot.org
New York Occupational Therapy Association: www.nysota.org
Occupational Therapy Association of California: www.call24online.com/otac
Occupational Therapy Association of Oregon: www.otao.com
Occupational Therapy Internet World: www.mother.com/~ktherapy/ot
Ohio Occupational Therapy Association: www.oota.org
Oklahoma Occupational Therapy Association: members.aol.com/OOTA1/Index.htm
Tennessee Occupational Therapy Association: www.tnota.org
Therapist's Guide to the Internet: otpt.ups.edu/Rehabilitation/TherapGuideInternet.html
Texas Occupational Therapy Association: www.tota.org
Utah Occupational Therapy Association: www.healthcaresource.com/uota
Vermont Occupational Therapy Association: www.healthcaresource.com/VOTA
Virginia Occupational Therapy Association: members.aol.com/VOTA1/index.htm
Washington Occupational Therapy Association: www.wota.org
World Federation of Occupational Therapists: www.who.int/ina-ngo/ngo/ngo170.htm

Occupational Therapist

Alabama

University of Alabama at Birmingham
School of Health Related Professions
900 South 19th Street/102 Bishop Building
Birmingham, AL 35294-2030

Contact Information:
Telephone: 612-626-4358
Fax: 612-625-7192
E-mail: jrowe@uab.edu
Web: www.uab.edu

Program Information:
Program begins: August
Duration of program: 24 months

Application Information:
Enrollment of program: 20

Financial Information:
Average cost of books: $800
% of students receiving aid: 95

Employment Profile:
% of students who pass the boards on their first try: 89
% employed within the first 6 months following graduation: 60
Average starting salary: $37,500

University of South Alabama
Springhill Academic Campus
1504 Springhill Avenue/Room 5108
Mobile, AL 36604

Contact Information:
Telephone: 334-434-3939
Fax: 334-434-3934
E-mail: mscaffa@jaguar1.usouthal.edu
Web: www.usouthal.edu

Program Information:
Program begins: August
Duration of program: 24 months

Application Information:
Enrollment of program: 60
Transfer students are accepted.

Financial Information:
Tuition, resident: $3,089
Tuition, non-resident: $5,937

Employment Profile:
% of students who pass the boards on their first try: 100

Arizona

Arizona School of Health Science—Kirksville College
3210 West Camelback Road
Phoenix, AZ 85017

Contact Information:
Telephone: 602-841-4077 ext. 1015
Fax: 602-841-4092
E-mail: melvinj@az.swc.kcom.edu
Web: www.kcom.com

Program Information:
Program begins: June
Duration of program: 33 months
Evening or weekend classes are available.

California

Loma Linda University
School of Allied Health Profession
Nichol Hall Room 903
Loma Linda, CA 92350-0001

Contact Information:
Telephone: 909-824-4628
Fax: 909-558-0239
E-mail: liane-hewitt@sahp.llu.edu
Web: www.llu.edu

Program Information:
Program begins: June
Duration of program: 24 months

Application Information:
Enrollment of program: 100
Transfer students are accepted.

Financial Information:
Average cost of books: $1,000
% of students receiving aid: 90

Employment Profile:
% of students who pass the boards on their first try: 85
Average starting salary: $46,000

Samuel Merritt College
370 Hawthorne Avenue
Oakland, CA 94609-3108

Contact Information:
Telephone: 510-869-8925
Fax: 510-869-6282
E-mail: guymccormack@samuelmerritt.edu
Web: www.samuelmerritt.edu

Program Information:
Program begins: September
Degrees offered: Master's, 27 months

Application Information:
Enrollment of program: 80
Transfer students are accepted.

Financial Information:
Average cost of books: $225
% of students receiving aid: 100

Employment Profile:
% of students who pass the boards on their first try: 95
% employed within the first 6 months following graduation: 100
Average starting salary: $52,500

San Jose State University
College of Applied Sciences and Arts
One Washington Square
San Jose, CA 95192-0059

Contact Information:
Telephone: 408-924-3070
Fax: 408-924-3088
E-mail: kschwart@email.sjsu.edu
Web: www.sjsu.edu

Program Information:
Program begins: June
Duration of program: 24 months
Evening or weekend classes are available.

Application Information:
Enrollment of program: 300
Transfer students are accepted.

Financial Information:
Tuition, resident: $1,584
Average cost of books: $600

Employment Profile:
% of students who pass the boards on their first try: 85
% employed within the first 6 months following graduation: 80
Average starting salary: $40,000

University of Southern California
1540 Alcazar
CHP 133
Los Angeles, CA 90033-1091

Contact Information:
Telephone: 213-342-2850
Fax: 213-342-1540
E-mail: otdept@usc.edu
Web: www.usd.edu

Program Information:
Program begins: September
Duration of program: 18 months
Evening or weekend classes are available.

Application Information:
Enrollment of program: 250
Transfer students are accepted.

Financial Information:
Average cost of books: $1,200

Employment Profile:
% of students who pass the boards on their first try: 98
Average starting salary: $45,000

Colorado

Colorado State University
228 Occupational Therapy Building
Ft. Collins, CO 80523

Contact Information:
Telephone: 970-491-6253
Fax: 970-491-6290
E-mail: hanzlik@cahs.colostate.edu
Web: www.colostate.edu

Program Information:
Program begins: August
Duration of program: 24 months

Application Information:
Enrollment of program: 250
Transfer students are accepted.

Financial Information:
Tuition, resident: $3,416
Tuition, non-resident: $11,182
Average cost of books: $700

Employment Profile:
% of students who pass the boards on their first try: 98

Connecticut

University of Hartford
College of Educational Nursing & Health Professions
200 Bloomfield Avenue
Dana Hall Room 232
West Hartford, CT 06117-1599

Contact Information:
Telephone: 205-934-3568
Fax: 205-934-0402
E-mail: bsmith@mail.hartford.edu
Web: www.hartford.edu

Program Information:
Program begins: August
Degrees offered: Bachelor's, 36 months

Application Information:
Enrollment of program: 160
Transfer students are accepted.

Financial Information:
Average cost of books: $800
% of students receiving aid: 90

Employment Profile:
% of students who pass the boards on their first try: 100
% employed within the first 6 months following graduation: 80
Average starting salary: $40,000

District of Columbia

Howard University
College of Allied Health Sciences
Sixth and Bryant Streets Northwest
Washington, DC 20059-0001

Contact Information:
Telephone: 202-806-7617
Fax: 202-806-7918
E-mail: sjackson@fac.howard.edu
Web: www.howard.edu

Program Information:
Program begins: August
Duration of program: 37 months

Application Information:
Enrollment of program: 150
Transfer students are accepted.

Financial Information:
Average cost of books: $2,400
% of students receiving aid: 90

Employment Profile:
% of students who pass the boards on their first try: 95
% employed within the first 6 months following graduation: 90
Average starting salary: $45,000

Florida

Florida A & M University
Division of Occupational Therapy
223 Ware-Rhaney Building
Tallahassee, FL 32307

Contact Information:
Telephone: 805-561-2014
Fax: 850-561-2457
E-mail: jbeck@nsi.famu.edu
Web: www.famu.edu

Program Information:
Program begins: August
Duration of program: 12 months

Application Information:
Enrollment of program: 45
Transfer students are accepted.

Financial Information:
Tuition, resident: $2,383
Tuition, non-resident: $8,591
Average cost of books: $400
% of students receiving aid: 90

Employment Profile:
% of students who pass the boards on their first try: 98
% employed within the first 6 months following graduation: 80
Average starting salary: $35,000

Florida International University
University Park Campus/CH101
Miami, FL 33199

Contact Information:
Telephone: 305-348-3510
Fax: 305-348-1240
E-mail: shaffner@fiu.edu
Web: www.fiu.edu

Program Information:
Program begins: September
Duration of program: 36 months

Financial Information:
Tuition, resident: $1,898
Tuition, non-resident: $7,597

Nova Southeastern University
Health Profession Division/College of Allied Health
3200 South University Drive
Ft. Lauderdale, FL 33328

Contact Information:
Telephone: 954-262-1242
Fax: 954-262-2290
E-mail: reba@nova.edu
Web: www.nova.edu

Program Information:
Program begins: January
Duration of program: 30 months

Application Information:
Enrollment of program: 150

Financial Information:
Tuition, resident: $18,500
Tuition, non-resident: $18,900
Average cost of books: $1,500
% of students receiving aid: 85

Employment Profile:
% of students who pass the boards on their first try: 96
% employed within the first 6 months following graduation: 60
Average starting salary: $54,000

University of Florida
PO Box 100164 JHMHC
Gainesville, FL 32610-0164

Contact Information:
Telephone: 919-966-2451
Fax: 919-966-9007
E-mail: kwalker@hp.ufl.edu
Web: www.hp.ufl.edu

Program Information:
Program begins: August
Duration of program: 30 months
Evening or weekend classes are available.

Application Information:
Enrollment of program: 225

Financial Information:
Tuition, resident: $2,140
Tuition, non-resident: $9,130
Average cost of books: $700
% of students receiving aid: 91

Employment Profile:
% of students who pass the boards on their first try: 100
% employed within the first 6 months following graduation: 85
Average starting salary: $34,000

Georgia

Brenau University
One Centennial Circle
Gainesville, GA 30501

Contact Information:
Telephone: 770-534-6139
Fax: 770-534-6186
E-mail: bschell@lib.brenau.edu
Web: www.brenau.edu/ot

Program Information:
Program begins: June
Duration of program: 33 months

Application Information:
Enrollment of program: 82
Transfer students are accepted.

Financial Information:
Tuition, resident: $17,890
Average cost of books: $700
% of students receiving aid: 87

Employment Profile:
% employed within the first 6 months following graduation: 75

Medical College of Georgia

School of Allied Health/EF 102
Augusta, GA 30912-0700

Contact Information:
Telephone: 706-721-3641
Fax: 706-721-9718
E-mail: kbradley@mail.mcg.edu
Web: www.mca.edu

Program Information:
Program begins: May
Duration of program: 36 months

Application Information:
Enrollment of program: 54

Financial Information:
Tuition, resident: $3,894
Tuition, non-resident: $14,289
Average cost of books: $600
% of students receiving aid: 49

Employment Profile:
% employed within the first 6 months following graduation: 90
Average starting salary: $36,500

Illinois

Chicago State University

9501 South King Drive
Chicago, IL 60628-1598

Contact Information:
Telephone: 773-995-2531
Fax: 773-995-2839
E-mail: bahzkks@csu.edu
Web: www.csu.edu

Program Information:
Program begins: June
Duration of program: 24 months

Application Information:
Enrollment of program: 80
Transfer students are accepted.

Financial Information:
Tuition, resident: $3,151
Tuition, non-resident: $7,735
Average cost of books: $600
% of students receiving aid: 90

Employment Profile:
% of students who pass the boards on their first try: 80
% employed within the first 6 months following graduation: 80
Average starting salary: $39,000

Governors State University

College of Health Professions
University Park, IL 60466-0975

Contact Information:
Telephone: 708-534-7293
Fax: 708-534-1647
E-mail: b-cada@govst.edu
Web: www.govst.edu/users/gsunhs/ot

Program Information:
Program begins: August
Duration of program: 27 months

Financial Information:
Tuition, resident: $1,233
Tuition, non-resident: $3,309

University of Illinois at Chicago

College of Health and Human Development Sciences
1919 West Taylor Street M/C 811
Chicago, IL 60612

Contact Information:
Telephone: 501-450-3192
Fax: 501-450-3622
E-mail: gfisher@uic.edu
Web: www.uic.edu

Program Information:
Program begins: August
Degrees offered: Master's, 28 months

Application Information:
Enrollment of program: 28
Transfer students are accepted.

Financial Information:
Tuition, resident: $5,500
Tuition, non-resident: $13,500
Average cost of books: $700
% of students receiving aid: 80

Employment Profile:
% of students who pass the boards on their first try: 97
% employed within the first 6 months following graduation: 100
Average starting salary: $35,000

Indiana

Indiana University School of Medicine

1140 West Michigan Street
Coleman Hall 316
Indianapolis, IN 46202-5119

Contact Information:
Telephone: 317-274-8006
Fax: 317-274-2150
E-mail: chamant@iupui.edu
Web: www.sahs.iupui.edu

Program Information:
Program begins: August
Duration of program: 25 months

Application Information:
Enrollment of program: 100

Financial Information:
Tuition, resident: $3,315
Tuition, non-resident: $4,503
Average cost of books: $1,700

Employment Profile:
% of students who pass the boards on their first try: 99
% employed within the first 6 months following graduation: 75
Average starting salary: $35,000

University of Southern Indiana

8600 University Boulevard/HP 2068
Evansville, IN 47712-3534

Contact Information:
Telephone: 812-465-1179
Fax: 812-465-7092
E-mail: otinfo@usi.edu
Web: www.usi.edu

Program Information:
Program begins: June
Duration of program: 22 months

Financial Information:
Tuition, resident: $5,446
Tuition, non-resident: $13,342

Iowa

St. Ambrose University

518 West Locust
Davenport, IA 52803

Contact Information:
Telephone: 319-333-6277
Fax: 319-333-6410
E-mail: pwenthe@saunix.sau.edu
Web: www.sau.edu

Program Information:
Program begins: August
Duration of program: 87 months

Application Information:
Enrollment of program: 40
Transfer students are accepted.

Financial Information:
Average cost of books: $800
% of students who pass the boards on their first try: 100
% employed within the first 6 months following graduation: 95
Average starting salary: $35,000

Kansas

Newman University

3100 McCormick Avenue
Wichita, KS 67213-2097

Contact Information:
Telephone: 316-942-4291
Fax: 316-942-4483
E-mail: sowerj@newman.edu
Web: www.newman.edu

Program Information:
Program begins: August
Duration of program: 33 months

Application Information:
Enrollment of program: 90
Transfer students are accepted.

Financial Information:
Tuition, resident: $8,500
Average cost of books: $200
% of students receiving aid: 90

Employment Profile:
% of students who pass the boards on their first try: 100

Kentucky

Eastern Kentucky University
Disney 103
Richmond, KY 40475-3135

Contact Information:
Telephone: 606-622-3300
Fax: 606-622-1140
E-mail: otsbenne@acs.eku.edu
Web: www.eku.edu

Program Information:
Program begins: January, June, August
Duration of program: 21 months
Evening or weekend classes are available.

Application Information:
Enrollment of program: 275
Transfer students are accepted.

Financial Information:
Tuition, resident: $1,010
Tuition, non-resident: $3,030
Average cost of books: $350
% of students receiving aid: 80

Employment Profile:
% of students who pass the boards on their first try: 98
% employed within the first 6 months following graduation: 50
Average starting salary: $35,000

Spalding University
851 South Fourth Street
Louisville, KY 40203-2188

Contact Information:
Telephone: 502-5857125
Fax: 502-588-7175
E-mail: rstrickland@spalding.edu

Program Information:
Program begins: September
Duration of program: 29 months

Application Information:
Enrollment of program: 120
Transfer students are accepted.

Financial Information:
Tuition, resident: $5,450

Maine

University of New England
College of Arts and Sciences
Biddeford, ME 04005-9599

Contact Information:
Telephone: 601-984-6350
Fax: 601-984-6344
E-mail: nmacme@mailbox.une.edu
Web: www.une.edu

Program Information:
Program begins: September, January
Duration of program: 36 months

Financial Information:
Tuition, resident: $14,320

University of Southern Maine
Lewiston-Auburn College
51 Westminster Street
Lewiston, ME 04240-3534

Contact Information:
Telephone: 207-753-6515
Fax: 207-753-6555
E-mail: rblack@usm.maine.edu
Web: www.usm.maine.edu

Program Information:
Program begins: September
Degrees offered: Master's, 30 months

Application Information:
Enrollment of program: 69

Financial Information:
Tuition, resident: $4,843
Tuition, non-resident: $13,659
Average cost of books: $250

Employment Profile:
% of students who pass the boards on their first try: 100
% employed within the first 6 months following graduation: 100

Maryland

Towson University
8000 York Road
Towson, MD 21252-0001

Contact Information:
Telephone: 410-830-2762
Fax: 410-830-2322
E-mail: mreitz@midget.towson.edu
Web: www.towson.edu

Program Information:
Program begins: January, September
Duration of program: 26 months
Evening or weekend classes are available.

Application Information:
Enrollment of program: 227
Transfer students are accepted.

Financial Information:
Tuition, resident: $4,520
Tuition, non-resident: $10,525
Average cost of books: $500

Massachusetts

Boston University
Sargent College of Health and Rehabilitation Sciences
635 Commonwealth Avenue
Boston, MA 02215

Contact Information:
Telephone: 617-353-2727 ext. 2727
Fax: 617-353-2926
E-mail: wjcoster@bu.edu
Web: www.bu.edu

Program Information:
Program begins: September
Degrees offered: Bachelor's, 54 months; Master's, 30 months; PhD, 42 months

Application Information:
Enrollment of program: 250
Transfer students are accepted.

Financial Information:
Average cost of books: $400
% of students receiving aid: 70

Employment Profile:
% of students who pass the boards on their first try: 98
% employed within the first 6 months following graduation: 85
Average starting salary: $33,000

Springfield College
263 Alden Street
Springfield, MA 01109-3797

Contact Information:
Telephone: 413-748-3762
Fax: 413-748-3796
E-mail: kpost@spfldcol.edu
Web: www.spfldcol.edu

Program Information:
Program begins: June
Duration of program: 22 months

Application Information:
Enrollment of program: 90

Financial Information:
Average cost of books: $900

Employment Profile:
% of students who pass the boards on their first try: 98

Tufts University
Boston School of Occupational Therapy
Medford, MA 02155-7084

Contact Information:
Telephone: 617-627-3720
Fax: 617-627-3722
E-mail: oolearof@emerald.tufts.edu
Web: www.ase.tufts.edu

Program Information:
Program begins: August
Duration of program: 18 months

Application Information:
Enrollment of program: 140

Financial Information:
Average cost of books: $500

Employment Profile:
% of students who pass the boards on their first try: 100
% employed within the first 6 months following graduation: 100

Worcester State College
486 Chandler Street
Worcester, MA 01602-2597

Contact Information:
Telephone: 508-929-8119
Fax: 508-929-8178
E-mail: djoss@worcester.edu
Web: www.worcester.edu

Program Information:
Program begins: January, June, August
Degrees offered: Bachelor's; Master's

Application Information:
Enrollment of program: 256
Transfer students are accepted.

Financial Information:
Tuition, resident: $2,458
Tuition, non-resident: $9,786
Average cost of books: $391

Employment Profile:
% of students who pass the boards on their first try: 89

Michigan

Baker College
1050 West Bristol Road
Flint, MI 48507-5508

Contact Information:
Telephone: 810-766-4192
Fax: 810-766-4049
E-mail: hagen_d@flint.baker.edu
Web: www.baker.edu

Program Information:
Program begins: September
Duration of program: 46 months

Application Information:
Transfer students are accepted.

Grand Valley State University
322 Henry Hall
One Campus Drive
Allendale, MI 49401-9403

Contact Information:
Telephone: 616-895-2734
Fax: 616-895-3350
E-mail: grapczyc@gvsu.edu
Web: www.gvsu.edu

Program Information:
Program begins: May
Degrees offered: Master's, 33 months
Evening or weekend classes are available.

Application Information:
Enrollment of program: 45
Transfer students are accepted.

Financial Information:
Tuition, resident: $5,312
Tuition, non-resident: $10,784

Employment Profile:
% of students who pass the boards on their first try: 100
% employed within the first 6 months following graduation: 100

Saginaw Valley State University
Ryder Center West Room 105
7400 Bay Rd
University Center, MI 48710-0001

Contact Information:
Telephone: 517-791-7355
Fax: 517-790-0545
E-mail: bracc@tardis.svsu.edu
Web: www.svsu.edu

Program Information:
Program begins: September
Duration of program: 26 months

Application Information:
Enrollment of program: 70
Transfer students are accepted.

Financial Information:
Tuition, resident: $4,261
Tuition, non-resident: $8,256
Average cost of books: $600
% of students receiving aid: 70

Employment Profile:
% of students who pass the boards on their first try: 100
% employed within the first 6 months following graduation: 50
Average starting salary: $35,000

Wayne State University
College of Pharmacy and Allied Health Professions
Detroit, MI 48202-3489

Contact Information:
Telephone: 313-577-5877
Fax: 313-577-5822
E-mail: susan-esdail@wayne.edu
Web: www.wayne.edu

Program Information:
Program begins: September
Duration of program: 32 months

Application Information:
Enrollment of program: 45
Transfer students are accepted.

Employment Profile:
% of students who pass the boards on their first try: 90

Western Michigan University
Kalamazoo, MI 49008-5051

Contact Information:
Telephone: 616-387-7263
Fax: 616-387-7262
E-mail: susan.meyers@wmich.edu
Web: www.wmich.edu

Program Information:
Program begins: May
Duration of program: 28 months
Evening or weekend classes are available.

Application Information:
Enrollment of program: 276
Transfer students are accepted.

Financial Information:
Tuition, resident: $3,948
Tuition, non-resident: $8,900

Employment Profile:
% of students who pass the boards on their first try: 98

Minnesota

College of St. Catherine
2004 Randolph Avenue
St. Paul, MN 55105-1794

Contact Information:
Telephone: 651-690-6602
Fax: 651-690-8804
E-mail: jdbasshaugenL@stkate.edu
Web: www.stkate.edu

Program Information:
Program begins: September
Degrees offered: Master's; Post-bachelor's Certificate
Evening or weekend classes are available.

Application Information:
Enrollment of program: 246
Transfer students are accepted.

Financial Information:
Average cost of books: $500
% of students receiving aid: 75

Employment Profile:
% of students who pass the boards on their first try: 95
Average starting salary: $26,500

College of St. Scholastica
1200 Kenwood Avenue
Duluth, MN 55811

Contact Information:
Telephone: 218-723-6713
Fax: 218-723-6472
E-mail: ngabres@css.edu
Web: www.css.edu

Program Information:
Program begins: August, June
Duration of program: 28 months

Application Information:
Enrollment of program: 91
Transfer students are accepted.

Financial Information:
Average cost of books: $1,537
% of students receiving aid: 90

Employment Profile:
% of students who pass the boards on their first try: 100

University of Minnesota—Twin Cities
Box 388 Mayo
420 Delaware Street Southeast
Minneapolis, MN 55455-0392

Contact Information:
Telephone: 317-788-3432
Fax: 317-788-3480
E-mail: reism001@tc.umn.edu
Web: www.med.umn.edu/ot

Program Information:
Duration of program: 30 months

Application Information:
Enrollment of program: 25
Transfer students are accepted.

Financial Information:
Tuition, resident: $6,878
Tuition, non-resident: $12,904
Average cost of books: $1,000

Employment Profile:
% of students who pass the boards on their first try: 100

Missouri

Rockhurst College
1100 Rockhurst Road
Kansas City, MO 64110-2561

Contact Information:
Telephone: 816-501-4635
Fax: 816-501-4643
E-mail: jan.rues@rockhurst.edu
Web: www.rockhurst.edu

Program Information:
Program begins: September
Duration of program: 27 months

Application Information:
Enrollment of program: 38
Transfer students are accepted.

Financial Information:
Tuition, resident: $9,490
Average cost of books: $500
% of students receiving aid: 75

Employment Profile:
% of students who pass the boards on their first try: 100
% employed within the first 6 months following graduation: 95
Average starting salary: $30,000

Washington University
School of Medicine/4444 Forest Park Avenue
Campus Box 8505
St. Louis, MO 63108

Contact Information:
Telephone: 314-286-1600
Fax: 314-286-1601
E-mail: cbaum@ot-link.wustl.edu

Program Information:
Program begins: September
Duration of program: 28 months

Application Information:
Enrollment of program: 271

Financial Information:
% of students receiving aid: 80

Employment Profile:
% of students who pass the boards on their first try: 99

New Hampshire

University of New Hampshire
School of Health and Human Services
Hewitt Hall/4 Library Way
Durham, NH 03824-3563

Contact Information:
Telephone: 573-882-3988
Fax: 573-884-2610
E-mail: acseidel@christa.unh.edu
Web: www.unh.edu

Program Information:
Program begins: September
Degrees offered: Bachelor's, 32 months; Master's, 24 months; Post-bachelor's Certificate, 24 months

Application Information:
Enrollment of program: 300
Transfer students are accepted.

Financial Information:
Tuition, resident: $3,870
Tuition, non-resident: $12,540

Employment Profile:
% of students who pass the boards on their first try: 96
% employed within the first 6 months following graduation: 95
Average starting salary: $35,000

New Jersey

Kean University
Willis Townsend 209
1000 Morris Avenue
Union, NJ 07083-9982

Contact Information:
Telephone: 908-527-2590
Fax: 908-354-2746
E-mail: pkramer@turbo.kean.edu
Web: www.kean.edu

Program Information:
Program begins: September
Degrees offered: Bachelor's, 46 months; Master's, 30 months
Evening or weekend classes are available.

Application Information:
Enrollment of program: 30
Transfer students are accepted.

Financial Information:
Tuition, resident: $4,384
Tuition, non-resident: $6,081
Average cost of books: $300

Employment Profile:
% of students who pass the boards on their first try: 97
% employed within the first 6 months following graduation: 100
Average starting salary: $40,000

New Mexico

University of New Mexico
School of Medicine
Health Science & Service Building Room 215
Albuquerque, NM 87131-5641

Contact Information:
Telephone: 207-283-0170 ext. 2233
Fax: 207-282-6379
E-mail: tkcrowe@unm.edu
Web: www.unm.edu

Program Information:
Program begins: May
Duration of program: 27 months

Application Information:
Enrollment of program: 72

Financial Information:
Tuition, resident: $4,075
Tuition, non-resident: $14,960
Average cost of books: $1,700

Employment Profile:
% of students who pass the boards on their first try: 100
% employed within the first 6 months following graduation: 100

New York

Columbia University
Neurological Institute 8th Floor
710 West 168th Street
New York, NY 10032

Contact Information:
Telephone: 212-305-3781
Fax: 212-305-4569
E-mail: chh14.@columbia.edu
Web: www.columbia.edu

Program Information:
Program begins: September
Degrees offered: Master's, 24 months

Application Information:
Enrollment of program: 110
Transfer students are accepted.

Financial Information:
Tuition, resident: $17,970
% of students receiving aid: 90

Employment Profile:
% of students who pass the boards on their first try: 100
% employed within the first 6 months following graduation: 75
Average starting salary: $46,000

Dominican College
10 Western Highway
Orangeburg, NY 10962-1299

Contact Information:
Telephone: 914-359-7800 ext. 209
Fax: 914-359-2313
Web: www.dc.edu

Program Information:
Program begins: September
Duration of program: 28 months
Evening or weekend classes are available.

Application Information:
Enrollment of program: 281
Transfer students are accepted.

Financial Information:
Tuition, resident: $8,775

Employment Profile:
% of students who pass the boards on their first try: 99
Average starting salary: $42,500

D'Youville College
One D'Youville Square
320 Porter Avenue
Buffalo, NY 14201-1084

Contact Information:
Telephone: 716-881-7624
Fax: 716-881-7790
E-mail: gingherm@dyc.edu
Web: www.dyc.edu

Program Information:
Program begins: September
Degrees offered: Bachelor's; Master's
Evening or weekend classes are available.

Application Information:
Enrollment of program: 270
Transfer students are accepted.

Employment Profile:
% of students who pass the boards on their first try: 97
Average starting salary: $38,000

Keuka College
Keuka Park, NY 14478-0098

Contact Information:
Telephone: 315-536-4411 ext. 5255
Fax: 315-536-5216
E-mail: ptalty@mail.keuka.edu
Web: www.keuka.edu

Program Information:
Program begins: September
Duration of program: 42 months

Application Information:
Enrollment of program: 180
Transfer students are accepted.

Financial Information:
Average cost of books: $300
% of students receiving aid: 90

Employment Profile:
% of students who pass the boards on their first try: 95
% employed within the first 6 months following graduation: 90
Average starting salary: $35,000

Russell Sage College
45 Ferry Street
Troy, NY 12180-4115

Contact Information:
Telephone: 518-244-2267
Fax: 518-244-4524
E-mail: frankm@sage.edu
Web: www.sage.edu

Program Information:
Program begins: August
Degrees offered: Bachelor's; Master's

Application Information:
Enrollment of program: 32
Transfer students are accepted.

Financial Information:
Average cost of books: $700
% of students receiving aid: 70

Employment Profile:
% of students who pass the boards on their first try: 100
% employed within the first 6 months following graduation: 90

SUNY at Buffalo
515 Stockton Kimball Tower
3435 Main Street
Buffalo, NY 14214-3079

Contact Information:
Telephone: 716-829-3141
Fax: 716-829-3217
E-mail: wmann@acus.buffalo.edu
Web: www.wings.buffalo.edu

Program Information:
Program begins: August
Duration of program: 24 months

Application Information:
Enrollment of program: 102
Transfer students are accepted.

Financial Information:
Tuition, resident: $3,400
Tuition, non-resident: $8,300
Average cost of books: $750

SUNY Health Science Center at Stony Brook
School of Health Technology and Management
Division of Rehabilitation Sciences
Stony Brook, NY 11794-8201

Contact Information:
Telephone: 631-444-8126
Fax: 631-444-7621
E-mail: dcosta@epo.hsc.sunysb.edu

Program Information:
Program begins: July
Degrees offered: Bachelor's, 24 months

Application Information:
Enrollment of program: 54
Transfer students are accepted.

Financial Information:
Tuition, resident: $3,884
Tuition, non-resident: $8,734
Average cost of books: $500
% of students receiving aid: 60

Employment Profile:
% of students who pass the boards on their first try: 100
% employed within the first 6 months following graduation: 100
Average starting salary: $40,000

Touro College—Bay Shore
1700 Union Boulevard
Bay Shore, NY 11706

Contact Information:
Telephone: 631-665-1600 ext. 231
Fax: 631-665-6084
Web: www.touro.edu

Program Information:
Program begins: August, September
Degrees offered: Bachelor's, 33 months; Master's, 33 months

Application Information:
Enrollment of program: 85
Transfer students are accepted.

Financial Information:
Average cost of books: $1,000
% of students receiving aid: 75

Employment Profile:
% of students who pass the boards on their first try: 99
% employed within the first 6 months following graduation: 100
Average starting salary: $47,000

North Carolina

East Carolina University
School of Allied Health Sciences
Greenville, NC 27858-4353

Contact Information:
Telephone: 919-328-4441
Fax: 919-328-4470
E-mail: dickersona@mail.ecu.edu
Web: www.ecu.edu

Program Information:
Program begins: August
Duration of program: 24 months

Application Information:
Transfer students are accepted.

Financial Information:
Tuition, resident: $876
Tuition, non-resident: $4,453

Employment Profile:
% of students who pass the boards on their first try: 100
Average starting salary: $37,000

Lenoir-Rhyne College
Box 7547
Hickory, NC 28603

Contact Information:
Telephone: 704-328-7367
Fax: 704-328-7364
E-mail: ssahler@lrc.edu
Web: www.lrc.edu

Program Information:
Program begins: July
Duration of program: 20 months

Application Information:
Enrollment of program: 55
Transfer students are accepted.

Financial Information:
Tuition, resident: $8,773
Tuition, non-resident: $6,155
Average cost of books: $400
% of students receiving aid: 70

Employment Profile:
% of students who pass the boards on their first try: 100
% employed within the first 6 months following graduation: 50
Average starting salary: $45,000

University of North Carolina at Chapel Hill
Medical School Wing East, CB 7120
Chapel Hill, NC 27599-7120

Contact Information:
Telephone: 603-862-3422
Fax: 603-862-0778
E-mail: rhumphry@css.unc.edu
Web: www.alliedhealth.unc.edu

Program Information:
Program begins: August
Duration of program: 24 months

Application Information:
Enrollment of program: 24

Financial Information:
Tuition, resident: $1,749
Tuition, non-resident: $13,491
Average cost of books: $500

Employment Profile:
% of students who pass the boards on their first try: 100
% employed within the first 6 months following graduation: 70
Average starting salary: $39,000

North Dakota

University of North Dakota School of Medicine and Health Science
Box 7126 University Station
Grand Forks, ND 58202-7126

Contact Information:
Telephone: 505-272-1753
Fax: 505-272-8079
E-mail: smcintyr@medicine.nodak.edu
Web: www.med.und.nodak.edu

Program Information:
Program begins: August
Degrees offered: Bachelor's, 24 months

Application Information:
Enrollment of program: 46
Transfer students are accepted.

Financial Information:
Tuition, resident: $2,956
Tuition, non-resident: $7,098
Average cost of books: $1,500
% of students receiving aid: 75

Employment Profile:
% of students who pass the boards on their first try: 98
% employed within the first 6 months following graduation: 95
Average starting salary: $35,000

Ohio

Medical College of Ohio
3015 Arlington Avenue
Toledo, OH 43614-5803

Contact Information:
Telephone: 419-383-4429
Fax: 419-383-5880
E-mail: jthomas@mco.edu
Web: www.mco.edu

Program Information:
Program begins: August
Duration of program: 27 months
Evening or weekend classes are available.

Application Information:
Enrollment of program: 20

Financial Information:
Tuition, resident: $5,544
Tuition, non-resident: $12,747
Average cost of books: $1,000
% of students receiving aid: 60

Employment Profile:
% of students who pass the boards on their first try: 100
% employed within the first 6 months following graduation: 50
Average starting salary: $40,000

Pennsylvania

Alvernia College
400 Saint Bernardine Street
Reading, PA 19607-1799

Contact Information:
Telephone: 610-796-8377
Fax: 610-796-8349
E-mail: pennyne@alvernia.edu
Web: www.alvernia.edu

Program Information:
Program begins: August
Duration of program: 30 months

Application Information:
Enrollment of program: 94
Transfer students are accepted.

Financial Information:
Tuition, resident: $11,720
Average cost of books: $200
% of students receiving aid: 60

Chatham College
Woodland Road
Pittsburgh, PA 15232-2826

Contact Information:
Telephone: 412-365-1109
Fax: 412-368-1213
E-mail: henry@chatham.edu
Web: www.chatham.edu

Program Information:
Program begins: September
Duration of program: 22 months

Financial Information:
Tuition, resident: $22,000

College Misericordia
Division of Health Sciences
301 Lake Street
Dallas, PA 18612-1098

Contact Information:
Telephone: 570-674-6412
Fax: 570-674-8902
E-mail: jciprian@miseri.edu
Web: www.miseri.edu

Program Information:
Program begins: August
Degrees offered: Bachelor's; Master's
Evening or weekend classes are available.

Application Information:
Enrollment of program: 400
Transfer students are accepted.

Financial Information:
Tuition, resident: $15,250

Employment Profile:
% of students who pass the boards on their first try: 98
Average starting salary: $38,000

Duquesne University
Rangos School of Health Sciences
Health Sciences Building/Room 234
Pittsburgh, PA 15282-0020

Contact Information:
Telephone: 412-396-5945
Fax: 412-396-4343
E-mail: crist@duq2.cc.duq.edu
Web: www.duq.edu

Program Information:
Program begins: May, September
Duration of program: 24 months
Evening or weekend classes are available.

Financial Information:
Average cost of books: $600
% of students receiving aid: 50

Employment Profile:
% of students who pass the boards on their first try: 100
% employed within the first 6 months following graduation: 20
Average starting salary: $35,000

Gannon University
University Square
Erie, PA 16541-0001

Contact Information:
Telephone: 814-871-7463
Fax: 814-871-5662
E-mail: dijoseph@gannon.edu
Web: www.gannon.edu

Program Information:
Program begins: August
Duration of program: 60 months

Application Information:
Enrollment of program: 150
Transfer students are accepted.

Financial Information:
Average cost of books: $500
% of students receiving aid: 90

Employment Profile:
% of students who pass the boards on their first try: 90

Temple University
College of Allied Health Professions
3307 North Broad Street
Philadelphia, PA 19140

Contact Information:
Telephone: 215-707-4881
Fax: 215-707-7656
E-mail: mkinneal@astro.temple.edu
Web: www.temple.edu

Program Information:
Program begins: August
Duration of program: 26 months

Application Information:
Enrollment of program: 200
Transfer students are accepted.

Financial Information:
Tuition, resident: $7,652
Tuition, non-resident: $13,490
Average cost of books: $200
% of students receiving aid: 80

Employment Profile:
% of students who pass the boards on their first try: 97
% employed within the first 6 months following graduation: 80
Average starting salary: $40,000

Thomas Jefferson University
130 South Ninth Street
Room 810 Edison Building
Philadelphia, PA 19107-5233

Contact Information:
Telephone: 215-503-9606
Fax: 215-503-3499
E-mail: janice.burke@mail.tju.edu
Web: www.tju.edu

Program Information:
Program begins: September
Degrees offered: Bachelor's, 27 months; Master's, 28 months

Application Information:
Enrollment of program: 77
Transfer students are accepted.

Financial Information:
Average cost of books: $1,150
% of students receiving aid: 82

Employment Profile:
% of students who pass the boards on their first try: 100
Average starting salary: $38,000

University of Pittsburgh
School of Health and Rehab Sciences
5022 Forbes Tower
Pittsburgh, PA 15260

Contact Information:
Telephone: 412-647-1183
Fax: 412-647-1255
E-mail: shrsadmit@pitt.edu
Web: www.shrs.upmc.edu

Program Information:
Program begins: August
Duration of program: 22 months

Application Information:
Transfer students are accepted.

Financial Information:
Tuition, resident: $10,256
Tuition, non-resident: $22,198

Puerto Rico

University of Puerto Rico
Medical Sciences Campus/PT & OT Departments
PO Box 365067
San Juan, PR 00936-5067

Contact Information:
Telephone: 787-758-2525 ext. 4200
Fax: 787-282-8174
Web: www.cprsweb.rcm.upr.edu

Program Information:
Program begins: August
Degrees offered: Bachelor's, 33 months

Application Information:
Enrollment of program: 120
Transfer students are accepted.

Financial Information:
Tuition, resident: $1,140
Tuition, non-resident: $2,400
Average cost of books: $900
% of students receiving aid: 99

Employment Profile:
% of students who pass the boards on their first try: 23
% employed within the first 6 months following graduation: 100
Average starting salary: $21,000

South Carolina

Medical University of South Carolina
College Health Related Professions
171 Ashley Avenue/Room 123-CHP
Charleston, SC 29425-2701

Contact Information:
Telephone: 803-792-2961
Fax: 803-792-0710
E-mail: trickeyb@musc.edu
Web: www.musc.edu

Program Information:
Program begins: June
Degrees offered: Master's, 36 months
Evening or weekend classes are available.

Application Information:
Enrollment of program: 140
Transfer students are accepted.

Financial Information:
Tuition, resident: $4,950
Tuition, non-resident: $7,967
Average cost of books: $800
% of students receiving aid: 80

Employment Profile:
% of students who pass the boards on their first try: 98
% employed within the first 6 months following graduation: 95
Average starting salary: $35,000

South Dakota

University of South Dakota
414 East Clark Street
Vermillion, SD 57069-2390

Contact Information:
Telephone: 605-677-5600
Fax: 605-677-6581

E-mail: usdot@usd.edu
Web: www.usd.edu

Program Information:
Program begins: May
Duration of program: 28 months

Application Information:
Enrollment of program: 78

Financial Information:
Tuition, resident: $6,467
Tuition, non-resident: $19,072

Texas

University of Texas—Pan American

1201 West University Drive
Edinburg, TX 78229-3900

Contact Information:
Telephone: 210-567-8881
Fax: 210-567-8893
E-mail: haradon@uthscsa.edu
Web: www.uthscsa.edu

Program Information:
Program begins: June
Duration of program: 28 months

Application Information:
Enrollment of program: 80
Transfer students are accepted.

Financial Information:
Tuition, resident: $1,344
Tuition, non-resident: $10,416
Average cost of books: $800

Employment Profile:
% of students who pass the boards on their first try: 95
% employed within the first 6 months following graduation: 20
Average starting salary: $32,000

University of Texas at El Paso

1101 North Campbell Street
El Paso, TX 79902

Contact Information:
Telephone: 915-747-7270
Fax: 915-747-8211
E-mail: gschmalz@utep.edu
Web: www.utep.edu

Program Information:
Program begins: August
Degrees offered: Bachelor's, 27 months

Application Information:
Enrollment of program: 65
Transfer students are accepted.

Financial Information:
Tuition, resident: $2,052
Tuition, non-resident: $5,904
Average cost of books: $800

Employment Profile:
% of students who pass the boards on their first try: 98
% employed within the first 6 months following graduation: 75
Average starting salary: $35,000

University of Texas Health Science Center at San Antonio

7703 Floyd Curl Drive
San Antonio, TX 78229-3900

Contact Information:
Telephone: 210-567-8881
Fax: 210-567-8893
E-mail: haradon@uthscsa.edu
Web: www.uthsca.edu

Program Information:
Program begins: September
Duration of program: 36 months

Application Information:
Enrollment of program: 80
Transfer students are accepted.

Financial Information:
Tuition, resident: $1,386
Tuition, non-resident: $9,144
Average cost of books: $800

Employment Profile:
% of students who pass the boards on their first try: 95
% employed within the first 6 months following graduation: 20
Average starting salary: $32,000

University of Texas Medical Branch

School of Allied Health Sciences
301 University Boulevard
Galveston, TX 77555-1028

Contact Information:
Telephone: 409-772-3001
Fax: 409-747-1623
E-mail: lprimeau@utmb.edu
Web: www.utmb.edu

Program Information:
Program begins: August
Duration of program: 24 months

Application Information:
Enrollment of program: 65
Transfer students are accepted.

Financial Information:
Tuition, resident: $988
Tuition, non-resident: $9,348
Average cost of books: $800

Employment Profile:
% of students who pass the boards on their first try: 98
% employed within the first 6 months following graduation: 75
Average starting salary: $35,000

Virginia

Shenandoah University

333 West Cork Street
Winchester, VA 22601

Contact Information:
Telephone: 540-665-5543
Fax: 540-665-5564
E-mail: gstone@su.edu
Web: www.su.edu

Program Information:
Program begins: January
Duration of program: 28 months
Evening or weekend classes are available.

Application Information:
Enrollment of program: 118

Financial Information:
Average cost of books: $900
% of students receiving aid: 90

Employment Profile:
% of students who pass the boards on their first try: 100
% employed within the first 6 months following graduation: 20
Average starting salary: $38,000

Virginia Commonwealth University, Medical College of VA Campus

PO Box 980008
Richmond, VA 23298-0008

Contact Information:
Telephone: 804-828-2219
Fax: 804-828-0782
E-mail: sjlane@vcu.edu
Web: www.views.vcu.edu

Program Information:
Program begins: May
Duration of program: 30 months

Application Information:
Enrollment of program: 110
Transfer students are accepted.

Financial Information:
Tuition, resident: $4,784
Tuition, non-resident: $12,268
Average cost of books: $800

Employment Profile:
% of students who pass the boards on their first try: 98
% employed within the first 6 months following graduation: 80
Average starting salary: $37,500

Washington

University of Puget Sound

School of Occupational Therapy
1500 North Warner
Tacoma, WA 98416-0510

Contact Information:
Telephone: 253-879-3281
Fax: 253-879-8309
E-mail: tomlin@ups.edu

Program Information:
Program begins: August
Duration of program: 30 months

Application Information:
Enrollment of program: 110
Transfer students are accepted.

Financial Information:
Average cost of books: $700
% of students receiving aid: 70

Employment Profile:
% of students who pass the boards on their first try: 98
% employed within the first 6 months following graduation: 80

Wisconsin

Concordia University Wisconsin
12800 North Lake Shore Drive
Mequon, WI 530972402

Contact Information:
Telephone: 414-243-4287
Fax: 414-243-4506
E-mail: peggy.denton@cuw.edu
Web: www.cuw.edu

Program Information:
Program begins: August
Duration of program: 36 months

University of Wisconsin—Milwaukee
School of Allied Health Professions
PO Box 413
Milwaukee, WI 53201-0413

Contact Information:
Telephone: 414-229-4713
Fax: 414-906-3930
E-mail: smithro@uwm.edu
Web: www.uwm.edu

Program Information:
Program begins: September
Degrees offered: Bachelor's, 22 months; Master's, 9 months
Evening or weekend classes are available.

Application Information:
Enrollment of program: 146
Transfer students are accepted.

Financial Information:
Tuition, resident: $3,740
Tuition, non-resident: $16,364
Average cost of books: $325

Employment Profile:
% of students who pass the boards on their first try: 96

Wyoming

Casper College
125 College Drive
Casper, WY 82601

Contact Information:
Telephone: 307-268-2867
Fax: 307-268-2891
E-mail: mwonser@acad.cc.whecn.edu
Web: www.cc.whecn.edu

Program Information:
Program begins: June
Degrees offered: Diploma, 15 months
Evening or weekend classes are available.

Application Information:
Enrollment of program: 22
Transfer students are accepted.

Financial Information:
Tuition, resident: $1,320
Tuition, non-resident: $1,920
Average cost of books: $500
% of students receiving aid: 80

Employment Profile:
% of students who pass the boards on their first try: 100
% employed within the first 6 months following graduation: 75
Average starting salary: $30,000

Occupational Therapy Assistant

Alabama

Wallace State Community College
PO Box 2000
Hanceville, AL 35077-2000

Contact Information:
Telephone: 256-352-8333
Fax: 256-352-8341
E-mail: hazard@bham.mindspring.com
Web: www.wscc.cc.al.us

Program Information:
Program begins: August
Duration of program: 12 months

Application Information:
Enrollment of program: 15

Financial Information:
Tuition, resident: $1,540
Average cost of books: $500
% of students receiving aid: 50

Employment Profile:
% of students who pass the boards on their first try: 97
% employed within the first 6 months following graduation: 3
Average starting salary: $20,000

California

Andon College at Modesto
Quest Education Corporation
1700 McHenry Village Way
Modesto, CA 95350

Contact Information:
Telephone: 209-571-8777
Fax: 209-571-9836
E-mail: andoncollege.com
Web: www.andoncollege.com

Program Information:
Program begins: March, October
Duration of program: 17 months
Evening or weekend classes are available.

Financial Information:
Average cost of books: $1,200
% of students receiving aid: 98

Employment Profile:
% of students who pass the boards on their first try: 100
% employed within the first 6 months following graduation: 50
Average starting salary: $33,960

Fresno City College
Loma Linda University
SAHP-Nichol Hall/Room A912
Loma Linda, CA 92350-0001

Contact Information:
Telephone: 909-824-4628 ext. 47473
Fax: 909-558-0239
E-mail: liane-hewitt@sahp.llu.edu
Web: www.llu.edu

Program Information:
Program begins: September
Duration of program: 15 months

Application Information:
Enrollment of program: 55
Transfer students are accepted.

Financial Information:
Average cost of books: $300
% of students receiving aid: 95

Employment Profile:
% of students who pass the boards on their first try: 93
% employed within the first 6 months following graduation: 75
Average starting salary: $31,000

Grossmont College
8800 Grossmont College Drive
El Cajon, CA 92020-1799

Contact Information:
Telephone: 619-644-7305
Fax: 619-644-7961
Web: www.grossmont.gcccd.cc.ca.us

Program Information:
Duration of program: 24 months
Evening or weekend classes are available.

Maric College of Medical Careers
3666 Kearny Villa Road
San Diego, CA 92123

Contact Information:
Telephone: 619-654-3650
Fax: 619-279-1620
Web: www.mariccollege.edu

Program Information:
Program begins: September, January, May
Duration of program: 20 months

Application Information:
Enrollment of program: 58
Transfer students are accepted.

Employment Profile:
% of students who pass the boards on their first try: 90

Mt. St. Mary's College

Doheny Campus
10 Chester Place
Los Angeles, CA 90007-2598

Contact Information:
Telephone: 213-477-2581
Fax: 213-477-2519
Web: www.msmc.la.edu

Program Information:
Program begins: September
Duration of program: 24 months
Evening or weekend classes are available.

Application Information:
Transfer students are accepted.

Financial Information:
Average cost of books: $450
% of students receiving aid: 95

Employment Profile:
% of students who pass the boards on their first try: 85
% employed within the first 6 months following graduation: 20
Average starting salary: $30,000

Sacramento City College

Allied Health Department
3835 Freeport Boulevard
Sacramento, CA 95822

Contact Information:
Telephone: 916-558-2297
Fax: 916-558-2392
Web: www.scc.losrios.cc.ca.us

Program Information:
Program begins: January
Duration of program: 24 months
Evening or weekend classes are available.

Application Information:
Enrollment of program: 30
Transfer students are accepted.

Financial Information:
Tuition, resident: $800
Tuition, non-resident: $8,750
Average cost of books: $400

Employment Profile:
% of students who pass the boards on their first try: 90
% employed within the first 6 months following graduation: 50
Average starting salary: $28,000

Santa Ana College

1530 West 17th Street
Santa Ana, CA 92706-3398

Contact Information:
Telephone: 714-564-6833
Fax: 714-564-6158
E-mail: sheabc@mail.rsccd.org
Web: www.rsccd.org

Program Information:
Program begins: January
Duration of program: 24 months

Application Information:
Enrollment of program: 36

Financial Information:
Tuition, resident: $660
Tuition, non-resident: $7,980
Average cost of books: $400
% of students receiving aid: 20

Employment Profile:
% of students who pass the boards on their first try: 100
% employed within the first 6 months following graduation: 60
Average starting salary: $32,000

Western Institute of Science & Health

130 Avram Avenue
Rohnert Park, CA 94928

Contact Information:
Telephone: 707-664-9267
Fax: 707-664-9237
Web: www.westerni.org

Program Information:
Program begins: August, January
Duration of program: 24 months

Application Information:
Enrollment of program: 10
Transfer students are accepted.

Financial Information:
Average cost of books: $550
% of students receiving aid: 100

Employment Profile:
% employed within the first 6 months following graduation: 20
Average starting salary: $30,000

Colorado

Arapahoe Community College

2500 West College Drive
PO Box 9002
Littleton, CO 80160-9002

Contact Information:
Telephone: 303-797-5939
Fax: 303-797-5935
E-mail: wfigueroaros@arapahoe.edu
Web: www.arapahoe.edu

Program Information:
Program begins: September
Duration of program: 24 months

Application Information:
Enrollment of program: 17
Transfer students are accepted.

Financial Information:
Tuition, resident: $3,506
Tuition, non-resident: $13,578

Employment Profile:
% of students who pass the boards on their first try: 100
Average starting salary: $22,000

Pueblo Community College

900 West Orman Avenue
Pueblo, CO 81004-1499

Contact Information:
Telephone: 719-549-3268
Fax: 719-549-3136
E-mail: terry.hawkins@pcc.cccoes.edu
Web: www.pcc.cccoes.edu/ota/welcome.htm

Program Information:
Program begins: August
Degrees offered: Associate's, 24 months
Evening or weekend classes are available.

Application Information:
Enrollment of program: 29
Transfer students are accepted.

Financial Information:
Tuition, resident: $2,567
Tuition, non-resident: $10,480
Average cost of books: $750

Employment Profile:
% of students who pass the boards on their first try: 100
% employed within the first 6 months following graduation: 80
Average starting salary: $28,000

Westwood College of Technology

Health Careers Division
7350 North Broadway
Denver, CO 80221

Contact Information:
Telephone: 303-426-7000 ext. 690
Fax: 303-657-5529
E-mail: kmcbride@westwood.edu
Web: www.westwood.edu

Program Information:
Program begins: March, May, August
Degrees offered: Associate's, 20 months

Application Information:
Enrollment of program: 32
Transfer students are accepted.

Financial Information:
Tuition, resident: $20,000
% of students receiving aid: 90

Employment Profile:
% of students who pass the boards on their first try: 90
% employed within the first 6 months following graduation: 80

Connecticut

Briarwood College

2279 Mt. Vernon Road
Southington, CT 06489

Contact Information:
Telephone: 860-628-4751
Fax: 860-628-6444
Web: www.briarwood.edu

Program Information:
Program begins: September
Duration of program: 18 months
Evening or weekend classes are available.

Application Information:
Enrollment of program: 45
Transfer students are accepted.

Financial Information:
Average cost of books: $800
% of students receiving aid: 87

Employment Profile:
% of students who pass the boards on their first try: 98

Manchester Community College

60 Bidwell Street MS 29
PO Box 1046
Manchester, CT 06045-1046

Contact Information:
Telephone: 860-647-6197
Fax: 860-647-6370
E-mail: ma_nieman@commnet.edu
Web: www.mctc.commnet.edu

Program Information:
Program begins: August
Degrees offered: Associate's, 24 months
Evening or weekend classes are available.

Application Information:
Enrollment of program: 25
Transfer students are accepted.

Financial Information:
Tuition, resident: $1,814
Tuition, non-resident: $5,438
Average cost of books: $500

Employment Profile:
% of students who pass the boards on their first try: 100

Delaware

Delaware Technical & Community College—Wilmington

333 Shipley Street
Wilmington, DE 19801-2499

Contact Information:
Telephone: 302-888-5298
Fax: 302-577-6431
E-mail: jgorecki@hopi.dtcc.edu
Web: www.dtcc.edu

Program Information:
Program begins: June
Duration of program: 28 months

Application Information:
Transfer students are accepted.

Financial Information:
Tuition, resident: $690
Tuition, non-resident: $1,725

Florida

Central Florida Community College

3001 Southwest College Road
Ocala, FL 34478

Contact Information:
Telephone: 352-854-2322 ext. 1327
E-mail: grabowsd@cfcc.cc.fl.us
Web: www.cfcc.cc.fl.us

Program Information:
Program begins: January
Duration of program: 16 months

Application Information:
Enrollment of program: 24

Financial Information:
Tuition, resident: $3,298
Tuition, non-resident: $12,047

Hillsborough Community College

PO Box 5096
Tampa, FL 33675-5096

Contact Information:
Telephone: 813-253-7431
Fax: 813-253-7506
Web: www.hcc.cc.fl.us

Program Information:
Program begins: September
Duration of program: 22 months

Application Information:
Enrollment of program: 20
Transfer students are accepted.

Financial Information:
Tuition, resident: $1,604
Tuition, non-resident: $5,831

Employment Profile:
% of students who pass the boards on their first try: 100
Average starting salary: $30,000

Palm Beach Community College

4200 South Congress Avenue
Lake Worth, FL 33461-4796

Contact Information:
Telephone: 561-439-8094
Fax: 561-434-5186
E-mail: munros@pbcc.cc.fl.us
Web: www.pbcc.cc.fl.us

Program Information:
Duration of program: 18 months

Application Information:
Enrollment of program: 30

Financial Information:
Tuition, resident: $3,230
Tuition, non-resident: $11,682

Idaho

American Institute of Health Technology

6600 Emerald
Boise, ID 83704-8738

Contact Information:
Telephone: 208-377-8080 ext. 27
Fax: 208-322-7658
E-mail: instrhlth@aol.com
Web: www.abhes.org/aiht

Program Information:
Program begins: August, January
Duration of program: 20 months

Application Information:
Enrollment of program: 25
Transfer students are accepted.

Financial Information:
% of students receiving aid: 95

Employment Profile:
% of students who pass the boards on their first try: 99
% employed within the first 6 months following graduation: 50
Average starting salary: $24,000

Illinois

College of DuPage

Occupational and Vocational Education
425 22nd Street
Glen Ellyn, IL 60137-6599

Contact Information:
Telephone: 630-942-2419
Fax: 630-858-5409
E-mail: mitalk@cdnet.cod.edu
Web: www.cod.edu

Program Information:
Program begins: April
Degrees offered: Associate's, 36 months
Evening or weekend classes are available.

Application Information:
Enrollment of program: 20
Transfer students are accepted.

Financial Information:
Tuition, resident: $3,200
Tuition, non-resident: $10,800
% of students receiving aid: 20

Employment Profile:
% of students who pass the boards on their first try: 100
% employed within the first 6 months following graduation: 75
Average starting salary: $28,000

South Suburban College of Cook County

15800 South State Street
South Holland, IL 60473-1262

Contact Information:
Telephone: 708-596-2000 ext. 2264
Fax: 708-210-5792
E-mail: jmyler@ssc.cc.il.us
Web: www.ssc.cc.il.us

Program Information:
Program begins: August
Duration of program: 20 months

Financial Information:
Tuition, resident: $3,060
Tuition, non-resident: $11,760

Wilbur Wright College

4300 North Narragansett Avenue
Chicago, IL 60634

Contact Information:
Telephone: 773-481-8875
Fax: 773-481-8892
E-mail: jwandel@ccc.edu
Web: www.ccc.edu

Program Information:
Program begins: August
Degrees offered: Associate's, 26 months

Application Information:
Enrollment of program: 26
Transfer students are accepted.

Financial Information:
Tuition, resident: $3,375
Tuition, non-resident: $15,000
Average cost of books: $500
% of students receiving aid: 77

Employment Profile:
% of students who pass the boards on their first try: 100
% employed within the first 6 months following graduation: 98
Average starting salary: $26,000

Kansas

Barton County Community College

245 Northeast 30th Road
Great Bend, KS 67530-9283

Contact Information:
Telephone: 316-792-9368
Fax: 316-786-1163
E-mail: fryel@barton.cc.ks.us
Web: www.barton.cc.ks.us

Program Information:
Program begins: August, January
Duration of program: 23 months

Application Information:
Enrollment of program: 52
Transfer students are accepted.

Financial Information:
Tuition, resident: $1,345
Tuition, non-resident: $2,208
Average cost of books: $230
% of students receiving aid: 75

Employment Profile:
% of students who pass the boards on their first try: 100
Average starting salary: $28,000

Kentucky

Jefferson Community College

109 East Broadway
Louisville, KY 40202

Contact Information:
Telephone: 502-584-0181 ext. 2342
Fax: 502-213-2491
E-mail: darcy.croghan@kctcs.net
Web: www.jefferson.cc.org

Program Information:
Program begins: June
Degrees offered: Associate's, 24 months

Application Information:
Enrollment of program: 20
Transfer students are accepted.

Financial Information:
Average cost of books: $500

Employment Profile:
% of students who pass the boards on their first try: 100
% employed within the first 6 months following graduation: 100

Louisiana

Northeast Louisiana University

College of Pharmacy and Health Sciences
School of Allied Health Sciences
Monroe, LA 71209-0430

Contact Information:
Telephone: 318-342-1610
Fax: 318-342-5584
E-mail: aldavis@alpha.nlu.edu

Program Information:
Program begins: August
Duration of program: 25 months

Application Information:
Enrollment of program: 35

Financial Information:
Tuition, resident: $1,925
Tuition, non-resident: $4,326

Maryland

Allegany College of Maryland

12401 Willowbrook Road Southeast
Cumberland, MD 21502-2596

Contact Information:
Telephone: 301-784-5536
Fax: 301-784-5015
E-mail: pam@ac.cc.md.us
Web: www.ac.cc.md.us

Program Information:
Program begins: September
Duration of program: 28 months

Application Information:
Enrollment of program: 16
Transfer students are accepted.

Financial Information:
Tuition, resident: $2,490
Tuition, non-resident: $7,470
Average cost of books: $250

Employment Profile:
% of students who pass the boards on their first try: 100
Average starting salary: $27,000

Massachusetts

Bay State College

122 Commonwealth Avenue
Boston, MA 02116

Contact Information:
Telephone: 617-375-0195
Fax: 617-375-0197
E-mail: sgelfman@baystate.edu
Web: www.baystate.edu

Program Information:
Program begins: September
Duration of program: 20 months

Application Information:
Enrollment of program: 30
Transfer students are accepted.

Financial Information:
Tuition, resident: $12,700
Average cost of books: $1,000
% of students receiving aid: 85

Employment Profile:
% of students who pass the boards on their first try: 100
Average starting salary: $28,000

Becker College

61 Sever Street Box 15071
Worcester, MA 01615-0071

Contact Information:
Telephone: 508-791-9241
Fax: 508-831-7505
E-mail: efenton@go.becker.edu
Web: www.becker.edu

Program Information:
Program begins: September
Duration of program: 18 months

Application Information:
Enrollment of program: 45
Transfer students are accepted.

Financial Information:
Average cost of books: $700
% of students receiving aid: 85

Employment Profile:
% of students who pass the boards on their first try: 92
Average starting salary: $32,000

Bristol Community College
777 Elsbree Street
Fall River, MA 02720-9960

Contact Information:
Telephone: 508-678-2811 ext. 2325
Fax: 508-675-2318
E-mail: jduponte@bristol.mass.edu
Web: www.bristol.mass.edu

Program Information:
Program begins: September
Duration of program: 24 months

Application Information:
Enrollment of program: 40

Financial Information:
Tuition, resident: $2,484
Tuition, non-resident: $8,292
Average cost of books: $750
% of students receiving aid: 43

Employment Profile:
% of students who pass the boards on their first try: 100
% employed within the first 6 months following graduation: 50
Average starting salary: $35,000

Lasell College
1844 Commonwealth Avenue
Auburndale, MA 02466

Contact Information:
Telephone: 617-243-2172
Fax: 617-243-2146
E-mail: mroberts@lasell.edu
Web: www.lasell.edu

Program Information:
Program begins: September
Duration of program: 18 months

Application Information:
Enrollment of program: 41

Massachusetts Bay Community College
Wellesley Hills Campus
50 Oakland Street
Wellesley Hills, MA 02181-5399

Contact Information:
Telephone: 781-239-2240
Fax: 781-416-1319
E-mail: leigh@mbcc.mass.edu
Web: www.mbcc.mass.edu

Program Information:
Program begins: September
Duration of program: 21 months
Evening or weekend classes are available.

Application Information:
Enrollment of program: 76
Transfer students are accepted.

Financial Information:
Tuition, resident: $4,250
Tuition, non-resident: $10,965

Employment Profile:
Average starting salary: $35,000

Mt. Ida College
Junior College Division
777 Dedham Street
Newton Centre, MA 02159-3310

Contact Information:
Telephone: 617-928-7343
Fax: 617-928-4760
E-mail: csacchetti@mountida.edu
Web: www.mountida.edu

Program Information:
Program begins: September
Duration of program: 18 months

Application Information:
Enrollment of program: 23
Transfer students are accepted.

Financial Information:
Average cost of books: $600

Springfield Technical Community College
One Armory Square
Springfield, MA 01101

Contact Information:
Telephone: 413-781-7822
Fax: 413-733-0688
E-mail: mjoyce@stcc.mass.edu
Web: www.stcc.mass.edu

Program Information:
Program begins: September
Duration of program: 18 months

Application Information:
Enrollment of program: 25
Transfer students are accepted.

Financial Information:
Tuition, resident: $1,200
Tuition, non-resident: $5,640
Average cost of books: $200

Michigan

Baker College of Muskegon
1903 Marquette
Muskegon, MI 49442

Contact Information:
Telephone: 231-775-5274
Fax: 231-777-5265
E-mail: andrew_k@muskegon.baker.edu
Web: www.baker.edu

Program Information:
Program begins: September, March
Duration of program: 24 months
Evening or weekend classes are available.

Minnesota

Lake Superior College
2101 Trinity Road
Duluth, MN 55811-3399

Contact Information:
Telephone: 218-733-7682
Fax: 218-723-4921
E-mail: j.dreher@lsc.mnscu.edu
Web: www.lsc.mnscu.edu

Program Information:
Program begins: August, January
Duration of program: 18 months

Application Information:
Transfer students are accepted.

Financial Information:
Tuition, resident: $4,914
Tuition, non-resident: $9,828

Employment Profile:
% of students who pass the boards on their first try: 100

Riverland Community College
1900 8th Avenue Northwest
Austin, MN 55912-1407

Contact Information:
Telephone: 507-433-0567
Fax: 507-433-0515
E-mail: davisca@au.cc.mn.us
Web: www.riverland.cc.mn.us

Program Information:
Program begins: September
Degrees offered: Associate's, 22 months
Evening or weekend classes are available.

Application Information:
Enrollment of program: 25
Transfer students are accepted.

Financial Information:
Tuition, resident: $2,209
Tuition, non-resident: $4,418
Average cost of books: $700
% of students receiving aid: 80

Employment Profile:
% of students who pass the boards on their first try: 100
% employed within the first 6 months following graduation: 90
Average starting salary: $23,000

Mississippi

Pearl River Community College—Hattiesburg
5448 US Highway 49 South
Hattiesburg, MS 39401

Contact Information:
Telephone: 601-554-9141
Fax: 601-554-9148
E-mail: bsutley@prcc.cc.ms.us
Web: www.prcc.ms.us

Program Information:
Program begins: June
Degrees offered: Associate's, 24 months

Application Information:
Enrollment of program: 40
Transfer students are accepted.

Financial Information:
Tuition, resident: $1,887
Average cost of books: $600

Employment Profile:
% of students who pass the boards on their first try: 100
% employed within the first 6 months following graduation: 100

Missouri

Missouri College
10121 Manchester Road
St. Louis, MO 63122-1583

Contact Information:
Telephone: 314-821-7703 ext. 2123
Fax: 314-984-0475
E-mail: susana@mocollege.org
Web: www.mocollege.org

Program Information:
Program begins: January, September
Duration of program: 19 months

Penn Valley Community College
3201 Southwest Trafficway
Kansas City, MO 64111-2764

Contact Information:
Telephone: 816-759-4235
Fax: 816-759-4553
E-mail: mcilnay@pennvalley.cc.mo.us
Web: www.kcmetro.cc.mo.us/pennvalley

Program Information:
Program begins: August
Duration of program: 22 months

Application Information:
Enrollment of program: 60

Financial Information:
Tuition, resident: $3,528
Tuition, non-resident: $8,424
Average cost of books: $306
% of students receiving aid: 30

Employment Profile:
% of students who pass the boards on their first try: 99
% employed within the first 6 months following graduation: 30
Average starting salary: $28,000

Sanford Brown College
Hazelwood Campus
75 Village Square
Hazelwood, MO 63042

Contact Information:
Telephone: 314-731-1101
Fax: 314-731-7044

Program Information:
Program begins: January
Duration of program: 18 months

Financial Information:
Tuition, resident: $11,600

St. Louis Community College at Meramec
11333 Big Bend Boulevard
St. Louis, MO 63122

Contact Information:
Telephone: 314-984-7364
Fax: 314-984-7250
Web: www.stlcc.mo.us

Program Information:
Program begins: August
Duration of program: 21 months

Financial Information:
Tuition, resident: $1,407
Tuition, non-resident: $1,776

Employment Profile:
% of students who pass the boards on their first try: 100

Montana

Montana State University College of Technology—Great Falls
Allied Health Department
PO Box 6010
Great Falls, MT 59406-6010

Contact Information:
Telephone: 406-771-4364
Fax: 406-771-4317
E-mail: hquarles@msucotgf.montana.edu
Web: www.msucotgf.montana.edu

Program Information:
Program begins: January
Duration of program: 24 months
Evening or weekend classes are available.

Application Information:
Enrollment of program: 20

Financial Information:
Tuition, resident: $1,872
Tuition, non-resident: $2,585
Average cost of books: $2,500

Employment Profile:
% of students who pass the boards on their first try: 100
% employed within the first 6 months following graduation: 75
Average starting salary: $25,000

New Hampshire

New Hampshire Community Technical College
One College Drive
Claremont, NH 03743-9707

Contact Information:
Telephone: 603-542-7744 ext. 2525
Fax: 603-543-1844
E-mail: jlarsen@tec.nh.us
Web: www.claremont.tec.nh.us

Program Information:
Program begins: August, January
Duration of program: 18 months
Evening or weekend classes are available.

Application Information:
Enrollment of program: 45
Transfer students are accepted.

Financial Information:
Tuition, resident: $3,960
Tuition, non-resident: $5,945
Average cost of books: $800
% of students receiving aid: 70

Employment Profile:
% of students who pass the boards on their first try: 100
% employed within the first 6 months following graduation: 50
Average starting salary: $25,000

New Mexico

Eastern New Mexico University—Roswell
Division of Health
52 University Boulevard/PO Box 6000
Roswell, NM 88202-6000

Contact Information:
Telephone: 505-624-7267
Fax: 505-624-7100
E-mail: herrerap@lib.enmuros.cc.nm.us
Web: www.roswell.enmu.edu

Program Information:
Program begins: August
Duration of program: 18 months

Application Information:
Transfer students are accepted.

Financial Information:
Tuition, resident: $1,018
Tuition, non-resident: $2,794

New York

Erie Community College—North Campus
6205 Main Street
Williamsville, NY 14221

Contact Information:
Telephone: 716-851-1320
Fax: 716-851-1429

E-mail: jones@ecc.edu
Web: www.ecc.edu

Program Information:
Program begins: September
Duration of program: 24 months

Application Information:
Enrollment of program: 70

Financial Information:
Tuition, resident: $2,475
Tuition, non-resident: $4,850
Average cost of books: $500

Employment Profile:
% of students who pass the boards on their first try: 96
Average starting salary: $18,500

Genesee Community College
One College Road
Batavia, NY 14020-9704

Contact Information:
Telephone: 716-345-3838
Fax: 716-343-0433
E-mail: mkhartman@sunygenesee.cc.ny.us
Web: www.sunygenesee.cc.ny.us

Program Information:
Program begins: August
Duration of program: 24 months

Application Information:
Enrollment of program: 55
Transfer students are accepted.

Financial Information:
Tuition, resident: $1,300
Tuition, non-resident: $1,500

Employment Profile:
% of students who pass the boards on their first try: 94

Herkimer County Community College
Reservoir Road
Herkimer, NY 13350-1598

Contact Information:
Telephone: 315-866-0300 ext. 356
Fax: 315-866-7253
E-mail: greeneme@hccc.suny.edu
Web: www.hccc.ntcnet.com

Program Information:
Program begins: August
Degrees offered: Associate's, 18 months

Application Information:
Enrollment of program: 55
Transfer students are accepted.

Financial Information:
Tuition, resident: $2,250
Tuition, non-resident: $4,200
Average cost of books: $315
% of students receiving aid: 78

Employment Profile:
% of students who pass the boards on their first try: 92
Average starting salary: $23,961

LaGuardia Community College
31-10 Thomson Avenue
Long Island City, NY 11101-3083

Contact Information:
Telephone: 718-482-5774
Fax: 718-482-6047
E-mail: ngreenbe@lagcc.cuny.edu
Web: www.lagcc.cuny.edu

Program Information:
Program begins: September, March
Duration of program: 24 months
Evening or weekend classes are available.

Application Information:
Enrollment of program: 120
Transfer students are accepted.

Financial Information:
Tuition, resident: $2,500
Tuition, non-resident: $3,076
Average cost of books: $250
% of students receiving aid: 75

Employment Profile:
% of students who pass the boards on their first try: 75
% employed within the first 6 months following graduation: 70
Average starting salary: $35,000

Mercy College
555 Broadway
Dobbs Ferry, NY 10522

Contact Information:
Telephone: 914-674-9331 ext. 604
Fax: 914-674-9457
E-mail: jparker@mercynet.edu
Web: www.mercynet.edu

Program Information:
Program begins: September
Duration of program: 12 months
Evening or weekend classes are available.

Application Information:
Enrollment of program: 30
Transfer students are accepted.

Financial Information:
Tuition, resident: $9,900
Average cost of books: $500

Employment Profile:
% of students who pass the boards on their first try: 95
% employed within the first 6 months following graduation: 80
Average starting salary: $35,000

Rockland Community College
145 College Road
Suffern, NY 10901-3699

Contact Information:
Telephone: 914-574-4312
Fax: 914-574-4462
E-mail: espergel@sunyrockland.edu
Web: www.sunyrockland.edu

Program Information:
Program begins: September, January
Duration of program: 24 months
Evening or weekend classes are available.

Application Information:
Enrollment of program: 120
Transfer students are accepted.

Financial Information:
Tuition, resident: $1,163
Tuition, non-resident: $2,325

North Carolina

Pitt Community College
PO Drawer 7007
Highway 11 South
Greenville, NC 27835-7007

Contact Information:
Telephone: 252-321-4370
Fax: 252-321-4451
E-mail: rarmstro@pcc.pitt.cc.nc.us

Program Information:
Program begins: January
Duration of program: 24 months

Application Information:
Enrollment of program: 48
Transfer students are accepted.

Financial Information:
Tuition, resident: $860
Tuition, non-resident: $7,009

Employment Profile:
% of students who pass the boards on their first try: 100
% employed within the first 6 months following graduation: 50
Average starting salary: $28,000

Southwestern Community College
447 College Drive
Sylva, NC 28779

Contact Information:
Telephone: 800-447-4091 ext. 395
Fax: 828-586-3129
E-mail: lynnj@southwest.cc.nc.us
Web: www.southwest.cc.nc.us

Program Information:
Program begins: August
Duration of program: 21 months

Application Information:
Enrollment of program: 23
Transfer students are accepted.

Financial Information:
Tuition, resident: $560
Tuition, non-resident: $4,564

Stanly Community College
141 College Drive
Albemarle, NC 28001-9402

Contact Information:
Telephone: 704-982-0121 ext. 209
Fax: 704-982-0819
E-mail: smithkb@stanly.cc.nc.us
Web: www.stanly.cc.nc.us

Program Information:
Program begins: August
Degrees offered: Diploma, 21 months

Application Information:
Enrollment of program: 30
Transfer students are accepted.

Financial Information:
Tuition, resident: $853
Tuition, non-resident: $6,588
Average cost of books: $700
% of students receiving aid: 30

Employment Profile:
% of students who pass the boards on their first try: 100
% employed within the first 6 months following graduation: 75
Average starting salary: $25,000

Ohio

Cincinnati State Technical and Community College

3520 Central Parkway
Cincinnati, OH 45223-2690

Contact Information:
Telephone: 513-569-1598
Fax: 513-569-1659
E-mail: millercl@cinstate.cc.oh.us
Web: www.cinstate.cc.oh.us

Program Information:
Program begins: September
Duration of program: 24 months

Financial Information:
Tuition, resident: $6,820
Tuition, non-resident: $13,750
% of students receiving aid: 50

Employment Profile:
% of students who pass the boards on their first try: 100
% employed within the first 6 months following graduation: 60
Average starting salary: $28,500

Lourdes College

6832 Convent Boulevard
Sylvania, OH 43560-2898

Contact Information:
Telephone: 419-885-3211
Fax: 419-882-3786
Web: www.lourdes.edu

Program Information:
Program begins: August, January
Duration of program: 36 months
Evening or weekend classes are available.

Application Information:
Enrollment of program: 65
Transfer students are accepted.

Financial Information:
Tuition, resident: $8,296
Average cost of books: $200
% of students receiving aid: 50

Employment Profile:
% of students who pass the boards on their first try: 99
% employed within the first 6 months following graduation: 75
Average starting salary: $23,000

Muskingum Area Technical College

1555 Newark Road
Zanesville, OH 43701-2694

Contact Information:
Telephone: 740-454-2501 ext. 1313
Fax: 740-454-0035
E-mail: marnold@matc.tec.oh.us
Web: www.matc.tec.oh.us

Program Information:
Program begins: September
Duration of program: 22 months

Application Information:
Enrollment of program: 50
Transfer students are accepted.

Financial Information:
Tuition, resident: $2,205

Owens Community College

PO Box 10,000
Oregon Road
Toledo, OH 43699-1947

Contact Information:
Telephone: 419-661-7000 ext. 7084
Fax: 419-661-7251
E-mail: bkneisley@owens.cc.oh.us
Web: www.owens.cc.oh.us

Program Information:
Program begins: August
Duration of program: 24 months
Evening or weekend classes are available.

Application Information:
Enrollment of program: 26
Transfer students are accepted.

Financial Information:
Tuition, resident: $2,032
Tuition, non-resident: $3,964

Employment Profile:
% of students who pass the boards on their first try: 100
% employed within the first 6 months following graduation: 50
Average starting salary: $26,000

Shawnee State University

940 Second Street
Portsmouth, OH 45662-4303

Contact Information:
Telephone: 740-355-2272
Fax: 740-355-2354
E-mail: swheeler@shawnee.edu
Web: www.shawnee.edu

Program Information:
Program begins: September
Duration of program: 21 months

Application Information:
Enrollment of program: 33

Financial Information:
Tuition, resident: $3,552
Tuition, non-resident: $6,676

Employment Profile:
% of students who pass the boards on their first try: 100

Oklahoma

Oklahoma City Community College

Health, Social Sciences & Human Services Division
7777 South May Avenue
Oklahoma City, OK 73159-4444

Contact Information:
Telephone: 405-682-7506
Fax: 405-682-7803
E-mail: phbaker@okc.cc.ok.us
Web: www.okc.cc.ok.us

Program Information:
Program begins: August, January
Duration of program: 20 months

Application Information:
Enrollment of program: 68

Financial Information:
Tuition, resident: $1,914
Tuition, non-resident: $3,501

Caddo-Kiowa Vocational Technical Center

PO Box 190
Fort Cobb, OK 73038

Contact Information:
Telephone: 405-643-5511 ext. 310
Fax: 405-643-2144
E-mail: kgillingham@ck.tec.ok.us

Program Information:
Program begins: August
Duration of program: 21 months

Application Information:
Enrollment of program: 15

Financial Information:
Tuition, resident: $4,000
Tuition, non-resident: $5,000
Average cost of books: $720
% of students receiving aid: 80

Employment Profile:
% of students who pass the boards on their first try: 100

% employed within the first 6 months following graduation: 80
Average starting salary: $30,000

Pennsylvania

Community College of Allegheny County

595 Beatty Road
Monroeville, PA 15146-1395

Contact Information:
Telephone: 410-455-4482
Fax: 410-719-6501
E-mail: lbriola@ccac.edu
Web: www.ccac.edu

Program Information:
Program begins: August
Duration of program: 25 months

Financial Information:
Tuition, resident: $2,040
Tuition, non-resident: $4,080
Average cost of books: $400

Employment Profile:
% of students who pass the boards on their first try: 100
% employed within the first 6 months following graduation: 20
Average starting salary: $25,000

Harcum College

750 Montgomery Avenue
Bryn Mawr, PA 19010-3476

Contact Information:
Telephone: 610-526-6115
Fax: 610-526-6031
E-mail: kpotter@harcum.edu
Web: www.harcum.edu

Program Information:
Program begins: September
Duration of program: 20 months
Evening or weekend classes are available.

Financial Information:
Tuition, resident: $10,390
Tuition, non-resident: $16,200

ICM School of Business and Medical Careers

10 Wood Street at Fort Pitt Boulevard
Pittsburgh, PA 15222-1977

Contact Information:
Telephone: 412-261-2647 ext. 254
Fax: 412-261-6491
E-mail: inquiry@icmschool.com
Web: www.icmschool.com

Program Information:
Program begins: Program begins quarterly.
Duration of program: 18 months

Lehigh Carbon Community College

4525 Education Park Drive
Schnecksville, PA 18078-2598

Contact Information:
Telephone: 610-799-1548
Fax: 610-799-1527
Web: www.lccc.edu

Program Information:
Program begins: August
Duration of program: 24 months
Evening or weekend classes are available.

Financial Information:
Tuition, resident: $2,142
Tuition, non-resident: $4,284

Mt. Aloysius College

7373 Admiral Peary Highway
Cresson, PA 16630

Contact Information:
Telephone: 814-886-6347
Fax: 814-886-4906
Web: www.mtaloy.edu

Program Information:
Program begins: August
Duration of program: 24 months
Evening or weekend classes are available.

Application Information:
Enrollment of program: 38
Transfer students are accepted.

Financial Information:
Average cost of books: $450
% of students receiving aid: 90

Employment Profile:
% of students who pass the boards on their first try: 98
% employed within the first 6 months following graduation: 85
Average starting salary: $22,000

Penn State Commonwealth College

Worthington Scranton Campus
120 Ridge View Drive
Dunmore, PA 18512-1699

Contact Information:
Telephone: 570-963-2547
Fax: 570-963-2535
E-mail: jwfs@psu.edu
Web: www.psu.edu

Program Information:
Program begins: August
Duration of program: 20 months

Application Information:
Transfer students are accepted.

Financial Information:
Tuition, resident: $6,222
Tuition, non-resident: $9,498
Average cost of books: $350

Employment Profile:
% of students who pass the boards on their first try: 95
% employed within the first 6 months following graduation: 50
Average starting salary: $30,000

Penn State University

Mont Alto Campus
1 Campus Drive
Mont Alto, PA 17237-9703

Contact Information:
Telephone: 814-375-4748
Fax: 814-375-4784
E-mail: jvd102@psu.edu
Web: www.ma.psu.edu/ot.htm

Program Information:
Program begins: August
Duration of program: 20 months
Evening or weekend classes are available.

Application Information:
Enrollment of program: 300
Transfer students are accepted.

Financial Information:
Tuition, resident: $5,832
Tuition, non-resident: $12,406
Average cost of books: $300

Employment Profile:
% of students who pass the boards on their first try: 98
Average starting salary: $25,000

Pennsylvania College of Technology

One College Avenue
Williamsport, PA 17701-5799

Contact Information:
Telephone: 717-321-5549
Fax: 717-321-5556
E-mail: bnatell@pct.edu
Web: www.pct.edu

Program Information:
Program begins: August
Duration of program: 22 months

Application Information:
Enrollment of program: 32
Transfer students are accepted.

Financial Information:
Tuition, resident: $5,740
Tuition, non-resident: $8,700
Average cost of books: $500
% of students receiving aid: 50

Employment Profile:
% of students who pass the boards on their first try: 100
Average starting salary: $24,000

Puerto Rico

Humacao University College

University of Puerto Rico
CUH Postal Station
Humacao, PR 00791-9998

Contact Information:
Telephone: 787-850-9392
Fax: 787-850-9434
E-mail: ce-alverio@cuhac.ur.clu.edu

Program Information:
Program begins: August
Degrees offered: Associate's, 22 months

Application Information:
Enrollment of program: 70
Transfer students are accepted.

Financial Information:
Tuition, resident: $1,408
Tuition, non-resident: $2,400
Average cost of books: $164
% of students receiving aid: 80

Employment Profile:
% of students who pass the boards on their first try: 65
% employed within the first 6 months following graduation: 80
Average starting salary: $24,000

South Dakota

Lake Area Technical Institute

230 11th Street Northeast
Watertown, SD 57201-0730

Contact Information:
Telephone: 605-882-5284 ext. 326
Fax: 605-882-6347
Web: www.lati.tech.sd.us

Program Information:
Program begins: September
Duration of program: 20 months

Application Information:
Enrollment of program: 44

Employment Profile:
% of students who pass the boards on their first try: 100
Average starting salary: $23,000

Tennessee

Nashville State Technical Institute

120 White Bridge Road
PO Box 90285
Nashville, TN 37209-4515

Contact Information:
Telephone: 615-353-3382
Fax: 615-353-3376
E-mail: twelves_l@nsti.tec.tn.us
Web: www.nsti.tec.tn.us

Program Information:
Program begins: August
Duration of program: 24 months

Application Information:
Enrollment of program: 30

Financial Information:
Tuition, resident: $1,300
Tuition, non-resident: $6,000
Average cost of books: $300

Employment Profile:
% of students who pass the boards on their first try: 98
% employed within the first 6 months following graduation: 50
Average starting salary: $30,000

Roane State Community College

276 Patton Lane
Harriman, TN 37748-5011

Contact Information:
Telephone: 423-481-2657 ext. 2011
Fax: 423-481-2019
E-mail: sain_s@a1.rscc.cc.tn.us
Web: www.rscc.cc.tn.us

Program Information:
Program begins: August
Duration of program: 20 months

Application Information:
Enrollment of program: 40
Transfer students are accepted.

Financial Information:
Tuition, resident: $1,024
Tuition, non-resident: $3,072

Texas

Army Medical Department Center and School

Academy of Health Sciences
3151 Scott Road Suite 1230
Ft. Sam Houston, TX 78234-6138

Contact Information:
Telephone: 210-221-3694
Fax: 210-221-4447
E-mail: patricia.hopkins@cen.amedd.army.mil
Web: www.cs.amedd.army.mil

Program Information:
Program begins: September, January, May
Duration of program: 7 months

Application Information:
Enrollment of program: 60

Employment Profile:
% of students who pass the boards on their first try: 93
Additional Information: Enrollment only open to active military personnel.

Austin Community College

Riverside Campus
1020 Grove Boulevard
Austin, TX 78741-3300

Contact Information:
Telephone: 512-223-6196
Fax: 512-223-6268
E-mail: scarrell@austin.cc.tx.us
Web: www.austin.cc.tx.us

Program Information:
Program begins: August
Duration of program: 24 months
Evening or weekend classes are available.

Application Information:
Enrollment of program: 40

Financial Information:
Tuition, resident: $759
Tuition, non-resident: $1,452

Navarro College

3200 West Seventh Avenue
Corsicana, TX 75110-4818

Contact Information:
Telephone: 903-874-6501 ext. 367
Fax: 903-874-4636
E-mail: alane@nav.cc.tx.us
Web: www.nav.cc.tx.us

Program Information:
Program begins: September
Duration of program: 24 months

Application Information:
Enrollment of program: 45
Transfer students are accepted.

Financial Information:
Tuition, resident: $540
Tuition, non-resident: $700

Employment Profile:
% of students who pass the boards on their first try: 100
% employed within the first 6 months following graduation: 94
Average starting salary: $28,000

North Central Texas College

601 East Hickory Street Suite B
Denton, TX 76201-4305

Contact Information:
Telephone: 940-380-0450
Fax: 940-380-9401
E-mail: khumbert@nctc.cc.tx.us
Web: www.nctc.cc.tx.us

Program Information:
Program begins: August
Duration of program: 24 months

Application Information:
Enrollment of program: 77

Financial Information:
Tuition, resident: $776
Tuition, non-resident: $1,252

Utah

Salt Lake Community College

4600 South Redwood Road
PO Box 30808
Salt Lake City, UT 84130-0808

Contact Information:
Telephone: 801-957-4314
Fax: 801-957-5708
E-mail: mancinle@slcc.edu
Web: www.slcc.edu

Program Information:
Duration of program: 24 months

Financial Information:
Tuition, resident: $1,588
Tuition, non-resident: $4,948

Vermont

Champlain College
163 South Willard Street
PO Box 670
Burlington, VT 05402-0670

Contact Information:
Telephone: 802-865-6490
Fax: 802-860-2750
E-mail: lepsic@champlain.edu
Web: www.champlain.edu

Program Information:
Program begins: August
Duration of program: 16 months

Application Information:
Enrollment of program: 40
Transfer students are accepted.

Financial Information:
Average cost of books: $500
% of students receiving aid: 85

Employment Profile:
% of students who pass the boards on their first try: 100
Average starting salary: $27,000

Virginia

College of Health Sciences
PO Box 13186
Roanoke, VA 24016

Contact Information:
Telephone: 540-985-4020
Fax: 540-985-9773
E-mail: dhaynes@health.chs.edu
Web: www.chs.edu

Program Information:
Program begins: August
Duration of program: 22 months
Evening or weekend classes are available.

Application Information:
Enrollment of program: 60

Financial Information:
Tuition, resident: $10,667
Tuition, non-resident: $19,734
Average cost of books: $800
% of students receiving aid: 70

Employment Profile:
% of students who pass the boards on their first try: 98
% employed within the first 6 months following graduation: 75
Average starting salary: $30,000

Tidewater Community College
Virginia Beach Campus
1700 College Crescent
Virginia Beach, VA 23456

Contact Information:
Telephone: 757-822-7273
Fax: 757-427-1338
E-mail: loriwc@yahoo.com
Web: www.tc.cc.va.us/vabeach/hstdiv/ota/index.htm

Program Information:
Program begins: May
Duration of program: 12 months

Application Information:
Enrollment of program: 16
Transfer students are accepted.

Financial Information:
Tuition, non-resident: $162
Average cost of books: $300

Employment Profile:
% of students who pass the boards on their first try: 99
% employed within the first 6 months following graduation: 20
Average starting salary: $28,000

Washington

Yakima Valley Community College
16th Avenue and Nob Hill Boulevard
PO Box 22520
Yakima, WA 98907-2520

Contact Information:
Telephone: 509-574-4951
Fax: 509-574-4734
E-mail: yakima.cc.wa.us
Web: www.yvcc.cc.wa.us

Program Information:
Program begins: September
Duration of program: 18 months

Financial Information:
Tuition, resident: $1,659
Tuition, non-resident: $6,309

Wisconsin

Fox Valley Technical College
1825 North Bluemound Drive
PO Box 2277
Appleton, WI 54912-2277

Contact Information:
Telephone: 920-735-4843
Fax: 920-735-2582
E-mail: holz@foxvalley.tec.wi.us
Web: www.foxvalley.tec.wi.us

Program Information:
Program begins: September, January
Duration of program: 21 months

Application Information:
Enrollment of program: 114
Transfer students are accepted.

Financial Information:
Tuition, resident: $2,100
Tuition, non-resident: $14,036
Average cost of books: $700

Employment Profile:
% of students who pass the boards on their first try: 95
% employed within the first 6 months following graduation: 33
Average starting salary: $24,000

Madison Area Technical College
211 North Carroll Street
Madison, WI 53703-2285

Contact Information:
Telephone: 608-258-2314
Fax: 608-258-2480
Web: www.madison.tec.wi.us

Program Information:
Program begins: August, January
Degrees offered: Associate's, 20 months

Application Information:
Transfer students are accepted.

Financial Information:
Tuition, resident: $3,200
Tuition, non-resident: $15,000
Average cost of books: $700

Employment Profile:
% of students who pass the boards on their first try: 100

Milwaukee Area Technical College
700 West State Street
Milwaukee, WI 53233-1443

Contact Information:
Telephone: 414-297-7158
Fax: 414-297-6851
E-mail: breakerj@milwaukee.tec
Web: www.matc.edu

Program Information:
Program begins: August, January
Duration of program: 18 months

Application Information:
Enrollment of program: 100
Transfer students are accepted.

Financial Information:
Tuition, resident: $1,639
Tuition, non-resident: $11,040

Employment Profile:
% of students who pass the boards on their first try: 95
Average starting salary: $23,000

Western Wisconsin Technical College
304 North Sixth Street
PO Box C 0908
LaCrosse, WI 54602-0908

Contact Information:
Telephone: 608-789-4757
Fax: 608-785-9194

E-mail: olsond@email.western.tec.wi.us
Web: www.western.tec.wi.us

Program Information:
Program begins: August
Duration of program: 20 months

Application Information:
Enrollment of program: 54
Transfer students are accepted.

Financial Information:
Tuition, resident: $2,364
Tuition, non-resident: $16,165
Average cost of books: $790
% of students receiving aid: 53

Employment Profile:
% of students who pass the boards on their first try: 100
Average starting salary: $23,500

Wyoming

Casper College
125 College Drive
Casper, WY 82601

Contact Information:
Telephone: 307-268-2867
Fax: 307-268-2891
E-mail: mwonser@acad.cc.whecn.edu
Web: www.cc.whecn.edu

Program Information:
Program begins: June
Duration of program: 12 months

Application Information:
Enrollment of program: 12
Transfer students are accepted.

Financial Information:
Tuition, resident: $410
Tuition, non-resident: $1,110
Average cost of books: $600
% of students receiving aid: 80

Employment Profile:
% of students who pass the boards on their first try: 60

Ophthalmic Dispensing Optician

Thomas M. Hunter, BA, ABOC, NCLC
Program Director
Ophthalmic Dispensing
Camden County College
Blackwood, New Jersey

Job Description

What Do They Do?

An optician is a healthcare professional who analyzes and interprets eyewear prescriptions written by ophthalmologists and optometrists in order to recommend and provide appropriate ophthalmic devices. These include eyeglasses, contact lenses and other types of optical goods. Opticians may also work with people who are nearly blind by fitting them with low vision devices to help them to read. The duty of the optician is to provide the patient or client with the best-informed choices for corrective eye care.

Most opticians are eyewear dispensers and work in a retail environment. It is the optician's job to greet the patient or customer and make them feel comfortable and ready to make important choices concerning their new eyewear. The optician analyzes the prescription and interviews clients to determine how their activities, job and hobbies may affect their eyewear needs. The optician then recommends the lenses that will be best for each wearer. He or she helps the client choose the right eyeglass frame by analyzing the client's facial shape and contour. It is important that the frame be the correct size and shape for both cosmetic and optical considerations. The optician then takes eye and facial measurements and formulates the frame and lenses to be made into eyeglasses. Many opticians fabricate the eyeglasses on their own, while others have them made at an optical laboratory. When the eyewear is completed, the optician fits and adjusts the glasses on the patient.

Type of Person

To be a successful optician, one must have the ability to interact and work closely with people and be able to solve problems. In many cases patient or clients may require time to grow accustomed to their new eyewear and will need to revisit the optician for refitting or other adjustments. The optician must have the patience to work with the person and resolve any difficulties expertly and efficiently.

Today's eyewear is a fashion statement. Opticians must be aware of this since many people wear eyewear because they desire a certain look or want to accessorize their wardrobes.

Optical professionals enjoy a career that consists of two worlds. As healthcare professionals, opticians can help people have the best vision possible. As members of the business world, they can experience the satisfaction of offering their patients or clients the best and most up-to-date optical products available.

With Whom Do They Work?

Opticians come in contact with other healthcare professionals such as ophthalmologists, optometrists, ophthalmic assistants, and ophthalmic medical technologists.

Employment

Places of Employment

Many opticians are independent business people who operate their own optical stores. Some fit eyeglasses; others choose to fit only contact lenses. Other places of employment for opticians include:

- doctor's offices, where they dispense eyeglasses and contact lenses exclusively to the doctor's patients
- large medical centers and eye hospitals
- frame and lens manufacturing companies, where they are employed as sales representatives

Employment Outlook

The employment opportunities for opticians are excellent. The *Jobs Rated Almanac* lists opticianry as number 76 out of the top 250 jobs.[1] In most areas of the country there are more jobs available than there are opticians to fill them.

There are many reasons why the need for opticians is great. First, millions of the Baby Boom generation are now reaching the age at which they will need eyewear to read. An increase in personal computer users has produced the need for special lenses to help people see screens clearly and comfortably. In addition, safety eyewear is now required for people who work wherever there is danger of eye injury. The demand for contact lenses is also greater than ever. Finally, new technology in both spectacle and contact lenses is developing at a rapid pace.

The expansion of large optical chains has created a great demand for qualified opticians. Recently, ophthalmologists have begun to open dispensaries in their offices creating even more positions for opticians.

Salary

Dispensing opticians earn an overall starting salary of $27,432. Owners, managers, and certified graduates of opticianry schools have higher earnings, as do opticians who work in states that require licensure.[2]

Educational Programs

Length

There are many community colleges and technical schools offering two-year opticianry programs. Students can earn an Associate's in Applied Science Degree, which is the terminal degree for opticianry.

Prerequisites

Candidates for these programs must have a high school diploma or equivalent and two years of high school algebra. They should also have good oral communication and writing skills. Some schools require SAT scores to be submitted, while others offer basic skills testing that will show the prospective student's level of math, reading, and writing skills.

Curriculum

The ophthalmic science curriculum consists of courses in optic principles, including the theory light, geometric optics, lens theory, anatomy of the eye, contact lens fitting, eyeglass dispensing, lens grinding and eyeglass assembly. Courses are generally fifty-percent classroom lecture and fifty-percent laboratory work. A clinical experience at the campus optical dispensary or an outside co-operative at an optical store or office is part of the course of study. This will give the student actual practice in the field. Upon graduation, the student may take a state licensing examination, national opticianry certification, and national contact lens certification examinations.

Accrediting Body

The Commission on Opticianry Accreditation
10341 Democracy Lane
Fairfax, VA 22030-2521
Telephone: 703-352-8028
Fax: 703-691-3929
E-mail: coa@erols.com

Certification Boards

There are two certification boards. Candidates for the American Board of Opticianry examination should have a minimum of one year of on the job training or one year of formal opticianry education. Candidates for the National Contact Lens Examiner examination should have a minimum of two years on the job training or two semesters of advanced contact lens classes.

The American Board of Opticianry
10341 Democracy Lane
Fairfax, VA 22030
Telephone: 800-296-1379
Fax: 703-691-3929
E-mail: aboncle@opticians.org
Web address: www.abo.org

National Contact Lens Examiners
10341 Democracy Lane
Fairfax, VA 22030
Telephone: 800-296-1379
Fax: 703-691-3929
E-mail: aboncle@opticians.org

Advice for Potential Students

Candidates should apply one year in advance of anticipated enrollment. Most programs have limited enrollment due to lab and classroom space. Have transcripts of previous college credit or high school available, as well as placement test or SAT scores if required. Schedule an interview with the program director of your school of choice as soon as possible. Speak to current students and graduates of the program for feedback and information about the program and the profession.

For Additional Information

Organizations

The National Federation of Opticianry Schools
10341 Democracy Lane
Fairfax, VA 22030-2521
Telephone: 703-691-8357

Opticians Association of America
10341 Democracy Lane
Fairfax, VA 22030-2521
Telephone: 703-691-8355

Publications

20/20 Magazine. Jobson Publishing Corporation LLC, 100 Avenue of the Americas, New York, NY 10013. www.2020mag.com.

A monthly publication that contains articles and advertisements about the latest frame fashions and lenses. Also includes articles on dispensing, sales, and communications.

Vision Monday. Jobson Publishing Corporation LLC, 100 Avenue of the Americas, New York, NY 10013. www.visionmonday.com

A biweekly business journal for the optical industry. Contains financial news, personnel changes, and general interest articles for the optical business community.

Contact Lens Spectrum. Boucher Communications, Inc., 535 Connecticut Avenue, Suite 104-A, Norwalk CT 06854-1722. www.clspectrum.com

Source for clinical contact lens information for ophthalmologists, optometrists, and opticians. Contains articles on fitting techniques, patient care, products, and news.

Internet Resources

The American Board of Opticianry: www.abo.org
The Commission on Opticianry Accreditation: www.coaccreditation.com/
Contact Lens Spectrum: www.clspectrum.com
OptiCareers: www.opticareers.com
Opticians Association of America: www.opticians.org
National Contact Lens Examiners: www.abo.org
National Federation of Opticianry Schools: www.nfos.org

Connecticut

Middlesex Community-Technical College

Ophthalmic Design and Dispensing
100 Training Hill Road
Middletown, CT 06457

Contact Information:
Telephone: 860-343-5845
E-mail: mx_dennis@commnet.edu

Program Information:
Program begins: September, March
Duration of program: 20 months
Evening or weekend classes are available.

Application Information:
Enrollment of program: 50
Transfer students are accepted.

Financial Information:
Tuition, resident: $907
Tuition, non-resident: $2,719
Average cost of books: $500
% of students receiving aid: 25

Employment Profile:
% of students who pass the boards on their first try: 95
% employed within the first 6 months following graduation: 100
Average starting salary: $30,000

Florida

Miami-Dade Community College

Vision Care Technology - Opticianry
950 Northwest 20th Street
Miami, FL 33127

Contact Information:
Telephone: 305-237-4039
Fax: 305-237-4278
E-mail: brownje@mdcc.edu
Web: www.mdcc.edu

Program Information:
Program begins: August
Degrees offered: Certificate program, 12 months; Associate's, 20 months

Application Information:
Enrollment of program: 50
Transfer students are accepted.

Financial Information:
Tuition, resident: $2,300
Tuition, non-resident: $7,800
Average cost of books: $400
% of students receiving aid: 50

Employment Profile:
% of students who pass the boards on their first try: 90
% employed within the first 6 months following graduation: 100
Average starting salary: $30,000

Georgia

DeKalb Technical Institute

495 North Indian Creek Drive
Clarkston, GA 30021

Contact Information:
Telephone: 404-297-9522 ext. 1207
Fax: 404-294-6496
E-mail: tschulz@mindspring.com
Web: www.dekalb.tec.ga.us

Program Information:
Program begins: October
Degrees offered: Associate's, 18 months

Application Information:
Enrollment of program: 16
Transfer students are accepted.

Financial Information:
Tuition, resident: $900
Tuition, non-resident: $1,656
Average cost of books: $700
% of students receiving aid: 90

Employment Profile:
% of students who pass the boards on their first try: 88
% employed within the first 6 months following graduation: 100
Average starting salary: $23,000

Massachusetts

Holyoke Community College

303 Homestead Avenue
Holyoke, MA 01040

Contact Information:
Telephone: 413-552-2474
Fax: 413-534-8975
E-mail: tsbalbi@hcc.mass.edu
Web: www.hcc..mass.edu

Program Information:
Program begins: September
Degrees offered: Certificate program, 8 months; Associate's, 16 months

Application Information:
Enrollment of program: 15
Transfer students are accepted.

Financial Information:
Tuition, resident: $2,859
Average cost of books: $300

Employment Profile:
% of students who pass the boards on their first try: 80
% employed within the first 6 months following graduation: 80
Average starting salary: $24,000

Michigan

Ferris State University

College of Allied Health Sciences
200 Ferris Drive
Big Rapids, MI 49307

Contact Information:
Telephone: 731-591-2224
Fax: 731-591-3788
Web: www.ferris.edu

Program Information:
Program begins: August
Duration of program: 20 months

Application Information:
Enrollment of program: 26
Transfer students are accepted.

Financial Information:
Tuition, resident: $4,560
Tuition, non-resident: $8,025
Average cost of books: $800
% of students receiving aid: 75

Employment Profile:
% of students who pass the boards on their first try: 98
% employed within the first 6 months following graduation: 100
Average starting salary: $22,300

New Jersey

Camden County College

PO Box 200
Blackwood, NJ 08012

Contact Information:
Telephone: 609-227-7200 ext. 4322
Fax: 609-227-4107
E-mail: tmhunter@bellatlantic.net
Web: www.camdencc.edu

Program Information:
Program begins: January
Degrees offered: Associate's, 24 months
Evening or weekend classes are available.

Application Information:
Enrollment of program: 100
Transfer students are accepted.

Financial Information:
Tuition, resident: $2,065
Tuition, non-resident: $2,205
Average cost of books: $250

Employment Profile:
% of students who pass the boards on their first try: 80
% employed within the first 6 months following graduation: 100
Average starting salary: $33,000

Essex County College

303 University Avenue
Newark, NJ 07102

Contact Information:
Telephone: 973-877-3367

Program Information:
Program begins: August, January
Duration of program: 24 months
Evening or weekend classes are available.

Application Information:
Enrollment of program: 24

Financial Information:
Tuition, resident: $1,600
Tuition, non-resident: $3,200

Raritan Valley Community College
Ophthalmic Science Program
PO Box 3300
Somerville, NJ 08876

Contact Information:
Telephone: 908-526-1200 ext. 8277
Fax: 908-526-0253
E-mail: bthomas@raritan.val.edu
Web: www.raritanual.edu

Program Information:
Program begins: August
Duration of program: 24 months

Application Information:
Enrollment of program: 250
Transfer students are accepted.

Financial Information:
Tuition, resident: $1,040
Average cost of books: $100

Employment Profile:
% of students who pass the boards on their first try: 90
% employed within the first 6 months following graduation: 100
Average starting salary: $35,000

New York

CUNY New York City Technical College
300 Jay Street
Brooklyn, NY 11201

Contact Information:
Telephone: 718-260-5298
Web: www.nyctc.cuny.edu

Program Information:
Program begins: September
Duration of program: 21 months
Evening or weekend classes are available.

Application Information:
Enrollment of program: 225
Transfer students are accepted.

Financial Information:
Tuition, resident: $3,200
Tuition, non-resident: $6,800
Average cost of books: $400
% of students receiving aid: 50

Employment Profile:
% of students who pass the boards on their first try: 90
% employed within the first 6 months following graduation: 90
Average starting salary: $25,000

Erie Community College—North Campus
6205 Main Street
Williamsville, NY 14221-7095

Contact Information:
Telephone: 716-851-1570
Fax: 716-851-1429
E-mail: well@ecc.edu
Web: www.suny.erie.edu

Program Information:
Program begins: Program begins quarterly.
Duration of program: 24 months

Application Information:
Enrollment of program: 55
Transfer students are accepted.

Financial Information:
Average cost of books: $200

Employment Profile:
% of students who pass the boards on their first try: 90
% employed within the first 6 months following graduation: 75
Average starting salary: $22,000

Tennessee

Roane State Community College
Opticianry
276 Patton Lane
Harriman, TN 37748

Contact Information:
Telephone: 423-882-4594
Fax: 423-882-4549
E-mail: goggin_mt@a1.rscc.cc.tn.us
Web: www.rscc.cc.tn.us

Program Information:
Program begins: August
Degrees offered: Diploma, 21 months

Application Information:
Enrollment of program: 40
Transfer students are accepted.

Financial Information:
Tuition, non-resident: $3,386
Average cost of books: $250

Employment Profile:
% of students who pass the boards on their first try: 95
% employed within the first 6 months following graduation: 95
Average starting salary: $25,000

Texas

El Paso Community College
Ophthalmic Technology
PO Box 20500
El Paso, TX 79998

Contact Information:
Telephone: 915-831-4075
Fax: 915-831-4114
E-mail: mannyb@epcc.edu
Web: www.epcc.edu

Program Information:
Program begins: September, January
Degrees offered: Certificate program, 12 months; Associate's, 24 months
Evening or weekend classes are available.

Application Information:
Enrollment of program: 20
Transfer students are accepted.

Financial Information:
Tuition, resident: $960
Tuition, non-resident: $1,400
Average cost of books: $400
% of students receiving aid: 70

Employment Profile:
% of students who pass the boards on their first try: 85
% employed within the first 6 months following graduation: 100
Average starting salary: $13,000

Virginia

Tri-Service Optician Schools (TOPS)
NWS PO Box 350
Yorktown, VA 23691-0350

Contact Information:
Telephone: 757-887-7148
Fax: 757-887-4511
E-mail: nbwatson@nos5.med.navy.mil
Web: www.nostra.med.navy.mil

Program Information:
Duration of program: 6 months

Physical Therapist

Risa Granick, EdD, MPA, PT
Professor and Chair
Department of Rehabilitation Sciences
MCP Hahnemann University
Philadelphia, Pennsylvania

Job Description

What Do They Do?

Physical therapists are healthcare professionals who evaluate and treat patients with long-term disabilities or acute type injuries as well as healthy clients who seek to maintain fitness and health. They assess muscle strength and endurance as well as joint flexibility, teach gait as well as activities required for daily living, and evaluate and provide exercises for cardiovascular and pulmonary problems.

Physical therapists assume roles in rehabilitation, prevention, and health maintenance programs. Their patients and clients range in age from newborn infants to the elderly.

Physical therapists can also specialize in specific areas of care, such as orthopedics, sports medicine, pediatrics, geriatrics, long-term rehabilitation, hand rehabilitation, acute care, aquatics, women's health issues, cardiopulmonary care, critical care, or private practice.

Physical therapists' responsibilities include:

- Examination of the patient/client through history taking and carrying out specific tests and measurements
- Evaluation based on the examination data
- Diagnosis to help determine the best strategies for treatment
- Prognosis to help determine a plan of care (anticipated level of improvement and the time required to reach that level
- Intervention in carrying out a plan of care
- Modification of the plans of care based on the patient's/client's response to treatment

Physical therapists also serve as consultants and educators to other healthcare personnel and families, participate in administrative activities, and carry out clinical research.

Type of Person

Physical therapists like to study in the sciences, are problem solvers and critical thinkers, have good interpersonal skills, and enjoy working with people.

With Whom Do They Work?

Physical therapists supervise physical therapist assistants and work with many other healthcare professionals, including physicians, speech language pathologists, nurses, athletic trainers, occupational therapists, exercise physiologists, respiratory therapists, psychologists, social workers, podiatrists, facility administrators, and case managers.

Employment

Places of Employment

Although many physical therapists practice in acute care hospitals or inpatient rehabilitation centers, more than 65 percent practice in private PT offices, community health centers, sports facilities, nursing homes, home health agencies, industrial health centers, schools, or pediatric centers.[1] They also work in research centers and teach in colleges or universities.

Employment Outlook

Currently, more than 90,000 physical therapists practice in the United States, treating nearly one million patients and clients a day. The American healthcare system has changed in recent years in the way it provides for and reimburses health services in a managed care environment. This change has created a slight decrease in the need for physical therapists. A recent American Physical Therapy Association (APTA) survey indicates there is currently a 2 percent surplus of physical therapists.[2] This situation will probably reverse in the next few years as an aging population puts more demands on the healthcare system. The redistribution of healthcare personnel and the development of creative and innovative new healthcare roles will also enhance employment opportunities in the future.

Salary

Average salary is approximately $55,000 per year. This varies depending on geographical location and practice setting. The APTA states that physical therapists have the potential to earn more than $100,000 annually as they progress through their careers.[3]

Educational Programs

Length

The APTA is encouraging students pursuing a career in PT to enter the profession with a post-baccalaureate degree. This degree will allow students to obtain a broad background in the liberal arts and allow for more time in the PT curriculum to integrate the vast amount of technology and scientific literature necessary to meet today's practice expectations. The majority of existing PT educational programs in the United States already offer a Master's degree. Although baccalaureate programs currently exist, the Commission on Accreditation in Physical Therapy Education will no longer accredit them as of January 1, 2002.

The minimum educational requirement in 2002 will be a Master's degree in PT (MPT or MSPT). Some programs have developed a clinical doctorate (PDT) as well. There are four different ways to earn a post-baccalaureate degree. All programs, regardless of their configuration and degree offered, are designed to provide a broad educational fouation in the discipline. Curricula vary based on the program's mission and strengths of its faculty. (The configuration numbers below refer to the number of years students spend taking prerequisite and professional course work or in earning a Bachelor's degree in a related field prior to beginning professional study.)

1. Integrative 5- or 6-Year Program: students are admitted as a freshman into the college or university and concurrently into the PT program. They complete the liberal arts, prerequisite sciences, and the professional curriculum to earn both a Bachelor's and Master's degree in PT.
2. 2+3 or 3+2 Programs: students complete the liberal arts and prerequisite science courses (2 or 3 years) before transferring into

the professional curriculum (2 or 3 years). The institution awards two degrees, the Bachelor's and Master's in PT.

3. 4+2 or 4+2.5 Program: students earn a Bachelor's degree (4 years) in a related area and fulfill liberal arts and science prerequisite courses for admission into a graduate program. The graduate curriculum provides 2 or 2.5 years of professional study in PT leading to the Master's degree.
4. 4+3 Program: students earn a Bachelor's degree (4 years) in a related area and fulfill liberal arts and science prerequisite courses for admission into graduate school. The graduate curriculum provides 3 years of professional education leading to the clinical doctorate in PT.

Prerequisites

1. Integrative 5- or 6-Year Program
   - High school diploma
2. 2+3 or 3+2 Programs. Prior to transferring into the professional curriculum, the following course work is required:
   - 2 courses in general biology with laboratory
   - 1–2 courses in anatomy and physiology
   - 2 courses in general chemistry with laboratory
   - 2 courses in general physics with laboratory
   - 1–3 courses in psychology
   - prescribed course work in English, mathematics, and speech and courses in humanities and social sciences (varies from program to program)
   - volunteer or work-related experience
   - Allied Health Admissions Test or Graduate Record Examination Test
3. 4+2, 4+2.5, and 4+3 Programs. Fulfill the following prerequisites:
   - Earn a Bachelor's degree
   - 3–5 courses in biology, which should include general biology with laboratory; human or mammalian physiology or combined courses in anatomy and; physiology with laboratory; other specific biology courses vary from program to program
   - 2 courses in general chemistry with laboratory
   - 2 courses in general physics with laboratory
   - 1-3 courses in psychology
   - statistics
   - 5–9 courses in the humanities and social sciences
   - volunteer or work-related experience
   - Graduate Record Examination Test

Curriculum

1. Integrative 5- or 6-Year Curriculum

   Follow a prescribed liberal arts and science-intensive pre-professional curriculum leading to professional coursework in the PT sciences such as gross anatomy, neuroscience, pathology, pharmacology, kinesiology, PT theory and practice, ethics, professional issues, organization and administration, and research. Clinical affiliation experiences are integrated throughout the professional curriculum.
2. 2+3 or 3+2 Programs

   Complete all liberal arts and science-intensive pre-professional courses before being admitted into the professional program. The PT curriculum consists of PT sciences, PT theory and practice, ethics, professional issues, organization and administration, and research. Clinical affiliation experiences are integrated throughout the professional curriculum.
3. 4+2, 4+2.5, 4+3 Programs

   Earn a Bachelor's degree and enter a program to complete the professional curriculum only. Course work includes PT sciences, PT theory and practice, ethics, professional issues, organization and administration, and research. Clinical affiliation experiences are integrated throughout the professional curriculum (4+2, 4+2.5). A clinical internship is the final clinical experience in the doctoral program (4+3).

Accrediting Body

The Commission on Accreditation in Physical Therapy Education of the American Physical Therapy Association is the accrediting body for all PT programs whether the terminal degree is at the Bachelor's, Master's, or Doctoral level. Beginning in 2002, the Commission will only accredit the master and clinical doctorate degree programs as the first degree to practice in the profession. Only graduates from accredited programs are eligible for licensure to practice.

Commission on Accreditation in Physical Therapy Education (CAPTE)
American Physical Therapy Association
1111 North Fairfax Street
Alexandria, VA 22314
Telephone: 800-999-APTA
Web address: www.apta.org

Licensure Board

After graduation, candidates must pass a state-administered national examination. Other requirements for PT practice vary from state to state according to PT practice acts or state regulations governing PT. Information can be obtained by contacting your state licensing board. Contact the Federation of State Boards of Physical Therapy (FSBPT) for a list of state agencies.

Federation of State Boards of Physical Therapy
509 Wythe Street
Alexandria, VA 22314
Telephone: 703-299-3100 or 800-200-3031
Fax: 703-299-3110 or 800-981-3031
Web address: www.fsbpt.org

Advice for Potential Students

Look for the "best fit" between student and program. If you are in high school and know you want to be a physical therapist, look at those programs that admit you as a college freshman. If you are not sure if you want a career in PT, start at a college or university as a biology, psychology, sports science, or pre-physical therapy major and begin doing some volunteer work in PT or work as a physical therapy aide. By doing this, you will begin to fulfill prerequisite course work and determine if PT is the right career choice for you. If your volunteer experiences reinforce your career decision, try to transfer as a junior or senior into a PT program; however, if you are happy in your undergraduate major, earn your Bachelor's degree then seek admission into a post-baccalaureate master or clinical doctorate degree program.

Admission into PT programs is competitive. You should maintain an undergraduate grade point average in the A–B range since students seeking admission into the post-baccalaureate programs need to show strong academic records. Admission committees look favorably at semester grade point increases with advancing levels of education. Some programs do not look favorably upon students repeating courses to earn a higher grade; they would rather see additional course work so check with the program that you plan on applying to before repeating a course. Admission committees look favorably on your volunteer or work-related experience as a PT aide and letters of recommendation from physical therapists and academic reference from your science professors.

Attend open houses or career days at the institutions you are considering. Try to meet with the program director or career counselor to evaluate your high school or college transcript. These individuals can offer advice to enhance a favorable admissions decision. Some programs require an interview for acceptance. If an interview is not required, ask permission from the program director to speak with some students to learn about the curriculum and its methods of instruction to determine if it meets your personal learning styles. Ask questions related to how many of the graduates pass the licensing examination on the first attempt as well as the second try. Also try to determine how long it takes the graduate to secure a position following graduation.

Talk to therapists at the facility(ies) at which you volunteered or worked about students from various programs. Determine their impressions of different programs in terms of preparing students for the clinical education experiences and first employment expectations.

For Additional Information

Organizations

American Physical Therapy Association
1111 North Fairfax Street
Alexandria, VA 22314
Telephone: 800-999-APTA
Web address: www.apta.org

Publications

Books

O'Sullivan: *Physical Rehabilitation—Assessment and Treatment,* 4th edition. Philadelphia: F.A. Davis Company, 2000.

Pagliarulo. *Introduction to Physical Therapy,* St. Louis: Mosby-Year Book, Inc., 1996.

A Future in Physical Therapy. Fairfax: American Physical Therapy Association. Order No. PR-23-A, APTA Service Center (800-999-2782, ext. 3395) or through Fax-on-Demand (800-399-2782).

Journals

Advance for Physical Therapists and Physical Therapist Assistants. Merion Publications, 2900 Horizon Drive, King of Prussia PA 19406. www.advanceforpt.com

A national, biweekly publication that reports on advances in research, reimbursement, and political and clinical news.

PT—Magazine. American Association of Physical Therapy, 1111 North Fairfax Street, Alexandria, VA 22314. www.apta.org/pt_magazine

The professional issues magazine of the American Physical Therapy Association (APTA). It provides legislative, healthcare, human interest, and association news and serves as a forum for discussion of professional issues and ideas in physical therapy practice.

Internet Resources

American Physical Therapy Association: www.apta.org
Federation of State Boards of Physical Therapy: www.fsbpt.org
MCP Hahnemann University, Department of Rehabilitation Sciences, Entry-Level Doctoral Program in Physical Therapy: www.mcphu.edu/shp/depts/rehab

Alabama

University of Alabama at Birmingham

School of Health Related Professions
900 South 19th Street/102 Bishop Building
Birmingham, AL 35294-2030

Contact Information:
Telephone: 701-777-2831
Fax: 701-777-4199
E-mail: sshaw@uab.edu
Web: www.uab.edu

Program Information:
Program begins: August
Duration of program: 24 months

Application Information:
Enrollment of program: 50

Financial Information:
Tuition, resident: $11,136
Tuition, non-resident: $22,272
Average cost of books: $560

Employment Profile:
% of students who pass the boards on their first try: 98
% employed within the first 6 months following graduation: 50
Average starting salary: $40,000

California

California State University—Fresno

2345 East San Ramon Avenue/MS-29
Fresno, CA 93740-8031

Contact Information:
Telephone: 559-278-2625
Fax: 559-278-3635
E-mail: robert_martin@csufresno.edu
Web: www.csufresno.edu

Program Information:
Program begins: August
Duration of program: 36 months

Financial Information:
Tuition, resident: $1,806
Tuition, non-resident: $3,690

California State University—Sacramento

College of Health and Human Services
Sacramento, CA 95819-6020

Contact Information:
Telephone: 916-278-6426
Fax: 916-278-5053
E-mail: mcgintys@csus.edu
Web: www.csus.edu

Program Information:
Program begins: September
Degrees offered: Certificate program, 6 months; Master's, 30 months

Application Information:
Enrollment of program: 32

Financial Information:
Tuition, resident: $1,934
Tuition, non-resident: $8,836
Average cost of books: $1,500

Employment Profile:
% of students who pass the boards on their first try: 90
% employed within the first 6 months following graduation: 100

Chapman University

School of Physical Therapy
One University Drive
Orange, CA 92666

Contact Information:
Telephone: 714-744-7620
Fax: 714-744-7621
Web: www.chapman.edu

Program Information:
Program begins: May, August
Duration of program: 24 months

Application Information:
Enrollment of program: 96

Financial Information:
Tuition, resident: $27,225
Average cost of books: $2,500
% of students receiving aid: 100

Employment Profile:
% of students who pass the boards on their first try: 90
% employed within the first 6 months following graduation: 80
Average starting salary: $45,000

Loma Linda University

Department of Physical Therapy
School of Allied Health Professions
Loma Linda, CA 92350

Contact Information:
Telephone: 909-824-4632 ext. 47251
Fax: 909-824-4291
E-mail: larry-chinnock@sahp.llu.edu
Web: www.llu.edu/llu/sahp

Program Information:
Program begins: September
Duration of program: 36 months

Application Information:
Enrollment of program: 52
Transfer students are accepted.

Financial Information:
Average cost of books: $150
% of students receiving aid: 98

Employment Profile:
% of students who pass the boards on their first try: 83
% employed within the first 6 months following graduation: 100
Average starting salary: $47,500

Samuel Merritt College

370 Hawthorne Avenue
Oakland, CA 94609

Contact Information:
Telephone: 510-869-6241
Fax: 510-869-6282
Web: www.samuelmerritt.edu

Program Information:
Program begins: August
Duration of program: 30 months

Application Information:
Enrollment of program: 120

Financial Information:
Average cost of books: $1,500
% of students receiving aid: 90

Employment Profile:
% of students who pass the boards on their first try: 99
% employed within the first 6 months following graduation: 100
Average starting salary: $50,455

San Fransico State University

374 Parnassus
San Francisco, CA 94143-0736

Contact Information:
Telephone: 904-826-0084
Fax: 904-826-4193
E-mail: byl@itsa.ucsf.edu

Program Information:
Program begins: May
Duration of program: 27 months
Evening or weekend classes are available.

Application Information:
Enrollment of program: 32

Financial Information:
Tuition, resident: $2,900
Tuition, non-resident: $7,000
Average cost of books: $2,000
% of students receiving aid: 70

Employment Profile:
% of students who pass the boards on their first try: 100
% employed within the first 6 months following graduation: 90
Average starting salary: $48,000

University of Southern California

Biokinesiology & Physical Therapy
1540 East Alcazar Street/CHP 155
Los Angeles, CA 90089-9006

Contact Information:
Telephone: 334-434-3575
Fax: 334-434-3822
E-mail: vorcas@hsc.usc.edu
Web: www.chp.hsc.usc.edu

Program Information:
Program begins: August, September
Duration of program: 32 months

Application Information:
Enrollment of program: 254

Western University of Health Sciences

Department of Physical Therapy Education
309 East Second Street
Pomona, CA 91766-1889

Contact Information:
Telephone: 909-469-5294
Fax: 909-469-5692
Web: www.westernu.edu

Program Information:
Program begins: September
Duration of program: 28 months

Application Information:
Enrollment of program: 108

Financial Information:
Average cost of books: $820
% of students receiving aid: 95

Employment Profile:
% of students who pass the boards on their first try: 94
% employed within the first 6 months following graduation: 90

Colorado

Regis University

Department of Physical Therapy
3333 Regis Boulevard G-4
Denver, CO 80221-1099

Contact Information:
Telephone: 303-458-4340
Fax: 303-964-5474
Web: www.regis.edu

Program Information:
Program begins: January
Degrees offered: Master's, 24 months

Application Information:
Enrollment of program: 100

Financial Information:
Average cost of books: $1,500

Employment Profile:
% of students who pass the boards on their first try: 90

University of Colorado Health Science Center

Health Sciences Center
4200 East Ninth Avenue/Box C244
Denver, CO 80262

Contact Information:
Telephone: 604-822-7404
Fax: 604-822-7624
E-mail: carolyn.heriza@uchsc.edu
Web: www.uchsc.edu

Program Information:
Program begins: January
Duration of program: 24 months

Application Information:
Enrollment of program: 114

Financial Information:
Tuition, resident: $17,425
Tuition, non-resident: $35,695
% of students receiving aid: 95

Employment Profile:
% of students who pass the boards on their first try: 98

Connecticut

Quinnipiac College

School of Health Sciences
Mt. Carmel Avenue
Hamden, CT 06518

Contact Information:
Telephone: 203-288-5251
Fax: 203-288-8706
E-mail: tantorski@quinnipiac.edu
Web: www.quinnipiac.edu

Program Information:
Program begins: June
Duration of program: 60 months

Application Information:
Enrollment of program: 500

Financial Information:
Tuition, resident: $14,160
Average cost of books: $600
% of students receiving aid: 69

District of Columbia

Howard University

College of Pharmacy, Nursing & Allied Health
6th and Bryant Streets Northwest
Washington, DC 20059

Contact Information:
Telephone: 202-806-7613
Fax: 202-462-6194
E-mail: jdanoff@howard.edu
Web: www.howard.edu

Program Information:
Program begins: August
Duration of program: 36 months

Florida

Florida International University

Department of Physical Therapy
College of Health
Miami, FL 33199

Contact Information:
Telephone: 305-348-3831
Fax: 305-348-1240
E-mail: stprix@fiu.edu
Web: www.fiu.edu

Program Information:
Program begins: January, May, September
Duration of program: 30 months

Application Information:
Enrollment of program: 123
Transfer students are accepted.

Financial Information:
Tuition, resident: $2,000
Average cost of books: $900
% of students receiving aid: 40

Employment Profile:
% employed within the first 6 months following graduation: 30

Nova Southeastern University

Health Professions Division
3200 South University Drive
Ft. Lauderdale, FL 33328

Contact Information:
Telephone: 954-262-1662
Fax: 954-262-1783
E-mail: hill@hpd.nova.edu
Web: www.nova.edu

Program Information:
Program begins: August
Duration of program: 24 months

Application Information:
Enrollment of program: 170

Financial Information:
Tuition, resident: $17,500
Tuition, non-resident: $19,850
Average cost of books: $1,500
% of students receiving aid: 98

Employment Profile:
Average starting salary: $41,000

University of Florida

Department of Physical Therapy
Box 100154 HSC
Gainesville, FL 32610-0154

Contact Information:
Telephone: 303-372-9143
Fax: 303-372-9016
Web: www.hp.ufl.edu

Program Information:
Program begins: August
Duration of program: 36 months

Financial Information:
Tuition, resident: $2,700

University of Miami

School of Medicine
5915 Ponce de Leon Boulevard/5th Floor
Coral Gables, FL 33146

Contact Information:
Telephone: 410-706-5658
Fax: 410-706-6387
E-mail: shayes@miami.edu
Web: www.miami.edu

Program Information:
Program begins: September
Duration of program: 31 months

Application Information:
Enrollment of program: 180

Financial Information:
Tuition, resident: $18,000
Average cost of books: $450
% of students receiving aid: 90

Employment Profile:
% of students who pass the boards on their first try: 96
% employed within the first 6 months following graduation: 20
Average starting salary: $38,500

Georgia

Armstrong Atlantic State University

11935 Abercorn Street
Savannah, GA 31419-1997

Contact Information:
Telephone: 912-921-2327

Fax: 912-921-5838
E-mail: lakedavi@mail.armstrong.edu
Web: www.armstrong.edu

Program Information:
Program begins: September
Duration of program: 16 months

Application Information:
Enrollment of program: 55
Transfer students are accepted.

Financial Information:
Tuition, resident: $2,460
Tuition, non-resident: $8,970
Average cost of books: $800

Employment Profile:
% of students who pass the boards on their first try: 88
% employed within the first 6 months following graduation: 66

Medical College of Georgia

Department of Physical Therapy
School of Allied Health Sciences
Augusta, GA 30912-0800

Contact Information:
Telephone: 514-398-4523
Fax: 514-398-6360
Web: www.mcg.edu

Program Information:
Program begins: August
Duration of program: 27 months

Application Information:
Enrollment of program: 174
Transfer students are accepted.

Financial Information:
Tuition, resident: $7,293
Tuition, non-resident: $29,172

Idaho

Idaho State University

Department of Physical and Occupational Therapy
College of Health Professions/Box 8002
Pocatello, ID 83209

Contact Information:
Telephone: 208-236-4095
Fax: 208-236-4962
Web: www.isu.edu

Program Information:
Program begins: May
Duration of program: 36 months

Application Information:
Enrollment of program: 72

Financial Information:
Tuition, resident: $6,200
Tuition, non-resident: $14,420
Average cost of books: $1,500
% of students receiving aid: 50

Employment Profile:
% of students who pass the boards on their first try: 100
% employed within the first 6 months following graduation: 30
Average starting salary: $41,000

Illinois

Bradley University

Department of Physical Therapy
1501 West Bradley Avenue
Peoria, IL 61625

Contact Information:
Telephone: 309-677-3489
Fax: 309-677-3445
E-mail: jun@bradley.edu
Web: www.bradley.edu/academics

Program Information:
Program begins: August
Duration of program: 27 months

Application Information:
Enrollment of program: 24

Financial Information:
Average cost of books: $1,500

Finch University of Health Science/ Chicago Medical School

School of Related Health Sciences
3333 Green Bay Road
North Chicago, IL 60064

Contact Information:
Telephone: 847-578-3307
Fax: 847-578-8816
E-mail: hoovenk@finchcms.edu
Web: www.finchcms.edu

Program Information:
Program begins: August
Duration of program: 36 months

Midwestern University

College of Health Sciences
555 31st Street
Downers Grove, IL 60515

Contact Information:
Telephone: 617-724-4841
Fax: 617-724-4854
Web: www.midwestern.edu

Program Information:
Program begins: August
Duration of program: 30 months

Financial Information:
Tuition, resident: $16,148
Tuition, non-resident: $18,492

Northwestern University Medical School

645 North Michigan Avenue/Suite 1100
Chicago, IL 60611-2814

Contact Information:
Telephone: 312-908-8160
Fax: 312-908-0741
E-mail: k-hayes@nwu.edu

Program Information:
Program begins: September
Degrees offered: Master's, 26 months

Application Information:
Enrollment of program: 60

Financial Information:
% of students receiving aid: 83

Employment Profile:
% of students who pass the boards on their first try: 95
% employed within the first 6 months following graduation: 95

University of Illinois at Chicago

College of Associated Health Professions
1919 West Taylor M/C 898/Department of Physical Therapy
Chicago, IL 60612

Contact Information:
Telephone: 302-831-8910
Fax: 302-831-4234
E-mail: sanlevi@uic.edu
Web: www.uic.edu

Program Information:
Program begins: June
Duration of program: 36 months

Application Information:
Enrollment of program: 48

Financial Information:
Tuition, resident: $4,481
Tuition, non-resident: $10,500
Average cost of books: $3,000

Employment Profile:
% employed within the first 6 months following graduation: 80

Indiana

Indiana University School of Medicine

1140 West Michigan Street/Room CF 326
Indianapolis, IN 46202-5119

Contact Information:
Telephone: 317-278-1875
Fax: 317-278-1876
E-mail: wsquille@iupui.edu
Web: www.sahs.iupui.edu

Program Information:
Program begins: August
Duration of program: 22 months

Application Information:
Enrollment of program: 120

Financial Information:
Average cost of books: $2,500
% of students receiving aid: 80

Employment Profile:
% of students who pass the boards on their first try: 90
% employed within the first 6 months following graduation: 50
Average starting salary: $35,000

University of Evansville

Department of Physical Therapy
1800 Lincoln Avenue
Evansville, IN 47722

Contact Information:
Telephone: 513-558-7477
Fax: 513-558-7474
E-mail: mk43@evansville.edu
Web: www.evansville.edu

Program Information:
Program begins: June
Degrees offered: Master's, 36 months

Application Information:
Enrollment of program: 113
Transfer students are accepted.

Financial Information:
Average cost of books: $850
% of students receiving aid: 90

Employment Profile:
% of students who pass the boards on their first try: 90
% employed within the first 6 months following graduation: 97

University of Indianapolis

Krannert School of Physical Therapy
1400 East Hanna Avenue
Indianapolis, IN 46227-3697

Contact Information:
Telephone: 812-479-2345
Fax: 812-479-2717
E-mail: pritzline@uindy.edu
Web: www.uindy.edu

Program Information:
Program begins: August
Duration of program: 24 months
Evening or weekend classes are available.

Application Information:
Enrollment of program: 80
Transfer students are accepted.

Employment Profile:
% of students who pass the boards on their first try: 88
% employed within the first 6 months following graduation: 95
Average starting salary: $33,000

Iowa

St. Ambrose University

Department of Physical Therapy
518 West Locust
Davenport, IA 52803

Contact Information:
Telephone: 319-333-6403
Fax: 319-333-6410
E-mail: jbarr@saunix.sau.edu
Web: www.sau.edu

Program Information:
Program begins: August
Duration of program: 27 months

Application Information:
Enrollment of program: 86
Transfer students are accepted.

Financial Information:
Average cost of books: $350
% of students receiving aid: 95

Employment Profile:
% of students who pass the boards on their first try: 97
% employed within the first 6 months following graduation: 50

University of Iowa

College of Medicine
2600 Steindler Building
Iowa City, IA 52242-1008

Contact Information:
Telephone: 352-846-2379
Fax: 352-392-6529
E-mail: david_nielsen@uiowa.edu
Web: www.uiowa.edu

Program Information:
Program begins: January
Duration of program: 30 months

Application Information:
Transfer students are accepted.

Financial Information:
Tuition, resident: $3,308
Tuition, non-resident: $10,662
Average cost of books: $800

Employment Profile:
% employed within the first 6 months following graduation: 80
Average starting salary: $39,000

University of Osteopathic Medicine and Health Sciences

3200 Grand Avenue
Des Moines, IA 50312

Contact Information:
Telephone: 904-620-2840
Fax: 904-620-2848
E-mail: ptadmit@uomhs.ed
Web: www.uomhs.ed

Program Information:
Program begins: August
Duration of program: 24 months

Application Information:
Enrollment of program: 79
Transfer students are accepted.

Financial Information:
Average cost of books: $2,500
% of students receiving aid: 97

Employment Profile:
% of students who pass the boards on their first try: 98
% employed within the first 6 months following graduation: 50

Kansas

University of Kansas Medical Center

3056 Robinson Hall
3901 Rainbow Boulevard
Kansas City, KS 66160-7601

Contact Information:
Telephone: 860-768-5303
Fax: 860-768-5244
E-mail: ptadmissions@kumc.edu
Web: www.kumc.edu

Program Information:
Program begins: June
Duration of program: 24 months

Application Information:
Enrollment of program: 88

Financial Information:
Tuition, resident: $4,800
Tuition, non-resident: $12,854

Employment Profile:
% of students who pass the boards on their first try: 100

Kentucky

University of Kentucky

213 CAHP Building
121 Washington Avenue
Lexington, KY 40506-0003

Contact Information:
Telephone: 312-996-1503
Fax: 312-996-4503
Web: www.uky.edu

Program Information:
Program begins: January
Degrees offered: Master's, 30 months

Application Information:
Enrollment of program: 192
Transfer students are accepted.

Financial Information:
Tuition, resident: $3,700
Tuition, non-resident: $11,000
Average cost of books: $900

Employment Profile:
% of students who pass the boards on their first try: 90
% employed within the first 6 months following graduation: 100
Average starting salary: $40,000

Maine

University of New England

Department of Physical Therapy
11 Hills Beach Road
Biddeford, ME 04005

Contact Information:
Telephone: 601-984-6330
Fax: 601-984-6344
Web: www.une.edu

Program Information:
Program begins: September
Duration of program: 60 months

Application Information:
Enrollment of program: 40
Transfer students are accepted.

Financial Information:
% of students receiving aid: 85

Maryland

University of Maryland Eastern Shore

Department of Physical Therapy
Kiah Hall First Floor
Princess Anne, MD 21853

Contact Information:
Telephone: 606-323-1100
Fax: 606-257-1816
E-mail: ptdept@umes-bird.umd.edu
Web: www.umes.edu

Program Information:
Program begins: August
Degrees offered: Master's, 36 months

Application Information:
Enrollment of program: 28
Transfer students are accepted.

Financial Information:
Average cost of books: $400
% of students receiving aid: 75

Employment Profile:
% of students who pass the boards on their first try: 100
% employed within the first 6 months following graduation: 100

Massachusetts

Boston University

Sargent College of Health and Rehabilitation Sciences
635 Commonwealth Avenue
Boston, MA 02215

Contact Information:
Telephone: 617-353-2720
Fax: 617-353-9463
E-mail: giallo@bu.edu
Web: www.bu.edu

Program Information:
Program begins: August
Duration of program: 24 months

MGH Institute of Health Professions

101 Merrimac Street
Boston, MA 02114

Contact Information:
Telephone: 914-674-9331 ext. 650
Fax: 914-674-9457
E-mail: lportney@partners.org
Web: www.mgh.harvard.edu

Program Information:
Program begins: September
Duration of program: 27 months

Application Information:
Enrollment of program: 96

Financial Information:
Tuition, resident: $23,000
Average cost of books: $500
% of students receiving aid: 15

Employment Profile:
% of students who pass the boards on their first try: 93
% employed within the first 6 months following graduation: 70
Average starting salary: $35,000

Simmons College

Graduate School for Health Sciences
300 The Fenway
Boston, MA 02115

Contact Information:
Telephone: 617-521-2635
Fax: 617-521-3137
Web: www.simmons.edu

Program Information:
Program begins: May
Duration of program: 36 months

Application Information:
Enrollment of program: 140

Financial Information:
Average cost of books: $960

Employment Profile:
% of students who pass the boards on their first try: 87

Springfield College

Department of Physical Therapy
263 Alden Street
Springfield, MA 01109

Contact Information:
Telephone: 413-748-3369
Fax: 413-748-3371
Web: www.spfldcol.edu

Program Information:
Program begins: August, September
Degrees offered: Master's, 66 months

Application Information:
Enrollment of program: 237

Financial Information:
Tuition, resident: $15,453
Average cost of books: $600
% of students receiving aid: 60

Employment Profile:
% of students who pass the boards on their first try: 98
% employed within the first 6 months following graduation: 65
Average starting salary: $38,000

University of Massachusetts—Lowell

Weed Hall 3 Solomont Way Sorte 5
Lowell, MA 01854-5124

Contact Information:
Telephone: 502-852-7816
Fax: 502-852-4597
E-mail: sally_healey@uml.edu
Web: www.uml.edu

Program Information:
Program begins: September
Duration of program: 27 months

Application Information:
Enrollment of program: 100

Financial Information:
Tuition, resident: $5,000
Tuition, non-resident: $11,000
Average cost of books: $800
% of students receiving aid: 70

Employment Profile:
% of students who pass the boards on their first try: 98
% employed within the first 6 months following graduation: 95
Average starting salary: $40,000

Michigan

Central Michigan University

134 Pearce Hall
Mt Pleasant, MI 48859

Contact Information:
Telephone: 517-774-2347
Fax: 517-774-2908
Web: www.cmich.edu

Program Information:
Program begins: August
Duration of program: 30 months

Application Information:
Enrollment of program: 145
Transfer students are accepted.

Financial Information:
Tuition, resident: $7,000
Tuition, non-resident: $12,000

Employment Profile:
% of students who pass the boards on their first try: 92

Grand Valley State University

Physical Therapy Program
1 Campus Drive, Henry Hall 328
Allendale, MI 49401

Contact Information:
Telephone: 616-895-3356
Fax: 616-895-3350

E-mail: peckj@gvsu.edu
Web: www.gvsu.edu

Program Information:
Program begins: September
Duration of program: 33 months

Application Information:
Enrollment of program: 180

Financial Information:
Tuition, resident: $14,467
Tuition, non-resident: $30,198
% of students receiving aid: 70

Employment Profile:
% of students who pass the boards on their first try: 87
% employed within the first 6 months following graduation: 20

Oakland University

School of Health Sciences
Rochester, MI 48309-4401

Contact Information:
Telephone: 248-370-4041
Fax: 248-370-4287
E-mail: marcoux@oakland.edu
Web: www.oakland.edu

Program Information:
Program begins: September
Duration of program: 36 months

Application Information:
Enrollment of program: 120
Transfer students are accepted.

Financial Information:
Tuition, resident: $8,000
Tuition, non-resident: $15,000
Average cost of books: $833

Employment Profile:
% of students who pass the boards on their first try: 85
% employed within the first 6 months following graduation: 50

Wayne State University

Department of Physical Therapy
439 Shapero Hall
Detroit, MI 48202

Contact Information:
Telephone: 313-577-1432
Fax: 313-577-8685
Web: www.wayne.edu

Program Information:
Program begins: June
Duration of program: 36 months

Application Information:
Enrollment of program: 110

Financial Information:
Tuition, resident: $5,780
Tuition, non-resident: $12,700

Minnesota

College of St. Catherine—Minneapolis

601 25th Avenue South
Minneapolis, MN 55454

Contact Information:
Telephone: 651-690-7828
Fax: 651-690-7876
E-mail: dosellheim@stkate.edu
Web: www.stkate.edu

Program Information:
Program begins: September
Duration of program: 27 months

Application Information:
Enrollment of program: 93
Transfer students are accepted.

Financial Information:
Tuition, resident: $43,200

Employment Profile:
% of students who pass the boards on their first try: 95

College of St. Scholastica

Department of Physical Therapy
1200 Kenwood Avenue
Duluth, MN 55811

Contact Information:
Telephone: 218-723-6786
Fax: 218-723-6472
Web: www.css.edu

Program Information:
Program begins: August
Duration of program: 28 months

Application Information:
Enrollment of program: 36
Transfer students are accepted.

Financial Information:
Average cost of books: $500

Employment Profile:
% of students who pass the boards on their first try: 86
% employed within the first 6 months following graduation: 95

Mayo Clinic-Mayo Foundation

Mayo School of Health Related Sciences
200 First Street Southwest
Rochester, MN 55905

Contact Information:
Telephone: 314-529-9523
Fax: 314-529-9946
Web: www.mayo.edu

Program Information:
Program begins: September
Degrees offered: Master's, 26 months

Application Information:
Enrollment of program: 72

Financial Information:
Average cost of books: $800
% of students receiving aid: 90

Employment Profile:
% of students who pass the boards on their first try: 95
% employed within the first 6 months following graduation: 98
Average starting salary: $42,000

Missouri

Rockhurst College

1100 Rockhurst Road
Kansas City, MO 64110

Contact Information:
Telephone: 816-501-4059
Fax: 816-501-4643
E-mail: pruitt@vaxl.rockhurst.edu
Web: www.rockhurst.edu

Program Information:
Program begins: June
Duration of program: 27 months

Application Information:
Enrollment of program: 120
Transfer students are accepted.

Financial Information:
Average cost of books: $600

Washington University

School of Medicine
4444 Forest Park Boulevard
Suite 1101
St. Louis, MO 63108

Contact Information:
Telephone: 314-286-1400
Fax: 314-286-1410
E-mail: ptprog@medicine.wustl.edu
Web: www.medicine.wustl.edu

Program Information:
Program begins: August
Duration of program: 28 months

Application Information:
Enrollment of program: 64

Financial Information:
Average cost of books: $1,000
% of students receiving aid: 90

Employment Profile:
% of students who pass the boards on their first try: 98
% employed within the first 6 months following graduation: 90
Average starting salary: $35,000

Montana

University of Montana—Missoula

Department of Physical Therapy
Missoula, MT 59812

Contact Information:
Telephone: 810-762-3373

Fax: 810-766-6668
Web: www.umt.edu

Program Information:
Program begins: August
Degrees offered: Master's, 25 months

Application Information:
Enrollment of program: 64

Financial Information:
Tuition, resident: $7,900
Tuition, non-resident: $15,300
Average cost of books: $1,000

Employment Profile:
% of students who pass the boards on their first try: 95
% employed within the first 6 months following graduation: 75
Average starting salary: $38,000

Nebraska

University of Nebraska

Nebraska Medical Center
984420 Medical Center
Omaha, NE 68198-4420

Contact Information:
Telephone: 612-626-5303
Fax: 612-625-7192
Web: www.unmc.edu/physicaltherapy

Program Information:
Program begins: August
Duration of program: 29 months

Application Information:
Enrollment of program: 120

Financial Information:
Tuition, resident: $4,500
Tuition, non-resident: $11,000
Average cost of books: $2,000
% of students receiving aid: 98

Employment Profile:
% of students who pass the boards on their first try: 97
% employed within the first 6 months following graduation: 25
Average starting salary: $39,000

New Jersey

Richard Stockton College of New Jersey

Jim Leeds Road
Pomona, NJ 08240

Contact Information:
Telephone: 609-652-4501 ext. 4638
Fax: 609-652-4858
E-mail: bkathrins@stockton.edu
Web: www.stockton.edu

Program Information:
Program begins: September
Degrees offered: Master's, 23 months

Application Information:
Enrollment of program: 108
Transfer students are accepted.

Financial Information:
Tuition, resident: $4,680
Tuition, non-resident: $6,282

Employment Profile:
% employed within the first 6 months following graduation: 100

University of Medicine & Dentistry of New Jersey

65 Bergen Street
SSB 319
Newark, NJ 07107-3001

Contact Information:
Telephone: 701-255-7500 ext. 501
Fax: 701-255-7687
Web: www.umdnj.edu

Program Information:
Program begins: June
Duration of program: 36 months

Application Information:
Enrollment of program: 150

Financial Information:
Average cost of books: $800

Employment Profile:
% of students who pass the boards on their first try: 90
Average starting salary: $45,000

New Mexico

University of New Mexico

Division of Physical Therapy
Health Sciences and Services Building/Room 204
Albuquerque, NM 87131-5661

Contact Information:
Telephone: 314-882-7103
Fax: 314-884-8000
E-mail: randrews@salud.unm.edu
Web: www.unm.edu

Program Information:
Program begins: June
Duration of program: 36 months

Application Information:
Enrollment of program: 30
Transfer students are accepted.

Financial Information:
Tuition, resident: $3,427
Tuition, non-resident: $10,899

New York

Columbia University

710 West168th Street/8th Floor
New York, NY 10032

Contact Information:
Telephone: 212-305-3781
Fax: 212-305-4569
E-mail: jee2@columbia.edu
Web: www.cpmcnet.columbia.edu

Program Information:
Program begins: August
Degrees offered: Master's, 22 months

Application Information:
Enrollment of program: 96

Financial Information:
Average cost of books: $1,500
% of students receiving aid: 85

CUNY College of Staten Island

2800 Victory Boulevard
Staten Island, NY 10314

Contact Information:
Telephone: 718-982-3153
Fax: 718-982-2984
E-mail: rothmanj@postbox.csi.cuny.edu
Web: www.csi.cuny.edu

Program Information:
Program begins: June
Degrees offered: Master's, 36 months

Application Information:
Enrollment of program: 75
Transfer students are accepted.

Financial Information:
Tuition, resident: $3,200
Tuition, non-resident: $7,800
Average cost of books: $700

Employment Profile:
% of students who pass the boards on their first try: 88
% employed within the first 6 months following graduation: 100
Average starting salary: $42,000

CUNY Hunter College

425 East Street 25th Street
New York, NY 10010

Contact Information:
Telephone: 212-481-4469
Fax: 212-481-7556
Web: www.hunter.cuny.edu/health/pt

Program Information:
Program begins: July
Duration of program: 36 months

Application Information:
Enrollment of program: 120
Transfer students are accepted.

Financial Information:
Tuition, resident: $3,300
Tuition, non-resident: $6,600
Average cost of books: $1,200

Employment Profile:
% of students who pass the boards on their first try: 75

Ithaca College
Department of Physical Therapy
335 Smiddy Hall
Ithaca, NY 14850-7183

Contact Information:
Telephone: 607-274-3342
Fax: 607-274-1900
E-mail: admission@ithaca.edu
Web: www.ithaca.edu

Program Information:
Program begins: May
Duration of program: 60 months

Application Information:
Enrollment of program: 418
Transfer students are accepted.

Financial Information:
Average cost of books: $750
% of students receiving aid: 88

Employment Profile:
% of students who pass the boards on their first try: 90

Long Island University—Brooklyn Campus
Zeckendorf Health Sciences Center
One University Plaza
Brooklyn, NY 11201-5372

Contact Information:
Telephone: 718-488-1011
Fax: 718-780-4524
Web: www.liu.edu

Program Information:
Program begins: June
Duration of program: 30 months

Application Information:
Enrollment of program: 133
Transfer students are accepted.

Financial Information:
Tuition, resident: $14,000
Average cost of books: $1,200
% of students receiving aid: 85

Employment Profile:
% of students who pass the boards on their first try: 90
% employed within the first 6 months following graduation: 75

Mercy College
Graduate Center
555 Broadway
Dobbs Ferry, NY 10522

Contact Information:
Telephone: 843-792-1267
Fax: 843-792-0710
E-mail: cfenderson@mercynet.edu
Web: www.mercynet.edu

Program Information:
Duration of program: 26 months
Evening or weekend classes are available.

Application Information:
Transfer students are accepted.

Financial Information:
Average cost of books: $1,000

Employment Profile:
% of students who pass the boards on their first try: 77
% employed within the first 6 months following graduation: 100

New York Medical College
Learning Center Room 302
Valhalla, NY 10595

Contact Information:
Telephone: 914-594-4531
Fax: 914-594-4292
E-mail: gshs_admission@nymc.edu
Web: www.nymc.edu

Program Information:
Program begins: May
Degrees offered: Master's, 24 months

Application Information:
Enrollment of program: 96

Financial Information:
Average cost of books: $700

Employment Profile:
% of students who pass the boards on their first try: 80
% employed within the first 6 months following graduation: 100

SUNY at Buffalo
Physical Therapy Exercise & Nutrition Sciences
405 Kimball Tower
Buffalo, NY 14214-3079

Contact Information:
Telephone: 716-829-2941 ext. 403
Fax: 716-829-2034
E-mail: dfish@acsu.buffalo.edu
Web: www.wings.buffalo.edu

Program Information:
Program begins: September
Duration of program: 24 months

Application Information:
Enrollment of program: 180
Transfer students are accepted.

Financial Information:
Tuition, resident: $4,188
Tuition, non-resident: $9,090

SUNY Health Science Center at Brooklyn
450 Clarkson Avenue
Box 16
Brooklyn, NY 11203-2098

Contact Information:
Telephone: 718-270-7720
Fax: 718-270-7439
E-mail: jkatz@netmail.hscbklyn.edu
Web: www.hscbklyn.edu

Program Information:
Program begins: June
Duration of program: 30 months

Application Information:
Enrollment of program: 30

Financial Information:
Tuition, resident: $5,279
Tuition, non-resident: $8,300
Average cost of books: $1,434

Employment Profile:
% of students who pass the boards on their first try: 88

SUNY Health Science Center at Syracuse
College of Health Professions
750 East Adams Street
Syracuse, NY 13210

Contact Information:
Telephone: 315-464-5101
Fax: 315-464-6887
Web: www.hscsyr.edu

Program Information:
Program begins: May
Duration of program: 36 months

Application Information:
Enrollment of program: 96
Transfer students are accepted.

Financial Information:
Tuition, resident: $4,537
Tuition, non-resident: $10,000
Average cost of books: $650
% of students receiving aid: 75

Employment Profile:
Average starting salary: $43,200

Touro College—Bay Shore
School of Health Sciences
1700 Union Boulevard
Bay Shore, NY 11706

Contact Information:
Telephone: 516-665-1600 ext. 245
Fax: 516-665-4986
Web: www.touro.edu

Program Information:
Program begins: June
Duration of program: 36 months

Application Information:
Enrollment of program: 110
Transfer students are accepted.

Financial Information:
Average cost of books: $300

Utica College of Syracuse University
Health & Human Studies Division
1600 Burrstone Road
Utica, NY 13502-4892

Contact Information:
Telephone: 315-792-3059

Fax: 315-792-3248
E-mail: dscalise-smith@utica.ucsu.edu
Web: www.utica.edu

Program Information:
Program begins: August
Degrees offered: Master's

Application Information:
Enrollment of program: 36
Transfer students are accepted.

Financial Information:
Average cost of books: $600
% of students receiving aid: 90

Employment Profile:
% employed within the first 6 months following graduation: 90
Average starting salary: $38,000

North Dakota

University of North Dakota

School of Medicine
PO Box 9037/501 North Columbia Road
Grand Forks, ND 58202-9037

Contact Information:
Telephone: 402-559-4259
Fax: 402-559-8626
E-mail: tommohr@mail.med.und.nodak.edu
Web: www.med.und.nodak.edu

Program Information:
Program begins: June
Duration of program: 29 months

Application Information:
Enrollment of program: 144

Financial Information:
Average cost of books: $1,000

Employment Profile:
% of students who pass the boards on their first try: 94

Ohio

The University of Findlay

1000 North Main Street
Findlay, OH 45840

Contact Information:
Telephone: 419-424-4863
Fax: 419-424-6977
E-mail: fry@lucy.findlay.edu
Web: www.findlay.edu

Program Information:
Program begins: May
Duration of program: 38 months

Application Information:
Enrollment of program: 96

Financial Information:
Average cost of books: $400
% of students receiving aid: 92

University of Cincinnati

Hastings and French Building
PO Box 670394
Cincinnati, OH 45267-0394

Contact Information:
Telephone: 205-934-3566
Fax: 205-975-7787
E-mail: talbotnr@uc.edu
Web: www.uc.edu

Program Information:
Program begins: May
Degrees offered: Master's, 23 months

Application Information:
Enrollment of program: 24

Financial Information:
Tuition, resident: $4,512
Tuition, non-resident: $14,498

Oregon

Pacific University

School of Physical Therapy
2043 College Way
Forest Grove, OR 97116

Contact Information:
Telephone: 800-933-9308
Fax: 503-359-2995
E-mail: banaitid@pacificu.edu
Web: www.pacificu.edu

Program Information:
Program begins: September
Duration of program: 27 months

Application Information:
Enrollment of program: 111

Financial Information:
Average cost of books: $1,100
% of students receiving aid: 80

Employment Profile:
% employed within the first 6 months following graduation: 33
Average starting salary: $36,000

Pennsylvania

Beaver College

Department of Physical Therapy
450 South Easton Road
Glenside, PA 19038-3295

Contact Information:
Telephone: 215-572-2950
Fax: 215-572-2157
E-mail: grad@beaver.edu
Web: www.ver.edu

Program Information:
Program begins: August
Duration of program: 33 months

Application Information:
Enrollment of program: 50

Financial Information:
Tuition: $17,440
Average cost of books: $500

Employment Profile:
% of students who pass the boards on their first try: 99
% employed within the first 6 months following graduation: 90
Average starting salary: $57,500

Duquesne University

Rangos School of Health Sciences
109 Health Sciences Building
Pittsburgh, PA 15282

Contact Information:
Telephone: 412-396-5541
Fax: 412-396-4399
Web: www.duq.edu

Program Information:
Program begins: August
Duration of program: 36 months

Application Information:
Enrollment of program: 202
Transfer students are accepted.

Financial Information:
Average cost of books: $500

Employment Profile:
% of students who pass the boards on their first try: 500
% employed within the first 6 months following graduation: 60
Average starting salary: $39,000

Gannon University

College of Sciences, Engineering & Health
109 University Square/AC 388
Erie, PA 16541-0001

Contact Information:
Telephone: 814-871-5639
Fax: 814-871-5662
E-mail: admissions@gannon.edu
Web: www.gannon.edu

Program Information:
Program begins: August
Duration of program: 27 months

Application Information:
Enrollment of program: 72
Transfer students are accepted.

Financial Information:
Tuition, resident: $20,740
% of students receiving aid: 99

Employment Profile:
% of students who pass the boards on their first try: 82
% employed within the first 6 months following graduation: 35
Average starting salary: $38,000

Temple University
College of Allied Health Professions
3307 North Broad Street
Philadelphia, PA 19140

Contact Information:
Telephone: 215-707-4815
Fax: 215-707-7500
Web: www.temple.edu

Program Information:
Program begins: September
Duration of program: 36 months

Application Information:
Enrollment of program: 150

Financial Information:
Tuition, resident: $10,332
Tuition, non-resident: $14,400
Average cost of books: $1,500
% of students receiving aid: 100

Employment Profile:
% of students who pass the boards on their first try: 95
% employed within the first 6 months following graduation: 100
Average starting salary: $42,000

University of Pittsburgh
School of Health and Rehab Sciences
4020 Forbes Tower
Pittsburgh, PA 15261

Contact Information:
Telephone: 405-271-2131
Fax: 405-271-2432
E-mail: shrsadmit@pitt.edu
Web: www.shrs.upmc.edu

Program Information:
Program begins: January
Duration of program: 24 months

University of Scranton
Department of Physical Therapy
800 Linden Street
Scranton, PA 18510-4586

Contact Information:
Telephone: 401-874-5001
Fax: 401-874-5630

Program Information:
Program begins: July
Duration of program: 43 months

Application Information:
Enrollment of program: 210

Financial Information:
Tuition, resident: $17,480
Average cost of books: $500

Employment Profile:
% of students who pass the boards on their first try: 99
% employed within the first 6 months following graduation: 90
Average starting salary: $38,500

Widener University
One University Place
Chester, PA 19013

Contact Information:
Telephone: 610-499-1277
Fax: 610-499-1231
Web: www.widener.edu

Program Information:
Program begins: August
Duration of program: 33 months

Application Information:
Enrollment of program: 120

Financial Information:
Average cost of books: $900
% of students receiving aid: 95

Employment Profile:
% of students who pass the boards on their first try: 93
% employed within the first 6 months following graduation: 13
Average starting salary: $40,000

South Dakota

University of South Dakota
Department of Physical Therapy
414 East Clark Street
Vermillion, SD 57069

Contact Information:
Telephone: 717-941-7499
Fax: 717-941-7940
Web: www.usd.edu/med/pt

Program Information:
Program begins: May
Duration of program: 24 months

Application Information:
Enrollment of program: 52

Financial Information:
Tuition, resident: $3,200
Tuition, non-resident: $9,600
Average cost of books: $1,200
% of students receiving aid: 90

Employment Profile:
% of students who pass the boards on their first try: 85
% employed within the first 6 months following graduation: 60

Tennessee

East Tennessee State University
Box 70624
Johnson City, TN 376140624

Contact Information:
Telephone: 423-439-8275
Fax: 423-439-8077
E-mail: epps@etsu.edu
Web: www.etsu.edu

Program Information:
Program begins: June
Degrees offered: Master's, 28 months

Application Information:
Enrollment of program: 47

Financial Information:
Tuition, resident: $1,500
Tuition, non-resident: $3,500
Average cost of books: $1,000

Employment Profile:
% of students who pass the boards on their first try: 100

University of Tennessee—Chattanooga
Physical Therapy Program Department 3253
615 McCallie Avenue
Chattanooga, TN 38163

Contact Information:
Telephone: 323-442-2900
Fax: 323-442-1515
E-mail: randy-walker@utc.edu
Web: www.utc.edu

Program Information:
Program begins: September
Duration of program: 32 months

Application Information:
Enrollment of program: 80

Financial Information:
Tuition, resident: $2,286
Tuition, non-resident: $6,109

University of Tennessee—Memphis
Department of Physical Therapy
822 Beale Street/Suite 337
Memphis, TN 38163

Contact Information:
Telephone: 423-755-4747
Fax: 423-785-2215
E-mail: bconnolly@utmem.edu
Web: www.utmem.edu

Program Information:
Program begins: July
Duration of program: 36 months

Application Information:
Enrollment of program: 170

Financial Information:
Tuition, resident: $3,200
Tuition, non-resident: $7,621

Employment Profile:
% of students who pass the boards on their first try: 92
Average starting salary: $40,000

Texas

Hardin-Simmons University
2200 Hickory
PO Box 16065
Abilene, TX 79698-6065

Contact Information:
Telephone: 915-670-5860

Fax: 915-670-5868
Web: www.hsutx.edu

Program Information:
Program begins: January
Duration of program: 24 months

Application Information:
Enrollment of program: 48

Financial Information:
Average cost of books: $800
% of students receiving aid: 50

Employment Profile:
% of students who pass the boards on their first try: 75
% employed within the first 6 months following graduation: 95
Average starting salary: $45,000

Southwest Texas State University

Health Science Center
601 University Drive
San Marcos, TX 78666

Contact Information:
Telephone: 512-245-8351
Fax: 512-245-8736
E-mail: bs04@swt.edu
Web: www.swt.edu

Program Information:
Program begins: September
Duration of program: 24 months

Application Information:
Enrollment of program: 75
Transfer students are accepted.

Financial Information:
Tuition, resident: $3,600
Tuition, non-resident: $12,000
Average cost of books: $2,500
% of students receiving aid: 75

Employment Profile:
% of students who pass the boards on their first try: 98
% employed within the first 6 months following graduation: 80
Average starting salary: $40,000

Texas Technical University Health Science Center

School of Allied Health
3601 4th Street
Lubbock, TX 79430

Contact Information:
Telephone: 806-743-3220
Fax: 806-743-1262
E-mail: alhhm@ttuhsc.edu
Web: www.ttuhsc.edu

Program Information:
Program begins: May, August
Duration of program: 27 months

Application Information:
Enrollment of program: 173

Financial Information:
Tuition, resident: $1,258
Tuition, non-resident: $9,176
Average cost of books: $200
% of students receiving aid: 80

Employment Profile:
% of students who pass the boards on their first try: 90
% employed within the first 6 months following graduation: 100
Average starting salary: $38,000

Texas Woman's University

School of Physical Therapy
PO Box 425766 TWU Station
Denton, TX 76204-5766

Contact Information:
Telephone: 940-898-2460
Fax: 940-898-2486
E-mail: s_3johnson@twu.edu
Web: www.twu.edu

Program Information:
Program begins: October
Duration of program: 26 months

Application Information:
Enrollment of program: 225

Financial Information:
Tuition, resident: $3,885
Tuition, non-resident: $12,083
Average cost of books: $800

Employment Profile:
% of students who pass the boards on their first try: 100
% employed within the first 6 months following graduation: 80
Average starting salary: $40,000

University of Texas Health Science Center at San Antonio

Department of Physical Therapy (MC624)
7703 Floyd Curl Drive
San Antonio, TX 78229-3900

Contact Information:
Telephone: 901-448-5888
Fax: 901-448-7545
Web: www.uthsca.edu

Program Information:
Program begins: August
Duration of program: 33 months

Application Information:
Enrollment of program: 108

Financial Information:
Tuition, resident: $2,555
Tuition, non-resident: $16,451

University of Texas Medical Branch

School of Allied Health Sciences
301 University Boulevard
Galveston, TX 77555-1028

Contact Information:
Telephone: 210-567-8750
Fax: 201-567-8774
E-mail: kmossber@utmb.edu
Web: www.utmb.edu

Program Information:
Program begins: September
Duration of program: 28 months

Application Information:
Enrollment of program: 120

Financial Information:
Tuition, resident: $1,300
Tuition, non-resident: $10,000
Average cost of books: $600

Employment Profile:
% of students who pass the boards on their first try: 85
% employed within the first 6 months following graduation: 40
Average starting salary: $40,000

University of Texas Southwestern Medical Center—Dallas

Southwestern Allied Health Sciences School
5323 Harry Hines Boulevard
Dallas, TX 75235-8876

Contact Information:
Telephone: 409-772-3068
Fax: 409-747-1613
E-mail: patricia.winchester@email.swmed.edu
Web: www.swmed.edu

Program Information:
Program begins: May
Degrees offered: Master's, 24 months

Application Information:
Enrollment of program: 40
Transfer students are accepted.

Financial Information:
Tuition, resident: $1,344
Tuition, non-resident: $10,332
Average cost of books: $630
% of students receiving aid: 50

Employment Profile:
% of students who pass the boards on their first try: 95
% employed within the first 6 months following graduation: 100
Average starting salary: $40,000

US Army/Baylor University

MCCS-HMT Physical Therapy Branch
Academy of Health Sciences/3151 Scott Road
Ft. Sam Houston, TX 78234-6138

Contact Information:
Telephone: 210-221-8410
Fax: 210-221-8612
Web: www.cs.amedd.army.mil

Program Information:
Program begins: August
Duration of program: 18 months

Employment Profile:
% of students who pass the boards on their first try: 99
% employed within the first 6 months following graduation: 100
Average starting salary: $29,600

Additional Information:
Military program: Students are commissioned officers. Salaried applications accepted from any qualified applicant.

Utah

University of Utah
Division of Physical Therapy
520 Wakara Way, Suite 302
Salt Lake City, UT 84108

Contact Information:
Telephone: 801-581-8681
Fax: 801-585-5629
Web: www.utah.edu

Program Information:
Program begins: August
Duration of program: 33 months

Application Information:
Enrollment of program: 108
Transfer students are accepted.

Financial Information:
Tuition, resident: $2,823
Tuition, non-resident: $8,841
Average cost of books: $600
% of students receiving aid: 60

Employment Profile:
% of students who pass the boards on their first try: 98
% employed within the first 6 months following graduation: 60
Average starting salary: $40,000

Virginia

Old Dominion University
Community Health Professions and Physical Therapy
Health Sciences Building
Norfolk, VA 23529-0288

Contact Information:
Telephone: 757-683-4519
Fax: 757-683-4410
E-mail: gcm100f@odu.edu
Web: www.odu.edu

Program Information:
Program begins: June
Degrees offered: Master's, 26 months

Application Information:
Enrollment of program: 60

Financial Information:
Tuition, resident: $9,100
Tuition, non-resident: $23,500
Average cost of books: $2,000
% of students receiving aid: 70

Employment Profile:
% of students who pass the boards on their first try: 86
% employed within the first 6 months following graduation: 90
Average starting salary: $46,750

Shenandoah University
333 West Cork Street
Winchester, VA 22601

Contact Information:
Telephone: 540-665-5520
Fax: 540-665-5530
E-mail: cwilson@su.edu
Web: www.su.edu

Program Information:
Program begins: August
Degrees offered: Master's, 30 months

Application Information:
Enrollment of program: 110

Financial Information:
Tuition, resident: $15,600

Employment Profile:
% of students who pass the boards on their first try: 98
% employed within the first 6 months following graduation: 100

Virginia Commonwealth University
Medical College of Virginia Campus
Box 980224
Richmond, VA 23298-0224

Contact Information:
Telephone: 804-828-0234
Fax: 804-828-8111
E-mail: rllamb@hsc.vcu.edu
Web: www.views.vcu.edu

Program Information:
Program begins: May
Duration of program: 27 months

Application Information:
Enrollment of program: 175
Transfer students are accepted.

Financial Information:
Tuition, resident: $5,112
Tuition, non-resident: $13,027

Employment Profile:
% of students who pass the boards on their first try: 100
% employed within the first 6 months following graduation: 50

Washington

Eastern Washington University
Department of Physical Therapy
526 Fifth Street/MS 4
Cheney, WA 99004-2431

Contact Information:
Telephone: 509-623-4305
Fax: 509-623-4321
E-mail: werikson@ewu.edu
Web: www.ewu.edu

Program Information:
Program begins: September
Duration of program: 27 months

Financial Information:
Tuition, resident: $4,200
Tuition, non-resident: $13,287

Employment Profile:
% of students who pass the boards on their first try: 97
Average starting salary: $33,000

University of Puget Sound
School of Physical Therapy
1500 North Warner
Tacoma, WA 98416

Contact Information:
Telephone: 412-647-1252
Fax: 412-647-1255
E-mail: hummel@ups.edu
Web: www.ups.edu

Program Information:
Program begins: September
Duration of program: 33 months

Application Information:
Enrollment of program: 30

Financial Information:
Average cost of books: $750
% of students receiving aid: 50

Employment Profile:
% of students who pass the boards on their first try: 99
% employed within the first 6 months following graduation: 100

West Virginia

Wheeling Jesuit University
Physical Therapy Department
316 Washington Avenue
Wheeling, WV 26003

Contact Information:
Telephone: 304-243-2432
Fax: 304-243-2042
E-mail: wjupt@wju.edu
Web: www.wju.edu

Program Information:
Program begins: September
Duration of program: 24 months

Application Information:
Enrollment of program: 60
Transfer students are accepted.

Employment Profile:
% of students who pass the boards on their first try: 96
% employed within the first 6 months following graduation: 91

Wisconsin

Concordia University Wisconsin

12800 North Lake Shore Drive
Mequon, WI 53092-7699

Contact Information:
Telephone: 414-243-4280
Fax: 414-243-4506
E-mail: terry.steffen@cuw.edu
Web: www.cuw.edu

Program Information:
Program begins: August
Degrees offered: Master's, 27 months

Application Information:
Enrollment of program: 70
Transfer students are accepted.

Financial Information:
Tuition, resident: $13,970
Average cost of books: $800

Marquette University

PO Box 1881
Milwaukee, WI 53201-1881

Contact Information:
Telephone: 310-954-4170
Fax: 310-954-4179
E-mail: go2marquette@marquette.edu
Web: www.marquette.edu

Program Information:
Program begins: July
Duration of program: 24 months

Application Information:
Enrollment of program: 70
Transfer students are accepted.

Financial Information:
Average cost of books: $650
% of students receiving aid: 90

University of Wisconsin—Madison

Department of Surgery/5185 MSC
1300 University Avenue
Madison, WI 53706-1532

Contact Information:
Telephone: 608-263-9427
Fax: 608-263-6434
E-mail: wall@surgery.wisc.edu
Web: www.surgery.wisc.edu

Program Information:
Program begins: August
Duration of program: 30 months

Application Information:
Enrollment of program: 98

Financial Information:
Tuition, resident: $5,400
Tuition, non-resident: $17,200
Average cost of books: $1,000

Employment Profile:
% of students who pass the boards on their first try: 95
% employed within the first 6 months following graduation: 95
Average starting salary: $40,000

University of Wisconsin—LaCrosse-Gundersen Mayo

Department of Physical Therapy
2032 Cowley Hall
La Crosse, WI 54601

Contact Information:
Telephone: 608-785-8470
Fax: 608-785-8460
E-mail: wilder.patr@uwlax.edu

Program Information:
Program begins: June
Degrees offered: Master's, 30 months

Application Information:
Enrollment of program: 90
Transfer students are accepted.

Financial Information:
Tuition, resident: $4,525
Tuition, non-resident: $13,761
Average cost of books: $800

Employment Profile:
% of students who pass the boards on their first try: 95
% employed within the first 6 months following graduation: 100

Physical Therapist Assistant

Risa Granick, EdD, MPA, PT
Professor and Chair
Department of Rehabilitation Sciences
MCP Hahnemann University
Philadelphia, Pennsylvania

Job Description

What Do They Do?

PTAs are skilled healthcare providers who work under the supervision of physical therapists. They assist the therapist by:

- implementing treatment programs
- training patients in exercise and activities of daily living
- conducting treatments developed by the physical therapist
- reporting to the therapist on the patient's responses to treatment
- working collaboratively with other healthcare providers
- interacting with members of the patient's or client's families and other caregivers

Type of Person

PTAs enjoy the satisfaction of helping patients with long-term disabilities or acute injuries. They also like working with clients who seek to maintain fitness and health. To perform their job successfully, they must have good organizational and interpersonal skills.

With Whom Do They Work?

PTAs work with the physical therapist and may supervise the physical therapy aide (non-licensed workers who have received on-the-job training to perform routine tasks related to the operation of the physical therapy department). These tasks may include maintaining equipment and supplies, cleaning and readying a treatment room for the next patient, supervising patients in hydrotherapy, or assisting patients in carrying out their exercises.

Employment

Places of Employment

PTAs work in hospitals, rehabilitation centers, private physical therapy practices, sports facilities, nursing homes, home health agencies, pediatric centers, schools, community health centers, and corporate or industrial health centers.

Employment Outlook

Despite changes in today's healthcare system in the way healthcare is administered and financed, there is still a need for the more cost-effective role of the PTA. Approximately 5,000 assistants graduate on a yearly basis.[1]

Salary

According to surveys conducted by the APTA, the mean income for an assistant is approximately $30,000. PTAs in the southern and western regions of the country earn the highest salaries since demand for them is greatest in this part of the country.

Educational Programs

Length

PTAs complete a 2-year education program, usually offered through a community or junior college. Candidates receive an Associate's degree upon graduation. There are three different ways to earn a degree. (The configuration numbers below refer to the number of years that students spend in classroom and clinical education.):

1. Integrated 2-Year Program: students are accepted into the institution and the program at the same time and concurrently (over 2 years) complete general education, physical therapy sciences, technical skills, and clinical education courses.
2. 1+1 Program: students are accepted into the assistant curriculum once they have demonstrated satisfactory completion of the general education and physical therapy science content (1 year). The assistant curriculum consists of technical skills and clinical education courses only (1 year).
3. 0.5 + 1.5 Program: students are accepted into the program once they have satisfactorily completed the general education content (one-half year). The assistant curriculum consists of the applied physical therapy sciences, technical skills, and clinical education courses (one and a half years).

Prerequisites

Applicants must have a high school diploma or a general education degree (GED). In addition, the following course work may be required prior to entering the program:

1. Integrated 2-Year Program
   - No prerequisite coursework is required. The curriculum is all-inclusive.
2. 1 + 1 Program. Students need to fulfill the following prerequisite course work before entering the program:
   - English
   - Psychology
   - Math/Algebra
   - Biology
   - Chemistry
   - Physics
   - Anatomy and physiology
3. 0.5 + 1.5 Program. Students need to fulfill the following prerequisites:
   - English
   - Psychology
   - Math/Algebra

Curriculum

PTA courses consist of kinesiology and applied biomechanics, medical-surgical conditions, life-span development, PTA techniques, therapeutic modalities, and rehabilitation principles. Three clinical education experiences in three different types of settings are usually required. These experiences correspond to the typical employment settings of the PTA. Students choose from a wide array of sites that usually include hospitals, rehabilitation centers, pediatric facilities, nursing homes, out-patient orthopedic centers, and private physical therapy offices.

Accrediting Body

The Commission on Accreditation in Physical Therapy Education of the American Physical Therapy Association is the accrediting body for all PTA programs.

Commission on Accreditation in Physical Therapy Education (CAPTE)
American Physical Therapy Association
1111 North Fairfax Street
Alexandria, VA 22314
Telephone: 703-706-3245
Web address: www.apta.org

Licensure, Registration, and Certification

Currently more than half of the states require PTAs to be licensed, registered, or certified. States requiring licensure stipulate specific educational and examination criteria. Information on practice acts and regulations may be obtained by contacting the licensing board in your state. Contact the Federation of State Boards of Physical Therapy (FSBPT) for a list of state agencies.

Federation of State Boards of Physical Therapy
509 Wythe Street
Alexandria, VA 22314
Telephone: 703-299-3100 or 800-200-3031
Fax: 703-299-3110 or 800-981-3031
Web address: www.fsbpt.org

Advice for Potential Students

Visit the schools you are interested in attending via open houses or career day conferences. Look at the job market in your geographical area by visiting local healthcare facilities that employ PTAs. Check local newspapers to see how many job openings are available. Volunteer experience is also helpful in formalizing a career choice. It is important to distinguish between a career as a PTA and one as a physical therapist. The assistant programs is not considered a stepping stone to a physical therapy program since the curriculum for the PTA does not provide the needed prerequisites required for acceptance into a physical therapy program. There are, however, a few accredited programs in California, Ohio, New York, and Pennsylvania designed to permit practicing PTAs to continue employment while attending a physical therapist master's degree program on the weekends.

For Additional Information

Organizations

American Physical Therapy Association
1111 North Fairfax Street
Alexandria, VA 22314
Telephone: 800-999-2782
Web address: www.apta.org

Publications

Books

A Future in Physical Therapy. Fairfax: American Physical Therapy Association. Order No. PR-23-A, APTA Service Center (800-999-2782, ext. 3395) or through Fax-on-Demand (800-399-2782).

Journals

Advance for Physical Therapists and Physical Therapist Assistants. Merion Publications, 2900 Horizon Drive, King of Prussia, PA 19406. www.advanceforpt.com

A national biweekly publication that reports on advances in research, reimbursement, and political and clinical news.

Internet Resources

American Physical Therapy Association: www.apta.org
Federation of State Boards of Physical Therapy: www.fsbpt.org
MCP Hahnemann University, Department of Rehabilitation Sciences, Physical Therapist Assistant Program: www.mcphu.edu/shp/depts/rehab

Alabama

Bishop State Community College

1365 Martin Luther King Jr. Avenue
Mobile, AL 36603-5362

Contact Information:
Telephone: 334-405-4441
Fax: 334-405-4427
Web: www.bscc.cc.al.us

Program Information:
Program begins: January
Degrees offered: Associate's, 24 months

Application Information:
Enrollment of program: 23
Transfer students are accepted.

Financial Information:
Tuition, resident: $2,132
Tuition, non-resident: $4,264
Average cost of books: $950

Employment Profile:
% of students who pass the boards on their first try: 85
% employed within the first 6 months following graduation: 50
Average starting salary: $25,000

George C. Wallace State Community College

Route 6 Box 62
Dothan, AL 36303-9234

Contact Information:
Telephone: 334-983-3521 ext. 306
Fax: 334-983-3600
E-mail: ptucker@www.wallace.edu
Web: www.wallace.edu

Program Information:
Program begins: June
Duration of program: 15 months

Application Information:
Enrollment of program: 16
Transfer students are accepted.

Financial Information:
Average cost of books: $1,350

Employment Profile:
% of students who pass the boards on their first try: 94
% employed within the first 6 months following graduation: 96
Average starting salary: $32,000

Jefferson State Community College

Division of Health Sciences
2601 Carson Road
Birmingham, AL 35215-3098

Contact Information:
Telephone: 205-856-8563
Fax: 205-856-7725
E-mail: bking@jscc.cc.al.us
Web: www.jscc.cc.al.us

Program Information:
Program begins: January
Degrees offered: Diploma, 12 months

Application Information:
Enrollment of program: 20
Transfer students are accepted.

Financial Information:
Tuition, resident: $2,200
Tuition, non-resident: $4,200
Average cost of books: $1,000
% of students receiving aid: 50

Employment Profile:
% of students who pass the boards on their first try: 90
Average starting salary: $25,000

Wallace State Community College

PO Box 2000
Hanceville, AL 35077-2000

Contact Information:
Telephone: 205-352-8332
Fax: 205-352-8320
Web: www.wscc.cc.al.us

Program Information:
Program begins: August
Degrees offered: Diploma, 12 months

Application Information:
Enrollment of program: 40
Transfer students are accepted.

Financial Information:
Tuition, resident: $807
Tuition, non-resident: $1,614

Employment Profile:
% of students who pass the boards on their first try: 88
% employed within the first 6 months following graduation: 90
Average starting salary: $25,000

Arkansas

Northwest Arkansas Community College

One College Drive
Bentonville, AR 72712-5091

Contact Information:
Telephone: 501-619-4253
Fax: 501-619-4254
Web: www.uark.edu

Program Information:
Program begins: June
Duration of program: 15 months

Financial Information:
Tuition, resident: $1,243
Tuition, non-resident: $2,308

California

Cerritos College

Health Occupations Division
11110 Alondra Boulevard
Norwalk, CA 90650

Contact Information:
Telephone: 562-860-2451 ext. 2550
Fax: 562-467-5077
E-mail: piorkowski@cerritos.edu
Web: www.cerritos.edu

Program Information:
Program begins: August
Duration of program: 24 months
Evening or weekend classes are available.

Application Information:
Enrollment of program: 30
Transfer students are accepted.

Financial Information:
Tuition, resident: $781
Tuition, non-resident: $1,534
Average cost of books: $400

Employment Profile:
% of students who pass the boards on their first try: 95
% employed within the first 6 months following graduation: 50
Average starting salary: $30,000

Loma Linda University

School of Allied Health Professions
Nichol Hall Room 1911
Loma Linda, CA 92350

Contact Information:
Telephone: 909-558-4634
Fax: 909-558-4291
E-mail: desmyrna-taylor@sahp.llu.edu
Web: www.llu.edu

Program Information:
Program begins: June
Duration of program: 15 months

Application Information:
Enrollment of program: 58
Transfer students are accepted.

Financial Information:
Average cost of books: $1,000

Employment Profile:
% of students who pass the boards on their first try: 82
% employed within the first 6 months following graduation: 15
Average starting salary: $32,000

Sacramento City College

Allied Health
3835 Freeport Boulevard
Sacramento, CA 95822

Contact Information:
Telephone: 916-558-2240
Fax: 916-558-2392
E-mail: chapee@mail.scc.losrios.cc.ca.us
Web: www.scc.losrios.cc.ca.us

Program Information:
Program begins: August
Degrees offered: Associate's, 22 months
Evening or weekend classes are available.

Application Information:
Enrollment of program: 60
Transfer students are accepted.

Financial Information:
Tuition, resident: $264
Average cost of books: $300

Employment Profile:
% of students who pass the boards on their first try: 84
% employed within the first 6 months following graduation: 80
Average starting salary: $28,000

Colorado

Pueblo Community College

900 West Orman Avenue
Pueblo, CO 81004

Contact Information:
Telephone: 719-543-8582
Fax: 719-543-8586
E-mail: mihelich@pcc.cccoes.edu
Web: www.pcc.cccoes.edu

Program Information:
Program begins: August
Degrees offered: Associate's, 20 months

Application Information:
Enrollment of program: 20
Transfer students are accepted.

Financial Information:
Tuition, resident: $1,558
Tuition, non-resident: $6,610
Average cost of books: $600
% of students receiving aid: 80

Employment Profile:
% of students who pass the boards on their first try: 80
% employed within the first 6 months following graduation: 50
Average starting salary: $25,000

Connecticut

Housatonic Community College

900 Lafayette Boulevard
Bridgeport, CT 06604-4704

Contact Information:
Telephone: 203-332-5107
Fax: 203-332-5123
E-mail: ho_reisa@commnet.edu

Program Information:
Program begins: September
Degrees offered: Associate's, 22 months
Evening or weekend classes are available.

Application Information:
Enrollment of program: 32
Transfer students are accepted.

Financial Information:
Tuition, resident: $1,814
Tuition, non-resident: $5,418
Average cost of books: $500

Employment Profile:
% of students who pass the boards on their first try: 95
% employed within the first 6 months following graduation: 100
Average starting salary: $32,000

Delaware

Delaware Technical & Community College—Wilmington

333 Shipley Street
Wilmington, DE 19801

Contact Information:
Telephone: 302-571-5355
Fax: 302-577-6431
E-mail: bancroft@hopi.dtcc.edu
Web: www.dtcc.edu

Program Information:
Program begins: May
Duration of program: 24 months

Financial Information:
Tuition, resident: $720
Tuition, non-resident: $1,800

Florida

Central Florida Community College

PO Box 1388
Ocala, FL 34478-1388

Contact Information:
Telephone: 352-854-2322 ext. 1255
Fax: 352-237-0510
E-mail: mccaulej@cfcc.cc.fl.us
Web: www.cfcc.cc.fl.us

Program Information:
Program begins: August
Degrees offered: Associate's, 27 months

Application Information:
Enrollment of program: 24
Transfer students are accepted.

Financial Information:
Tuition, resident: $3,660
Tuition, non-resident: $13,510
Average cost of books: $100

Employment Profile:
% of students who pass the boards on their first try: 96
% employed within the first 6 months following graduation: 100
Average starting salary: $28,000

St. Petersburg Junior College

PO Box 13489
St. Petersburg, FL 33733

Contact Information:
Telephone: 813-341-3611
Fax: 813-341-3744
E-mail: ericksond@spjc.edu
Web: www.spj.edu

Program Information:
Program begins: August
Degrees offered: Associate's, 18 months

Application Information:
Enrollment of program: 70
Transfer students are accepted.

Financial Information:
Tuition, resident: $3,900
Tuition, non-resident: $13,588
Average cost of books: $500

Georgia

Middle Georgia College

1100 Second Street Southeast
Cochran, GA 31014

Contact Information:
Telephone: 912-734-3409
Fax: 912-934-3461
E-mail: lshere@warrior.mgc.peachnet.edu
Web: www.mgc.peachnet.edu

Program Information:
Program begins: August
Duration of program: 24 months

Application Information:
Enrollment of program: 26

Hawaii

Kapiolani Community College

Health Science Department
4303 Diamond Head Road
Honolulu, HI 96816

Contact Information:
Telephone: 808-734-9398
Fax: 808-734-9126
E-mail: marilynm@hawaii.edu
Web: www.kcc.hawaii.edu

Program Information:
Program begins: August
Duration of program: 24 months
Evening or weekend classes are available.

Application Information:
Enrollment of program: 26
Transfer students are accepted.

Financial Information:
Tuition, resident: $960
Tuition, non-resident: $5,600
Average cost of books: $1,000
% of students receiving aid: 50

Employment Profile:
% of students who pass the boards on their first try: 80
% employed within the first 6 months following graduation: 100
Average starting salary: $25,000

Illinois

Belleville Area College

2500 Carlyle Avenue
Belleville, IL 62221

Contact Information:
Telephone: 618-235-2700 ext. 5362
Fax: 618-235-2052
E-mail: muertzja@bacnet.edu
Web: www.bacnet.edu

Program Information:
Program begins: August
Duration of program: 21 months

Application Information:
Transfer students are accepted.

Financial Information:
Tuition, resident: $3,160
Tuition, non-resident: $7,952

Illinois Central College

201 Southwest Adams Street
Peoria, IL 61635-0001

Contact Information:
Telephone: 309-999-4672
Fax: 309-673-9626
E-mail: p.beck@icc.cc.il.us
Web: www.icc.cc.il.us

Program Information:
Program begins: August
Duration of program: 19 months

Application Information:
Enrollment of program: 43
Transfer students are accepted.

Financial Information:
Tuition, resident: $2,792
Average cost of books: $1,200

Employment Profile:
% of students who pass the boards on their first try: 90
% employed within the first 6 months following graduation: 86
Average starting salary: $27,000

Kaskaskia College
27210 College Road
Centralia, IL 62801

Contact Information:
Telephone: 618-545-3308 ext. 394
Fax: 618-532-1990
E-mail: srdewhirst@kccn.kc.cc.il.us
Web: www.lc.cc.il.us

Program Information:
Program begins: August
Degrees offered: Associate's, 23 months

Application Information:
Enrollment of program: 50

Financial Information:
Tuition, resident: $1,332
Average cost of books: $450
% of students receiving aid: 25

Employment Profile:
% of students who pass the boards on their first try: 80
% employed within the first 6 months following graduation: 90
Average starting salary: $25,000

Lake Land College
LLC Kluthe Center
1204 Network Center Drive
Effingham, IL 62401

Contact Information:
Telephone: 217-342-0951
Fax: 217-342-0999
E-mail: mmioux@lakeland.cc.il.us
Web: www.lakeland.cc.il.us

Program Information:
Program begins: August
Duration of program: 30 months

Application Information:
Enrollment of program: 48

Financial Information:
Tuition, resident: $3,500

Lincoln Land Community College
5250 Shepherd Road
PO Box 19256
Springfield, IL 62794-9256

Contact Information:
Telephone: 217-786-2498
Fax: 217-786-2824
E-mail: debragray@llcc.cc.il.us
Web: www.llcc.cc.il.us

Program Information:
Program begins: June
Duration of program: 24 months

Application Information:
Enrollment of program: 26

Financial Information:
Tuition, resident: $2,814
Average cost of books: $800
% of students receiving aid: 60

Employment Profile:
% of students who pass the boards on their first try: 86
% employed within the first 6 months following graduation: 75
Average starting salary: $24,000

Oakton Community College
1600 East Golf Road
Des Plaines, IL 60016

Contact Information:
Telephone: 847-635-1857
Fax: 847-635-1764
E-mail: maryd@oakton.edu
Web: www.oakton.edu

Program Information:
Program begins: August
Duration of program: 20 months

Application Information:
Enrollment of program: 60

Financial Information:
Tuition, resident: $12,025
Tuition, non-resident: $4,485

Employment Profile:
% of students who pass the boards on their first try: 80
Average starting salary: $27,000

Southern Illinois University—Carbondale
SIU Clinical Center
Clinical Center - 4602
Carbondale, IL 62901-4602

Contact Information:
Telephone: 618-453-6143
Fax: 618-453-6126
E-mail: jrogers@siu.edu
Web: www.siue.edu

Program Information:
Program begins: August
Degrees offered: Associate's, 24 months

Application Information:
Enrollment of program: 48
Transfer students are accepted.

Financial Information:
Tuition, resident: $1,500
Tuition, non-resident: $3,500

Employment Profile:
% of students who pass the boards on their first try: 85
% employed within the first 6 months following graduation: 80
Average starting salary: $30,000

Indiana

Ivy Tech State College—Northwest
1440 East 35th Avenue
Gary, IN 46409

Contact Information:
Telephone: 219-981-1111 ext. 430
Fax: 219-981-4415
Web: www.ivy.tec.in.us

Program Information:
Program begins: August
Duration of program: 24 months

Application Information:
Enrollment of program: 35
Transfer students are accepted.

Financial Information:
Tuition, resident: $5,448
Tuition, non-resident: $8,695
Average cost of books: $150
% of students receiving aid: 60

Employment Profile:
% of students who pass the boards on their first try: 70
% employed within the first 6 months following graduation: 90
Average starting salary: $33,000

Ivy Tech State College EC—Muncie
4301 South Cowan Road
PO Box 3100
Muncie, IN 47307

Contact Information:
Telephone: 765-289-2291 ext. 404
Fax: 765-289-2291
E-mail: kbusha@ivy.tec.in.us
Web: www.ivy.tec.in.us

Program Information:
Program begins: August
Duration of program: 20 months

Application Information:
Enrollment of program: 63

Financial Information:
Tuition, resident: $5,974
Tuition, non-resident: $8,836
Average cost of books: $450

Michiana College
1030 East Jefferson Boulevard
South Bend, IN 46617

Contact Information:
Telephone: 219-237-0774
Fax: 219-237-3585
Web: www.michianacollege.com

Program Information:
Program begins: June, November
Duration of program: 29 months

Application Information:
Enrollment of program: 111
Transfer students are accepted.

Financial Information:
Average cost of books: $1,800
% of students receiving aid: 80

Employment Profile:
% of students who pass the boards on their first try: 100

University of Indianapolis
Krannert School of Physical Therapy
1400 East Hanna Avenue
Indianapolis, IN 46227-3697

Contact Information:
Telephone: 317-788-3500
Fax: 317-788-3542
E-mail: pritzline@unidy.edu
Web: www.uindy.edu

Program Information:
Program begins: August
Degrees offered: Associate's, 24 months; Master's, 28 months; PhD, 36 months

Application Information:
Transfer students are accepted.

Employment Profile:
% of students who pass the boards on their first try: 88
% employed within the first 6 months following graduation: 95
Average starting salary: $33,000

University of Saint Francis
2701 Spring Street
Ft. Wayne, IN 46408

Contact Information:
Telephone: 217-434-7662
Fax: 217-434-7601
Web: www.sf.edu

Program Information:
Program begins: August
Duration of program: 21 months

Application Information:
Enrollment of program: 18
Transfer students are accepted.

Financial Information:
Tuition, resident: $11,360

Employment Profile:
% of students who pass the boards on their first try: 88
% employed within the first 6 months following graduation: 95
Average starting salary: $28,000

Vincennes University
Health Occupations Department
Vincennes, IN 47591

Contact Information:
Telephone: 812-888-4416
E-mail: rschneid@vunet.vinu.edu
Web: www.vinu.edu

Program Information:
Program begins: August
Degrees offered: Associate's, 24 months

Application Information:
Enrollment of program: 48
Transfer students are accepted.

Financial Information:
Tuition, resident: $3,024
Tuition, non-resident: $7,200
Average cost of books: $500
% of students receiving aid: 50

Employment Profile:
% of students who pass the boards on their first try: 99
% employed within the first 6 months following graduation: 95
Average starting salary: $27,500

Iowa

Kirkwood Community College
6301 Kirkwood Boulevard
Cedar Rapids, IA 52406

Contact Information:
Telephone: 319-398-5566
Fax: 319-398-1293
E-mail: mthomas@kirkwood.cc.ia.us
Web: www.kirkwood.ccia.us

Program Information:
Program begins: August
Degrees offered: Diploma, 21 months
Evening or weekend classes are available.

Application Information:
Enrollment of program: 48
Transfer students are accepted.

Financial Information:
Tuition, resident: $2,200
Tuition, non-resident: $4,400
Average cost of books: $600

Employment Profile:
% of students who pass the boards on their first try: 95
% employed within the first 6 months following graduation: 75
Average starting salary: $23,000

Western Iowa Technology Community College
4647 Stone Avenue
PO Box 5199
Sioux City, IA 51102-5199

Contact Information:
Telephone: 712-274-6400 ext. 1321
Fax: 712-274-6412
E-mail: huculab@witcc.cc.ia.us
Web: www.witcc.cc.ia.us

Program Information:
Program begins: August, January
Duration of program: 24 months

Application Information:
Enrollment of program: 24
Transfer students are accepted.

Financial Information:
Tuition, resident: $2,300
Tuition, non-resident: $4,600

Employment Profile:
% of students who pass the boards on their first try: 83

Kansas

Colby Community College
1255 South Range
Colby, KS 67701

Contact Information:
Telephone: 913-462-4797
Fax: 913-462-4699
E-mail: pate@katie.colby.cc.ks.us
Web: www.colby.cc.ks.us

Program Information:
Program begins: August
Duration of program: 12 months

Application Information:
Enrollment of program: 40
Transfer students are accepted.

Financial Information:
Tuition, resident: $2,509
Tuition, non-resident: $3,969
Average cost of books: $600
% of students receiving aid: 85

Employment Profile:
% of students who pass the boards on their first try: 80
Average starting salary: $25,000

Washburn University of Topeka
School of Applied Studies
1700 Southwest College Avenue
Topeka, KS 66621

Contact Information:
Telephone: 785-231-1010 ext. 1406
Fax: 785-231-1027
E-mail: zzbahn@washburn.edu
Web: www.washburn.edu

Program Information:
Program begins: August

Degrees offered: Associate's, 22 months
Evening or weekend classes are available.

Application Information:
Enrollment of program: 24
Transfer students are accepted.

Financial Information:
Tuition, resident: $3,090
Tuition, non-resident: $8,340
Average cost of books: $200
% of students receiving aid: 33

Employment Profile:
% of students who pass the boards on their first try: 90
% employed within the first 6 months following graduation: 75
Average starting salary: $30,000

Kentucky

Midway College

School for Career Development
512 East Stephens Street
Midway, KY 40347-1120

Contact Information:
Telephone: 606-846-5772
Fax: 606-846-5876
Web: www.midway.edu

Program Information:
Duration of program: 18 months
Evening or weekend classes are available.

Application Information:
Enrollment of program: 14
Transfer students are accepted.

Financial Information:
Average cost of books: $500

Employment Profile:
% of students who pass the boards on their first try: 91

Paducah Community College

PO Box 7380
Paducah, KY 42002-7380

Contact Information:
Telephone: 502-554-6274
Fax: 502-554-6227
E-mail: pegblock@yahoo.com

Program Information:
Program begins: August
Degrees offered: Associate's, 20 months
Evening or weekend classes are available.

Application Information:
Enrollment of program: 16
Transfer students are accepted.

Financial Information:
Tuition, resident: $1,156
Tuition, non-resident: $3,276
Average cost of books: $800

Employment Profile:
% of students who pass the boards on their first try: 85
% employed within the first 6 months following graduation: 75
Average starting salary: $22,000

Maine

Kennebec Valley Technical College

92 Western Avenue
Fairfield, ME 04937-1367

Contact Information:
Telephone: 207-453-5147
Fax: 207-453-5011
E-mail: knchandl@kvtc.net
Web: www.kvtc.net

Program Information:
Duration of program: 22 months

Application Information:
Enrollment of program: 48

Financial Information:
Tuition, resident: $2,508
Tuition, non-resident: $9,581
Average cost of books: $250
% of students receiving aid: 70

Employment Profile:
% of students who pass the boards on their first try: 90
% employed within the first 6 months following graduation: 20
Average starting salary: $26,000

Maryland

Allegany College of Maryland

12401 Willowbrook Road Southeast
Cumberland, MD 21502-2596

Contact Information:
Telephone: 301-784-5538
Fax: 301-784-5015
E-mail: beth@ac.cc.md.us
Web: www.ac.cc.md.us

Program Information:
Program begins: June
Degrees offered: Certificate program, 15 months; Associate's, 12 months

Application Information:
Enrollment of program: 16
Transfer students are accepted.

Financial Information:
Tuition, resident: $3,360
Tuition, non-resident: $6,636
Average cost of books: $1,000

Employment Profile:
% of students who pass the boards on their first try: 75
% employed within the first 6 months following graduation: 75
Average starting salary: $30,000

Montgomery College

7600 Takoma Avenue
Takoma Park, MD 20912

Contact Information:
Telephone: 301-650-1450
Fax: 301-650-1446
E-mail: jcepeda@mc.cc.md.us
Web: www.mc.cc.md.us

Program Information:
Program begins: September
Duration of program: 20 months
Evening or weekend classes are available.

Application Information:
Enrollment of program: 20
Transfer students are accepted.

Financial Information:
Tuition, resident: $2,210
Tuition, non-resident: $6,018

Employment Profile:
% of students who pass the boards on their first try: 98
% employed within the first 6 months following graduation: 90
Average starting salary: $28,000

Massachusetts

Becker College

61 Sever Street
Worcester, MA 01615-0071

Contact Information:
Telephone: 508-791-9241 ext. 362
Fax: 508-849-5194
E-mail: fuller@go.becker.edu
Web: www.becker.edu

Program Information:
Program begins: August
Duration of program: 24 months

Application Information:
Enrollment of program: 100
Transfer students are accepted.

Financial Information:
% of students receiving aid: 85

Berkshire Community College

1350 West Street
Pittsfield, MA 01201-5786

Contact Information:
Telephone: 413-499-4660 ext. 313
Fax: 413-447-7840
E-mail: mdarroch@cc.berkshire.org
Web: www.cc.berkshire.org

Program Information:
Program begins: August
Degrees offered: Associate's, 19 months
Evening or weekend classes are available.

Application Information:
Enrollment of program: 26
Transfer students are accepted.

Financial Information:
Tuition, resident: $1,088
Tuition, non-resident: $6,528
Average cost of books: $300
% of students receiving aid: 90

Employment Profile:
% of students who pass the boards on their first try: 88
% employed within the first 6 months following graduation: 75
Average starting salary: $25,000

Cape Cod Community College
2240 Iyanough Road
West Barnstable, MA 02668-1599

Contact Information:
Telephone: 508-362-2131 ext. 4335
Fax: 508-362-3988
E-mail: eprice@capecod.mass.edu
Web: www.cfcc.net

Program Information:
Program begins: August
Degrees offered: Associate's, 20 months

Application Information:
Enrollment of program: 18

Financial Information:
Tuition, resident: $6,700

Employment Profile:
% of students who pass the boards on their first try: 100

Endicott College
376 Hale Street
Beverly, MA 01915

Contact Information:
Telephone: 978-232-2311
Fax: 978-232-2600
E-mail: kbarnes@endicott.edu
Web: www.endicott.edu

Program Information:
Program begins: September
Duration of program: 24 months

Application Information:
Transfer students are accepted.

Financial Information:
Average cost of books: $500
% of students receiving aid: 76

Massachusetts Bay Community College
Wellesley Hills Campus
50 Oakland Street
Wellesley Hills, MA 02181-5399

Contact Information:
Telephone: 781-239-2500
Fax: 781-416-1319
E-mail: dentpatr@mbcc.mass.edu
Web: www.mbcc.mass.edu

Program Information:
Program begins: September
Duration of program: 24 months

Financial Information:
Tuition, resident: $2,790

Newbury College
PO Box 508
129 Fisher Avenue
Brookline, MA 02445-5796

Contact Information:
Telephone: 617-730-7061
Fax: 617-738-2430
E-mail: m_smutok@newbury.edu
Web: www.newbury.edu

Program Information:
Program begins: September
Duration of program: 24 months
Evening or weekend classes are available.

Application Information:
Enrollment of program: 77

Financial Information:
Average cost of books: $200
% of students receiving aid: 76

Employment Profile:
% of students who pass the boards on their first try: 80
% employed within the first 6 months following graduation: 30
Average starting salary: $30,000

North Shore Community College
One Ferncroft Road
PO Box 3344
Danvers, MA 01923-0840

Contact Information:
Telephone: 978-762-4000 ext. 4165
Fax: 978-762-4022
E-mail: jjames@nscc.mass.edu
Web: www.nscc.cc.ma.us

Program Information:
Program begins: September
Degrees offered: Associate's, 24 months

Financial Information:
Tuition, resident: $2,365
Tuition, non-resident: $6,468
Average cost of books: $400

Employment Profile:
% of students who pass the boards on their first try: 98

Springfield Technical Community College
Building 20
One Armory Square
Springfield, MA 01101

Contact Information:
Telephone: 413-755-4844
Fax: 413-733-0688
E-mail: ldesmarais@stcc.mass.edu
Web: www.stcc.mass.edu

Program Information:
Program begins: September
Duration of program: 24 months
Evening or weekend classes are available.

Application Information:
Enrollment of program: 18
Transfer students are accepted.

Financial Information:
Tuition, resident: $2,500
Tuition, non-resident: $7,850
Average cost of books: $550

Employment Profile:
% of students who pass the boards on their first try: 95
% employed within the first 6 months following graduation: 60
Average starting salary: $26,000

Michigan

Baker College
1050 West Bristol Road
Flint, MI 48507-5508

Contact Information:
Telephone: 810-766-4100
Fax: 810-766-4049
Web: www.baker.edu

Program Information:
Program begins: September, January
Duration of program: 24 months
Evening or weekend classes are available.

Application Information:
Transfer students are accepted.

Delta College
F-56 Allied Health Building
University Center, MI 48710

Contact Information:
Telephone: 517-686-9478
Fax: 517-686-8736
E-mail: amspitz@alpha.delta.edu
Web: www.delta.edu

Program Information:
Program begins: August
Duration of program: 16 months
Evening or weekend classes are available.

Financial Information:
Tuition, resident: $1,400

Employment Profile:
% employed within the first 6 months following graduation: 25
Average starting salary: $25,000

Henry Ford Community College
5101 Evergreen Road
Dearborn, MI 48128

Contact Information:
Telephone: 313-845-9877
Fax: 313-317-6569
E-mail: robinson@mail.hfcc.net
Web: www.hfcc.net

Program Information:
Program begins: September
Degrees offered: Associate's, 24 months

Application Information:
Enrollment of program: 30
Transfer students are accepted.

Financial Information:
Tuition, resident: $1,590
Tuition, non-resident: $2,550

Employment Profile:
% of students who pass the boards on their first try: 100
% employed within the first 6 months following graduation: 100
Average starting salary: $29,000

Kellogg Community College

450 North Avenue
Battle Creek, MI 49017

Contact Information:
Telephone: 616-965-3931 ext. 2313
Fax: 616-965-4133
E-mail: millerd@kellogg.cc.mi.us
Web: www.kellogg.cc.mi.us

Program Information:
Program begins: August
Duration of program: 24 months

Financial Information:
Tuition, resident: $3,885

Minnesota

Anoka-Hennepin Technical College

1355 West Highway 10
Anoka, MN 55303

Contact Information:
Telephone: 612-576-4700 ext. 4899
Fax: 612-576-4715
E-mail: mhull@ank.tec.mn.us
Web: www.ank.tec.mn.us

Program Information:
Program begins: August
Degrees offered: Associate's, 24 months

Application Information:
Enrollment of program: 60
Transfer students are accepted.

Financial Information:
Tuition, resident: $2,874
Tuition, non-resident: $5,760
Average cost of books: $400
% of students receiving aid: 25

Employment Profile:
% of students who pass the boards on their first try: 85
% employed within the first 6 months following graduation: 87
Average starting salary: $20,000

Lake Superior College

2101 Trinity Road
Duluth, MN 55811

Contact Information:
Telephone: 218-733-7632
Fax: 218-723-4921
E-mail: j.worley@lsc.mnscu.edu
Web: www.lsc.mnscu.edu

Program Information:
Program begins: August
Duration of program: 24 months

Application Information:
Enrollment of program: 30

Financial Information:
Tuition, resident: $2,200
Tuition, non-resident: $4,400

Mississippi

Pearl River Community College—Hattiesburg

5448 US Highway 49 South
Hattiesburg, MS 39401

Contact Information:
Telephone: 601-554-9087
Fax: 601-554-9148
E-mail: fingram@prcc.cc.mo.us
Web: www.prcc.ms.us

Program Information:
Program begins: August
Duration of program: 22 months

Application Information:
Enrollment of program: 40
Transfer students are accepted.

Financial Information:
Tuition, resident: $1,286
Tuition, non-resident: $2,500
Average cost of books: $500

Employment Profile:
% of students who pass the boards on their first try: 89
% employed within the first 6 months following graduation: 90
Average starting salary: $32,000

Missouri

Linn State Technical College

One Technology Drive
Linn, MO 65051

Contact Information:
Telephone: 573-632-5625
Fax: 573-632-5623
E-mail: medin@linnstate.edu
Web: www.linnstate.edu

Program Information:
Program begins: May
Degrees offered: Associate's, 20 months
Evening or weekend classes are available.

Application Information:
Enrollment of program: 23
Transfer students are accepted.

Financial Information:
Tuition, resident: $3,348
Tuition, non-resident: $4,572

Employment Profile:
Average starting salary: $29,000

Penn Valley Community College

3201 Southwest Trafficway
Kansas City, MO 64111-2764

Contact Information:
Telephone: 816-759-4241
Fax: 816-759-4553
E-mail: robertsn@pennvalley.cc.mo.us
Web: www.kcmetro.cc.mo.us/pennvalley

Program Information:
Program begins: August
Duration of program: 22 months

Application Information:
Enrollment of program: 27

Financial Information:
Tuition, resident: $1,669

Sanford Brown College—Hazelwood Campus

75 Village Square
Hazelwood, MO 63042

Contact Information:
Telephone: 314-731-1101
Fax: 314-731-7044

Program Information:
Program begins: May
Duration of program: 19 months

Application Information:
Enrollment of program: 48
Transfer students are accepted.

St. Louis Community College at Meramec

11333 Big Bend Boulevard
St. Louis, MO 63122

Contact Information:
Telephone: 314-984-7385
Fax: 314-984-7250
Web: www.stlcc.mo.us

Program Information:
Program begins: August
Duration of program: 20 months
Evening or weekend classes are available.

Application Information:
Enrollment of program: 32

Financial Information:
Tuition, resident: $1,428
Tuition, non-resident: $1,904

Montana

Montana State University—Great Falls

College of Technology
2100 16th Avenue South
Great Falls, MT 59405

Contact Information:
Telephone: 406-771-4359
Fax: 406-771-4317
E-mail: ckowalski@msugf.edu
Web: www.montana.edu

Program Information:
Program begins: August
Duration of program: 22 months

Nebraska

Northeast Community College

801 East Benjamin Avenue
PO Box 469
Norfolk, NE 68702-0469

Contact Information:
Telephone: 402-371-2020
Fax: 402-644-0650
E-mail: marvin@alpha.necc.cc.ne.us
Web: www.alpha.necc.cc.ne.us

Program Information:
Program begins: August
Duration of program: 21 months

Application Information:
Enrollment of program: 35
Transfer students are accepted.

Financial Information:
Tuition, resident: $1,718
Tuition, non-resident: $2,066
Average cost of books: $750

Employment Profile:
% of students who pass the boards on their first try: 90
% employed within the first 6 months following graduation: 40
Average starting salary: $25,000

Nevada

Community College of Southern Nevada

6375 West Charleston Boulevard
Las Vegas, NV 89102

Contact Information:
Telephone: 702-651-5588
Fax: 702-651-5506
E-mail: joe_cracraft@ccsn.Nevada.edu
Web: www.ccsn.Nevada.edu

Program Information:
Program begins: August
Degrees offered: Associate's, 21 months

Application Information:
Enrollment of program: 32
Transfer students are accepted.

Financial Information:
Tuition, resident: $1,525
Tuition, non-resident: $2,525
Average cost of books: $300
% of students receiving aid: 20

Employment Profile:
% of students who pass the boards on their first try: 98
% employed within the first 6 months following graduation: 90
Average starting salary: $31,000

New Hampshire

New Hampshire Community Technical College

One College Drive
Claremont, NH 03743-9707

Contact Information:
Telephone: 603-542-7744
Fax: 603-543-1844
E-mail: lclute@tec.nh.us
Web: www.nhctcs.tec.nh.us

Program Information:
Program begins: August
Duration of program: 24 months
Evening or weekend classes are available.

Application Information:
Enrollment of program: 45
Transfer students are accepted.

Financial Information:
Tuition, resident: $4,000
Tuition, non-resident: $7,500
Average cost of books: $375
% of students receiving aid: 80

Employment Profile:
% of students who pass the boards on their first try: 60
% employed within the first 6 months following graduation: 100
Average starting salary: $25,000

New Jersey

Atlantic Cape Community College

5100 Black Horse Pike
Mays Landing, NJ 08330

Contact Information:
Telephone: 609-343-5037
Fax: 609-343-5122
E-mail: handler@atlantic.edu
Web: www.atlantic.edu

Program Information:
Program begins: January
Degrees offered: Associate's, 18 months

Application Information:
Enrollment of program: 30
Transfer students are accepted.

Financial Information:
Tuition, resident: $1,785
Tuition, non-resident: $3,571
Average cost of books: $300
% of students receiving aid: 40

Employment Profile:
% of students who pass the boards on their first try: 95
% employed within the first 6 months following graduation: 75
Average starting salary: $30,000

Bergen Community College

400 Paramus Road
Paramus, NJ 07652-1595

Contact Information:
Telephone: 201-447-7944
Fax: 201-612-3876
Web: www.bergen.cc.nj.us

Program Information:
Program begins: August, September
Degrees offered: Associate's, 22 months

Application Information:
Enrollment of program: 21
Transfer students are accepted.

Financial Information:
Tuition, resident: $2,485
Tuition, non-resident: $5,250
Average cost of books: $400
% of students receiving aid: 30

Employment Profile:
% of students who pass the boards on their first try: 80
% employed within the first 6 months following graduation: 74
Average starting salary: $30,000

New Mexico

San Juan College

4601 College Boulevard
Farmington, NM 87402-4699

Contact Information:
Telephone: 505-599-0407
Fax: 505-599-0385
E-mail: bircher@sjc.cc.nm.us
Web: www.sic.cc.nm.us

Program Information:
Program begins: January
Duration of program: 24 months

Application Information:
Enrollment of program: 12
Transfer students are accepted.

Financial Information:
Tuition, resident: $1,080
Tuition, non-resident: $1,800
Average cost of books: $1,000
% of students receiving aid: 25

Employment Profile:
% of students who pass the boards on their first try: 90
% employed within the first 6 months following graduation: 75
Average starting salary: $30,000

New York

Broome Community College

Decker Building
PO Box 1017
Binghamton, NY 13902

Contact Information:
Telephone: 607-778-5211
Fax: 607-778-5467
E-mail: abrams_d@sunybroome.edu
Web: www.sunybroome.edu

Program Information:
Program begins: August
Duration of program: 24 months

Application Information:
Enrollment of program: 48

Financial Information:
Tuition, resident: $2,268
Tuition, non-resident: $4,536
Average cost of books: $500
% of students receiving aid: 93

Employment Profile:
% employed within the first 6 months following graduation: 100
Average starting salary: $22,000

Genesee Community College

One College Road
Batavia, NY 14020-9704

Contact Information:
Telephone: 716-343-0055 ext. 6366
Fax: 716-343-0433
E-mail: pckerr@sunygenesee.cc.ny.us
Web: www.sunygenesee.cc.ny.us

Program Information:
Program begins: September
Duration of program: 24 months

Application Information:
Enrollment of program: 100
Transfer students are accepted.

Financial Information:
Tuition, resident: $2,500
Tuition, non-resident: $2,850
Average cost of books: $600
% of students receiving aid: 75

Employment Profile:
% of students who pass the boards on their first try: 100

Herkimer County Community College

Reservoir Road
Herkimer, NY 13350

Contact Information:
Telephone: 315-866-0300 ext. 340
Fax: 315-866-7523
E-mail: delormece@hccc.suny.edu
Web: www.hccc.ntcnet.com

Program Information:
Program begins: August
Duration of program: 20 months

Application Information:
Enrollment of program: 49
Transfer students are accepted.

Financial Information:
Tuition, resident: $2,450
Tuition, non-resident: $3,600
Average cost of books: $650
% of students receiving aid: 80

Maria College

700 New Scotland Avenue
Albany, NY 12208-1798

Contact Information:
Telephone: 518-489-7436 ext. 244
Fax: 518-438-7170
E-mail: lindas@mariacollege.org
Web: www.mariacollege.org

Program Information:
Program begins: August
Duration of program: 24 months
Evening or weekend classes are available.

Application Information:
Enrollment of program: 110
Transfer students are accepted.

Financial Information:
Tuition, resident: $5,400
Tuition, non-resident: $5,700
Average cost of books: $300

Nassau Community College

One Education Drive
Garden City, NY 11530

Contact Information:
Telephone: 516-572-7550
Fax: 516-572-7565
Web: www.sunynassau.edu

Program Information:
Program begins: September
Degrees offered: Associate's, 24 months

Application Information:
Enrollment of program: 80
Transfer students are accepted.

Financial Information:
Tuition, resident: $2,700
Tuition, non-resident: $5,400
Average cost of books: $400
% of students receiving aid: 50

Employment Profile:
% of students who pass the boards on their first try: 90
% employed within the first 6 months following graduation: 90
Average starting salary: $30,000

New York University

School of Contract Education/11 West 42nd Street
Room 518
New York, NY 10036

Contact Information:
Telephone: 212-790-1633
Fax: 212-790-1669
E-mail: mat2@is4.nyu.edu
Web: www.nyu.edu

Program Information:
Program begins: September
Degrees offered: Associate's, 48 months
Evening or weekend classes are available.

Application Information:
Enrollment of program: 30
Transfer students are accepted.

Financial Information:
Tuition, resident: $14,186
Average cost of books: $300
% of students receiving aid: 60

Employment Profile:
% employed within the first 6 months following graduation: 70
Average starting salary: $35,000

Niagara County Community College

Division of Life Sciences
3111 Saunders Settlement Road
Sanborn, NY 14132

Contact Information:
Telephone: 716-731-3271 ext. 319
Fax: 716-731-4053
E-mail: matuch@alpha.sunyniagara.cc.ny.us
Web: www.sunyniagara.cc.ny.us

Program Information:
Program begins: September
Duration of program: 24 months

Financial Information:
Tuition, resident: $2,250
Tuition, non-resident: $3,375
Average cost of books: $500

Employment Profile:
% employed within the first 6 months following graduation: 40
Average starting salary: $23,000

Orange County Community College

115 South Street
Middletown, NY 10940

Contact Information:
Telephone: 914-341-4290
Fax: 914-343-1228
E-mail: lschneide@sunyorange.edu
Web: www.sunyorange.edu

Program Information:
Program begins: September
Duration of program: 24 months

Financial Information:
Tuition, resident: $2,300

North Carolina

Caldwell Community College & Technical Institute
2855 Hickory Boulevard
Hudson, NC 28638

Contact Information:
Telephone: 828-726-2605
Fax: 828-726-2216
E-mail: mzimmerman@caldwell.cc.nc.us
Web: www.caldwell.cc.nc.us

Program Information:
Program begins: May
Degrees offered: Associate's, 24 months

Application Information:
Enrollment of program: 24
Transfer students are accepted.

Financial Information:
Tuition, resident: $900
Tuition, non-resident: $7,000
Average cost of books: $400
% of students receiving aid: 25

Employment Profile:
% of students who pass the boards on their first try: 86
% employed within the first 6 months following graduation: 65
Average starting salary: $28,000

Southwestern Community College
447 College Drive
Sylva, NC 28779

Contact Information:
Telephone: 828-586-4091 ext. 331
Fax: 828-586-3129
E-mail: debm@southwest.cc.nc.us
Web: www.southwest.cc.nc.us

Program Information:
Program begins: August
Duration of program: 18 months

Application Information:
Enrollment of program: 16

Financial Information:
Tuition, resident: $950
Tuition, non-resident: $8,000
Average cost of books: $300

Employment Profile:
% of students who pass the boards on their first try: 98
Average starting salary: $25,000

Stanly Community College
141 College Drive
Albemarle, NC 28001

Contact Information:
Telephone: 704-982-0121 ext. 303
Fax: 704-982-0819
E-mail: morettmt@stanly.cc.nc.us
Web: www.stanly.cc.nc.us

Program Information:
Program begins: August
Duration of program: 24 months

Application Information:
Enrollment of program: 24
Transfer students are accepted.

Financial Information:
Tuition, resident: $720
Tuition, non-resident: $5,868
Average cost of books: $300
% of students receiving aid: 40

Employment Profile:
% of students who pass the boards on their first try: 95
% employed within the first 6 months following graduation: 89
Average starting salary: $29,000

North Dakota

Williston State College
PO Box 1326
1410 University Avenue
Williston, ND 58802-1326

Contact Information:
Telephone: 701-774-4291
Fax: 701-774-4265
E-mail: rbenson@mail.wsc.nodak.edu
Web: www.wsc.nodak.edu

Program Information:
Duration of program: 26 months

Application Information:
Enrollment of program: 15
Transfer students are accepted.

Financial Information:
Tuition, resident: $1,806
Tuition, non-resident: $4,398
Average cost of books: $800
% of students receiving aid: 70

Employment Profile:
% of students who pass the boards on their first try: 57
% employed within the first 6 months following graduation: 53
Average starting salary: $20,000

Ohio

Central Ohio Technical College
Department of Allied Health and Public Service
1179 University Drive
Newark, OH 43055

Contact Information:
Telephone: 614-366-9360
Fax: 614-366-5047
E-mail: dsmith@cotc.tec.oh.us
Web: www.cotc.tec.oh.us

Program Information:
Program begins: September
Duration of program: 21 months

Application Information:
Enrollment of program: 26
Transfer students are accepted.

Financial Information:
Tuition, resident: $780
Tuition, non-resident: $1,080
Average cost of books: $200
% of students receiving aid: 30

Employment Profile:
% of students who pass the boards on their first try: 98
Average starting salary: $28,000

Cuyahoga Community College
2900 Community College Avenue/S & T 126
Cleveland, OH 44115

Contact Information:
Telephone: 216-987-4247
Fax: 216-987-4386
E-mail: toby.sternheimer@tri_c.cc.oh.us
Web: www.cypress.cc.ca.us

Program Information:
Program begins: August
Degrees offered: Associate's, 24 months

Application Information:
Enrollment of program: 32
Transfer students are accepted.

Financial Information:
Tuition, resident: $2,214
Tuition, non-resident: $5,868
Average cost of books: $250

Employment Profile:
% of students who pass the boards on their first try: 98
Average starting salary: $28,500

Lima Technical College
4240 Campus Drive
Lima, OH 45804

Contact Information:
Telephone: 419-995-8256
Fax: 419-995-8818
E-mail: metryma@ltc.tec.oh.us
Web: www.ltc.tec.oh.us

Program Information:
Program begins: September
Duration of program: 17 months
Evening or weekend classes are available.

Application Information:
Enrollment of program: 30
Transfer students are accepted.

Financial Information:
Tuition, resident: $3,200
Tuition, non-resident: $6,152
Average cost of books: $900
% of students receiving aid: 62

Employment Profile:
% of students who pass the boards on their first try: 80
% employed within the first 6 months following graduation: 30
Average starting salary: $29,000

North Central State College
2441 Kenwood Circle
PO Box 698
Mansfield, OH 44901-0698

Contact Information:
Telephone: 419-755-4773
Fax: 419-755-5630
E-mail: jhull@nctc.tec.oh.us
Web: www.nctc.tec.oh.us

Program Information:
Program begins: June
Degrees offered: Associate's, 24 months

Application Information:
Enrollment of program: 44

Financial Information:
Tuition, resident: $2,915
Tuition, non-resident: $5,511
Average cost of books: $600
% of students receiving aid: 60

Employment Profile:
% of students who pass the boards on their first try: 85
% employed within the first 6 months following graduation: 50
Average starting salary: $26,000

Owens Community College
PO Box 10,000
Oregon Road
Toledo, OH 43699-1947

Contact Information:
Telephone: 419-661-7084
Fax: 419-661-7251
E-mail: lgrinonneau@owens.cc.oh.us
Web: www.owens.cc.oh.us

Program Information:
Program begins: August
Duration of program: 24 months

Application Information:
Enrollment of program: 50

Financial Information:
Tuition, resident: $2,000
Tuition, non-resident: $4,000

Oklahoma

Carl Albert State College
1507 South McKenna
Poteau, OK 74953-5208

Contact Information:
Telephone: 918-647-1357
Fax: 918-647-1327
E-mail: bcarroll@casc.cc.ok.us
Web: www.casc.cc.ok.us

Program Information:
Program begins: August
Degrees offered: Associate's, 24 months

Application Information:
Enrollment of program: 32
Transfer students are accepted.

Financial Information:
Tuition, resident: $896
Tuition, non-resident: $2,816
Average cost of books: $400
% of students receiving aid: 50

Employment Profile:
% of students who pass the boards on their first try: 90
% employed within the first 6 months following graduation: 80
Average starting salary: $28,000

Murray State College
One Murray Campus
NAH 116
Tishomingo, OK 73460

Contact Information:
Telephone: 580-371-2371 ext. 341
Fax: 580-371-9844
E-mail: grobinson@msc.cc.ok.us
Web: www.msc.cc.ok.us

Program Information:
Program begins: May
Duration of program: 14 months

Application Information:
Enrollment of program: 40

Financial Information:
Average cost of books: $700
% of students receiving aid: 90

Employment Profile:
% of students who pass the boards on their first try: 90
% employed within the first 6 months following graduation: 60
Average starting salary: $28,000

Tulsa Community College
909 South Boston Avenue
Tulsa, OK 74119

Contact Information:
Telephone: 918-595-7002
Fax: 918-595-7091
E-mail: sreese@tulsa.cc.ok.us
Web: www.tulsa.cc.ok.us

Program Information:
Program begins: August
Duration of program: 24 months

Application Information:
Enrollment of program: 69

Financial Information:
Tuition, resident: $912
Tuition, non-resident: $1,960
Average cost of books: $600
% of students receiving aid: 50

Employment Profile:
% of students who pass the boards on their first try: 100
% employed within the first 6 months following graduation: 60
Average starting salary: $25,000

Pennsylvania

Alvernia College
400 Saint Bernardine Street
Reading, PA 19607

Contact Information:
Telephone: 610-796-8226
Fax: 610-796-8349
Web: www.alvernia.edu

Program Information:
Program begins: August
Duration of program: 18 months

Application Information:
Enrollment of program: 45
Transfer students are accepted.

Financial Information:
Average cost of books: $400

Employment Profile:
% of students who pass the boards on their first try: 95
Average starting salary: $23,000

Butler County Community College
PO Box 1203
Butler, PA 16003-1203

Contact Information:
Telephone: 412-287-8711 ext. 372
Fax: 412-285-6047
E-mail: barb@isrv.com
Web: www.bc3.pa.us

Program Information:
Program begins: August
Degrees offered: Associate's, 27 months

Application Information:
Enrollment of program: 25
Transfer students are accepted.

Financial Information:
Tuition, resident: $1,572
Tuition, non-resident: $3,157
Average cost of books: $400

Employment Profile:
% of students who pass the boards on their first try: 95
% employed within the first 6 months following graduation: 75
Average starting salary: $25,000

Central Pennsylvania College
Campus on College Hill
Summerdale, PA 17093-0309

Contact Information:
Telephone: 717-732-0702 ext. 2231
Fax: 717-732-5254
E-mail: joannelafferty@centralpenn.edu
Web: www.centralpenn.edu

Program Information:
Program begins: August
Duration of program: 20 months

Community College of Allegheny County

595 Beatty Road
Monroeville, PA 15146

Contact Information:
Telephone: 724-325-6663
Fax: 724-325-6701
Web: www.ccac.edu

Program Information:
Program begins: August
Duration of program: 24 months

Application Information:
Enrollment of program: 70
Transfer students are accepted.

Financial Information:
Tuition, resident: $1,632
Tuition, non-resident: $4,896
Average cost of books: $200

Employment Profile:
% of students who pass the boards on their first try: 90
% employed within the first 6 months following graduation: 100
Average starting salary: $24,000

Harcum College

750 Montgomery Avenue
Bryn Mawr, PA 19010

Contact Information:
Telephone: 610-526-6039
Fax: 610-526-6031
E-mail: sfeather@harcum.edu
Web: www.harcum.edu

Program Information:
Program begins: May
Degrees offered: Associate's, 24 months
Evening or weekend classes are available.

Application Information:
Enrollment of program: 96
Transfer students are accepted.

Financial Information:
Tuition, resident: $8,840
Average cost of books: $150
% of students receiving aid: 90

Employment Profile:
% of students who pass the boards on their first try: 80
% employed within the first 6 months following graduation: 95
Average starting salary: $32,000

Keystone College

Allied Health and Environmental Science Division
One College Green
La Plume, PA 18440-0200

Contact Information:
Telephone: 800-824-2764
Fax: 570-945-6770
E-mail: admissns@keystone.edu
Web: www.keystone.edu

Program Information:
Program begins: August
Duration of program: 25 months

Application Information:
Enrollment of program: 61
Transfer students are accepted.

Financial Information:
Average cost of books: $700
% of students receiving aid: 88

Lehigh Carbon Community College

4525 Education Park Drive
Schnecksville, PA 18078-2598

Contact Information:
Telephone: 610-799-1525
Fax: 610-799-1527
Web: www.lccc.edu

Program Information:
Program begins: September
Degrees offered: Associate's, 24 months

Application Information:
Enrollment of program: 72
Transfer students are accepted.

Financial Information:
Tuition, resident: $1,400
Tuition, non-resident: $3,600

Employment Profile:
% of students who pass the boards on their first try: 96
% employed within the first 6 months following graduation: 90
Average starting salary: $25,000

Mercyhurst College

16 West Division Street
North East, PA 16428

Contact Information:
Telephone: 814-725-6134
Fax: 814-725-6133
E-mail: glabrozz@mercyhurst.edu
Web: www.mercyhurst.edu

Program Information:
Program begins: September
Duration of program: 24 months
Evening or weekend classes are available.

Application Information:
Enrollment of program: 24
Transfer students are accepted.

Financial Information:
Tuition, resident: $8,712
Average cost of books: $400
% of students receiving aid: 95

Employment Profile:
% of students who pass the boards on their first try: 91
% employed within the first 6 months following graduation: 100
Average starting salary: $30,000

Penn State University—DuBois

College Place
DuBois, PA 15801

Contact Information:
Telephone: 814-375-4700
Fax: 814-375-4724
E-mail: ber125@psu.edu
Web: www.psu.edu

Program Information:
Program begins: August
Duration of program: 24 months

Financial Information:
Tuition, resident: $5,024
Tuition, non-resident: $7,808

Penn State University—Hazleton

Box 704-A
Hazleton, PA 18201

Contact Information:
Telephone: 717-749-6217
Fax: 717-749-6166
Web: www.hn.psu.edu/programs

Program Information:
Program begins: September
Duration of program: 19 months

Application Information:
Enrollment of program: 39
Transfer students are accepted.

Financial Information:
Average cost of books: $550
% of students receiving aid: 90

Employment Profile:
% of students who pass the boards on their first try: 85
Average starting salary: $30,000

Penn State University—Mont Alto

Campus Drive
Mont Alto, PA 17237-9703

Contact Information:
Telephone: 724-983-2866
Fax: 724-983-2820
E-mail: txg3@psu.edu
Web: www.ma.psu.edu

Program Information:
Program begins: August
Degrees offered: Associate's, 24 months
Evening or weekend classes are available.

Application Information:
Enrollment of program: 70
Transfer students are accepted.

Financial Information:
Tuition, resident: $5,654
Tuition, non-resident: $8,678
Average cost of books: $300
% of students receiving aid: 60

Employment Profile:
% of students who pass the boards on their first try: 75
% employed within the first 6 months following graduation: 50
Average starting salary: $20,000

Penn State University—Shenango
147 Shenango Avenue
Sharon, PA 161461597

Contact Information:
Telephone: 717-450-3043
Fax: 717-450-3182
E-mail: rlh18@psu.edu
Web: www.psu.edu

Program Information:
Program begins: August
Duration of program: 27 months

Application Information:
Transfer students are accepted.

Financial Information:
Tuition, resident: $6,222
Tuition, non-resident: $9,498

Employment Profile:
% of students who pass the boards on their first try: 81

University of Pittsburgh—Titusville
504 East Main Street
Titusville, PA 16354-2097

Contact Information:
Telephone: 814-827-4441
Fax: 814-827-4487
E-mail: jmexleyt@pitt.edu
Web: www.pitt.edu

Program Information:
Program begins: August, January
Duration of program: 20 months

Application Information:
Enrollment of program: 32
Transfer students are accepted.

Financial Information:
Tuition, resident: $2,822
Tuition, non-resident: $6,199
Average cost of books: $800
% of students receiving aid: 90

Employment Profile:
% of students who pass the boards on their first try: 75
Average starting salary: $26,000

Puerto Rico

Ponce University College
University of Puerto Rico Regional College Administration
PO Box 7186
Ponce, PR 00732

Contact Information:
Telephone: 787-844-8484 ext. 2414
Fax: 787-844-8108
E-mail: 1-nieves@cutpo.upr.clu.edu
Web: www.cutpo.upr.clu.edu

Program Information:
Program begins: August
Degrees offered: Associate's, 21 months

Application Information:
Enrollment of program: 124
Transfer students are accepted.

Financial Information:
Tuition, resident: $1,250
Average cost of books: $350
% of students receiving aid: 86

Employment Profile:
% of students who pass the boards on their first try: 100
% employed within the first 6 months following graduation: 95

Rhode Island

Community College of Rhode Island
275 Broadway
Newport, RI 02840-2612

Contact Information:
Telephone: 401-847-9800
Fax: 401-846-9051
Web: www.ccri.cc.ri.us

Program Information:
Program begins: September
Duration of program: 21 months

Financial Information:
Tuition, resident: $783
Tuition, non-resident: $2,292

South Carolina

Trident Technical College
PO Box 118067 AH-M
Charleston, SC 29423-8067

Contact Information:
Telephone: 843-574-6141
Fax: 843-574-6585
E-mail: zpsosal@trident.tec.sc.us
Web: www.trident.tec.sc.us

Program Information:
Program begins: May
Degrees offered: Associate's, 16 months

Application Information:
Enrollment of program: 25
Transfer students are accepted.

Financial Information:
Tuition, resident: $1,584
Tuition, non-resident: $4,899
Average cost of books: $500

Employment Profile:
% of students who pass the boards on their first try: 80
% employed within the first 6 months following graduation: 75
Average starting salary: $25,000

Tennessee

Chattanooga State Technical Community College
4501 Amnicola Highway
Chattanooga, TN 37406-1097

Contact Information:
Telephone: 423-697-4450 ext. 4730
Fax: 423-634-3071
E-mail: lwarren@cstcc.cc.tn.us

Program Information:
Program begins: August
Degrees offered: Associate's, 18 months
Evening or weekend classes are available.

Application Information:
Enrollment of program: 4

Financial Information:
Tuition, resident: $1,010
Tuition, non-resident: $4,116
Average cost of books: $700
% of students receiving aid: 50

Employment Profile:
% of students who pass the boards on their first try: 95
% employed within the first 6 months following graduation: 95
Average starting salary: $26,500

Shelby State Community College
PO Box 40568
Memphis, TN 38174-0568

Contact Information:
Telephone: 901-544-5394
Fax: 901-544-5391
Web: www.sscc.cc.tn.us

Program Information:
Program begins: May
Duration of program: 24 months

Application Information:
Enrollment of program: 20
Transfer students are accepted.

Financial Information:
Tuition, resident: $1,575
Tuition, non-resident: $5,670

Volunteer State Community College
1480 Nashville Pike
Gallatin, TN 37066

Contact Information:
Telephone: 615-452-8600 ext. 3336
Fax: 615-230-3224
E-mail: ddipert@vscc.tn.us
Web: www.vscc.cc.tn.us

Program Information:
Program begins: May
Duration of program: 24 months

Application Information:
Enrollment of program: 22
Transfer students are accepted.

Financial Information:
Tuition, resident: $1,786
Tuition, non-resident: $6,878
% of students receiving aid: 50

Employment Profile:
% of students who pass the boards on their first try: 83
% employed within the first 6 months following graduation: 30
Average starting salary: $25,000

Texas

El Paso Community College

Rio Grande Campus
PO Box 20500
El Paso, TX 79998

Contact Information:
Telephone: 915-831-4172
Fax: 915-831-4114
E-mail: debrat@epcc.edu
Web: www.epcc.edu

Program Information:
Program begins: September
Duration of program: 24 months

Application Information:
Enrollment of program: 24
Transfer students are accepted.

Financial Information:
Tuition, resident: $800
Tuition, non-resident: $1,500
Average cost of books: $300
% of students receiving aid: 80

Employment Profile:
% of students who pass the boards on their first try: 50
% employed within the first 6 months following graduation: 80
Average starting salary: $26,000

Kilgore College

1100 Broadway
Kilgore, TX 75662

Contact Information:
Telephone: 903-983-8148
Fax: 903-983-8600
E-mail: gleaton@kilgore.cc.tx.us
Web: www.kings.edu

Program Information:
Program begins: September
Duration of program: 21 months

Application Information:
Enrollment of program: 30
Transfer students are accepted.

Financial Information:
Tuition, resident: $2,108
Tuition, non-resident: $4,852
Average cost of books: $950

Employment Profile:
% of students who pass the boards on their first try: 95
% employed within the first 6 months following graduation: 80
Average starting salary: $29,000

McLennan Community College

1400 College Drive
Waco, TX 76708

Contact Information:
Telephone: 254-299-8825
Fax: 254-299-8814
E-mail: jap@mcc.cc.tx.us
Web: www.mcc.cc.tx.us

Program Information:
Program begins: July
Duration of program: 23 months

Application Information:
Enrollment of program: 46

Financial Information:
Tuition, resident: $2,900
Tuition, non-resident: $7,200
Average cost of books: $750

Employment Profile:
% of students who pass the boards on their first try: 94

Odessa College

201 West University Boulevard
Odessa, TX 79764

Contact Information:
Telephone: 915-335-6842
Fax: 915-335-6846
E-mail: ldammann@odessa.edu
Web: www.odessa.edu

Program Information:
Program begins: August
Duration of program: 21 months

Application Information:
Enrollment of program: 30
Transfer students are accepted.

Financial Information:
Tuition, resident: $3,800
Tuition, non-resident: $5,000
Average cost of books: $1,000

Employment Profile:
% of students who pass the boards on their first try: 98
% employed within the first 6 months following graduation: 85
Average starting salary: $31,500

St. Philip's College

1801 Martin Luther King Jr. Drive
San Antonio, TX 78203-2098

Contact Information:
Telephone: 512-531-3416
Fax: 512-531-4811
Web: www.accd.edu

Program Information:
Program begins: August
Degrees offered: Associate's, 16 months

Application Information:
Enrollment of program: 50
Transfer students are accepted.

Financial Information:
Tuition, resident: $600
Tuition, non-resident: $1,000
Average cost of books: $200

Employment Profile:
% of students who pass the boards on their first try: 85
% employed within the first 6 months following graduation: 50
Average starting salary: $24,000

Wharton County Junior College

911 Boling Highway
Wharton, TX 77488

Contact Information:
Telephone: 409-532-6491
Fax: 409-532-6489
Web: www.whatcom.ctc.edu

Program Information:
Program begins: August
Duration of program: 21 months

Financial Information:
Tuition, resident: $1,967
Tuition, non-resident: $3,278

Utah

Salt Lake Community College

PO Box 30808
4600 South Redwood Road
Salt Lake City, UT 84130-0808

Contact Information:
Telephone: 801-957-4054
Fax: 801-957-5708
E-mail: ploegedi@slcc.edu
Web: www.slcc.edu

Program Information:
Program begins: August
Degrees offered: Associate's, 16 months

Application Information:
Enrollment of program: 24
Transfer students are accepted.

Financial Information:
Tuition, resident: $2,004
Tuition, non-resident: $6,240
Average cost of books: $600
% of students receiving aid: 40

Employment Profile:
% of students who pass the boards on their first try: 99
% employed within the first 6 months following graduation: 100
Average starting salary: $30,000

Virginia

John Tyler Community College
13101 Jefferson Davis Highway
Chester, VA 23831

Contact Information:
Telephone: 804-796-4040
Fax: 804-796-4361
E-mail: dbowman@jt.cc.va.us
Web: www.jt.cc.va.us

Program Information:
Program begins: January, August
Degrees offered: Associate's, 22 months
Evening or weekend classes are available.

Application Information:
Enrollment of program: 12
Transfer students are accepted.

Financial Information:
Tuition, resident: $1,400
Tuition, non-resident: $5,100
Average cost of books: $400
% of students receiving aid: 25

Employment Profile:
% of students who pass the boards on their first try: 90
% employed within the first 6 months following graduation: 75
Average starting salary: $28,000

Tidewater Community College
1700 College Crescent
Building East/Room E101
Virginia Beach, VA 23456-1918

Contact Information:
Telephone: 757-822-7251
Fax: 757-427-1338
E-mail: tcjacok@tc.cc.va.us
Web: www.tc.cc.va.us/campuses/vabeach.htm

Program Information:
Program begins: August
Duration of program: 21 months

Financial Information:
Tuition, resident: $3,500
Average cost of books: $650

Wytheville Community College
1000 East Main Street
Wytheville, VA 24382

Contact Information:
Telephone: 540-223-4717
Fax: 540-223-4778
E-mail: wcheimd@wc.cc.va.us
Web: www.wc.cc.va.us

Program Information:
Program begins: August
Duration of program: 21 months

Application Information:
Enrollment of program: 25

Financial Information:
Tuition, resident: $1,408
Tuition, non-resident: $6,007

Washington

Spokane Falls Community College
3410 West Fort George Wright Drive
MS3160
Spokane, WA 99224-5288

Contact Information:
Telephone: 509-533-4144
Fax: 509-533-41432
E-mail: debbies@sfcc.spokane.cc.wa.us
Web: www.sfcc.spokane.cc.wa.us

Program Information:
Program begins: September
Degrees offered: Associate's, 18 months

Application Information:
Enrollment of program: 48
Transfer students are accepted.

Financial Information:
Tuition, resident: $1,575
Tuition, non-resident: $4,150
Average cost of books: $900
% of students receiving aid: 50

Employment Profile:
% employed within the first 6 months following graduation: 90

Whatcom Community College
237 West Kellogg Road
Bellingham, WA 98226

Contact Information:
Telephone: 360-676-2170 ext. 3311
Fax: 360-752-6767
E-mail: bgraves@whatcom.ctc.edu
Web: www.whatcom.ctc.edu

Program Information:
Program begins: September
Degrees offered: Associate's, 15 months

Financial Information:
Tuition, resident: $2,250
Tuition, non-resident: $4,000

West Virginia

College of West Virginia
609 South Kanawha Street
Beckley, WV 25802-2830

Contact Information:
Telephone: 304-253-7351 ext. 421
Fax: 304-253-0789
E-mail: front@cwv.edu
Web: www.cwv.edu

Program Information:
Program begins: July
Duration of program: 12 months

Application Information:
Enrollment of program: 20

Financial Information:
Average cost of books: $1,000
% of students receiving aid: 62

Employment Profile:
% of students who pass the boards on their first try: 55
% employed within the first 6 months following graduation: 65
Average starting salary: $30,000

Fairmont State College
School of Health Careers
501 West Main Street
Clarksburg, WV 26301

Contact Information:
Telephone: 304-623-5721
Fax: 304-624-5587
Web: www.fscwv.edu

Program Information:
Program begins: August
Duration of program: 22 months

Application Information:
Enrollment of program: 40
Transfer students are accepted.

Financial Information:
Tuition, resident: $2,244
Tuition, non-resident: $5,228

Marshall University
Marshall Community & Technical College
2000 Seventh Avenue
Huntington, WV 25703-1527

Contact Information:
Telephone: 304-696-3008
Fax: 304-696-2396
E-mail: mitchelp@marshall.edu
Web: www.marshall.edu

Program Information:
Program begins: July
Duration of program: 24 months

Application Information:
Enrollment of program: 24
Transfer students are accepted.

Financial Information:
Tuition, resident: $3,500
Tuition, non-resident: $5,800
Average cost of books: $1,000
% of students receiving aid: 50

Employment Profile:
% of students who pass the boards on their first try: 90
% employed within the first 6 months following graduation: 50
Average starting salary: $30,000

Wisconsin

Blackhawk Technical College

6004 Prairie Road
County Trunk G
Janesville, WI 53547-5009

Contact Information:
Telephone: 608-757-7698
Fax: 608-743-4407
E-mail: ilarson@blackhawk.tec.wi.us
Web: www.blackhawk.tec.wi.us

Program Information:
Program begins: August
Duration of program: 25 months
Evening or weekend classes are available.

Application Information:
Enrollment of program: 36
Transfer students are accepted.

Financial Information:
Tuition, resident: $2,200
Average cost of books: $400
% of students receiving aid: 50

Employment Profile:
% of students who pass the boards on their first try: 95
% employed within the first 6 months following graduation: 100
Average starting salary: $26,000

Milwaukee Area Technical College

Health Occupations Division
700 West State Street
Milwaukee, WI 53233

Contact Information:
Telephone: 414-297-7148
Fax: 414-297-6851
Web: www.matc.edu

Program Information:
Program begins: September
Degrees offered: Diploma, 24 months

Application Information:
Enrollment of program: 72
Transfer students are accepted.

Financial Information:
Tuition, resident: $1,789
Tuition, non-resident: $14,104

Northeast Wisconsin Technical College

2740 West Mason Street
Green Bay, WI 54307

Contact Information:
Telephone: 920-498-5543
Fax: 920-498-5673
Web: www.nwtc.tec.wi.us

Program Information:
Program begins: August
Duration of program: 24 months

Application Information:
Enrollment of program: 72
Transfer students are accepted.

Financial Information:
Tuition, resident: $2,000
Average cost of books: $560

Employment Profile:
Average starting salary: $26,000

Wyoming

Central Wyoming College

Allied Health Division
2660 Peck Avenue
Riverton, WY 82501

Contact Information:
Telephone: 307-855-2136
Fax: 307-855-2099
E-mail: ddye@interservel.cwc.whecn.edu
Web: www.cwc.whecn.edu

Program Information:
Program begins: September
Duration of program: 24 months

Application Information:
Enrollment of program: 16
Transfer students are accepted.

Financial Information:
Tuition, resident: $1,448
Tuition, non-resident: $3,552
Average cost of books: $600
% of students receiving aid: 63

Employment Profile:
% of students who pass the boards on their first try: 80
% employed within the first 6 months following graduation: 50
Average starting salary: $26,000

Physician Assistant

Michael Dryer, PA-C, MPH
Chair
Department of Physician Assistant Studies
Beaver College

Job Description

What Do They Do?

Physician assistants are healthcare professionals licensed to practice medicine under the supervision of a physician. Their specific responsibilities vary based upon training, specialty and state laws. Within the physician/ PA relationship, PAs exercise autonomy in medical decision-making. In general, PAs are able to perform 80–90 percent of the services that are typically provided by a primary care physician. Physician assistants perform the following duties:

- take patient histories and do physical exams
- diagnose illnesses
- develop and carry out treatment plans
- order and interpret diagnostic tests
- perform minor surgical procedures
- assist in surgery
- prescribe appropriate medications (in 46 states and the District of Columbia)
- counsel and educate patients concerning their medical problems

Type of Person

Physician assistants must be able to work in very stressful situations. They need to be empathetic, flexible and have strong communication skills. Most of all they must be compassionate and genuinely enjoy caring for people.

With Whom Do They Work?

Teamwork is a vital component of all physician assistant practices. They work closely and collaboratively with physicians, registered nurses, licensed practical nurses, medical assistants and medical administrators as well as other healthcare professionals.

Employment

Places of Employment

Physician assistants are employed in all of the medical specialties. They work in hospitals, emergency departments, medical offices, health maintenance organizations, occupational health centers, urgent care centers, surgical centers, and clinics. There are even PAs working in the White House who are responsible for caring for the President and the executive staff.

Employment Outlook

The rapid growth in managed care in the 1990s significantly expanded the opportunities for PA practice. Eighty-three percent of 1997 PA program graduates were employed as PAs within six months of graduation. The U.S. Bureau of Labor Statistics projects that the number of PA jobs will increase by nearly 47 percent between 1996 and 2005.[1]

Salary

The 1999 American Academy of Physician Assistant census survey reported that the average annual income for PAs who were not self-employed or employed by the government and who worked at least 32 hours per week was $68,164. Typically, those PAs who have on-call or supervisory responsibility earn an additional 10 to15 percent. That same study showed that the average annual starting salary (PAs in clinical practice for less than one year) was $57,982.[2]

Educational Programs

Length

Medical schools, universities, colleges and medical centers sponsor PA programs. The typical program is 24–25 months long. These programs offer a wide variety of degrees including Associate, Baccalaureate, and Master's, as well as graduate certificates. The trend is rapidly moving towards the Master's as the entry-level degree. Post-graduate residency programs are available for most specialties, but they are optional and are not required for licensure. During a residency the PA is typically paid a salary.

Prerequisites

Physician assistant programs typically require applicants to have at least two years of college with course work in biology and chemistry. The majority of students (70 percent) possess a BA or BS degree prior to entering a PA program. Most PA programs require that students have some prior clinical experience. While the minimum requirement varies from several hundred hours to a year or more, the average amount of prior clinical experience is 49 months.

Curriculum

The first phase of the typical PA program has 9 to 12 months of classroom and laboratory training in the basic and clinical sciences. The second phase, which is usually 12 to 15 months, includes clinical rotations in hospitals, clinics and physician's offices.

Accrediting Body

Commission on Accreditation of Allied Health Education Programs
35 East Wacker Drive, Suite 1930
Chicago, IL 60601-2208
Telephone: 312-553-9355
Fax: 312-553-9616
Web address: www.caahep.org

Certification Board

In order to practice in most states, PAs are required to take the Physician Assistant National Certification Exam. The organization that administers this exam is the National Commission on Certification of Physician Assistants (NCCPA). In addition, physician assistants must complete 100 hours of continuing medical education every two years and pass a recertification exam every six years.

National Commission on Certification of Physician Assistants (NCCPA)
157 Technology Parkway, Suite 800
Norcross, GA 30092-2913
Telephone: 770-734-4500
Fax: 770-734-4535
Web address: www.nccpa.org

Advice for Potential Students

Entrance into PA programs is highly competitive, with most programs receiving five to ten applications for each available seat. It is usually a good idea to apply to several programs and to apply as early as possible. Contact programs early in your decision-making process to find out the specific prerequisites and entrance requirements. Spend some time shadowing a practicing PA to develop a better understanding of the occupation. Contact your state physician assistant chapter to help identify PAs willing to be shadowed.

For Additional Information

Organizations

American Academy of Physician Assistants
950 North Washington Street
Alexandria, VA 22314-1552
Telephone: 703-836-2272
Fax: 703-684-1924
Web address: www.aapa.org

Publications

Books

Hooker, R. & Cawley, J. *Physician Assistants in American Medicine.* Philadelphia: Churchill Livingstone, 1997.

Provides an in-depth history of the physician assistant profession.

Journals

Clinician Reviews. Clinicians Publishing Group, 2 Brighton Road, Clifton, NJ 07012.

Provides information on advances in healthcare for physician assistants and nurse practitioners.

Journal of the American Academy of Physician Assistants. Medical Economics Company, 5 Paragon Drive, Montvale, NJ 07645.

This is the official scientific publication of the American Academy of Physician Assistants.

Physician Assistant Journal. Springhouse Corporation, 1111 Bethlehem Pike, Springhouse, PA 19477.

Provides clinical and professional information for PA practice.

Internet Resources

American Academy of Physician Assistants: www.aapa.org
National Commission on Certification of Physician Assistants: www.nccpa.org
Commission on Accreditation of Allied Health Education Programs: www.caahep.org
Student Academy of the American Academy of Physician Assistants: www.saaapa.aapa.org

Alabama

University of Alabama at Birmingham

School of Health Related Professions
1715 9th Avenue South, UAB Station
Birmingham, AL 35294-1270

Contact Information:
Telephone: 606-323-1100 ext. 292
Fax: 606-257-2454
E-mail: geraldj@admin.shrp.uab.edu
Web: www.uab.edu.

Program Information:
Program begins: June
Duration of program: 24 months

Application Information:
Enrollment of program: 49

Financial Information:
Tuition, resident: $7,200
Tuition, non-resident: $14,800
Average cost of books: $800
% of students receiving aid: 100

Employment Profile:
% of students who pass the boards on their first try: 95
% employed within the first 6 months following graduation: 80
Average starting salary: $60,000

University of South Alabama

Department of Physician Assistant Studies
1504 Springhill Avenue/Suite 4410
Mobile, AL 36604-3273

Contact Information:
Telephone: 515-571-1603
Fax: 515-271-1603
E-mail: pastudies@usamail.usouthal.edu
Web: www.usouthal.edu

Program Information:
Program begins: June
Duration of program: 27 months

Application Information:
Enrollment of program: 69

Financial Information:
Tuition, resident: $17,110
Tuition, non-resident: $21,025

Employment Profile:
% of students who pass the boards on their first try: 97
% employed within the first 6 months following graduation: 50
Average starting salary: $54,000

California

Charles R. Drew University of Medicine & Science

1731 East 120th Street/MP#42
Los Angeles, CA 90059-3025

Contact Information:
Telephone: 323-563-5879
Fax: 323-563-4833
E-mail: belassit@cdrewu.edu
Web: www.cdrewu.edu

Program Information:
Program begins: June
Duration of program: 24 months

Financial Information:
Average cost of books: $3,500
% of students receiving aid: 85

Employment Profile:
% employed within the first 6 months following graduation: 80
Average starting salary: $50,000

University of Southern California

Health Sciences Campus
The Keck School of Medicine 1975 Zonal Park KAM-B29
Los Angeles, CA 900899038

Contact Information:
Telephone: 334-434-3641
Fax: 334-434-3646
E-mail: skern@hsc.usc.edu
Web: www.usc.edu/hsc/medicine/family_med/pa/index.html

Program Information:
Program begins: August
Duration of program: 24 months

Western University of Health Sciences

Primary Care
450 East Second Street
Pomona, CA 91766-1854

Contact Information:
Telephone: 909-469-5445
Fax: 909-469-5407
E-mail: roygrac@weternu.edu
Web: www.western.edu

Program Information:
Program begins: August
Degrees offered: Master's, 24 months

Application Information:
Enrollment of program: 200
Transfer students are accepted.

Financial Information:
Tuition, resident: $13,110
Average cost of books: $1,500
% of students receiving aid: 95

Employment Profile:
% of students who pass the boards on their first try: 94
% employed within the first 6 months following graduation: 96
Average starting salary: $54,000

Colorado

Red Rocks Community College

Campus Box 38
13300 West 6th Avenue
Lakewood, CO 80228

Contact Information:
Telephone: 303-914-6386
Fax: 303-914-6804
E-mail: kathie.mcalpine@rrcc.cccoes.edu
Web: www.rrcc.cccoes.edu

Program Information:
Program begins: August
Degrees offered: Certificate program, 24 months; Master's, 24-27 months

Application Information:
Enrollment of program: 50
Transfer students are accepted.

Financial Information:
Tuition, resident: $8,265
Tuition, non-resident: $11,625
Average cost of books: $1,500

Employment Profile:
% of students who pass the boards on their first try: 90

University of Colorado Health Science Center

Child Health Associated Physician Assistant Program
4200 East Ninth Avenue/PO Box C219
Denver, CO 80262-0001

Contact Information:
Telephone: 505-272-9678
Fax: 505-272-9828
E-mail: gerald.merenstein@uchsc.edu
Web: www.uchsc.edu

Program Information:
Program begins: June
Duration of program: 33 months

Application Information:
Enrollment of program: 90

Financial Information:
Tuition, resident: $11,000
Tuition, non-resident: $25,000
Average cost of books: $1,800
% of students receiving aid: 90

Employment Profile:
% of students who pass the boards on their first try: 100
% employed within the first 6 months following graduation: 80
Average starting salary: $50,000

Florida

Barry University

11300 Northeast 2nd Avenue
Miami Shores, FL 33161

Contact Information:
Telephone: 305-899-3777
Fax: 305-899-3253
E-mail: cobrew@mail.barry.edu
Web: www.barry.edu

Program Information:
Program begins: August
Duration of program: 27 months

Financial Information:
% of students receiving aid: 100

Nova Southeastern University

3200 South University Drive
Ft. Lauderdale, FL 33328

Contact Information:
Telephone: 954-262-1250
Fax: 954-262-2285
E-mail: dpalmer@hpd.nova.edu
Web: www.nova.edu

Program Information:
Program begins: June
Degrees offered: Bachelor's, 27 months; Master's, 27 months

Application Information:
Enrollment of program: 75

Financial Information:
Tuition, resident: $15,800
Tuition, non-resident: $16,000
Average cost of books: $500
% of students receiving aid: 85

Employment Profile:
% of students who pass the boards on their first try: 96
% employed within the first 6 months following graduation: 90
Average starting salary: $54,500

University of Florida

College of Medicine
PO Box 100176
Gainesville, FL 32610-0176

Contact Information:
Telephone: 801-581-7764
Fax: 801-581-7766
E-mail: ops@pap.ufl.edu
Web: www.medinfo.ufl.edu

Program Information:
Program begins: June, July
Degrees offered: Certificate program, 24 months; Master's, 24 months

Application Information:
Enrollment of program: 60

Financial Information:
Tuition, resident: $5,768

Tuition, non-resident: $20,197
Average cost of books: $950
% of students receiving aid: 79

Employment Profile:
% of students who pass the boards on their first try: 96
% employed within the first 6 months following graduation: 100
Average starting salary: $58,561

Georgia

Emory University
School of Medicine
1462 Clifton Road/Suite 280
Atlanta, GA 30322

Contact Information:
Telephone: 404-727-7825
Fax: 404-727-7836
E-mail: kmarshal@pa.emory.edu
Web: www.emory.edu

Program Information:
Program begins: August
Degrees offered: Master's, 28 months

Financial Information:
Average cost of books: $1,500
% of students receiving aid: 98

Employment Profile:
% of students who pass the boards on their first try: 100
% employed within the first 6 months following graduation: 100
Average starting salary: $56,000

Medical College of Georgia
1120 15th Street/AE 1032
Augusta, GA 30912

Contact Information:
Telephone: 706-721-3246
Fax: 706-721-3990
E-mail: bdadig@mail.mcg.edu
Web: www.mcg.edu

Program Information:
Program begins: June
Degrees offered: Bachelor's, 24 months

Application Information:
Enrollment of program: 80

Financial Information:
Tuition, resident: $3,213
Tuition, non-resident: $10,121
Average cost of books: $350
% of students receiving aid: 70

Employment Profile:
% of students who pass the boards on their first try: 98
% employed within the first 6 months following graduation: 90
Average starting salary: $58,000

South College
709 Mall Boulevard
Savannah, GA 31406

Contact Information:
Telephone: 912-691-6024
Fax: 912-691-6082
E-mail: mvacala@southcollege.edu

Program Information:
Program begins: August
Duration of program: 28 months

Application Information:
Enrollment of program: 40
Transfer students are accepted.

Financial Information:
Tuition, non-resident: $17,200
Average cost of books: $2,000

Illinois

Finch University of Health Science—Chicago Medical School
3333 Green Bay Road
Building #51
North Chicago, IL 60064-3095

Contact Information:
Telephone: 847-578-3312
Fax: 847-578-8690
E-mail: finchcms.edu/rhs/msphysass
Web: www.finchcms.edu

Program Information:
Program begins: May
Duration of program: 24 months

Application Information:
Enrollment of program: 100

Financial Information:
Average cost of books: $2,199
% of students receiving aid: 88

Employment Profile:
% of students who pass the boards on their first try: 98
% employed within the first 6 months following graduation: 75
Average starting salary: $55,000

Midwestern University
555 31st Street
Downers Grove, IL 60515-1235

Contact Information:
Telephone: 630-515-6034
Fax: 630-971-6402
Web: www.midwestern.edu

Program Information:
Program begins: June
Degrees offered: Bachelor's, 24 months; Master's, 27 months

Application Information:
Enrollment of program: 165
Transfer students are accepted.

Financial Information:
Tuition, resident: $13,289
Tuition, non-resident: $14,575

Employment Profile:
% of students who pass the boards on their first try: 90
% employed within the first 6 months following graduation: 94

Iowa

University of Iowa
School of Medicine
5167 Westlawn
Iowa City, IA 52242-1008

Contact Information:
Telephone: 205-934-4605
Fax: 205-934-3780
E-mail: david-asprey@uiowa.edu
Web: www.uiowa.edu

Program Information:
Program begins: September
Duration of program: 25 months

Financial Information:
Tuition, resident: $4,572
Tuition, non-resident: $14,730
Average cost of books: $800

Employment Profile:
% of students who pass the boards on their first try: 100
% employed within the first 6 months following graduation: 65
Average starting salary: $51,399

University of Osteopathic Medicine and Health Sciences
3200 Grand Avenue
Des Moines, IA 50312-4198

Contact Information:
Telephone: 817-735-2301
Fax: 817-735-2529
E-mail: jcahalan@uomhs.edu
Web: www.uomhs.edu

Program Information:
Program begins: May
Duration of program: 24 months

Application Information:
Enrollment of program: 64
Transfer students are accepted.

Financial Information:
Average cost of books: $3,200
% of students receiving aid: 97

Employment Profile:
% of students who pass the boards on their first try: 94
% employed within the first 6 months following graduation: 50
Average starting salary: $55,000

Kansas

Wichita State University
Campus Box 43
1845 North Fairmount
Wichita, KS 67260-0043

Contact Information:
Telephone: 316-978-3011
Fax: 316-978-3025
E-mail: lary@chp.twsu.edu
Web: www.wichita.edu

Program Information:
Program begins: August
Duration of program: 24 months

Application Information:
Enrollment of program: 92
Transfer students are accepted.

Financial Information:
Tuition, resident: $6,852
Tuition, non-resident: $24,276
Average cost of books: $1,300
% of students receiving aid: 5

Employment Profile:
% of students who pass the boards on their first try: 95
% employed within the first 6 months following graduation: 90
Average starting salary: $51,500

Maryland

Anne Arundel Community College

101 College Parkway
Arnold, MD 21012

Contact Information:
Telephone: 410-315-7037
Fax: 410-315-7000
E-mail: pdfalkenstein@aacc.cc.ms.us
Web: www.aacc.cc.ms.us

Program Information:
Program begins: May
Duration of program: 26 months

Application Information:
Enrollment of program: 58
Transfer students are accepted.

Financial Information:
Tuition, resident: $16,323
Tuition, non-resident: $33,666
Average cost of books: $1,200
% of students receiving aid: 100

Employment Profile:
% of students who pass the boards on their first try: 964
% employed within the first 6 months following graduation: 20
Average starting salary: $52,300

Essex Community College

7201 Rossville Boulevard
Baltimore, MD 21237

Contact Information:
Telephone: 410-789-6579
Fax: 410-780-6504
E-mail: sshaw@essex.cc.md.us

Program Information:
Program begins: June
Duration of program: 26 months

Application Information:
Enrollment of program: 60

Financial Information:
Tuition, resident: $6,000
Tuition, non-resident: $17,000
Average cost of books: $2,000

Employment Profile:
% of students who pass the boards on their first try: 98
% employed within the first 6 months following graduation: 95
Average starting salary: $48,000

Massachusetts

Northeastern University

360 Huntington Avenue/202 Robinson
Boston, MA 021155000

Contact Information:
Telephone: 617-373-3195
Fax: 617-373-3338
Web: www.dac.neu.edu

Program Information:
Program begins: September
Degrees offered: Master's, 24 months

Application Information:
Enrollment of program: 64

Employment Profile:
% of students who pass the boards on their first try: 100
% employed within the first 6 months following graduation: 100
Average starting salary: $55,000

Michigan

Central Michigan University

101 Foust Hall
Mt Pleasant, MI 48859

Contact Information:
Telephone: 517-774-2478
Fax: 517-774-2433
Web: www.cmich.edu

Program Information:
Program begins: May
Duration of program: 27 months

Application Information:
Enrollment of program: 80

Financial Information:
Average cost of books: $2,000
% of students receiving aid: 98

Employment Profile:
% of students who pass the boards on their first try: 100
% employed within the first 6 months following graduation: 60
Average starting salary: $54,000

Grand Valley State University

Cook Institute for Medical Education and Research
251 Michigan Northeast
Grand Rapids, MI 49403

Contact Information:
Telephone: 616-391-9550
Fax: 616-391-9559
Web: www.gvsu.edu

Program Information:
Program begins: August
Duration of program: 32 months
Evening or weekend classes are available.

Application Information:
Enrollment of program: 89

Financial Information:
Tuition, resident: $6,000
Tuition, non-resident: $12,000
Average cost of books: $600

Employment Profile:
% of students who pass the boards on their first try: 100
% employed within the first 6 months following graduation: 60
Average starting salary: $55,000

University of Detroit—Mercy

8200 West Outer Drive
Detroit, MI 48219

Contact Information:
Telephone: 214-648-1701
Fax: 214-648-1003
E-mail: abdelnol@udmercy.edu
Web: www.llids.udmercy.edu/paprogram

Program Information:
Program begins: September
Duration of program: 24 months
Evening or weekend classes are available.

Application Information:
Enrollment of program: 86
Transfer students are accepted.

Financial Information:
Average cost of books: $900
% of students receiving aid: 92

Employment Profile:
% of students who pass the boards on their first try: 97
% employed within the first 6 months following graduation: 98
Average starting salary: $59,000

Wayne State University

College of Pharmacy and Allied Health Professions
Rackham Building #102, 60 East Farnsworth
Detroit, MI 48202

Contact Information:
Telephone: 313-577-7597
Fax: 313-577-5467
E-mail: h.normile@wayne.edu
Web: www.pa.wayne.edu

Program Information:
Program begins: May
Degrees offered: Master's, 24 months

Application Information:
Enrollment of program: 96
Transfer students are accepted.

Financial Information:
Tuition, resident: $3,912
Tuition, non-resident: $8,520
Average cost of books: $300
% of students receiving aid: 50

Employment Profile:
% of students who pass the boards on their first try: 99
% employed within the first 6 months following graduation: 100
Average starting salary: $55,000

Western Michigan University
Kalamazoo, MI 49008-5138

Contact Information:
Telephone: 616-387-5311
Fax: 616-387-5319
E-mail: jim.vanrhee@ismich.edu
Web: www.wmich.edu

Program Information:
Program begins: August
Duration of program: 24 months
Evening or weekend classes are available.

Application Information:
Enrollment of program: 36

Financial Information:
Tuition, resident: $13,265
Tuition, non-resident: $35,740
Average cost of books: $1,000

Employment Profile:
% of students who pass the boards on their first try: 100

Minnesota

Augsburg College
2211 Riverside Avenue, CB 149
Minneapolis, MN 55454

Contact Information:
Telephone: 621-330-1039
Fax: 612-330-1757
E-mail: paprog@augsburg.edu

Program Information:
Duration of program: 27 months

Application Information:
Enrollment of program: 56
Transfer students are accepted.

Employment Profile:
% of students who pass the boards on their first try: 97
% employed within the first 6 months following graduation: 60
Average starting salary: $50,000

Missouri

Saint Louis University Health Sciences Center
3437 Caroline Street
St. Louis, MO 63104

Contact Information:
Telephone: 314-577-8521
Fax: 314-577-8503
E-mail: mumard@slu.edu
Web: www.slu.edu

Program Information:
Program begins: May
Degrees offered: Certificate program, 27 months; Bachelor's, 27 months; Master's, 31 months

Application Information:
Enrollment of program: 61

Financial Information:
Average cost of books: $1,400
% of students receiving aid: 95

Employment Profile:
% of students who pass the boards on their first try: 100
Average starting salary: $52,194

Montana

Rocky Mountain College
1511 Poly Drive
Billings, MT 59102-1796

Contact Information:
Telephone: 406-657-1190
Fax: 406-657-1194
Web: www.rocky.edu

Program Information:
Program begins: August
Duration of program: 24 months

Application Information:
Enrollment of program: 40
Transfer students are accepted.

Financial Information:
Average cost of books: $1,500
% of students receiving aid: 65

Employment Profile:
% of students who pass the boards on their first try: 100
% employed within the first 6 months following graduation: 80
Average starting salary: $45,000

Nebraska

Union College
3800 South 48th Street
Lincoln, NE 68506

Contact Information:
Telephone: 402-486-2527
Fax: 402-486-2559
E-mail: paprog@ucollege.edu
Web: www.ucollege.edu/pa

Program Information:
Program begins: June
Duration of program: 27 months

Application Information:
Enrollment of program: 50
Transfer students are accepted.

Financial Information:
Average cost of books: $1,500

University of Nebraska Medical Center
984300 Nebraska Medical Center
Omaha, NE 68198-4300

Contact Information:
Telephone: 313-993-6057
Fax: 313-993-6175
E-mail: dklanden@unmc.edu
Web: www.unmc.edu/alliedhealth/pa

Program Information:
Program begins: August
Degrees offered: Master's, 28 months

Application Information:
Enrollment of program: 40

Financial Information:
Tuition, resident: $6,121
Tuition, non-resident: $15,119

Employment Profile:
% of students who pass the boards on their first try: 98
% employed within the first 6 months following graduation: 100
Average starting salary: $57,000

New Hampshire

Notre Dame College
2321 Elm Street
Manchester, NH 03104-2299

Contact Information:
Telephone: 603-647-5500 ext. 220
Fax: 603-669-6968
E-mail: admissions@notredame.edu
Web: ww.notredame.edu

Program Information:
Program begins: January
Duration of program: 24 months

Application Information:
Enrollment of program: 1500

Financial Information:
Average cost of books: $1,000
% of students receiving aid: 100

New Jersey

University of Medicine & Dentistry of New Jersey
Robert Wood Johnson Medical School
675 Hoes Lane
Piscataway, NJ 08854-5635

Contact Information:
Telephone: 303-315-7963
Fax: 303-315-6976
Web: www.umdnj.edu

Program Information:
Program begins: May
Degrees offered: Master's, 36 months

Application Information:
Enrollment of program: 105

Financial Information:
Tuition, resident: $9,756
Tuition, non-resident: $14,634
Average cost of books: $400
% of students receiving aid: 97

Employment Profile:
% of students who pass the boards on their first try: 98
% employed within the first 6 months following graduation: 100
Average starting salary: $55,000

New York

Bronx Lebanon Hospital Center
1650 Selwyn Avenue
Suite 11D
Bronx, NY 10457

Contact Information:
Telephone: 718-960-1255
Fax: 718-960-1329

Program Information:
Duration of program: 27 months

Employment Profile:
% of students who pass the boards on their first try: 95
% employed within the first 6 months following graduation: 75
Average starting salary: $55,000

Daemen College
4380 Main Street
Amherst, NY 14226-3592

Contact Information:
Telephone: 716-839-8551
Fax: 716-839-8252
Web: www.daemen.edu

Program Information:
Program begins: September
Degrees offered: Bachelor's, 57 months; Master's, 57 months

Application Information:
Enrollment of program: 160
Transfer students are accepted.

Financial Information:
Average cost of books: $1,000
% of students receiving aid: 81

Employment Profile:
% of students who pass the boards on their first try: 100
% employed within the first 6 months following graduation: 95
Average starting salary: $45,000

D'Youville College
320 Porter Avenue
Buffalo, NY 14201

Contact Information:
Telephone: 716-881-7607
Fax: 716-881-7732
E-mail: rudoffm.@dyc.edu
Web: www.dyc.edu

Program Information:
Program begins: July
Duration of program: 48 months

Application Information:
Enrollment of program: 80
Transfer students are accepted.

Financial Information:
Average cost of books: $600

Employment Profile:
% of students who pass the boards on their first try: 98
% employed within the first 6 months following graduation: 75

Hudson Valley Community College
Albany Medical College Mail Code 4
47 New Scotland Avenue
Albany, NY 12208

Contact Information:
Telephone: 518-262-5251
Fax: 518-262-6698
E-mail: bauersal@hvcc.edu
Web: www.hucc.edu

Program Information:
Program begins: August
Degrees offered: Certificate program, 24 months; Post-bachelor's Certificate, 24 months

Application Information:
Enrollment of program: 80

Financial Information:
Tuition, resident: $3,525
Tuition, non-resident: $8,100
Average cost of books: $2,400
% of students receiving aid: 55

Employment Profile:
% of students who pass the boards on their first try: 100
% employed within the first 6 months following graduation: 50
Average starting salary: $55,000

Le Moyne College
1419 Salt Springs Road
Syracuse, NY 13214-1399

Contact Information:
Telephone: 315-445-4745
Fax: 315-445-4602
E-mail: simonepa@lemoyne.edu
Web: www.lemoyne.edu

Program Information:
Program begins: August
Duration of program: 24 months

Rochester Institute of Technology
85 Lomb Memorial Drive
Rochester, NY 14623-5604

Contact Information:
Telephone: 716-475-5945
Fax: 716-475-5809
E-mail: sjtscl@rit.edu
Web: www.rit.edu

Program Information:
Program begins: August
Duration of program: 48 months

Application Information:
Enrollment of program: 101
Transfer students are accepted.

Financial Information:
Average cost of books: $1,500
% of students receiving aid: 75

Employment Profile:
% of students who pass the boards on their first try: 96
% employed within the first 6 months following graduation: 50
Average starting salary: $45,000

Sisters of Charity Medical Center—Bayley Seton Camp
75 Vanderbilt Avenue
Staten Island, NY 10304-3850

Contact Information:
Telephone: 718-354-5570
Fax: 718-354-6146

Program Information:
Program begins: August
Degrees offered: Certificate program, 23 months

Application Information:
Enrollment of program: 90

Financial Information:
Average cost of books: $1,800
% of students receiving aid: 99

Employment Profile:
% of students who pass the boards on their first try: 99
% employed within the first 6 months following graduation: 80
Average starting salary: $55,000

SUNY Health Science Center at Brooklyn
450 Clarkson Avenue
PO Box 1222
Brooklyn, NY 11203

Contact Information:
Telephone: 718-270-2324
Fax: 718-270-7459
Web: www.hscbklyn.edu

Program Information:
Program begins: June
Degrees offered: Bachelor's, 27 months

Application Information:
Enrollment of program: 30
Transfer students are accepted.

Financial Information:
Tuition, resident: $4,903
Tuition, non-resident: $8,300
Average cost of books: $300

Employment Profile:
% of students who pass the boards on their first try: 95
% employed within the first 6 months following graduation: 90
Average starting salary: $55,000

SUNY Health Science Center at Stony Brook
SHTM-HSC/L2-052
Stony Brook, NY 11794-8202

Contact Information:
Telephone: 516-444-3190
Fax: 516-444-7621
E-mail: plombardo@epo.hsc.sunysb.edu
Web: www.sunysb.edu/shtm

Program Information:
Program begins: September
Duration of program: 24 months

Application Information:
Enrollment of program: 96
Transfer students are accepted.

Financial Information:
Tuition, resident: $4,141
Tuition, non-resident: $9,041
Average cost of books: $2,500

Employment Profile:
% of students who pass the boards on their first try: 100
% employed within the first 6 months following graduation: 70
Average starting salary: $55,000

North Carolina

East Carolina University
School of Allied Health Sciences
Carol Belk Building Annex 6
Greenville, NC 27858-4353

Contact Information:
Telephone: 252-328-2096
Fax: 252-328-2098
E-mail: huechtkere@mail.ecu.edu
Web: www.ecu.edu

Program Information:
Program begins: August
Duration of program: 24 months

Application Information:
Transfer students are accepted.

Financial Information:
Tuition, resident: $3,500

Ohio

Cuyahoga Community College
11000 Pleasant Valley Road
Parma, OH 44130

Contact Information:
Telephone: 216-987-5123
Fax: 216-987-5066
E-mail: joyce.janicek@tri-c.cc.oh.us
Web: www.tri-c.cc.us

Program Information:
Program begins: August, January
Duration of program: 22 months

Application Information:
Enrollment of program: 47

Financial Information:
Tuition, resident: $4,700
Tuition, non-resident: $12,300

Employment Profile:
% of students who pass the boards on their first try: 100
% employed within the first 6 months following graduation: 50
Average starting salary: $40,000

Oklahoma

University of Oklahoma Health Sciences Center
PO Box 26901
Oklahoma City, OK 73190

Contact Information:
Telephone: 207-283-0171 ext. 2812
Fax: 207-286-9493
Web: www.ouhsc.edu

Program Information:
Program begins: September
Duration of program: 30 months

Application Information:
Enrollment of program: 50

Financial Information:
Tuition, resident: $5,326
Tuition, non-resident: $15,763
Average cost of books: $2,000

Employment Profile:
% of students who pass the boards on their first try: 95
% employed within the first 6 months following graduation: 50
Average starting salary: $50,000

Oregon

Oregon Health Sciences University
3181 Southwest Sam Jackson Park Road/GH 219
Portland, OR 97201

Contact Information:
Telephone: 503-494-1484
Fax: 503-494-1409
E-mail: ruback@ohsu.edu
Web: www.ohsu.edu

Program Information:
Program begins: August
Duration of program: 26 months

Application Information:
Enrollment of program: 45

Financial Information:
Tuition, resident: $15,000
Tuition, non-resident: $18,900
Average cost of books: $1,500
% of students receiving aid: 80

Employment Profile:
% of students who pass the boards on their first try: 97

Pacific University
2043 College Way
Forest Grove, OR 97116

Contact Information:
Telephone: 503-359-2898
Fax: 503-359-2977
Web: www.pacific.edu

Program Information:
Program begins: June
Duration of program: 27 months

Application Information:
Enrollment of program: 300

Employment Profile:
% employed within the first 6 months following graduation: 80
Average starting salary: $52,000

Pennsylvania

Duquesne University
Rangos School of Health Sciences
Health Sciences Building/Room 323
Pittsburgh, PA 15282-0010

Contact Information:
Telephone: 412-396-5914
Fax: 412-396-5554
E-mail: pinevich@duq.edu
Web: www.duq.edu

Program Information:
Program begins: August
Duration of program: 27 months

Application Information:
Enrollment of program: 68
Transfer students are accepted.

Financial Information:
Average cost of books: $1,500

Employment Profile:
% of students who pass the boards on their first try: 100

Gannon University
109 University Square
Erie, PA 16541-0001

Contact Information:
Telephone: 814-871-5643

Fax: 814-871-5662
E-mail: rothkauf001@mail1.gannon.edu
Web: www.gannon.edu

Program Information:
Program begins: August
Duration of program: 48 months
Evening or weekend classes are available.

Application Information:
Enrollment of program: 150
Transfer students are accepted.

Financial Information:
Tuition, resident: $12,710
Tuition, non-resident: $14,310
Average cost of books: $630
% of students receiving aid: 80

Employment Profile:
% of students who pass the boards on their first try: 90
Average starting salary: $43,500

King's College

133 North River Street
Wilkes Barre, PA 18711

Contact Information:
Telephone: 570-208-5853
Fax: 570-208-6018
E-mail: esbaboni@kings.edu
Web: www.kings.edu

Program Information:
Program begins: August
Duration of program: 24 months

Application Information:
Enrollment of program: 44
Transfer students are accepted.

Financial Information:
Average cost of books: $800
% of students receiving aid: 100

Employment Profile:
% of students who pass the boards on their first try: 90
% employed within the first 6 months following graduation: 90
Average starting salary: $50,000

Lock Haven University

401 North Fairview Street
G22 Stevenson Library
Lock Haven, PA 17745

Contact Information:
Telephone: 570-893-2541
Fax: 570-893-2540
E-mail: lbeers@eagle.lhup.edu
Web: www.lhup.edu

Program Information:
Program begins: May
Degrees offered: Master's, 24 months

Application Information:
Enrollment of program: 60

Financial Information:
Tuition, resident: $4,122
Tuition, non-resident: $7,492
Average cost of books: $600
% of students receiving aid: 80

Employment Profile:
% of students who pass the boards on their first try: 94
% employed within the first 6 months following graduation: 100

Pennsylvania College of Technology

One College Avenue #123
Williamsport, PA 17701

Contact Information:
Telephone: 570-327-4779
Fax: 570-321-5557
E-mail: eklinger@pct.edu
Web: www.pct.edu

Program Information:
Program begins: August
Degrees offered: Bachelor's, 24 months

Application Information:
Enrollment of program: 25
Transfer students are accepted.

Financial Information:
Tuition, resident: $12,656
Tuition, non-resident: $13,900
Average cost of books: $1,800

Employment Profile:
% of students who pass the boards on their first try: 96
% employed within the first 6 months following graduation: 100
Average starting salary: $50,000

Philadelphia College of Osteopathic Medicine

Evans Hall 005
4170 City Avenue
Philadelphia, PA 19131

Contact Information:
Telephone: 215-871-6772
Fax: 215-871-6702
Web: www.pcom.edu

Program Information:
Program begins: August
Degrees offered: Certificate program, 25 months; Master's, 25 months

Application Information:
Enrollment of program: 50

Financial Information:
Tuition, resident: $14,930
Average cost of books: $1,000
% of students receiving aid: 35

Employment Profile:
% of students who pass the boards on their first try: 94
% employed within the first 6 months following graduation: 100
Average starting salary: $51,000

Philadelphia College of Textiles and Science

School of Science and Health
School House Lane and Henry Avenue
Philadelphia, PA 19144

Contact Information:
Telephone: 215-951-2908
Fax: 215-951-2526
E-mail: bakerm@philad.edu
Web: www.philad.edu

Program Information:
Program begins: June
Duration of program: 25 months

Application Information:
Enrollment of program: 86
Transfer students are accepted.

Financial Information:
Tuition, resident: $18,646
Tuition, non-resident: $18,696
Average cost of books: $2,500

Employment Profile:
% of students who pass the boards on their first try: 97

Seton Hill College

Seton Hill Drive
Greensburg, PA 15601

Contact Information:
Telephone: 724-838-7846
Fax: 724-830-1295
E-mail: admit@setonhill.edu
Web: www.setonhill.edu

Program Information:
Program begins: September
Duration of program: 23 months

Application Information:
Enrollment of program: 75
Transfer students are accepted.

Financial Information:
Average cost of books: $750
% of students receiving aid: 94

St. Francis College

Sullivan Hall Room 104
Loretto, PA 15940

Contact Information:
Telephone: 814-472-3134
Fax: 814-472-3137
E-mail: bsimon@sfcpa.edu
Web: www.secpa.edu

Program Information:
Program begins: August
Duration of program: 24 months

Application Information:
Enrollment of program: 45
Transfer students are accepted.

Financial Information:
Average cost of books: $800
% of students receiving aid: 96

Employment Profile:
% of students who pass the boards on their first try: 93
Average starting salary: $48,000

South Carolina

Medical University of South Carolina
PO Box 250856
165 Cannon Street, Suite 403
Charleston, SC 29425

Contact Information:
Telephone: 843-792-4690
Fax: 843-792-0506
E-mail: metzae@musc.edu
Web: www.musc.edu/pa-program

Program Information:
Program begins: May
Degrees offered: Bachelor's, 27 months; Master's

Application Information:
Enrollment of program: 36

Financial Information:
Tuition, resident: $8,900
Tuition, non-resident: $25,948
Average cost of books: $400

Employment Profile:
% of students who pass the boards on their first try: 98
% employed within the first 6 months following graduation: 90
Average starting salary: $55,000

South Dakota

University of South Dakota
414 East Clark Street
Vermillion, SD 57069

Contact Information:
Telephone: 219-458-2483
Fax: 219-458-3077
E-mail: gstewart@usd.edu
Web: www.usd.edu

Program Information:
Program begins: August
Degrees offered: Certificate program, 24 months; Associate's, 24 months

Application Information:
Enrollment of program: 40

Financial Information:
Tuition, resident: $3,400
Tuition, non-resident: $11,000
Average cost of books: $2,000

Employment Profile:
% of students who pass the boards on their first try: 97
% employed within the first 6 months following graduation: 100
Average starting salary: $47,500

Tennessee

Trevecca Nazarene University
333 Murfreesboro Road
Nashville, TN 37210-2877

Contact Information:
Telephone: 615-248-1225
Fax: 615-248-1622
E-mail: dlennon@trevecca.edu
Web: www.treveca.com

Program Information:
Program begins: September
Duration of program: 27 months

Application Information:
Enrollment of program: 99
Transfer students are accepted.

Financial Information:
Average cost of books: $1,200
% of students receiving aid: 100

Employment Profile:
% of students who pass the boards on their first try: 95
Average starting salary: $55,000

Texas

Army Medical Department Center and School
MCCS HMP (PA Br)
Ft. Sam Houston, TX 78234-6138

Contact Information:
Telephone: 210-221-8765
Fax: 210-221-8493
Web: www.cs.amedd.army.mil/ipap

Program Information:
Program begins: Quarterly
Degrees offered: Certificate program, 24 months; Associate's, 24 months

Application Information:
Enrollment of program: 360

Employment Profile:
% of students who pass the boards on their first try: 98
% employed within the first 6 months following graduation: 100
Additional Information: Enrollment only open to active military personnel

Baylor College of Medicine
One Baylor Plaza, Room 633E
Houston, TX 77030

Contact Information:
Telephone: 713-798-4619
Fax: 713-798-6128
E-mail: melodym@bcm.tmc.edu
Web: www.bcm.tmc.edu

Program Information:
Program begins: May
Duration of program: 30 months

Application Information:
Enrollment of program: 90

Financial Information:
Average cost of books: $2,000

Employment Profile:
% of students who pass the boards on their first try: 100

University of North Texas Health Science Center at Ft. Worth
3500 Camp Bowie Boulevard
Ft. Worth, TX 76107-2699

Contact Information:
Telephone: 402-559-7953
Fax: 402-559-5356
Web: www.hsc.unit.edu

Program Information:
Program begins: August
Duration of program: 31 months

Application Information:
Enrollment of program: 43

Financial Information:
Tuition, resident: $6,700
Tuition, non-resident: $36,000

University of Texas Medical Branch
School of Allied Health Sciences
301 University Boulevard
Galveston, TX 77555-1028

Contact Information:
Telephone: 605-677-5128
Fax: 605-677-6569
E-mail: rrahr@utmb.edu
Web: www.utmb.edu

Program Information:
Program begins: June
Duration of program: 24 months
Evening or weekend classes are available.

Application Information:
Enrollment of program: 122

Financial Information:
Tuition, resident: $900
Tuition, non-resident: $5,700
Average cost of books: $2,000
% of students receiving aid: 85

Employment Profile:
% of students who pass the boards on their first try: 95
% employed within the first 6 months following graduation: 75
Average starting salary: $50,000

University of Texas Southwestern Medical Center—Dallas
5323 Harry Hines Boulevard
Dallas, TX 75235-9090

Contact Information:
Telephone: 323-442-1328
Fax: 323-442-1260

E-mail: ejones@mednet.swmed.edu
Web: www.swmed.edu

Program Information:
Program begins: May
Duration of program: 27 months

Application Information:
Enrollment of program: 110

Financial Information:
Tuition, resident: $4,370
Tuition, non-resident: $28,520
Average cost of books: $1,500
% of students receiving aid: 67

Employment Profile:
% of students who pass the boards on their first try: 100
% employed within the first 6 months following graduation: 90
Average starting salary: $56,000

Utah

University of Utah Health Sciences Center

520 Wakara Way
Salt Lake City, UT 84108

Contact Information:
Telephone: 801-585-9135
Fax: 801-585-1001
E-mail: dpedersen@upap.utah.edu
Web: www.utah.edu

Program Information:
Program begins: August
Degrees offered: Master's, 24 months

Application Information:
Enrollment of program: 32

Financial Information:
Tuition, resident: $11,887
Tuition, non-resident: $13,841
Average cost of books: $1,000
% of students receiving aid: 80

Employment Profile:
% of students who pass the boards on their first try: 97
% employed within the first 6 months following graduation: 100
Average starting salary: $56,000

Virginia

College of Health Sciences

PO Box 13186
Roanoke, VA 24031-3186

Contact Information:
Telephone: 540-985-4016
Fax: 540-224-4551
E-mail: pa@chs.edu
Web: www.chs.edu

Program Information:
Program begins: August
Degrees offered: Bachelor's, 24 months

Application Information:
Enrollment of program: 48

Wisconsin

University of Wisconsin—Madison

1300 University Avenue/1050 MSC
Madison, WI 53706

Contact Information:
Telephone: 608-263-5620
Fax: 608-263-6434
E-mail: jjnoack@facstaff.wisc.edu
Web: www.medsch.wisc.edu

Program Information:
Program begins: September
Duration of program: 24 months

Application Information:
Enrollment of program: 60
Transfer students are accepted.

Financial Information:
Tuition, resident: $4,588
Tuition, non-resident: $15,939
Average cost of books: $2,300

Employment Profile:
% of students who pass the boards on their first try: 100
Average starting salary: $50,000

University Wisconsin—LaCrosse-Gundersen Mayo

116 Cowley Hall/1725 State Street
La Crosse, WI 54601-3767

Contact Information:
Telephone: 608-785-6620
Fax: 608-785-6647
E-mail: zellmermark@uwlax.edu
Web: www.uwlax.edu/sah/physicianassistant

Program Information:
Program begins: June
Degrees offered: Certificate program, 28 months; Bachelor's, 28 months

Application Information:
Enrollment of program: 24
Transfer students are accepted.

Financial Information:
Tuition, resident: $7,371
Tuition, non-resident: $17,528
Average cost of books: $1,200
% of students receiving aid: 90

Employment Profile:
% of students who pass the boards on their first try: 100
% employed within the first 6 months following graduation: 1000
Average starting salary: $51,000

Radiation Therapist

Patricia J. Giordano, MS, RT(R)(T)
Assistant Professor/Program Director
Radiation Therapy
Gwynedd-Mercy College
School of Allied Health
Gwynedd Valley, Pennsylvania

Job Description

What Do They Do?

A radiographer uses low energy X-rays to diagnose disease whereas a radiation therapist uses high energy X-rays and radioactive materials to treat cancer patients. (See Chapter 17 for more information on Radiography). Radiation therapists care for cancer patients of all ages by using high energy X-rays, radioactive materials and other sources of ionizing radiation. Radiation affects the DNA and disrupts the cell cycle and cell division and either shrinks the size of or completely eradicates a tumor. Radiation therapists assist the radiation oncologist (a physician who specializes in the treatment of cancer) and radiation physicist in administering the prescribed radiation procedures that include

- simulation—the procedure in which the treatment parameters are set
- dosimetry—the procedure in which the patient's treatment dosage is calculated
- treatment administration
- performance of quality assurance
- nursing
- follow-up care of the patient

The radiation therapist operates sophisticated state-of-the-art equipment in providing this care.

Radiation therapists are responsible for the following tasks:

- Participating as an essential member of the radiation oncology team
- Evaluating and assessing treatment delivery equipment
- Delivering an accurate prescribed course of treatment
- Evaluating and assessing the physiologic and psychological conditions of their patients
- Adhering to their professional code of ethics and the boundaries within which radiation therapists practice

Radiation therapists work under the direction of radiation oncologists.

Type of Person

Radiation therapists tend to be highly motivated individuals who possess good communication skills, have an aptitude for science and math, are task-oriented, and enjoy working as team members.

With Whom Do They Work?

Radiation therapists are members of the radiation oncology team. They work with radiation oncologists, radiation physicists, oncology nurses, and social workers as well as other members of the medical profession.

Employment

Places of Employment

Radiation therapists primarily work in hospitals and freestanding radiation oncology centers. They also may work in research facilities and with manufacturers of radiation oncology equipment.

Employment Outlook

In the last few years employment opportunities in radiation therapy had not been plentiful due to changes in healthcare reimbursement. Unfortunately, hospital administrators were often forced to stop hiring in order to keep costs down. An oversupply of therapists led to the reduction in applications to many schools in the United States and many programs closed as a result. Currently, however, there is a shortage of radiation therapists throughout the country so entry into the educational programs is competitive. Salaries are good and jobs are highly competitive.

Salary

The annual entry-level salary ranges from approximately $29,000 to $36,122; the median salary for the profession is $34,000 annually.[1]

Educational Programs

Length

Radiation therapy educational programs may be one, two or four years in length. The one-year programs are certificate programs offered primarily for registered radiographers who wish to specialize in radiation therapy. It is not necessary to be a registered radiographer to enter the field of radiation therapy. The one-year programs are primarily offered for the radiographer because there is an overlap in some of the core courses and radiographers do not need to retake them. The two-year programs are either certificate or Associate's degree programs, and the four-year programs award Baccalaureate degrees. In 1993 the American Society of Radiologic Technologists' (ASRT's) House of Delegates passed a resolution requiring entry-level education be a baccalaureate degree; however, implementation of the entry-level baccalaureate program has not yet been completed.

Prerequisites

Applicants must have a high school diploma or GED and have successfully completed course work in biology, chemistry, physics, algebra I, II, geometry and trigonometry. Computer literacy is essential because of the state-of the-art equipment, scheduling, record keeping and billing systems that are used.

Curriculum

The radiation therapy student will study both general education and professional component courses. General education requirements include:

- Language, literature, and fine arts courses to include English composition, literature, speech, and language arts
- Biological, behavioral and physical sciences to include anatomy and physiology, pathophysiology, histopathology, psychology, sociology, statistics, mathematics, chemistry, physics, and computer information technology
- Healthcare studies, to include healthcare administration, finances, education and public policy, and regulatory agencies

- Professional practice, to include pharmacology, patient care, radiation physics, radiation biology and protection, medical ethics and legal issues, medical terminology, instrumentation, application of radiologic sciences theory and techniques, quality assessment, and competency-based clinical education

Accrediting Body

The accrediting agency is the organization that conducts peer review evaluations of educational programs to assure that they are providing their students with a well-rounded, comprehensive didactic and clinical education and that they make available to their students the appropriate resources and support services. The accrediting agency for radiation therapy programs is:

The Joint Review Committee on Education in Radiologic Technology (JRCERT)
20 N. Wacker Drive, Suite 900
Chicago, IL 60606-2901
Telephone: 312-704-5300
Fax: 312-704-5304
E-mail: mail @jrcert.org
Web address: www.jrcert.org

Certification Board

The certifying agency is responsible for creating and administering the certification examination that all graduating students must take in order to practice. The organization that is responsible for administering the examination in radiation therapy is:

The American Registry of Radiologic Technology (ARRT)
1255 Northland Drive
St. Paul, MN 55120-1155
Telephone: 651-687-0048
Web address: www.arrt.org

Advice for Potential Students

Visit the school in which you are interested in attending and speak with the program director and currently enrolled students. Ask the program director about the job placement rate of his/her graduates immediately after graduation and where the jobs they find are located. Additionally, schedule a shadow visit to a radiation oncology department for a minimum of one day and observe the radiation therapists as they work. Ask questions about the employment opportunities in your area. Call or write the American Society of Radiologic Technologists (ASRT) for additional information regarding employment opportunities as a radiation therapist.

For Additional Information

Organizations

American Society of Radiologic Technologists
15000 Central Avenue, SE
Albuquerque, NM 87123-3917
Telephone: 505-298-4500
Web address: www.asrt.org

Publications

Books

Campeau, Frances E. *Radiography: Technology, Environment, Professionalism.* Philadelphia: Lippincott, Williams & Wilkins, 1999.

Radiation Therapy Professional Curriculum. Albuquerque: American Society of Radiologic Technologists Task Force on Educational Standards in Radiation Therapy, 1997.

Standards for an Accredited Educational Program in Radiologic Sciences. Chicago: The Joint Review Committee on Education in Radiologic Technology, 1996.

Stanfield, Peggy & Hui, Y.H. *Introduction to the Health Professions, 3rd ed.* Sudbury, MA: Jones & Bartlett Publishers, Inc, 1998.

Tolley-Gurley, LaVerne & Callaway, William J. *Introduction to Radiologic Technology.* St. Louis: Mosby/Yearbook, Inc., 1996.

Washington, Charles & Leaver, Dennis. *Principles and Practices of Radiation Therapy, Vol. I.* St. Louis: Mosby-Year Book Inc., 1996.

Journals

Radiation Therapist. American Society of Radiologic Technologists, 15000 Central Avenue, SE, Albuquerque, NM 87123-3917. www.asrt.org

Internet Resources

American Registry of Radiologic Technologists: www.arrt.org
American Society of Radiologic Technologists: www.asrt.org
The Joint Review Committee on Education in Radiologic Technology: www.jrcert.org

Alabama

University of Alabama at Birmingham

LRC 354
1714 9th Avenue South
Birmingham, AL 35294-1270

Contact Information:
Telephone: 508-856-5551
Fax: 508-856-5006
E-mail: bsrtt@uab.edu
Web: www.uab.edu/radtherap

Program Information:
Duration of program: 18 months

Application Information:
Enrollment of program: 15
Transfer students are accepted.

Financial Information:
Tuition, resident: $7,952
Tuition, non-resident: $15,904
Average cost of books: $500

Employment Profile:
% of students who pass the boards on their first try: 99
% employed within the first 6 months following graduation: 100
Average starting salary: $32,000

California

California State University—Long Beach

1250 Bellflower Boulevard
Long Beach, CA 90840-4902

Contact Information:
Telephone: 562-985-7507

Fax: 562-985-2384
E-mail: seatmon@csulb.edu

Program Information:
Program begins: September
Degrees offered: Bachelor's, 48 months

Financial Information:
Tuition, resident: $2,334
Tuition, non-resident: $7,626
Average cost of books: $500

Employment Profile:
% of students who pass the boards on their first try: 100
% employed within the first 6 months following graduation: 100

City College of San Francisco
50 Phelan Avenue Box S91
San Francisco, CA 94112

Contact Information:
Telephone: 415-239-3458
Fax: 415-239-3930
Web: www.ccsf.cc.ca.us

Program Information:
Program begins: August, January
Degrees offered: Associate's, 26 months

Application Information:
Enrollment of program: 15
Transfer students are accepted.

Financial Information:
Average cost of books: $170

Employment Profile:
% of students who pass the boards on their first try: 98
% employed within the first 6 months following graduation: 100
Average starting salary: $45,000

City of Hope National Medical Center
1500 East Duarte Road
Duarte, CA 91010-0269

Contact Information:
Telephone: 626-301-8247
Fax: 626-930-5334
E-mail: cforell@smtplink.coh.org

Program Information:
Program begins: August, May
Degrees offered: Certificate program, 12 months

Application Information:
Enrollment of program: 10

Financial Information:
Tuition, resident: $2,000
Average cost of books: $300

Employment Profile:
% of students who pass the boards on their first try: 100
Average starting salary: $22,000

Loma Linda University
Nichol Hall Room A29
Loma Linda, CA 92350

Contact Information:
Telephone: 909-824-4378
Fax: 909-478-4264
E-mail: cdavis@prolit.ccu.edu
Web: www.llu.edu

Program Information:
Program begins: October
Degrees offered: Certificate program, 12 months

Application Information:
Enrollment of program: 13
Transfer students are accepted.

Financial Information:
Average cost of books: $500
% of students receiving aid: 100

Employment Profile:
% of students who pass the boards on their first try: 96
Average starting salary: $39,000

Connecticut

Gateway Community Technical College
88 Bassett Road
North Haven, CT 06473

Contact Information:
Telephone: 203-234-3364
Fax: 203-234-3353
E-mail: gw_bellemove@commnet.edu
Web: www.gwctc.commnet.edu

Program Information:
Program begins: August
Duration of program: 23 months

Application Information:
Enrollment of program: 10
Transfer students are accepted.

Financial Information:
Tuition, resident: $1,814
Tuition, non-resident: $5,438

Employment Profile:
% of students who pass the boards on their first try: 100
% employed within the first 6 months following graduation: 100
Average starting salary: $36,000

Hartford Hospital
80 Seymour Street
Hartford, CT 06115-0729

Contact Information:
Telephone: 860-545-3956
Fax: 860-545-6461
Web: www.harthosp.org

Program Information:
Program begins: October
Duration of program: 24 months

Application Information:
Enrollment of program: 8
Transfer students are accepted.

Financial Information:
Average cost of books: $700

Employment Profile:
% of students who pass the boards on their first try: 100
% employed within the first 6 months following graduation: 100
Average starting salary: $35,000

Florida

Halifax Medical Center
303 North Clyde Morris Boulevard
PO Box 2830
Daytona Beach, FL 32120-2830

Contact Information:
Telephone: 904-254-4075
Fax: 904-254-4231

Program Information:
Program begins: September
Duration of program: 12 months

Application Information:
Enrollment of program: 4

Financial Information:
Tuition, resident: $1,400
Average cost of books: $400

Employment Profile:
% of students who pass the boards on their first try: 99
% employed within the first 6 months following graduation: 100
Average starting salary: $33,500

Hillsborough Community College
PO Box 30030
Tampa, FL 33630

Contact Information:
Telephone: 813-253-7372
Fax: 813-253-7491
E-mail: knelson@hcc.cc.fl.us
Web: www.hcc.cc.fl.us

Program Information:
Program begins: August
Duration of program: 24 months

Application Information:
Enrollment of program: 35

Financial Information:
Tuition, resident: $1,087
Tuition, non-resident: $4,048

Miami-Dade Community College
Medical Center Campus
950 Northwest 20th Street
Miami, FL 33127

Contact Information:
Telephone: 305-237-4205
Fax: 305-237-4278

E-mail: cabrerf@mdcc.edu
Web: www.mdcc.edu

Program Information:
Program begins: September
Duration of program: 24 months

Application Information:
Enrollment of program: 27
Transfer students are accepted.

Financial Information:
Tuition, resident: $1,833
Tuition, non-resident: $6,458
Average cost of books: $500
% of students receiving aid: 60

Employment Profile:
% of students who pass the boards on their first try: 75
% employed within the first 6 months following graduation: 80
Average starting salary: $34,000

Radiation Therapy Regional Center

Lakes Park Office
7341 Gladiolas Drive
Ft. Meyers, FL 33908

Contact Information:
Telephone: 941-489-3420
Fax: 941-489-3219
E-mail: dmoody@rtsx.com
Web: www.dmoody@rtsx.com

Program Information:
Program begins: September
Duration of program: 14 months

Application Information:
Enrollment of program: 4
Transfer students are accepted.

Financial Information:
Tuition, resident: $500
Tuition, non-resident: $1,000
Average cost of books: $350

Employment Profile:
% of students who pass the boards on their first try: 98
% employed within the first 6 months following graduation: 100

Georgia

Armstrong Atlantic State University

11935 Abercorn Street
Savannah, GA 31419-1997

Contact Information:
Telephone: 912-927-5360
Fax: 912-921-7429
E-mail: demarc@mail.armstrong.edu
Web: www.armstrong.edu

Program Information:
Program begins: August
Duration of program: 21 months
Evening or weekend classes are available.

Application Information:
Enrollment of program: 16
Transfer students are accepted.

Financial Information:
Tuition, resident: $2,885
Tuition, non-resident: $8,564
Average cost of books: $100

Employment Profile:
% employed within the first 6 months following graduation: 100
Average starting salary: $35,000

Grady Health System

80 Butler Street Southeast
PO Box 26095
Atlanta, GA 30335

Contact Information:
Telephone: 404-616-5024
Fax: 404-616-3512

Program Information:
Program begins: September
Degrees offered: Diploma, 12 months

Application Information:
Enrollment of program: 5

Financial Information:
Tuition, resident: $3,200
Average cost of books: $400
% of students receiving aid: 75

Employment Profile:
% of students who pass the boards on their first try: 100
% employed within the first 6 months following graduation: 100
Average starting salary: $35,000

Medical College of Georgia

Building HK
Augusta, GA 30912-3965

Contact Information:
Telephone: 706-721-2971
Fax: 706-721-7248
Web: www.mcg.edu/centers

Program Information:
Program begins: September
Duration of program: 21 months
Evening or weekend classes are available.

Application Information:
Enrollment of program: 7
Transfer students are accepted.

Financial Information:
Tuition, resident: $2,596
Tuition, non-resident: $9,526
Average cost of books: $450

Employment Profile:
% of students who pass the boards on their first try: 100
% employed within the first 6 months following graduation: 95
Average starting salary: $35,000

Illinois

National-Louis University

2840 North Sheridan Road
Evanston, IL 60201

Contact Information:
Telephone: 847-475-1100
Fax: 847-256-1057
Web: www.nl.edu

Program Information:
Program begins: August
Duration of program: 48 months

Application Information:
Transfer students are accepted.

Financial Information:
Tuition, resident: $14,000
Tuition, non-resident: $15,000
Average cost of books: $300

Employment Profile:
% employed within the first 6 months following graduation: 50
Average starting salary: $35,000

Swedish American Hospital

1400 Charles Street
Rockford, IL 61104-2298

Contact Information:
Telephone: 815-489-4862
Fax: 815-966-3966
E-mail: amenkeswedam.com

Program Information:
Program begins: June
Duration of program: 20 months

Financial Information:
Tuition, resident: $1,500
Average cost of books: $950

Employment Profile:
% of students who pass the boards on their first try: 100
% employed within the first 6 months following graduation: 90
Average starting salary: $34,000

Indiana

Indiana University Northwest

3400 Broadway
Gary, IN 46408-1197

Contact Information:
Telephone: 219-981-4204
Fax: 219-980-6649
E-mail: spiehl@iunhaw1.iun.indiana.edu
Web: www.iun.indiana.edu

Program Information:
Program begins: September
Duration of program: 22 months

Application Information:
Enrollment of program: 12
Transfer students are accepted.

Financial Information:
Tuition, resident: $6,912
Tuition, non-resident: $17,568
Average cost of books: $500

Employment Profile:
% of students who pass the boards on their first try: 100

Indiana University School of Medicine

1140 West Michigan Street
Coleman Hall 120
Indianapolis, IN 46202-5119

Contact Information:
Telephone: 317-274-1302
Fax: 317-274-4723
E-mail: dodunn@iupui.edu
Web: www.iupui.edu

Program Information:
Program begins: May
Duration of program: 48 months

Application Information:
Enrollment of program: 19
Transfer students are accepted.

Financial Information:
Tuition, resident: $4,945
Tuition, non-resident: $12,900
Average cost of books: $520

Employment Profile:
% of students who pass the boards on their first try: 100
% employed within the first 6 months following graduation: 100

Methodist Hospital

1701 North Senate Boulevard/PO Box 1367
Wile Hall Room 645
Indianapolis, IN 46206-1367

Contact Information:
Telephone: 317-929-3377
Fax: 317-929-2102
E-mail: dstrahan@clarian.com

Program Information:
Program begins: August
Duration of program: 24 months

Application Information:
Transfer students are accepted.

Financial Information:
Tuition, resident: $3,200
Average cost of books: $350

Employment Profile:
% of students who pass the boards on their first try: 98
Average starting salary: $34,000

Iowa

The University of Iowa Hospitals and Clinics

200 Hawkins Drive West 1892 GH
Iowa City, IA 52242-1009

Contact Information:
Telephone: 319-356-8286
Fax: 319-356-1530
E-mail: pam-jones@uiowa.edu
Web: www.vh.org

Program Information:
Program begins: September
Duration of program: 12 months

Application Information:
Enrollment of program: 6

Financial Information:
Average cost of books: $400
% of students receiving aid: 80

Employment Profile:
% of students who pass the boards on their first try: 100
% employed within the first 6 months following graduation: 100
Average starting salary: $34,000

Kansas

Washburn University of Topeka

1700 College Avenue Southwest
Topeka, KS 66621

Contact Information:
Telephone: 785-231-1010 ext. 1398
Fax: 785-231-1027
E-mail: zzfrye@washburn.edu
Web: www.washburn.edu

Program Information:
Program begins: August
Degrees offered: Certificate program, 11 months

Application Information:
Enrollment of program: 15

Financial Information:
Tuition, resident: $2,976
Tuition, non-resident: $6,541
Average cost of books: $350
% of students receiving aid: 90

Employment Profile:
% of students who pass the boards on their first try: 93
% employed within the first 6 months following graduation: 100
Average starting salary: $30,000

Maine

Southern Maine Technical College

Two Fort Road
South Portland, ME 04106

Contact Information:
Telephone: 207-767-9593
Fax: 207-767-9690
E-mail: dleaver@smtc.net
Web: www.smtc.net

Program Information:
Program begins: September

Application Information:
Enrollment of program: 5
Transfer students are accepted.

Financial Information:
Tuition, resident: $3,572
Tuition, non-resident: $11,938
Average cost of books: $600
% of students receiving aid: 80

Employment Profile:
% of students who pass the boards on their first try: 90
% employed within the first 6 months following graduation: 50
Average starting salary: $34,000

Massachusetts

University of Mass Medical Center—Worcester State College

55 Lake Avenue North
Worcester, MA 01655

Contact Information:
Telephone: 612-273-6393
Fax: 612-273-8459
E-mail: websterp@ummhc.org

Program Information:
Program begins: September
Duration of program: 15 months

Application Information:
Enrollment of program: 5

Michigan

Baker College of Owosso

1020 South Washington Street
Owosso, MI 48867-4400

Contact Information:
Telephone: 517-729-3420
Fax: 517-729-3411
E-mail: smith_s@owosso.baker.edu
Web: www.baker.edu

Program Information:
Program begins: October
Duration of program: 48 months
Evening or weekend classes are available.

Application Information:
Enrollment of program: 25
Transfer students are accepted.

Financial Information:
Average cost of books: $1,200
% of students receiving aid: 73

Employment Profile:
% of students who pass the boards on their first try: 75
% employed within the first 6 months following graduation: 100

University of Michigan—Flint

1500 East Medical Center Drive
Box 0010 Room B2C490
Ann Arbor, MI 48109

Contact Information:
Telephone: 205-934-3443
Fax: 205-975-7302
Web: www.med.umich.edu/radone/therapy

Program Information:
Program begins: September
Duration of program: 24 months

Application Information:
Enrollment of program: 5
Transfer students are accepted.

Financial Information:
Tuition, resident: $3,600
Tuition, non-resident: $8,600
Average cost of books: $400
% of students receiving aid: 100

William Beaumont Hospital

3601 West13 Mile Road
Royal Oak, MI 48073-6769

Contact Information:
Telephone: 248-551-7156
Fax: 248-551-7166
E-mail: lochs@beaumont.edu
Web: www.beaumont/edu

Program Information:
Program begins: September
Duration of program: 24 months

Financial Information:
Tuition, resident: $2,730
Average cost of books: $600

Employment Profile:
% of students who pass the boards on their first try: 100
% employed within the first 6 months following graduation: 100
Average starting salary: $33,000

Minnesota

Mayo Clinic—Mayo Foundation

School of Health Related Sciences
200 First Street Southwest
Rochester, MN 55905

Contact Information:
Telephone: 507-284-4148
Fax: 507-284-0079
E-mail: bussmanyeakel.leila@mayo.edu
Web: www.mayo.edu

Program Information:
Program begins: September
Duration of program: 12 months

Financial Information:
Average cost of books: $450
% of students receiving aid: 33

Employment Profile:
% of students who pass the boards on their first try: 100
% employed within the first 6 months following graduation: 100
Average starting salary: $34,900

University of Minnesota Hospital and Clinic

Harvard Street at East River Road
PO Box 494
Minneapolis, MN 55455

Contact Information:
Telephone: 810-237-6502
Fax: 810-762-3003
E-mail: jschmid3@fairview.org
Web: www.fairview.org

Program Information:
Program begins: August
Duration of program: 12 months

Financial Information:
Average cost of books: $200
% of students receiving aid: 90

Employment Profile:
% of students who pass the boards on their first try: 100
% employed within the first 6 months following graduation: 95
Average starting salary: $34,500

Nebraska

University of Nebraska Medical Center

981045 Nebraska Medical Center
Department of Radiology
Omaha, NE 68198-1045

Contact Information:
Telephone: 402-559-7604
Fax: 402-559-4667
E-mail: csanders@unmc.edu
Web: www.unme.edu/alliedhealth/rste

Program Information:
Program begins: September
Duration of program: 12 months

Application Information:
Transfer students are accepted.

Financial Information:
Tuition, resident: $3,840
Average cost of books: $1,000
% of students receiving aid: 100

Employment Profile:
% of students who pass the boards on their first try: 99
% employed within the first 6 months following graduation: 100
Average starting salary: $37,000

New Jersey

Cooper Hospital—University Medical Center

One Cooper Plaza
Camden, NJ 08103

Contact Information:
Telephone: 609-342-2734
Fax: 609-365-8504
Web: www.cooperhealth.org

Program Information:
Program begins: September
Duration of program: 12 months

Application Information:
Enrollment of program: 4

Financial Information:
Average cost of books: $450
% of students receiving aid: 100

Employment Profile:
% of students who pass the boards on their first try: 100
% employed within the first 6 months following graduation: 100
Average starting salary: $41,000

New York

Erie Community College—City Campus

121 Ellicott Street
Buffalo, NY 14203

Contact Information:
Telephone: 716-851-1129
Web: www.ecc.edu

Program Information:
Program begins: August
Duration of program: 24 months

Application Information:
Transfer students are accepted.

Financial Information:
Tuition, resident: $1,250
Tuition, non-resident: $2,500

Employment Profile:
% of students who pass the boards on their first try: 80
Average starting salary: $34,000

Montefiore Medical Center

Moses Division/111 East 210th Street
Bronx, NY 10467

Contact Information:
Telephone: 718-920-5083
Fax: 718-882-6913

Program Information:
Program begins: August
Duration of program: 24 months

Application Information:
Enrollment of program: 25

Financial Information:
Average cost of books: $400
% of students receiving aid: 100

Employment Profile:
% of students who pass the boards on their first try: 97
% employed within the first 6 months following graduation: 75
Average starting salary: $48,000

Nassau Community College
One Education Drive
Garden City, NY 11530

Contact Information:
Telephone: 516-572-7551
Fax: 516-572-7092

Program Information:
Program begins: August
Duration of program: 24 months

Application Information:
Enrollment of program: 28

Financial Information:
Tuition, resident: $1,400
Tuition, non-resident: $2,800
Average cost of books: $400
% of students receiving aid: 60

Employment Profile:
% of students who pass the boards on their first try: 95
% employed within the first 6 months following graduation: 90
Average starting salary: $42,000

New York Methodist Hospital
506 Sixth Street
Box 159008
Brooklyn, NY 11215-9008

Contact Information:
Telephone: 718-780-3677
Fax: 718-780-3688

Program Information:
Program begins: September
Degrees offered: Certificate program; Diploma, 24 months

Application Information:
Enrollment of program: 14

Employment Profile:
% of students who pass the boards on their first try: 100
% employed within the first 6 months following graduation: 100
Average starting salary: $45,000

SUNY Health Science Center at Syracuse
750 East Adams Street
Syracuse, NY 13210

Contact Information:
Telephone: 315-464-6937
Fax: 315-464-6914
E-mail: obrienj@hscsyr.edu
Web: www.ec.hscsyr.edu/chrp/college/

Program Information:
Program begins: July
Duration of program: 20 months

Application Information:
Enrollment of program: 20
Transfer students are accepted.

Financial Information:
Tuition, resident: $3,200
Tuition, non-resident: $8,300

Employment Profile:
% of students who pass the boards on their first try: 96
% employed within the first 6 months following graduation: 99
Average starting salary: $32,000

North Carolina

Pitt Community College
PO Drawer 7007
Greenville, NC 27835-7007

Contact Information:
Telephone: 252-321-4452
Fax: 252-321-4451
Web: www.pitt.cc.nc.us

Program Information:
Program begins: August
Duration of program: 12 months

Financial Information:
Tuition, resident: $758
Tuition, non-resident: $6,036

Ohio

Arthur G. James Cancer Hospital
300 West Tenth Avenue
Columbus, OH 43210

Contact Information:
Telephone: 614-293-8415
Fax: 614-293-4044
E-mail: hackworth-1@medctr.osu.edu
Web: www.radonc.med.ohio-state.edu

Program Information:
Program begins: July
Degrees offered: Certificate program, 12 months

Application Information:
Enrollment of program: 7

Financial Information:
Average cost of books: $350

Employment Profile:
% of students who pass the boards on their first try: 100
% employed within the first 6 months following graduation: 100
Average starting salary: $28,000

Oklahoma

University of Oklahoma Health Sciences Center
801 Northeast 13th
CHB 451
Oklahoma City, OK 73190

Contact Information:
Telephone: 405-271-6477
Fax: 405-271-1424
E-mail: stacy-anderson@ouhsc.edu
Web: www.ouhsc.edu

Program Information:
Program begins: August
Degrees offered: Bachelor's, 24 months

Application Information:
Enrollment of program: 12
Transfer students are accepted.

Financial Information:
Tuition, resident: $2,300
Tuition, non-resident: $6,476
Average cost of books: $800
% of students receiving aid: 75

Employment Profile:
% of students who pass the boards on their first try: 97
% employed within the first 6 months following graduation: 100
Average starting salary: $40,000

Oregon

Oregon Health Sciences University
3181 Southwest Sam Jackson Park Road
L37
Portland, OR 97201-3098

Contact Information:
Telephone: 503-494-6708
Fax: 503-494-2730
E-mail: maddefoa@ohsu.edu
Web: www.ohsu.edu/alliedhealth/radiation_therapy

Program Information:
Program begins: August
Duration of program: 24 months

Financial Information:
Tuition, resident: $8,300
Tuition, non-resident: $14,446

Employment Profile:
% of students who pass the boards on their first try: 100
% employed within the first 6 months following graduation: 100

Pennsylvania

Community College of Allegheny County
808 Ridge Avenue
Pittsburgh, PA 15212-6097

Contact Information:
Telephone: 412-237-2752
Fax: 412-237-4521
E-mail: eharkay@ccac.edu
Web: www.ccac.edu

Program Information:
Program begins: September
Duration of program: 24 months

Financial Information:
Tuition, resident: $2,400
Tuition, non-resident: $4,000

Gwynedd–Mercy College

PO Box 901
Sumneytown Pike
Gwynedd Valley, PA 19437

Contact Information:

Telephone: 215-646-7300 ext. 465
Fax: 215-641-5559
E-mail: giordano.p@gmc.edu
Web: www.gmc.edu

Program Information:

Program begins: July, August, September
Degrees offered: Certificate program, 20 months; Bachelor's, 40 months

Application Information:

Enrollment of program: 25
Transfer students are accepted.

Financial Information:

Average cost of books: $300

Employment Profile:

% of students who pass the boards on their first try: 81
% employed within the first 6 months following graduation: 100
Average starting salary: $32,500

Tennessee

Vanderbilt University Medical Center

Center for Radiation Oncology
The Vanderbilt Clinic B 902
Nashville, TN 37232-5671

Contact Information:

Telephone: 615-322-2555
Fax: 615-343-0161
Web: www.mc.vanderbilt.edu

Program Information:

Program begins: September
Degrees offered: Certificate program, 12 months

Application Information:

Enrollment of program: 4

Financial Information:

Average cost of books: $300

Employment Profile:

Average starting salary: $32,000

Texas

Amarillo College

PO Box 447
Amarillo, TX 79178

Contact Information:

Telephone: 806-354-6063
Fax: 806-356-6076
E-mail: tmtackit@actx.edu
Web: www.actx.edu

Program Information:

Program begins: July
Duration of program: 24 months

Application Information:

Enrollment of program: 17
Transfer students are accepted.

Financial Information:

Tuition, resident: $747
Tuition, non-resident: $1,101
Average cost of books: $400

Employment Profile:

% of students who pass the boards on their first try: 100
% employed within the first 6 months following graduation: 100
Average starting salary: $34,000

Galveston College—University of Texas

4015 Avenue Q
Galveston, TX 77550-2782

Contact Information:

Telephone: 409-772-1631
Fax: 409-772-3014
E-mail: kcrumple@utmb.edu
Web: www.gc.edu

Program Information:

Program begins: September
Duration of program: 20 months

Application Information:

Enrollment of program: 8
Transfer students are accepted.

Financial Information:

Tuition, resident: $859
Tuition, non-resident: $1,524

Employment Profile:

% of students who pass the boards on their first try: 100
% employed within the first 6 months following graduation: 100
Average starting salary: $32,000

University of Texas MD Anderson Cancer Center

1515 Holcombe Boulevard
PO Box 701
Houston, TX 77030

Contact Information:

Telephone: 713-792-3455
Fax: 713-792-0956
E-mail: dbolik@notes.mdocc.tmc.edu
Web: www.mdanderson.org

Program Information:

Program begins: September

Financial Information:

Tuition, resident: $2,000

Vermont

University of Vermont

302 Rowell Building
Burlington, VT 05405

Contact Information:

Telephone: 802-656-3811
Fax: 802-656-2191
E-mail: ahuot@cosmos.uvm.edu
Web: www.uvm.edu

Program Information:

Program begins: June
Degrees offered: Bachelor's, 48 months; Master's, 24 months

Application Information:

Enrollment of program: 22
Transfer students are accepted.

Financial Information:

Tuition, resident: $7,464
Tuition, non-resident: $18,672
Average cost of books: $714

Wisconsin

St. Luke's Medical Center

2900 West Oklahoma Avenue
PO Box 2901
Milwaukee, WI 53201-2901

Contact Information:

Telephone: 414-649-6420
Fax: 414-649-5309
E-mail: amy_pelikan@aurora.org

Program Information:

Program begins: July
Duration of program: 12 months

University of Wisconsin Hospital & Clinics

1725 State Street
La Crosse, WI 54601

Contact Information:

Telephone: 608-785-6979
Fax: 608-785-6647
E-mail: saeger@mail.humonc.wisc.edu
Web: www.hosp.wisc.edu

Program Information:

Program begins: September
Duration of program: 42 months

Application Information:

Enrollment of program: 24
Transfer students are accepted.

Financial Information:

Tuition, resident: $3,000
Tuition, non-resident: $9,300

Radiographer, Diagnostic Medical Sonographer, Nuclear Medicine Technologist

Kathryn S. Durand, RT(R), AS
Director
Inservice Education for Radiology
Lawrence and Memorial Hospital
New London, Connecticut

Job Description

Radiographers use radiation to produce diagnostic images. Their job is to produce a radiographic image that will give the radiologist enough information to diagnose a patient's condition.

The radiation that is used passes through the patient's body but is not absorbed into the body's tissues. This radiation is produced by accelerating electrons (tiny negatively charged particles) that smash into a stationary target. Matter is thus converted into energy, and that energy is released in the form of X-rays and heat. X-rays are classified as ionizing radiation, meaning they have enough energy to change the electrical charge that is found within atoms. (Ionization is the same effect that you feel when you scuff your feet on a carpet on a cold winter's day and then touch a metal doorknob.) While major ionization of the body can be harmful, the minor ionization caused by diagnostic X-rays is outweighed by the benefits that come from an accurate diagnosis of the patient's condition. Radiographers are instructed in the proper methods for producing and controlling X-rays. If used properly and safely, X-rays are not dangerous to either the patient or radiographer.

Radiographers work with all types of people, from newborn infants to the elderly. To produce a diagnostic radiograph, they use the following tools:

- radiographic units—machines designed to produce ionizing radiation
- patient assistance devices—used to help patients keep, move to and from the X-ray table, and make a patient in distress more comfortable during the procedure
- radiographic film and cassettes to store the image
- automatic film processors to develop the image

Radiographers must possess a varied set of skills. They must be able to:

- correctly determine the amount and the minimum strength of radiation that should be used to produce a diagnostically acceptable radiograph
- care for the patient during the procedure
- evaluate the patient's abilities to determine the best method by which to obtain the radiographic images. (Since patients come in different shapes and sizes and have different degrees of illness and mobility, a radiographer must be able to assess a patient's abilities to complete each radiographic procedure. He or she must know how to modify the steps in the procedure to accommodate the abilities of each patient.)
- provide radiation protection for their patients, other health care workers and themselves
- provide patient education

The types of diagnostic radiographic procedures that radiographers frequently perform include:

- routine radiographs—chest X-rays, hand X-rays, etc.
- surgical radiographs—taken during orthopedic procedures. These radiographs will assist the orthopedic surgeon in determining correct alignment during procedures where metal plates and rods are used to hold fractured bones together.
- trauma radiographs—performed on patients with multiple injuries in the emergency department
- gastrointestinal (stomach and intestines) radiographs
- urinary (kidneys and urinary bladder) radiographs
- portable radiographs using a portable X-ray machine

Type of Person

Radiographers tend to be good at problem-solving and creative thinking. These skills allow radiographers to tailor examinations to meet the needs of their patients. Additionally, radiographers should possess good organizational skills and have high ethical standards.

With Whom Do They Work?

Radiographers work most frequently with radiologists. They also work with nurses, physicians and other health care personnel.

Employment

Places of Employment

Radiographers work in hospitals, health centers, physician offices and clinics.

Employment Outlook

Job seekers are currently finding a competitive market for positions in this field. Hospitals have merged, and as a cost-cutting measure, other health professionals are now being trained to perform simple radiographic procedures. In addition, qualified new technologists continue to enter the job market. Despite these trends, job opportunities for radiographers are expected to grow faster than the average for all occupations. This trend is predicted to continue through the year 2006.[1]

Salary

The median annual base salary for a full-time radiographer in 1997 was $28,800.[2]

Educational Programs

Length

There are two basic types of educational programs in radiography: the hospital-based program and the college-based program.

1. The hospital-based program is commonly two years in length (24 months). Students receive the academic and clinical components of

the program at the hospital. Upon graduation, students receive a certificate of completion, but do not earn a degree. Students are then eligible to take the American Registry of Radiologic Technologists examination and become a Registered Technologist, Radiography (RTR).

2. The college-based program can be two or four years in length. Students who attend these programs earn a degree rather than a certificate of completion. Two-year programs offer an Associate's degree; four-year programs offer a Bachelor's degree. Students in a college program take all of their courses at the college and fulfill their clinical components at various hospitals or other clinical sites that are affiliated with the college. Students who have successfully completed these programs are also eligible to take the American Registry of Radiologic Technology examination and become a Registered Technologist, Radiography (RTR).

Hospital-based programs are generally less expensive to attend than college-based programs and students get more clinical experience. By attending college-based programs, however, students will be better prepared for roles in management and higher education. Those who have earned certificates from a hospital-based program can begin working in the field while they then attend a college program to earn a degree.

Prerequisites

Applicants for both program types must have a high school diploma. It is important that the applicant contact the program prior to application, since additional prerequisites vary from institution to institution.

Curriculum

Radiography students commonly take the following courses prior to or during their clinical experience: introduction to radiography; radiographic exposure and technique; radiation physics; anatomy and physiology; medical terminology; pathology; radiographic positioning and procedures; basic nursing techniques (such as blood pressure measurement, treatment for shock, proper movement techniques, etc.); and ethics.

Accrediting Body

There are two types of accreditation. The individual program can be accredited or the entire school can be accredited. The Joint Review Committee on Education in Radiologic Technology (JRCERT) accredits radiologic technology programs. Some college-based radiography programs may be accredited by a regional accreditation agency. This type of accreditation applies to the entire college, not just the radiography program. These agencies are too numerous to list.

JRCERT
20 North Wacker Drive, Suite 900
Chicago, IL 60606-2901
Telephone: 312-704-5300
Fax: 312-704-5304
E-mail: mail@jrcert.org
Web address: www.jrcert.org

Certification Board

The American Registry of Radiologic Technology (ARRT) is the nationally recognized organization for certification in the radiologic sciences. Applicants must have successfully completed an accredited radiography program in order to sit for this examination.

American Registry of Radiology Technology
1255 Northland Drive
St. Paul, MN 55120
Phone: 651-687-0048
Web address: www.arrt.org

Advice for Potential Students

Visit the program that you are interested in and set up an appointment with the program director. Some of the questions that you might want to ask in order to determine how well the program prepares its students include:

- How many students successfully graduate from your program, compared with the number that start the program?
- How many graduates from the last program successfully passed the registry examination?
- How many graduates from your last class found work in radiography that includes a salary as well as employee benefits (insurance, vacation time, etc.)?

Other research that you should do may include:

- Contact your state's department of licensing and find out what the requirements are in your state to practice as a radiographer.
- Contact your state's department of labor and inquire about the field of radiography. Is there a shortage or an excess of radiographers in the geographic area in which you intend to work?
- Contact some hospitals in the area. Inquire how many radiographers are on staff. Also ask the last time a radiographer was hired.
- Contact the ARRT and ask about their requirements for registry.

Accredited Programs That Offer Additional Areas of Specialization in Radiography

Radiographers can choose to specialize in several different areas. Specialization requires additional certifications that are administered by certification bodies similar in nature to the ARRT. Two areas of specialization, diagnostic medical sonography and nuclear medicine technology, have accredited educational programs and are therefore included in this book.

Diagnostic Medical Sonography (Diagnostic Ultrasound)

This modality uses high-frequency sound waves instead of radiation. The sound, far beyond the level at which humans can hear, is focused into the patient's body and reflected back. The returning reflection (or echo) produces images with the help of a computer. The image is formed due to the differences between the densities of the bodily structures. Some of the sonographic examinations that are performed include vascular (blood flows), echocardiography (heart), abdominal scans (that show the spleen, liver and pancreas), obstetrics and gynecological studies.

Accrediting Body

The following organization accredits educational programs in diagnostic medical sonography:

The Joint Review Committee on Education in Diagnostic Medical Sonography
71085 Alton Way—Building C
Englewood, CO 80112
Telephone: 303-741-3533
Fax: 303-741-3655
E-mail: CoA@ast.org
Web address: www. caahep.org

Certification Board

Certification in sonography is administered by the American Registry of Diagnostic Medical Sonographers (ARDMS).

For more information contact:

The American Registry of Diagnostic Medical Sonographers
600 Jefferson Plaza, Suite 360
Rockville, MD 20852-1150
Telephone: 800-541-9754
Fax: 301-738-0312/0313
Web address: www.ardms.org

or

Society of Diagnostic Medical Sonographers
127700 Coit Road, Suite 708
Dallas, TX 75251
Telephone: 972-239-7367
Fax: 972-239-7378
Web address: www.sdms.org

Nuclear Medicine Technologist

This modality uses radiation, but instead of the radiation passing through the patient (as it does with diagnostic radiography), the radiation is emitted from a substance injected into, swallowed or inhaled by the patient. The image that is produced on a computer screen or film is caused by the radiation emitted from the patient. Therapeutic doses of radiation, as opposed to diagnostic doses, are sometimes given. The dosage will be determined by the radiologist and administered by the nuclear medicine technologist.

Accrediting Body

The Joint Review Committee on Educational Programs in Nuclear Medicine Technology
One 2nd Avenue East, Suite C
Polson, MT 59860-2320
Telephone: 406-883-0003
Fax: 406-883-0022
Web address: www.caheep.org

Certification Board

Certification may be obtained from the ARRT, as well as the Nuclear Medicine Technology Certification Board (NMTCB).

For more information contact:

The American Registry of Radiologic Technologists
1255 Northland Drive
St. Paul, MN 55120
Telephone: 651-687-0048
Web address: www.arrt.org

Nuclear Medicine Technology Certification Board
2970 Clairmont Road Suite 935
Atlanta, GA 30329-4421
Telephone: 404-315-1739
Fax: 404-315-6502
Web address: www.nmtcb.org

Additional Areas of Specialization in Radiography

Radiographers can choose to specialize in other areas as well as diagnostic medical sonography and nuclear medicine. The few educational programs that exist in the following areas are not accredited by any particular group and are not listed in this book. In most cases, radiographers learn about these areas of specialty on the job and prepare for the ARRT specialty certifications through self-study.

Mammography

This modality uses radiation to show breast tissue. Specialized radiographic equipment is used and attention to detail is critical. Quality management (see below) plays a large role in mammography.

Interventional Radiology

This modality uses sophisticated equipment to show blood vessels within the body by using contrast media (a type of solution that shows up on a radiograph). Conditions such as stenosis (narrowing of a vessel), aneurysms (weakened arterial walls), and arteriovenous malformations (congenital anomalies) are commonly demonstrated. This modality also allows the radiologist to intervene in the treatment of many of these conditions where at one time the only course of treatment was surgery. With this procedure the patient is often able to resume normal activities within days of the procedure rather than weeks.

Interventional radiology uses specialized catheters. Angioplasty is performed by introducing these catheters into an artery and then snaking them through the vessels of the body until the area of occlusion has been located. At this point, the catheter is inflated. This causes the plaque that was occluding the vessel to be pressed against the wall of the vessel, thus increasing blood flow to the part.

There are many other procedures that can be accomplished using this modality. Some inject medications through the catheter directly into the area of a vessel. Still other procedures inject an occluding agent to block an artery so tumors can be removed with less blood loss during surgery. The interventional radiographer works closely with the radiologist, assisting the radiologist throughout these complex procedures.

Radiographers who want to practice in this area must first pass the ARRT's examination for interventional radiography.

Computed Tomography (CT)

This modality uses radiation and a highly specialized computer. The radiographic tube moves around the patient and the computer produces a radiation absorption image from the data received. Some of the common procedures performed with CT include brain scans, chest/lung scans, abdomen studies and biopsy localizations. CT often deals with patients who have severe trauma. A CT scan will show a complex image of the body part in question. If you imagine putting a baloney in a meat slicer, slicing the baloney into fine slices and then holding up and examining the individual slices, you have envisioned what a CT scan looks like.

Magnetic Resonance Imaging (MRI)

This modality does not use radiation. Instead, it produces digital images using a powerful magnetic field and changing radio frequencies. Images are obtained using a computer. MRI is used to demonstrate many types of pathologies.

Quality Management

This specialized area involves the management of quality assurance in imaging departments. This involves testing and measurement of equipment output, film quality, processor control and other vital aspects of an imaging center.

For Additional Information

Organizations

American Society of Radiologic Technologists
15000 Central Avenue SE
Albuquerque, NM 87123
Web address: www.asrt.org

Publications

Radiologic Technology. American Society of Radiologic Technologists, 15000 Central Avenue SE, Albuquerque, NM 87123. www.asrt.org.

A peer-reviewed, scholarly journal written for and by technologists. It includes articles for all disciplines of the radiologic sciences and professions.

ASRT Scanner. American Society of Radiologic Technologists, 15000 Central Avenue SE, Albuquerque, NM 87123. www.asrt.org.

The ASRT Scanner is a newsmagazine that looks at issues affecting the radiologic professions. It is geared more toward articles on current events (healthcare reform, job outlooks, etc.) and future trends.

Radiographer

Alabama

Baptist Medical Center

2190 East South Boulevard
Montgomery, AL 36116

Contact Information:
Telephone: 334-286-3028
Fax: 334-281-7793
E-mail: phlrjl@msn.com

Program Information:
Program begins: September
Duration of program: 24 months

Application Information:
Enrollment of program: 39

Financial Information:
Average cost of books: $410
% of students receiving aid: 10

Employment Profile:
% of students who pass the boards on their first try: 90
% employed within the first 6 months following graduation: 100
Average starting salary: $27,500

Carraway Methodist Medical Center

1600 Carraway Boulevard
Birmingham, AL 35234

Contact Information:
Telephone: 205-502-6920
Fax: 205-502-5365
E-mail: harrisa@mail.carraway.com
Web: www.carraway.org

Program Information:
Program begins: August
Duration of program: 24 months

Application Information:
Enrollment of program: 14

Financial Information:
Tuition, resident: $500
Average cost of books: $600

Employment Profile:
% of students who pass the boards on their first try: 80
% employed within the first 6 months following graduation: 100
Average starting salary: $26,000

DCH Regional Medical Center

809 University Boulevard East
Tuscaloosa, AL 35401

Contact Information:
Telephone: 205-759-6266
Fax: 205-759-6012
Web: www.noblood.com

Program Information:
Program begins: October
Duration of program: 24 months

Application Information:
Enrollment of program: 28

Financial Information:
Average cost of books: $450

Employment Profile:
% of students who pass the boards on their first try: 90
% employed within the first 6 months following graduation: 100
Average starting salary: $21,580

Jefferson State Community College

2601 Carson Road
Birmingham, AL 35215-3098

Contact Information:
Telephone: 205-856-6026
Fax: 205-856-7725
E-mail: tleesbg@jscc.cc.al.us
Web: www.jscc.cc.al.us

Program Information:
Program begins: August
Duration of program: 24 months

Application Information:
Enrollment of program: 52
Transfer students are accepted.

Financial Information:
Tuition, resident: $4,256
Tuition, non-resident: $8,056

Employment Profile:
% of students who pass the boards on their first try: 91
% employed within the first 6 months following graduation: 90
Average starting salary: $23,500

Southern Union State Community College
1701 Lafayette Parkway
Opelika, AL 36801

Contact Information:
Telephone: 334-745-6437
Fax: 334-741-9795
E-mail: csouthern@suscc.cc.al.us
Web: www.suscc.cc.al.us

Program Information:
Program begins: June
Degrees offered: Associate's, 24 months

Application Information:
Enrollment of program: 30
Transfer students are accepted.

Financial Information:
Tuition, resident: $2,902
Tuition, non-resident: $4,502
Average cost of books: $650

Employment Profile:
% of students who pass the boards on their first try: 89
% employed within the first 6 months following graduation: 100
Average starting salary: $25,000

Arizona

Gateway Community College
108 North 40th Street
Phoenix, AZ 85034

Contact Information:
Telephone: 602-392-5033
Fax: 602-392-5244
Web: www.gwc.maricopa.edu

Program Information:
Program begins: August
Degrees offered: Certificate program; Associate's, 23 months

Application Information:
Enrollment of program: 32

Financial Information:
Tuition, resident: $1,740
Tuition, non-resident: $6,786
Average cost of books: $500

Employment Profile:
% of students who pass the boards on their first try: 98
% employed within the first 6 months following graduation: 100
Average starting salary: $29,000

Pima Medical Institute—Tucson
3350 East Grant Road
Tucson, AZ 85716

Contact Information:
Telephone: 520-326-1600
Web: www.pimamedical.com

Program Information:
Program begins: July
Degrees offered: Associate's, 24 months

Application Information:
Enrollment of program: 36
Transfer students are accepted.

Financial Information:
Average cost of books: $750
% of students receiving aid: 95

Employment Profile:
% of students who pass the boards on their first try: 90
% employed within the first 6 months following graduation: 100
Average starting salary: $26,000

Arkansas

Arkansas State University
PO Box 910
State University, AR 72467-0069

Contact Information:
Telephone: 870-972-3073
Fax: 870-972-2004
E-mail: rwinters@crow.astate.edu
Web: www.atu.edu

Program Information:
Program begins: June
Degrees offered: Associate's, 24 months; Bachelor's, 48 months
Evening or weekend classes are available.

Application Information:
Enrollment of program: 80
Transfer students are accepted.

Financial Information:
Tuition, resident: $3,000
Tuition, non-resident: $5,000
Average cost of books: $120

Employment Profile:
% of students who pass the boards on their first try: 90
% employed within the first 6 months following graduation: 100
Average starting salary: $26,000

Baptist Health
11900 Colonel Glenn Road
Suite 1000
Little Rock, AR 72210-2820

Contact Information:
Telephone: 501-202-7942
Fax: 501-202-7406

Program Information:
Program begins: June
Degrees offered: Certificate program, 24 months; Bachelor's, 48 months

Application Information:
Enrollment of program: 30

Financial Information:
Tuition, resident: $2,500
Tuition, non-resident: $3,600
Average cost of books: $800

Employment Profile:
% of students who pass the boards on their first try: 100
% employed within the first 6 months following graduation: 100
Average starting salary: $27,000

North Arkansas College
1515 Pioneer Drive
Harrison, AR 72601

Contact Information:
Telephone: 870-391-3318
Fax: 870-391-3250
E-mail: srichard@northark.cc.ar.us
Web: www.pioneer.northark.cc.ar.us

Program Information:
Program begins: July
Degrees offered: Associate's, 24 months

Application Information:
Enrollment of program: 24
Transfer students are accepted.

Financial Information:
Tuition, resident: $2,120
Tuition, non-resident: $3,770
Average cost of books: $600
% of students receiving aid: 50

Employment Profile:
% of students who pass the boards on their first try: 98
% employed within the first 6 months following graduation: 100
Average starting salary: $24,000

Northwest Technical Institute
PO Box 2000
Springdale, AR 72765

Contact Information:
Telephone: 501-751-8824 ext. 115
Fax: 501-751-7780
E-mail: rjones@nti.tec.ar.us
Web: www.nti.tec.ar.us

Program Information:
Program begins: August
Degrees offered: Diploma

Application Information:
Enrollment of program: 20
Transfer students are accepted.

Financial Information:
Tuition, resident: $1,050
Tuition, non-resident: $1,500
Average cost of books: $500

Employment Profile:
% of students who pass the boards on their first try: 97
% employed within the first 6 months following graduation: 100
Average starting salary: $18,750

South Arkansas Community College

300 South West Avenue
PO Box 7010 West Campus
El Dorado, AR 71731-7010

Contact Information:
Telephone: 605-333-6466
Fax: 605-333-1554
E-mail: edney@eagle.saccw.cc.ar.us
Web: www.saccw.cc.ar.us

Program Information:
Program begins: June
Duration of program: 24 months

Application Information:
Enrollment of program: 26
Transfer students are accepted.

Financial Information:
Tuition, resident: $1,527
Tuition, non-resident: $4,087
Average cost of books: $275

Employment Profile:
% of students who pass the boards on their first try: 86
% employed within the first 6 months following graduation: 100
Average starting salary: $22,000

University of Arkansas for Medical Sciences

AHEC-Northwest
2907 East Joyce Street
Fayetteville, AR 72703

Contact Information:
Telephone: 513-745-5689
Fax: 513-558-8736
E-mail: stano@nwark.com
Web: www.uams.edu

Program Information:
Program begins: August
Degrees offered: Bachelor's, 48 months

Application Information:
Enrollment of program: 14

Financial Information:
Tuition, resident: $2,813
Tuition, non-resident: $6,989
Average cost of books: $500
% of students receiving aid: 50

Employment Profile:
% of students who pass the boards on their first try: 100
% employed within the first 6 months following graduation: 100
Average starting salary: $22,880

California

Bakersfield College

1801 Panorama Drive
Bakersfield, CA 93305

Contact Information:
Telephone: 661-395-4284
Fax: 661-395-4295
Web: www.bc.cc.us

Program Information:
Program begins: August
Duration of program: 24 months
Evening or weekend classes are available.

Application Information:
Enrollment of program: 40

Financial Information:
Tuition, resident: $400
Tuition, non-resident: $4,000

Cabrillo College

6500 Soquel Drive
Aptos, CA 95003

Contact Information:
Telephone: 831-479-6461
Fax: 831-479-5748
E-mail: anoconno@cabrillo.cc.ca.us
Web: www.cabrillo.cc.ca.us

Program Information:
Program begins: August
Duration of program: 22 months

Application Information:
Enrollment of program: 44
Transfer students are accepted.

Financial Information:
Tuition, resident: $725
Tuition, non-resident: $8,250
Average cost of books: $700

Employment Profile:
% of students who pass the boards on their first try: 100
% employed within the first 6 months following graduation: 100
Average starting salary: $40,000

California State University—Northridge

18111 Nordhoff Street
Northridge, CA 91330-8285

Contact Information:
Telephone: 818-677-2475
Fax: 818-677-2045
E-mail: anita.slechta@csun.edu
Web: www.csun.edu

Program Information:
Program begins: July
Degrees offered: Bachelor's, 55 months
Evening or weekend classes are available.

Application Information:
Enrollment of program: 90
Transfer students are accepted.

Financial Information:
Tuition, resident: $965
Tuition, non-resident: $1,500
Average cost of books: $900
% of students receiving aid: 50

Employment Profile:
% of students who pass the boards on their first try: 100
% employed within the first 6 months following graduation: 80
Average starting salary: $30,000

Canada College

4200 Farm Hill Boulevard
Redwood City, CA 94061

Contact Information:
Telephone: 650-306-3283
Fax: 650-306-3149

Program Information:
Program begins: August
Degrees offered: Certificate program, 23 months; Diploma, 23 months

Application Information:
Enrollment of program: 20

Financial Information:
Tuition, resident: $397
Tuition, non-resident: $4,240
Average cost of books: $500

Employment Profile:
% of students who pass the boards on their first try: 80
% employed within the first 6 months following graduation: 90
Average starting salary: $40,000

Chaffey Community College

5885 Haven Avenue
Rancho Cucamonga, CA 91737

Contact Information:
Telephone: 909-941-2359
Fax: 909-466-2887
E-mail: tnorcutt@chaffey.cc.ca.us
Web: www.chaffey.cc.ca.us

Program Information:
Program begins: August
Duration of program: 24 months

Application Information:
Enrollment of program: 50
Transfer students are accepted.

Financial Information:
Tuition, resident: $468
Tuition, non-resident: $4,644
Average cost of books: $450
% of students receiving aid: 87

Employment Profile:
% of students who pass the boards on their first try: 100

% employed within the first 6 months following graduation: 92
Average starting salary: $30,000

Cypress College

9200 Valley View Street
Cypress, CA 90630-5897

Contact Information:
Telephone: 714-484-7286
Fax: 714-527-2175
Web: www.cypress.cc.ca.us

Program Information:
Program begins: August
Duration of program: 30 months
Evening or weekend classes are available.

Application Information:
Enrollment of program: 72
Transfer students are accepted.

Financial Information:
Tuition, resident: $377
Tuition, non-resident: $3,306
Average cost of books: $300

Employment Profile:
% of students who pass the boards on their first try: 100
% employed within the first 6 months following graduation: 100
Average starting salary: $28,000

Daniel Freeman Memorial Hospital

333 North Prairie Avenue
Inglewood, CA 90301

Contact Information:
Telephone: 310-674-7050 ext. 3413
Fax: 310-671-8968

Program Information:
Program begins: September
Duration of program: 24 months

Financial Information:
Average cost of books: $450

Employment Profile:
% of students who pass the boards on their first try: 100
% employed within the first 6 months following graduation: 95
Average starting salary: $34,000

Kaiser Permanente Medical Center

901 Nevin Avenue
Richmond, CA 94801-3195

Contact Information:
Telephone: 510-307-2320
Fax: 510-307-2327
E-mail: phillip.fong@kp.org
Web: www.kpscal.org

Program Information:
Program begins: October
Duration of program: 24 months

Application Information:
Enrollment of program: 23
Transfer students are accepted.

Financial Information:
Tuition, resident: $972
Tuition, non-resident: $11,097
Average cost of books: $600

Employment Profile:
% of students who pass the boards on their first try: 97

Long Beach City College

4901 East Carson Street
Long Beach, CA 90808-1076

Contact Information:
Telephone: 562-938-4176
Fax: 562-938-4191
E-mail: vgoodsonclhcc.cc.ca.us
Web: www.lbcc.cc.ca.us

Program Information:
Program begins: January
Duration of program: 30 months

Application Information:
Enrollment of program: 30
Transfer students are accepted.

Financial Information:
Tuition, resident: $566
Tuition, non-resident: $5,525
Average cost of books: $500
% of students receiving aid: 50

Employment Profile:
% of students who pass the boards on their first try: 90
% employed within the first 6 months following graduation: 72
Average starting salary: $34,000

Los Angeles City College

855 North Vermont Avenue
Los Angeles, CA 90029

Contact Information:
Telephone: 213-953-4325
Fax: 213-953-4294
Web: www.lacc.cc.ca.us

Program Information:
Program begins: August
Duration of program: 27 months
Evening or weekend classes are available.

Application Information:
Enrollment of program: 35
Transfer students are accepted.

Financial Information:
Average cost of books: $500

Employment Profile:
% of students who pass the boards on their first try: 100
% employed within the first 6 months following graduation: 80
Average starting salary: $34,000

Los Angeles County Harbor—UCLA Medical Center

1000 West Carson Street
PO Box 27
Torrance, CA 90509-2910

Contact Information:
Telephone: 310-222-2825
Fax: 310-618-9500

Program Information:
Program begins: August
Degrees offered: Certificate program, 24 months

Application Information:
Enrollment of program: 17

Financial Information:
Average cost of books: $300

Employment Profile:
% of students who pass the boards on their first try: 95
% employed within the first 6 months following graduation: 100
Average starting salary: $30,000

Merced College

3600 M Street
Merced, CA 95348-2898

Contact Information:
Telephone: 209-384-6132
Fax: 209-384-6167
E-mail: rosej@merced.cc.ca.us
Web: www.merced.cc.ca.us

Program Information:
Program begins: June
Duration of program: 29 months

Application Information:
Enrollment of program: 16
Transfer students are accepted.

Financial Information:
Tuition, resident: $338
Tuition, non-resident: $2,964
Average cost of books: $300

Employment Profile:
% of students who pass the boards on their first try: 85
% employed within the first 6 months following graduation: 80
Average starting salary: $29,000

Merritt College

12500 Campus Drive
Oakland, CA 94619

Contact Information:
Telephone: 510-436-2484
Fax: 510-434-3870
E-mail: vrussell@merritt.edu
Web: www.merritt.edu/radte

Program Information:
Program begins: August
Duration of program: 24 months

Application Information:
Enrollment of program: 45

Financial Information:
Tuition, resident: $780
Tuition, non-resident: $1,600

Moorpark College

7075 Campus Road
Moorpark, CA 93021

Contact Information:
Telephone: 805-378-1535
Fax: 805-378-1548
E-mail: jmoore@vcccd.cc.ca.us
Web: www.moorpark.cc.ca.us

Program Information:
Program begins: June
Duration of program: 24 months

Application Information:
Enrollment of program: 25

Financial Information:
Tuition, resident: $585
Tuition, non-resident: $5,130
Average cost of books: $1,000

Employment Profile:
% of students who pass the boards on their first try: 90
% employed within the first 6 months following graduation: 50
Average starting salary: $35,000

Mt. San Antonio College

1100 North Grand Avenue
Walnut, CA 91789-1399

Contact Information:
Telephone: 909-594-5611 ext. 4527
Fax: 909-468-3938
E-mail: rkirchma@mtsac.edu
Web: www.mtsac.edu

Program Information:
Program begins: June
Duration of program: 26 months

Application Information:
Enrollment of program: 50
Transfer students are accepted.

Financial Information:
Tuition, resident: $416
Tuition, non-resident: $4,736

Employment Profile:
% of students who pass the boards on their first try: 90
% employed within the first 6 months following graduation: 85

Orange Coast College

2701 Fairview Road
PO Box 5005
Costa Mesa, CA 92628-5005

Contact Information:
Telephone: 714-432-5540
Fax: 714-432-5534
E-mail: lvisinta@mail.occ.ccd.edu
Web: www.occ.cccd.edu

Program Information:
Program begins: September
Duration of program: 24 months

Application Information:
Enrollment of program: 36
Transfer students are accepted.

Financial Information:
Tuition, resident: $683
Tuition, non-resident: $6,195
Average cost of books: $1,000
% of students receiving aid: 40

Employment Profile:
% of students who pass the boards on their first try: 95
% employed within the first 6 months following graduation: 89
Average starting salary: $40,000

Pasadena City College

1570 East Colorado Boulevard
Pasadena, CA 91106-2003

Contact Information:
Telephone: 626-585-7469
Fax: 626-585-7978
E-mail: lxpires@paced.cc.ca.us
Web: www.paccd.cc.ca.us

Program Information:
Program begins: August
Duration of program: 24 months

Application Information:
Transfer students are accepted.

Financial Information:
Tuition, resident: $332
Tuition, non-resident: $2,808
Average cost of books: $800
% of students receiving aid: 25

Employment Profile:
% of students who pass the boards on their first try: 99
% employed within the first 6 months following graduation: 100
Average starting salary: $46,000

San Joaquin General Hospital

PO Box 1020
Stockton, CA 95201

Contact Information:
Telephone: 713-476-1871
Fax: 713-478-2364

Program Information:
Program begins: July
Duration of program: 24 months

Application Information:
Enrollment of program: 10

Financial Information:
Tuition, resident: $465
Tuition, non-resident: $4,683
Average cost of books: $500

Employment Profile:
% of students who pass the boards on their first try: 100
% employed within the first 6 months following graduation: 100
Average starting salary: $30,000

Santa Barbara City College

721 Cliff Drive
Santa Barbara, CA 93109-2394

Contact Information:
Telephone: 816-472-7400 ext. 3025
Web: www.sbcc.net

Program Information:
Program begins: June
Duration of program: 24 months
Evening or weekend classes are available.

Application Information:
Enrollment of program: 51
Transfer students are accepted.

Financial Information:
Average cost of books: $400
% of students receiving aid: 50

Employment Profile:
% of students who pass the boards on their first try: 90
% employed within the first 6 months following graduation: 75
Average starting salary: $33,000

Santa Rosa Junior College

1501 Mendocino Avenue
Santa Rosa, CA 95401-4395

Contact Information:
Telephone: 352-395-5702
Fax: 352-395-5711
E-mail: xho@santarosa.edu
Web: www.santarosa.edu

Program Information:
Program begins: August
Duration of program: 25 months

Application Information:
Enrollment of program: 30
Transfer students are accepted.

Financial Information:
Tuition, resident: $399
Tuition, non-resident: $4,053
Average cost of books: $450
% of students receiving aid: 50

Employment Profile:
% of students who pass the boards on their first try: 90
% employed within the first 6 months following graduation: 80
Average starting salary: $36,000

Colorado

Centura-St. Anthony Hospitals

1601 Lowell Boulevard
Denver, CO 80204-1597

Contact Information:
Telephone: 303-899-5267

Fax: 303-595-6097
E-mail: joycesnyder@centura.org
Web: www.centura.org

Program Information:
Program begins: January, August
Degrees offered: Certificate program, 24 months

Application Information:
Enrollment of program: 30
Transfer students are accepted.

Financial Information:
Average cost of books: $150

Employment Profile:
% of students who pass the boards on their first try: 95
% employed within the first 6 months following graduation: 100
Average starting salary: $27,000

Community College of Denver—Auraria Campus

Health Education Center
1070 Yosemite Street
Denver, CO 80230

Contact Information:
Telephone: 303-365-8372
Fax: 303-365-8396
E-mail: lindaf@cccs.cccoes.edu
Web: www.ccd.rightchoice.org

Program Information:
Program begins: August
Degrees offered: Associate's, 20 months

Application Information:
Enrollment of program: 32
Transfer students are accepted.

Financial Information:
Tuition, resident: $2,147
Tuition, non-resident: $8,618
Average cost of books: $700
% of students receiving aid: 90

Employment Profile:
% of students who pass the boards on their first try: 98
% employed within the first 6 months following graduation: 60
Average starting salary: $25,000

ConCorde Career Institute

770 Grant Street
Denver, CO 80203

Contact Information:
Telephone: 303-861-1151
Fax: 303-839-5478
Web: www.concordecareercolleges.com

Program Information:
Program begins: April, October
Degrees offered: Certificate program, 24 months

Application Information:
Enrollment of program: 15

Financial Information:
Tuition, resident: $8,500
Average cost of books: $300
% of students receiving aid: 90

Employment Profile:
% of students who pass the boards on their first try: 100
% employed within the first 6 months following graduation: 100
Average starting salary: $26,000

Memorial Hospital

2790 North Academy Boulevard Suite 201
Colorado Springs, CO 80917

Contact Information:
Telephone: 719-365-6819
Fax: 719-365-5374

Program Information:
Program begins: June
Duration of program: 24 months

Financial Information:
Average cost of books: $600
% of students receiving aid: 25

Employment Profile:
% of students who pass the boards on their first try: 100
% employed within the first 6 months following graduation: 100
Average starting salary: $26,000

Pima Medical Institute—Denver

1701 West 72nd Avenue
Denver, CO 80221

Contact Information:
Telephone: 303-426-1800
Fax: 303-430-4048
Web: www.pimamedical.com

Program Information:
Program begins: September
Duration of program: 24 months

Application Information:
Enrollment of program: 20

Financial Information:
Average cost of books: $1,545
% of students receiving aid: 90

Employment Profile:
% of students who pass the boards on their first try: 94
% employed within the first 6 months following graduation: 90
Average starting salary: $30,000

Red Rocks Community College

4851 Independence
Suite 218
Wheat Ridge, CO 80033

Contact Information:
Telephone: 303-420-6879
Fax: 303-940-9967
Web: www.rrcc.cccoes.edu

Program Information:
Program begins: September
Degrees offered: Diploma, 24 months

Application Information:
Enrollment of program: 25
Transfer students are accepted.

Financial Information:
Tuition, resident: $3,000
Tuition, non-resident: $7,500
Average cost of books: $300
% of students receiving aid: 40

Employment Profile:
% of students who pass the boards on their first try: 80
% employed within the first 6 months following graduation: 100
Average starting salary: $28,000

Connecticut

Capital Community Technical College

61 Woodland Street
Hartford, CT 06105

Contact Information:
Telephone: 860-520-7940
Fax: 860-520-7906
E-mail: creech@apollo.commnet.edu
Web: www.cctc.commnet.edu

Program Information:
Duration of program: 22 months

Application Information:
Enrollment of program: 30
Transfer students are accepted.

Financial Information:
Tuition, resident: $1,800
Tuition, non-resident: $2,800
Average cost of books: $250
% of students receiving aid: 40

Employment Profile:
% of students who pass the boards on their first try: 90
% employed within the first 6 months following graduation: 90
Average starting salary: $30,000

Danbury Hospital

24 Hospital Avenue
Danbury, CT 06810

Contact Information:
Telephone: 203-797-7182
Fax: 203-797-7721
Web: www.danhosp.org

Program Information:
Program begins: September
Degrees offered: Certificate program, 24 months

Application Information:
Enrollment of program: 14

Financial Information:
Average cost of books: $600

Employment Profile:
% of students who pass the boards on their first try: 90
% employed within the first 6 months following graduation: 100
Average starting salary: $32,000

Gateway Community Technical College
88 Bassett Road
North Haven, CT 06473

Contact Information:
Telephone: 203-234-3342
Fax: 203-234-3343
E-mail: gw_taylor@commnet.edu
Web: www.gwctc.commnet.edu

Program Information:
Program begins: August
Degrees offered: Associate's, 23 months
Evening or weekend classes are available.

Application Information:
Enrollment of program: 40
Transfer students are accepted.

Financial Information:
Tuition, resident: $1,814
Tuition, non-resident: $5,438
Average cost of books: $375
% of students receiving aid: 35

Employment Profile:
% of students who pass the boards on their first try: 90
% employed within the first 6 months following graduation: 100
Average starting salary: $30,000

Hartford Hospital
560 Hudson Street
Hartford, CT 06106

Contact Information:
Telephone: 860-545-3955
Fax: 860-545-6461
E-mail: pcooke@harthosp.org
Web: www.harthosp.org

Program Information:
Program begins: September
Duration of program: 24 months

Application Information:
Enrollment of program: 8
Transfer students are accepted.

Financial Information:
Average cost of books: $500

Employment Profile:
Average starting salary: $33,000

Middlesex Community Technical College
100 Training Hill Road
Middletown, CT 06457

Contact Information:
Telephone: 860-344-6505
Fax: 860-347-3176
Web: www.commnet.edu

Program Information:
Program begins: June
Duration of program: 27 months

Application Information:
Enrollment of program: 26
Transfer students are accepted.

Financial Information:
Average cost of books: $500
% of students receiving aid: 50

Employment Profile:
% of students who pass the boards on their first try: 100
% employed within the first 6 months following graduation: 80

Naugatuck Valley Community Technical College
750 Chase Parkway
Waterbury, CT 06708

Contact Information:
Telephone: 203-575-8266
Fax: 203-596-8779
E-mail: jpronovost@nvctc5.commnet.edu
Web: www.nvctc.commnet.edu

Program Information:
Program begins: September
Degrees offered: Associate's, 22 months

Application Information:
Enrollment of program: 21
Transfer students are accepted.

Financial Information:
Tuition, resident: $1,814
Tuition, non-resident: $5,438

Employment Profile:
% of students who pass the boards on their first try: 100
% employed within the first 6 months following graduation: 100
Average starting salary: $27,000

Quinnipiac College
Mt. Carmel Avenue
Hamden, CT 06518-0008

Contact Information:
Telephone: 203-281-8683
Fax: 203-281-8706
E-mail: conbaum@aol.com
Web: www.quinnipiac.edu

Program Information:
Program begins: September
Degrees offered: Certificate program, 27 months; Bachelor's, 36 months
Evening or weekend classes are available.

Application Information:
Enrollment of program: 60

Financial Information:
Average cost of books: $130

Employment Profile:
% of students who pass the boards on their first try: 100
% employed within the first 6 months following graduation: 100
Average starting salary: $30,000

Stamford Hospital
Shelburne Road and West Broad Street
Box 9317
Stamford, CT 06904-9317

Contact Information:
Telephone: 203-325-7877
Fax: 203-325-7352
E-mail: dorothy_saia@stamhosp.chime.org
Web: www.stamfordhospital.org

Program Information:
Program begins: July
Duration of program: 24 months

Application Information:
Enrollment of program: 9
Transfer students are accepted.

Financial Information:
Average cost of books: $500

Employment Profile:
% of students who pass the boards on their first try: 100
% employed within the first 6 months following graduation: 95
Average starting salary: $31,000

University of Hartford
200 Bloomfield Avenue
Dana Hall Room 267
West Hartford, CT 06117

Contact Information:
Telephone: 205-934-7382
Fax: 205-975-7302
E-mail: morison@mail.hartford.edu
Web: www.hartford.edu

Program Information:
Program begins: September
Degrees offered: Certificate program, Bachelor's, 50 months

Application Information:
Enrollment of program: 30
Transfer students are accepted.

Financial Information:
Average cost of books: $300
% of students receiving aid: 50

Employment Profile:
% of students who pass the boards on their first try: 92
% employed within the first 6 months following graduation: 80
Average starting salary: $30,000

Windham Community Memorial Hospital

112 Mansfield Avenue
Willimantic, CT 06226

Contact Information:
Telephone: 860-456-6713
Fax: 860-456-6883
E-mail: mpatros@wcmh.org
Web: www.wcmh.org

Program Information:
Program begins: July
Duration of program: 24 months

Financial Information:
Average cost of books: $650
% of students receiving aid: 58

Delaware

Delaware Technical & Community College—Owens Campus

PO Box 610
Georgetown, DE 19947

Contact Information:
Telephone: 302-856-5400 ext. 5517
Fax: 302-856-5773
E-mail: dludema@outland.dtcc.edu
Web: www.dtcc.edu

Program Information:
Program begins: January
Degrees offered: Associate's, 23 months

Application Information:
Enrollment of program: 30

Financial Information:
Tuition, resident: $1,595
Tuition, non-resident: $3,987
Average cost of books: $600
% of students receiving aid: 75

Employment Profile:
% of students who pass the boards on their first try: 90
% employed within the first 6 months following graduation: 98
Average starting salary: $28,000

Delaware Technical & Community College—Wilmington

333 Shipley Street
Wilmington, DE 19801

Contact Information:
Telephone: 302-428-6945
Fax: 302-428-2691
E-mail: tfoy@christiancare.org
Web: www.dtcc.edu

Program Information:
Program begins: May
Duration of program: 24 months

Application Information:
Enrollment of program: 32
Transfer students are accepted.

Financial Information:
Tuition, resident: $1,890
Tuition, non-resident: $4,725
Average cost of books: $300
% of students receiving aid: 30

Employment Profile:
% of students who pass the boards on their first try: 95
% employed within the first 6 months following graduation: 100
Average starting salary: $29,000

District of Columbia

Washington Hospital Center

110 Irving Street, NW
Washington, DC 20010

Contact Information:
Telephone: 202-877-6343
Web: www.midlantic.mhg.edu

Program Information:
Program begins: September
Degrees offered: Certificate program, 22-24 months

Application Information:
Enrollment of program: 24

Financial Information:
Average cost of books: $500

Employment Profile:
% of students who pass the boards on their first try: 90
% employed within the first 6 months following graduation: 91
Average starting salary: $29,000

Florida

Bethesda Memorial Hospital

2815 South Seacrest Boulevard
Boynton Beach, FL 33435

Contact Information:
Telephone: 561-737-7733 ext. 4574
Fax: 561-737-6758
Web: www.bethesdaweb.com

Program Information:
Program begins: July
Degrees offered: Certificate program, 24 months

Application Information:
Enrollment of program: 16

Employment Profile:
% of students who pass the boards on their first try: 98
% employed within the first 6 months following graduation: 100
Average starting salary: $25,000

Brevard Community College

1519 Clearlake Road
Cocoa, FL 32922

Contact Information:
Telephone: 407-632-1111 ext. 63552
Fax: 407-634-3731
E-mail: sheehans@brenard.cc.fl.us
Web: www.brevard.cc.fl.us

Program Information:
Program begins: February, June, October
Duration of program: 24 months

Application Information:
Enrollment of program: 40

Financial Information:
Tuition, resident: $3,465
Tuition, non-resident: $8,046
Average cost of books: $700

Employment Profile:
% employed within the first 6 months following graduation: 95
Average starting salary: $27,000

Edison Community College

PO Box 60210
Ft. Myers, FL 33906-6210

Contact Information:
Telephone: 941-637-5617
Fax: 603-963-0760
E-mail: rcrabb@edison.edu
Web: www.edison.edu

Program Information:
Program begins: July
Duration of program: 24 months

Application Information:
Transfer students are accepted.

Financial Information:
Tuition, resident: $2,496
Tuition, non-resident: $9,234
Average cost of books: $500

Employment Profile:
% of students who pass the boards on their first try: 100
% employed within the first 6 months following graduation: 75
Average starting salary: $26,000

Halifax Medical Center

303 North Clyde Morris Boulevard
PO Box 2830
Daytona Beach, FL 32120-2830

Contact Information:
Telephone: 904-254-4075 ext. 3509
Fax: 904-254-4231
Web: www.halif.org

Program Information:
Program begins: January
Degrees offered: Certificate program, 30 months

Application Information:
Enrollment of program: 20

Financial Information:
Average cost of books: $400
% of students receiving aid: 80

Employment Profile:
% of students who pass the boards on their first try: 100
% employed within the first 6 months following graduation: 100
Average starting salary: $25,000

Manatee Community College
5840 26th Street West
PO Box 1849
Bradenton, FL 32406-1849

Contact Information:
Telephone: 813-755-1511
Fax: 813-727-8304
E-mail: randleg@bc.mcc.cc.fl.us
Web: www.mcc.cc.fl.us

Program Information:
Program begins: June
Degrees offered: Associate's, 23 months

Application Information:
Enrollment of program: 30
Transfer students are accepted.

Financial Information:
Tuition, resident: $2,878
Tuition, non-resident: $6,542
Average cost of books: $1,040
% of students receiving aid: 80

Employment Profile:
% of students who pass the boards on their first try: 100
% employed within the first 6 months following graduation: 100
Average starting salary: $27,000

Marion County School of Radiologic Technology
1014 Southwest Seventh Road
Ocala, FL 34474

Contact Information:
Telephone: 352-620-7582
Fax: 352-629-1117
E-mail: richart5@worldnet.att.net
Web: www.mcctae.com

Program Information:
Program begins: July
Duration of program: 24 months

Application Information:
Enrollment of program: 40
Transfer students are accepted.

Financial Information:
Tuition, resident: $1,020
Tuition, non-resident: $2,040
Average cost of books: $550
% of students receiving aid: 30

Employment Profile:
% employed within the first 6 months following graduation: 100
Average starting salary: $25,000

Miami-Dade Community College
Medical Center Campus
950 Northwest 20th Street
Miami, FL 33127

Contact Information:
Telephone: 305-237-4034
Fax: 305-237-4116
E-mail: gferench@mdcc.edu
Web: www.mdcc.edu

Program Information:
Program begins: June
Duration of program: 24 months

Application Information:
Enrollment of program: 80
Transfer students are accepted.

Financial Information:
Tuition, resident: $1,539
Tuition, non-resident: $5,200
Average cost of books: $275
% of students receiving aid: 98

Employment Profile:
% of students who pass the boards on their first try: 85
% employed within the first 6 months following graduation: 90
Average starting salary: $29,000

Palm Beach Community College
3160 PGA Boulevard
Palm Beach Gardens, FL 33418-2893

Contact Information:
Telephone: 561-625-2511
Fax: 561-625-2305
Web: www.pbcc.cc.fl.us

Program Information:
Program begins: October
Duration of program: 24 months

Financial Information:
Tuition, resident: $1,598
Tuition, non-resident: $5,126

Employment Profile:
% of students who pass the boards on their first try: 100

Santa Fe Community College
3000 Northwest 83rd Street
Gainesville, FL 32602-6200

Contact Information:
Telephone: 805-965-0581
Fax: 805-963-7222
E-mail: ed.dice@santafe.cc.fl.us
Web: www.inst.santafe.cc.fl.us

Program Information:
Program begins: August
Duration of program: 22 months

Application Information:
Transfer students are accepted.

Financial Information:
Tuition, resident: $3,195
Tuition, non-resident: $11,893
Average cost of books: $415
% of students receiving aid: 50

Employment Profile:
% of students who pass the boards on their first try: 100
% employed within the first 6 months following graduation: 90
Average starting salary: $25,500

Shands-Jacksonville
655 West Eighth Street
Jacksonville, FL 32209

Contact Information:
Telephone: 412-749-4230
Fax: 412-749-4203

Program Information:
Program begins: July
Degrees offered: Certificate program, 24 months

Application Information:
Enrollment of program: 20
Transfer students are accepted.

Financial Information:
Average cost of books: $250
% of students receiving aid: 10

Employment Profile:
% of students who pass the boards on their first try: 88
% employed within the first 6 months following graduation: 100
Average starting salary: $25,000

University of Central Florida
4000 Central Florida Boulevard
PO Box 25000
Orlando, FL 32816-2220

Contact Information:
Telephone: 210-544-8248
Fax: 210-844-8910
E-mail: tedwards@mail.ucf.edu
Web: www.ucf.edu

Program Information:
Program begins: August
Degrees offered: Bachelor's, 48 months

Application Information:
Enrollment of program: 52

Financial Information:
Tuition, resident: $2,894
Tuition, non-resident: $11,769

Employment Profile:
% of students who pass the boards on their first try: 100
% employed within the first 6 months following graduation: 100

University of Miami/Jackson Memorial Hospital
1611 North 12th Avenue
Miami, FL 33136

Contact Information:
Telephone: 304-357-4854
Fax: 304-357-4965

Program Information:
Program begins: June
Degrees offered: Certificate program, 15 months

Application Information:
Enrollment of program: 20

Financial Information:
Tuition, resident: $1,225
Tuition, non-resident: $1,525
Average cost of books: $600

Employment Profile:
% of students who pass the boards on their first try: 90
% employed within the first 6 months following graduation: 60
Average starting salary: $31,000

Valencia Community College
PO Box 3028
Orlando, FL 32802

Contact Information:
Telephone: 407-299-5000 ext. 1288
Web: www.valencia.cc.fl.us

Program Information:
Program begins: August
Duration of program: 24 months

Application Information:
Enrollment of program: 20

Financial Information:
Tuition, resident: $1,821
Tuition, non-resident: $6,609

Employment Profile:
% of students who pass the boards on their first try: 100
% employed within the first 6 months following graduation: 90
Average starting salary: $29,000

West Boca Medical Center
21644 State Road 7
Boca Raton, FL 33428

Contact Information:
Telephone: 561-488-8173
Fax: 561-488-8347
Web: www.mindspring.com

Program Information:
Program begins: October
Degrees offered: Certificate program, 24 months

Application Information:
Enrollment of program: 28

Financial Information:
Average cost of books: $350

Employment Profile:
% of students who pass the boards on their first try: 100
% employed within the first 6 months following graduation: 100

Georgia

Athens Area Technical Institute
800 US Highway 29 North
Athens, GA 30601-1500

Contact Information:
Telephone: 706-355-5052
Fax: 706-369-5753
E-mail: cummings@aati.edu
Web: www.athens.tec.ga.us

Program Information:
Program begins: July
Duration of program: 24 months

Application Information:
Enrollment of program: 24
Transfer students are accepted.

Financial Information:
Tuition, resident: $1,132
Tuition, non-resident: $2,264
Average cost of books: $400
% of students receiving aid: 75

Employment Profile:
% of students who pass the boards on their first try: 100
% employed within the first 6 months following graduation: 100
Average starting salary: $30,000

Carroll Technical Institute
4600 Timber Ridge Drive
Douglasville, GA 30135

Contact Information:
Telephone: 770-947-7222
Fax: 770-947-7216
E-mail: psaylors@falcon.carroll.tec.ga.us
Web: www.carroll.tec.ga.us

Program Information:
Program begins: July
Degrees offered: Associate's, 24 months

Application Information:
Enrollment of program: 34

Financial Information:
Tuition, resident: $1,172
Average cost of books: $500

Employment Profile:
% of students who pass the boards on their first try: 85
% employed within the first 6 months following graduation: 100
Average starting salary: $25,000

Emory University
1364 Clifton Road Northeast
Atlanta, GA 30322

Contact Information:
Telephone: 404-712-5005
Fax: 404-712-7256
E-mail: dawn_moore@emory.edu
Web: www.emory.edu

Program Information:
Program begins: March
Duration of program: 24 months

Application Information:
Enrollment of program: 35
Transfer students are accepted.

Financial Information:
Average cost of books: $700
% of students receiving aid: 100

Employment Profile:
% of students who pass the boards on their first try: 95
% employed within the first 6 months following graduation: 85
Average starting salary: $26,000

Georgia Baptist Medical Center
303 Parkway Northeast/Box 51
Atlanta, GA 30312-1206

Contact Information:
Telephone: 404-265-4299
Fax: 404-265-4983
Web: www.tenethealth.com/georgiabaptist

Program Information:
Program begins: March
Duration of program: 24 months

Application Information:
Enrollment of program: 10

Financial Information:
Average cost of books: $500
% of students receiving aid: 10

Employment Profile:
% of students who pass the boards on their first try: 100
% employed within the first 6 months following graduation: 100
Average starting salary: $30,000

Grady Health System
80 Butler Street Southeast
PO Box 26095
Atlanta, GA 30335-3801

Contact Information:
Telephone: 404-616-3610
Fax: 404-616-3512

Program Information:
Program begins: September
Degrees offered: Diploma, 24 months

Application Information:
Enrollment of program: 43

Financial Information:
Average cost of books: $300
% of students receiving aid: 75

Employment Profile:
% of students who pass the boards on their first try: 100
% employed within the first 6 months following graduation: 100
Average starting salary: $30,000

Griffin Technical Institute

501 Varsity Road
Griffin, GA 30223-2042

Contact Information:
Telephone: 770-229-3225
Fax: 770-229-3227
E-mail: rogersd@admin1.griffin.tec.ga.us
Web: www.griffin.tec.ga.us

Program Information:
Program begins: September
Duration of program: 24 months

Application Information:
Enrollment of program: 18
Transfer students are accepted.

Financial Information:
Average cost of books: $650
% of students receiving aid: 96

Employment Profile:
% employed within the first 6 months following graduation: 100
Average starting salary: $30,000

Gwinnett Technical Institute

5150 Sugarloaf Parkway
PO Box 1505
Lawrenceville, GA 30046

Contact Information:
Telephone: 770-962-7580 ext. 326
Fax: 770-962-7985
E-mail: jsass@gwinnett.tec.ga.us
Web: www.gwinnett.tech.org

Program Information:
Program begins: June
Duration of program: 20 months

Application Information:
Enrollment of program: 30
Transfer students are accepted.

Financial Information:
Tuition, resident: $1,350
Tuition, non-resident: $2,500
Average cost of books: $400
% of students receiving aid: 95

Employment Profile:
% of students who pass the boards on their first try: 100
% employed within the first 6 months following graduation: 100
Average starting salary: $25,000

Heart of Georgia Technical Institute

560 Pinehill Road
Dublin, GA 31021

Contact Information:
Telephone: 912-274-7882
Fax: 912-275-6642
E-mail: billj@heartga.tec.ga.us
Web: www.gain.mercer.edu

Program Information:
Program begins: July
Duration of program: 24 months

Application Information:
Enrollment of program: 20
Transfer students are accepted.

Financial Information:
Tuition, resident: $2,160
Average cost of books: $1,200
% of students receiving aid: 95

Employment Profile:
% of students who pass the boards on their first try: 100
% employed within the first 6 months following graduation: 100
Average starting salary: $26,000

Medical Center Incorporated

727 Center Street
PO Box 951
Columbus, GA 31902-0951

Contact Information:
Telephone: 706-571-1155
Fax: 706-660-2887
Web: www.accc-cancer.org

Program Information:
Program begins: June
Duration of program: 24 months

Application Information:
Enrollment of program: 30

Financial Information:
Average cost of books: $800

Employment Profile:
% of students who pass the boards on their first try: 94

Medical Center of Central Georgia

777 Hemlock Street
PO Box 6000
Macon, GA 31208

Contact Information:
Telephone: 912-633-1258
Fax: 912-633-2378
Web: www.mccg.org/radiology

Program Information:
Program begins: July
Duration of program: 24 months

Application Information:
Enrollment of program: 19

Financial Information:
Average cost of books: $500
% of students receiving aid: 50

Employment Profile:
% of students who pass the boards on their first try: 98
% employed within the first 6 months following graduation: 100
Average starting salary: $30,000

Moultrie Area Technical Institute

361 Industrial Drive
Moultrie, GA 31768

Contact Information:
Telephone: 912-891-7000
Fax: 912-891-7010
Web: www.collegeedge.com

Program Information:
Program begins: July
Duration of program: 24 months

Application Information:
Transfer students are accepted.

Financial Information:
Tuition, resident: $1,152
Tuition, non-resident: $2,304
Average cost of books: $600
% of students receiving aid: 100

Employment Profile:
% of students who pass the boards on their first try: 93
% employed within the first 6 months following graduation: 100
Average starting salary: $24,000

Thomas Technical Institute

15689 US Highway 19 North
Thomasville, GA 31792

Contact Information:
Telephone: 912-225-3957
Fax: 912-225-5289
E-mail: wwaldron@ttin1.thomas.tec.ga.us
Web: www.thomas-tech.com

Program Information:
Program begins: August
Duration of program: 21 months

Application Information:
Enrollment of program: 27
Transfer students are accepted.

Financial Information:
Tuition, resident: $1,128
Tuition, non-resident: $2,256
Average cost of books: $200
% of students receiving aid: 80

Employment Profile:
% of students who pass the boards on their first try: 100
% employed within the first 6 months following graduation: 100
Average starting salary: $22,000

Well Star Kennestone Hospital

60 Lacy Street
Marietta, GA 30060

Contact Information:
Telephone: 770-793-5571
Fax: 770-793-7796
E-mail: tamplin_barbara@promina.org

Program Information:
Program begins: June
Duration of program: 24 months

Application Information:
Enrollment of program: 19

Financial Information:
Average cost of books: $700

Employment Profile:
% employed within the first 6 months following graduation: 100

Idaho

Boise State University

College of Health Sciences
1910 University Drive
Boise, ID 83725

Contact Information:
Telephone: 208-426-3290
Fax: 208-426-4459
E-mail: dtravis@boisestate.edu
Web: www.idbsu.edu

Program Information:
Program begins: August
Degrees offered: Bachelor's

Application Information:
Enrollment of program: 24
Transfer students are accepted.

Financial Information:
Tuition, resident: $2,104
Tuition, non-resident: $7,450
Average cost of books: $334

Employment Profile:
% of students who pass the boards on their first try: 100
% employed within the first 6 months following graduation: 90
Average starting salary: $25,000

Illinois

Blessing Hospital

Box 7005/Broadway at 14th Street
Quincy, IL 623017005

Contact Information:
Telephone: 217-223-1200 ext. 4292
Fax: 217-223-3906
E-mail: upper@blessinghospital.com
Web: www.urop.uci.edu

Program Information:
Program begins: July
Duration of program: 24 months

Application Information:
Enrollment of program: 20

Financial Information:
Average cost of books: $400

Employment Profile:
% of students who pass the boards on their first try: 100
% employed within the first 6 months following graduation: 100
Average starting salary: $27,000

Bloomington-Normal School of Radiography

900 Franklin Avenue
Normal, IL 61761

Contact Information:
Telephone: 309-452-2834
Fax: 309-392-2835

Program Information:
Program begins: July
Duration of program: 24 months

Application Information:
Enrollment of program: 20
Transfer students are accepted.

Financial Information:
Average cost of books: $600
% of students receiving aid: 10

Employment Profile:
% of students who pass the boards on their first try: 100
% employed within the first 6 months following graduation: 100
Average starting salary: $23,500

College of DuPage

19351 West Washington Street
Glen Ellyn, IL 60137-6599

Contact Information:
Telephone: 630-942-2434
Fax: 630-858-5409
E-mail: rigoni@cdnet.cod.edu
Web: www.dupage.edu

Program Information:
Program begins: September
Duration of program: 24 months

Application Information:
Enrollment of program: 55

Financial Information:
Tuition, resident: $1,440
Tuition, non-resident: $4,416

Employment Profile:
% of students who pass the boards on their first try: 92
% employed within the first 6 months following graduation: 100
Average starting salary: $28,000

College of Lake County

19351 West Washington Street
Grayslake, IL 60030-1198

Contact Information:
Telephone: 847-543-2313
Fax: 847-223-1357
E-mail: tomvogl@clc.cc.il.us
Web: www.clc.cc.il.us

Program Information:
Program begins: June
Duration of program: 22 months

Application Information:
Enrollment of program: 35
Transfer students are accepted.

Financial Information:
Tuition, resident: $1,734
Tuition, non-resident: $6,592

Employment Profile:
% of students who pass the boards on their first try: 91
% employed within the first 6 months following graduation: 97
Average starting salary: $27,500

Illinois Central College

Health and Public Services Building
201 Southwest Adams Street
Peoria, IL 61635-0001

Contact Information:
Telephone: 309-999-4659
Fax: 309-673-9626
E-mail: dschulz@icc.cc.il.us
Web: www.icc.cc.il.us

Program Information:
Program begins: January
Duration of program: 23 months

Financial Information:
Tuition, resident: $2,856
Tuition, non-resident: $5,587

Employment Profile:
% of students who pass the boards on their first try: 98

Kaskaskia College

27210 College Road
Centralia, IL 62801

Contact Information:
Telephone: 618-545-3363 ext. 333
Fax: 618-532-1990
E-mail: plbrinkman@kc.cc.il.us
Web: www.kc.cc.il.us

Program Information:
Program begins: June
Duration of program: 18 months

Application Information:
Enrollment of program: 44
Transfer students are accepted.

Financial Information:
Tuition, resident: $3,135
Tuition, non-resident: $7,837

Employment Profile:
% employed within the first 6 months following graduation: 100
Average starting salary: $23,500

Moraine Valley Community College

10900 South 88th Avenue
Palos Hills, IL 60465

Contact Information:
Telephone: 708-974-5316
Fax: 708-974-1184
E-mail: hein@moraine.cc.il.us
Web: www.mv.cc.il.us./alliedhealth

Program Information:
Program begins: June
Degrees offered: Associate's, 26 months

Application Information:
Enrollment of program: 52
Transfer students are accepted.

Financial Information:
Tuition, resident: $1,320
Tuition, non-resident: $5,070
Average cost of books: $150
% of students receiving aid: 10

Employment Profile:
% of students who pass the boards on their first try: 95
% employed within the first 6 months following graduation: 100
Average starting salary: $29,000

Parkland College

2400 West Bradley Avenue
Champaign, IL 61821-1899

Contact Information:
Telephone: 217-351-2436
Fax: 217-373-3830
E-mail: twagner@parkland.cc.il.us
Web: www.parkland.cc.il.us

Program Information:
Program begins: August
Degrees offered: Associate's, 24 months

Application Information:
Enrollment of program: 17
Transfer students are accepted.

Financial Information:
Tuition, resident: $1,620
Tuition, non-resident: $4,860
Average cost of books: $500

Employment Profile:
% of students who pass the boards on their first try: 90
% employed within the first 6 months following graduation: 100
Average starting salary: $28,000

Provena United Samaritans Medical Center

812 North Logan Avenue
Danville, IL 61832-3788

Contact Information:
Telephone: 217-443-5245
Fax: 217-443-1965
E-mail: bobverkler@provena.org
Web: www.provenausmc.org

Program Information:
Program begins: June
Duration of program: 24 months

Application Information:
Enrollment of program: 12

Financial Information:
% of students receiving aid: 30

Employment Profile:
% of students who pass the boards on their first try: 100
% employed within the first 6 months following graduation: 100
Average starting salary: $28,000

Rockford Memorial Hospital

2400 North Rockton Avenue
Rockford, IL 61103

Contact Information:
Telephone: 815-971-5480
Fax: 815-968-3407
Web: www.rhsnet.org

Program Information:
Program begins: June
Duration of program: 24 months

Application Information:
Enrollment of program: 16
Transfer students are accepted.

Financial Information:
Tuition, resident: $1,600
Tuition, non-resident: $2,400
Average cost of books: $375

Employment Profile:
% of students who pass the boards on their first try: 100
% employed within the first 6 months following graduation: 100
Average starting salary: $28,000

Sauk Valley Community College

173 Illinois Route 2
Dixon, IL 61021-9112

Contact Information:
Telephone: 707-527-4346
Fax: 707-527-4426
E-mail: shippes@hpuxl.svcc.edu
Web: www.succ.edu

Program Information:
Program begins: August
Degrees offered: Diploma, 22 months

Application Information:
Enrollment of program: 56
Transfer students are accepted.

Financial Information:
Tuition, resident: $1,645
Tuition, non-resident: $4,621
Average cost of books: $250
% of students receiving aid: 50

Employment Profile:
% of students who pass the boards on their first try: 100
% employed within the first 6 months following graduation: 100
Average starting salary: $27,000

St. Francis Hospital

355 Ridge Avenue
Evanston, IL 60202

Contact Information:
Telephone: 315-798-8258
Fax: 315-798-8382
Web: www.saintfrancis.com

Program Information:
Program begins: August
Degrees offered: Certificate program, 24 months

Application Information:
Transfer students are accepted.

Financial Information:
Tuition, resident: $735
Average cost of books: $350
% of students receiving aid: 50

Employment Profile:
% of students who pass the boards on their first try: 98
% employed within the first 6 months following graduation: 100
Average starting salary: $31,200

St. Francis Medical Center

530 Northeast Glen Oak Avenue
Peoria, IL 61637

Contact Information:
Telephone: 309-655-2782
Fax: 309-655-3480
E-mail: suzanne.m.yezek.osfhealthcare.org
Web: www.osfsaintfrancis.org

Program Information:
Program begins: July
Duration of program: 24 months

Application Information:
Enrollment of program: 18
Transfer students are accepted.

Financial Information:
Average cost of books: $350

Employment Profile:
% of students who pass the boards on their first try: 95
% employed within the first 6 months following graduation: 75
Average starting salary: $23,000

Swedish American Hospital

1400 Charles Street
Rockford, IL 61104-2298

Contact Information:
Telephone: 815-489-4966 ext. 4966
Fax: 815-966-3979

Program Information:
Program begins: August
Duration of program: 21 months

Application Information:
Enrollment of program: 18

Financial Information:
Tuition, resident: $10,000
Average cost of books: $420

Employment Profile:
% of students who pass the boards on their first try: 100

% employed within the first 6 months following graduation: 100
Average starting salary: $28,000

Trinity Medical Center
555 6th Street
Moline, IL 61265-1216

Contact Information:
Telephone: 701-857-5000 ext. 5620
E-mail: fohte@trinitygc.com
Web: www.tinityqc.com

Program Information:
Program begins: June
Duration of program: 24 months

Application Information:
Enrollment of program: 12
Transfer students are accepted.

Employment Profile:
% employed within the first 6 months following graduation: 95
Average starting salary: $22,500

Triton College
2000 North Fifth Avenue
River Grove, IL 60171

Contact Information:
Telephone: 708-456-0300 ext. 3370
Fax: 708-583-3336
E-mail: clekosta@triton.cc.il.us
Web: www.triton.cc.il.us

Program Information:
Program begins: August
Duration of program: 24 months

Application Information:
Enrollment of program: 42

Financial Information:
Tuition, resident: $1,505
Tuition, non-resident: $6,762

Employment Profile:
Average starting salary: $30,000

Indiana

Ball Memorial Hospital
2401 University Avenue
Muncie, IN 47303-3499

Contact Information:
Telephone: 765-747-4372
Fax: 765-747-4415
E-mail: shinds@cam13.com
Web: www.cardinalhealthsystem.org

Program Information:
Program begins: June
Degrees offered: Associate's, 24 months

Application Information:
Enrollment of program: 10

Financial Information:
Average cost of books: $500
% of students receiving aid: 67

Employment Profile:
% of students who pass the boards on their first try: 100
% employed within the first 6 months following graduation: 100
Average starting salary: $26,000

Columbus Regional Hospital
2400 East 17th Street
Columbus, IN 47201

Contact Information:
Telephone: 812-376-5354
Fax: 812-378-5988
E-mail: kfrazier@crh.org
Web: www.crg.org

Program Information:
Program begins: July
Degrees offered: Certificate program, 24 months

Application Information:
Enrollment of program: 10

Financial Information:
Average cost of books: $275

Employment Profile:
% of students who pass the boards on their first try: 96
% employed within the first 6 months following graduation: 100

Community Hospitals of Indianapolis
1500 North Ritter Avenue
Indianapolis, IN 46219

Contact Information:
Telephone: 317-355-5867
Fax: 317-351-7864
Web: www.commhospindy.org

Program Information:
Program begins: June
Duration of program: 24 months

Financial Information:
Average cost of books: $550

Employment Profile:
% of students who pass the boards on their first try: 95

Ft. Wayne School of Radiography
700 Broadway
Ft. Wayne, IN 46802

Contact Information:
Telephone: 219-425-3990
Fax: 219-425-3975
E-mail: fwsr@fw1.com
Web: www.iupui.edu

Program Information:
Program begins: June
Duration of program: 24 months

Application Information:
Transfer students are accepted.

Financial Information:
Tuition, resident: $2,000
Tuition, non-resident: $4,000
Average cost of books: $1,500

Employment Profile:
% of students who pass the boards on their first try: 100
% employed within the first 6 months following graduation: 100
Average starting salary: $26,009

Hancock Memorial Hospital
801 North State Street
Greenfield, IN 46140

Contact Information:
Telephone: 317-462-0468
Fax: 317-462-0549
E-mail: vsutton@hmhhs.org

Program Information:
Program begins: July
Duration of program: 24 months

Application Information:
Enrollment of program: 14

Employment Profile:
% of students who pass the boards on their first try: 100
% employed within the first 6 months following graduation: 98
Average starting salary: $24,500

Indiana University Northwest
3400 Broadway
Gary, IN 46408-1197

Contact Information:
Telephone: 219-980-6540
Fax: 219-980-6649
E-mail: mledbett@junhaw1.iun.indiana.edu
Web: www.iun.indiana.edu

Program Information:
Program begins: August
Duration of program: 24 months

Application Information:
Transfer students are accepted.

Financial Information:
Tuition, resident: $7,110
Tuition, non-resident: $18,717
Average cost of books: $600

Employment Profile:
% of students who pass the boards on their first try: 95
% employed within the first 6 months following graduation: 95

Ivy Tech State College—Indianapolis
Central Indiana Region
One West 26th Street/PO Box 1763
Indianapolis, IN 46206-1763

Contact Information:
Telephone: 317-921-4414
Fax: 317-921-4753
E-mail: lmcgloth@ivy.tec.in.us
Web: www.infonet.ivy.tec.in.us

Program Information:
Program begins: June
Duration of program: 24 months

Application Information:
Enrollment of program: 28
Transfer students are accepted.

Financial Information:
Tuition, resident: $2,780
Tuition, non-resident: $5,187
Average cost of books: $725

Employment Profile:
% of students who pass the boards on their first try: 92
% employed within the first 6 months following graduation: 100
Average starting salary: $26,200

King's Daughter's Hospital
One King's Daughter's Drive
PO Box 447
Madison, IN 47250

Contact Information:
Telephone: 812-265-5211 ext. 633
Fax: 812-265-0474

Program Information:
Program begins: July
Degrees offered: Certificate program, 24 months

Application Information:
Enrollment of program: 12

Financial Information:
Average cost of books: $600

Employment Profile:
% of students who pass the boards on their first try: 100
% employed within the first 6 months following graduation: 100
Average starting salary: $26,000

Reid Hospital & Health Care Services
1401 Chester Boulevard
Richmond, IN 47374

Contact Information:
Telephone: 765-983-3167
Fax: 765-983-3176
E-mail: prestoro@reidhosp.com
Web: www.reidhosp.com

Program Information:
Program begins: October
Degrees offered: Certificate program, 24 months

Application Information:
Enrollment of program: 16

Financial Information:
Average cost of books: $600

Employment Profile:
% of students who pass the boards on their first try: 99
% employed within the first 6 months following graduation: 100
Average starting salary: $26,000

St. Joseph Hospital & Health Center
1907 West Sycamore Street
Kokomo, IN 46904-9010

Contact Information:
Telephone: 317-456-5144
Fax: 317-456-5812
Web: www.stjhhc.org

Program Information:
Program begins: October
Degrees offered: Certificate program, 24 months

Application Information:
Enrollment of program: 12

Financial Information:
Average cost of books: $500

Employment Profile:
% of students who pass the boards on their first try: 100
% employed within the first 6 months following graduation: 100
Average starting salary: $26,000

University of Saint Francis
2701 Spring Street
Ft. Wayne, IN 46808

Contact Information:
Telephone: 412-647-3528
Fax: 412-647-6512
E-mail: dlyke @sf.edu
Web: www.sf.edu

Program Information:
Program begins: August
Duration of program: 2 months
Evening or weekend classes are available.

Application Information:
Enrollment of program: 44
Transfer students are accepted.

Financial Information:
Tuition, resident: $10,700

Employment Profile:
% of students who pass the boards on their first try: 99
% employed within the first 6 months following graduation: 93
Average starting salary: $28,000

Iowa

Allen College
1825 Logan Avenue
Waterloo, IA 50703

Contact Information:
Telephone: 319-274-6731
Web: www.allencollege.edu

Program Information:
Program begins: August
Duration of program: 24 months

Application Information:
Enrollment of program: 17
Transfer students are accepted.

Iowa Central Community College
330 Avenue M
Ft. Dodge, IA 50501

Contact Information:
Telephone: 515-576-0099 ext. 2306
Fax: 515-576-7206
E-mail: lee@duke.iccc.cc.ia.us
Web: www.duke.iccc.cc.ia.us

Program Information:
Program begins: August
Duration of program: 22 months

Application Information:
Transfer students are accepted.

Financial Information:
Tuition, resident: $2,596
Tuition, non-resident: $3,994

Employment Profile:
% of students who pass the boards on their first try: 100
% employed within the first 6 months following graduation: 98
Average starting salary: $22,000

Iowa Methodist Medical Center
1200 Pleasant Street
Des Moines, IA 50309-1453

Contact Information:
Telephone: 515-241-6171
Fax: 515-241-8015
E-mail: pagemj@ihs.org
Web: www.insdesmoines.org

Program Information:
Program begins: July
Duration of program: 24 months

Application Information:
Enrollment of program: 19
Transfer students are accepted.

Financial Information:
Average cost of books: $1,000
% of students receiving aid: 22

Employment Profile:
% of students who pass the boards on their first try: 100
% employed within the first 6 months following graduation: 100
Average starting salary: $24,000

Mercy-St. Luke's Hospitals
1026 A Avenue Northeast
Cedar Rapids, IA 52402

Contact Information:
Telephone: 319-369-7097
Web: www.isrt.org

Program Information:
Program begins: June, July
Degrees offered: Diploma, 24 months

Application Information:
Enrollment of program: 38
Transfer students are accepted.

Financial Information:
Average cost of books: $400

Employment Profile:
% of students who pass the boards on their first try: 100
% employed within the first 6 months following graduation: 100
Average starting salary: $25,000

Mercy Health Center—North Iowa

1000 Fourth Street Southwest
Mason City, IA 50401

Contact Information:
Telephone: 515-422-7200
Fax: 515-422-7916
E-mail: simek@mercyhealth.com
Web: www.northiowamercy.com

Program Information:
Program begins: July
Duration of program: 24 months

Application Information:
Enrollment of program: 15

Financial Information:
Average cost of books: $750

Employment Profile:
% of students who pass the boards on their first try: 100
% employed within the first 6 months following graduation: 100
Average starting salary: $24,000

The University of Iowa Hospitals and Clinics

200 Hawkins Drive C-723 GH
Iowa City, IA 52242-1077

Contact Information:
Telephone: 319-356-4332
Fax: 319-384-9574
E-mail: kathy-martensen@uiowa.edu
Web: www.radiology.uiowa.edu

Program Information:
Program begins: August
Duration of program: 24 months

Financial Information:
Average cost of books: $300

Employment Profile:
% of students who pass the boards on their first try: 100
% employed within the first 6 months following graduation: 98
Average starting salary: $26,000

Kansas

Ft. Hays State University

600 Park Street
Hays, KS 67601-4099

Contact Information:
Telephone: 913-628-5678
Fax: 913-628-4076
E-mail: mmadden@fhsu.edu
Web: www.fhsu.edu

Program Information:
Program begins: August
Duration of program: 24 months

Application Information:
Enrollment of program: 70
Transfer students are accepted.

Financial Information:
Tuition, resident: $4,882
Tuition, non-resident: $15,358
Average cost of books: $1,000
% of students receiving aid: 90

Employment Profile:
% of students who pass the boards on their first try: 95
% employed within the first 6 months following graduation: 100
Average starting salary: $27,000

Hutchinson Community College and Area Vocational School

815 North Walnut
Hutchinson, KS 67501

Contact Information:
Telephone: 316-665-4954 ext. 4954
Fax: 316-665-4924
E-mail: kautzerr@hutchcc.edu

Program Information:
Program begins: August
Duration of program: 24 months

Application Information:
Enrollment of program: 45

Financial Information:
Tuition, resident: $1,419
Tuition, non-resident: $3,201
Average cost of books: $850

Employment Profile:
% of students who pass the boards on their first try: 99
% employed within the first 6 months following graduation: 90
Average starting salary: $23,000

Labette Community College

200 South 14th Street
Parsons, KS 67357

Contact Information:
Telephone: 316-421-6700 ext. 59
Fax: 316-421-0180
E-mail: paulb@labette.cc.ks.us
Web: www.labette.cc.ks.us

Program Information:
Program begins: July
Degrees offered: Associate's, 23 months
Evening or weekend classes are available.

Application Information:
Enrollment of program: 50
Transfer students are accepted.

Financial Information:
Tuition, resident: $1,619
Tuition, non-resident: $3,792
Average cost of books: $450
% of students receiving aid: 77

Employment Profile:
% of students who pass the boards on their first try: 100
% employed within the first 6 months following graduation: 100
Average starting salary: $28,500

Washburn University of Topeka

1700 Southwest College Avenue
Topeka, KS 66621

Contact Information:
Telephone: 785-231-1010 ext. 1281
Fax: 785-231-1027
E-mail: zzrobe@washburn.edu
Web: www.wuacc.edu

Program Information:
Program begins: August
Degrees offered: Associate's, 23 months

Application Information:
Enrollment of program: 36
Transfer students are accepted.

Financial Information:
Tuition, resident: $3,150
Tuition, non-resident: $6,867
Average cost of books: $400
% of students receiving aid: 50

Employment Profile:
% of students who pass the boards on their first try: 98
% employed within the first 6 months following graduation: 100
Average starting salary: $27,000

Kentucky

Bowling Green Technical College

1845 Loop Drive
Bowling Green, KY 42101

Contact Information:
Telephone: 502-746-7461 ext. 2180
Fax: 502-746-7466
E-mail: diane.button@kctcs.net
Web: www.kctcs.net

Program Information:
Program begins: August
Degrees offered: Diploma, 20 months

Application Information:
Enrollment of program: 44
Transfer students are accepted.

Financial Information:
Tuition, resident: $870
Tuition, non-resident: $1,740
Average cost of books: $350

Employment Profile:
% of students who pass the boards on their first try: 84
% employed within the first 6 months following graduation: 100

Central Kentucky Technical College

308 Vocational -Technical Road
Lexington, KY 40511

Contact Information:
Telephone: 606-246-2400
Fax: 606-246-2504
Web: www.kctcs.net

Program Information:
Program begins: August
Duration of program: 24 months

Financial Information:
Tuition, resident: $800
Tuition, non-resident: $1,600

Elizabethtown Technical College

505 University Drive
Elizabethtown, KY 42701

Contact Information:
Telephone: 270-766-5133 ext. 164
Fax: 270-766-5224
E-mail: penelope.logsdon@kctcs.net
Web: www.state.ky.us

Program Information:
Program begins: August
Duration of program: 22 months

Application Information:
Enrollment of program: 25
Transfer students are accepted.

Financial Information:
Tuition, resident: $820
Average cost of books: $650
% of students receiving aid: 25

Employment Profile:
% of students who pass the boards on their first try: 90
% employed within the first 6 months following graduation: 90
Average starting salary: $23,920

King's Daughter's Medical Center

2201 Lexington Avenue
Ashland, KY 41105-0151

Contact Information:
Telephone: 606-327-4637
Fax: 606-327-4707
E-mail: tdobbins@kdmc.com
Web: www.kdmc.com

Program Information:
Program begins: August
Degrees offered: Certificate program, 24 months

Application Information:
Enrollment of program: 8

Financial Information:
Average cost of books: $475

Employment Profile:
% of students who pass the boards on their first try: 100
% employed within the first 6 months following graduation: 100
Average starting salary: $26,000

Madisonville Technical College

750 North Laffoon Street
Madisonville, KY 42431

Contact Information:
Telephone: 270-824-7552
Web: www.madtechcollege.com

Program Information:
Program begins: August
Duration of program: 22 months

Application Information:
Enrollment of program: 30
Transfer students are accepted.

Financial Information:
Tuition, resident: $760
Tuition, non-resident: $1,520
Average cost of books: $500
% of students receiving aid: 40

Employment Profile:
% of students who pass the boards on their first try: 99
% employed within the first 6 months following graduation: 98
Average starting salary: $21,000

Northern Kentucky University

227 Albright Health Center
Highland Heights, KY 41099-2104

Contact Information:
Telephone: 606-527-5606
Fax: 606-572-6592
Web: www.nku.edu

Program Information:
Program begins: August
Duration of program: 22 months

Financial Information:
Tuition, resident: $1,160
Tuition, non-resident: $3,180

Employment Profile:
% employed within the first 6 months following graduation: 90
Average starting salary: $21,000

Owensboro Community College

4800 New Hartford Road
Owensboro, KY 42303

Contact Information:
Telephone: 502-686-4498
Fax: 502-686-4662
E-mail: debbie.poelhuis@kctcs.net
Web: www.owecc.net

Program Information:
Program begins: June
Duration of program: 24 months

Application Information:
Enrollment of program: 22
Transfer students are accepted.

Financial Information:
Tuition, resident: $1,151
Tuition, non-resident: $3,548

Employment Profile:
% employed within the first 6 months following graduation: 100

St. Joseph Hospital

One St. Joseph Drive
Lexington, KY 40504

Contact Information:
Telephone: 606-254-1177 ext. 123
Fax: 606-313-3115
Web: www.sjhiex.org

Program Information:
Program begins: September
Degrees offered: Certificate program, 24 months

Application Information:
Enrollment of program: 19

Financial Information:
Average cost of books: $425

Employment Profile:
% of students who pass the boards on their first try: 75
% employed within the first 6 months following graduation: 100
Average starting salary: $22,880

University of Louisville

School of Allied Health Science / Health Science Center
4055 K Building
555 South Floyd Street HSC
Louisville, KY 40292

Contact Information:
Telephone: 407-823-2747
Fax: 407-823-6509
E-mail: fecamp01@gwise.louisville.edu
Web: www.louisville.edu

Program Information:
Program begins: June
Duration of program: 21 months

Application Information:
Enrollment of program: 46
Transfer students are accepted.

Financial Information:
Tuition, resident: $4,260
Tuition, non-resident: $11,985
Average cost of books: $500

Employment Profile:
% of students who pass the boards on their first try: 93

% employed within the first 6 months following graduation: 100
Average starting salary: $20,800

West Kentucky Technical College
5200 Blandville Road
PO Box 7408
Paducah, KY 42002-7408

Contact Information:
Telephone: 502-554-6232
Fax: 502-554-6227
Web: www.wkytech.com

Program Information:
Program begins: August
Degrees offered: Diploma, 24 months

Application Information:
Enrollment of program: 30
Transfer students are accepted.

Financial Information:
Tuition, resident: $620
Tuition, non-resident: $1,240
Average cost of books: $350
% of students receiving aid: 25

Employment Profile:
% of students who pass the boards on their first try: 100
% employed within the first 6 months following graduation: 98
Average starting salary: $23,000

Louisiana

Baton Rouge General Medical Center
3600 Florida Boulevard
PO Box 2511
Baton Rouge, LA 70806

Contact Information:
Telephone: 504-387-7157
Fax: 504-381-6168
E-mail: cathy_lennier@generalhealth.org
Web: www.generalhealth.org

Program Information:
Program begins: July
Duration of program: 24 months

Application Information:
Enrollment of program: 12

Financial Information:
Average cost of books: $450
% of students receiving aid: 45

Employment Profile:
% of students who pass the boards on their first try: 100
% employed within the first 6 months following graduation: 100
Average starting salary: $22,700

Delgado Community College
615 City Park Avenue
New Orleans, LA 70119-4399

Contact Information:
Telephone: 504-483-4015
Fax: 504-483-4609
E-mail: rgiscl@dcc.edu
Web: www.dcc.edu

Program Information:
Program begins: September
Duration of program: 26 months

Application Information:
Enrollment of program: 95
Transfer students are accepted.

Financial Information:
Tuition, resident: $1,500
Tuition, non-resident: $3,700
Average cost of books: $400
% of students receiving aid: 50

Employment Profile:
% of students who pass the boards on their first try: 100
% employed within the first 6 months following graduation: 100
Average starting salary: $22,000

Lafayette General Medical Center
1214 Coolidge Avenue
PO Box 52009 OCS
Lafayette, LA 70505

Contact Information:
Telephone: 318-289-8457
Fax: 318-289-8136
E-mail: cpowell@lgmc.com
Web: www.lgmc.com

Program Information:
Program begins: July
Duration of program: 24 months

Application Information:
Enrollment of program: 61

Financial Information:
Average cost of books: $600

Employment Profile:
% of students who pass the boards on their first try: 100
% employed within the first 6 months following graduation: 90
Average starting salary: $21,000

Louisiana State University at Eunice
PO Box 1129
Eunice, LA 70535

Contact Information:
Telephone: 318-550-1340
Fax: 318-550-1289
E-mail: rmclaugh@lsue.edu
Web: www.lsue.edu

Program Information:
Program begins: June
Duration of program: 24 months

Application Information:
Enrollment of program: 661
Transfer students are accepted.

Financial Information:
Tuition, resident: $1,746
Tuition, non-resident: $5,706
Average cost of books: $400
% of students receiving aid: 63

Employment Profile:
% of students who pass the boards on their first try: 94
% employed within the first 6 months following graduation: 82
Average starting salary: $23,000

McNeese State University
PO Box 92000
Lake Charles, LA 70609-2000

Contact Information:
Telephone: 318-475-5657
Fax: 318-475-5677
E-mail: gbradley@mail.mcneese.edu
Web: www.mcneese.edu

Program Information:
Program begins: August
Degrees offered: Bachelor's, 45 months

Application Information:
Enrollment of program: 150
Transfer students are accepted.

Financial Information:
Tuition, resident: $2,178
Tuition, non-resident: $3,530

Employment Profile:
% of students who pass the boards on their first try: 100
Average starting salary: $26,000

North Oaks Health System
PO Box 2668 Highway 51 South
Hammond, LA 70404

Contact Information:
Telephone: 504-345-9805
Fax: 504-345-9894
E-mail: radschool@northoaks.org
Web: www.northoaks.org

Program Information:
Program begins: July
Duration of program: 24 months

Application Information:
Enrollment of program: 14

Financial Information:
Tuition, resident: $4,000
Average cost of books: $550

Employment Profile:
% employed within the first 6 months following graduation: 100
Average starting salary: $24,000

Northwestern State University
1800 Line Avenue
Shreveport, LA 71101-4653

Contact Information:
Telephone: 318-677-3066
Fax: 318-677-3068
E-mail: carwile@alpha.nsula.edu
Web: www.nsula.edu

Program Information:
Program begins: July
Degrees offered: Bachelor's, 45 months

Application Information:
Transfer students are accepted.

Financial Information:
Tuition, resident: $2,000
Tuition, non-resident: $5,226

Southern University at Shreveport—Bossier City

610 Texas Street
Shreveport, LA 71101

Contact Information:
Telephone: 318-674-3339
Fax: 318-676-5308
E-mail: sgreen@sus.edu
Web: www.sus.edu

Program Information:
Program begins: August
Duration of program: 24 months

Application Information:
Enrollment of program: 40
Transfer students are accepted.

Financial Information:
Tuition, resident: $1,110
Average cost of books: $500
% of students receiving aid: 90

Employment Profile:
% of students who pass the boards on their first try: 89
% employed within the first 6 months following graduation: 100
Average starting salary: $25,000

Maine

Central Maine Medical Center

300 Main Street
Lewiston, ME 04240-0305

Contact Information:
Telephone: 207-795-2428
Fax: 207-795-5539
E-mail: ripleyj@cmhc.org
Web: www.cmmc.org

Program Information:
Program begins: August
Duration of program: 24 months

Application Information:
Enrollment of program: 14
Transfer students are accepted.

Financial Information:
Average cost of books: $400
% of students receiving aid: 63

Employment Profile:
% of students who pass the boards on their first try: 100
% employed within the first 6 months following graduation: 100
Average starting salary: $25,000

Southern Maine Technical College

Two Fort Road
South Portland, ME 04106

Contact Information:
Telephone: 207-767-9596
E-mail: sdoe@smtc.net
Web: www.smtc.net

Program Information:
Program begins: January
Duration of program: 23 months

Application Information:
Enrollment of program: 35

Financial Information:
Tuition, resident: $6,000
Tuition, non-resident: $12,000
Average cost of books: $600

Employment Profile:
% of students who pass the boards on their first try: 96
% employed within the first 6 months following graduation: 100
Average starting salary: $28,000

Maryland

Allegany College of Maryland

12401 Willowbrook Road Southeast
Cumberland, MD 21502-2596

Contact Information:
Telephone: 301-784-5560
Fax: 301-784-5015
E-mail: ester@ac.cc.md.us
Web: www.ac.cc.md.us

Program Information:
Program begins: August
Duration of program: 22 months

Application Information:
Enrollment of program: 30
Transfer students are accepted.

Financial Information:
Tuition, resident: $3,320
Tuition, non-resident: $6,640
Average cost of books: $300
% of students receiving aid: 80

Employment Profile:
% employed within the first 6 months following graduation: 50
Average starting salary: $27,000

Chesapeake College

PO Box 8
Wye Mills, MD 21679

Contact Information:
Telephone: 410-822-5400 ext. 707
Fax: 410-770-3764
E-mail: lblythe@chesapeake.edu
Web: www.chesapeake.edu

Program Information:
Program begins: August
Duration of program: 24 months

Application Information:
Enrollment of program: 9
Transfer students are accepted.

Financial Information:
Tuition, resident: $2,243
Tuition, non-resident: $6,281
Average cost of books: $500

Employment Profile:
% of students who pass the boards on their first try: 100
% employed within the first 6 months following graduation: 100
Average starting salary: $25,000

Essex Community College

7201 Rossville Boulevard
Baltimore, MD 21237-9987

Contact Information:
Telephone: 410-682-7414
Fax: 410-682-7987
E-mail: linda@helix.org
Web: www.ccbc.cc.md.us

Program Information:
Program begins: August
Duration of program: 24 months

Application Information:
Enrollment of program: 32
Transfer students are accepted.

Financial Information:
Tuition, resident: $1,980
Tuition, non-resident: $3,498
Average cost of books: $450
% of students receiving aid: 29

Employment Profile:
% of students who pass the boards on their first try: 100
% employed within the first 6 months following graduation: 90
Average starting salary: $27,000

Greater Baltimore Medical Center

6701 North Charles Street
Baltimore, MD 21204

Contact Information:
Telephone: 410-828-2463
Fax: 410-828-2866
Web: www.gbmc.org

Program Information:
Program begins: August
Degrees offered: Certificate program

Application Information:
Enrollment of program: 24

Financial Information:
Average cost of books: $450

Employment Profile:
% of students who pass the boards on their first try: 100
% employed within the first 6 months following graduation: 100
Average starting salary: $29,000

Hagerstown Community College

11400 Robinwood Drive
Hagerstown, MD 21742-6590

Contact Information:
Telephone: 301-790-2800 ext. 205
Fax: 301-739-0737
E-mail: hassinger.b@hjc.cc.md.us
Web: www.hcc.cc.md.us

Program Information:
Program begins: September
Duration of program: 24 months

Financial Information:
Tuition, resident: $2,565
Tuition, non-resident: $4,735

Holy Cross Hospital

1500 Forest Glen Road
Silver Spring, MD 20910

Contact Information:
Telephone: 301-754-7367
Fax: 301-754-7371
Web: www.careermosaic.com

Program Information:
Program begins: September
Degrees offered: Certificate program, 24 months

Application Information:
Enrollment of program: 22
Transfer students are accepted.

Financial Information:
Average cost of books: $400

Employment Profile:
% of students who pass the boards on their first try: 89
% employed within the first 6 months following graduation: 100
Average starting salary: $30,000

Johns Hopkins Hospital

600 North Wolfe Street
Baltimore, MD 21287

Contact Information:
Telephone: 410-955-9089
Fax: 410-955-0589
E-mail: semoore.jhmi.edu
Web: www.imagingschools.rad.jhmi.edu

Program Information:
Program begins: July
Duration of program: 18 months

Application Information:
Enrollment of program: 17
Transfer students are accepted.

Financial Information:
Average cost of books: $250

Employment Profile:
% of students who pass the boards on their first try: 98
% employed within the first 6 months following graduation: 95
Average starting salary: $30,000

Prince George's Community College

301 Largo Road
Largo, MD 20772-2199

Contact Information:
Telephone: 301-322-0648
Fax: 301-386-7528
Web: www.pg.cc.md.us

Program Information:
Program begins: September
Duration of program: 24 months

Application Information:
Enrollment of program: 48
Transfer students are accepted.

Financial Information:
Tuition, resident: $1,794
Tuition, non-resident: $3,432

Employment Profile:
% of students who pass the boards on their first try: 95
% employed within the first 6 months following graduation: 85
Average starting salary: $28,000

Wor-Wic Community College

32000 Campus Drive
Salisbury, MD 21804

Contact Information:
Telephone: 410-572-8740
Fax: 410-572-8730
E-mail: awoodward@mail.workwk.cc.maus
Web: www.worwic.cc.md.us

Program Information:
Program begins: June
Duration of program: 24 months
Evening or weekend classes are available.

Application Information:
Enrollment of program: 32

Financial Information:
Tuition, resident: $2,255
Tuition, non-resident: $6,437

Massachusetts

Bunker Hill Community College

Medical Imaging Program
250 New Rutherford Ave
Boston, MA 02129-2991

Contact Information:
Telephone: 617-228-2197
Fax: 617-228-2052
E-mail: dmisrati@bhcc.state.ma.us
Web: www.bhcc.state.ma.us

Program Information:
Program begins: June
Duration of program: 24 months
Evening or weekend classes are available.

Application Information:
Enrollment of program: 30
Transfer students are accepted.

Financial Information:
Tuition, resident: $3,767
Tuition, non-resident: $1,117
Average cost of books: $500

Employment Profile:
% of students who pass the boards on their first try: 88
% employed within the first 6 months following graduation: 60
Average starting salary: $30,000

Holyoke Community College

303 Homestead Avenue
Holyoke, MA 01040

Contact Information:
Telephone: 413-552-2460
E-mail: kroot@hcc.mass.edu
Web: www.hcc.mass.edu

Program Information:
Program begins: July
Duration of program: 23 months

Application Information:
Enrollment of program: 14
Transfer students are accepted.

Financial Information:
Tuition, resident: $2,859
Tuition, non-resident: $6,747
Average cost of books: $200

Employment Profile:
% of students who pass the boards on their first try: 100
% employed within the first 6 months following graduation: 100
Average starting salary: $28,000

Massachusetts Bay Community College

Wellesley Hills Campus
50 Oakland Street
Wellesley Hills, MA 02181-5399

Contact Information:
Telephone: 617-239-2238
Web: www.mbcc.mass.edu

Program Information:
Program begins: September
Degrees offered: Diploma, 20 months
Evening or weekend classes are available.

Application Information:
Enrollment of program: 30
Transfer students are accepted.

Financial Information:
Tuition, resident: $3,200
Average cost of books: $350
% of students receiving aid: 80

Employment Profile:
% of students who pass the boards on their first try: 100
% employed within the first 6 months following graduation: 100
Average starting salary: $28,000

Massasoit Community College

One Massasoit Boulevard
Brockton, MA 02402

Contact Information:
Telephone: 508-588-9100 ext. 1784
Fax: 508-427-1250
E-mail: nsutcliffe@massasoit.mass.edu
Web: www.massasoit.mass.edu

Program Information:
Program begins: September
Duration of program: 21 months

Application Information:
Transfer students are accepted.

Financial Information:
Tuition, resident: $3,081
Tuition, non-resident: $7,644

North Shore Community College

One Ferncroft Road
PO Box 3340
Danvers, MA 01923-0840

Contact Information:
Telephone: 508-762-4163
Fax: 508-762-4022
E-mail: cwiley@seahawk.nscc.mass.edu
Web: www.nscc.ma.edu

Program Information:
Program begins: September
Duration of program: 21 months

Application Information:
Enrollment of program: 20

Financial Information:
Tuition, resident: $2,400
Tuition, non-resident: $7,260
Average cost of books: $800

Employment Profile:
% of students who pass the boards on their first try: 100
% employed within the first 6 months following graduation: 100
Average starting salary: $28,000

Northern Essex Community College

45 Franklin Street
Lawrence, MA 01841

Contact Information:
Telephone: 978-738-7516
Fax: 978-738-7450
E-mail: cwallace@necc.mass.edu
Web: www.necc.mass.edu

Program Information:
Program begins: August
Duration of program: 22 months

Application Information:
Transfer students are accepted.

Employment Profile:
% of students who pass the boards on their first try: 100
% employed within the first 6 months following graduation: 100
Average starting salary: $24,000

Quinsigamond Community College

670 West Boylston Street
Worcester, MA 01606-2092

Contact Information:
Telephone: 508-854-4289
Fax: 508-852-6943
E-mail: sandieo@qcc.mass.edu
Web: www.worcesterphoenix.com

Program Information:
Program begins: June
Duration of program: 22 months

Application Information:
Enrollment of program: 18
Transfer students are accepted.

Financial Information:
Tuition, resident: $1,000
Tuition, non-resident: $3,000
Average cost of books: $400

Employment Profile:
% of students who pass the boards on their first try: 98
% employed within the first 6 months following graduation: 97
Average starting salary: $26,000

Michigan

Baker College of Owosso

1020 South Washington Street
Owosso, MI 48867-4400

Contact Information:
Telephone: 517-729-3422
Fax: 517-729-3411
E-mail: pickfo_b@owosso.baker.edu
Web: www.baker.edu

Program Information:
Program begins: September
Duration of program: 24 months
Evening or weekend classes are available.

Application Information:
Enrollment of program: 35
Transfer students are accepted.

Financial Information:
Average cost of books: $1,200
% of students receiving aid: 73

Employment Profile:
% of students who pass the boards on their first try: 90
% employed within the first 6 months following graduation: 91
Average starting salary: $29,000

Henry Ford Community College

Health Careers Division
5101 Evergreen Road
Dearborn, MI 48128

Contact Information:
Telephone: 313-317-6595
Fax: 313-317-6569
Web: www.hfcc.net

Program Information:
Program begins: August
Duration of program: 24 months

Application Information:
Enrollment of program: 23

Financial Information:
Tuition, resident: $3,000
Tuition, non-resident: $4,646

Employment Profile:
% employed within the first 6 months following graduation: 92
Average starting salary: $29,000

Henry Ford Hospital

2799 West Grand Boulevard
Detroit, MI 48202

Contact Information:
Telephone: 313-876-1348
Fax: 313-876-9119
E-mail: kathy@rad.hfh.edu
Web: www.henry.org

Program Information:
Program begins: May
Duration of program: 24 months

Financial Information:
Average cost of books: $600

Employment Profile:
% of students who pass the boards on their first try: 96
% employed within the first 6 months following graduation: 100
Average starting salary: $27,000

Hurley Medical Center

One Hurley Plaza
Flint, MI 48503-5993

Contact Information:
Telephone: 810-257-9835
Fax: 810-257-9009
E-mail: dsturkl@hurleymc.com
Web: www.hurleymc.com

Program Information:
Program begins: August
Degrees offered: Certificate program, 24 months

Application Information:
Enrollment of program: 20

Financial Information:
Tuition, resident: $1,250
Average cost of books: $500
% of students receiving aid: 10

Employment Profile:
% of students who pass the boards on their first try: 75
% employed within the first 6 months following graduation: 90
Average starting salary: $25,000

Kellogg Community College

450 North Avenue
Battle Creek, MI 49017-3397

Contact Information:
Telephone: 616-965-3931 ext. 2315
Fax: 616-965-4144
E-mail: schollj@kellogg.cc.mi.us
Web: www.db.mde.state.mi.us

Program Information:
Program begins: June
Duration of program: 24 months

Application Information:
Enrollment of program: 15
Transfer students are accepted.

Financial Information:
Tuition, resident: $3,870
Tuition, non-resident: $6,205

Employment Profile:
% of students who pass the boards on their first try: 97
% employed within the first 6 months following graduation: 75
Average starting salary: $27,000

Lake Michigan College

2755 East Napier Avenue
Benton Harbor, MI 49022-1899

Contact Information:
Telephone: 616-927-8100
Fax: 616-927-8616
E-mail: holmes@lmc.cc.mi.us
Web: www.lmc.cc.mi.us

Program Information:
Program begins: August
Degrees offered: Diploma, 24 months
Evening or weekend classes are available.

Application Information:
Enrollment of program: 18
Transfer students are accepted.

Financial Information:
Tuition, resident: $1,320
Tuition, non-resident: $1,560

Employment Profile:
% of students who pass the boards on their first try: 100
% employed within the first 6 months following graduation: 100
Average starting salary: $30,000

Lansing Community College

Department 3400
PO Box 40010
Lansing, MI 48901-7210

Contact Information:
Telephone: 517-783-1423
E-mail: rowens@lansing.cc.mi.us
Web: www.lansing.cc.mi.us

Program Information:
Program begins: August
Degrees offered: Associate's, 24 months

Application Information:
Transfer students are accepted.

Financial Information:
Tuition, resident: $2,983
Tuition, non-resident: $4,085
Average cost of books: $600

Employment Profile:
% of students who pass the boards on their first try: 90
% employed within the first 6 months following graduation: 95
Average starting salary: $24,000

Marquette General Hospital

420 West Magnetic Street
Marquette, MI 49855

Contact Information:
Telephone: 906-225-3470
Fax: 906-225-3037
E-mail: jhowko@mgh.com
Web: www.mgh.org

Program Information:
Program begins: September
Duration of program: 24 months

Application Information:
Enrollment of program: 12
Transfer students are accepted.

Financial Information:
Average cost of books: $550
% of students receiving aid: 25

Employment Profile:
% of students who pass the boards on their first try: 100
% employed within the first 6 months following graduation: 70
Average starting salary: $30,000

Marygrove College

8425 West McNichols Road
Detroit, MI 48221-2599

Contact Information:
Telephone: 313-927-1200
Fax: 313-927-1345
E-mail: jhigh@marygrove.edu
Web: www.marygrove.edu

Program Information:
Program begins: August
Duration of program: 24 months
Evening or weekend classes are available.

Application Information:
Enrollment of program: 25
Transfer students are accepted.

Financial Information:
Tuition, resident: $8,294
% of students receiving aid: 85

Employment Profile:
% of students who pass the boards on their first try: 90
% employed within the first 6 months following graduation: 100
Average starting salary: $27,000

Mid-Michigan Community College

1375 South Clare Avenue
Harrison, MI 48625-9447

Contact Information:
Telephone: 517-386-6646
Fax: 517-386-2411
E-mail: jskinner@midmich.cc.mi.us
Web: www.midmich.cc.mi.us

Program Information:
Program begins: August
Degrees offered: Associate's, 23 months

Application Information:
Enrollment of program: 40
Transfer students are accepted.

Financial Information:
Tuition, resident: $2,657
Tuition, non-resident: $3,554
Average cost of books: $325

Employment Profile:
% of students who pass the boards on their first try: 89
% employed within the first 6 months following graduation: 95
Average starting salary: $25,000

Oakwood-Hospitals—Annapolis Center

33155 Annapolis Road
Wayne, MI 48184

Contact Information:
Telephone: 734-467-4115
Fax: 734-467-6911
E-mail: porcall@oakwood.org
Web: www.springnet.com

Program Information:
Program begins: July
Duration of program: 24 months

Financial Information:
Average cost of books: $700

Employment Profile:
% of students who pass the boards on their first try: 100
% employed within the first 6 months following graduation: 100
Average starting salary: $28,000

Washtenaw Community College

4800 East Huron River Drive
Ann Arbor, MI 48106-0978

Contact Information:
Telephone: 734-973-3336
Fax: 734-617-5078
E-mail: jbaker@orchard.washtenaw.cc.mi.us
Web: www.washtenaw.cc.mi.us

Program Information:
Program begins: August
Duration of program: 24 months

Application Information:
Enrollment of program: 60
Transfer students are accepted.

Financial Information:
Tuition, resident: $1,976
Tuition, non-resident: $2,850
Average cost of books: $500
% of students receiving aid: 20

Employment Profile:
% of students who pass the boards on their first try: 98
% employed within the first 6 months following graduation: 100
Average starting salary: $28,000

William Beaumont Hospital

3601 West 13 Mile Road
Royal Oak, MI 48073

Contact Information:
Telephone: 248-551-6048
Fax: 248-551-5490
E-mail: ttrost@beaumont.edu
Web: www.beaumont.edu

Program Information:
Program begins: July
Degrees offered: Certificate program, 24 months

Application Information:
Enrollment of program: 32

Financial Information:
Average cost of books: $750

Employment Profile:
% of students who pass the boards on their first try: 90
% employed within the first 6 months following graduation: 100
Average starting salary: $31,000

Minnesota

Century Community and Technical College

3300 Century Avenue North
White Bear Lake, MN 55110

Contact Information:
Telephone: 612-779-3334
Fax: 612-779-3417
E-mail: d.fleury@cctc.cc.mn.us
Web: www.century.cc.mn.us

Program Information:
Program begins: August
Degrees offered: Associate's, 24 months
Evening or weekend classes are available.

Application Information:
Enrollment of program: 55
Transfer students are accepted.

Financial Information:
Tuition, resident: $4,697
Tuition, non-resident: $8,858
Average cost of books: $600
% of students receiving aid: 40

Employment Profile:
% of students who pass the boards on their first try: 100
% employed within the first 6 months following graduation: 100
Average starting salary: $26,500

Fairview University—Normandale Community College

420 Dearware Street Southeast
Minneapolis, MN 55455

Contact Information:
Telephone: 612-626-5098
Fax: 612-273-6887
E-mail: pskundbi@fairview.org
Web: www.fairview.org

Program Information:
Program begins: August
Duration of program: 25 months

Financial Information:
Tuition, resident: $3,145

Employment Profile:
% of students who pass the boards on their first try: 95
% employed within the first 6 months following graduation: 100
Average starting salary: $28,000

Mayo Clinic—Mayo Foundation

School of Health Related Sciences
Siebens 1119
Rochester, MN 55905

Contact Information:
Telephone: 507-284-3169
Fax: 507-284-3640
E-mail: efrank@mayo.edu
Web: www.mayo.edu

Program Information:
Program begins: September
Duration of program: 24 months

Application Information:
Enrollment of program: 36

Financial Information:
Tuition, resident: $2,200
Average cost of books: $700
% of students receiving aid: 75

Employment Profile:
% of students who pass the boards on their first try: 100
% employed within the first 6 months following graduation: 100
Average starting salary: $29,000

Minneapolis Veterans Affairs Medical Center

One Veterans Drive
Minneapolis, MN 55417

Contact Information:
Telephone: 612-725-2000 ext. 2546
Fax: 612-727-5635
E-mail: heywood.kristin@minneapolis.va.gov
Web: www.internshipprograms.com

Program Information:
Program begins: July
Duration of program: 24 months

Application Information:
Transfer students are accepted.

Financial Information:
Average cost of books: $1,000

Employment Profile:
% of students who pass the boards on their first try: 100
% employed within the first 6 months following graduation: 100

Northwest Technical College—East Grand Forks

2022 Central Avenue Northeast
East Grand Forks, MN 56721

Contact Information:
Telephone: 218-773-3441
Fax: 218-773-4502
E-mail: deb.king@mail.ntc.mnsu.edu
Web: www.ntc-online.com

Program Information:
Program begins: August
Duration of program: 24 months

Financial Information:
Tuition, resident: $3,000
Tuition, non-resident: $6,000

Employment Profile:
% employed within the first 6 months following graduation: 100

Rice Memorial Hospital

301 Becker Avenue Southwest
Willmar, MN 56201-3395

Contact Information:
Telephone: 320-231-4530
Fax: 320-231-4865
E-mail: ilinn@rice.willmar.mn.us
Web: www.richhospital.com

Program Information:
Program begins: August
Degrees offered: Certificate program

Financial Information:
Average cost of books: $400

Employment Profile:
% of students who pass the boards on their first try: 100
% employed within the first 6 months following graduation: 100
Average starting salary: $29,000

Mississippi

Itawamba Community College
Department of Applied Science and Technology
602 West Hill Street
Fulton, MS 38843-0999

Contact Information:
Telephone: 662-862-8345
Fax: 662-862-8350
E-mail: whmay@icc.cc.ms.us
Web: www.icc.cc.ms.us

Program Information:
Program begins: August
Duration of program: 22 months

Application Information:
Enrollment of program: 18
Transfer students are accepted.

Financial Information:
Tuition, resident: $2,600
Tuition, non-resident: $5,480
Average cost of books: $700
% of students receiving aid: 65

Employment Profile:
% of students who pass the boards on their first try: 100
% employed within the first 6 months following graduation: 100
Average starting salary: $30,000

Jones County Junior College
900 South Court Street
Ellisville, MS 39437

Contact Information:
Telephone: 601-477-4159
Fax: 601-477-4152
E-mail: sandy.cchran@jcjc.cc.ms.us
Web: www.jcjc.cc.ms.us

Program Information:
Program begins: July
Duration of program: 24 months

Application Information:
Enrollment of program: 20
Transfer students are accepted.

Financial Information:
Tuition, resident: $900
Tuition, non-resident: $2,300
Average cost of books: $600

Employment Profile:
% employed within the first 6 months following graduation: 100
Average starting salary: $23,000

Meridian Community College
910 Highway 19 North
Meridian, MS 39307

Contact Information:
Telephone: 601-483-8241 ext. 757
Fax: 601-482-3936
E-mail: dshell@mcc.cc.ms.us
Web: www.mcc.cc.ms.us

Program Information:
Program begins: August
Duration of program: 24 months

Financial Information:
Tuition, resident: $1,310
Tuition, non-resident: $2,700

Mississippi Delta Community College
PO Box 668
Moorhead, MS 38761

Contact Information:
Telephone: 601-2466507
Fax: 601-246-6517
E-mail: apyles@mdcc.cc.ms.us
Web: www.mdcc.cc.ms.us

Program Information:
Program begins: August
Duration of program: 24 months

Application Information:
Enrollment of program: 40
Transfer students are accepted.

Financial Information:
Tuition, resident: $920
Tuition, non-resident: $2,370
Average cost of books: $350
% of students receiving aid: 43

Employment Profile:
% of students who pass the boards on their first try: 93
% employed within the first 6 months following graduation: 100
Average starting salary: $26,000

Northeast Mississippi Community College
Cunningham Boulevard
Booneville, MS 38829

Contact Information:
Telephone: 662-720-7364
Fax: 662-728-1165
E-mail: csimms@necc.cc.ms.us
Web: www.necc.cc.ms.us

Program Information:
Program begins: August
Duration of program: 23 months

Application Information:
Enrollment of program: 24

Financial Information:
Tuition, resident: $515
Tuition, non-resident: $1,210
Average cost of books: $250
% of students receiving aid: 50

Employment Profile:
% of students who pass the boards on their first try: 100
% employed within the first 6 months following graduation: 90
Average starting salary: $21,000

Missouri

Jewish Hospital College of Nursing and Allied Health
306 South Kings Highway
St. Louis, MO 63110

Contact Information:
Telephone: 314-454-7597
Fax: 314-454-5239
E-mail: jbm0623@bjcmail.carenet.org
Web: www.jhconah.org

Program Information:
Program begins: July
Duration of program: 24 months

Application Information:
Transfer students are accepted.

Mineral Area School of Radiologic Technology
1212 Weber Road
Farmington, MO 63640-3398

Contact Information:
Telephone: 573-756-4581 ext. 387
Fax: 573-756-6007
E-mail: h.cashion@marmc.org
Web: www.marmc.org

Program Information:
Program begins: August
Duration of program: 23 months

Application Information:
Enrollment of program: 20
Transfer students are accepted.

Financial Information:
Average cost of books: $900

Employment Profile:
% of students who pass the boards on their first try: 100
% employed within the first 6 months following graduation: 100
Average starting salary: $25,000

Missouri Southern State College
3950 East Newman Road
Joplin, MO 64801-1595

Contact Information:
Telephone: 417-625-9322 ext. 3118
Web: www.mssc.com

Program Information:
Program begins: August
Duration of program: 24 months

Financial Information:
Tuition, resident: $2,772
Tuition, non-resident: $5,544

Nichols Career Center
609 Union Street
Jefferson City, MO 65101

Contact Information:
Telephone: 573-659-3238
Fax: 573-659-3154
E-mail: ronda.wahl@hs.jcps.kq.mo.us

Program Information:
Program begins: August
Duration of program: 24 months

Employment Profile:
% of students who pass the boards on their first try: 100
% employed within the first 6 months following graduation: 90

Penn Valley Community College
3201 Southwest Trafficway
Kansas City, MO 64111

Contact Information:
Telephone: 816-759-4243
Fax: 816-759-4553

Program Information:
Program begins: June
Degrees offered: Associate's, 24 months

Application Information:
Enrollment of program: 27
Transfer students are accepted.

Financial Information:
Tuition, resident: $3,400
Tuition, non-resident: $8,100
Average cost of books: $100

Employment Profile:
% employed within the first 6 months following graduation: 100
Average starting salary: $23,000

Research Medical Center
2316 East Meyer Boulevard
Kansas City, MO 64132-1199

Contact Information:
Telephone: 816-276-3390
Fax: 816-276-3138

Program Information:
Program begins: July
Duration of program: 24 months

Application Information:
Enrollment of program: 27
Transfer students are accepted.

Financial Information:
Average cost of books: $650
% of students receiving aid: 60

Employment Profile:
% of students who pass the boards on their first try: 100
% employed within the first 6 months following graduation: 100
Average starting salary: $28,000

Rolla Technical Center
500 Forum Drive
Rolla, MO 65401-3699

Contact Information:
Telephone: 573-368-4782 ext. 16190
Fax: 573-368-4741
E-mail: mogden@rolla.k12.me.us

Program Information:
Program begins: August
Degrees offered: Diploma, 23 months

Application Information:
Enrollment of program: 27

Financial Information:
Tuition, resident: $3,150
Tuition, non-resident: $3,400
Average cost of books: $600

Employment Profile:
% of students who pass the boards on their first try: 100
% employed within the first 6 months following graduation: 100
Average starting salary: $23,000

Sanford Brown College
12006 Manchester Road
Des Peres, MO 63131

Contact Information:
Telephone: 910-695-3841
Fax: 910-692-2756
E-mail: linda.pressley@sanford-brown.edu
Web: www.sanford-brown.edu

Program Information:
Program begins: December
Duration of program: 19 months

Application Information:
Enrollment of program: 29
Transfer students are accepted.

Financial Information:
Tuition, resident: $10,401
Average cost of books: $600
% of students receiving aid: 99

Employment Profile:
% of students who pass the boards on their first try: 70
% employed within the first 6 months following graduation: 100
Average starting salary: $27,500

University of Missouri—Columbia
School of Health Related Professions
518 Lewis Hall
Columbia, MO 65211

Contact Information:
Telephone: 502-852-5629
Fax: 502-852-4597
E-mail: sebacherm@health.missouri.edu
Web: www.missouri.edu

Program Information:
Program begins: August
Degrees offered: Bachelor's

Application Information:
Enrollment of program: 17
Transfer students are accepted.

Financial Information:
Tuition, resident: $4,280
Tuition, non-resident: $11,723
Average cost of books: $450
% of students receiving aid: 75

Employment Profile:
% of students who pass the boards on their first try: 99
% employed within the first 6 months following graduation: 80

Montana

Benefis Health Care—West Campus
500 15th Avenue South
Great Falls, MT 59405

Contact Information:
Telephone: 406-455-2146
Fax: 406-455-2162

Program Information:
Program begins: July
Duration of program: 24 months

Application Information:
Enrollment of program: 12

Financial Information:
Average cost of books: $500

Employment Profile:
% of students who pass the boards on their first try: 100
% employed within the first 6 months following graduation: 100
Average starting salary: $20,000

Nebraska

Alegent Health/Immanuel Medical Center
6901 North 72nd Street
Omaha, NE 68122

Contact Information:
Telephone: 402-572-2043
Fax: 402-572-2422
E-mail: lbaylor@alegent.org
Web: www.accc-cancer.org

Program Information:
Program begins: August
Duration of program: 24 months

Application Information:
Enrollment of program: 16
Transfer students are accepted.

Financial Information:
Average cost of books: $700

Employment Profile:
% of students who pass the boards on their first try: 100
% employed within the first 6 months following graduation: 100
Average starting salary: $23,000

Clarkson College
101 South 42nd Street
Omaha, NE 68131-2739

Contact Information:
Telephone: 402-552-6140
Fax: 402-552-6019
E-mail: collins@clrkcol.crhsnet.edu
Web: www.clarksonrdkge.edu

Program Information:
Program begins: July
Degrees offered: Bachelor's

Application Information:
Enrollment of program: 16
Transfer students are accepted.

Financial Information:
Average cost of books: $500
% of students receiving aid: 85

Employment Profile:
% of students who pass the boards on their first try: 90
% employed within the first 6 months following graduation: 100
Average starting salary: $24,000

Mary Lanning Memorial Hospital
715 North Street Joseph Avenue
Hastings, NE 68901

Contact Information:
Telephone: 402-461-5177
Fax: 402-461-5059
E-mail: mlmh-radschool@tcgcs.com
Web: www.mlmh.org

Program Information:
Program begins: August
Degrees offered: Certificate program, 24 months

Application Information:
Enrollment of program: 13

Financial Information:
Average cost of books: $300
% of students receiving aid: 70

Employment Profile:
% of students who pass the boards on their first try: 99
% employed within the first 6 months following graduation: 100

Regional West Medical Center
4021 Avenue B
Scottsbluff, NE 69361

Contact Information:
Telephone: 308-632-1155
Fax: 308-630-1983
Web: www.rwmc.net

Program Information:
Program begins: August
Degrees offered: Diploma, 24 months

Application Information:
Enrollment of program: 5
Transfer students are accepted.

Financial Information:
Average cost of books: $300
% of students receiving aid: 60

Employment Profile:
% of students who pass the boards on their first try: 100
% employed within the first 6 months following graduation: 100

University of Nebraska Medical Center
981045 Nebraska Medical Center
Omaha, NE 68198-1045

Contact Information:
Telephone: 305-585-6811 ext. 1
Fax: 305-326-7982
E-mail: jtemme@unmc.edu
Web: www.unmc.pdu

Program Information:
Program begins: August
Degrees offered: Bachelor's

Application Information:
Transfer students are accepted.

Financial Information:
Tuition, resident: $3,225
Tuition, non-resident: $8,772
Average cost of books: $1,000

Employment Profile:
% employed within the first 6 months following graduation: 100

New Hampshire

New Hampshire Technical Institute
11 Institute Drive
Concord, NH 03301-7412

Contact Information:
Telephone: 603-271-7154
Fax: 603-271-7182
E-mail: kbarry@tecinst.us
Web: www.nhti.net

Program Information:
Program begins: September
Duration of program: 24 month

Application Information:
Enrollment of program: 52
Transfer students are accepted.

Financial Information:
Tuition, resident: $3,300
Tuition, non-resident: $7,590
Average cost of books: $600
% of students receiving aid: 80

Employment Profile:
% of students who pass the boards on their first try: 90
% employed within the first 6 months following graduation: 100
Average starting salary: $24,000

New Jersey

Burlington County College
County Route 530
Pemberton, NJ 08068

Contact Information:
Telephone: 609-894-9311 ext. 7407
Fax: 609-726-1781
E-mail: lprice@bcc.edu
Web: www.bcc.edu

Program Information:
Program begins: May
Duration of program: 24 months

Financial Information:
Average cost of books: $600

Employment Profile:
% employed within the first 6 months following graduation: 80

Cooper Hospital—University Medical Center
One Cooper Plaza
Camden, NJ 08103

Contact Information:
Telephone: 609-342-2397
Fax: 609-968-8532
E-mail: williams-frank@cooperhealth.edu
Web: www.cooperhealth.org

Program Information:
Program begins: August
Duration of program: 24 months

Application Information:
Enrollment of program: 17
Transfer students are accepted.

Financial Information:
Average cost of books: $700
% of students receiving aid: 30

Employment Profile:
% of students who pass the boards on their first try: 90
% employed within the first 6 months following graduation: 75
Average starting salary: $36,000

Cumberland County College

PO Box 517
College Drive
Vineland, NJ 08362-0517

Contact Information:
Telephone: 856-691-8600 ext. 344
Fax: 856-691-9489
E-mail: leggieri@cccnj.net
Web: www.cccnj.net

Program Information:
Program begins: July
Degrees offered: Associate's, 24 months

Application Information:
Enrollment of program: 26
Transfer students are accepted.

Financial Information:
Tuition, resident: $2,388
Tuition, non-resident: $4,777
Average cost of books: $250
% of students receiving aid: 64

Employment Profile:
% of students who pass the boards on their first try: 95
% employed within the first 6 months following graduation: 67
Average starting salary: $25,000

Englewood Hospital and Medical Center

350 Engle Street
Englewood, NJ 07631

Contact Information:
Telephone: 201-894-3481
Fax: 201-894-1924
Web: www.egmc.org

Program Information:
Program begins: July
Degrees offered: Diploma, 24 months

Application Information:
Enrollment of program: 8

Financial Information:
Average cost of books: $550

Employment Profile:
% of students who pass the boards on their first try: 100
% employed within the first 6 months following graduation: 100
Average starting salary: $22,600

Hudson Area School of Radiologic Technology

29 East 29th Street
Bayonne, NJ 07002

Contact Information:
Telephone: 201-858-5348
Fax: 201-858-7363

Program Information:
Program begins: September
Duration of program: 24 months

Application Information:
Enrollment of program: 16

Financial Information:
Tuition, resident: $5,500
Average cost of books: $1,000

Employment Profile:
% of students who pass the boards on their first try: 98
% employed within the first 6 months following graduation: 97
Average starting salary: $30,000

Middlesex County College

2600 Woodbridge Avenue
PO Box 3050
Edison, NJ 08818-3050

Contact Information:
Telephone: 732-906-2583
Fax: 732-906-7784
E-mail: snopek@pilot.njin.net
Web: www.middlesex.cc.nj.us

Program Information:
Program begins: September
Duration of program: 24 months

Application Information:
Enrollment of program: 70
Transfer students are accepted.

Financial Information:
Tuition, resident: $1,950
Tuition, non-resident: $3,930
Average cost of books: $450
% of students receiving aid: 25

Employment Profile:
% of students who pass the boards on their first try: 100
% employed within the first 6 months following graduation: 85
Average starting salary: $34,000

Muhlenberg Regional Medical Center

Park Avenue and Randolph Road
Plainfield, NJ 07061

Contact Information:
Telephone: 908-668-2844
Fax: 908-226-4568
Web: www.rwj-obgyn.umdnj.edu

Program Information:
Program begins: September, January
Duration of program: 27 months

Application Information:
Enrollment of program: 35
Transfer students are accepted.

Financial Information:
Tuition, resident: $2,600
Tuition, non-resident: $5,200
Average cost of books: $600
% of students receiving aid: 75

Employment Profile:
% of students who pass the boards on their first try: 100
% employed within the first 6 months following graduation: 75
Average starting salary: $27,500

Pascack Valley Hospital

Old Hook Road
Westwood, NJ 07675-3181

Contact Information:
Telephone: 201-358-3219
Fax: 201-358-3216
Web: www.pvhospital.org

Program Information:
Program begins: September
Duration of program: 24 months

Application Information:
Enrollment of program: 10

Financial Information:
Tuition, resident: $2,000
Average cost of books: $450

Employment Profile:
% of students who pass the boards on their first try: 100
% employed within the first 6 months following graduation: 100
Average starting salary: $40,000

Shore Memorial Hospital

644 Shore Road
Somers Point, NJ 08244

Contact Information:
Telephone: 901-544-5417
Fax: 901-544-5391
E-mail: eric_olson@smh1.ccmail.compuserve.com
Web: www.shorememorial.org

Program Information:
Program begins: August
Degrees offered: Certificate program, 24 months

Application Information:
Enrollment of program: 10
Transfer students are accepted.

Financial Information:
Average cost of books: $700

Employment Profile:
% of students who pass the boards on their first try: 100
% employed within the first 6 months following graduation: 90
Average starting salary: $28,000

South Jersey Hospital—Bridgeton Hospital Division

333 Irving Avenue
Bridgeton, NJ 08302

Contact Information:
Telephone: 870-862-8131 ext. 226
Fax: 870-864-7122
E-mail: rodguez@sjhs.com

Program Information:
Program begins: September
Duration of program: 24 months

Application Information:
Enrollment of program: 14
Transfer students are accepted.

Financial Information:
Average cost of books: $600

Employment Profile:
% of students who pass the boards on their first try: 100
% employed within the first 6 months following graduation: 100

St. Francis Medical Center
601 Hamilton Avenue
Trenton, NJ 08629-1986

Contact Information:
Telephone: 309-655-2782
Fax: 309-655-3480
E-mail: terrilevitsky@chi-east.org
Web: www.osfsaintfrancis.org

Program Information:
Program begins: July
Duration of program: 24 months

Application Information:
Transfer students are accepted.

Financial Information:
Average cost of books: $650

Employment Profile:
% of students who pass the boards on their first try: 97
Average starting salary: $29,000

New Mexico

Northern New Mexico Community College
921 Paseo de Onate
Espanola, NM 87532

Contact Information:
Telephone: 505-747-2218
Fax: 505-747-2180
E-mail: foster@nnm.cc.nm.us
Web: www.nnm.cc.nm.us

Program Information:
Program begins: August
Duration of program: 24 months

Application Information:
Enrollment of program: 24

Financial Information:
Tuition, resident: $720
Tuition, non-resident: $1,745

Employment Profile:
% of students who pass the boards on their first try: 80
% employed within the first 6 months following graduation: 80

Pima Medical Institute—Albuquerque
2201 San Pedro Northeast
Building 3 Suite 100
Albuquerque, NM 87110

Contact Information:
Telephone: 505-881-1234
Fax: 505-884-8371
E-mail: pimaabq@flash.net

Program Information:
Program begins: August, January
Degrees offered: Diploma, 24 months

Application Information:
Enrollment of program: 97
Transfer students are accepted.

Financial Information:
Average cost of books: $740
% of students receiving aid: 92

Employment Profile:
% of students who pass the boards on their first try: 98
% employed within the first 6 months following graduation: 100
Average starting salary: $28,000

New York

Arnot Ogden Medical Center
600 Roe Avenue
Elmira, NY 14905-1676

Contact Information:
Telephone: 607-737-4289
Fax: 607-737-4116
Web: www.aomc.org

Program Information:
Program begins: August
Degrees offered: Certificate program

Application Information:
Enrollment of program: 14
Transfer students are accepted.

Financial Information:
Average cost of books: $600
% of students receiving aid: 75

Employment Profile:
% of students who pass the boards on their first try: 98
% employed within the first 6 months following graduation: 100
Average starting salary: $22,000

Broome Community College
Upper Front Street
PO Box 1017
Binghamton, NY 13902

Contact Information:
Telephone: 607-778-5070
Fax: 607-778-5467
E-mail: button-n@sunybroome.edu
Web: www.sunybroome.edu

Program Information:
Program begins: September
Duration of program: 22 months

Application Information:
Transfer students are accepted.

Financial Information:
Tuition, resident: $2,168
Tuition, non-resident: $4,336
Average cost of books: $600
% of students receiving aid: 85

Employment Profile:
% of students who pass the boards on their first try: 100
% employed within the first 6 months following graduation: 100

Catholic Medical Center of Brooklyn & Queens
175-05 Horace Harding Expressway
Fresh Meadows, NY 11365

Contact Information:
Telephone: 718-357-0500 ext. 109
Fax: 718-357-4575
E-mail: a.kish@cmc.ny.com

Program Information:
Program begins: September
Duration of program: 24 months

Financial Information:
Tuition, resident: $5,000
Average cost of books: $700

Central Suffolk Hospital
1300 Roanoke Avenue
Riverhead, NY 11901

Contact Information:
Telephone: 516-548-6173
Fax: 516-548-6751
Web: www.centralsuffolkhospital.org

Program Information:
Program begins: September
Duration of program: 24 months

Financial Information:
Average cost of books: $550

Employment Profile:
% employed within the first 6 months following graduation: 100

Champlain Valley Physician Hospital Medical Center
75 Beekman Street
Plattsburgh, NY 12901

Contact Information:
Telephone: 518-562-7510
Fax: 518-562-7486
E-mail: fashline@cvph.org
Web: www.cvph.org

Program Information:
Program begins: July
Duration of program: 24 months

Application Information:
Enrollment of program: 24

Financial Information:
Tuition, resident: $4,000

Tuition, non-resident: $6,160
Average cost of books: $500
% of students receiving aid: 70

Employment Profile:
% of students who pass the boards on their first try: 100
% employed within the first 6 months following graduation: 100
Average starting salary: $30,000

CUNY Bronx Community College

University Avenue and West 181st Street
Bronx, NY 10453

Contact Information:
Telephone: 718-289-5396
Fax: 718-289-6373
Web: www.bcc.cuny.edu

Program Information:
Program begins: September
Duration of program: 24 months

Application Information:
Enrollment of program: 56
Transfer students are accepted.

Financial Information:
Tuition, resident: $2,500
Tuition, non-resident: $3,076
Average cost of books: $600
% of students receiving aid: 90

Employment Profile:
% of students who pass the boards on their first try: 96
% employed within the first 6 months following graduation: 100
Average starting salary: $39,500

Glens Falls Hospital

100 Park Street
Glens Falls, NY 12801

Contact Information:
Telephone: 518-792-3151 ext. 5495
Fax: 518-761-5288

Program Information:
Program begins: September
Duration of program: 24 months

Financial Information:
Tuition, resident: $4,700
Average cost of books: $700
% of students receiving aid: 30

Employment Profile:
% of students who pass the boards on their first try: 100
% employed within the first 6 months following graduation: 100
Average starting salary: $25,000

Harlem Hospital Center

506 Lenox Avenue
Kountz Pavilion Room 415
New York, NY 10037

Contact Information:
Telephone: 212-939-3475
Fax: 212-939-3479
E-mail: cglenn47@aol.com
Web: www.harlemxray.com

Program Information:
Program begins: October
Duration of program: 24 months

Application Information:
Enrollment of program: 28
Transfer students are accepted.

Financial Information:
Average cost of books: $600
% of students receiving aid: 80

Employment Profile:
% of students who pass the boards on their first try: 93
% employed within the first 6 months following graduation: 90
Average starting salary: $36,000

Long Island College Hospital

339 Hicks Street
Brooklyn, NY 11201

Contact Information:
Telephone: 718-780-1681
Fax: 718-858-8586

Program Information:
Program begins: September
Duration of program: 24 months

Application Information:
Enrollment of program: 12
Transfer students are accepted.

Financial Information:
Tuition, resident: $5,000
Average cost of books: $500
% of students receiving aid: 50

Employment Profile:
% of students who pass the boards on their first try: 89
% employed within the first 6 months following graduation: 50
Average starting salary: $39,000

Long Island University—CW Post Campus

720 Northern Boulevard
Brookville, NY 11548-1300

Contact Information:
Telephone: 516-299-3075
Fax: 516-299-3081
E-mail: radtech@titan.liunet.edu
Web: www.liu.edu

Program Information:
Program begins: September
Degrees offered: Bachelor's, 48 months
Evening or weekend classes are available.

Application Information:
Enrollment of program: 68
Transfer students are accepted.

Financial Information:
Tuition, resident: $15,340
Average cost of books: $400
% of students receiving aid: 78

Employment Profile:
% of students who pass the boards on their first try: 98
% employed within the first 6 months following graduation: 95
Average starting salary: $34,000

Monroe Community College

1000 East Henrietta Road
Rochester, NY 14623-5780

Contact Information:
Telephone: 716-292-2379
Fax: 719-292-3834
E-mail: edoyle@monroecc.edu
Web: www.monroecc.edu

Program Information:
Program begins: September
Duration of program: 21 months

Application Information:
Enrollment of program: 55
Transfer students are accepted.

Financial Information:
Tuition, resident: $2,500
Tuition, non-resident: $5,000
Average cost of books: $500

Employment Profile:
% of students who pass the boards on their first try: 95
% employed within the first 6 months following graduation: 100
Average starting salary: $24,000

Northport VA Medical Center

#632C
79 Middleville Road (632/153)
Northport, NY 11768

Contact Information:
Telephone: 516-261-4400 ext. 2015
Fax: 516-266-6092
Web: www.va.gov.edu

Program Information:
Program begins: September
Duration of program: 24 months

Application Information:
Enrollment of program: 15

Financial Information:
Average cost of books: $800

Employment Profile:
% of students who pass the boards on their first try: 93
% employed within the first 6 months following graduation: 100
Average starting salary: $40,000

St. Elizabeth Hospital

2209 Genesee Street
Utica, NY 13501

Contact Information:
Telephone: 330-480-3265

Fax: 330-480-2912
E-mail: mecret@stemc
Web: www.stemc.org

Program Information:
Program begins: July
Duration of program: 24 months

Application Information:
Transfer students are accepted.

Financial Information:
Average cost of books: $550
% of students receiving aid: 70

Employment Profile:
% of students who pass the boards on their first try: 98
% employed within the first 6 months following graduation: 85
Average starting salary: $20,000

St. James Mercy Hospital

411 Canisteo Street
Hornell, NY 14843

Contact Information:
Telephone: 609-599-5234
Fax: 609-599-6370

Program Information:
Program begins: July
Degrees offered: Diploma, 24 months

Application Information:
Enrollment of program: 12
Transfer students are accepted.

Financial Information:
Average cost of books: $375

Employment Profile:
% of students who pass the boards on their first try: 100
% employed within the first 6 months following graduation: 100
Average starting salary: $26,000

SUNY Health Science Center at Syracuse

750 East Adams Street
Syracuse, NY 13210

Contact Information:
Telephone: 315-464-4464
Fax: 315-464-6914
E-mail: duffyp@vax.cs.hscsyr.edu
Web: www.hscsyr.edu

Program Information:
Program begins: September
Duration of program: 23 months

Application Information:
Enrollment of program: 29

Financial Information:
Tuition, resident: $4,604
Tuition, non-resident: $11,665
Average cost of books: $1,040
% of students receiving aid: 100

Employment Profile:
% of students who pass the boards on their first try: 100
% employed within the first 6 months following graduation: 80
Average starting salary: $29,072

United Hospital Medical Center

406 Boston Post Road
Port Chester, NY 10573

Contact Information:
Telephone: 914-934-3164
Fax: 914-934-3168
Web: www.unmc.com

Program Information:
Program begins: October
Degrees offered: Diploma, 24 months

Application Information:
Enrollment of program: 20
Transfer students are accepted.

Financial Information:
Tuition, resident: $7,000
Average cost of books: $700
% of students receiving aid: 20

Employment Profile:
% of students who pass the boards on their first try: 100
% employed within the first 6 months following graduation: 100
Average starting salary: $35,000

Winthrop University Hospital

259 First Street
Mineola, NY 11501

Contact Information:
Telephone: 516-663-2536
Fax: 516-663-2587
Web: www.winthrop.org

Program Information:
Program begins: September
Degrees offered: Certificate program, 24 months

Application Information:
Enrollment of program: 10

Financial Information:
Average cost of books: $500
% of students receiving aid: 10

Employment Profile:
% of students who pass the boards on their first try: 90
% employed within the first 6 months following graduation: 100
Average starting salary: $32,000

Woman's Christian Association Hospital

207 Foote Avenue
Jamestown, NY 14701-0840

Contact Information:
Telephone: 716-664-8238
Fax: 716-664-8312

Program Information:
Program begins: August
Duration of program: 24 months

Application Information:
Transfer students are accepted.

Financial Information:
Average cost of books: $600

Employment Profile:
% of students who pass the boards on their first try: 95
% employed within the first 6 months following graduation: 100
Average starting salary: $23,000

North Carolina

Carolinas College of Health Sciences

PO Box 32861
Charlotte, NC 28232-2861

Contact Information:
Telephone: 704-355-2446
Fax: 704-355-5967
E-mail: sstricker@carolinas.org
Web: www.carolinas.org

Program Information:
Program begins: August
Degrees offered: Diploma, 21 months

Application Information:
Enrollment of program: 20
Transfer students are accepted.

Financial Information:
Average cost of books: $400
% of students receiving aid: 81

Employment Profile:
% of students who pass the boards on their first try: 100
% employed within the first 6 months following graduation: 1000
Average starting salary: $27,000

Fayetteville Technical Community College

PO Box 35236
Fayetteville, NC 28303-0236

Contact Information:
Telephone: 910-678-8303
Fax: 910-678-8500
E-mail: gentrym@ftccmail.faytech.cc.nc.us
Web: www.fayech.cc.nc.us

Program Information:
Program begins: August
Duration of program: 21 months

Application Information:
Enrollment of program: 29

Financial Information:
Tuition, resident: $1,632
Tuition, non-resident: $10,355

Forsyth Technical Community College

2100 Silas Creek Parkway
Winston-Salem, NC 27103

Contact Information:
Telephone: 336-723-0371 ext. 7291
Fax: 336-748-9395
E-mail: cholland@yadtel.net
Web: www.forsyth.tec.nc.us

Program Information:
Program begins: August
Duration of program: 21 months

Application Information:
Enrollment of program: 50
Transfer students are accepted.

Financial Information:
Tuition, resident: $840
Tuition, non-resident: $6,709
Average cost of books: $1,500

Employment Profile:
% employed within the first 6 months following graduation: 100
Average starting salary: $25,000

Moses H. Cone Memorial Hospital

1200 North Elm Street
Greensboro, NC 27401-1020

Contact Information:
Telephone: 336-832-7628
Fax: 336-832-7381
E-mail: betsy.shields@mosescone.com

Program Information:
Program begins: July
Degrees offered: Certificate program, 24 months

Application Information:
Enrollment of program: 20

Financial Information:
Average cost of books: $400

Employment Profile:
% of students who pass the boards on their first try: 100
% employed within the first 6 months following graduation: 100
Average starting salary: $25,000

Presbyterian Hospital

200 Hawthorne Lane
PO Box 33549
Charlotte, NC 28233-3549

Contact Information:
Telephone: 704-384-5104
Fax: 704-384-5693
Web: www.presbyterian.org

Program Information:
Program begins: July
Duration of program: 24 months

Financial Information:
Average cost of books: $510

Employment Profile:
% of students who pass the boards on their first try: 94
% employed within the first 6 months following graduation: 100
Average starting salary: $25,000

Southwestern Community College

447 College Drive
Sylva, NC 28779

Contact Information:
Telephone: 704-586-4091 ext. 359
Fax: 704-586-3129
Web: www.southwest.cc.nc.us

Program Information:
Program begins: July
Duration of program: 21 months

Application Information:
Enrollment of program: 31
Transfer students are accepted.

Financial Information:
Tuition, resident: $560
Tuition, non-resident: $4,480
Average cost of books: $115
% of students receiving aid: 55

Employment Profile:
% employed within the first 6 months following graduation: 80
Average starting salary: $24,500

University of North Carolina at Chapel Hill

Medical School
CB 7130 East Wing
Chapel Hill, NC 27599-7130

Contact Information:
Telephone: 402-559-6954
Fax: 402-559-1011
E-mail: jrenner@css.unc.edu
Web: www.uncess.edu

Program Information:
Program begins: July
Degrees offered: Bachelor's, 48 months

Application Information:
Enrollment of program: 24
Transfer students are accepted.

Financial Information:
Tuition, resident: $1,450
Tuition, non-resident: $10,622
Average cost of books: $800

Employment Profile:
% of students who pass the boards on their first try: 100
% employed within the first 6 months following graduation: 100
Average starting salary: $29,000

Wake Technical Community College

9101 Fayetteville Road
Raleigh, NC 27603

Contact Information:
Telephone: 919-231-4500
Fax: 919-250-4329
E-mail: arphilli@mail.wake.tec.nc.us
Web: www.wake.tec.nc.us

Program Information:
Program begins: June
Duration of program: 21 months

Application Information:
Enrollment of program: 42
Transfer students are accepted.

Financial Information:
Tuition, resident: $450
Tuition, non-resident: $3,668
Average cost of books: $600

Employment Profile:
% of students who pass the boards on their first try: 100
% employed within the first 6 months following graduation: 80
Average starting salary: $24,000

Wilkes Regional Medical Center

West D Street
PO Box 609
North Wilkesboro, NC 28659

Contact Information:
Telephone: 336-651-8431
Fax: 336-651-8432
Web: www.wfubmc.edu

Program Information:
Program begins: June
Degrees offered: Certificate program, 24 months

Application Information:
Enrollment of program: 19

Financial Information:
Tuition, resident: $600
Tuition, non-resident: $2,500
Average cost of books: $1,200
% of students receiving aid: 50

Employment Profile:
% of students who pass the boards on their first try: 100
% employed within the first 6 months following graduation: 85
Average starting salary: $24,000

Ohio

Central Ohio Technical College

1179 University Drive
Newark, OH 43055-1767

Contact Information:
Telephone: 614-366-9387
Fax: 614-366-5047
E-mail: hopewell@cotc.tec.oh.us
Web: www.cotc.tec.oh.us

Program Information:
Program begins: August
Duration of program: 22 months

Application Information:
Enrollment of program: 25
Transfer students are accepted.

Financial Information:
Tuition, resident: $2,950
Tuition, non-resident: $5,100
Average cost of books: $500

Employment Profile:
% of students who pass the boards on their first try: 97
% employed within the first 6 months following graduation: 100
Average starting salary: $26,000

Children's Hospital Medical Center of Akron

One Perkins Square
Akron, OH 44308

Contact Information:
Telephone: 330-379-8849
Fax: 330-258-3250
E-mail: dwhipple@chmca.org
Web: www.akronchildrens.org

Program Information:
Program begins: July
Duration of program: 24 months

Application Information:
Enrollment of program: 7
Transfer students are accepted.

Financial Information:
Average cost of books: $350

Employment Profile:
% of students who pass the boards on their first try: 99
% employed within the first 6 months following graduation: 100
Average starting salary: $23,000

Cuyahoga Community College

Western Campus
11000 Pleasant Valley Road
Parma, OH 44130-5199

Contact Information:
Telephone: 216-987-5264
Fax: 216-987-5066
Web: www.tri-c.cc.us

Program Information:
Program begins: August, January
Duration of program: 24 months
Evening or weekend classes are available.

Application Information:
Enrollment of program: 67
Transfer students are accepted.

Financial Information:
Tuition, resident: $2,248
Tuition, non-resident: $2,986
Average cost of books: $750

Employment Profile:
% of students who pass the boards on their first try: 100
% employed within the first 6 months following graduation: 60
Average starting salary: $30,500

Jefferson Community College

4000 Sunset Boulevard
Steubenville, OH 43952-3598

Contact Information:
Telephone: 740-264-5591 ext. 168
Fax: 740-264-1338
Web: www.jeffersoncc.org

Program Information:
Program begins: June
Duration of program: 24 months

Financial Information:
Tuition, resident: $2,065
Tuition, non-resident: $3,120

Kent State University

2491 SR 45 South
Salem, OH 44460-9412

Contact Information:
Telephone: 330-332-0361
Fax: 330-332-9256
E-mail: gibson@salem.kent.edu
Web: www.salem.kent.edu

Program Information:
Program begins: August, January
Duration of program: 24 months

Application Information:
Enrollment of program: 24

Financial Information:
Tuition, resident: $4,321
Tuition, non-resident: $8,781
Average cost of books: $500

Employment Profile:
% of students who pass the boards on their first try: 100
% employed within the first 6 months following graduation: 75
Average starting salary: $24,000

Kettering College of Medical Arts

3737 Southern Boulevard
Kettering, OH 45429

Contact Information:
Telephone: 937-298-3399 ext. 5696
Fax: 937-296-4238
E-mail: larry_beneke@ketthealth.com
Web: www.kcma.edu

Program Information:
Program begins: September
Duration of program: 20 months

Application Information:
Enrollment of program: 38
Transfer students are accepted.

Financial Information:
Average cost of books: $788
% of students receiving aid: 60

Employment Profile:
% of students who pass the boards on their first try: 89
% employed within the first 6 months following graduation: 80
Average starting salary: $25,000

Lakeland Community College

7700 Clocktower Drive
Kirtland, OH 44094-5198

Contact Information:
Telephone: 440-953-7074
Fax: 440-975-4733
E-mail: jthomas@lakeland.cc.oh.us
Web: www.lakeland.cc.oh.us

Program Information:
Program begins: August
Degrees offered: Associate's, 24 months

Application Information:
Enrollment of program: 58
Transfer students are accepted.

Financial Information:
Tuition, resident: $2,377
Tuition, non-resident: $6,222
Average cost of books: $540

Employment Profile:
% of students who pass the boards on their first try: 90
% employed within the first 6 months following graduation: 94
Average starting salary: $28,000

Lorain County Community College

1005 North Abbe Road, HS223
Elyria, OH 44035

Contact Information:
Telephone: 440-365-5222 ext. 7197
Fax: 440-366-4116
E-mail: jwalmsle@lorainccc.edu
Web: www.lorainccc.edu

Program Information:
Program begins: August
Degrees offered: Associate's, 21 months

Financial Information:
Tuition, resident: $5,200
Tuition, non-resident: $6,200

Marion General Hospital

McKinley Park Drive
Marion, OH 43302

Contact Information:
Telephone: 740-383-8417
Fax: 740-375-8105

Program Information:
Program begins: August
Duration of program: 23 months

Application Information:
Enrollment of program: 14

Financial Information:
Tuition, resident: $2,310
Average cost of books: $440

Employment Profile:
% of students who pass the boards on their first try: 100
% employed within the first 6 months following graduation: 100
Average starting salary: $25,000

Mercy College of Northwest Ohio
2221 Madison Avenue
Toledo, OH 43608-2691

Contact Information:
Telephone: 419-251-2851
Fax: 419-251-1730
E-mail: beverly_lower@mhsnr.org
Web: www.mercycollege.edu

Program Information:
Program begins: September
Duration of program: 24 months

Meridia Health System
18901 Lakeshore Boulevard
Euclid, OH 44119

Contact Information:
Telephone: 216-692-8708
Fax: 216-692-7453

Program Information:
Program begins: August
Degrees offered: Certificate program, 24 months

Application Information:
Enrollment of program: 30

Financial Information:
Average cost of books: $575

Employment Profile:
% of students who pass the boards on their first try: 100
% employed within the first 6 months following graduation: 100
Average starting salary: $14,000

Muskingum Area Technical College
1555 Newark Road
Zanesville, OH 43701

Contact Information:
Telephone: 740-454-2501 ext. 1241
Fax: 740-454-0035
E-mail: jgill@matc.tec.oh.us
Web: www.matc.tec.oh.us

Program Information:
Program begins: June
Degrees offered: Diploma, 24 months
Evening or weekend classes are available.

Application Information:
Enrollment of program: 35
Transfer students are accepted.

Financial Information:
Tuition, resident: $2,650
Tuition, non-resident: $4,160
Average cost of books: $400

Employment Profile:
% of students who pass the boards on their first try: 99
% employed within the first 6 months following graduation: 100
Average starting salary: $24,000

North Central State College
2441 Kenwood Circle
PO Box 698
Mansfield, OH 44901-0698

Contact Information:
Telephone: 419-755-4886
Fax: 419-755-5630
E-mail: atac735166@aol.com
Web: www.ncstate.tec.oh.us

Program Information:
Program begins: July
Degrees offered: Associate's, 24 months
Evening or weekend classes are available.

Application Information:
Enrollment of program: 22
Transfer students are accepted.

Financial Information:
Tuition, resident: $2,934
Tuition, non-resident: $5,511
Average cost of books: $961

Employment Profile:
% of students who pass the boards on their first try: 100
% employed within the first 6 months following graduation: 100
Average starting salary: $27,000

Ohio State University
1583 Perry Street
Columbus, OH 43210-1234

Contact Information:
Telephone: 614-292-0571
Fax: 614-292-0210
E-mail: finney.1@osu.edu
Web: www.amp.ohio-state.edu

Program Information:
Program begins: September
Degrees offered: Bachelor's, 48 months

Application Information:
Enrollment of program: 34
Transfer students are accepted.

Financial Information:
Tuition, resident: $5,516
Tuition, non-resident: $16,116
Average cost of books: $400

Employment Profile:
% of students who pass the boards on their first try: 100
% employed within the first 6 months following graduation: 80
Average starting salary: $27,500

Owens Community College
PO Box 10,000
Oregon Road
Toledo, OH 43699-1947

Contact Information:
Telephone: 419-661-7261
Fax: 419-661-7251
E-mail: lmyers@owens.cc.oh.us
Web: www.owens.cc.oh.us

Program Information:
Program begins: January, June
Duration of program: 23 months

Application Information:
Enrollment of program: 50

Financial Information:
Tuition, resident: $2,060
Tuition, non-resident: $3,860

Shawnee State University
940 Second Street
Portsmouth, OH 45662-4344

Contact Information:
Telephone: 724-983-5603
Fax: 724-983-5614
E-mail: bsykes@shawnee.edu
Web: www.shawnee.edu

Program Information:
Program begins: July
Duration of program: 24 months

Application Information:
Enrollment of program: 15
Transfer students are accepted.

Financial Information:
Tuition, resident: $3,753
Tuition, non-resident: $6,288
Average cost of books: $250
% of students receiving aid: 78

Employment Profile:
% of students who pass the boards on their first try: 100
% employed within the first 6 months following graduation: 100

Sinclair Community College
444 West Third Street
Dayton, OH 45402-1460

Contact Information:
Telephone: 609-653-3924
Fax: 609-926-1987
E-mail: dmoore@sinclair.edu
Web: www.sinclair.edu

Program Information:
Program begins: September
Duration of program: 24 months

Application Information:
Enrollment of program: 35
Transfer students are accepted.

Financial Information:
Tuition, resident: $3,410
Tuition, non-resident: $5,610
Average cost of books: $750
% of students receiving aid: 60

Employment Profile:
% of students who pass the boards on their first try: 96
% employed within the first 6 months following graduation: 94
Average starting salary: $25,000

University of Cincinnati

Raymond Walters College
9555 Plainfield Road
Blue Ash, OH 45236

Contact Information:
Telephone: 706-774-8646
Fax: 706-774-5079
E-mail: tracy.herrmann@uc.edu
Web: www.uc.edu

Program Information:
Program begins: September
Degrees offered: Associate's, 24 months

Application Information:
Enrollment of program: 20
Transfer students are accepted.

Financial Information:
Tuition, resident: $4,628
Tuition, non-resident: $11,660

Employment Profile:
% of students who pass the boards on their first try: 90
% employed within the first 6 months following graduation: 100
Average starting salary: $25,000

Xavier University

3800 Victory Parkway
Cincinnati, OH 45207-4331

Contact Information:
Telephone: 513-745-3358
Fax: 513-745-1954
E-mail: endicott@admin.xu.edu
Web: www.xu.edu

Program Information:
Program begins: June
Duration of program: 23 months

Application Information:
Enrollment of program: 22
Transfer students are accepted.

Financial Information:
Average cost of books: $350

Employment Profile:
% of students who pass the boards on their first try: 100
% employed within the first 6 months following graduation: 100
Average starting salary: $25,000

Oklahoma

Autry Technology Center

1201 West Willow
Enid, OK 73703

Contact Information:
Telephone: 405-242-2750 ext. 127
Fax: 405-233-8262
E-mail: vrodriguez@autrytec.com

Program Information:
Program begins: July
Duration of program: 12 months

Application Information:
Enrollment of program: 10
Transfer students are accepted.

Financial Information:
Tuition, resident: $1,675
Tuition, non-resident: $5,745
Average cost of books: $600
% of students receiving aid: 45

Employment Profile:
% of students who pass the boards on their first try: 95
% employed within the first 6 months following graduation: 80
Average starting salary: $24,000

Great Plains Technology Center

4500 West Lee Boulevard
Lawton, OK 73505

Contact Information:
Telephone: 580-250-5577
Fax: 580-250-5583
E-mail: cbaxter@gpv.org
Web: www.gpv.org

Program Information:
Program begins: August
Degrees offered: Certificate program, 24 months

Application Information:
Enrollment of program: 26
Transfer students are accepted.

Financial Information:
Tuition, resident: $1,550
Tuition, non-resident: $2,550
Average cost of books: $450
% of students receiving aid: 50

Employment Profile:
% of students who pass the boards on their first try: 90
% employed within the first 6 months following graduation: 90
Average starting salary: $26,500

Meridian Technology Center

1312 South Sangre Road
Stillwater, OK 74074

Contact Information:
Telephone: 405-377-3333
Fax: 405-377-9604
E-mail: maryp@meridian-technology.com
Web: www.okstate.edu

Program Information:
Program begins: August
Duration of program: 24 months

Application Information:
Enrollment of program: 20
Transfer students are accepted.

Financial Information:
Tuition, resident: $2,000
Tuition, non-resident: $4,000
Average cost of books: $400
% of students receiving aid: 50

Employment Profile:
% of students who pass the boards on their first try: 90
% employed within the first 6 months following graduation: 90
Average starting salary: $24,000

Rose State College

6420 Southeast 15th Street
Midwest City, OK 73110-2799

Contact Information:
Telephone: 405-733-7568
Fax: 405-736-0338
E-mail: htownsend@ms.rose.cc.ok.us
Web: www.rose.cc.ok.us

Program Information:
Program begins: August
Duration of program: 24 months

Application Information:
Enrollment of program: 37

Financial Information:
Tuition, resident: $1,162
Tuition, non-resident: $3,174
Average cost of books: $330
% of students receiving aid: 40

Employment Profile:
% of students who pass the boards on their first try: 88
% employed within the first 6 months following graduation: 95
Average starting salary: $21,000

Southwestern Oklahoma State University

409 East Mississippi
Sayre, OK 73662-1236

Contact Information:
Telephone: 405-928-5533 ext. 155
Fax: 405-928-5533
E-mail: stuffle@swosu.edu
Web: www.swosu.edu

Program Information:
Program begins: September
Degrees offered: Associate's, 24 months

Application Information:
Enrollment of program: 24
Transfer students are accepted.

Financial Information:
Tuition, resident: $2,100
Tuition, non-resident: $5,040

Average cost of books: $700
% of students receiving aid: 70

Employment Profile:
% of students who pass the boards on their first try: 85
% employed within the first 6 months following graduation: 93
Average starting salary: $28,000

Tulsa Community College
909 South Boston Avenue
Tulsa, OK 74119-2094

Contact Information:
Telephone: 918-595-7004
Fax: 918-595-2798
E-mail: rboodt@tulsa.cc.ok.us
Web: www.tulsa.cc.ok.us

Program Information:
Program begins: June
Degrees offered: Associate's, 24 months
Evening or weekend classes are available.

Application Information:
Enrollment of program: 40
Transfer students are accepted.

Financial Information:
Tuition, resident: $1,360
Tuition, non-resident: $3,400
Average cost of books: $500
% of students receiving aid: 25

Employment Profile:
% of students who pass the boards on their first try: 90
% employed within the first 6 months following graduation: 90
Average starting salary: $25,000

Tulsa Technology Center
3420 South Memorial Drive
Tulsa, OK 74145-1390

Contact Information:
Telephone: 918-579-3288
Fax: 918-828-1009
Web: www.tulsatech.com

Program Information:
Program begins: August
Duration of program: 24 months

Application Information:
Enrollment of program: 10

Financial Information:
Average cost of books: $325
% of students receiving aid: 80

Employment Profile:
% of students who pass the boards on their first try: 100
% employed within the first 6 months following graduation: 100
Average starting salary: $22,500

Oregon

Oregon Institute of Technology
3201 Campus Drive
Klamath Falls, OR 97601-8801

Contact Information:
Telephone: 541-885-1808
Fax: 541-885-1849
E-mail: schultzs@oit.edu
Web: www.oit.edu

Program Information:
Program begins: July
Degrees offered: Bachelor's, 48 months

Financial Information:
Tuition, resident: $3,000
Tuition, non-resident: $9,000

Portland Community College
12000 Southwest 49th Avenue
PO Box 19000
Portland, OR 97280-0990

Contact Information:
Telephone: 503-977-4907
Fax: 503-977-4869
E-mail: dbiddle@pcc.edu
Web: www.pcc.edu

Program Information:
Program begins: August
Duration of program: 24 months

Financial Information:
Tuition, resident: $2,300
Tuition, non-resident: $7,500
Average cost of books: $1,400

Employment Profile:
% of students who pass the boards on their first try: 100
% employed within the first 6 months following graduation: 100

Pennsylvania

Bradford Regional Medical Center
116 Interstate Parkway
Bradford, PA 16701

Contact Information:
Telephone: 814-362-8292
Fax: 814-368-7750
Web: www.bfdmed.org

Program Information:
Program begins: September
Duration of program: 24 months

Application Information:
Enrollment of program: 8
Transfer students are accepted.

Financial Information:
Average cost of books: $580

Employment Profile:
% of students who pass the boards on their first try: 100
% employed within the first 6 months following graduation: 100
Average starting salary: $20,500

College Misericordia
19351 West Washington Street
Dallas, PA 18612

Contact Information:
Telephone: 570-674-6480
Fax: 570-675-2441
E-mail: ehalesey@miseri.edu
Web: www.miseri.edu

Program Information:
Program begins: July
Degrees offered: Bachelor's, 42 months
Evening or weekend classes are available.

Application Information:
Enrollment of program: 50
Transfer students are accepted.

Financial Information:
Average cost of books: $600
% of students receiving aid: 93

Employment Profile:
% of students who pass the boards on their first try: 100
% employed within the first 6 months following graduation: 40
Average starting salary: $24,591

Community College of Allegheny County
595 Beatty Road
Monroeville, PA 15146-1395

Contact Information:
Telephone: 724-325-6734
Fax: 724-325-6701
E-mail: akellerm@ccac.edu
Web: www.ccac.edu

Program Information:
Program begins: September
Duration of program: 24 months
Evening or weekend classes are available.

Application Information:
Enrollment of program: 63
Transfer students are accepted.

Financial Information:
Tuition, resident: $1,020
Tuition, non-resident: $2,020
Average cost of books: $650
% of students receiving aid: 60

Employment Profile:
% of students who pass the boards on their first try: 93
% employed within the first 6 months following graduation: 80
Average starting salary: $29,500

Community College of Philadelphia

1700 Spring Garden Street
Philadelphia, PA 19130

Contact Information:
Telephone: 215-751-8424
Fax: 215-751-8937
E-mail: wwesolowski@ccpp.cc.pa.us
Web: www.ccp.cc.pa.us

Program Information:
Program begins: July
Duration of program: 24 months

Application Information:
Enrollment of program: 31

Financial Information:
Tuition, resident: $5,520
Tuition, non-resident: $11,040

Employment Profile:
% of students who pass the boards on their first try: 100
% employed within the first 6 months following graduation: 90
Average starting salary: $30,000

Conemaugh Valley Memorial Hospital

1086 Franklin Street
Johnstown, PA 15905-4398

Contact Information:
Telephone: 814-534-9582
Fax: 814-534-3110
Web: www.conemaugh.org

Program Information:
Program begins: September
Duration of program: 24 months

Application Information:
Enrollment of program: 18

Financial Information:
Average cost of books: $450
% of students receiving aid: 53

Employment Profile:
% of students who pass the boards on their first try: 100
Average starting salary: $22,000

Gannon University

109 University Square
Erie, PA 165410001

Contact Information:
Telephone: 814-871-5644
Fax: 814-871-5662
E-mail: liotta@gannon.edu
Web: www.gannon.edu

Program Information:
Program begins: September
Degrees offered: Bachelor's

Application Information:
Enrollment of program: 25

Financial Information:
Tuition, resident: $11,520
Tuition, non-resident: $13,000

Employment Profile:
% of students who pass the boards on their first try: 87
Average starting salary: $25,000

Hazleton-St. Joseph Medical Center

687 North Church Street
Hazleton, PA 18201-3198

Contact Information:
Telephone: 570-501-6506
Fax: 570-501-6177
Web: www.ghha.org

Program Information:
Program begins: July
Duration of program: 24 months

Application Information:
Enrollment of program: 13

Holy Family College

Grant and Frankford Avenues
Philadelphia, PA 19114

Contact Information:
Telephone: 215-637-7202
Fax: 215-637-7377
E-mail: jniewood@hfc.edu
Web: www.hfc.edu

Program Information:
Program begins: July
Degrees offered: Associate's, 22 months; Bachelor's
Evening or weekend classes are available.

Application Information:
Enrollment of program: 18
Transfer students are accepted.

Financial Information:
Average cost of books: $1,000
% of students receiving aid: 89

Employment Profile:
% of students who pass the boards on their first try: 100
% employed within the first 6 months following graduation: 90
Average starting salary: $28,000

Holy Spirit Hospital

503 North 21st Street
Camp Hill, PA 17011-2288

Contact Information:
Telephone: 717-763-2123
E-mail: gconrad@hsh.org
Web: www.collmed.psu.edu

Program Information:
Program begins: January
Duration of program: 30 months

Financial Information:
Average cost of books: $500

Employment Profile:
% of students who pass the boards on their first try: 95
% employed within the first 6 months following graduation: 100
Average starting salary: $25,000

Lancaster Institute for Health Education

Lancaster General Hospital
143 East Lemon Street
Lancaster, PA 17602

Contact Information:
Telephone: 717-290-4912
Fax: 717-290-5970
Web: www.lha.org

Program Information:
Program begins: August
Duration of program: 24 months

Application Information:
Enrollment of program: 35
Transfer students are accepted.

Financial Information:
Average cost of books: $500
% of students receiving aid: 50

Employment Profile:
% of students who pass the boards on their first try: 100
% employed within the first 6 months following graduation: 100
Average starting salary: $25,000

Monsour Medical Center

70 Lincoln Way East
Jeannette, PA 15644

Contact Information:
Telephone: 724-527-0427
Fax: 724-527-3711

Program Information:
Program begins: August
Duration of program: 24 months

Application Information:
Enrollment of program: 11

Financial Information:
Tuition, resident: $650

Employment Profile:
% of students who pass the boards on their first try: 100
% employed within the first 6 months following graduation: 80

Northampton Community College

3835 Green Pond Road
Bethlehem, PA 18020

Contact Information:
Telephone: 610-861-5387
Fax: 610-861-4581
E-mail: szile@northhampton.edu
Web: www.northampton.edu

Program Information:
Program begins: July
Duration of program: 24 months

Application Information:
Enrollment of program: 56
Transfer students are accepted.

Financial Information:
Tuition, resident: $5,451
Tuition, non-resident: $17,043
Average cost of books: $1,000
% of students receiving aid: 57

Employment Profile:
% employed within the first 6 months following graduation: 100
Average starting salary: $24,000

Northwest Medical Center—Franklin Campus

One Spruce Street
Franklin, PA 16323

Contact Information:
Telephone: 814-437-7000 ext. 5373
Fax: 814-437-3038

Program Information:
Program begins: August
Duration of program: 24 months

Application Information:
Transfer students are accepted.

Financial Information:
Average cost of books: $500

Employment Profile:
% of students who pass the boards on their first try: 100
% employed within the first 6 months following graduation: 100
Average starting salary: $22,500

Penn State University—Schuylkill

200 University Drive
Schuylkill Haven, PA 17972-0308

Contact Information:
Telephone: 570-385-6108
Fax: 717-385-3672
E-mail: cxm34@psu.edu
Web: www.psu.edu

Program Information:
Program begins: September
Duration of program: 28 months

Application Information:
Enrollment of program: 20
Transfer students are accepted.

Financial Information:
Tuition, resident: $15,000
Tuition, non-resident: $22,000
Average cost of books: $900
% of students receiving aid: 80

Employment Profile:
% of students who pass the boards on their first try: 90
% employed within the first 6 months following graduation: 93
Average starting salary: $24,000

Pennsylvania College of Technology

One College Avenue
Williamsport, PA 17701-5799

Contact Information:
Telephone: 570-326-3761 ext. 7409
Fax: 570-321-5556
E-mail: rslothus@pct.edu
Web: www.pct.edu

Program Information:
Program begins: August
Duration of program: 24 months

Application Information:
Enrollment of program: 32
Transfer students are accepted.

Financial Information:
Tuition, resident: $7,696
Average cost of books: $1,200

Employment Profile:
% of students who pass the boards on their first try: 93
% employed within the first 6 months following graduation: 60
Average starting salary: $24,000

Reading Hospital and Medical Center

PO Box 16052
Reading, PA 19612-6052

Contact Information:
Telephone: 610-988-8993
Fax: 610-998-8400
Web: www.internshipprograms.com

Program Information:
Program begins: September
Duration of program: 24 months

Robert Morris College—Ohio Valley General Hospital

Ohio Valley General Hospital
Heckel Road
McKees Rocks, PA 15136

Contact Information:
Telephone: 412-777-6210
Fax: 412-777-6866
Web: www.ohiovalleyhospital.org

Program Information:
Program begins: September
Duration of program: 24 months

Application Information:
Transfer students are accepted.

Financial Information:
Tuition, resident: $7,800

Employment Profile:
% of students who pass the boards on their first try: 99
Average starting salary: $23,000

Sharon Regional Health System

740 East State Street
Sharon, PA 16146-3395

Contact Information:
Telephone: 904-549-3274
Fax: 904-549-3186
Web: www.srhsschoolofnursing.com

Program Information:
Program begins: September
Duration of program: 24 months

Application Information:
Transfer students are accepted.

Financial Information:
Average cost of books: $600

Employment Profile:
% employed within the first 6 months following graduation: 100

St. Joseph Medical Center

12th and Walnut Streets
PO Box 316
Reading, PA 19603

Contact Information:
Telephone: 610-378-2230
Fax: 610-378-2803
E-mail: cynthiakeane@chi-east.org
Web: www.sjrhs.org

Program Information:
Program begins: July
Duration of program: 24 months

Financial Information:
Tuition, resident: $1,000
Average cost of books: $440

Employment Profile:
% of students who pass the boards on their first try: 100
% employed within the first 6 months following graduation: 100
Average starting salary: $26,000

Thomas Jefferson University

130 South Ninth Street/Suite 1010
Philadelphia, PA 19107-5233

Contact Information:
Telephone: 215-503-1865
Fax: 215-503-1031
E-mail: frances.gilman@mail.edu
Web: www.tju.edu

Program Information:
Program begins: September
Degrees offered: Bachelor's

University of Pittsburgh Medical Center

Health Systems
200 Lothrop Street
Pittsburgh, PA 15213-2582

Contact Information:
Telephone: 505-272-5254
Fax: 505-272-8079
Web: www.upmc.edu

Program Information:
Program begins: July
Degrees offered: Certificate program

Application Information:
Enrollment of program: 30
Transfer students are accepted.

Financial Information:
Average cost of books: $550

Employment Profile:
% of students who pass the boards on their first try: 100
% employed within the first 6 months following graduation: 100
Average starting salary: $22,000

Valley Medical Facilities—Sewickley Valley Hospital
720 Blackburn Road
Sewickley, PA 15143

Contact Information:
Telephone: 412-749-7245
Fax: 412-749-7713
E-mail: imagingschools@vhsnet.org

Program Information:
Program begins: June
Duration of program: 24 months

Application Information:
Enrollment of program: 20

Financial Information:
Average cost of books: $600
% of students receiving aid: 47

Employment Profile:
% of students who pass the boards on their first try: 80
% employed within the first 6 months following graduation: 40
Average starting salary: $25,600

Washington Hospital
155 Wilson Avenue
Washington, PA 15301

Contact Information:
Telephone: 724-223-3326
Fax: 724-229-2018

Program Information:
Program begins: July
Degrees offered: Diploma, 24 months

Application Information:
Enrollment of program: 24

Financial Information:
Average cost of books: $300
% of students receiving aid: 80

Employment Profile:
% of students who pass the boards on their first try: 90
% employed within the first 6 months following graduation: 100
Average starting salary: $26,000

Western School of Health & Business Careers
421 Seventh Avenue
Pittsburgh, PA 15219

Contact Information:
Telephone: 412-281-2600 ext. 137
Fax: 412-281-0319
Web: www.westernschool.com

Program Information:
Program begins: September
Duration of program: 24 months

Application Information:
Enrollment of program: 40
Transfer students are accepted.

Financial Information:
Average cost of books: $1,715
% of students receiving aid: 100

Employment Profile:
% of students who pass the boards on their first try: 75
% employed within the first 6 months following graduation: 75
Average starting salary: $24,000

Wyoming Valley Health Care System
575 North River Street
Wilkes-Barre, PA 18764

Contact Information:
Telephone: 717-552-1760
Fax: 717-552-1707

Program Information:
Program begins: June
Duration of program: 24 months

Application Information:
Enrollment of program: 16
Transfer students are accepted.

Financial Information:
Average cost of books: $600

Employment Profile:
% of students who pass the boards on their first try: 98
% employed within the first 6 months following graduation: 100
Average starting salary: $20,000

Puerto Rico

Universidad Central del Caribe
Call Box 60 327
Bayamon, PR 00960-6032

Contact Information:
Telephone: 501-587-2668
Fax: 501-587-2611
E-mail: jmoscoso@uccaribe.edu
Web: www.uccaribe.edu

Program Information:
Program begins: August
Duration of program: 24 months

Application Information:
Enrollment of program: 70

Financial Information:
Tuition, resident: $5,500
Average cost of books: $600
% of students receiving aid: 80

Employment Profile:
% employed within the first 6 months following graduation: 20
Average starting salary: $24,000

University of Puerto Rico
GPO Box 5067
San Juan, PR 00936

Contact Information:
Telephone: 405-271-6477
Fax: 405-271-1424
Web: www.cprsweb.rcm.upr.edu

Program Information:
Program begins: August
Degrees offered: Associate's, 24 months

Application Information:
Enrollment of program: 25

Financial Information:
Tuition, resident: $2,000
Tuition, non-resident: $2,500
Average cost of books: $450
% of students receiving aid: 78

Employment Profile:
% of students who pass the boards on their first try: 97
% employed within the first 6 months following graduation: 98
Average starting salary: $22,000

Rhode Island

Rhode Island Hospital
593 Eddy Street
SWP 107
Providence, RI 02903

Contact Information:
Telephone: 401-444-5505
Fax: 401-444-6308

Program Information:
Program begins: July
Duration of program: 24 months

Application Information:
Transfer students are accepted.

Financial Information:
Average cost of books: $550

Employment Profile:
% employed within the first 6 months following graduation: 100

South Carolina

Greenville Technical College

PO Box 5616
Greenville, SC 29606-5616

Contact Information:

Telephone: 864-250-8316
Fax: 864-250-8462
E-mail: hirtjkh@gvltec.edu
Web: www.greenvilletech.com

Program Information:

Program begins: August
Duration of program: 28 months
Evening or weekend classes are available.

Application Information:

Transfer students are accepted.

Financial Information:

Tuition, resident: $4,375
Tuition, non-resident: $11,200
Average cost of books: $1,000

Employment Profile:

% of students who pass the boards on their first try: 100
% employed within the first 6 months following graduation: 100
Average starting salary: $23,920

Horry-Georgetown Technical College

Highway 501 East
PO Box 261966
Conway, SC 29528-6066

Contact Information:

Telephone: 843-349-5321
Fax: 843-347-4207
E-mail: galbraith@hor.tee.sc.us
Web: www.hor.tec.sc.us

Program Information:

Program begins: June
Duration of program: 24 months

Application Information:

Enrollment of program: 30

Financial Information:

Tuition, resident: $600
Tuition, non-resident: $1,431
Average cost of books: $500
% of students receiving aid: 70

Employment Profile:

% of students who pass the boards on their first try: 80
% employed within the first 6 months following graduation: 100
Average starting salary: $22,000

Midlands Technical College

PO Box 2408
Columbia, SC 29202

Contact Information:

Telephone: 803-434-6343
Fax: 803-434-4500
Web: www.mid.tec.sc.us

Program Information:

Program begins: June
Duration of program: 24 months

Application Information:

Enrollment of program: 20
Transfer students are accepted.

Financial Information:

Tuition, resident: $1,800
Tuition, non-resident: $3,600
Average cost of books: $400
% of students receiving aid: 35

Employment Profile:

% employed within the first 6 months following graduation: 100

Orangeburg Calhoun Technical College

3250 St. Matthews Road
Orangeburg, SC 29118

Contact Information:

Telephone: 803-535-1356
Fax: 803-535-1350
E-mail: andrewsf@org.tec.sc.us
Web: www.octech.org

Program Information:

Program begins: August
Duration of program: 24 months

Application Information:

Enrollment of program: 22
Transfer students are accepted.

Financial Information:

Tuition, resident: $2,088
Tuition, non-resident: $5,004
Average cost of books: $870
% of students receiving aid: 50

Employment Profile:

% of students who pass the boards on their first try: 100
% employed within the first 6 months following graduation: 100
Average starting salary: $21,000

Spartanburg Technical College

PO Drawer 4386
Spartanburg, SC 29305-4386

Contact Information:

Telephone: 864-591-3720
Fax: 864-591-3708
E-mail: kiserd@spt.tec.sc.us
Web: www.spt.tec.sc.us

Program Information:

Program begins: June
Degrees offered: Associate's, 24 months

Application Information:

Enrollment of program: 21
Transfer students are accepted.

Financial Information:

Tuition, resident: $1,300
Tuition, non-resident: $3,140
Average cost of books: $500
% of students receiving aid: 50

Employment Profile:

% of students who pass the boards on their first try: 100
% employed within the first 6 months following graduation: 100
Average starting salary: $30,000

York Technical College

452 South Anderson Road
Rock Hill, SC 29730

Contact Information:

Telephone: 803-981-7036
Fax: 803-327-8059
E-mail: dcaldwell@york.tec.sc.us
Web: www.yorktech.com

Program Information:

Program begins: July
Duration of program: 24 months

Application Information:

Enrollment of program: 16
Transfer students are accepted.

Financial Information:

Tuition, resident: $945
Tuition, non-resident: $4,480
Average cost of books: $400
% of students receiving aid: 58

Employment Profile:

% of students who pass the boards on their first try: 100
% employed within the first 6 months following graduation: 100
Average starting salary: $24,000

South Dakota

Rapid City Regional Hospital

353 Fairmont Boulevard
PO Box 6000
Rapid City, SD 57709-6000

Contact Information:

Telephone: 605-341-8433
Fax: 605-341-8983
E-mail: dmartin@rcrh.org
Web: www.rcrh.org

Program Information:

Program begins: June
Degrees offered: Certificate program, 24 months

Application Information:

Enrollment of program: 20

Financial Information:

Average cost of books: $400
% of students receiving aid: 50

Employment Profile:

% of students who pass the boards on their first try: 50
% employed within the first 6 months following graduation: 100
Average starting salary: $25,000

Sacred Heart Hospital
501 Summit Street
Yankton, SD 57078-9967

Contact Information:
Telephone: 609-451-8700 ext. 2236
Fax: 609-451-0335
Web: www.shh.org

Program Information:
Program begins: September
Duration of program: 24 months

Application Information:
Enrollment of program: 12
Transfer students are accepted.

Financial Information:
Average cost of books: $300
% of students receiving aid: 100

Employment Profile:
% of students who pass the boards on their first try: 98
% employed within the first 6 months following graduation: 75
Average starting salary: $23,000

Sioux Valley Hospital
1100 South Euclid Avenue
PO Box 5039
Sioux Falls, SD 57117-5039

Contact Information:
Telephone: 937-512-2842
Fax: 937-512-2058
Web: www.siouxvalley.org

Program Information:
Program begins: July
Degrees offered: Certificate program, 24 months

Application Information:
Enrollment of program: 21

Financial Information:
Average cost of books: $550
% of students receiving aid: 80

Employment Profile:
% of students who pass the boards on their first try: 100
% employed within the first 6 months following graduation: 100
Average starting salary: $26,000

Tennessee

Columbia State Community College
PO Box 1315, Highway 412 West
Columbia, TN 38402-1315

Contact Information:
Telephone: 931-540-2745
Fax: 931-540-2798
E-mail: coleman@coscc.cc.tn.us
Web: www.coscc.cc.tn.us

Program Information:
Program begins: July
Degrees offered: Associate's, 22 months

Application Information:
Enrollment of program: 50

Financial Information:
Tuition, resident: $1,398
Tuition, non-resident: $5,577
Average cost of books: $250
% of students receiving aid: 75

Employment Profile:
% of students who pass the boards on their first try: 90
% employed within the first 6 months following graduation: 100
Average starting salary: $22,000

Methodist Healthcare
1265 Union Avenue
Memphis, TN 38104

Contact Information:
Telephone: 901-726-7358
Fax: 901-726-7490
E-mail: franklip@methodisthealth.org
Web: www.methodisthealth.org

Program Information:
Program begins: July
Duration of program: 24 months

Financial Information:
Average cost of books: $800

Employment Profile:
% employed within the first 6 months following graduation: 100
Average starting salary: $29,500

Roane State Community College
701 Briarcliff
Oak Ridge, TN 37830

Contact Information:
Telephone: 423-481-2015
Fax: 423-481-2019
Web: www.rscc.cc.tn.us

Program Information:
Program begins: August
Duration of program: 24 months

Application Information:
Enrollment of program: 60
Transfer students are accepted.

Financial Information:
Tuition, resident: $1,882
Tuition, non-resident: $5,079

Employment Profile:
% of students who pass the boards on their first try: 95
% employed within the first 6 months following graduation: 95
Average starting salary: $25,000

University of Tennessee Medical Center at Knoxville
Radiology Department
1924 Alcoa Highway
Knoxville, TN 37920

Contact Information:
Telephone: 334-434-3456
Web: www.utmck.edu

Program Information:
Program begins: June
Degrees offered: Certificate program, 24 months

Application Information:
Enrollment of program: 20

Financial Information:
Tuition, resident: $500
Average cost of books: $350

Employment Profile:
% of students who pass the boards on their first try: 90
% employed within the first 6 months following graduation: 100

Volunteer State Community College
1480 Nashville Pike
Gallatin, TN 37066-3188

Contact Information:
Telephone: 615-452-8600 ext. 3651
Fax: 615-230-3224
E-mail: mwhite@vscc.cc.tn.us
Web: www.vscc.tn.us

Program Information:
Program begins: July
Degrees offered: Associate's, 24 months

Application Information:
Enrollment of program: 50
Transfer students are accepted.

Financial Information:
Tuition, resident: $1,845
Tuition, non-resident: $6,924
Average cost of books: $700
% of students receiving aid: 30

Employment Profile:
% of students who pass the boards on their first try: 97
% employed within the first 6 months following graduation: 100
Average starting salary: $26,000

Texas

Amarillo College
PO Box 447
Amarillo, TX 79178

Contact Information:
Telephone: 806-354-6072 ext. 6072
Fax: 806-354-6076
E-mail: kmwoody@actx.edu
Web: www.actx.edu

Program Information:
Program begins: August
Degrees offered: Associate's, 24 months

Application Information:
Enrollment of program: 50
Transfer students are accepted.

Financial Information:
Tuition, resident: $1,350
Tuition, non-resident: $2,600
Average cost of books: $200
% of students receiving aid: 80

Employment Profile:
% of students who pass the boards on their first try: 95
% employed within the first 6 months following graduation: 90
Average starting salary: $22,000

Angelina College
PO Box 1768
Lufkin, TX 75902-1768

Contact Information:
Telephone: 406-633-5267
Fax: 409-639-4299
E-mail: jheck@angelina.cc.tx.us
Web: www.angelina.cc.tx.us

Program Information:
Program begins: August
Degrees offered: Associate's, 20 months

Application Information:
Enrollment of program: 43
Transfer students are accepted.

Financial Information:
Tuition, resident: $834
Tuition, non-resident: $1,614
Average cost of books: $600
% of students receiving aid: 80

Employment Profile:
% of students who pass the boards on their first try: 100
% employed within the first 6 months following graduation: 100
Average starting salary: $22,000

Army Medical Department Center and School
HSHA-ML (Radiology Branch)
3151 Scott Road
Ft. Sam Houston, TX 78234-6137

Contact Information:
Telephone: 210-221-8597
Fax: 210-221-7611
E-mail: carlos.solivan@cen.amedd.mil
Web: www.cs.amedd.army.mil

Program Information:
Duration of program: 12 months
Additional Information: Enrollment only open to active military personnel.

Baptist Health System
111 Dallas Street
San Antonio, TX 78205-1230

Contact Information:
Telephone: 210-297-9160
Fax: 210-297-0716

Program Information:
Program begins: September
Duration of program: 12 months

Application Information:
Enrollment of program: 39

Financial Information:
Average cost of books: $400

Employment Profile:
% of students who pass the boards on their first try: 90
% employed within the first 6 months following graduation: 100
Average starting salary: $26,500

Baptist Hospital of Southeast Texas
PO Drawer 1591
Beaumont, TX 77704

Contact Information:
Telephone: 409-654-5726
Fax: 409-654-5743
E-mail: carolyn-nicholas@mhhs.org
Web: www.tx-cancer-connection.com

Program Information:
Program begins: June
Duration of program: 24 months

Application Information:
Enrollment of program: 28

Financial Information:
Average cost of books: $1,500
% of students receiving aid: 10

Employment Profile:
% of students who pass the boards on their first try: 95
% employed within the first 6 months following graduation: 90
Average starting salary: $25,000

Baylor University Medical Center
3500 Gaston Avenue
Dallas, TX 75246

Contact Information:
Telephone: 214-820-3780
Fax: 214-820-7773
E-mail: Irenec@baylordallas.edu
Web: www.baylorhealth.com

Program Information:
Program begins: July
Degrees offered: Certificate program, 24 months

Application Information:
Enrollment of program: 20
Transfer students are accepted.

Financial Information:
Average cost of books: $600

Employment Profile:
% of students who pass the boards on their first try: 100
% employed within the first 6 months following graduation: 100

Blinn College
PO Box 6030
Bryan, TX 77805-6030

Contact Information:
Telephone: 409-823-0366
Fax: 409-821-0289
Web: www.blinncol.edu

Program Information:
Duration of program: 24 months

Application Information:
Enrollment of program: 38
Transfer students are accepted.

Financial Information:
Average cost of books: $600
% of students receiving aid: 30

Employment Profile:
% of students who pass the boards on their first try: 100
% employed within the first 6 months following graduation: 100
Average starting salary: $22,500

Citizens Medical Center
2701 Hospital Drive
Victoria, TX 77901

Contact Information:
Telephone: 512-572-5062
Fax: 512-572-5091
Web: www.citizensmedicalcenter.org

Program Information:
Program begins: July
Degrees offered: Certificate program, 24 months

Application Information:
Enrollment of program: 15

Financial Information:
Average cost of books: $200

Employment Profile:
% of students who pass the boards on their first try: 80
% employed within the first 6 months following graduation: 100
Average starting salary: $24,500

Galveston College—University of Texas
4015 Avenue Q
Galveston, TX 77550-2782

Contact Information:
Telephone: 409-772-9467
Fax: 409-772-3014
E-mail: pstinson@utmb.edu
Web: www.utmb.edu

Program Information:
Program begins: August
Degrees offered: Certificate program, 22 months; Associate's, 22 months

Application Information:
Enrollment of program: 30
Transfer students are accepted.

Financial Information:
Tuition, resident: $1,100
Tuition, non-resident: $1,568
Average cost of books: $630
% of students receiving aid: 40

Employment Profile:
% of students who pass the boards on their first try: 100
% employed within the first 6 months following graduation: 100
Average starting salary: $30,000

Harris County Hospital District—Ben Taub Hospital

1504 Taub Loop
Houston, TX 77030

Contact Information:
Telephone: 713-793-2276
Fax: 713-793-2416

Program Information:
Program begins: August, January
Duration of program: 24 months

Financial Information:
Tuition, resident: $600
Tuition, non-resident: $650
Average cost of books: $600
% of students receiving aid: 5

Employment Profile:
% of students who pass the boards on their first try: 97
% employed within the first 6 months following graduation: 100
Average starting salary: $26,000

Hendrick Medical Center

1242 North 19th
Abilene, TX 79601-2316

Contact Information:
Telephone: 915-670-2427
Fax: 915-670-2575
E-mail: rbower@hendrickmed.org
Web: www.abilene.com

Program Information:
Program begins: January, July
Duration of program: 24 months

Application Information:
Enrollment of program: 20
Transfer students are accepted.

Financial Information:
Average cost of books: $550

Employment Profile:
% of students who pass the boards on their first try: 96
Average starting salary: $26,000

Lamar Institute of Technology—Beaumont

PO Box 10061
Beaumont, TX 77710

Contact Information:
Telephone: 409-880-8845
Fax: 409-880-8955
E-mail: shortwd@hal.lamar.edu
Web: www.hal.lamar.edu

Program Information:
Program begins: June
Duration of program: 48 months

Application Information:
Enrollment of program: 30
Transfer students are accepted.

Financial Information:
Tuition, resident: $1,800
Tuition, non-resident: $7,000

Employment Profile:
% of students who pass the boards on their first try: 93
% employed within the first 6 months following graduation: 95
Average starting salary: $25,000

McLennan Community College

1400 College Drive
Waco, TX 76708

Contact Information:
Telephone: 254-299-8342
Fax: 254-299-8435
E-mail: bjd@mcc.cc.tx.us
Web: www.mcc.cc.tx.us

Program Information:
Program begins: August
Degrees offered: Associate's, 24 months

Application Information:
Enrollment of program: 50
Transfer students are accepted.

Financial Information:
Tuition, resident: $756
Tuition, non-resident: $2,916
Average cost of books: $400
% of students receiving aid: 90

Employment Profile:
% of students who pass the boards on their first try: 97
% employed within the first 6 months following graduation: 100
Average starting salary: $27,000

Methodist/St. Mary Health Systems

3801 19th, Suite 500
Lubbock, TX 79410

Contact Information:
Telephone: 806-793-4056
Fax: 806-784-5046

Program Information:
Program begins: July
Duration of program: 24 months

Financial Information:
Average cost of books: $600

Employment Profile:
% of students who pass the boards on their first try: 90
% employed within the first 6 months following graduation: 100
Average starting salary: $22,000

Midland College

3600 North Garfield
Midland, TX 79705-6399

Contact Information:
Telephone: 915-685-4600
Fax: 915-685-4762
E-mail: eskimo@mc.midland.tx.us
Web: www.midland.cc.tx.us

Program Information:
Program begins: August
Degrees offered: Associate's, 23 months

Application Information:
Enrollment of program: 22
Transfer students are accepted.

Financial Information:
Tuition, resident: $1,238
Tuition, non-resident: $1,466
Average cost of books: $700
% of students receiving aid: 30

Employment Profile:
% of students who pass the boards on their first try: 99
% employed within the first 6 months following graduation: 99
Average starting salary: $23,000

Midwestern State University

3410 Taft Boulevard
Wichita Falls, TX 76308-2099

Contact Information:
Telephone: 940-397-4608
Fax: 940-397-4845
E-mail: fshwltrv@nexus.mwsu.edu
Web: www.mwsu.edu

Program Information:
Program begins: July
Degrees offered: Bachelor's, Master's

Application Information:
Enrollment of program: 48
Transfer students are accepted.

Financial Information:
Tuition, resident: $2,100
Tuition, non-resident: $7,500
Average cost of books: $800
% of students receiving aid: 50

Employment Profile:
% of students who pass the boards on their first try: 95
% employed within the first 6 months following graduation: 90
Average starting salary: $21,000

Scenic Mountain Medical Center

1601 West 11th Place
Big Spring, TX 79720-9990

Contact Information:
Telephone: 815-288-5511 ext. 342
Fax: 815-288-5651
E-mail: vgordon@apex2000.net
Web: www.smmccares.com

Program Information:
Program begins: May
Duration of program: 24 months

Application Information:
Enrollment of program: 7
Transfer students are accepted.

Financial Information:
Average cost of books: $500
% of students receiving aid: 30

Employment Profile:
% of students who pass the boards on their first try: 95
% employed within the first 6 months following graduation: 90
Average starting salary: $34,000

South Plains College

1302 Main Street
Lubbock, TX 79401

Contact Information:
Telephone: 806-747-0576 ext. 4629
Fax: 806-765-2775
E-mail: dbarnes@spc.cc.tx.us
Web: www.spc.cc.tx.us

Program Information:
Program begins: August
Degrees offered: Associate's, 24 months

Application Information:
Enrollment of program: 32
Transfer students are accepted.

Financial Information:
Tuition, resident: $688
Tuition, non-resident: $1,376
Average cost of books: $1,000

Employment Profile:
% of students who pass the boards on their first try: 94
% employed within the first 6 months following graduation: 100
Average starting salary: $28,000

Tarrant County College—Northeast

828 Harwood Road
Hurst, TX 76054

Contact Information:
Telephone: 817-515-6569
Fax: 817-515-6700
E-mail: mholt@tcjc.cc.tx.us
Web: www.tccd.net

Program Information:
Program begins: July
Duration of program: 24 months

Application Information:
Enrollment of program: 54
Transfer students are accepted.

Financial Information:
Tuition, resident: $2,700
Tuition, non-resident: $10,080

Employment Profile:
% of students who pass the boards on their first try: 99
% employed within the first 6 months following graduation: 99
Average starting salary: $24,000

Tyler Junior College

PO Box 9020
Tyler, TX 75711

Contact Information:
Telephone: 903-510-2346
Fax: 903-510-2880
E-mail: nwar1@tjc.tyler.cc.tx.us
Web: www.tyler.cc.tx.us

Program Information:
Program begins: July
Duration of program: 24 months

Application Information:
Enrollment of program: 31

Financial Information:
Tuition, resident: $2,022
Tuition, non-resident: $3,822
Average cost of books: $800

Employment Profile:
% of students who pass the boards on their first try: 100
% employed within the first 6 months following graduation: 90
Average starting salary: $24,000

Wharton County Junior College

911 Boling Highway
Suite J230
Wharton, TX 77488

Contact Information:
Telephone: 409-532-6379
Fax: 409-532-6489
Web: www.whatcom.ctc.edu

Program Information:
Program begins: July
Duration of program: 24 months

Financial Information:
Tuition, resident: $685
Tuition, non-resident: $1,140

Employment Profile:
% of students who pass the boards on their first try: 100
% employed within the first 6 months following graduation: 100
Average starting salary: $25,000

Utah

Salt Lake Community College

South City Campus
1575 South State Street
Salt Lake City, UT 84121

Contact Information:
Telephone: 605-668-8758
Fax: 605-668-8153
E-mail: tuckerma@slcc.edu
Web: www.slcc.edu

Program Information:
Program begins: August
Duration of program: 21 months

Application Information:
Enrollment of program: 52
Transfer students are accepted.

Financial Information:
Tuition, resident: $1,446
Tuition, non-resident: $4,506

Employment Profile:
% of students who pass the boards on their first try: 94
% employed within the first 6 months following graduation: 90
Average starting salary: $28,000

Utah Valley Regional Medical Center

1034 North 500 West
Provo, UT 84605

Contact Information:
Telephone: 801-357-7850 ext. 2484
Fax: 801-357-7997
E-mail: uvdwinte@ihc.com
Web: www.orem.ut.us

Program Information:
Program begins: September
Duration of program: 24 months

Application Information:
Enrollment of program: 20

Employment Profile:
% employed within the first 6 months following graduation: 50
Average starting salary: $26,000

Vermont

Champlain College

163 South Willard Street
PO Box 670
Burlington, VT 05402-0670

Contact Information:
Telephone: 802-860-2728
Fax: 802-860-2750
E-mail: miller@champlain.edu
Web: www.champlain.edu

Program Information:
Program begins: June
Duration of program: 21 months

Application Information:
Enrollment of program: 29
Transfer students are accepted.

Financial Information:
Tuition, resident: $10,485
Average cost of books: $500
% of students receiving aid: 85

Employment Profile:
% of students who pass the boards on their first try: 95
% employed within the first 6 months following graduation: 100
Average starting salary: $27,000

Rutland Regional Medical Center
160 Allen Street
Rutland, VT 05701-4595

Contact Information:
Telephone: 802-747-1712
Fax: 802-747-6200

Program Information:
Program begins: July
Duration of program: 24 months

Application Information:
Enrollment of program: 12

Financial Information:
Average cost of books: $400
% of students receiving aid: 50

Employment Profile:
% of students who pass the boards on their first try: 95
% employed within the first 6 months following graduation: 90
Average starting salary: $26,000

Virginia

Central Virginia Community College
3506 Wards Road
Lynchburg, VA 24502-2498

Contact Information:
Telephone: 804-386-4695
Fax: 804-386-4681
E-mail: blairg@cv.cc.va.us
Web: www.cv.cc.vc.us

Program Information:
Program begins: June
Duration of program: 23 months

Application Information:
Enrollment of program: 34

Financial Information:
Tuition, resident: $1,679
Tuition, non-resident: $5,616
Average cost of books: $275

Employment Profile:
% of students who pass the boards on their first try: 100
% employed within the first 6 months following graduation: 95
Average starting salary: $27,000

Mary Washington Hospital
1001 Sam Perry Boulevard
Fredericksburg, VA 22401

Contact Information:
Telephone: 540-899-1892
Fax: 540-899-2560
E-mail: jclark@medicorpihn.com

Program Information:
Program begins: July
Degrees offered: Certificate program, 23 months

Application Information:
Enrollment of program: 14

Financial Information:
Average cost of books: $600

Employment Profile:
% of students who pass the boards on their first try: 96
% employed within the first 6 months following graduation: 100
Average starting salary: $28,700

Riverside School of Health Occupations
12420 Warwick Boulevard
Suite 6-G
Newport News, VA 23606

Contact Information:
Telephone: 757-594-2722
Fax: 757-594-3067

Program Information:
Duration of program: 24 months

Application Information:
Enrollment of program: 10
Transfer students are accepted.

Financial Information:
Tuition, resident: $2,200
Tuition, non-resident: $2,550
Average cost of books: $440
% of students receiving aid: 30

Employment Profile:
% of students who pass the boards on their first try: 100
% employed within the first 6 months following graduation: 100
Average starting salary: $20,000

Rockingham Memorial Hospital
235 Cantrell Avenue
Harrisonburg, VA 22801-3293

Contact Information:
Telephone: 540-433-4532
Fax: 540-433-4423
E-mail: jlough@rhcc.ccm
Web: www.accc-cancer.org

Program Information:
Program begins: June
Duration of program: 24 months
Evening or weekend classes are available.

Application Information:
Enrollment of program: 20
Transfer students are accepted.

Financial Information:
Tuition, resident: $2,300
Tuition, non-resident: $4,000

Southside Regional Medical Center
801 South Adams Street
Petersburg, VA 23803

Contact Information:
Telephone: 804-862-5883
Fax: 804-862-5937
E-mail: pshelton@ssrmc.org
Web: www.srmconline.com

Program Information:
Program begins: August
Duration of program: 23 months

Application Information:
Enrollment of program: 16
Transfer students are accepted.

Financial Information:
Tuition, resident: $2,250
Tuition, non-resident: $3,500
Average cost of books: $800
% of students receiving aid: 40

Employment Profile:
% of students who pass the boards on their first try: 100
% employed within the first 6 months following graduation: 100
Average starting salary: $25,000

Southwest Virginia Community College
PO Box SVCC
Richlands, VA 24641-1510

Contact Information:
Telephone: 540-964-7306
Fax: 540-964-9307
Web: www.sw.cc.va.us

Program Information:
Program begins: August
Degrees offered: Associate's, 24 months

Application Information:
Enrollment of program: 24
Transfer students are accepted.

Financial Information:
Tuition, resident: $2,126
Tuition, non-resident: $7,007
Average cost of books: $250
% of students receiving aid: 80

Employment Profile:
% of students who pass the boards on their first try: 99
% employed within the first 6 months following graduation: 95
Average starting salary: $22,900

St. Mary's Hospital
5801 Bremo Road
Richmond, VA 23226

Contact Information:
Telephone: 414-527-5149
Fax: 414-527-5156
E-mail: joyce-hawkins@hshsi.com
Web: www.st-marys.org

Program Information:
Program begins: August
Duration of program: 24 months

Application Information:
Enrollment of program: 9
Transfer students are accepted.

Financial Information:
Average cost of books: $500

Employment Profile:
% of students who pass the boards on their first try: 100
% employed within the first 6 months following graduation: 100
Average starting salary: $21,000

Tidewater Community College

1700 College Crescent
Virginia Beach, VA 23456

Contact Information:
Telephone: 757-822-7253
Fax: 757-427-1338
E-mail: tcutlek@tc.cc.va.us
Web: www.tc.cc.va.us

Program Information:
Program begins: September
Duration of program: 24 months

Application Information:
Enrollment of program: 75
Transfer students are accepted.

Financial Information:
Tuition, resident: $3,165
Tuition, non-resident: $12,360
Average cost of books: $400
% of students receiving aid: 65

Employment Profile:
% of students who pass the boards on their first try: 97
% employed within the first 6 months following graduation: 90
Average starting salary: $21,000

Virginia Commonwealth University—Medical College of VA Campus

Box 980495
1200 East Broad Street Room 632
Richmond, VA 23298-0495

Contact Information:
Telephone: 804-828-9104
Fax: 804-828-5778
E-mail: tfauber@hsc.vcu.edu

Program Information:
Program begins: June
Duration of program: 33 months

Financial Information:
Tuition, resident: $3,575
Tuition, non-resident: $13,029

Winchester Medical Center

1840 Amherst Street
PO Box 3340
Winchester, VA 22603

Contact Information:
Telephone: 540-722-8750
Fax: 540-722-8827
E-mail: jorndorf@valleyheathlink.com
Web: www.vvalley.com

Program Information:
Program begins: June
Duration of program: 24 months

Application Information:
Transfer students are accepted.

Financial Information:
Average cost of books: $700
% of students receiving aid: 15

Employment Profile:
% of students who pass the boards on their first try: 100
% employed within the first 6 months following graduation: 60
Average starting salary: $25,000

Washington

Holy Family Hospital

North 5633 Lidgerwood Avenue
Spokane, WA 99207

Contact Information:
Telephone: 509-482-2384
Fax: 509-482-2176
Web: www.holyfamilyhosp.org

Program Information:
Program begins: August
Duration of program: 22 months

Application Information:
Enrollment of program: 17
Transfer students are accepted.

Financial Information:
Average cost of books: $300

Employment Profile:
% of students who pass the boards on their first try: 100
% employed within the first 6 months following graduation: 84
Average starting salary: $31,000

Pima Medical Institute—Seattle

1627 Eastlake Avenue East
Seattle, WA 98102

Contact Information:
Telephone: 206-322-6100 ext. 22
Fax: 206-324-1985

Program Information:
Program begins: March, July, November
Degrees offered: Associate's, 24 months

Application Information:
Enrollment of program: 32
Transfer students are accepted.

Financial Information:
% of students receiving aid: 90

Employment Profile:
% of students who pass the boards on their first try: 93
% employed within the first 6 months following graduation: 100
Average starting salary: $31,000

Tacoma Community College

6501 South 19th Street
Tacoma, WA 98466

Contact Information:
Telephone: 253-566-5168
Fax: 253-566-5273
E-mail: mmixdorf@tcc.tacoma.ctc.edu
Web: www.tacoma.ctc.edu

Program Information:
Program begins: March, July, October
Duration of program: 24 months

Financial Information:
Tuition, resident: $2,222
Tuition, non-resident: $8,420
Average cost of books: $800

Yakima Valley Community College

PO Box 22520
Yakima, WA 98907

Contact Information:
Telephone: 509-574-4928
Fax: 509-574-4606
E-mail: mbarnes@yakima.cc.wa.us
Web: www.yvcc.cc.wa.us

Program Information:
Program begins: July
Duration of program: 24 months

Application Information:
Transfer students are accepted.

Financial Information:
Tuition, resident: $1,590
Tuition, non-resident: $2,012
Average cost of books: $800
% of students receiving aid: 75

Employment Profile:
% of students who pass the boards on their first try: 83
% employed within the first 6 months following graduation: 30
Average starting salary: $28,000

West Virginia

Bluefield State College

219 Rock Street
Bluefield, WV 24701

Contact Information:
Telephone: 304-327-4145
Fax: 304-327-4219
E-mail: mhaye@bscvax.wvnet.edu
Web: www.bluefield.wvnet.edu

Program Information:
Program begins: August
Duration of program: 24 months

Application Information:
Enrollment of program: 39

Financial Information:
Tuition, resident: $3,041
Tuition, non-resident: $7,661
Average cost of books: $614
% of students receiving aid: 70

Employment Profile:
% employed within the first 6 months following graduation: 78
Average starting salary: $22,000

Camden-Clark Memorial Hospital

PO Box 718
Parkersburg, WV 26102

Contact Information:
Telephone: 304-424-2974
Fax: 304-424-2722
Web: www.ccmh.org

Program Information:
Program begins: July
Degrees offered: Certificate program, 24 months

Application Information:
Enrollment of program: 10

Financial Information:
Average cost of books: $500

Employment Profile:
% employed within the first 6 months following graduation: 100
Average starting salary: $24,000

United Hospital Center

3 Hospital Plaza
PO Box 1680
Clarksburg, WV 26301

Contact Information:
Telephone: 304-624-2895
Fax: 304-624-2856

Program Information:
Program begins: August
Duration of program: 24 months

Financial Information:
Average cost of books: $350

Employment Profile:
% of students who pass the boards on their first try: 100
% employed within the first 6 months following graduation: 100

University of Charleston

2300 MacCorkle Avenue Southeast
Charleston, WV 25304

Contact Information:
Telephone: 787-798-3006
Fax: 787-785-3425
E-mail: dgoddin@uchaswv.edu
Web: www.uchaswv.edu

Program Information:
Program begins: July
Degrees offered: Bachelor's, 48 months
Evening or weekend classes are available.

Application Information:
Enrollment of program: 45
Transfer students are accepted.

Financial Information:
% of students receiving aid: 85

Employment Profile:
% of students who pass the boards on their first try: 99
% employed within the first 6 months following graduation: 98
Average starting salary: $28,000

West Virginia University Hospitals Inc

Box 8062
Morgantown, WV 26505-8062

Contact Information:
Telephone: 304-598-4251
Fax: 304-598-4702
E-mail: morrisj@rcbhsc.wvu.edu
Web: www.hsc.wvu.edu

Program Information:
Program begins: July
Degrees offered: Certificate program, 24 months

Application Information:
Enrollment of program: 30

Financial Information:
Average cost of books: $600
% of students receiving aid: 30

Employment Profile:
% of students who pass the boards on their first try: 98
% employed within the first 6 months following graduation: 100
Average starting salary: $25,000

Wheeling Hospital

Medical Park
Wheeling, WV 26003

Contact Information:
Telephone: 304-243-3173
Fax: 304-243-3130
Web: www.wheelinghosp.com

Program Information:
Program begins: July
Duration of program: 24 months

Application Information:
Enrollment of program: 18

Financial Information:
Average cost of books: $350

Employment Profile:
% of students who pass the boards on their first try: 98
% employed within the first 6 months following graduation: 85
Average starting salary: $21,000

Wisconsin

Affinity Health System

631 Hazel Street
PO Box 1100
Oshkosh, WI 54902

Contact Information:
Telephone: 414-236-2253
Fax: 414-236-1373

Program Information:
Program begins: September
Degrees offered: Certificate program, 24 months

Application Information:
Transfer students are accepted.

Financial Information:
% of students receiving aid: 45

Employment Profile:
% of students who pass the boards on their first try: 100
% employed within the first 6 months following graduation: 100
Average starting salary: $28,000

All Saints Healthcare System Inc.

1320 Wisconsin Avenue
Racine, WI 53403

Contact Information:
Telephone: 414-636-2846
Fax: 414-636-8834
E-mail: cheridyke@allsaintshealthcare.org

Program Information:
Program begins: July
Duration of program: 24 months

Application Information:
Enrollment of program: 18

Financial Information:
Average cost of books: $625

Employment Profile:
% of students who pass the boards on their first try: 100
% employed within the first 6 months following graduation: 100
Average starting salary: $27,300

Chippewa Valley Technical College

620 West Clairemont Avenue
Eau Claire, WI 54701-6162

Contact Information:
Telephone: 715-833-6428
Fax: 715-833-6470
E-mail: sschreiner@mail.chippewa.tec.wi.us
Web: www.chippewa.tech.wi.us

Program Information:
Program begins: September
Degrees offered: Associate's, 22 months
Evening or weekend classes are available.

Application Information:
Enrollment of program: 32
Transfer students are accepted.

Financial Information:
Tuition, resident: $2,385
Tuition, non-resident: $18,797
Average cost of books: $440

Employment Profile:
% of students who pass the boards on their first try: 100
% employed within the first 6 months following graduation: 98
Average starting salary: $24,000

Froedtert Memorial Lutheran Hospital

9200 West Wisconsin Avenue
Milwaukee, WI 53226

Contact Information:
Telephone: 414-257-6115
Fax: 414-257-9290
E-mail: ssann@fmlh.edu
Web: www.froedtert.com

Program Information:
Program begins: September
Duration of program: 24 months

Application Information:
Enrollment of program: 15
Transfer students are accepted.

Financial Information:
Average cost of books: $700

Employment Profile:
% of students who pass the boards on their first try: 100
% employed within the first 6 months following graduation: 100
Average starting salary: $28,000

Lakeshore Technical College

1290 North Avenue
Cleveland, WI 53015-1414

Contact Information:
Telephone: 920-458-4183 ext. 840
Fax: 920-693-8955
Web: www.ltc.tcc.edu

Program Information:
Program begins: September
Duration of program: 22 months

Application Information:
Enrollment of program: 26
Transfer students are accepted.

Financial Information:
Tuition, resident: $4,320
Tuition, non-resident: $12,960
Average cost of books: $550
% of students receiving aid: 80

Employment Profile:
% of students who pass the boards on their first try: 100
% employed within the first 6 months following graduation: 100
Average starting salary: $24,000

Madison Area Technical College

3550 Anderson Street
Madison, WI 53704-2599

Contact Information:
Telephone: 608-258-2478
Fax: 608-258-2480
E-mail: jmoe@madison.tec.wi.us
Web: www.madison.tec.wi.us

Program Information:
Program begins: August
Duration of program: 24 months

Application Information:
Transfer students are accepted.

Financial Information:
Tuition, resident: $5,860
Tuition, non-resident: $26,775
Average cost of books: $850

Employment Profile:
% of students who pass the boards on their first try: 93
% employed within the first 6 months following graduation: 71
Average starting salary: $24,000

St. Luke's Medical Center

2900 West Oklahoma Avenue
PO Box 2901
Milwaukee, WI 53201-2901

Contact Information:
Telephone: 414-649-6762
Fax: 414-649-6046
E-mail: maramont@execpc.com
Web: www.aurorahealthcare.org

Program Information:
Program begins: August
Duration of program: 24 months

Application Information:
Enrollment of program: 20
Transfer students are accepted.

Financial Information:
Average cost of books: $800
% of students receiving aid: 10

Employment Profile:
% of students who pass the boards on their first try: 100
% employed within the first 6 months following graduation: 100
Average starting salary: $27,000

St. Michael Hospital

2400 West Villard Avenue
Milwaukee, WI 53209

Contact Information:
Telephone: 406-329-5829
Fax: 406-329-5690

Program Information:
Program begins: October
Degrees offered: Certificate program, 24 months

Application Information:
Enrollment of program: 15

Financial Information:
Average cost of books: $600

Employment Profile:
% of students who pass the boards on their first try: 100
% employed within the first 6 months following graduation: 100
Average starting salary: $28,700

University of Wisconsin Hospital & Clinics

600 Highland Avenue
E3/311 Radiology
Madison, WI 53792-3252

Contact Information:
Telephone: 301-459-7867
Fax: 202-274-5952
E-mail: glspicer@facstaff.wisc.edu
Web: www.hosp.wisc.edu

Program Information:
Program begins: July
Duration of program: 24 months

Application Information:
Enrollment of program: 32
Transfer students are accepted.

Financial Information:
Average cost of books: $600
% of students receiving aid: 25

Employment Profile:
% of students who pass the boards on their first try: 100
% employed within the first 6 months following graduation: 100
Average starting salary: $32,000

Western Wisconsin Technical College

304 North Sixth Street
PO Box C-0908
LaCrosse, WI 54601-0908

Contact Information:
Telephone: 608-785-9255
Fax: 608-785-9194
Web: www.western.tec.wi.us

Program Information:
Duration of program: 23 months

Application Information:
Enrollment of program: 28
Transfer students are accepted.

Financial Information:
Tuition, resident: $2,168
Tuition, non-resident: $14,920
Average cost of books: $500

Employment Profile:
% of students who pass the boards on their first try: 100
% employed within the first 6 months following graduation: 50
Average starting salary: $24,000

Wyoming

Laramie County Community College

1400 East College Drive
Cheyenne, WY 82007

Contact Information:
Telephone: 307-778-1391
Fax: 307-778-4386
E-mail: smason@mail.lcc.whecn.edu
Web: www.lcc.whecn.edu

Program Information:
Program begins: October
Duration of program: 24 months

Application Information:
Transfer students are accepted.

Financial Information:
Tuition, resident: $1,648
Tuition, non-resident: $4,177
Average cost of books: $100

Employment Profile:
% employed within the first 6 months following graduation: 100
Average starting salary: $25,000

Diagnostic Medical Sonographer

Arizona

Gateway Community College

108 North 40th Street
Phoenix, AZ 85034

Contact Information:
Telephone: 602-392-5039
Fax: 602-392-5244
E-mail: murphy@gwc.maricopa.edu
Web: www.gwc.maricopa.edu

Program Information:
Program begins: August, January
Duration of program: 24 months
Evening or weekend classes are available.

Application Information:
Enrollment of program: 12

Financial Information:
Tuition, resident: $2,600
Average cost of books: $600

Employment Profile:
% employed within the first 6 months following graduation: 80

California

Loma Linda University

School of Allied Health Professions
Loma Linda, CA 92350

Contact Information:
Telephone: 909-824-4416
Fax: 909-558-4166
E-mail: mdelange@ahs.llumc.edu
Web: www.llu.edu

Program Information:
Program begins: September
Duration of program: 24 months

Employment Profile:
% of students who pass the boards on their first try: 80
% employed within the first 6 months following graduation: 100

Colorado

University of Colorado Health Science Center

Department of Ultrasound/Box C-277
4200 East Ninth Avenue
Denver, CO 80262

Contact Information:
Telephone: 303-372-6190
Fax: 303-372-6626
E-mail: carolyn.coffin@uhcolorado.edu
Web: www.uchsc.edu

Program Information:
Program begins: September
Degrees offered: Certificate program, 12 months

Application Information:
Enrollment of program: 10

Financial Information:
Average cost of books: $350

Employment Profile:
% of students who pass the boards on their first try: 85
% employed within the first 6 months following graduation: 100

District of Columbia

George Washington University

2300 K Street, NW
Washington, DC 20037

Contact Information:
Telephone: 202-994-3650
Fax: 202-994-0247
E-mail: hspcxi@gwumc.edu
Web: www.gwumc.edu/healthsci/rs.htm

Program Information:
Program begins: August
Duration of program: 45 months

Application Information:
Enrollment of program: 18
Transfer students are accepted.

Financial Information:
Average cost of books: $1,200
% of students receiving aid: 78

Employment Profile:
% employed within the first 6 months following graduation: 100

Florida

Broward Community College

North Campus Building 41
1000 Coconut Creek Boulevard
Coconut Creek, FL 33066

Contact Information:
Telephone: 954-969-2089
Fax: 954-973-2348
Web: www.broward.ce.fl.us

Program Information:
Program begins: September
Degrees offered: Certificate program, 15 months; Associate's, 24 months

Application Information:
Enrollment of program: 12

Financial Information:
Tuition, resident: $1,548
Tuition, non-resident: $6,120
Average cost of books: $400

Employment Profile:
% of students who pass the boards on their first try: 97
% employed within the first 6 months following graduation: 100
Average starting salary: $32,500

Florida Hospital College of Health Sciences

800 Lake Estelle Drive
Orlando, FL 32803

Contact Information:
Telephone: 407-303-5733
Fax: 407-303-7820
Web: www.fhchs.edu

Program Information:
Program begins: May
Duration of program: 24 months

Valencia Community College

PO Box 3028
Orlando, FL 32802

Contact Information:
Telephone: 407-299-5000 ext. 1191
Fax: 407-299-5000
Web: www.valencia.cc.fl.us

Program Information:
Program begins: September
Duration of program: 24 months

Application Information:
Enrollment of program: 10

Financial Information:
Tuition, resident: $1,702
Tuition, non-resident: $6,179

Average cost of books: $700
% of students receiving aid: 20

Employment Profile:
% of students who pass the boards on their first try: 95
% employed within the first 6 months following graduation: 100
Average starting salary: $28,000

Georgia

Grady Health System
80 Butler Street Southeast
PO Box 26095
Atlanta, GA 30335

Contact Information:
Telephone: 404-616-5032
Fax: 404-616-3512

Program Information:
Program begins: September
Degrees offered: Certificate program, 12 months

Application Information:
Enrollment of program: 9

Financial Information:
Average cost of books: $400
% of students receiving aid: 85

Employment Profile:
% of students who pass the boards on their first try: 90
% employed within the first 6 months following graduation: 100
Average starting salary: $36,000

Medical College of Georgia
AE-1003
Augusta, GA 30912-0600

Contact Information:
Telephone: 706-721-3691
Fax: 706-721-8293
E-mail: ireyes@mail.mcg.edu
Web: www.mcg.edu

Program Information:
Program begins: August
Duration of program: 12 months

Financial Information:
Tuition, resident: $2,700
Tuition, non-resident: $9,942

Iowa

The University of Iowa Hospitals and Clinics
Radiology Department/C726 GH
200 Hawkins Drive
Iowa City, IA 52242-1077

Contact Information:
Telephone: 319-356-4871
Fax: 319-384-9574
E-mail: stephanie-ellingson@uiowa.edu
Web: www.vh.org

Program Information:
Program begins: September
Duration of program: 18 months

Application Information:
Enrollment of program: 7

Financial Information:
Tuition, resident: $3,000
Tuition, non-resident: $3,750
Average cost of books: $600

Employment Profile:
% of students who pass the boards on their first try: 95
% employed within the first 6 months following graduation: 100
Average starting salary: $31,000

Kentucky

West Kentucky Technical College
5200 Blandville Road
PO Box 7408
Paducah, KY 42002-7408

Contact Information:
Telephone: 502-554-6229
Fax: 502-554-6227
E-mail: avaughn@kctcs.net
Web: www.wkytech.com

Program Information:
Program begins: June
Degrees offered: Diploma, 18 months

Application Information:
Enrollment of program: 7
Transfer students are accepted.

Financial Information:
Tuition, resident: $960
Tuition, non-resident: $1,920
Average cost of books: $450
% of students receiving aid: 20

Employment Profile:
% of students who pass the boards on their first try: 100
% employed within the first 6 months following graduation: 100
Average starting salary: $30,000

Maryland

Johns Hopkins Hospital
Radiology Admin B-179
600 North Wolfe Street
Baltimore, MD 21287

Contact Information:
Telephone: 410-955-6198
Fax: 410-955-0059
E-mail: nyanke@jhmi.edu

Program Information:
Program begins: July
Duration of program: 14 months

Montgomery College
7600 Takoma Avenue
Takoma Park, MD 20912

Contact Information:
Telephone: 301-650-1431
Fax: 301-650-1335
E-mail: lzanin@mc.cc.md.us
Web: www.mc.cc.md.us

Program Information:
Program begins: September
Duration of program: 22 months
Evening or weekend classes are available.

Application Information:
Enrollment of program: 18
Transfer students are accepted.

Financial Information:
Tuition, resident: $2,380
Tuition, non-resident: $4,080
Average cost of books: $1,000
% of students receiving aid: 40

Employment Profile:
% of students who pass the boards on their first try: 87
% employed within the first 6 months following graduation: 100
Average starting salary: $40,000

University of Maryland Baltimore County
1000 Hilltop Circle
Baltimore, MD 21250

Contact Information:
Telephone: 410-455-2766
Fax: 410-455-1322
E-mail: dolk@umbc.edu
Web: www.gl.umbc.edu

Program Information:
Program begins: July
Degrees offered: Certificate program, 14 months

Application Information:
Enrollment of program: 30
Transfer students are accepted.

Financial Information:
Average cost of books: $500
% of students receiving aid: 50

Employment Profile:
% of students who pass the boards on their first try: 70
% employed within the first 6 months following graduation: 93
Average starting salary: $35,000

Massachusetts

Bunker Hill Community College
250 New Rutherford Avenue
Boston, MA 02129-2991

Contact Information:
Telephone: 617-228-2407
Fax: 617-228-2052
Web: www.bhcc.state.ma.us

Program Information:
Program begins: September
Duration of program: 24 months

Application Information:
Enrollment of program: 10

Financial Information:
Tuition, resident: $3,613
Tuition, non-resident: $10,718
Average cost of books: $500

Employment Profile:
% employed within the first 6 months following graduation: 80
Average starting salary: $30,000

Middlesex Community College—Bedford
Springs Road
Bedford, MA 01730

Contact Information:
Telephone: 781-280-3983
Web: www.middlesex.cc.ma.us

Program Information:
Program begins: September
Degrees offered: Certificate program, 12 months; Associate's, 24 months

Application Information:
Enrollment of program: 32
Transfer students are accepted.

Financial Information:
Tuition, resident: $3,060
Tuition, non-resident: $3,366
Average cost of books: $250
% of students receiving aid: 20

Employment Profile:
% of students who pass the boards on their first try: 90
% employed within the first 6 months following graduation: 100
Average starting salary: $35,000

Springfield Technical Community College
One Armory Square
Springfield, MA 01105

Contact Information:
Telephone: 413-755-4915
Fax: 413-733-0688
E-mail: dsloan@stcc.mass.edu
Web: www.stcc.mass.edu

Program Information:
Program begins: September
Duration of program: 22 months

Application Information:
Enrollment of program: 16

Financial Information:
Tuition, resident: $1,296
Tuition, non-resident: $7,056

Employment Profile:
% employed within the first 6 months following graduation: 86
Average starting salary: $34,000

Michigan

Henry Ford Hospital
2799 West Grand Boulevard
Detroit, MI 48202

Contact Information:
Telephone: 313-916-3514
Fax: 313-916-9450
E-mail: mike@rad.hfh.edu
Web: www.henryfordhealthsystem.org

Program Information:
Program begins: September
Duration of program: 15 months

Financial Information:
Average cost of books: $660

Employment Profile:
% of students who pass the boards on their first try: 75
% employed within the first 6 months following graduation: 100
Average starting salary: $32,000

Jackson Community College
2111 Emmons Road
Jackson, MI 49201

Contact Information:
Telephone: 517-796-8535
Fax: 517-796-8633
E-mail: lynne_schreiber@jackson.cc.mi.us

Program Information:
Program begins: May
Degrees offered: Certificate program, 15 months; Associate's, 30 months

Application Information:
Enrollment of program: 40
Transfer students are accepted.

Financial Information:
Tuition, resident: $1,881
Tuition, non-resident: $2,451
Average cost of books: $400
% of students receiving aid: 50

Employment Profile:
% of students who pass the boards on their first try: 90
% employed within the first 6 months following graduation: 100
Average starting salary: $32,000

Providence Hospital and Medical Centers
16001 West Nine Mile Road
Southfield, MI 48037

Contact Information:
Telephone: 248-424-5385
Fax: 248-424-5395

Program Information:
Program begins: September
Duration of program: 15 months

Application Information:
Enrollment of program: 4

Employment Profile:
% of students who pass the boards on their first try: 90
% employed within the first 6 months following graduation: 100
Average starting salary: $31,500

Minnesota

Mayo Clinic—Mayo Foundation
200 First Street Southwest
Rochester, MN 55905

Contact Information:
Telephone: 507-284-3169
Fax: 507-284-0656
E-mail: kuntz.kathryn@mayo.edu
Web: www.mayo.edu/hrs

Program Information:
Program begins: September
Degrees offered: Certificate program, 18-20 months

Application Information:
Enrollment of program: 40

Financial Information:
Average cost of books: $700
% of students receiving aid: 50

Employment Profile:
% of students who pass the boards on their first try: 100
% employed within the first 6 months following graduation: 100
Average starting salary: $35,000

Missouri

St. Louis Community College at Forest Park
5600 Oakland Avenue
St. Louis, MO 63110

Contact Information:
Telephone: 314-644-9399
Fax: 314-644-9752
E-mail: banderhub@fpmail.stlcc.cc.mo.us
Web: www.stlcc.mu.us

Program Information:
Program begins: August
Degrees offered: Certificate program, 12 months

Application Information:
Enrollment of program: 12

Financial Information:
Tuition, resident: $1,344
Tuition, non-resident: $2,144
Average cost of books: $500
% of students receiving aid: 40

Employment Profile:
% of students who pass the boards on their first try: 80-90
% employed within the first 6 months following graduation: 100
Average starting salary: $30,000

Nebraska

Nebraska Methodist College
8501 West Dodge Road
Omaha, NE 68114

Contact Information:
Telephone: 402-354-4851
Fax: 402-354-8875
E-mail: psulliv@nmhs.org
Web: www.methodistcollege.edu

Program Information:
Program begins: September
Degrees offered: Associate's, 24 months; Bachelor's, 48 months
Evening or weekend classes are available.

Application Information:
Enrollment of program: 10
Transfer students are accepted.

Financial Information:
Tuition, resident: $7,100
Tuition, non-resident: $8,900
Average cost of books: $300

Employment Profile:
% of students who pass the boards on their first try: 100
% employed within the first 6 months following graduation: 95
Average starting salary: $33,000

University of Nebraska Medical Center
Radiology Department/Ultrasound
981045 Nebraska Medical Center
Omaha, NE 68198-1045

Contact Information:
Telephone: 402-559-1189
Fax: 402-559-1011
Web: www.unmc.edu/alliedhealth/rste

Program Information:
Program begins: September
Duration of program: 12 months

Application Information:
Transfer students are accepted.

Financial Information:
Tuition, resident: $2,826
Tuition, non-resident: $7,677
Average cost of books: $770

Employment Profile:
% of students who pass the boards on their first try: 100
% employed within the first 6 months following graduation: 180
Average starting salary: $26,000

New Jersey

Gloucester County College
1400 Tanyard Road
Sewell, NJ 08080

Contact Information:
Telephone: 609-468-5000
Fax: 609-464-8463
Web: www.gccnj.edu

Program Information:
Program begins: September
Duration of program: 22 months

Financial Information:
Tuition, resident: $1,809
Tuition, non-resident: $7,236
Average cost of books: $600

Employment Profile:
% of students who pass the boards on their first try: 87
% employed within the first 6 months following graduation: 70
Average starting salary: $31,000

University of Medicine & Dentistry of New Jersey
School of Health Related Professions
65 Bergen Street
Newark, NJ 07107-3006

Contact Information:
Telephone: 908-889-2521
Fax: 908-889-2527
E-mail: silkowcy@umdnj.edu
Web: www.umdnj.edu

Program Information:
Program begins: July, December
Duration of program: 15 months

Financial Information:
Tuition, resident: $6,084
Tuition, non-resident: $8,112
Average cost of books: $850

Employment Profile:
% of students who pass the boards on their first try: 100
% employed within the first 6 months following graduation: 80
Average starting salary: $36,000

New York

Hudson Valley Community College
80 Vandenburgh Avenue
Troy, NY 12180

Contact Information:
Telephone: 518-629-7345
Fax: 518-629-7542
Web: www.hvcc.edu

Program Information:
Program begins: August
Duration of program: 12 months

Application Information:
Enrollment of program: 18

Financial Information:
Tuition, resident: $3,200
Tuition, non-resident: $6,400
Average cost of books: $600
% of students receiving aid: 100

Employment Profile:
% of students who pass the boards on their first try: 95
% employed within the first 6 months following graduation: 100
Average starting salary: $28,000

New York University
11 West 42nd Street
Room 518
New York, NY 10036

Contact Information:
Telephone: 212-790-1663
Fax: 212-790-1669
E-mail: weinberg.kerry@nyu.edu
Web: www.nyu.edu

Program Information:
Program begins: September
Degrees offered: Associate's, 21 months

Application Information:
Enrollment of program: 30
Transfer students are accepted.

Financial Information:
Average cost of books: $400
% of students receiving aid: 100

Employment Profile:
% of students who pass the boards on their first try: 85
% employed within the first 6 months following graduation: 100
Average starting salary: $36,000

Rochester Institute of Technology
85 Lomb Memorial Drive
Rochester, NY 14623-5603

Contact Information:
Telephone: 716-475-2241
Fax: 716-475-5809
E-mail: hhgscl@rit.edu
Web: www.rit.edu

Program Information:
Program begins: September
Degrees offered: Certificate program, 12 months; Bachelor's, 48 months
Evening or weekend classes are available.

Application Information:
Enrollment of program: 20

Financial Information:
Tuition: $15,375

Employment Profile:
% of students who pass the boards on their first try: 95
% employed within the first 6 months following graduation: 99
Average starting salary: $33,500

SUNY Health Science Center—Brooklyn

College of Health Related Professions
450 Clarkson Avenue, Box 1192
Brooklyn, NY 11203

Contact Information:
Telephone: 718-270-7765
Fax: 718-270-7746
E-mail: jmiller@netmail.hscbklyn.edu
Web: www.hscbklyn.edu

Program Information:
Program begins: August
Duration of program: 22 months

Financial Information:
Tuition, resident: $4,496
Tuition, non-resident: $11,068

Employment Profile:
% employed within the first 6 months following graduation: 99
Average starting salary: $40,000

Western Suffolk BOCES

Northport VA Medical Center
79 Middleville Road/Building 62
Northport, NY 11768

Contact Information:
Telephone: 516-261-4400 ext. 7670
Fax: 516-266-6092

Program Information:
Program begins: July
Duration of program: 24 months

Financial Information:
Tuition: $4,140

North Carolina

Caldwell Community College & Technical Institute

2855 Hickory Boulevard
Hudson, NC 28638

Contact Information:
Telephone: 828-726-2322
Fax: 828-726-2489
E-mail: cccti.kwatts@caldwell.cc.nc.us
Web: www.caldwell.cc.nc.us

Program Information:
Program begins: August
Duration of program: 21 months

Application Information:
Enrollment of program: 15
Transfer students are accepted.

Financial Information:
Tuition, resident: $1,873
Tuition, non-resident: $1,883
Average cost of books: $600
% of students receiving aid: 50

Employment Profile:
% of students who pass the boards on their first try: 75
% employed within the first 6 months following graduation: 100
Average starting salary: $32,000

Forsyth Technical Community College

2100 Silas Creek Parkway
Winston-Salem, NC 27103

Contact Information:
Telephone: 336-723-0371 ext. 7291
Fax: 336-748-9395
Web: www.forsyth.tec.nc.us

Program Information:
Program begins: August
Duration of program: 21 months

Application Information:
Enrollment of program: 8
Transfer students are accepted.

Financial Information:
Tuition, resident: $1,000
Tuition, non-resident: $7,500
Average cost of books: $600
% of students receiving aid: 20

Employment Profile:
% employed within the first 6 months following graduation: 100
Average starting salary: $32,000

Pitt Community College

PO Drawer 7007
Highway 11 South
Greenville, NC 27835-7007

Contact Information:
Telephone: 919-321-4254
Fax: 919-321-4451
E-mail: ljacobso@pcc.pitt.cc.nc.us

Program Information:
Program begins: August
Duration of program: 12 months

Application Information:
Enrollment of program: 28

Financial Information:
Tuition, resident: $720
Tuition, non-resident: $6,031

Ohio

Kettering College of Medical Arts

3737 Southern Boulevard
Kettering, OH 45429

Contact Information:
Telephone: 937-296-7201 ext. 5662
Fax: 937-297-8059
E-mail: susan.price@ketthealth.com
Web: www.kcma.edu

Program Information:
Program begins: August
Duration of program: 24 months

Application Information:
Enrollment of program: 34

Financial Information:
Average cost of books: $600

Employment Profile:
% of students who pass the boards on their first try: 95
% employed within the first 6 months following graduation: 100
Average starting salary: $31,200

Lorain County Community College

1005 North Abbe Road
Elyria, OH 44035

Contact Information:
Telephone: 440-365-5222 ext. 4032
Fax: 440-366-9116
E-mail: cpeneff@lorain.ccc.edu
Web: www.lorain.ccc.edu

Program Information:
Program begins: August
Degrees offered: Associate's, 22 months

Application Information:
Enrollment of program: 75
Transfer students are accepted.

Financial Information:
Tuition, resident: $5,500
Tuition, non-resident: $14,000
Average cost of books: $600

Employment Profile:
% of students who pass the boards on their first try: 80
% employed within the first 6 months following graduation: 100
Average starting salary: $31,000

Owens Community College

PO Box 10,000
Oregon Road
Toledo, OH 43699-1947

Contact Information:
Telephone: 419-661-7260
Fax: 419-661-7251
E-mail: pbutler@owens.cc.oh.us
Web: www.owens.cc.oh.us

Program Information:
Program begins: June
Duration of program: 24 months
Evening or weekend classes are available.

Financial Information:
Tuition, resident: $2,060
Tuition, non-resident: $3,860
Average cost of books: $675
% of students receiving aid: 100

Employment Profile:
% employed within the first 6 months following graduation: 100
Average starting salary: $32,500

Oklahoma

University of Oklahoma Health Sciences Center

PO Box 26901
Oklahoma City, OK 73190

Contact Information:
Telephone: 405-271-6477
Fax: 405-271-1424
E-mail: jean-spitz@uohsc.edu
Web: www.uohsc.edu

Program Information:
Program begins: August
Degrees offered: Bachelor's, 24 months

Application Information:
Enrollment of program: 20
Transfer students are accepted.

Financial Information:
Tuition, resident: $2,300
Tuition, non-resident: $6,476
Average cost of books: $600

Employment Profile:
% of students who pass the boards on their first try: 90
% employed within the first 6 months following graduation: 100
Average starting salary: $40,000

Pennsylvania

Community College of Allegheny County

595 Beatty Road
Monroeville, PA 15146

Contact Information:
Telephone: 724-325-6731
Fax: 724-325-6701
E-mail: lgigande@ccac.edu
Web: www.ccac.edu

Program Information:
Program begins: August
Duration of program: 20 months

Application Information:
Enrollment of program: 38
Transfer students are accepted.

Financial Information:
Tuition, resident: $2,108
Tuition, non-resident: $6,324
Average cost of books: $88
% of students receiving aid: 60

Employment Profile:
% of students who pass the boards on their first try: 65
% employed within the first 6 months following graduation: 90
Average starting salary: $28,000

Lancaster Institute for Health Education

Lancaster General Hospital
143 East Lemon Street
Lancaster, PA 17602

Contact Information:
Telephone: 717-290-4912 ext. 7045
Fax: 717-290-5970
E-mail: rmhess@lha.org
Web: www.lha.org

Program Information:
Program begins: July
Duration of program: 12 months

Application Information:
Enrollment of program: 5

Financial Information:
Average cost of books: $500

Employment Profile:
% of students who pass the boards on their first try: 100
Average starting salary: $32,000

Thomas Jefferson University

130 South Ninth Street/Suite 1008
Philadelphia, PA 19107

Contact Information:
Telephone: 215-503-8724
Fax: 215-503-1031
E-mail: michael.hartman@mail.tju.edu
Web: www.jeffline.tju.edu

Program Information:
Program begins: September
Duration of program: 12 months

Tennessee

Chattanooga State Technical Community College

535 Chestnut Street
Suite 112
Chattanooga, TN 37402

Contact Information:
Telephone: 423-697-3341
Fax: 423-697-3325
E-mail: arnold@cstcc.cc.tn.us
Web: www.cstcc.cc.tn.us

Program Information:
Program begins: August
Duration of program: 12 months

Application Information:
Enrollment of program: 15
Transfer students are accepted.

Financial Information:
Tuition, resident: $1,533
Tuition, non-resident: $5,594
Average cost of books: $750
% of students receiving aid: 30

Employment Profile:
% of students who pass the boards on their first try: 89
% employed within the first 6 months following graduation: 95
Average starting salary: $30,000

Texas

Austin Community College

1020 Grove Boulevard
Austin, TX 78741-3300

Contact Information:
Telephone: 512-223-6286
Fax: 512-223-6700
E-mail: ginas@austin.cc.tx.us
Web: www.austin.cc.tx.us

Program Information:
Program begins: August
Duration of program: 16 months

Application Information:
Enrollment of program: 20
Transfer students are accepted.

Financial Information:
Tuition, resident: $1,100
Average cost of books: $650

Employment Profile:
% of students who pass the boards on their first try: 83
% employed within the first 6 months following graduation: 100
Average starting salary: $36,000

Del Mar College

101 Baldwin and Ayers Streets
Corpus Christi, TX 78404

Contact Information:
Telephone: 361-698-1909
Fax: 361-698-1598
Web: www.delmar.edu

Program Information:
Program begins: August
Degrees offered: Diploma, 24 months

Application Information:
Enrollment of program: 11
Transfer students are accepted.

Financial Information:
Tuition, resident: $512
Tuition, non-resident: $768
Average cost of books: $875

Employment Profile:
% of students who pass the boards on their first try: 60
% employed within the first 6 months following graduation: 98
Average starting salary: $30,000

El Centro College

Main and Lamar Streets
Dallas, TX 75202

Contact Information:
Telephone: 214-860-2303
Fax: 214-860-2268
E-mail: jdb5529@dcccd.edu
Web: www.dcccd.edu

Program Information:
Program begins: August
Degrees offered: Certificate program, 18 months; Diploma, 28 months

Application Information:
Enrollment of program: 10
Transfer students are accepted.

Financial Information:
Tuition, resident: $1,767
Tuition, non-resident: $2,287
Average cost of books: $800
% of students receiving aid: 20

Employment Profile:
% of students who pass the boards on their first try: 85
% employed within the first 6 months following graduation: 100
Average starting salary: $40,000

Tyler Junior College
PO Box 9020
Tyler, TX 75711

Contact Information:
Telephone: 903-510-2668
Fax: 903-510-2880
E-mail: pbro@tyler.tic.cc.tx.us
Web: www.tyler.cc.tx.us

Program Information:
Program begins: May
Duration of program: 16 months

Financial Information:
Tuition, resident: $637
Tuition, non-resident: $817
% of students receiving aid: 25

Employment Profile:
% of students who pass the boards on their first try: 90
% employed within the first 6 months following graduation: 90
Average starting salary: $30,000

Virginia

Southwest Virginia Community College
PO Box SVCC
Richlands, VA 24641-1510

Contact Information:
Telephone: 540-964-7642
Fax: 540-964-7715
E-mail: linda_brewster@sw.cc.va.us
Web: www.sw.cc.va.us

Program Information:
Program begins: August
Duration of program: 21 months

Financial Information:
Tuition, resident: $2,035
Tuition, non-resident: $6,628

Tidewater Community College
1700 College Cresent
Virginia Beach, VA 23456

Contact Information:
Telephone: 757-822-7271
Fax: 757-427-1338
E-mail: fcjonef@tc.cc.va.us
Web: www.tc.cc.va.us

Program Information:
Program begins: August
Degrees offered: Diploma, 16 months

Application Information:
Enrollment of program: 15
Transfer students are accepted.

Financial Information:
Tuition, resident: $2,184
Tuition, non-resident: $6,777
Average cost of books: $350

Employment Profile:
% of students who pass the boards on their first try: 85
% employed within the first 6 months following graduation: 100
Average starting salary: $30,000

Washington

Bellevue Community College
3000 Landerholm Circle Southeast
Room B243
Bellevue, WA 98007-6484

Contact Information:
Telephone: 425-641-2316
Fax: 425-603-4193
E-mail: apolin@bcc.ctc.edu

Program Information:
Program begins: April, October
Duration of program: 24 months

Application Information:
Enrollment of program: 40

Financial Information:
Tuition, resident: $4,344
Tuition, non-resident: $16,744
Average cost of books: $450
% of students receiving aid: 25

Employment Profile:
% employed within the first 6 months following graduation: 100
Average starting salary: $36,000

Seattle University
900 Broadway
Seattle, WA 98122-4460

Contact Information:
Telephone: 206-296-5960
Fax: 206-296-6429
E-mail: jpope@seattleu.edu
Web: www.seattleu.edu

Program Information:
Program begins: September
Duration of program: 39 months

Application Information:
Enrollment of program: 45
Transfer students are accepted.

Financial Information:
Tuition: $16,110
Average cost of books: $600
% of students receiving aid: 70

Employment Profile:
% of students who pass the boards on their first try: 90
% employed within the first 6 months following graduation: 30
Average starting salary: $39,000

West Virginia

College of West Virginia
PO Box AG
Beckley, WV 25801

Contact Information:
Telephone: 304-253-7351
Fax: 304-253-0789
E-mail: mhdeib@cwv.edu
Web: www.cwv.edu

Program Information:
Program begins: September
Duration of program: 14 months

Application Information:
Enrollment of program: 30
Transfer students are accepted.

Financial Information:
Tuition, resident: $7,790
Tuition, non-resident: $9,690
Average cost of books: $600
% of students receiving aid: 90

Employment Profile:
% of students who pass the boards on their first try: 90
% employed within the first 6 months following graduation: 25
Average starting salary: $14,000

West Virginia University Hospitals
PO Box 8062
Medical Center Drive
Morgantown, WV 26506

Contact Information:
Telephone: 304-598-4254
Fax: 304-598-4702
E-mail: williamsd@rcbhsc.wvu.edu
Web: www.hsc.wvu.edu

Program Information:
Program begins: July, December
Duration of program: 18 months

Application Information:
Enrollment of program: 3

Financial Information:
Average cost of books: $700
% of students receiving aid: 50

Employment Profile:
% of students who pass the boards on their first try: 80
% employed within the first 6 months following graduation: 95
Average starting salary: $31,000

Wisconsin

Chippewa Valley Technical College
620 West Clairemont Avenue
Eau Claire, WI 54701

Contact Information:
Telephone: 715-833-6430
Fax: 715-833-6470
E-mail: tsalava@chippewa.tec.wi.us
Web: www.chippewa.tec.wi.us

Program Information:
Program begins: August
Duration of program: 24 months

Application Information:
Enrollment of program: 34
Transfer students are accepted.

Financial Information:
Tuition, resident: $2,124
Tuition, non-resident: $16,344
Average cost of books: $1,000

Employment Profile:
% employed within the first 6 months following graduation: 95
Average starting salary: $34,000

Columbia-St. Mary's Hospital
2323 North Lake Drive
Milwaukee, WI 53201

Contact Information:
Telephone: 414-291-1156
Fax: 414-291-1720

Program Information:
Program begins: October
Degrees offered: Certificate program, 18 months

Application Information:
Enrollment of program: 6
Transfer students are accepted.

Financial Information:
Tuition, resident: $2,000
Average cost of books: $900

Employment Profile:
% of students who pass the boards on their first try: 75
% employed within the first 6 months following graduation: 100
Average starting salary: $40,000

St. Luke's Medical Center
2900 West Oklahoma Avenue
Milwaukee, WI 53215

Contact Information:
Telephone: 414-649-6689
Fax: 414-649-7981

Program Information:
Program begins: September
Degrees offered: Certificate program, 24 months

Application Information:
Enrollment of program: 11

Financial Information:
Average cost of books: $600

Employment Profile:
% employed within the first 6 months following graduation: 100
Average starting salary: $40,000

University of Wisconsin Hospital & Clinics
Department of Radiology
600 Highland Avenue
Madison, WI 537923252

Contact Information:
Telephone: 608-263-9033
Fax: 608-263-9208
Web: www.hosp.wisc.edu

Program Information:
Program begins: January, April
Duration of program: 16 months

Financial Information:
Tuition, resident: $2,143
Tuition, non-resident: $2,457

Nuclear Medicine Technologist

Arkansas

University of Arkansas for Medical Sciences
4301 West Markham Street
Little Rock, AR 72205

Contact Information:
Telephone: 501-686-6848
Fax: 501-686-6513
E-mail: pickettmarthaw@exchange.uams.edu
Web: www.uams.edu/chrp/nuc_med.htm

Program Information:
Program begins: August
Duration of program: 12 months

Application Information:
Transfer students are accepted.

Financial Information:
Tuition, resident: $3,210
Tuition, non-resident: $8,010
Average cost of books: $500
% of students receiving aid: 80

Employment Profile:
% of students who pass the boards on their first try: 95
% employed within the first 6 months following graduation: 90
Average starting salary: $35,000

Connecticut

Gateway Community-Technical College
88 Bassett Road
North Haven, CT 06473

Contact Information:
Telephone: 203-234-3360
Fax: 203-234-3343
E-mail: gw_murphy@commnet.edu
Web: www.gwctc.commnet.edu

Program Information:
Program begins: July, September
Duration of program: 24 months

Application Information:
Transfer students are accepted.

Financial Information:
Tuition, resident: $1,814
Tuition, non-resident: $5,438

Employment Profile:
% of students who pass the boards on their first try: 100
% employed within the first 6 months following graduation: 100
Average starting salary: $37,000

Florida

Broward Community College
Center for Health Sciences Education Building 41-137
1000 Coconut Creek Boulevard
Coconut Creek, FL 33066

Contact Information:
Telephone: 954-969-2083
Fax: 954-973-2348
E-mail: lharriso@broward.cc.fl.us
Web: www.broward.cc.fl.us

Program Information:
Program begins: September
Duration of program: 12 months

Application Information:
Enrollment of program: 15
Transfer students are accepted.

Financial Information:
Tuition, resident: $1,103
Tuition, non-resident: $4,020
Average cost of books: $500
% of students receiving aid: 50

Employment Profile:
% of students who pass the boards on their first try: 80
% employed within the first 6 months following graduation: 75
Average starting salary: $30,000

Hillsborough Community College
PO Box 30030
Tampa, FL 33630

Contact Information:
Telephone: 813-253-7418
Fax: 813-253-7491
E-mail: lgibson@hcc.cc.fl.us
Web: www.hcc.cc.fl.us

Program Information:
Program begins: August
Duration of program: 24 months

Application Information:
Transfer students are accepted.

Financial Information:
Tuition, resident: $1,719
Tuition, non-resident: $6,247

Employment Profile:
% of students who pass the boards on their first try: 90
% employed within the first 6 months following graduation: 100
Average starting salary: $30,500

Santa Fe Community College
3000 Northwest 83rd Street
Gainesville, FL 32606-6200

Contact Information:
Telephone: 352-395-5702
Fax: 352-395-5711
E-mail: ed.dice@santafe.cc.fl.us
Web: www.inst.santafe.cc.fl.us

Program Information:
Program begins: August
Duration of program: 22 months

Application Information:
Enrollment of program: 22
Transfer students are accepted.

Financial Information:
Tuition, resident: $3,112
Tuition, non-resident: $11,584
Average cost of books: $415
% of students receiving aid: 50

Employment Profile:
% of students who pass the boards on their first try: 100
% employed within the first 6 months following graduation: 90
Average starting salary: $27,000

University of Miami/Jackson Memorial Hospital
1611 Northwest 12th Avenue
Miami, FL 33136

Contact Information:
Telephone: 502-852-5624
Fax: 502-852-4597

Program Information:
Program begins: July
Degrees offered: Certificate program, 15 months

Application Information:
Enrollment of program: 9

Financial Information:
Tuition, resident: $1,800
Tuition, non-resident: $2,000
Average cost of books: $300

Employment Profile:
% employed within the first 6 months following graduation: 100
Average starting salary: $30,000

Georgia

Medical College of Georgia
1120 15th Street Building AE 1003
Augusta, GA 30912

Contact Information:
Telephone: 706-721-3691
Fax: 706-721-8293
E-mail: gpassmor@mail.mcg.edu
Web: www.mcg.edu

Program Information:
Program begins: September
Duration of program: 12 months
Evening or weekend classes are available.

Application Information:
Enrollment of program: 12
Transfer students are accepted.

Financial Information:
Tuition, resident: $3,621
Tuition, non-resident: $14,484
Average cost of books: $600

Employment Profile:
% of students who pass the boards on their first try: 90
% employed within the first 6 months following graduation: 100
Average starting salary: $38,000

Illinois

Edward Hines Jr. VA Hospital
Fifth Avenue and Roosevelt Road/115 F
Hines, IL 60141

Contact Information:
Telephone: 708-202-8387 ext. 21984
Fax: 708-202-2390
E-mail: mcdonald.nancy@hines.va.gov
Web: www.unis.luc.edu

Program Information:
Program begins: June
Duration of program: 12 months

Application Information:
Enrollment of program: 6
Transfer students are accepted.

Financial Information:
Average cost of books: $200
% of students receiving aid: 50

Employment Profile:
% of students who pass the boards on their first try: 98
% employed within the first 6 months following graduation: 100
Average starting salary: $34,000

Triton College
2000 North Fifth Avenue
River Grove, IL 60171

Contact Information:
Telephone: 708-456-0300
Fax: 708-583-3336
E-mail: cchett@triton.cc.il.us
Web: www.triton.cc.il.us

Program Information:
Program begins: August
Degrees offered: Associate's, 22 months

Application Information:
Enrollment of program: 34
Transfer students are accepted.

Financial Information:
Tuition, resident: $1,618
Tuition, non-resident: $4,973
Average cost of books: $80
% of students receiving aid: 15

Employment Profile:
% of students who pass the boards on their first try: 95
% employed within the first 6 months following graduation: 100
Average starting salary: $35,000

Iowa

The University of Iowa Hospitals and Clinics
Department of Radiology
Iowa City, IA 52242-1009

Contact Information:
Telephone: 319-356-2954
Fax: 319-356-2220
E-mail: anthony-knight@uiowa.edu
Web: www.uiowa.edu

Program Information:
Program begins: July
Duration of program: 12 months

Application Information:
Enrollment of program: 8

Financial Information:
Tuition, resident: $3,088
Tuition, non-resident: $11,336
Average cost of books: $400
% of students receiving aid: 100

Employment Profile:
% of students who pass the boards on their first try: 100
% employed within the first 6 months following graduation: 87
Average starting salary: $36,000

Kansas

University of Kansas Medical Center

3901 Rainbow Boulevard
Kansas City, KS 661607234

Contact Information:
Telephone: 801-581-2369
Fax: 801-585-2403
E-mail: tcrain@kumc.edu
Web: www.kumc.edu

Program Information:
Program begins: August
Duration of program: 12 months

Financial Information:
Average cost of books: $400
% of students receiving aid: 30

Employment Profile:
Average starting salary: $38,000

Louisiana

Delgado Community College

501 City Park Avenue
New Orleans, LA 70119

Contact Information:
Telephone: 504-483-4015
Fax: 504-483-4609
E-mail: ethoma@pop3.dcc.edu
Web: www.dcc.edu

Program Information:
Program begins: January, August
Duration of program: 12 months

Application Information:
Enrollment of program: 8
Transfer students are accepted.

Financial Information:
Tuition, resident: $1,600
Tuition, non-resident: $4,300
Average cost of books: $200

Employment Profile:
% of students who pass the boards on their first try: 100
% employed within the first 6 months following graduation: 100
Average starting salary: $36,000

Maine

Central Maine Medical Center

300 Main Street
Lewiston, ME 04240

Contact Information:
Telephone: 207-795-2431

Program Information:
Program begins: September
Duration of program: 12 months

Application Information:
Enrollment of program: 10

Maryland

Johns Hopkins Hospital

600 North Wolfe Street
Radiology Admin Block B179
Baltimore, MD 21287

Contact Information:
Telephone: 410-955-8422
Fax: 410-955-0059
E-mail: jkrhine@rad.jhu.edu
Web: www.imagingschools.rad.jhmi.edu

Program Information:
Program begins: August
Duration of program: 14 months

Application Information:
Transfer students are accepted.

Financial Information:
Average cost of books: $300

Employment Profile:
% of students who pass the boards on their first try: 90
% employed within the first 6 months following graduation: 100
Average starting salary: $27,000

Naval School of Health Sciences—Maryland

8903 Wisconsin Avenue
Bethesda, MD 20889-5611

Contact Information:
Telephone: 301-319-4715
Fax: 301-295-0621
E-mail: fcarroll@nsh10.med.navy.mil
Web: nshs.med.navy.mil

Program Information:
Program begins: October
Duration of program: 12 months

Employment Profile:
% of students who pass the boards on their first try: 99
% employed within the first 6 months following graduation: 100

Prince George's Community College

301 Largo Road
Largo, MD 20774

Contact Information:
Telephone: 301-322-0733
Fax: 301-386-7528
E-mail: jh326@pgstumail.pg.cc.md.us
Web: www.pg.cc.md.us

Program Information:
Program begins: August, September
Duration of program: 13 months
Evening or weekend classes are available.

Application Information:
Transfer students are accepted.

Financial Information:
Tuition, resident: $2,800
Tuition, non-resident: $4,700
Average cost of books: $350

Employment Profile:
% of students who pass the boards on their first try: 95
% employed within the first 6 months following graduation: 75
Average starting salary: $33,000

Massachusetts

Massachusetts College of Pharmacy & Allied Health Science

179 Longwood Avenue
Boston, MA 02115

Contact Information:
Telephone: 617-732-2933
Fax: 617-732-2801
E-mail: gamtelli@mcp.edu
Web: www.mcp.edu

Program Information:
Program begins: August
Duration of program: 36 months
Evening or weekend classes are available.

Application Information:
Enrollment of program: 50
Transfer students are accepted.

Financial Information:
% of students receiving aid: 76

University of Mass Medical Center—Worcester State College

55 Lake Avenue North
Worcester, MA 01655

Contact Information:
Telephone: 513-558-2018
Fax: 513-558-6002
Web: www.worc.mass.edu

Program Information:
Program begins: August
Duration of program: 12 months

Application Information:
Enrollment of program: 7
Transfer students are accepted.

Financial Information:
Tuition, resident: $2,978
Tuition, non-resident: $6,450

Employment Profile:
% of students who pass the boards on their first try: 95
% employed within the first 6 months following graduation: 50
Average starting salary: $33,000

Michigan

William Beaumont Hospital

3601 West 13 Mile Road
Royal Oak, MI 48073-6769

Contact Information:
Telephone: 248-551-4125
Fax: 248-551-0768
E-mail: mpremo@beaumont.edu
Web: www.beaumont.edu

Program Information:
Program begins: August
Duration of program: 14 months

Application Information:
Enrollment of program: 8

Employment Profile:
% of students who pass the boards on their first try: 100
% employed within the first 6 months following graduation: 100
Average starting salary: $32,000

Minnesota

Mayo Clinic—Mayo Foundation

School of Health Related Sciences
200 First Street Southwest
Rochester, MN 55905

Contact Information:
Telephone: 507-284-3245
Fax: 507-284-0656
E-mail: hockert.nancy@mayo.edu
Web: www.mayo.edu

Program Information:
Program begins: June
Duration of program: 12 months

Application Information:
Enrollment of program: 8
Transfer students are accepted.

Financial Information:
Average cost of books: $125

Employment Profile:
% employed within the first 6 months following graduation: 100

St. Mary's University of Minnesota

700 Terrace Heights #10
Winona, MN 55987-1399

Contact Information:
Telephone: 507-457-1546
Fax: 507-457-6986
E-mail: dalsum@smumn.edu
Web: www.smumn.edu

Program Information:
Program begins: August
Duration of program: 48 months

Application Information:
Enrollment of program: 6
Transfer students are accepted.

Financial Information:
Average cost of books: $250
% of students receiving aid: 10

Employment Profile:
% of students who pass the boards on their first try: 85
% employed within the first 6 months following graduation: 90
Average starting salary: $34,000

Mississippi

University of Mississippi Medical Center

2500 North State Street
Jackson, MS 39216

Contact Information:
Telephone: 973-972-6422
Fax: 973-972-7024
E-mail: jvanders@radiology.umsmed.edu

Program Information:
Program begins: September
Duration of program: 12 months

Employment Profile:
% of students who pass the boards on their first try: 100
% employed within the first 6 months following graduation: 100

Missouri

Research Medical Center

2316 East Meyer Boulevard
Kansas City, MO 64132

Contact Information:
Telephone: 816-276-4235
Fax: 816-276-3138
Web: www.healthmidwest.org

Program Information:
Program begins: January, July
Duration of program: 12 months

Application Information:
Enrollment of program: 6

Employment Profile:
% of students who pass the boards on their first try: 98
% employed within the first 6 months following graduation: 99

University of Missouri—Columbia

504 Lewis Hall
Columbia, MO 65211

Contact Information:
Telephone: 601-984-2585
Fax: 601-984-2502
E-mail: galenj@health.missouri.edu
Web: www.hsc.missouri.edu

Program Information:
Program begins: August
Duration of program: 24 months
Evening or weekend classes are available.

Application Information:
Enrollment of program: 9
Transfer students are accepted.

Financial Information:
Tuition, resident: $4,280
Tuition, non-resident: $11,723
% of students receiving aid: 75

Employment Profile:
% of students who pass the boards on their first try: 100
% employed within the first 6 months following graduation: 100
Average starting salary: $37,000

Nebraska

University of Nebraska Medical Center

981045 Nebraska Medical Center
Omaha, NE 68198-1045

Contact Information:
Telephone: 573-882-8011
Fax: 573-884-1490
E-mail: cldworak@unmc.edu
Web: www.unmc.edu/alliedhealth/rste

Program Information:
Program begins: August
Degrees offered: Bachelor's, 24 months

Application Information:
Enrollment of program: 10
Transfer students are accepted.

Financial Information:
Tuition, resident: $3,490
Tuition, non-resident: $9,500
Average cost of books: $1,500
% of students receiving aid: 100

Employment Profile:
% of students who pass the boards on their first try: 100
% employed within the first 6 months following graduation: 100
Average starting salary: $30,000

New Jersey

Gloucester County College

1400 Tanyard Road
Sewell, NJ 08080

Contact Information:
Telephone: 609-468-5000
Fax: 609-464-8463
Web: www.gcc.cc.nj.us

Program Information:
Program begins: August
Duration of program: 21 months

Financial Information:
Tuition, resident: $2,322
Tuition, non-resident: $2,365
Average cost of books: $400

Employment Profile:
% of students who pass the boards on their first try: 100
% employed within the first 6 months following graduation: 90
Average starting salary: $34,000

University of Medicine & Dentistry of New Jersey
School of Health Related Professions
65 Bergen Street
Newark, NJ 07107-3006

Contact Information:
Telephone: 913-588-6858
Fax: 915-588-1823
E-mail: tetersms@umdnj.edu
Web: www.umdnj.edu/shrpweb

Program Information:
Program begins: September
Duration of program: 15 months

Application Information:
Enrollment of program: 8

Financial Information:
Average cost of books: $600
% of students receiving aid: 50

Employment Profile:
Average starting salary: $36,000

New York

Institute of Allied Medical Professions
405 Park Avenue
Suite 501
New York, NY 10022-4405

Contact Information:
Telephone: 212-758-1410
Fax: 212-758-1424

Program Information:
Program begins: August
Duration of program: 12 months
Evening or weekend classes are available.

Application Information:
Enrollment of program: 24

Employment Profile:
% of students who pass the boards on their first try: 99
% employed within the first 6 months following graduation: 86
Average starting salary: $49,500

Molloy College
1000 Hempstead Avenue
Rockville Centre, NY 11571-5002

Contact Information:
Telephone: 516-678-5000 ext. 6462
Fax: 516-256-2252
Web: www.molloy.edu

Program Information:
Program begins: September
Degrees offered: Associate's, 21 months

Application Information:
Enrollment of program: 24

Financial Information:
Tuition: $11,900
Average cost of books: $200
% of students receiving aid: 75

Employment Profile:
% of students who pass the boards on their first try: 100
% employed within the first 6 months following graduation: 100
Average starting salary: $42,000

Northport VA Medical Center
79 Middleville Road
Northport, NY 11768

Contact Information:
Telephone: 516-261-4400 ext. 7359

Program Information:
Program begins: July
Duration of program: 24 months

Application Information:
Enrollment of program: 7

Financial Information:
Tuition, resident: $750

Rochester Institute of Technology
Department of Allied Health Sciences
85 Lomb Memorial Drive
Rochester, NY 14623

Contact Information:
Telephone: 716-475-5117
Fax: 716-475-5809
E-mail: kmw4088@rit.edu
Web: www.rit.edu

Program Information:
Program begins: July
Duration of program: 12 months

Application Information:
Transfer students are accepted.

Financial Information:
Average cost of books: $700
% of students receiving aid: 70

Employment Profile:
% of students who pass the boards on their first try: 96
% employed within the first 6 months following graduation: 95
Average starting salary: $34,000

St. Vincent's Hospital & Medical Center of New York
153 West 11th Street
New York, NY 10011

Contact Information:
Telephone: 212-604-8716
Fax: 212-604-3119
E-mail: samy@nucmedicine.com
Web: www.nucmedicine.com

Program Information:
Program begins: January, August
Duration of program: 15 months

SUNY at Buffalo
105 Parker Hall
Buffalo, NY 14214-3007

Contact Information:
Telephone: 716-838-5889 ext. 115
Fax: 716-838-4918
E-mail: elpida@nucmed.buffalo.edu
Web: www.nucmed.buffalo.edu/nmt

Program Information:
Program begins: September
Duration of program: 18 months

Application Information:
Enrollment of program: 24
Transfer students are accepted.

Financial Information:
Tuition, resident: $4,510
Tuition, non-resident: $9,410
Average cost of books: $300

Employment Profile:
% of students who pass the boards on their first try: 100
% employed within the first 6 months following graduation: 75
Average starting salary: $42,000

North Carolina

Caldwell Community College & Technical Institute
2855 Hickory Boulevard
Hudson, NC 28638

Contact Information:
Telephone: 828-726-2356
Fax: 828-726-2489
E-mail: jcouncil@caldwell.cc.nc.us
Web: www.caldwell.cc.nc.us

Program Information:
Program begins: September
Duration of program: 21 months

Application Information:
Transfer students are accepted.

Financial Information:
Tuition, resident: $1,739
Tuition, non-resident: $11,034
Average cost of books: $150

Employment Profile:
% of students who pass the boards on their first try: 100
% employed within the first 6 months following graduation: 85
Average starting salary: $32,000

Ohio

St. Elizabeth Health Center
1044 Belmont Avenue
Youngstown, OH 44501

Contact Information:
Telephone: 330-480-3266
Web: www.stemc.org

Program Information:
Program begins: September
Degrees offered: Certificate program, 24 months

Application Information:
Enrollment of program: 10

Financial Information:
Average cost of books: $350

Employment Profile:
% of students who pass the boards on their first try: 100
% employed within the first 6 months following graduation: 100
Average starting salary: $32,000

The University of Findlay
1000 North Main Street
Findlay, OH 45840

Contact Information:
Telephone: 419-424-4708
Fax: 419-424-4822
E-mail: nmi@findlay.edu
Web: www.findlay.edu

Program Information:
Program begins: August
Duration of program: 12 months

Application Information:
Enrollment of program: 17
Transfer students are accepted.

Financial Information:
Average cost of books: $500

Employment Profile:
% employed within the first 6 months following graduation: 50
Average starting salary: $30,000

University of Cincinnati
College of Allied Health Sciences
PO Box 670394
Cincinnati, OH 45267

Contact Information:
Telephone: 305-585-6345
Fax: 305-585-8538
E-mail: alan.vespie@uc.edu
Web: www.uc.edu

Program Information:
Program begins: September
Degrees offered: Bachelor's, 48 months

Application Information:
Enrollment of program: 15
Transfer students are accepted.

Financial Information:
Tuition, resident: $4,998
Tuition, non-resident: $12,879
Average cost of books: $250

Employment Profile:
% of students who pass the boards on their first try: 90
% employed within the first 6 months following graduation: 100
Average starting salary: $30,000

Oklahoma

University of Oklahoma Health Sciences Center
PO Box 26901
Oklahoma City, OK 73190

Contact Information:
Telephone: 919-966-5233
Fax: 919-966-6645
E-mail: jan-winn@ouhsc.edu
Web: www.ouhsc.edu/ahealth

Program Information:
Program begins: January, August
Duration of program: 48 months

Application Information:
Enrollment of program: 22
Transfer students are accepted.

Financial Information:
Tuition, resident: $3,103
Tuition, non-resident: $5,101
Average cost of books: $1,000
% of students receiving aid: 75

Employment Profile:
% of students who pass the boards on their first try: 98
% employed within the first 6 months following graduation: 100
Average starting salary: $34,000

Pennsylvania

Lancaster Institute for Health Education
Lancaster General Hospital
143 East Lemon Street
Lancaster, PA 17602

Contact Information:
Telephone: 717-290-5668
Fax: 717-290-5970
E-mail: platen@lha.org
Web: www.lha.org

Program Information:
Program begins: September
Duration of program: 12 months

Financial Information:
Average cost of books: $550

Employment Profile:
% of students who pass the boards on their first try: 100
% employed within the first 6 months following graduation: 100

Wyoming Valley Health Care System
North River and Auburn Streets
Wilkes Barre, PA 18764

Contact Information:
Telephone: 717-552-1740
Fax: 717-552-1758
E-mail: ctuchin@wvhcs.org

Program Information:
Program begins: September
Duration of program: 12 months

Financial Information:
Average cost of books: $550

Employment Profile:
% employed within the first 6 months following graduation: 90

Puerto Rico

University of Puerto Rico
PO Box 365067
San Juan, PR 009365067

Contact Information:
Telephone: 405-271-6477
Fax: 405-271-1424
E-mail: miriamespada@cprs.rcm.upr.edu
Web: www.cprsweb.rcm.upr.edu

Program Information:
Program begins: July
Duration of program: 12 months

Application Information:
Enrollment of program: 7
Transfer students are accepted.

Financial Information:
Tuition, resident: $1,080
Tuition, non-resident: $2,400
Average cost of books: $500
% of students receiving aid: 100

Employment Profile:
% of students who pass the boards on their first try: 86
% employed within the first 6 months following graduation: 100
Average starting salary: $19,200

South Carolina

Midlands Technical College
PO Box 2408
Columbia, SC 29202

Contact Information:
Telephone: 803-434-6343
Fax: 803-434-4500
E-mail: Hatchert@mtc.mid.tec.sc.us
Web: www.mid.tec.sc.us

Program Information:
Program begins: September
Degrees offered: Certificate program, 12 months

Application Information:
Transfer students are accepted.

Financial Information:
Tuition, resident: $1,728
Tuition, non-resident: $5,184
Average cost of books: $400
% of students receiving aid: 30

Employment Profile:
% of students who pass the boards on their first try: 100

% employed within the first 6 months following graduation: 80
Average starting salary: $32,500

South Dakota

Southeast Technical Institute
2301 Career Place
Sioux Falls, SD 57107

Contact Information:
Telephone: 605-367-8459 ext. 275
Fax: 605-367-6108
E-mail: southcaa@seti.tec.sd.us
Web: www.seti.tec.sd.us

Program Information:
Program begins: August
Duration of program: 27 months

Application Information:
Enrollment of program: 40
Transfer students are accepted.

Financial Information:
Average cost of books: $1,755

Employment Profile:
% of students who pass the boards on their first try: 100
% employed within the first 6 months following graduation: 71
Average starting salary: $32,000

Tennessee

Chattanooga State Technical Community College
4501 Amnicola Highway
Chattanooga, TN 37406

Contact Information:
Telephone: 423-697-3335
Fax: 423-697-3324
E-mail: kallen@cstcc.cc.tn.us

Program Information:
Program begins: August
Degrees offered: Certificate program, 12 months

Application Information:
Enrollment of program: 15

Financial Information:
Tuition, resident: $1,200
Tuition, non-resident: $5,100
Average cost of books: $300
% of students receiving aid: 20

Employment Profile:
% of students who pass the boards on their first try: 100
% employed within the first 6 months following graduation: 100
Average starting salary: $35,000

University of Tennessee Medical Center at Knoxville
1924 Alcoa Highway
Knoxville, TN 37920

Contact Information:
Telephone: 787-758-2525 ext. 4607
Fax: 787-764-1760
E-mail: ghathawa@mc.utmck.edu
Web: www.utmck.edu

Program Information:
Program begins: September
Duration of program: 12 months

Vanderbilt University Medical Center
Radiology Department 21st and Garland
CCC-1124 MCN
Nashville, TN 37232-2675

Contact Information:
Telephone: 615-322-0508
Fax: 615-322-3764
E-mail: jim.patton@mcmail.vanderbilt.edu
Web: www.mc.vanderbilt.edu

Program Information:
Program begins: August
Duration of program: 12 months

Application Information:
Enrollment of program: 7

Financial Information:
Tuition: $1,900
Average cost of books: $100
% of students receiving aid: 70

Employment Profile:
% of students who pass the boards on their first try: 90
% employed within the first 6 months following graduation: 100
Average starting salary: $32,000

Texas

Amarillo College
PO Box 447
Amarillo, TX 79178

Contact Information:
Telephone: 806-354-6056
Fax: 806-354-6076
E-mail: csnorton@actx.edu
Web: www.actx.edu

Program Information:
Program begins: August
Duration of program: 24 months

Application Information:
Transfer students are accepted.

Financial Information:
Tuition, resident: $1,100
Tuition, non-resident: $2,743
Average cost of books: $650
% of students receiving aid: 72

Employment Profile:
% of students who pass the boards on their first try: 94
% employed within the first 6 months following graduation: 100
Average starting salary: $20,000

Galveston College—University of Texas
4015 Avenue Q
Galveston, TX 77550

Contact Information:
Telephone: 409-772-3042
Fax: 409-772-3014
E-mail: bobrown@utmb.edu
Web: www.sahs.utmb.edu

Program Information:
Program begins: August
Degrees offered: Certificate program; Diploma

Application Information:
Enrollment of program: 10
Transfer students are accepted.

Financial Information:
Tuition, resident: $1,146
Tuition, non-resident: $1,674
Average cost of books: $400
% of students receiving aid: 35

Employment Profile:
% of students who pass the boards on their first try: 100
% employed within the first 6 months following graduation: 100
Average starting salary: $30,000

Vermont

University of Vermont
302 Rowell Building
Burlington, VT 05405

Contact Information:
Telephone: 210-829-3991
Fax: 210-829-3174
E-mail: louis.izzo@uvm.edu
Web: www.uvm.edu

Program Information:
Program begins: September
Duration of program: 48 months

Financial Information:
Tuition, resident: $7,464
Tuition, non-resident: $18,672

Washington

Bellevue Community College
Box 900
Seattle, WA 98111

Contact Information:
Telephone: 206-223-6951
Fax: 206-344-7959
E-mail: radjlp@vmmc.org

Program Information:
Program begins: July
Duration of program: 12 months

Application Information:
Enrollment of program: 2

Financial Information:
Average cost of books: $400

Employment Profile:
% of students who pass the boards on their first try: 100
% employed within the first 6 months following graduation: 95

West Virginia

Wheeling Jesuit University
316 Washington Avenue
Wheeling, WV 26003

Contact Information:
Telephone: 304-243-2387
Fax: 304-243-4441
E-mail: amaacci@wjv.edu
Web: www.wju.edu

Program Information:
Program begins: September
Duration of program: 48 months

Application Information:
Enrollment of program: 38
Transfer students are accepted.

Financial Information:
Tuition, resident: $15,000
% of students receiving aid: 91

Employment Profile:
% of students who pass the boards on their first try: 100
% employed within the first 6 months following graduation: 100

Wisconsin

Froedtert Memorial Lutheran Hospital
9200 West Wisconsin Avenue
PO Box 26099
Milwaukee, WI 53226

Contact Information:
Telephone: 414-259-2071
Fax: 414-771-3460

Program Information:
Program begins: June
Duration of program: 12 months

Application Information:
Enrollment of program: 6

Employment Profile:
% of students who pass the boards on their first try: 100
% employed within the first 6 months following graduation: 100

Gundersen Lutheran Medical Center
1836 South Avenue
La Crosse, WI 54601

Contact Information:
Telephone: 608-782-7300 ext. 5074
Fax: 608-791-6642
E-mail: rloeffel@gundluth.org
Web: www.gundluth.org

Program Information:
Program begins: September
Degrees offered: Certificate program, 12 months; Bachelor's

Financial Information:
Tuition, resident: $3,242

Employment Profile:
% of students who pass the boards on their first try: 100
% employed within the first 6 months following graduation: 100
Average starting salary: $40,000

St. Joseph's Hospital
611 St. Joseph Avenue
Marshfield, WI 54449

Contact Information:
Telephone: 715-387-7787
E-mail: johnsoje@mfldclin.edu

Program Information:
Program begins: August
Degrees offered: Certificate program, 12 months

Application Information:
Enrollment of program: 5

Financial Information:
Tuition, resident: $1,700
Tuition, non-resident: $5,000
Average cost of books: $300

Employment Profile:
% of students who pass the boards on their first try: 100
% employed within the first 6 months following graduation: 90
Average starting salary: $35,000

St. Luke's Medical Center
2900 West Oklahoma Avenue
Milwaukee, WI 53215

Contact Information:
Telephone: 414-649-6418
Fax: 414-649-5118

Program Information:
Program begins: June
Degrees offered: Certificate program, 12 months

Application Information:
Enrollment of program: 7

Financial Information:
Tuition: $1,000

Employment Profile:
% of students who pass the boards on their first try: 100
% employed within the first 6 months following graduation: 100
Average starting salary: $38,000

Respiratory Care Practitioner

Thomas J. Butler, MS, RRT, RPFT
Director of Clinical Education
Respiratory Care Program
SUNY Rockland Community College
Suffern, New York
and
Manager of Respiratory Care
Kessler Rehabilitation Corporation
West Orange, New Jersey

Job Description

What Do They Do?

Respiratory care practitioners (RCPs), also called respiratory therapists, play important roles in any situation in which breathing becomes difficult. In addition to providing life support functions, RCPs help assess, diagnose and treat cardiopulmonary diseases. They work with life support equipment such as ventilators, administer respiratory medications and perform tests to assess lung and heart function. Other key responsibilities of the RCP include rehabilitation, community education, and disease prevention programs, such as anti-smoking campaigns. Thorough knowledge of respiratory physiology, familiarity with complex medical equipment and patient assessment skills are some of the tools used by RCPs in clinical decision making, cost containment, and patient education. These skills make RCPs an integral part of the healthcare team.

Type of Person

RCPs need to be comfortable working with sophisticated medical equipment. In addition, they should have excellent communication and problem-solving skills. They work independently, so they must have excellent time management skills. Physical requirements include standing for long hours, bending, lifting and transporting heavy objects such as ventilators and medical gas cylinders.

With Whom Do They Work?

RCPs work under the supervision of a physician. They work alongside other physicians, nurses, social workers and physical and occupational therapists.

Employment

Places of Employment

In the past, RCPs worked almost exclusively in acute care hospitals. Recent changes in healthcare, however, have shifted the focus of healthcare away from acute care and toward managed care. This has changed the places in which RCPs work. Although they can still be found in acute care, RCPs also work in delivery rooms at the birth of premature infants, with children suffering from asthma or cystic fibrosis, managing ventilators in the intensive care unit, retraining breathing techniques in rehabilitation facilities, testing for sleep disorders in sleep centers, assisting in testing and performing patient education in physicians' offices and supervising the delivery of respiratory care in the home care setting. They also work in non-clinical jobs by serving as educators, product specialists, or sales representatives for the manufacturers of medical equipment and devices.

Employment Outlook

As with all healthcare professions, Medicare cutbacks and the emergence of managed care have affected the number of respiratory care jobs available in acute care facilities. However, the aging of our population and the growing number of individuals with cardiopulmonary diseases will likely increase the demand for employment in the non-acute care setting. The U.S. Bureau of Labor Statistics Outlook 1998–1999 reported that there will be a 46 percent increase in the number of new respiratory care jobs from 1996 to 2006.[1]

Salary

The median annual base salary for respiratory therapists was $32,500 in 1997. There is no clear difference in pay between a certified respiratory therapist and a registered respiratory therapist. Some employers may pay a higher salary to a registered respiratory therapist, but that is not always the case. Therapists who are willing to work nights and weekends may be able to increase their salaries by as much as 10 percent. The mean salary for managers of respiratory care departments, who are generally registered respiratory therapists, is $59,700.[2]

Educational Programs

Length

An Associate's degree is the minimum level of education required to enter the profession. These programs are generally two years in length.

Approximately 9 percent of respiratory therapy programs offer a Bachelor's degree. These programs are generally four years in length and are recommended for those students who are interested in pursuing a career in management or higher education.

Prerequisites

Applicants to respiratory care programs must be high school graduates and have an aptitude for science. Students entering clinical rotations must be able to pass state health requirements for healthcare workers.

Curriculum

In addition to the respiratory care content, the curriculum consists of anatomy and physiology, chemistry, physics or physical science, English, general psychology and microbiology. Laboratory and clinical hours are also required. The clinical hours include, but are not limited to, intensive and coronary care units, neonatal and pediatrics, operating room, home care and rehabilitation rotations.

Accrediting Body

Educational programs are evaluated and accredited by the Committee on Accreditation for Respiratory Care. There is no distinct difference in regard to accreditation for entry-level versus advanced practitioner programs; however, those programs that prepare students at the advanced practitioner level will teach the core concepts that are tested in the entry-level certification examination as well as the more advanced topics that are addressed in the advanced respiratory therapist examination. Since advanced practitioner programs cover more information, they are generally, but not necessarily, longer programs than the entry-level ones.

Committee on Accreditation for Respiratory Care (CoARC)
1248 Harwood Road
Bedford, TX 76021-4244
Telephone: 817-283-2835
Fax: 817-354-8519
Web address: www.coarc.com

Certification Board

Upon completion of an accredited program, graduates of both Associate's and Bachelor's degree programs are eligible to sit for the entry-level certification examination to earn the certified respiratory therapist (CRT) credential. This examination, offered nationwide by the National Board for Respiratory Care, sets the minimal standard for practice in most states.

Students who graduate from advanced practitioner programs are also eligible to take the advanced practitioner examination, following successful completion of the entry-level examination. The advanced practitioner examination consists of two parts: a 100-question multiple choice examination and a clinical simulation examination. It tests many of the same topics as the entry-level examination as well as several more advanced procedures. It also focuses more on developing care plans rather than simply implementing them. The registered respiratory therapist (RRT) credential is awarded when a person passes both parts of this examination.

Therapists with expertise in pulmonary function testing and neonatal/pediatric respiratory care may also sit for specialty examinations for credentials in certified pulmonary function technologist (CPFT), registered pulmonary function technologist (RPFT), or neonatal/pediatric specialist designation. Earning these additional credentials indicates that the therapist has a particular expertise in these areas.

These examinations are administered by:

National Board for Respiratory Care (NBRC)
830 Nieman Road
Lenexa, KS 66214
Telephone: 913-599-4200
Fax: 913-541-0156
Web address: www.nbrc.org

Licensure

New practitioners are also obligated to meet licensure requirements for the state in which they will practice. The requirements for the individual states can be obtained from the state's licensure board; a listing of the state licensure boards and the requirements can be obtained from the American Association for Respiratory Care (AARC).

Advice for Potential Students

Since the academic and clinical requirements are quite rigorous, potential students should consider observing a respiratory therapist during his or her working hours. Contact the director or manager of the respiratory care department at a local hospital and ask for an appointment. You should ask questions about the nature of the job and about job availability. Also, try to arrange an interview with the respiratory care program director at the college in which you are interested. Ask about the academic requirements, graduate pass rates on the credentialing examination and the employment rate of new graduates.

For Additional Information

Organizations

American Association for Respiratory Care (AARC)
11030 Ables Lane
Dallas, TX 75229-4593
Telephone: 972-243-2272
Fax: 972-484-2720
Web address: www.aarc.org

Publications

Advance for Respiratory Care Practitioners. Merion Publications, 2900 Horizon Drive, King of Prussia, PA 19406. www.advanceweb.com

AARC Times. American Association for Respiratory Care. www.aarc.org

Internet Resources

American Association for Respiratory Care: www.aarc.org
The AARC lists sites for all of its state affiliates as well as other respira tory care sites.
Committee on Accreditation for Respiratory Care: www.coarc.com
National Board for Respiratory Care: www.nbrc.org

Entry-Level Respiratory Therapist

Alabama

Tuskegee University

Basil O'Connor Hall
Tuskegee, AL 36088-1696

Contact Information:
Telephone: 334-727-8696
Fax: 334-727-8259
Web: www.tusk.edu

Program Information:
Program begins: June
Duration of program: 28 months

Application Information:
Enrollment of program: 55
Transfer students are accepted.

Financial Information:
Average cost of books: $300
% of students receiving aid: 80

Employment Profile:
% of students who pass the boards on their first try: 95
Average starting salary: $35,000

University of Alabama at Birmingham

Webb Building Room 423
Birmingham, AL 35294-3361

Contact Information:
Telephone: 205-934-1678
Fax: 205-934-5980
E-mail: grostics@shrp.uab.edu
Web: www.uab.edu

Program Information:
Program begins: August
Duration of program: 12 months

Application Information:
Enrollment of program: 28
Transfer students are accepted.

Financial Information:
Tuition, resident: $4,452
Tuition, non-resident: $8,904
Average cost of books: $750

Employment Profile:
% of students who pass the boards on their first try: 90
% employed within the first 6 months following graduation: 90
Average starting salary: $29,500

Arizona

Gateway Community College

108 North 40th Street
Phoenix, AZ 85034

Contact Information:
Telephone: 602-392-5234
Fax: 602-392-5244
E-mail: rodriguez@gwc.maricopa.edu
Web: www.gwc.maricopa.edu

Program Information:
Program begins: August
Degrees offered: Associate's, 24 months

Application Information:
Enrollment of program: 30
Transfer students are accepted.

Financial Information:
Tuition, resident: $925
Tuition, non-resident: $4,050
Average cost of books: $200
% of students receiving aid: 60

Employment Profile:
% of students who pass the boards on their first try: 75
% employed within the first 6 months following graduation: 80

Long Technical College

13450 North Black Canyon Highway #104
Phoenix, AZ 85029

Contact Information:
Telephone: 602-548-1955
Fax: 602-548-1956
Web: www.longtechnicalcollege.com

Program Information:
Program begins: January, June, September
Degrees offered: Associate's, 21 months
Evening or weekend classes are available.

Application Information:
Enrollment of program: 33
Transfer students are accepted.

Financial Information:
Average cost of books: $812
% of students receiving aid: 94

Employment Profile:
% of students who pass the boards on their first try: 50
% employed within the first 6 months following graduation: 91
Average starting salary: $27,560

Pima Medical Institute—Mesa

957 South Dobson Road
Mesa, AZ 85202

Contact Information:
Telephone: 602-345-7777
Fax: 602-649-5249
Web: www.pimamedical.com

Program Information:
Program begins: August
Degrees offered: Associate's, 18 months

Application Information:
Enrollment of program: 50
Transfer students are accepted.

Financial Information:
Tuition: $15,990
Average cost of books: $1,434
% of students receiving aid: 95

Employment Profile:
% of students who pass the boards on their first try: 85
% employed within the first 6 months following graduation: 85
Average starting salary: $28,000

Arkansas

Pulaski Technical College

3000 West Scenic Drive
North Little Rock, AR 72118

Contact Information:
Telephone: 501-771-1000 ext. 223
Fax: 501-812-2316

Program Information:
Program begins: August
Degrees offered: Certificate program, 9 months; Associate's, 18 months

Application Information:
Enrollment of program: 24
Transfer students are accepted.

Financial Information:
Tuition, resident: $2,500
Average cost of books: $400
% of students receiving aid: 50

Employment Profile:
% of students who pass the boards on their first try: 60
% employed within the first 6 months following graduation: 99
Average starting salary: $25,000

University of Arkansas Community College at Hope

Highway 29 South
PO Box 140
Hope, AR 71801

Contact Information:
Telephone: 501-777-5722
Fax: 501-777-5957
E-mail: klejeune@mail.uacch.cc.ar.us

Program Information:
Program begins: June
Degrees offered: Associate's, 18 months

Application Information:
Enrollment of program: 25
Transfer students are accepted.

Financial Information:
Tuition, resident: $912
Tuition, non-resident: $960
Average cost of books: $400
% of students receiving aid: 30

Employment Profile:
% of students who pass the boards on their first try: 80
% employed within the first 6 months following graduation: 98
Average starting salary: $40,000

California

ConCorde Career Institute

12412 Victory Boulevard
North Hollywood, CA 91606

Contact Information:
Telephone: 818-766-8151 ext. 253
Fax: 818-766-1587
E-mail: mhaberwood@concordecareercolleges.com
Web: www.concordecareercolleges.com

Program Information:
Program begins: Quarterly
Degrees offered: Associate's, 18 months

Application Information:
Enrollment of program: 104
Transfer students are accepted.

Financial Information:
Average cost of books: $485
% of students receiving aid: 97

Employment Profile:
% of students who pass the boards on their first try: 90

Crafton Hills College

11711 Sand Canyon Road
Yucaipa, CA 92399

Contact Information:
Telephone: 909-389-3286
Fax: 909-794-0423
E-mail: kbryson@crafton.sbccd.cc.ca.us
Web: www.sbccd.cc.ca.us

Program Information:
Program begins: August, September
Degrees offered: Certificate program, 15 months; Diploma, 24 months; Associate's, 18 months

Application Information:
Enrollment of program: 50
Transfer students are accepted.

Financial Information:
Tuition, resident: $777
Tuition, non-resident: $7,050
Average cost of books: $350

Employment Profile:
% of students who pass the boards on their first try: 95
% employed within the first 6 months following graduation: 100
Average starting salary: $30,000

Hacienda LaPuente Adult Education
15325 East Los Robles Avenue
Hacienda Heights, CA 91744

Contact Information:
Telephone: 626-855-3138
Fax: 626-855-3141
E-mail: jhunt@hlpusd.k12.ca.us
Web: www.hlpusd.k12.ca.us

Program Information:
Degrees offered: Associate's, 24 months
Evening or weekend classes are available.

Application Information:
Enrollment of program: 75
Transfer students are accepted.

Financial Information:
Average cost of books: $400
% of students receiving aid: 25

Employment Profile:
% of students who pass the boards on their first try: 96
% employed within the first 6 months following graduation: 95
Average starting salary: $30,000

Florida

Broward Community College
1000 Coconut Creek Boulevard
Coconut Creek, FL 33066

Contact Information:
Telephone: 954-969-2082
Fax: 954-973-2348
E-mail: jprince@Broward.cc.fl.us
Web: www.broward.cc.fl.us

Program Information:
Program begins: August
Duration of program: 12 months
Evening or weekend classes are available.

Application Information:
Enrollment of program: 25

Financial Information:
Tuition, resident: $1,700
Tuition, non-resident: $5,325
Average cost of books: $150
% of students receiving aid: 50

Employment Profile:
% of students who pass the boards on their first try: 85
% employed within the first 6 months following graduation: 100
Average starting salary: $35,000

Miami-Dade Community College
Medical Center Campus
950 Northwest 20th Street
Miami, FL 33127

Contact Information:
Telephone: 305-237-4031
Fax: 305-237-4278
E-mail: millec@mdcc.edu
Web: www.mdcc.edu

Program Information:
Program begins: August
Duration of program: 16 months

Application Information:
Enrollment of program: 40

Financial Information:
Tuition, resident: $1,939
Tuition, non-resident: $6,815
Average cost of books: $400

Employment Profile:
% of students who pass the boards on their first try: 90
Average starting salary: $21,000

Palm Beach Community College
3160 PGA Boulevard
Palm Beach Gardens, FL 33410

Contact Information:
Telephone: 561-625-2588
Fax: 561-625-2305
E-mail: rogersj@pbcc.cc.fl.us
Web: www.pbcc.cc.fl.us

Program Information:
Program begins: January, August
Duration of program: 10 months

Application Information:
Enrollment of program: 10
Transfer students are accepted.

Financial Information:
Tuition, resident: $1,862
Tuition, non-resident: $5,587
Average cost of books: $450
% of students receiving aid: 38

Employment Profile:
% of students who pass the boards on their first try: 100
Average starting salary: $21,000

Georgia

Coosa Valley Technical Institute
One Maurice Culberson Drive
Rome, GA 30161-6757

Contact Information:
Telephone: 706-295-6910
Fax: 706-295-6894
E-mail: lpapp@adminl.coosa.tec.ga.us

Program Information:
Program begins: July
Duration of program: 18 months

Application Information:
Enrollment of program: 18

Financial Information:
Tuition, resident: $1,656
Tuition, non-resident: $3,312

Gwinnett Technical Institute
5150 Sugarloaf Parkway
PO Box 1505
Lawrenceville, GA 30046-1505

Contact Information:
Telephone: 770-962-7580 ext. 158
Fax: 770-962-7985
E-mail: bdelorme@gwinnett.tec.ga.us
Web: www.gwinnett-tech.org

Program Information:
Program begins: July
Duration of program: 24 months

Application Information:
Enrollment of program: 18

Financial Information:
Tuition, resident: $2,712
Tuition, non-resident: $4,920

Employment Profile:
% employed within the first 6 months following graduation: 100
Average starting salary: $30,000

Okefenokee Technical Institute
1701 Carswell Avenue
Waycross, GA 31501

Contact Information:
Telephone: 912-287-6515
Fax: 912-284-2508
E-mail: faye@admin1.waycross-tec.ga.us
Web: oti.waycross.tcc.ga.us

Program Information:
Program begins: September

Application Information:
Transfer students are accepted.

Financial Information:
Tuition, resident: $252
Tuition, non-resident: $504

Employment Profile:
% of students who pass the boards on their first try: 50
% employed within the first 6 months following graduation: 80
Average starting salary: $19,000

Idaho

Boise State University
College of Technology
1910 University Drive
Boise, ID 83725

Contact Information:
Telephone: 208-426-4708

Fax: 208-466-2933
E-mail: jpukstas@boisestate.edu
Web: www.idbsu.edu

Program Information:
Program begins: August
Degrees offered: Associate's, 21 months

Application Information:
Enrollment of program: 20
Transfer students are accepted.

Financial Information:
Tuition, resident: $2,472
Tuition, non-resident: $8,174
Average cost of books: $300
% of students receiving aid: 50

Employment Profile:
% of students who pass the boards on their first try: 75
% employed within the first 6 months following graduation: 92
Average starting salary: $25,000

Illinois

College of DuPage
425 22nd Street
Glen Ellyn, IL 60137-6599

Contact Information:
Telephone: 630-942-2518
Fax: 630-858-9399
E-mail: bretlk@cdnet.cod.edu
Web: www.cod.edu

Program Information:
Program begins: June, September
Degrees offered: Certificate program, 18 months

Application Information:
Enrollment of program: 30
Transfer students are accepted.

Financial Information:
Tuition, resident: $1,500
Tuition, non-resident: $4,600
Average cost of books: $400

Employment Profile:
% of students who pass the boards on their first try: 95
% employed within the first 6 months following graduation: 100
Average starting salary: $30,000

Kaskaskia College
27210 College Road
Centralia, IL 62801

Contact Information:
Telephone: 618-545-3352
Fax: 618-532-1990
E-mail: bsurban@kc.cc.il.us
Web: www.kc.cc.il.us

Program Information:
Program begins: June
Degrees offered: Diploma, 12 months

Application Information:
Enrollment of program: 20
Transfer students are accepted.

Financial Information:
Tuition, resident: $1,760
Tuition, non-resident: $4,708
Average cost of books: $600

Employment Profile:
% of students who pass the boards on their first try: 87
% employed within the first 6 months following graduation: 100
Average starting salary: $19,720

St. Augustine College
1345 West Argyle
Chicago, IL 60640

Contact Information:
Telephone: 773-878-8756
Fax: 773-878-0937

Program Information:
Program begins: January, August
Degrees offered: Diploma, 28 months; Associate's, 18 months
Evening or weekend classes are available.

Application Information:
Enrollment of program: 96
Transfer students are accepted.

Financial Information:
Average cost of books: $95
% of students receiving aid: 30

Employment Profile:
% of students who pass the boards on their first try: 35
% employed within the first 6 months following graduation: 99
Average starting salary: $28,000

St. John's Hospital
800 East Carpenter Street
Springfield, IL 62769

Contact Information:
Telephone: 217-544-6464 ext. 44255
Fax: 217-535-3881
E-mail: jszoke@st-johns.org
Web: www.st-johns.org

Program Information:
Program begins: June
Degrees offered: Associate's, 18 months

Employment Profile:
% employed within the first 6 months following graduation: 100

Trinity Hospital
2320 East 93rd Street
Chicago, IL 60617

Contact Information:
Telephone: 773-978-2000 ext. 5320
Fax: 773-933-6436
E-mail: goldie.belk@advocatehealth.com

Program Information:
Program begins: August
Degrees offered: Certificate program, 14 months

Application Information:
Enrollment of program: 20
Transfer students are accepted.

Financial Information:
Average cost of books: $500
% of students receiving aid: 70

Employment Profile:
% of students who pass the boards on their first try: 80
% employed within the first 6 months following graduation: 100
Average starting salary: $30,000

Waubonsee Community College
Route 47 at Harter Road
Sugar Grove, IL 60554

Contact Information:
Telephone: 630-466-7900 ext. 2592
Fax: 630-466-7784
E-mail: csolarski@mail.wcc.cc.il.us
Web: www.wcc.cc.il.us

Program Information:
Program begins: August
Degrees offered: Associate's, 24 months

Application Information:
Enrollment of program: 10
Transfer students are accepted.

Financial Information:
Tuition, resident: $3,010
Tuition, non-resident: $16,458
Average cost of books: $400

Employment Profile:
% of students who pass the boards on their first try: 85
% employed within the first 6 months following graduation: 75
Average starting salary: $26,000

Indiana

Ivy Tech State College—Michigan City
3714 Franklin Street
Michigan City, IN 46360

Contact Information:
Telephone: 219-879-9137
Fax: 219-879-9157
E-mail: slayhew@ivy.tec.in.us
Web: www.gar.ivy.tec.in.us

Program Information:
Degrees offered: Certificate program, 12 months

Financial Information:
Tuition, resident: $3,400
Tuition, non-resident: $6,300
Average cost of books: $450

Employment Profile:
% of students who pass the boards on their first try: 80

% employed within the first 6 months following graduation: 85
Average starting salary: $25,000

Iowa

Hawkeye Community College

151 East Orange Road
PO Box 8015
Waterloo, IA 50704

Contact Information:
Telephone: 319-296-2320
Fax: 319-296-2874
E-mail: ldahl@hawkeye.cc.ia.us
Web: www.hawkeye.cc.ia.us

Program Information:
Program begins: August
Degrees offered: Associate's, 22 months

Application Information:
Enrollment of program: 26
Transfer students are accepted.

Financial Information:
Tuition, resident: $5,325
Tuition, non-resident: $10,560
Average cost of books: $500
% of students receiving aid: 75

Employment Profile:
% employed within the first 6 months following graduation: 84
Average starting salary: $21,000

Kansas

Kansas City, Kansas Community College—Bethany Medical Center

51 North 12th Street
Kansas City, KS 66102

Contact Information:
Telephone: 913-281-8768
Fax: 913-281-7875
Web: www.kckcc.cc.ks.us

Program Information:
Program begins: September
Duration of program: 12 months

Financial Information:
Tuition, resident: $3,850
Tuition, non-resident: $5,200

Washburn University of Topeka

1700 College Avenue Southwest
Topeka, KS 66621

Contact Information:
Telephone: 785-231-1010 ext. 1404
Fax: 785-231-1027
E-mail: zzmunz@washburn.edu
Web: www.washburn.edu

Program Information:
Program begins: August
Degrees offered: Certificate program, 15 months

Application Information:
Enrollment of program: 18
Transfer students are accepted.

Financial Information:
Tuition, resident: $2,976
Tuition, non-resident: $6,541
Average cost of books: $1,200
% of students receiving aid: 80

Employment Profile:
% of students who pass the boards on their first try: 95
% employed within the first 6 months following graduation: 100
Average starting salary: $28,000

Kentucky

Bowling Green Technical College

1845 Loop Drive
Bowling Green, KY 42101

Contact Information:
Telephone: 502-746-7461 ext. 2182
Fax: 502-746-7466
E-mail: brian.harlan@kctcs.net
Web: www.state.ky.us

Program Information:
Program begins: August
Degrees offered: Diploma, 15 months

Application Information:
Enrollment of program: 24
Transfer students are accepted.

Financial Information:
Tuition, resident: $1,305
Tuition, non-resident: $2,295
Average cost of books: $250
% of students receiving aid: 60

Employment Profile:
% of students who pass the boards on their first try: 90
% employed within the first 6 months following graduation: 100
Average starting salary: $21,000

Central Kentucky Technical College

308 Vocational -Technical Road, Region 15
Lexington, KY 40511-2626

Contact Information:
Telephone: 606-246-2400 ext. 273
Fax: 606-246-2504
E-mail: rebecca.simms@kctcs.net
Web: www.ktcc.state.ky.us

Program Information:
Program begins: August
Degrees offered: Diploma, 24 months

Application Information:
Enrollment of program: 20
Transfer students are accepted.

Financial Information:
Tuition, resident: $660
Tuition, non-resident: $1,320
Average cost of books: $400
% of students receiving aid: 50

Employment Profile:
% of students who pass the boards on their first try: 89
% employed within the first 6 months following graduation: 100
Average starting salary: $19,200

Cumberland Technical College Rockcastle Consortium

PO Box 275
Mt. Vernon, KY 40456

Contact Information:
Telephone: 606-256-4346
Fax: 606-256-4337

Program Information:
Degrees offered: Diploma, 15 months

Application Information:
Enrollment of program: 30
Transfer students are accepted.

Financial Information:
Tuition, resident: $800
Average cost of books: $500
% of students receiving aid: 80

Employment Profile:
% of students who pass the boards on their first try: 36
% employed within the first 6 months following graduation: 100
Average starting salary: $20,000

Louisiana

Delgado Community College

615 City Park Avenue
New Orleans, LA 70119

Contact Information:
Telephone: 504-483-4114 ext. 4007
Fax: 504-483-4609
E-mail: dolsen@dcc.edu
Web: www.dcc.edu

Program Information:
Program begins: August
Duration of program: 24 months

Application Information:
Enrollment of program: 20
Transfer students are accepted.

Financial Information:
Tuition, resident: $1,455
Tuition, non-resident: $3,255
Average cost of books: $500
% of students receiving aid: 50

Employment Profile:
% of students who pass the boards on their first try: 70
% employed within the first 6 months following graduation: 90
Average starting salary: $27,000

Louisiana State University at Eunice
PO Box 1129
Eunice, LA 70535

Contact Information:
Telephone: 318-457-7311 ext. 311
Fax: 318-546-6620
E-mail: jbush@lsue.edu
Web: www.lsue.edu

Program Information:
Program begins: June
Degrees offered: Diploma, 24 months
Evening or weekend classes are available.

Application Information:
Enrollment of program: 20
Transfer students are accepted.

Financial Information:
Tuition, resident: $1,320
Tuition, non-resident: $2,820
Average cost of books: $480
% of students receiving aid: 80

Employment Profile:
% of students who pass the boards on their first try: 95
% employed within the first 6 months following graduation: 100
Average starting salary: $29,000

Massachusetts

Northern Essex Community College
45 Franklin Street
Lawrence, MA 01841-4911

Contact Information:
Telephone: 978-738-7514
Fax: 978-738-7450
E-mail: crowse@necc.mass.edu
Web: www.necc.mass.edu

Program Information:
Program begins: August
Duration of program: 14 months

Application Information:
Enrollment of program: 18
Transfer students are accepted.

Financial Information:
Tuition, resident: $2,739
Tuition, non-resident: $8,349

Employment Profile:
% of students who pass the boards on their first try: 90
% employed within the first 6 months following graduation: 90
Average starting salary: $29,000

Minnesota

Northwest Technical College—East Grand Forks
2022 Central Avenue Northwest
East Grand Forks, MN 56721

Contact Information:
Telephone: 218-773-3441
Fax: 218-773-4502
E-mail: tony.sorum@mail.ntc.mnscu.edu
Web: www.ntc-online.com

Program Information:
Program begins: Program begins quarterly.
Duration of program: 16 months

Application Information:
Enrollment of program: 20
Transfer students are accepted.

Financial Information:
Tuition, resident: $4,505
Tuition, non-resident: $9,010
Average cost of books: $580

Employment Profile:
% of students who pass the boards on their first try: 85
% employed within the first 6 months following graduation: 100
Average starting salary: $27,500

Mississippi

Copiah-Lincoln Community College
Natchez Campus Vocational/Technical
30 Campus Drive
Natchez, MS 39120-5398

Contact Information:
Telephone: 601-442-9111
Fax: 601-446-1298

Program Information:
Program begins: January
Duration of program: 16 months

Application Information:
Enrollment of program: 15

Financial Information:
Tuition, resident: $1,250
Tuition, non-resident: $2,500
Average cost of books: $600
% of students receiving aid: 80

Employment Profile:
% of students who pass the boards on their first try: 90
% employed within the first 6 months following graduation: 70
Average starting salary: $24,000

Hinds Community College
1750 Chadwick Drive
Jackson, MS 39204

Contact Information:
Telephone: 601-372-6517
Fax: 601-371-3508
E-mail: dsylveter@hinds.cc.ms.us
Web: www.hinds.cc.ms.us

Program Information:
Program begins: August
Duration of program: 33 months

Financial Information:
Tuition, resident: $1,405
Tuition, non-resident: $4,171

Missouri

Cape Girardeau Area Vocational Technical School
301 North Clark Avenue
Cape Girardeau, MO 63701

Contact Information:
Telephone: 573-334-0826 ext. 35
Fax: 573-334-5930
E-mail: kpfau@votech.cape.k12.mo.us

Program Information:
Program begins: August
Duration of program: 12 months

ConCorde Career Institute
3239 Broadway
Kansas City, MO 64111

Contact Information:
Telephone: 816-531-5223
Fax: 816-756-3231
E-mail: lbass@concordecolleges.com
Web: www.concordecareercolleges.com

Program Information:
Program begins: August
Duration of program: 18 months

Missouri Southern State College
3950 E Newman Road
Joplin, MO 64801

Contact Information:
Telephone: 417-659-4423
Fax: 417-659-4408
E-mail: ajo-po.erwin_j@mail.mssc.edu
Web: www.mssc.edu

Program Information:
Program begins: August
Duration of program: 24 months

Application Information:
Enrollment of program: 27
Transfer students are accepted.

Employment Profile:
% of students who pass the boards on their first try: 90
% employed within the first 6 months following graduation: 100
Average starting salary: $30,000

Rolla Technical Institute
1304 East 10th Street
Rolla, MO 654014678

Contact Information:
Telephone: 573-368-4782
Fax: 573-368-4741
E-mail: jjoiner@rollanet.org

Program Information:
Program begins: August
Duration of program: 12 months

Application Information:
Enrollment of program: 18
Transfer students are accepted.

Financial Information:
Tuition: $4,800
Average cost of books: $1,541
% of students receiving aid: 75

Employment Profile:
% employed within the first 6 months following graduation: 90
Average starting salary: $24,000

Montana

University of Montana—Missoula

College of Technology
Missoula, MT 59801

Contact Information:
Telephone: 210-544-8262
Fax: 210-544-8910
E-mail: bwafstet@selway.umt.edu
Web: www.umt.edu

Program Information:
Program begins: September
Duration of program: 13 months

Financial Information:
Tuition, resident: $7,000
Tuition, non-resident: $14,000
Average cost of books: $1,500

Employment Profile:
% of students who pass the boards on their first try: 90
% employed within the first 6 months following graduation: 60
Average starting salary: $24,000

New Jersey

Gloucester County College

1400 Tanyard Road
Sewell, NJ 08080

Contact Information:
Telephone: 856-415-2192 ext. 495
Fax: 856-464-8463
E-mail: aleder@accnj.edu
Web: www.accnj.edu

Program Information:
Program begins: August
Duration of program: 10 months

Application Information:
Enrollment of program: 16
Transfer students are accepted.

Financial Information:
Tuition, resident: $2,000
Average cost of books: $700
% of students receiving aid: 25

Employment Profile:
% of students who pass the boards on their first try: 89
% employed within the first 6 months following graduation: 100
Average starting salary: $36,000

New York

Mohawk Valley Community College

1101 Sherman Drive
Payne Hall 351
Utica, NY 13501

Contact Information:
Telephone: 315-792-5664
Fax: 315-792-5666
E-mail: lphillips@mvcc.edu
Web: www.mvcc.edu

Program Information:
Program begins: September
Duration of program: 12 months
Evening or weekend classes are available.

Application Information:
Transfer students are accepted.

Financial Information:
Tuition, resident: $3,590
Tuition, non-resident: $7,180
Average cost of books: $600
% of students receiving aid: 80

Employment Profile:
% employed within the first 6 months following graduation: 100
Average starting salary: $22,000

Onondaga Community College

Route 173
Syracuse, NY 13215

Contact Information:
Telephone: 315-469-2458
Fax: 315-469-2593
Web: www.sunyocc.edu

Program Information:
Program begins: March
Duration of program: 12 months

Financial Information:
Tuition, resident: $2,500
Tuition, non-resident: $5,000

Employment Profile:
% of students who pass the boards on their first try: 90
% employed within the first 6 months following graduation: 80
Average starting salary: $30,000

Ohio

Collins Career Center

11627 State Route 243
Chesapeake, OH 45619

Contact Information:
Telephone: 614-867-6641 ext. 411
Fax: 614-867-2009
E-mail: katerry@collins-cc.k12.oh.us

Program Information:
Program begins: August
Degrees offered: Diploma, 22 months
Evening or weekend classes are available.

Application Information:
Enrollment of program: 40

Financial Information:
Average cost of books: $250
% of students receiving aid: 60

Employment Profile:
% of students who pass the boards on their first try: 69
% employed within the first 6 months following graduation: 100
Average starting salary: $24,000

University of Toledo

College of Health and Human Services
2801 West Bancroft Street
Toledo, OH 43606

Contact Information:
Telephone: 210-567-8850
Fax: 210-567-8852
Web: www.utoledo.edu

Program Information:
Program begins: August
Duration of program: 22 months

Application Information:
Enrollment of program: 20
Transfer students are accepted.

Financial Information:
Tuition, resident: $5,275
Tuition, non-resident: $12,325
Average cost of books: $750

Employment Profile:
% of students who pass the boards on their first try: 90
% employed within the first 6 months following graduation: 100
Average starting salary: $22,000

Oklahoma

Francis Tuttle

12777 North Rockwell Avenue
Oklahoma City, OK 73142

Contact Information:
Telephone: 405-717-4269
Fax: 405-717-4789
E-mail: lheyland@francistuttle.com
Web: www.francistuttle.com

Program Information:
Program begins: August
Duration of program: 18 months

Application Information:
Enrollment of program: 60
Transfer students are accepted.

Financial Information:
Tuition: $1,500
Average cost of books: $450

Employment Profile:
% of students who pass the boards on their first try: 85
% employed within the first 6 months following graduation: 90

Great Plains Technology Center
4500 West Lee Boulevard
Lawton, OK 73505

Contact Information:
Telephone: 580-250-5572
Fax: 580-250-5583
E-mail: powers@gpv.org
Web: www.gpv.org

Program Information:
Program begins: August
Degrees offered: Associate's, 18 months

Application Information:
Enrollment of program: 12
Transfer students are accepted.

Financial Information:
Tuition, resident: $1,640
Tuition, non-resident: $2,640
Average cost of books: $400

Employment Profile:
% employed within the first 6 months following graduation: 95
Average starting salary: $22,000

Tulsa Community College
909 South Boston Avenue
Tulsa, OK 74119

Contact Information:
Telephone: 918-595-7016
Fax: 918-595-7298
Web: www.tulsa.cc.ok.us

Program Information:
Program begins: August
Duration of program: 24 months

Application Information:
Enrollment of program: 35
Transfer students are accepted.

Financial Information:
Tuition, resident: $1,558
Tuition, non-resident: $4,069
Average cost of books: $250
% of students receiving aid: 50

Employment Profile:
% of students who pass the boards on their first try: 80
% employed within the first 6 months following graduation: 75
Average starting salary: $22,000

Pennsylvania

Gwynedd-Mercy College
Sumneytown Pike
Gwynedd Valley, PA 19437

Contact Information:
Telephone: 610-641-5536
Fax: 610-641-5559
E-mail: galvin.w@gmc.edu
Web: www.gmc.edu

Program Information:
Program begins: August
Degrees offered: Certificate program, 13 months; Diploma, 20 months; Associate's, 18 months; Bachelor's, 4 years
Evening or weekend classes are available.

Application Information:
Enrollment of program: 40
Transfer students are accepted.

Financial Information:
Average cost of books: $250
% of students receiving aid: 100

Employment Profile:
% of students who pass the boards on their first try: 95
% employed within the first 6 months following graduation: 100
Average starting salary: $37,000

York College of Pennsylvania
Country Club Road
York, PA 17403

Contact Information:
Telephone: 717-851-2464
Fax: 717-851-2487
E-mail: msimmons@yorkhospital.edu
Web: www.ycp.edu

Program Information:
Program begins: September
Duration of program: 24 months

Application Information:
Enrollment of program: 32
Transfer students are accepted.

Employment Profile:
% of students who pass the boards on their first try: 95
% employed within the first 6 months following graduation: 100

South Carolina

Greenville Technical College
PO Box 5616
Greenville, SC 29606

Contact Information:
Telephone: 864-250-8308
Fax: 864-250-8462
Web: www.greenvilletech.com

Program Information:
Program begins: August
Duration of program: 15 months

Financial Information:
Tuition, resident: $2,500
Tuition, non-resident: $6,400

Midlands Technical College
PO Box 2408
Columbia, SC 29202

Contact Information:
Telephone: 803-822-3433
Fax: 803-822-3079
E-mail: ackermanl@mtc.mid.tcc.sc.us
Web: www.mid.tec.sc.us

Program Information:
Program begins: August
Degrees offered: Diploma, 15 months
Evening or weekend classes are available.

Application Information:
Enrollment of program: 53
Transfer students are accepted.

Financial Information:
Tuition, resident: $1,620
Tuition, non-resident: $3,240
Average cost of books: $800
% of students receiving aid: 80

Employment Profile:
% of students who pass the boards on their first try: 100
% employed within the first 6 months following graduation: 100
Average starting salary: $31,000

Orangeburg Calhoun Technical College
3250 St. Matthews Road
Orangeburg, SC 29118

Contact Information:
Telephone: 803-536-0311
Fax: 803-535-1388
E-mail: stinchcomba@org.tec.sc.us
Web: www.octech.org

Program Information:
Program begins: January
Degrees offered: Associate's, 18 months

Application Information:
Enrollment of program: 17
Transfer students are accepted.

Financial Information:
Tuition, resident: $1,104
Tuition, non-resident: $1,392
Average cost of books: $240
% of students receiving aid: 50

Employment Profile:
% of students who pass the boards on their first try: 65
% employed within the first 6 months following graduation: 92
Average starting salary: $24,000

Tennessee

Tennessee Technology Center—Memphis

550 Alabama Avenue
Memphis, TN 38105

Contact Information:
Telephone: 901-543-6100 ext. 6186
Fax: 901-543-6197
E-mail: bfaulkner@memphis.tec.tn.us
Web: www.memphis.tec.tn.us

Program Information:
Program begins: September
Duration of program: 12 months

Application Information:
Enrollment of program: 30

Financial Information:
Tuition, resident: $1,000
Average cost of books: $300
% of students receiving aid: 30

Employment Profile:
% of students who pass the boards on their first try: 55
% employed within the first 6 months following graduation: 50
Average starting salary: $26,000

Texas

Alvin Community College

3110 Mustang Road
Alvin, TX 77511

Contact Information:
Telephone: 281-388-4695
Fax: 281-388-4936
E-mail: dflatlan@alvin.cc.tx.us
Web: www.alvin.cc.tx.us

Program Information:
Program begins: August
Duration of program: 18 months

Application Information:
Enrollment of program: 16
Transfer students are accepted.

Financial Information:
Tuition, resident: $1,295
Tuition, non-resident: $3,234
Average cost of books: $600
% of students receiving aid: 25

Employment Profile:
% of students who pass the boards on their first try: 100
% employed within the first 6 months following graduation: 100
Average starting salary: $25,000

Army Medical Department Center and School

Medical Science Division
PE Branch Building 1151
Ft. Sam Houston, TX 78234-6100

Contact Information:
Telephone: 210-295-4411
Fax: 210-295-4304
Web: www.cs.amedd.army.mil

Program Information:
Program begins: August
Duration of program: 8 months

Application Information:
Enrollment of program: 60
Transfer students are accepted.

Employment Profile:
% employed within the first 6 months following graduation: 98
Additional Information: Enrollment only open to active military personnel.

Lamar Institute of Technology—Beaumont

PO Box 10061
Beaumont, TX 77710

Contact Information:
Telephone: 409-880-8852
Fax: 409-880-8955
E-mail: bronsonpa@hal.lamar.edu
Web: www.lamar.edu

Program Information:
Program begins: August
Duration of program: 24 months

Application Information:
Enrollment of program: 75

Financial Information:
Tuition, resident: $2,298
Tuition, non-resident: $9,796

Employment Profile:
% of students who pass the boards on their first try: 96
% employed within the first 6 months following graduation: 100

Midland College

3600 North Garfield
Midland, TX 79705

Contact Information:
Telephone: 915-685-4601
Fax: 915-685-4762
E-mail: rweidmann@midland.cc.tx
Web: www.midland.cc.tx.us

Program Information:
Program begins: September
Degrees offered: Certificate program, 24 months
Evening or weekend classes are available.

Application Information:
Enrollment of program: 20
Transfer students are accepted.

Financial Information:
Tuition, resident: $1,095
Tuition, non-resident: $1,550
Average cost of books: $800
% of students receiving aid: 60

Employment Profile:
% of students who pass the boards on their first try: 73
% employed within the first 6 months following graduation: 94
Average starting salary: $24,000

St. Philip's College

1801 Martin Luther King Jr. Drive
San Antonio, TX 78203-2098

Contact Information:
Telephone: 210-531-3473
Fax: 210-531-3459
E-mail: bfisher@accd.edu
Web: www.accd.edu

Program Information:
Program begins: June
Degrees offered: Associate's, 18 months

Application Information:
Enrollment of program: 30
Transfer students are accepted.

Financial Information:
Tuition, resident: $1,000
Tuition, non-resident: $4,000
Average cost of books: $350
% of students receiving aid: 90

Employment Profile:
% of students who pass the boards on their first try: 90
% employed within the first 6 months following graduation: 90
Average starting salary: $27,000

University of Texas Health Science Center at San Antonio

7703 Floyd Curl Drive
Mail Code 6248
San Antonio, TX 782293900

Contact Information:
Telephone: 406-243-7821
Fax: 406-243-7899
E-mail: shelledy@uthscsa.edu
Web: www.uthscsa.edu

Program Information:
Duration of program: 23 months

Application Information:
Enrollment of program: 40
Transfer students are accepted.

Financial Information:
Tuition, resident: $1,800
Tuition, non-resident: $11,000
Average cost of books: $400

Employment Profile:
% of students who pass the boards on their first try: 100
% employed within the first 6 months following graduation: 100
Average starting salary: $32,000

Victoria College
2220 East Red River
Victoria, TX 77901

Contact Information:
Telephone: 361-572-6491
Fax: 361-582-2585
E-mail: ckallus@vc.cc.tx.us
Web: www.vc.cc.tx.us

Program Information:
Program begins: July
Duration of program: 16 months

Application Information:
Enrollment of program: 18

Financial Information:
Tuition, resident: $996
Tuition, non-resident: $4,233

Employment Profile:
% of students who pass the boards on their first try: 100
% employed within the first 6 months following graduation: 100

Utah

Weber State University
3750 Harrison Boulevard
Ogden, UT 84408-3904

Contact Information:
Telephone: 801-626-7071
Fax: 801-626-7683
E-mail: gbills@weber.edu
Web: www.weber.edu

Program Information:
Program begins: May
Duration of program: 10 months
Evening or weekend classes are available.

Application Information:
Enrollment of program: 12

Financial Information:
Average cost of books: $700

Employment Profile:
% of students who pass the boards on their first try: 90
% employed within the first 6 months following graduation: 100
Average starting salary: $24,000

Virginia

Central Virginia Community College
3506 Wards Road
Lynchburg, VA 24502

Contact Information:
Telephone: 804-832-7685
Fax: 804-832-7835
E-mail: crawleym@cv.cc.va.us
Web: www.cv.cc.va.us

Program Information:
Program begins: August
Duration of program: 12 months

Application Information:
Enrollment of program: 20
Transfer students are accepted.

Financial Information:
Tuition, resident: $1,879
Tuition, non-resident: $8,008
Average cost of books: $450
% of students receiving aid: 67

Employment Profile:
% of students who pass the boards on their first try: 100
% employed within the first 6 months following graduation: 100
Average starting salary: $24,000

Mountain Empire Community College
Drawer 700
Big Stone Gap, VA 24219

Contact Information:
Telephone: 540-523-2400 ext. 277
Fax: 540-523-8220
E-mail: mcook@me.cc.va.us

Program Information:
Program begins: August
Degrees offered: Certificate program, 12 months; Diploma, 14 months

Application Information:
Enrollment of program: 25
Transfer students are accepted.

Financial Information:
Tuition, resident: $2,826
Tuition, non-resident: $9,042
Average cost of books: $700

Employment Profile:
% of students who pass the boards on their first try: 88
% employed within the first 6 months following graduation: 70
Average starting salary: $18,000

Wyoming

Western Wyoming Community College
2500 College Drive
PO Box 428
Rock Springs, WY 82901-0428

Contact Information:
Telephone: 307-382-1799
Fax: 307-382-7665
E-mail: klizzi@wwcc.cc.wy.us

Program Information:
Program begins: June
Degrees offered: Certificate program, 10 months; Associate's, 10 months

Application Information:
Enrollment of program: 6
Transfer students are accepted.

Financial Information:
Tuition, resident: $1,098
Tuition, non-resident: $2,886
Average cost of books: $400
% of students receiving aid: 70

Employment Profile:
% of students who pass the boards on their first try: 80
% employed within the first 6 months following graduation: 100
Average starting salary: $21,840

Advanced Respiratory Therapist

Alabama

Shelton State Community College
3401 Martin Luther King Jr. Boulevard
Tuscaloosa, AL 35401

Contact Information:
Telephone: 205-391-2641
Fax: 205-391-2658
E-mail: bspruell@shelton.cc.al.us
Web: www.shelton.cc.al.us

Program Information:
Program begins: September
Degrees offered: Associate's, 18 months

Application Information:
Enrollment of program: 15
Transfer students are accepted.

Financial Information:
Tuition, resident: $1,260
Tuition, non-resident: $2,520
Average cost of books: $350
% of students receiving aid: 46

Employment Profile:
% of students who pass the boards on their first try: 75
% employed within the first 6 months following graduation: 100

University of Alabama at Birmingham
LRC 317
1714 9th Avenue South
Birmingham, AL 35294-1270

Contact Information:
Telephone: 787-766-1717 ext. 6596
Fax: 787-759-7663
E-mail: grangerw@shrp.uab.edu
Web: www.uab.edu.

Program Information:
Program begins: September
Degrees offered: Bachelor's

Financial Information:
Tuition, resident: $3,840
Tuition, non-resident: $7,680

Arizona

Apollo College

630 West Southern Avenue
Mesa, AZ 85210

Contact Information:

Telephone: 480-831-6585
Fax: 480-827-0022
Web: www.apollocollege.com

Program Information:

Degrees offered: Diploma, 20 months
Evening or weekend classes are available.

Application Information:

Enrollment of program: 50
Transfer students are accepted.

Financial Information:

% of students receiving aid: 85

Employment Profile:

% of students who pass the boards on their first try: 65
% employed within the first 6 months following graduation: 100
Average starting salary: $30,000

Gateway Community College

108 North 40th Street
Phoenix, AZ 85034

Contact Information:

Telephone: 602-392-5234
Fax: 602-392-5300
E-mail: rodriguez@gwc.maricopa.edu
Web: www.gwc.maricopa.edu

Program Information:

Program begins: September
Degrees offered: Associate's

Application Information:

Enrollment of program: 60
Transfer students are accepted.

Financial Information:

Tuition, resident: $1,147
Tuition, non-resident: $5,022
Average cost of books: $200
% of students receiving aid: 30

Employment Profile:

% of students who pass the boards on their first try: 75
% employed within the first 6 months following graduation: 90
Average starting salary: $38,000

Pima Medical Institute—Mesa

957 South Dobson Road
Mesa, AZ 85202

Contact Information:

Telephone: 602-345-7777
Fax: 602-649-5249
Web: www.pimamedical.com

Program Information:

Program begins: January, August
Degrees offered: Associate's, 15 months

Application Information:

Enrollment of program: 50
Transfer students are accepted.

Financial Information:

Tuition: $15,990
Average cost of books: $1,435
% of students receiving aid: 95

Employment Profile:

% of students who pass the boards on their first try: 85
% employed within the first 6 months following graduation: 85
Average starting salary: $28,000

Pima Medical Institute—Tucson

3350 East Grant Road
Tucson, AZ 85716

Contact Information:

Telephone: 520-326-1600
Fax: 520-795-3463
Web: www.pimamedical.com

Program Information:

Program begins: Quarterly
Degrees offered: Associate's, 26 months

Application Information:

Enrollment of program: 20

Financial Information:

Tuition: $11,185
% of students receiving aid: 90

Employment Profile:

% of students who pass the boards on their first try: 80
% employed within the first 6 months following graduation: 98

Arkansas

University of Arkansas for Medical Sciences

AHEC-Southwest, PO Box 2871
300 East 6th Street
Texarkana, AR 71854

Contact Information:

Telephone: 330-972-7906
Fax: 330-972-7906
E-mail: p_evans@ahersw.uams.edu
Web: www.uams.edu

Program Information:

Program begins: September
Degrees offered: Bachelor's, 24 months

Application Information:

Enrollment of program: 12

Financial Information:

Tuition, resident: $3,036
Tuition, non-resident: $7,590
Average cost of books: $650
% of students receiving aid: 70

Employment Profile:

% of students who pass the boards on their first try: 90
% employed within the first 6 months following graduation: 100
Average starting salary: $26,000

California

American River College

4700 College Oak Drive
Sacramento, CA 95841

Contact Information:

Telephone: 916-484-8876
Fax: 916-484-8030
E-mail: warmanj@arc.losrios.cc.ca.us
Web: www.arc.losrios.cc.ca.us

Program Information:

Program begins: August
Degrees offered: Associate's, 21 months
Evening or weekend classes are available.

Application Information:

Enrollment of program: 48
Transfer students are accepted.

Financial Information:

Tuition, resident: $416
Tuition, non-resident: $3,900
Average cost of books: $150
% of students receiving aid: 23

Employment Profile:

% of students who pass the boards on their first try: 95
% employed within the first 6 months following graduation: 100
Average starting salary: $38,000

Crafton Hills College

11711 Sand Canyon Road
Yucaipa, CA 92399

Contact Information:

Telephone: 909-389-3286
Fax: 909-794-0423
E-mail: kbryson@crafton.sbccd.cc.ca.us
Web: www.sbccd.cc.ca.us

Program Information:

Program begins: August
Degrees offered: Certificate program, 24 months; Diploma, 24 months

Application Information:

Enrollment of program: 30
Transfer students are accepted.

Financial Information:

Tuition, resident: $1,589
Tuition, non-resident: $13,570
Average cost of books: $350

Employment Profile:

% of students who pass the boards on their first try: 70
% employed within the first 6 months following graduation: 100
Average starting salary: $35,000

El Camino College

16007 South Crenshaw Boulevard
Torrance, CA 90506

Contact Information:
Telephone: 310-660-3248
Fax: 310-660-3378
E-mail: sinepoli@elcamino.cc.ca.us
Web: www.elcamino.cc.ca.us

Program Information:
Program begins: January
Degrees offered: Certificate program, 24 months; Associate's, 24 months

Application Information:
Enrollment of program: 15
Transfer students are accepted.

Financial Information:
Tuition, resident: $100
Tuition, non-resident: $1,000
Average cost of books: $100
% of students receiving aid: 50

Employment Profile:
% of students who pass the boards on their first try: 95
% employed within the first 6 months following graduation: 100
Average starting salary: $35,000

Foothill College

12345 El Monte Road
Los Altos Hills, CA 94022

Contact Information:
Telephone: 650-949-7292
Fax: 650-949-7375
E-mail: treanor@admin.fhda.edu
Web: www.foothill.fhda.edu

Program Information:
Program begins: September
Degrees offered: Associate's, 22 months; Post-bachelor's Certificate, 22 months

Application Information:
Enrollment of program: 45
Transfer students are accepted.

Financial Information:
Tuition, resident: $576
Tuition, non-resident: $5,184
Average cost of books: $450

Employment Profile:
% of students who pass the boards on their first try: 100
% employed within the first 6 months following graduation: 100
Average starting salary: $47,000

Fresno City College

1101 East University Avenue
Fresno, CA 93741

Contact Information:
Telephone: 554-442-4600
Fax: 554-244-2626
Web: www.fcc.cc.ca.us

Program Information:
Degrees offered: Associate's, 18 months

Application Information:
Enrollment of program: 48

Financial Information:
Tuition, resident: $332
Tuition, non-resident: $3,456
Average cost of books: $250

Employment Profile:
% of students who pass the boards on their first try: 88
% employed within the first 6 months following graduation: 86
Average starting salary: $25,000

Grossmont College

8800 Grossmont College Drive
El Cajon, CA 92020

Contact Information:
Telephone: 619-465-1700 ext. 7448
Fax: 619-644-7961
E-mail: lorenda_seibold_phalan@gcccd.net
Web: www.grossmont.gcccd.cc.ca.us

Program Information:
Program begins: August
Duration of program: 18 months

Financial Information:
Tuition, resident: $325
Tuition, non-resident: $2,775

Los Angeles Valley College

5800 Fulton Avenue
Valley Glen, CA 91401-4096

Contact Information:
Telephone: 818-947-2600 ext. 2845
Fax: 818-947-2850
E-mail: ettingvm@laccd.ca.us.ed
Web: www.lavc.cc.ca.us

Program Information:
Program begins: June
Degrees offered: Certificate program, 24 months; Associate's, 24 months

Application Information:
Enrollment of program: 27
Transfer students are accepted.

Financial Information:
Tuition, resident: $364
Tuition, non-resident: $3,724
Average cost of books: $500

Employment Profile:
% of students who pass the boards on their first try: 97
% employed within the first 6 months following graduation: 88
Average starting salary: $31,000

Modesto Junior College

435 College Avenue
Modesto, CA 95350

Contact Information:
Telephone: 209-575-6388
E-mail: lylet@yosenite.cc.ca.us

Program Information:
Program begins: August
Degrees offered: Associate's, 20 months

Financial Information:
Tuition, resident: $300
Tuition, non-resident: $3,000

Mt. San Antonio College

1100 North Grand Avenue
Walnut, CA 91789

Contact Information:
Telephone: 909-594-5611 ext. 4527
Fax: 909-468-3938
E-mail: zin@earthlink.net

Program Information:
Program begins: August
Duration of program: 22 months

Application Information:
Enrollment of program: 50
Transfer students are accepted.

Financial Information:
Tuition, resident: $400
Tuition, non-resident: $3,540

Employment Profile:
% of students who pass the boards on their first try: 90
% employed within the first 6 months following graduation: 85

Orange Coast College

2701 Fairview Road
PO Box 5005
Costa Mesa, CA 92628

Contact Information:
Telephone: 714-432-5541
Fax: 714-432-5534
E-mail: dadelman@cccd.edu
Web: www.occ.cccd.edu

Program Information:
Program begins: June
Degrees offered: Certificate program, 21 months; Diploma, 36 months

Application Information:
Enrollment of program: 37

Financial Information:
Tuition, resident: $330
Tuition, non-resident: $5,520
Average cost of books: $600
% of students receiving aid: 33

Employment Profile:
% of students who pass the boards on their first try: 98
% employed within the first 6 months following graduation: 100

San Joaquin Valley College—Visalia Campus
8400 West Mineral King
Visalia, CA 93291

Contact Information:
Telephone: 559-651-2500
Fax: 559-651-3645
Web: www.sjvc.com

Program Information:
Degrees offered: Associate's, 21 months

Application Information:
Enrollment of program: 30
Transfer students are accepted.

Financial Information:
Tuition, resident: $7,200
% of students receiving aid: 90

Employment Profile:
% of students who pass the boards on their first try: 94
% employed within the first 6 months following graduation: 99
Average starting salary: $31,200

Santa Monica College
Health Science Department
1900 Pico Boulevard
Santa Monica, CA 90405-1628

Contact Information:
Telephone: 310-434-3463
Fax: 310-434-0377
E-mail: melwelch@prodigy.net
Web: www.smc.edu

Program Information:
Program begins: January, June, August
Degrees offered: Certificate program, 24 months; Associate's, 24 months
Evening or weekend classes are available.

Application Information:
Transfer students are accepted.

Financial Information:
Tuition, resident: $455
Tuition, non-resident: $4,515
Average cost of books: $350

Employment Profile:
% of students who pass the boards on their first try: 90
% employed within the first 6 months following graduation: 100
Average starting salary: $38,000

Skyline College
3300 College Drive
San Bruno, CA 94066

Contact Information:
Telephone: 415-738-4382
Fax: 415-738-4299
E-mail: williamsonm@smcccd.cc.ca.us
Web: www.smcccd.cc.ca.us

Program Information:
Program begins: August
Degrees offered: Diploma, 24 months

Application Information:
Enrollment of program: 40
Transfer students are accepted.

Financial Information:
Tuition, resident: $416
Tuition, non-resident: $4,000
Average cost of books: $500
% of students receiving aid: 25

Employment Profile:
% of students who pass the boards on their first try: 94
% employed within the first 6 months following graduation: 100

Colorado

Front Range Community College—Westminster
3645 West 112th Avenue
Westminster, CO 80030

Contact Information:
Telephone: 303-404-5217
Fax: 303-404-2178

Program Information:
Program begins: August
Degrees offered: Certificate program; Associate's, 18 months

Application Information:
Enrollment of program: 15
Transfer students are accepted.

Financial Information:
Tuition, resident: $2,035
Tuition, non-resident: $9,640

Employment Profile:
% of students who pass the boards on their first try: 86
% employed within the first 6 months following graduation: 98

Connecticut

Manchester Community Technical College
60 Bidwell Street
Manchester, CT 06045-1046

Contact Information:
Telephone: 860-647-6193
Fax: 860-647-6370
E-mail: ma_milikowsk@commnet.edu
Web: www.mctc.commnet.edu

Program Information:
Program begins: August
Duration of program: 20 months

Application Information:
Transfer students are accepted.

Financial Information:
Tuition, resident: $2,131
Tuition, non-resident: $5,755

Employment Profile:
% of students who pass the boards on their first try: 90
% employed within the first 6 months following graduation: 100
Average starting salary: $40,000

University of Hartford
200 Bloomfield Avenue
West Hartford, CT 06117-1559

Contact Information:
Telephone: 860-768-4823
Fax: 860-768-5706
E-mail: pkennedy@mail.harford.edu
Web: www.hartford.edu

Program Information:
Program begins: September
Duration of program: 48 months

Application Information:
Enrollment of program: 40
Transfer students are accepted.

Financial Information:
Tuition: $17,900

Employment Profile:
% of students who pass the boards on their first try: 85
% employed within the first 6 months following graduation: 90

Delaware

Delaware Technical & Community College—Owens Campus
PO Box 610
Georgetown, DE 19947

Contact Information:
Telephone: 302-856-5400
Fax: 302-856-5773
E-mail: jlittle@outland.dtcc.edu
Web: www.dtcc.edu

Program Information:
Program begins: August
Duration of program: 23 months
Evening or weekend classes are available.

Application Information:
Enrollment of program: 18
Transfer students are accepted.

Financial Information:
Tuition, resident: $2,070
Tuition, non-resident: $5,175

Employment Profile:
% of students who pass the boards on their first try: 100
% employed within the first 6 months following graduation: 100
Average starting salary: $27,000

Delaware Technical & Community College—Wilmington
333 Shipley Street
Wilmington, DE 19801

Contact Information:
Telephone: 302-428-2678
Fax: 302-428-2691
E-mail: rlang@christianacare.org
Web: www.dtcc.edu

Program Information:
Program begins: August
Degrees offered: Associate's, 23 months

Application Information:
Enrollment of program: 15
Transfer students are accepted.

Financial Information:
Tuition, resident: $1,890
Tuition, non-resident: $4,725

Employment Profile:
% of students who pass the boards on their first try: 90
% employed within the first 6 months following graduation: 100

Florida

Broward Community College

1000 Coconut Creek Boulevard
Coconut Creek, FL 33066

Contact Information:
Telephone: 954-969-2082
Fax: 954-973-2348
E-mail: jprince@broward.cc.fl.us
Web: www.broward.cc.fl.us

Program Information:
Program begins: August
Duration of program: 24 months
Evening or weekend classes are available.

Application Information:
Enrollment of program: 25

Financial Information:
Tuition, resident: $1,700
Tuition, non-resident: $5,325
Average cost of books: $150
% of students receiving aid: 50

Employment Profile:
% of students who pass the boards on their first try: 85
% employed within the first 6 months following graduation: 100
Average starting salary: $35,000

Daytona Beach Community College

1200 West International Speedway Boulevard
PO Box 2811
Daytona Beach, FL 32120-2811

Contact Information:
Telephone: 904-255-8131
Fax: 904-254-4491
E-mail: mccumbm@dbcc.cc.fl.us
Web: www.dbcc.cc.fl.us

Program Information:
Program begins: August
Degrees offered: Associate's, 21 months

Application Information:
Enrollment of program: 28
Transfer students are accepted.

Financial Information:
Tuition, resident: $1,800
Tuition, non-resident: $6,500
Average cost of books: $500

Employment Profile:
% of students who pass the boards on their first try: 98
% employed within the first 6 months following graduation: 85
Average starting salary: $19,200

Edison Community College

8099 College Parkway Southwest
PO Box 06210
Ft. Myers, FL 33906-6210

Contact Information:
Telephone: 941-489-9252
Fax: 941-489-9037
E-mail: bkenney@edison.edu
Web: www.edison.edu

Program Information:
Program begins: August
Degrees offered: Diploma, 22 months

Application Information:
Enrollment of program: 25
Transfer students are accepted.

Financial Information:
Tuition, resident: $1,483
Tuition, non-resident: $5,943
Average cost of books: $275
% of students receiving aid: 50

Employment Profile:
% of students who pass the boards on their first try: 90
% employed within the first 6 months following graduation: 100
Average starting salary: $23,000

Indian River Community College

3209 Virginia Avenue
Ft. Pierce, FL 34981-5599

Contact Information:
Telephone: 561-462-4358
Fax: 561-462-4900
E-mail: grosenfe@ircc.cc.fl.us
Web: www.ircc.cc.fl.us

Program Information:
Program begins: August
Duration of program: 21 months

Application Information:
Enrollment of program: 15

Financial Information:
Tuition, resident: $1,443
Average cost of books: $500

Employment Profile:
% of students who pass the boards on their first try: 100
% employed within the first 6 months following graduation: 100

Manatee Community College

5840 26th Street West
PO Box 1849
Bradenton, FL 34206

Contact Information:
Telephone: 941-755-1511
E-mail: hainesl@bc.mcc.cc.fl.us
Web: www.mcc.cc.fl.us

Program Information:
Program begins: August
Duration of program: 20 months

Application Information:
Enrollment of program: 20
Transfer students are accepted.

Financial Information:
Tuition, resident: $2,904
Tuition, non-resident: $7,260
Average cost of books: $700
% of students receiving aid: 60

Employment Profile:
% of students who pass the boards on their first try: 98
% employed within the first 6 months following graduation: 70
Average starting salary: $25,000

Miami-Dade Community College

Medical Center Campus
950 Northwest 20th Street
Miami, FL 33127

Contact Information:
Telephone: 305-237-4031
Fax: 305-237-4278
E-mail: cmiller@mdcc.edu
Web: www.mdcc.edu

Program Information:
Program begins: August
Degrees offered: Certificate program, 16 months; Diploma, 24 months

Application Information:
Enrollment of program: 35
Transfer students are accepted.

Financial Information:
Tuition, resident: $1,939
Tuition, non-resident: $6,815
Average cost of books: $530
% of students receiving aid: 60

Employment Profile:
% of students who pass the boards on their first try: 95
% employed within the first 6 months following graduation: 100
Average starting salary: $26,000

Palm Beach Community College

3160 PGA Boulevard
Palm Beach Gardens, FL 33410-2893

Contact Information:
Telephone: 561-625-2588

Fax: 561-625-2305
E-mail: rogersj@pbcc.cc.fl.us
Web: www.pbcc.fl.us

Program Information:
Program begins: August
Degrees offered: Certificate program, 10 months; Associate's, 18 months

Application Information:
Enrollment of program: 19
Transfer students are accepted.

Financial Information:
Tuition, resident: $3,369
Tuition, non-resident: $10,109
Average cost of books: $450
% of students receiving aid: 38

Employment Profile:
% of students who pass the boards on their first try: 85
% employed within the first 6 months following graduation: 100
Average starting salary: $21,000

Santa Fe Community College
3000 Northwest 83rd Street
Gainesville, FL 32606-6200

Contact Information:
Telephone: 352-395-5706
Fax: 352-395-5711
E-mail: dave.yonutas@santafe.cc.fl.us

Program Information:
Program begins: August
Degrees offered: Associate's, 18 months

Application Information:
Enrollment of program: 14
Transfer students are accepted.

Financial Information:
Tuition, resident: $3,504
Tuition, non-resident: $13,087
Average cost of books: $450

Employment Profile:
% of students who pass the boards on their first try: 98
% employed within the first 6 months following graduation: 93
Average starting salary: $28,000

University of Central Florida
Department of Health Professions and Physical Therapy
Orlando, FL 32816

Contact Information:
Telephone: 407-823-2214
Fax: 407-823-6138
E-mail: worrell@pegasus.cc.ucf.edu
Web: www.ucf.edu

Program Information:
Program begins: May
Degrees offered: Bachelor's, 20 months
Evening or weekend classes are available.

Application Information:
Enrollment of program: 32
Transfer students are accepted.

Financial Information:
Tuition, resident: $2,400
Tuition, non-resident: $4,541
Average cost of books: $300

Employment Profile:
% of students who pass the boards on their first try: 95
% employed within the first 6 months following graduation: 95
Average starting salary: $26,000

Valencia Community College
PO Box 3028
Orlando, FL 32802-9961

Contact Information:
Telephone: 407-299-5000 ext. 1550
Fax: 407-293-8839
E-mail: lcapraun@valencia.cc.fl.us
Web: www.valencia.cc.fl.us

Program Information:
Program begins: August
Degrees offered: Associate's, 22 months
Evening or weekend classes are available.

Application Information:
Enrollment of program: 48
Transfer students are accepted.

Financial Information:
Tuition, resident: $1,690
Tuition, non-resident: $6,160
Average cost of books: $300
% of students receiving aid: 25

Employment Profile:
% of students who pass the boards on their first try: 90
% employed within the first 6 months following graduation: 95
Average starting salary: $26,000

Georgia

Augusta Technical Institute
3116 Deans Bridge Road
Augusta, GA 30906

Contact Information:
Telephone: 706-771-4194
Fax: 706-771-4181
Web: www.augusta.tec.ga.us

Program Information:
Program begins: September
Degrees offered: Diploma, 24 months

Application Information:
Enrollment of program: 42

Financial Information:
Average cost of books: $910
% of students receiving aid: 40

Employment Profile:
% of students who pass the boards on their first try: 85
% employed within the first 6 months following graduation: 85
Average starting salary: $26,000

Columbus State University
4225 University Avenue
Columbus, GA 31907-5645

Contact Information:
Telephone: 706-568-2130
Fax: 706-569-3101
E-mail: chang_david@colstate.edu
Web: www.colstate.edu

Program Information:
Program begins: June
Degrees offered: Bachelor's, 48 months

Application Information:
Enrollment of program: 60
Transfer students are accepted.

Financial Information:
Tuition, resident: $2,595
Tuition, non-resident: $7,830

Employment Profile:
% of students who pass the boards on their first try: 100
% employed within the first 6 months following graduation: 100
Average starting salary: $28,000

Georgia State University
University Plaza
Atlanta, GA 30303

Contact Information:
Telephone: 404-651-3037
Fax: 404-651-1531
Web: www.gsu.edu

Program Information:
Program begins: August
Duration of program: 22 months

Application Information:
Enrollment of program: 60
Transfer students are accepted.

Financial Information:
Tuition, resident: $3,283
Tuition, non-resident: $13,098
Average cost of books: $700

Employment Profile:
% of students who pass the boards on their first try: 86
Average starting salary: $30,000

Gwinnett Technical Institute
5150 Sugarloaf Parkway
PO Box 1505
Lawrenceville, GA 30246-1505

Contact Information:
Telephone: 770-962-7580 ext. 158
Fax: 770-962-7985
E-mail: bdelorme@gwinnett.tec.ga.us
Web: www.gwinnett-tech.org

Program Information:
Program begins: August
Duration of program: 24 months

Application Information:
Enrollment of program: 18

Financial Information:
Tuition, resident: $1,356
Tuition, non-resident: $2,460

Employment Profile:
% employed within the first 6 months following graduation: 100
Average starting salary: $30,000

Medical College of Georgia
815 St. Sebastian Way
Room HM-143
Augusta, GA 30912

Contact Information:
Telephone: 706-721-3554
Fax: 706-721-0495
E-mail: smishoe@mail.mcg.edu
Web: www.mcg.edu

Program Information:
Program begins: September
Degrees offered: Bachelor's, 22 months

Application Information:
Enrollment of program: 40
Transfer students are accepted.

Financial Information:
Tuition, resident: $1,870
Tuition, non-resident: $5,327
Average cost of books: $810
% of students receiving aid: 66

Employment Profile:
% of students who pass the boards on their first try: 100
% employed within the first 6 months following graduation: 100
Average starting salary: $34,000

Idaho

Boise State University
College of Health Science
1910 University Drive Room HSR 116
Boise, ID 83725

Contact Information:
Telephone: 208-426-3383
Fax: 208-426-4093
E-mail: lashwor@boisestate.edu
Web: www.idbsu.edu

Program Information:
Program begins: May
Duration of program: 33 months

Financial Information:
Tuition, resident: $2,300
Tuition, non-resident: $8,174

Employment Profile:
% of students who pass the boards on their first try: 95
% employed within the first 6 months following graduation: 100
Average starting salary: $30,000

Illinois

College of DuPage
Advanced Practitioner
425 22nd Street
Glen Ellyn, IL 60137-6599

Contact Information:
Telephone: 630-942-2518
Fax: 630-858-9399
E-mail: bretlk@cdnet.cod.edu
Web: www.cod.edu

Program Information:
Program begins: June, September
Degrees offered: Diploma, 24 months
Evening or weekend classes are available.

Application Information:
Enrollment of program: 20
Transfer students are accepted.

Financial Information:
Tuition, resident: $2,880
Tuition, non-resident: $8,832
Average cost of books: $400

Employment Profile:
% of students who pass the boards on their first try: 95
% employed within the first 6 months following graduation: 100
Average starting salary: $30,000

Illinois Central College
201 Southwest Adams Street
Peoria, IL 61635-0001

Contact Information:
Telephone: 309-999-4663
Fax: 309-673-9626
E-mail: mswanson@icc.cc.il.us
Web: www.icc.cc.il.us

Program Information:
Program begins: August
Degrees offered: Associate's, 21 months

Application Information:
Enrollment of program: 35
Transfer students are accepted.

Financial Information:
Tuition, resident: $1,680
Tuition, non-resident: $6,400

Employment Profile:
% employed within the first 6 months following graduation: 100

Kankakee Community College
River Road
PO Box 888
Kankakee, IL 60901

Contact Information:
Telephone: 815-933-0276
Fax: 815-933-0217
E-mail: nfrey@kcc.cc.il.us
Web: www.kcc.cc.il.us

Program Information:
Program begins: August
Degrees offered: Associate's, 21 months

Application Information:
Enrollment of program: 32
Transfer students are accepted.

Financial Information:
Tuition, resident: $1,140
Tuition, non-resident: $2,310
Average cost of books: $800
% of students receiving aid: 50

Employment Profile:
% of students who pass the boards on their first try: 95
% employed within the first 6 months following graduation: 100
Average starting salary: $27,000

Lincoln Land Community College
PO Box 19256
Shepherd Road
Springfield, IL 62794-9256

Contact Information:
Telephone: 217-786-2814
Fax: 217-786-2824
E-mail: randy.prather@llcc.cc.il.us
Web: www.llcc.cc.il.us

Program Information:
Program begins: June
Degrees offered: Certificate program, 22 months; Associate's, 22 months

Application Information:
Enrollment of program: 20
Transfer students are accepted.

Financial Information:
Tuition, resident: $1,575
Average cost of books: $800
% of students receiving aid: 25

Employment Profile:
% of students who pass the boards on their first try: 93
% employed within the first 6 months following graduation: 100
Average starting salary: $25,000

National-Louis University
2840 North Sheridan Road
Evanston, IL 60201

Contact Information:
Telephone: 847-256-5150 ext. 2539
Fax: 847-256-1057
E-mail: stho@evan1.nl.edu
Web: www.nl.edu

Program Information:
Program begins: August
Duration of program: 15 months

Application Information:
Enrollment of program: 12
Transfer students are accepted.

Financial Information:
Average cost of books: $400

Employment Profile:
% of students who pass the boards on their first try: 90
% employed within the first 6 months following graduation: 90
Average starting salary: $30,000

Rock Valley College
3301 North Mulford Road
Rockford, IL 61114-5699

Contact Information:
Telephone: 815-654-4413
Fax: 815-654-4408
E-mail: fahe3js@rvc.cc.il.us
Web: www.rvc.cc.il.us

Program Information:
Program begins: August
Duration of program: 22 months

Application Information:
Enrollment of program: 18
Transfer students are accepted.

Financial Information:
Tuition, resident: $1,435
Tuition, non-resident: $4,674
Average cost of books: $350
% of students receiving aid: 60

Employment Profile:
% of students who pass the boards on their first try: 95
% employed within the first 6 months following graduation: 100
Average starting salary: $25,000

Indiana

Indiana University School of Medicine
1140 West Michigan Street/CF 224
Indianapolis, IN 46202

Contact Information:
Telephone: 317-274-7381
Fax: 317-278-7383
E-mail: rtstaff@iupui.edu
Web: www.saha.iupui.edu

Program Information:
Program begins: September
Degrees offered: Bachelor's, 44 months

Application Information:
Enrollment of program: 60
Transfer students are accepted.

Financial Information:
Tuition, resident: $3,672
Tuition, non-resident: $11,268
Average cost of books: $1,000
% of students receiving aid: 25

Employment Profile:
% of students who pass the boards on their first try: 90
% employed within the first 6 months following graduation: 95
Average starting salary: $33,500

Ivy Tech State College—Lafayette
3208 Ross Road
PO Box 6299
Lafayette, IN 47903

Contact Information:
Telephone: 765-772-9219
Fax: 765-772-9248
E-mail: pjames@ivytec.in.us
Web: www.laf.ivy.tec.in.us

Program Information:
Program begins: August
Degrees offered: Associate's, 20 months
Evening or weekend classes are available.

Application Information:
Enrollment of program: 20
Transfer students are accepted.

Financial Information:
Tuition, resident: $3,570
Tuition, non-resident: $5,819

Employment Profile:
% of students who pass the boards on their first try: 96
% employed within the first 6 months following graduation: 100

Ivy Tech State College NE—Fort Wayne
3800 North Anthony Boulevard
Ft. Wayne, IN 46805

Contact Information:
Telephone: 219-482-9171 ext. 4270
Fax: 219-480-4149
E-mail: cschlade@ivy.tec.in.us

Program Information:
Program begins: August
Degrees offered: Associate's, 21 months
Evening or weekend classes are available.

Application Information:
Enrollment of program: 28
Transfer students are accepted.

Financial Information:
Tuition, resident: $2,819
Tuition, non-resident: $5,135
Average cost of books: $750
% of students receiving aid: 85

Employment Profile:
% of students who pass the boards on their first try: 93
% employed within the first 6 months following graduation: 100
Average starting salary: $27,000

Iowa

Des Moines Area Community College
2006 Ankeny Boulevard
Ankeny, IA 50021

Contact Information:
Telephone: 515-964-6298
Fax: 515-964-6327
E-mail: kegeorge@dmacc.cc.ia.us
Web: www.dmacc.cc.ia.us

Program Information:
Program begins: August
Degrees offered: Associate's, 23 months

Application Information:
Enrollment of program: 40
Transfer students are accepted.

Financial Information:
Tuition, resident: $2,640
Tuition, non-resident: $5,280

Employment Profile:
% of students who pass the boards on their first try: 95
% employed within the first 6 months following graduation: 100
Average starting salary: $28,700

Kirkwood Community College
6301 Kirkwood Boulevard Southwest
PO Box 2068
Cedar Rapids, IA 52406-9973

Contact Information:
Telephone: 319-398-5411
Fax: 319-398-1293
E-mail: kbronkh@kirkwood.cc.ia.us
Web: www.kirkwood.cc.ia.us

Program Information:
Program begins: August
Degrees offered: Associate's, 21 months
Evening or weekend classes are available.

Application Information:
Enrollment of program: 30
Transfer students are accepted.

Financial Information:
Tuition, resident: $2,393
Tuition, non-resident: $4,785
Average cost of books: $550
% of students receiving aid: 40

Employment Profile:
% of students who pass the boards on their first try: 75-80
% employed within the first 6 months following graduation: 100
Average starting salary: $28,500

Kansas

Bethany Medical Center
Kansas City Kansas Community College
7250 State Avenue
Kansas City, KS 66112

Contact Information:
Telephone: 913-334-1100 ext. 245
Fax: 913-281-7875
Web: www.kckcc.cc.ks.us

Financial Information:
Tuition, resident: $3,850
Tuition, non-resident: $5,200

Seward County Community College

PO Box 1137
Liberal, KS 67905-1137

Contact Information:

Telephone: 316-626-3080
Fax: 316-626-3026
E-mail: eanderso@sccc.cc.ks.us
Web: www.sccc.cc.ks.us

Program Information:

Program begins: August
Degrees offered: Associate's, 24 months

Application Information:

Enrollment of program: 16
Transfer students are accepted.

Financial Information:

Tuition, resident: $1,134
Tuition, non-resident: $2,100
Average cost of books: $300
% of students receiving aid: 95

Employment Profile:

% of students who pass the boards on their first try: 75
% employed within the first 6 months following graduation: 100
Average starting salary: $30,000

Washburn University of Topeka

1700 College Avenue Southwest
Topeka, KS 66621

Contact Information:

Telephone: 785-231-1010 ext. 1404
Fax: 785-231-1027
E-mail: zzmunz@washburn.edu
Web: www.washburn.edu

Program Information:

Program begins: August
Degrees offered: Associate's, 24 months

Application Information:

Enrollment of program: 18
Transfer students are accepted.

Financial Information:

Tuition, resident: $3,456
Tuition, non-resident: $8,018
Average cost of books: $1,200
% of students receiving aid: 80

Employment Profile:

% of students who pass the boards on their first try: 100
Average starting salary: $28,000

Kentucky

Cumberland Valley—Southeast Community College Consortium

US 25E South PO Box 187
Pineville, KY 40977

Contact Information:

Telephone: 606-337-3106
Fax: 606-337-5662
E-mail: mike.good@kctcs.net
Web: www.kctcs.net

Program Information:

Program begins: August
Degrees offered: Associate's, 24 months

Application Information:

Enrollment of program: 24
Transfer students are accepted.

Financial Information:

Average cost of books: $500
% of students receiving aid: 80

Employment Profile:

% of students who pass the boards on their first try: 100
% employed within the first 6 months following graduation: 100
Average starting salary: $24,000

Northern Kentucky University

Nunn Drive
AHC-225
Highland Heights, KY 41099-8002

Contact Information:

Telephone: 606-572-5557
Fax: 606-572-6592
E-mail: langenderfer@nku.edu
Web: www.nku.edu

Program Information:

Program begins: August
Degrees offered: Associate's, 21 months

Application Information:

Enrollment of program: 28
Transfer students are accepted.

Financial Information:

Tuition, resident: $2,615
Tuition, non-resident: $7,040
Average cost of books: $300
% of students receiving aid: 48

Employment Profile:

% of students who pass the boards on their first try: 98
% employed within the first 6 months following graduation: 100
Average starting salary: $30,000

Louisiana

Delgado Community College

615 City Park Avenue
New Orleans, LA 70119

Contact Information:

Telephone: 504-483-4114 ext. 4007
Fax: 504-483-4609
E-mail: dolsen@dcc.edu
Web: www.dcc.edu

Program Information:

Program begins: August
Duration of program: 24 months

Application Information:

Enrollment of program: 11
Transfer students are accepted.

Financial Information:

Tuition, resident: $1,455
Tuition, non-resident: $3,255
Average cost of books: $500
% of students receiving aid: 50

Employment Profile:

% of students who pass the boards on their first try: 70
% employed within the first 6 months following graduation: 90
Average starting salary: $27,000

Maine

Southern Maine Technical College

Two Fort Road
South Portland, ME 04106

Contact Information:

Telephone: 207-767-9592
Fax: 207-767-9690
E-mail: wchop@smtc.net
Web: www.smtc.net

Program Information:

Program begins: August, September
Duration of program: 21 months

Application Information:

Enrollment of program: 25
Transfer students are accepted.

Financial Information:

Tuition, resident: $2,800
Tuition, non-resident: $5,600
Average cost of books: $300
% of students receiving aid: 60

Employment Profile:

% of students who pass the boards on their first try: 90
% employed within the first 6 months following graduation: 100
Average starting salary: $28,000

Maryland

Allegany College of Maryland

12401 Willowbrook Road Southeast
Cumberland, MD 21502-2596

Contact Information:

Telephone: 301-784-5521
Fax: 301-784-5015
E-mail: brocks@acc7.ac.cc.md.us
Web: www.ac.cc.md.us

Program Information:

Program begins: September
Duration of program: 17 months

Application Information:

Enrollment of program: 24
Transfer students are accepted.

Financial Information:

Tuition, resident: $3,600
Tuition, non-resident: $11,376

Employment Profile:

% of students who pass the boards on their first try: 95

% employed within the first 6 months following graduation: 90
Average starting salary: $30,000

Frederick Community College
7932 Opossumtown Pike
Frederick, MD 21702

Contact Information:
Telephone: 301-846-2528
Fax: 301-846-2498
Web: www.fcc.cc.md.us

Program Information:
Program begins: May
Duration of program: 21 months

Application Information:
Transfer students are accepted.

Financial Information:
Tuition, resident: $4,899
Tuition, non-resident: $16,077
Average cost of books: $500

Employment Profile:
% of students who pass the boards on their first try: 100
% employed within the first 6 months following graduation: 100
Average starting salary: $32,000

Prince George's Community College
301 Largo Road
Largo, MD 20774

Contact Information:
Telephone: 301-322-0740
Fax: 301-386-7528
E-mail: smithla1@pg.cc.md.us

Program Information:
Program begins: August
Degrees offered: Associate's, 21 months

Application Information:
Enrollment of program: 24
Transfer students are accepted.

Financial Information:
Tuition, resident: $2,967
Tuition, non-resident: $7,349
Average cost of books: $200
% of students receiving aid: 50

Employment Profile:
% of students who pass the boards on their first try: 90
% employed within the first 6 months following graduation: 100
Average starting salary: $30,000

Salisbury State University
1101 Camden Avenue
Salisbury, MD 21801

Contact Information:
Telephone: 410-543-6365
Fax: 410-548-9185
E-mail: srschneider@ssu.edu
Web: www.ssu.edu

Program Information:
Program begins: September
Duration of program: 24 months

Application Information:
Enrollment of program: 20
Transfer students are accepted.

Financial Information:
Tuition, resident: $2,972
Tuition, non-resident: $7,366
% of students receiving aid: 63

Employment Profile:
% employed within the first 6 months following graduation: 95
Average starting salary: $30,000

Massachusetts

Northeastern University
100 Dockser Hall
360 Huntington Ave
Boston, MA 021155000

Contact Information:
Telephone: 617-373-3667
Fax: 617-373-2968
E-mail: tbarnes@lynx.neu.edu
Web: www.neu.edu

Program Information:
Program begins: September
Degrees offered: Bachelor's, 57 months

Application Information:
Enrollment of program: 75
Transfer students are accepted.

Financial Information:
Average cost of books: $350
% of students receiving aid: 75

Employment Profile:
% of students who pass the boards on their first try: 100
% employed within the first 6 months following graduation: 100
Average starting salary: $35,000

Northern Essex Community College
45 Franklin Street
Lawrence, MA 01841-4911

Contact Information:
Telephone: 978-738-7000
Fax: 978-738-1667
E-mail: crowse@necc.mass.edu
Web: www.necc.mass.edu

Program Information:
Program begins: August
Degrees offered: Certificate program, 16 months; Associate's, 22 months
Evening or weekend classes are available.

Application Information:
Enrollment of program: 25
Transfer students are accepted.

Financial Information:
Tuition, resident: $2,673
Tuition, non-resident: $8,283
Average cost of books: $200
% of students receiving aid: 20

Employment Profile:
% of students who pass the boards on their first try: 85
% employed within the first 6 months following graduation: 85
Average starting salary: $27,000

Michigan

Delta College
F-56 Allied Health Building
University Center, MI 48710

Contact Information:
Telephone: 517-686-9489
Fax: 517-686-8736
E-mail: ebgregor@alpha.delta.edu
Web: www.delta.edu

Program Information:
Program begins: September
Duration of program: 24 months
Evening or weekend classes are available.

Application Information:
Enrollment of program: 15
Transfer students are accepted.

Financial Information:
Tuition, resident: $1,717
Tuition, non-resident: $3,100

Employment Profile:
% employed within the first 6 months following graduation: 90
Average starting salary: $30,000

Kalamazoo Valley Community College
Texas Township Campus
6767 West O Avenue, PO Box 4070
Kalamazoo, MI 49003-4070

Contact Information:
Telephone: 616-372-5288
Fax: 616-372-5458
E-mail: amoss@kvcc.edu
Web: www.kvcc.edu

Program Information:
Program begins: August
Degrees offered: Associate's, 19 months
Evening or weekend classes are available.

Application Information:
Enrollment of program: 24
Transfer students are accepted.

Financial Information:
Tuition, resident: $1,476

Tuition, non-resident: $3,852
Average cost of books: $400

Employment Profile:
% of students who pass the boards on their first try: 98
% employed within the first 6 months following graduation: 100
Average starting salary: $28,000

Macomb Community College
44575 Garfield Road
East Building Room 219
Clinton Township, MI 48038-1139

Contact Information:
Telephone: 810-286-2150
Fax: 810-286-2098
E-mail: alsteadm@macomb.cc.mi.us
Web: www.macomb.cc.mi.us

Program Information:
Program begins: August
Duration of program: 21 months

Application Information:
Enrollment of program: 23
Transfer students are accepted.

Financial Information:
Tuition, resident: $3,348
Tuition, non-resident: $5,084
Average cost of books: $682

Employment Profile:
% of students who pass the boards on their first try: 90
% employed within the first 6 months following graduation: 97
Average starting salary: $26,600

Marygrove College
8425 West McNicholos Road
Detroit, MI 48221-2599

Contact Information:
Telephone: 313-927-1421
Fax: 313-927-1345
E-mail: kmiller@marygrove.edu
Web: www.marygrove.edu

Program Information:
Program begins: January
Duration of program: 24 months
Evening or weekend classes are available.

Application Information:
Enrollment of program: 9
Transfer students are accepted.

Employment Profile:
% of students who pass the boards on their first try: 40
% employed within the first 6 months following graduation: 40
Average starting salary: $26,000

Muskegon Community College
221 South Quarterline Road
Muskegon, MI 49442

Contact Information:
Telephone: 616-777-0370
Fax: 231-777-0490
E-mail: knued@muskegon.cc.mi.us
Web: www.muskegon.cc.mi.us

Program Information:
Program begins: January, September
Duration of program: 28 months
Evening or weekend classes are available.

Application Information:
Enrollment of program: 40
Transfer students are accepted.

Financial Information:
Tuition, resident: $1,900
Tuition, non-resident: $2,800
Average cost of books: $500
% of students receiving aid: 80

Employment Profile:
% of students who pass the boards on their first try: 80
% employed within the first 6 months following graduation: 100
Average starting salary: $35,000

Oakland Community College
2480 Opdyke Road
Bloomfield Hills, MI 48304-2266

Contact Information:
Telephone: 248-552-2655
Fax: 248-552-2661
E-mail: mltroxel@occ.cc.mi.us
Web: www.occ.cc.mi.us

Program Information:
Program begins: May
Duration of program: 16 months

Application Information:
Transfer students are accepted.

Financial Information:
Tuition, resident: $2,250
Tuition, non-resident: $3,900
Average cost of books: $400

Employment Profile:
% of students who pass the boards on their first try: 95
% employed within the first 6 months following graduation: 90
Average starting salary: $32,000

Minnesota

Lake Superior College
2101 Trinity Road
Duluth, MN 55811

Contact Information:
Telephone: 218-733-5925
Fax: 218-723-4921
E-mail: c.annable@lsc.cc.mn.us
Web: www.lsc.cc.mn.us

Program Information:
Program begins: August
Duration of program: 21 months

Northwest Technical College—East Grand Forks
2022 Central Avenue Northeast
East Grand Forks, MN 56721

Contact Information:
Telephone: 218-773-3441 ext. 415
Fax: 218-773-4502
E-mail: tony.sorum@mail.ntc.mnscu.edu
Web: www.ntc-online.com

Program Information:
Program begins: August
Degrees offered: Associate's, 18 months; Bachelor's, 36 months

Application Information:
Enrollment of program: 25
Transfer students are accepted.

Financial Information:
Tuition, resident: $6,618
Tuition, non-resident: $13,236
Average cost of books: $580

Employment Profile:
% of students who pass the boards on their first try: 85
% employed within the first 6 months following graduation: 100

Mississippi

Mississippi Gulf Coast Community College
PO Box 100
Gautier, MS 39553

Contact Information:
Telephone: 601-497-7711 ext. 290
Fax: 601-497-7670
Web: www.mgccc.cc.ms.us

Program Information:
Program begins: August
Degrees offered: Certificate program, 24 months; Associate's, 24 months

Application Information:
Enrollment of program: 20
Transfer students are accepted.

Financial Information:
Tuition, resident: $1,400
Tuition, non-resident: $2,800
Average cost of books: $100
% of students receiving aid: 75

Employment Profile:
% employed within the first 6 months following graduation: 100
Average starting salary: $29,000

Northwest Mississippi Community College
5197 West Ross Parkway
Southaven, MS 38671

Contact Information:
Telephone: 662-280-6151 ext. 137

Fax: 601-280-4677
E-mail: r_clark@nwcc.cc.ms.us
Web: www.nwcc.cc.ms.us

Program Information:
Program begins: August
Degrees offered: Associate's, 20 months

Application Information:
Enrollment of program: 20
Transfer students are accepted.

Financial Information:
Tuition, resident: $1,000
Tuition, non-resident: $2,400
Average cost of books: $250

Employment Profile:
% of students who pass the boards on their first try: 100
% employed within the first 6 months following graduation: 100
Average starting salary: $33,000

Missouri

St. Louis Community College at Forest Park

5600 Oakland Avenue
St. Louis, MO 63110

Contact Information:
Telephone: 314-644-9079
Fax: 314 644-9752
E-mail: jbrennan@fpmail.stlcc.cc.mo.us
Web: www.stlcc.cc.mo.us

Program Information:
Program begins: August
Degrees offered: Associate's, 22 months

Application Information:
Transfer students are accepted.

Financial Information:
Tuition, resident: $2,000
Tuition, non-resident: $27,000
Average cost of books: $350
% of students receiving aid: 65

Employment Profile:
% of students who pass the boards on their first try: 95
% employed within the first 6 months following graduation: 100
Average starting salary: $25,000

Montana

Montana State University College of Technology—Great Falls

2100 16th Avenue South
PO Box 6010
Great Falls, MT 59405

Contact Information:
Telephone: 406-771-4360
Fax: 406-771-4313
E-mail: lbates@msucotgf.montana.edu
Web: www.msucotgf.montana.edu

Program Information:
Program begins: August
Degrees offered: Associate's, 27 months

Application Information:
Enrollment of program: 18
Transfer students are accepted.

Financial Information:
Tuition, resident: $2,074
Tuition, non-resident: $5,172
Average cost of books: $300
% of students receiving aid: 75

Employment Profile:
% of students who pass the boards on their first try: 89
% employed within the first 6 months following graduation: 98

Nebraska

Nebraska Methodist College

8501 West Dodge Road
Omaha, NE 68114

Contact Information:
Telephone: 402-354-4913
Fax: 402-354-8875
E-mail: chamil1@nmhs.org
Web: www.methodistcollege.edu

Program Information:
Program begins: August
Duration of program: 24 months
Evening or weekend classes are available.

Application Information:
Enrollment of program: 20
Transfer students are accepted.

Financial Information:
Average cost of books: $400
% of students receiving aid: 100

Employment Profile:
% of students who pass the boards on their first try: 92
% employed within the first 6 months following graduation: 100
Average starting salary: $30,000

Southeast Community College

8800 O Street
Lincoln, NE 68520-1299

Contact Information:
Telephone: 402-437-2782
Web: www.sccm.cc.ne.us

Program Information:
Program begins: July
Degrees offered: Associate's, 27 months
Evening or weekend classes are available.

Application Information:
Transfer students are accepted.

Financial Information:
Tuition, resident: $1,987
Tuition, non-resident: $2,700

Employment Profile:
% of students who pass the boards on their first try: 100
% employed within the first 6 months following graduation: 100
Average starting salary: $26,000

New Hampshire

New Hampshire Community Technical College

One College Drive
Claremont, NH 03743

Contact Information:
Telephone: 603-542-7744
Fax: 603-543-1844
E-mail: jmarcley@tec.nh.us

Program Information:
Program begins: September
Degrees offered: Associate's, 21 months

Application Information:
Enrollment of program: 13
Transfer students are accepted.

Financial Information:
Tuition, resident: $3,080
Tuition, non-resident: $7,084
Average cost of books: $300
% of students receiving aid: 80

Employment Profile:
% of students who pass the boards on their first try: 90
% employed within the first 6 months following graduation: 100
Average starting salary: $27,000

New Jersey

Bergen Community College

400 Paramus Road
Paramus, NJ 07652

Contact Information:
Telephone: 201-447-7944
Fax: 201-612-3876
E-mail: rmuller@mailhost.bergen.cc.nj.us
Web: www.bergen.cc.nj.us

Program Information:
Program begins: September
Duration of program: 22 months

Application Information:
Enrollment of program: 25
Transfer students are accepted.

Financial Information:
Tuition, resident: $2,908
Tuition, non-resident: $5,816

Employment Profile:
% of students who pass the boards on their first try: 95
% employed within the first 6 months following graduation: 100

Brookdale Community College

765 Newman Springs Road
Lincroft, NJ 07738

Contact Information:
Telephone: 732-224-2606
Fax: 732-224-2772
E-mail: pfusaru@brookdale.cc.nj.us
Web: www.brookdale.cc.nj.us

Program Information:
Program begins: September
Degrees offered: Diploma, 16 months

Application Information:
Enrollment of program: 20
Transfer students are accepted.

Financial Information:
Tuition, resident: $2,168
Tuition, non-resident: $4,335
Average cost of books: $250
% of students receiving aid: 30

Employment Profile:
% of students who pass the boards on their first try: 95
% employed within the first 6 months following graduation: 90
Average starting salary: $32,000

Mansfield University

St. Clares Hospital
400 West Blackwell Street
Dover, NJ 07801

Contact Information:
Telephone: 973-537-3906
Fax: 973-537-3996
E-mail: dadams@saintclares.org
Web: www.mnsfld.edu

Program Information:
Program begins: September
Duration of program: 24 months
Evening or weekend classes are available.

Application Information:
Transfer students are accepted.

Financial Information:
Tuition, resident: $3,028
Tuition, non-resident: $7,566

Employment Profile:
% employed within the first 6 months following graduation: 80

Northwest NJ Consortium Respiratory Care Education

St. Clares Hospital
400 West Blackweil Street
Dover, NJ 07801

Contact Information:
Telephone: 973-537-3906
Fax: 973-537-3996
E-mail: dadamas@saintclares.org

Program Information:
Program begins: September
Duration of program: 24 months
Evening or weekend classes are available.

Application Information:
Transfer students are accepted.

Financial Information:
Tuition, resident: $3,028
Tuition, non-resident: $7,566

Employment Profile:
% of students who pass the boards on their first try: 100
% employed within the first 6 months following graduation: 80

Union County College

East Second Street
Plainfield, NJ 07060

Contact Information:
Telephone: 908-412-3577
Fax: 908-754-2798

Program Information:
Program begins: May
Duration of program: 20 months

Application Information:
Enrollment of program: 20
Transfer students are accepted.

Financial Information:
Tuition, resident: $2,085
Tuition, non-resident: $4,170
Average cost of books: $250
% of students receiving aid: 40

Employment Profile:
% of students who pass the boards on their first try: 93
% employed within the first 6 months following graduation: 80
Average starting salary: $29,000

University of Medicine & Dentistry of New Jersey

School of Health Related Professions
65 Bergen Street
Newark, NJ 07107-3006

Contact Information:
Telephone: 973-972-5503
Fax: 973-972-5258
E-mail: scanlan@umdnj.edu
Web: www.umdnj.edu

Program Information:
Program begins: June
Duration of program: 21 months

Application Information:
Enrollment of program: 27
Transfer students are accepted.

Financial Information:
Tuition, resident: $75
Tuition, non-resident: $150
Average cost of books: $400
% of students receiving aid: 70

Employment Profile:
% of students who pass the boards on their first try: 99
% employed within the first 6 months following graduation: 50
Average starting salary: $37,000

New Mexico

Albuquerque Technical Vocational Institute

525 Buena Vista Southeast
Albuquerque, NM 87106

Contact Information:
Telephone: 505-224-4111 ext. 4123
Fax: 505-224-4120
E-mail: rgentile@tvi.cc.nm.us
Web: www.tvi.cc.nm.us

Program Information:
Program begins: September
Duration of program: 20 months

Financial Information:
Tuition, resident: $496
Tuition, non-resident: $3,743
Average cost of books: $1,000

Employment Profile:
% of students who pass the boards on their first try: 100
% employed within the first 6 months following graduation: 100
Average starting salary: $25,000

New York

Hudson Valley Community College

80 Vandenburgh Avenue
Troy, NY 12180

Contact Information:
Telephone: 518-629-7454
Fax: 518-629-7594
E-mail: hylanpat@hvcc.edu
Web: www.hvcc.edu

Program Information:
Program begins: August
Duration of program: 21 months

Application Information:
Enrollment of program: 30
Transfer students are accepted.

Financial Information:
Tuition, resident: $2,350
Tuition, non-resident: $6,134
Average cost of books: $1,500

Employment Profile:
% of students who pass the boards on their first try: 100
% employed within the first 6 months following graduation: 100
Average starting salary: $27,000

Nassau Community College

One Education Drive
Garden City, NY 11530

Contact Information:
Telephone: 516-572-7560
Web: www.sunynassau.edu

Program Information:
Program begins: August
Degrees offered: Associate's, 24 months

Application Information:
Enrollment of program: 48
Transfer students are accepted.

Financial Information:
Tuition, resident: $2,120
Tuition, non-resident: $4,240
Average cost of books: $623
% of students receiving aid: 60

Employment Profile:
% of students who pass the boards on their first try: 84
% employed within the first 6 months following graduation: 100
Average starting salary: $32,000

Onondaga Community College

Route 173
Syracuse, NY 13215

Contact Information:
Telephone: 315-469-2458
Fax: 315-469-2593
E-mail: clevelad@aurora.sunyocc.edu
Web: www.sunyocc.edu

Program Information:
Program begins: January
Duration of program: 24 months

Financial Information:
Tuition, resident: $1,250
Tuition, non-resident: $2,500

Employment Profile:
% of students who pass the boards on their first try: 90
% employed within the first 6 months following graduation: 80
Average starting salary: $35,000

SUNY Health Science Center at Syracuse

750 East Adams Street
Syracuse, NY 13210

Contact Information:
Telephone: 315-464-5580
Fax: 315-464-6876
E-mail: wiezalic@vax.cs.hscsyr.edu
Web: www.ec.hscsyr.edu

Program Information:
Program begins: September
Duration of program: 16 months

Application Information:
Enrollment of program: 34
Transfer students are accepted.

Financial Information:
Tuition, resident: $3,400
Tuition, non-resident: $8,300
Average cost of books: $995
% of students receiving aid: 44

Employment Profile:
% of students who pass the boards on their first try: 100
% employed within the first 6 months following graduation: 95
Average starting salary: $32,000

North Carolina

Carteret Community College

3505 Arendell Street
Morehead City, NC 28557

Contact Information:
Telephone: 252-247-6000
Fax: 252-247-2514
E-mail: lap@carteret.cc.nc.us
Web: www.carteret.cc.nc.us

Program Information:
Program begins: August
Degrees offered: Associate's, 24 months

Application Information:
Enrollment of program: 20
Transfer students are accepted.

Financial Information:
Tuition, resident: $840
Tuition, non-resident: $6,846
Average cost of books: $610
% of students receiving aid: 20

Employment Profile:
% of students who pass the boards on their first try: 93
% employed within the first 6 months following graduation: 100
Average starting salary: $28,000

Catawba Valley Community College

2550 Highway 70 Southeast
Hickory, NC 28602

Contact Information:
Telephone: 828-327-7000 ext. 4391
Fax: 828-327-7276
E-mail: cbitsche@cvcc.cc.nc.us
Web: www.cvcc.cc.nc.us

Program Information:
Program begins: September
Degrees offered: Associate's, 21 months

Application Information:
Enrollment of program: 15
Transfer students are accepted.

Financial Information:
Tuition, resident: $771
Tuition, non-resident: $6,049
Average cost of books: $400
% of students receiving aid: 50

Employment Profile:
% of students who pass the boards on their first try: 95
% employed within the first 6 months following graduation: 100
Average starting salary: $24,000

Central Piedmont Community College

PO Box 35009
Charlotte, NC 28235

Contact Information:
Telephone: 704-330-6274
Fax: 704-330-5930
E-mail: tom.morris@cpcc.cc.nc.us
Web: www.cpcc.cc.nc.us

Program Information:
Program begins: August
Duration of program: 21 months

Application Information:
Enrollment of program: 77
Transfer students are accepted.

Financial Information:
Tuition, resident: $1,054
Tuition, non-resident: $6,488
Average cost of books: $450

Employment Profile:
% of students who pass the boards on their first try: 95
% employed within the first 6 months following graduation: 90

Forsyth Technical Community College

2100 Silas Creek Parkway
Winston-Salem, NC 27103

Contact Information:
Telephone: 336-723-0371 ext. 7427
Fax: 336-761-2399
E-mail: psheppard@forsyth.cc.nc.us
Web: www.forsyth.tec.nc.us

Program Information:
Program begins: September
Degrees offered: Associate's, 21 months

Application Information:
Enrollment of program: 18
Transfer students are accepted.

Financial Information:
Tuition, resident: $1,124
Tuition, non-resident: $7,130
Average cost of books: $600
% of students receiving aid: 25

Employment Profile:
% of students who pass the boards on their first try: 100
% employed within the first 6 months following graduation: 100
Average starting salary: $32,000

Sandhills Community College

2200 Airport Road
Pinehurst, NC 28374

Contact Information:
Telephone: 910-695-3836
Fax: 910-692-6918
E-mail: crofb@email.sandhills.cc.nc.us
Web: www.sandhills.cc.nc.us

Program Information:
Program begins: August
Degrees offered: Associate's, 20 months
Evening or weekend classes are available.

Application Information:
Enrollment of program: 20
Transfer students are accepted.

Financial Information:
Tuition, resident: $988
Tuition, non-resident: $6,279
Average cost of books: $1,500
% of students receiving aid: 50

Employment Profile:
% of students who pass the boards on their first try: 80
% employed within the first 6 months following graduation: 100
Average starting salary: $30,000

Southwestern Community College

447 College Drive
Sylva, NC 28779-9578

Contact Information:
Telephone: 828-586-4091 ext. 317
Fax: 828-586-3129
E-mail: billp@southwest.cc.nc.us
Web: www.southwest.cc.nc.us

Program Information:
Program begins: August
Degrees offered: Diploma, 24 months

Application Information:
Enrollment of program: 29
Transfer students are accepted.

Financial Information:
Tuition, resident: $742
Tuition, non-resident: $6,020
Average cost of books: $1,500

Employment Profile:
% of students who pass the boards on their first try: 100
% employed within the first 6 months following graduation: 100
Average starting salary: $26,000

North Dakota

NDSU—Merit Care Hospital Consortium

720 Fourth Street North
Fargo, ND 58122

Contact Information:
Telephone: 701-234-6147
Fax: 701-234-6942
Web: www.ndsu.nodak.edu

Program Information:
Program begins: August
Degrees offered: Certificate program, 12 months; Bachelor's, 48 months

Application Information:
Enrollment of program: 12
Transfer students are accepted.

Financial Information:
Tuition, resident: $2,480
Tuition, non-resident: $6,622
Average cost of books: $600
% of students receiving aid: 80

Employment Profile:
% of students who pass the boards on their first try: 97
% employed within the first 6 months following graduation: 100
Average starting salary: $26,520

St. Alexius Medical Center—University of Mary

North Dakota School of Respiratory Care
900 East Broadway/PO Box 5510
Bismarck, ND 58506

Contact Information:
Telephone: 701-530-7757
Fax: 701-530-7701
E-mail: Wbeachey@primecare.org
Web: www.st.alexius.org

Program Information:
Program begins: September
Degrees offered: Bachelor's, 48 months

Application Information:
Enrollment of program: 20
Transfer students are accepted.

Financial Information:
Average cost of books: $350
% of students receiving aid: 90

Employment Profile:
% of students who pass the boards on their first try: 75
% employed within the first 6 months following graduation: 100
Average starting salary: $30,000

Ohio

Bowling Green State University

One University Drive
901 Rye Beach Road
Huron, OH 44839-9791

Contact Information:
Telephone: 419-433-5560
Fax: 419-433-9696
E-mail: rroark@bgnet.bgsu.edu
Web: www.bgsu.edu

Program Information:
Program begins: August
Duration of program: 24 months

Application Information:
Enrollment of program: 33
Transfer students are accepted.

Financial Information:
Tuition, resident: $3,354
Tuition, non-resident: $8,902
Average cost of books: $400
% of students receiving aid: 45

Employment Profile:
% of students who pass the boards on their first try: 91
% employed within the first 6 months following graduation: 90
Average starting salary: $25,000

Cuyahoga Community College

11000 Pleasant Valley Road
Parma, OH 44130

Contact Information:
Telephone: 216-987-5267
Fax: 216-987-5066
E-mail: dave.lucas@tri-c.cc.oh.us
Web: www.tri-c.cc.us

Program Information:
Program begins: August
Duration of program: 21 months

Application Information:
Transfer students are accepted.

Financial Information:
Tuition, resident: $2,228
Tuition, non-resident: $2,960
Average cost of books: $500
% of students receiving aid: 15

Employment Profile:
% of students who pass the boards on their first try: 18
% employed within the first 6 months following graduation: 50
Average starting salary: $32,000

Jefferson Community College

4000 Sunset Boulevard
Steubenville, OH 43952

Contact Information:
Telephone: 502-584-0181 ext. 2199
Fax: 502-584-0181
E-mail: ccarducci@jefferson.cc.org
Web: www.jefferson.cc.org

Program Information:
Program begins: September
Duration of program: 21 months

Application Information:
Enrollment of program: 6
Transfer students are accepted.

Financial Information:
Tuition, resident: $2,240
Tuition, non-resident: $2,870

Employment Profile:
% of students who pass the boards on their first try: 80
% employed within the first 6 months following graduation: 90

Kettering College of Medical Arts

3737 Southern Boulevard
Kettering, OH 45429

Contact Information:
Telephone: 937-298-3399 ext. 5645
Fax: 937-296-4238
E-mail: tom.hill@ketthealth.com
Web: www.kcma.edu

Program Information:
Program begins: August
Duration of program: 22 months

Application Information:
Enrollment of program: 15
Transfer students are accepted.

Financial Information:
Tuition, resident: $8,120
Average cost of books: $500
% of students receiving aid: 60

Employment Profile:
% of students who pass the boards on their first try: 98
% employed within the first 6 months following graduation: 90
Average starting salary: $26,000

Lakeland Community College

7700 Clocktower Drive
Kirtland, OH 44094-5198

Contact Information:
Telephone: 216-953-7343
Fax: 216-975-4733
E-mail: ckenny@lakeland.c.oh.us
Web: www.lakeland.cc.oh.us

Program Information:
Program begins: September
Duration of program: 21 months
Evening or weekend classes are available.

Application Information:
Enrollment of program: 23

Financial Information:
Tuition, resident: $2,680
Tuition, non-resident: $3,238
Average cost of books: $300
% of students receiving aid: 35

Employment Profile:
% of students who pass the boards on their first try: 93
% employed within the first 6 months following graduation: 100
Average starting salary: $30,000

North Central State College

2441 Kenwood Circle
PO Box 698
Mansfield, OH 44901

Contact Information:
Telephone: 419-755-4800
Fax: 419-755-5630
E-mail: rslabod@nctc.tec.oh.us
Web: www.nctc.tec.oh.us

Program Information:
Program begins: September
Degrees offered: Associate's, 21 months
Evening or weekend classes are available.

Application Information:
Enrollment of program: 20
Transfer students are accepted.

Financial Information:
Tuition, resident: $3,414
Tuition, non-resident: $6,413

Employment Profile:
% employed within the first 6 months following graduation: 100
Average starting salary: $26,000

Ohio State University

1583 Perry Street
Columbus, OH 43210

Contact Information:
Telephone: 614-292-8445
Fax: 614-292-0210
E-mail: douce.2@osu.edu
Web: www.amp.ohio-state.edu

Program Information:
Program begins: September
Duration of program: 45 months

Application Information:
Enrollment of program: 30
Transfer students are accepted.

Financial Information:
Tuition, resident: $3,468
Tuition, non-resident: $10,335
Average cost of books: $400

Employment Profile:
% of students who pass the boards on their first try: 100
% employed within the first 6 months following graduation: 100
Average starting salary: $33,970

Shawnee State University

940 Second Street
Portsmouth, OH 45662

Contact Information:
Telephone: 614-355-2235
Fax: 614-355-2354
E-mail: dthomas@shawnee.edu
Web: www.shawnee.edu

Program Information:
Program begins: August
Degrees offered: Diploma, 21 months

Application Information:
Enrollment of program: 20

Financial Information:
Tuition, resident: $4,276
Tuition, non-resident: $7,176
Average cost of books: $500
% of students receiving aid: 80

Employment Profile:
% of students who pass the boards on their first try: 90
% employed within the first 6 months following graduation: 100
Average starting salary: $31,000

Sinclair Community College

444 West Third Street
Dayton, OH 45402

Contact Information:
Telephone: 937-512-2849
Fax: 937-512-2058
E-mail: cbeckett@sinclair.edu
Web: www.sinclair.edu

Program Information:
Program begins: September
Duration of program: 21 months

Application Information:
Enrollment of program: 70
Transfer students are accepted.

Financial Information:
Tuition, resident: $1,674
Tuition, non-resident: $2,700

Employment Profile:
% of students who pass the boards on their first try: 100
% employed within the first 6 months following graduation: 90
Average starting salary: $24,000

University of Akron

302 East Buchtel Avenue
Akron, OH 44325

Contact Information:
Telephone: 787-834-9595
Fax: 787-834-9597
E-mail: lavarne@uakron.edu
Web: www.uakron.edu

Program Information:
Program begins: August
Duration of program: 22 months

Application Information:
Enrollment of program: 25
Transfer students are accepted.

Financial Information:
Tuition, resident: $3,279
Tuition, non-resident: $9,033
Average cost of books: $600

Employment Profile:
% of students who pass the boards on their first try: 95
% employed within the first 6 months following graduation: 100
Average starting salary: $33,000

University of Toledo

College of Health and Human Services
2801 West Bancroft Street
Toledo, OH 43606

Contact Information:
Telephone: 419-530-5308
Fax: 419-530-5514
Web: www.utoledo.edu

Program Information:
Program begins: August
Degrees offered: Bachelor's, 48 months

Application Information:
Enrollment of program: 20
Transfer students are accepted.

Financial Information:
Tuition, resident: $5,275
Tuition, non-resident: $12,325
Average cost of books: $750

Employment Profile:
% of students who pass the boards on their first try: 90
% employed within the first 6 months following graduation: 100
Average starting salary: $22,000

Youngstown State University
One University Plaza
Youngstown, OH 44555

Contact Information:
Telephone: 330-742-1764
Fax: 330-742-2921
E-mail: lnharris@cc.ysu.edu
Web: www.ysu.edu

Program Information:
Program begins: September
Duration of program: 46 months
Evening or weekend classes are available.

Application Information:
Enrollment of program: 18
Transfer students are accepted.

Financial Information:
Tuition, resident: $3,865
Tuition, non-resident: $6,553

Employment Profile:
% of students who pass the boards on their first try: 100
% employed within the first 6 months following graduation: 90
Average starting salary: $34,000

Oregon

Lane Community College
4000 East 30th Avenue
Eugene, OR 97405

Contact Information:
Telephone: 541-747-4501
Fax: 541-744-4151
E-mail: hechtr@lanecc.edu
Web: www.lanecc.edu

Program Information:
Program begins: September
Degrees offered: Associate's, 21 months

Application Information:
Enrollment of program: 30
Transfer students are accepted.

Financial Information:
Tuition, resident: $1,782
Tuition, non-resident: $5,742
Average cost of books: $500

Employment Profile:
% of students who pass the boards on their first try: 90
% employed within the first 6 months following graduation: 90

Mount Hood Community College
26000 Southeast Stark Street
Gresham, OR 97030

Contact Information:
Telephone: 503-667-7172
Fax: 503-492-6047
E-mail: hicksg@mhcc.cc.or.us
Web: www.mhcc.cc.or.us

Program Information:
Program begins: September
Degrees offered: Associate's, 18 months

Application Information:
Enrollment of program: 40
Transfer students are accepted.

Financial Information:
Tuition, resident: $1,733
Tuition, non-resident: $5,670
Average cost of books: $350
% of students receiving aid: 35

Employment Profile:
% of students who pass the boards on their first try: 90
% employed within the first 6 months following graduation: 90
Average starting salary: $29,000

Rogue Community College
202 South Riverside
Medford, OR 97501

Contact Information:
Telephone: 541-245-7504 ext. 1404
Fax: 541-774-4203
E-mail: jhulse@rogue.cc.or.us
Web: www.rogue.cc.or.us

Program Information:
Program begins: September
Degrees offered: Certificate program, 22 months; Associate's, 22 months

Application Information:
Enrollment of program: 26
Transfer students are accepted.

Financial Information:
Tuition, resident: $3,456
Tuition, non-resident: $10,464

Employment Profile:
% of students who pass the boards on their first try: 95
% employed within the first 6 months following graduation: 100

Pennsylvania

Community College of Allegheny County
808 Ridge Avenue
Pittsburgh, PA 15212

Contact Information:
Telephone: 412-237-2607
Fax: 412-237-4521
E-mail: troop@ccac.edu
Web: www.ccac.edu

Program Information:
Program begins: September
Degrees offered: Associate's, 21 months

Application Information:
Enrollment of program: 25
Transfer students are accepted.

Financial Information:
Tuition, resident: $2,040
Tuition, non-resident: $4,040
Average cost of books: $100

Employment Profile:
% of students who pass the boards on their first try: 92
% employed within the first 6 months following graduation: 100
Average starting salary: $28,000

Crozer-Chester Medical Center Delaware County Community College
One Medical Center Boulevard
Chester, PA 19013

Contact Information:
Telephone: 610-447-2440
Fax: 610-447-6353
E-mail: kday@dcccnet.dccc.edu
Web: www.dccc.edu

Program Information:
Program begins: September
Duration of program: 22 months

Application Information:
Enrollment of program: 16
Transfer students are accepted.

Financial Information:
Tuition, resident: $2,088
Tuition, non-resident: $6,264
Average cost of books: $700

Employment Profile:
% of students who pass the boards on their first try: 95
% employed within the first 6 months following graduation: 100
Average starting salary: $38,000

Gannon University
University Square
Erie, PA 16541

Contact Information:
Telephone: 814-871-5637

Fax: 814-871-5662
E-mail: cornfiel001@mail1.gannon.edu
Web: www.gannon.edu

Program Information:
Program begins: August
Duration of program: 48 months
Evening or weekend classes are available.

Application Information:
Enrollment of program: 22
Transfer students are accepted.

Financial Information:
Average cost of books: $150

Employment Profile:
% of students who pass the boards on their first try: 85
% employed within the first 6 months following graduation: 97
Average starting salary: $27,000

Gwynedd-Mercy College

Sumneytown Pike
Gwynedd Valley, PA 19437

Contact Information:
Telephone: 215-641-5536
Fax: 215-641-5559
E-mail: galvin.w@gmc.edu
Web: www.gmc.edu

Program Information:
Program begins: September
Duration of program: 21 months

Application Information:
Enrollment of program: 20
Transfer students are accepted.

Financial Information:
Average cost of books: $400
% of students receiving aid: 85

Employment Profile:
% of students who pass the boards on their first try: 90
% employed within the first 6 months following graduation: 100
Average starting salary: $37,000

Harrisburg Area Community College

One HACC Drive
Harrisburg, PA 17110

Contact Information:
Telephone: 717-780-2315
Fax: 717-780-2551
E-mail: baleidic@hacc.edu
Web: www.hacc.edu

Program Information:
Program begins: August
Degrees offered: Associate's, 28 months
Evening or weekend classes are available.

Application Information:
Enrollment of program: 25
Transfer students are accepted.

Financial Information:
Tuition, resident: $2,448
Tuition, non-resident: $4,896

Employment Profile:
% of students who pass the boards on their first try: 98
% employed within the first 6 months following graduation: 100
Average starting salary: $26,500

Indiana University of Pennsylvania

4800 Friendship Avenue
Pittsburgh, PA 15224

Contact Information:
Telephone: 412-578-7000
Fax: 412-578-4651
E-mail: r.hartman@grove.iup.edu
Web: www.westpenn.hospital.com

Program Information:
Program begins: August
Degrees offered: Bachelor's, 36 months

Application Information:
Enrollment of program: 90

Financial Information:
Tuition, resident: $5,040
Average cost of books: $500
% of students receiving aid: 75

Employment Profile:
% of students who pass the boards on their first try: 100
% employed within the first 6 months following graduation: 100
Average starting salary: $31,000

Lehigh Carbon Community College

4525 Education Park Drive
Schnecksville, PA 18078-2598

Contact Information:
Telephone: 610-799-1504
Fax: 610-799-1537
Web: www.lccc.edu

Program Information:
Program begins: August
Duration of program: 21 months

Application Information:
Enrollment of program: 20
Transfer students are accepted.

Financial Information:
Tuition, resident: $2,600
Tuition, non-resident: $5,290
Average cost of books: $700
% of students receiving aid: 90

Employment Profile:
% employed within the first 6 months following graduation: 95
Average starting salary: $28,000

Millersville University of Pennsylvania

Millersville, PA 17551

Contact Information:
Telephone: 717-290-5511 ext. 7105
Fax: 717-290-5970
E-mail: jhughes@marauder.millersu.edu
Web: www.milersu.edu

Program Information:
Program begins: August
Duration of program: 16 months

Financial Information:
Tuition, resident: $3,468
Tuition, non-resident: $8,824
Average cost of books: $503

Employment Profile:
% of students who pass the boards on their first try: 77
% employed within the first 6 months following graduation: 100
Average starting salary: $35,550

University of Pittsburgh—Johnstown

227 Krebs Hall
Johnstown, PA 15904

Contact Information:
Telephone: 814-269-2960 ext. 2958
Fax: 814-269-7255
E-mail: bcolbert@pitt.edu
Web: www.pitt.edu

Program Information:
Program begins: September
Duration of program: 20 months

Financial Information:
Tuition, resident: $10,848
Tuition, non-resident: $21,696

Employment Profile:
% of students who pass the boards on their first try: 95
% employed within the first 6 months following graduation: 90

York College of Pennsylvania

Country Club Road
York, PA 17405

Contact Information:
Telephone: 717-851-2464
Fax: 717-851-2487
E-mail: msimmons@yorkhospital.edu
Web: www.ycp.edu

Program Information:
Program begins: August
Degrees offered: Bachelor's, 48 months

Application Information:
Enrollment of program: 32
Transfer students are accepted.

Employment Profile:
% of students who pass the boards on their first try: 95
% employed within the first 6 months following graduation: 100

Puerto Rico

Universidad Metropolitana
PO Box 21150
San Juan, PR 009281150

Contact Information:
Telephone: 501-661-1202 ext. 4203
Fax: 501-370-6691
E-mail: um_ltorres@suagm4.suagm.edu

Program Information:
Program begins: August
Degrees offered: Bachelor's, 40 months

Application Information:
Enrollment of program: 50
Transfer students are accepted.

Financial Information:
Tuition, resident: $4,154
% of students receiving aid: 100

Employment Profile:
% of students who pass the boards on their first try: 31
% employed within the first 6 months following graduation: 89

South Carolina

Greenville Technical College
PO Box 5616
Greenville, SC 29606

Contact Information:
Telephone: 864-250-8308
Fax: 864-250-8308
E-mail: conrylac@gvltec.edu
Web: www.greenvilletech.com

Program Information:
Program begins: August, September
Duration of program: 24 months
Evening or weekend classes are available.

Financial Information:
Tuition, resident: $3,750
Tuition, non-resident: $9,600

Midlands Technical College
PO Box 2408
Columbia, SC 29202

Contact Information:
Telephone: 803-822-3433
Fax: 803-822-3079
E-mail: ackermanl@mtc.mid.tec.sc.us
Web: www.mid.tec.sc.us

Program Information:
Program begins: June
Degrees offered: Associate's, 24 months
Evening or weekend classes are available.

Application Information:
Enrollment of program: 30
Transfer students are accepted.

Financial Information:
Tuition, resident: $1,620
Tuition, non-resident: $3,240
Average cost of books: $800
% of students receiving aid: 75

Employment Profile:
% of students who pass the boards on their first try: 100
% employed within the first 6 months following graduation: 100
Average starting salary: $30,000

Trident Technical College
PO Box 118067
Charleston, SC 29423

Contact Information:
Telephone: 843-574-6101
Fax: 843-574-6585
E-mail: zpmoorea@trident.tec.sc.us

Program Information:
Program begins: August
Degrees offered: Associate's, 21 months

Application Information:
Enrollment of program: 48

Financial Information:
Tuition, resident: $1,056
Tuition, non-resident: $3,226
Average cost of books: $250
% of students receiving aid: 85

Employment Profile:
% of students who pass the boards on their first try: 100
% employed within the first 6 months following graduation: 100
Average starting salary: $31,000

South Dakota

Dakota State University
Science Center
Madison, SD 57042-1799

Contact Information:
Telephone: 605-322-8613
Fax: 605-322-6666
E-mail: feistneb@dsu03.dsu.edu
Web: www.dsu.edu

Program Information:
Program begins: August
Degrees offered: Associate's, 21 months; Bachelor's, 44 months

Application Information:
Enrollment of program: 37
Transfer students are accepted.

Financial Information:
Tuition, resident: $1,850
Tuition, non-resident: $5,895
Average cost of books: $300

Employment Profile:
% of students who pass the boards on their first try: 95
% employed within the first 6 months following graduation: 100
Average starting salary: $25,000

Tennessee

Jackson State Community College
2046 North Parkway Street
Jackson, TN 38301-3797

Contact Information:
Telephone: 901-425-2612
Fax: 901-425-9551
E-mail: cgarner@jscc.cc.tn.us
Web: www.jscc.cc.tn.us

Program Information:
Program begins: August
Degrees offered: Associate's, 21 months

Application Information:
Enrollment of program: 12

Financial Information:
Tuition, resident: $1,971
Tuition, non-resident: $5,382
Average cost of books: $650

Employment Profile:
% of students who pass the boards on their first try: 100
% employed within the first 6 months following graduation: 80
Average starting salary: $23,000

Volunteer State Community College
1480 Nashville Pike
Gallatin, TN 37066

Contact Information:
Telephone: 615-452-8600 ext. 3340
Fax: 615-230-3224
Web: www.vscc.tn.us

Program Information:
Program begins: August
Degrees offered: Certificate program, 9 months

Application Information:
Enrollment of program: 20
Transfer students are accepted.

Financial Information:
Tuition, resident: $700
Tuition, non-resident: $2,688
Average cost of books: $160
% of students receiving aid: 50

Employment Profile:
% of students who pass the boards on their first try: 90
% employed within the first 6 months following graduation: 99
Average starting salary: $29,000

Texas

Alvin Community College
3110 Mustang Road
Alvin, TX 77511

Contact Information:
Telephone: 281-388-4695
Fax: 281-388-4936
E-mail: dflatlan@alvin.cc.tx.us
Web: www.alvin.cc.tx.us

Program Information:
Program begins: August
Degrees offered: Certificate program, 9 months; Associate's, 18 months

Application Information:
Enrollment of program: 12
Transfer students are accepted.

Financial Information:
Tuition, resident: $1,563
Tuition, non-resident: $3,996
Average cost of books: $800
% of students receiving aid: 25

Employment Profile:
% employed within the first 6 months following graduation: 100
Average starting salary: $35,000

Amarillo College
PO Box 447
Amarillo, TX 79178

Contact Information:
Telephone: 806-354-6058
Fax: 806-354-6076
E-mail: wayoung@actx.edu
Web: www.actx.edu

Program Information:
Program begins: August
Degrees offered: Associate's, 22 months

Application Information:
Enrollment of program: 20
Transfer students are accepted.

Financial Information:
Tuition, resident: $786
Tuition, non-resident: $1,119
Average cost of books: $400

Employment Profile:
% of students who pass the boards on their first try: 93
% employed within the first 6 months following graduation: 97
Average starting salary: $24,000

El Paso Community College
PO Box 20500
El Paso, TX 79998

Contact Information:
Telephone: 915-831-4199
Fax: 915-831-4114
E-mail: paula@epcc.edu
Web: www.epcc.edu

Program Information:
Program begins: May
Duration of program: 24 months

Application Information:
Enrollment of program: 24

Financial Information:
Tuition, resident: $1,128
Tuition, non-resident: $3,503

Employment Profile:
% of students who pass the boards on their first try: 80
% employed within the first 6 months following graduation: 80
Average starting salary: $19,000

Houston Community College
1900 Galen Drive
Houston, TX 77030

Contact Information:
Telephone: 713-718-7378
Fax: 713-718-7401
E-mail: bartel_r.hccs.cc.tx.us
Web: www.hccs.cc.tx.us

Program Information:
Program begins: August
Duration of program: 24 months

Application Information:
Enrollment of program: 23
Transfer students are accepted.

Financial Information:
Tuition, resident: $1,260
Tuition, non-resident: $2,115
Average cost of books: $200
% of students receiving aid: 20

Employment Profile:
% of students who pass the boards on their first try: 80
% employed within the first 6 months following graduation: 100
Average starting salary: $25,000

Lamar Institute of Technology—Beaumont
PO Box 10061
Beaumont, TX 77710

Contact Information:
Telephone: 409-880-8852
Fax: 409-880-8955
E-mail: bronsonpa@hal.lamar.edu
Web: www.lamar.edu

Program Information:
Program begins: June
Degrees offered: Associate's, 24 months

Application Information:
Enrollment of program: 50
Transfer students are accepted.

Financial Information:
Tuition, resident: $2,298
Tuition, non-resident: $9,796
Average cost of books: $350
% of students receiving aid: 60

Employment Profile:
% of students who pass the boards on their first try: 90
% employed within the first 6 months following graduation: 100
Average starting salary: $30,000

Midland College
3600 North Garfield
Midland, TX 79705

Contact Information:
Telephone: 915-685-4601
Fax: 915-685-4762
E-mail: rweidmann@midland.cc.tx.us
Web: www.midland.cc.tx.us

Program Information:
Program begins: September
Degrees offered: Associate's, 23 months
Evening or weekend classes are available.

Application Information:
Enrollment of program: 20
Transfer students are accepted.

Financial Information:
Tuition, resident: $1,369
Tuition, non-resident: $2,097
Average cost of books: $800
% of students receiving aid: 60

Employment Profile:
% of students who pass the boards on their first try: 64
% employed within the first 6 months following graduation: 93
Average starting salary: $26,000

Midwestern State University
3410 Taft Boulevard
Wichita Falls, TX 76308

Contact Information:
Telephone: 940-397-4652
Fax: 940-397-4933
E-mail: burkew@nexus.mwsu.edu
Web: www.mwsu.edu

Program Information:
Program begins: June
Duration of program: 45 months

Application Information:
Enrollment of program: 75

Financial Information:
Tuition, resident: $2,200
Tuition, non-resident: $9,000

Employment Profile:
% of students who pass the boards on their first try: 70
% employed within the first 6 months following graduation: 100

Odessa College

201 West University Boulevard
Odessa, TX 79764

Contact Information:
Telephone: 915-335-6456
Fax: 915-335-6846
E-mail: jsullivan@odessa.edu
Web: www.coyote.odessa.edu

Program Information:
Program begins: August
Degrees offered: Certificate program, 22 months; Associate's, 22 months

Application Information:
Enrollment of program: 14
Transfer students are accepted.

Financial Information:
Tuition, resident: $964
Tuition, non-resident: $1,124
Average cost of books: $1,000
% of students receiving aid: 20

Employment Profile:
% of students who pass the boards on their first try: 80
% employed within the first 6 months following graduation: 100
Average starting salary: $22,500

San Jacinto College Central Campus

8060 Spencer Highway
PO Box 2007
Pasadena, TX 77505-2007

Contact Information:
Telephone: 281-476-1864
Fax: 281-478-2754
E-mail: ivandi@central.sjc.cc.tx.us
Web: www.sjc.cc.tx.us

Program Information:
Program begins: August
Degrees offered: Diploma, 21 months

Application Information:
Enrollment of program: 32
Transfer students are accepted.

Financial Information:
Tuition, resident: $598
Tuition, non-resident: $978
Average cost of books: $250
% of students receiving aid: 10

Employment Profile:
% of students who pass the boards on their first try: 80
% employed within the first 6 months following graduation: 100
Average starting salary: $30,000

South Plains College

1302 Main Street
Lubbock, TX 79401

Contact Information:
Telephone: 806-747-0576 ext. 4625
Fax: 806-765-2775
E-mail: scollier@spc.cc.tx.us
Web: www.spc.cc.tx.us

Program Information:
Program begins: September
Degrees offered: Diploma, 24 months
Evening or weekend classes are available.

Application Information:
Enrollment of program: 25
Transfer students are accepted.

Financial Information:
Tuition, resident: $1,900
Tuition, non-resident: $2,200
Average cost of books: $450

Employment Profile:
% of students who pass the boards on their first try: 95
% employed within the first 6 months following graduation: 100
Average starting salary: $24,000

Tarrant County College—Northeast

828 Harwood Road
Hurst, TX 76054

Contact Information:
Telephone: 817-515-6574
Fax: 817-515-6426
Web: www.tccd.net

Program Information:
Program begins: August
Duration of program: 21 months

Application Information:
Transfer students are accepted.

Financial Information:
Tuition, resident: $1,100
Tuition, non-resident: $1,500
Average cost of books: $250

Employment Profile:
% of students who pass the boards on their first try: 90
% employed within the first 6 months following graduation: 100
Average starting salary: $38,000

University of Texas Health Science Center at San Antonio

7703 Floyd Curl Drive
Mail Code 6248
San Antonio, TX 78284-6248

Contact Information:
Telephone: 210-567-8850
Fax: 210-567-8852
E-mail: shelledy@uthscsa.edu
Web: www.uthsca.edu

Program Information:
Program begins: August
Degrees offered: Bachelor's, 23 months

Application Information:
Enrollment of program: 40
Transfer students are accepted.

Financial Information:
Tuition, resident: $1,800
Tuition, non-resident: $11,000
Average cost of books: $400

Employment Profile:
% of students who pass the boards on their first try: 100
% employed within the first 6 months following graduation: 100
Average starting salary: $32,000

University of Texas Medical Branch

School of Allied Health Sciences
301 University Boulevard
Galveston, TX 77555-1028

Contact Information:
Telephone: 409-772-5693
Fax: 409-772-3014
E-mail: jnilsest@utmb.edu
Web: www.utmb.edu

Program Information:
Program begins: August
Degrees offered: Bachelor's, 24 months

Application Information:
Enrollment of program: 25
Transfer students are accepted.

Financial Information:
Tuition, resident: $1,536
Tuition, non-resident: $11,904
Average cost of books: $305
% of students receiving aid: 70

Employment Profile:
% of students who pass the boards on their first try: 90
% employed within the first 6 months following graduation: 100
Average starting salary: $25,000

Victoria College

2200 East Red River
Victoria, TX 77901

Contact Information:
Telephone: 361-572-6491
Fax: 361-582-2542
E-mail: ckallus@vc.cc.tx.us
Web: www.vc.cc.tx.us

Program Information:
Program begins: August
Degrees offered: Associate's, 21 months

Application Information:
Enrollment of program: 18
Transfer students are accepted.

Financial Information:
Tuition, resident: $996
Tuition, non-resident: $4,233
Average cost of books: $500
% of students receiving aid: 50

Employment Profile:
% of students who pass the boards on their first try: 90
% employed within the first 6 months following graduation: 100
Average starting salary: $26,000

Vermont

Champlain College

163 South Willard Street
Burlington, VT 05401

Contact Information:

Telephone: 802-865-6491
Fax: 802-860-2750
E-mail: baconf@champlain.edu
Web: www.champlain.edu/clnd/repiratory.htm

Program Information:

Program begins: August
Duration of program: 21 months
Evening or weekend classes are available.

Application Information:

Enrollment of program: 15
Transfer students are accepted.

Financial Information:

Average cost of books: $100
% of students receiving aid: 90

Employment Profile:

% of students who pass the boards on their first try: 95
% employed within the first 6 months following graduation: 100
Average starting salary: $30,000

Virginia

College of Health Sciences

920 South Jefferson Street
PO Box 13186
Roanoke, VA 24031

Contact Information:

Telephone: 540-985-8263
Fax: 540-985-8773
E-mail: kroe@health.chs.edu
Web: www.chs.edu

Program Information:

Program begins: August
Degrees offered: Bachelor's, 42 months
Evening or weekend classes are available.

Application Information:

Enrollment of program: 25
Transfer students are accepted.

Financial Information:

Tuition, resident: $7,800
Average cost of books: $550
% of students receiving aid: 95

Employment Profile:

% of students who pass the boards on their first try: 85
% employed within the first 6 months following graduation: 95
Average starting salary: $27,000

Northern Virginia Community College

8333 Little River Turnpike
Annandale, VA 22003

Contact Information:

Telephone: 703-323-3435
Fax: 703-323-4576
E-mail: lstone@nv.cc.va.us
Web: www.nv.cc.va.us

Program Information:

Program begins: August
Duration of program: 22 months

Application Information:

Enrollment of program: 24
Transfer students are accepted.

Financial Information:

Tuition, resident: $2,160
Tuition, non-resident: $7,080
Average cost of books: $400

Employment Profile:

% employed within the first 6 months following graduation: 95
Average starting salary: $28,000

Shenandoah University

1775 North Sector Court
Winchester, VA 22601-5195

Contact Information:

Telephone: 540-665-5516
Fax: 540-665-5519
E-mail: kschultz@su.edu
Web: www.su.edu

Program Information:

Program begins: August
Duration of program: 20 months

Application Information:

Enrollment of program: 18
Transfer students are accepted.

Financial Information:

Average cost of books: $700
% of students receiving aid: 89

Southwest Virginia Community College

Box SVCC
Richlands, VA 24641-1510

Contact Information:

Telephone: 540-964-2555
Fax: 540-964-9307
E-mail: joe_dipietro@sw.cc.va.us
Web: www.sw.cc.va.us

Program Information:

Program begins: August
Duration of program: 22 months

Application Information:

Enrollment of program: 48
Transfer students are accepted.

Financial Information:

Tuition, resident: $1,446
Tuition, non-resident: $4,836
Average cost of books: $1,500
% of students receiving aid: 80

Employment Profile:

% of students who pass the boards on their first try: 92
% employed within the first 6 months following graduation: 100

Washington

Highline Community College

2400 South 240th Street
Des Moines, WA 98198-9800

Contact Information:

Telephone: 206-878-3710 ext. 3471
Fax: 206-870-3780
E-mail: bhirnle@hcc.ctc.edu
Web: www.highline.ctc.edu

Program Information:

Program begins: June
Degrees offered: Associate's, 21 months

Application Information:

Enrollment of program: 27
Transfer students are accepted.

Financial Information:

Tuition, resident: $1,848
Tuition, non-resident: $7,273
Average cost of books: $540

Employment Profile:

% of students who pass the boards on their first try: 90
% employed within the first 6 months following graduation: 95
Average starting salary: $34,000

Tacoma Community College

6501 South 19th Street
Tacoma, WA 98466

Contact Information:

Telephone: 253-566-5231
Fax: 253-566-5273
E-mail: bleffler@tcc.tacoma.ctc.edu
Web: www.tcc.tacoma.ctc.edu

Program Information:

Program begins: August
Degrees offered: Associate's, 24 months

Application Information:

Enrollment of program: 31
Transfer students are accepted.

Financial Information:

Tuition, resident: $2,337
Tuition, non-resident: $9,185
Average cost of books: $200

Employment Profile:

% of students who pass the boards on their first try: 75
% employed within the first 6 months following graduation: 100
Average starting salary: $35,000

West Virginia

University of Charleston

2300 MacCorkle Avenue Southeast
Charleston, WV 25304

Contact Information:
Telephone: 304-357-4837
Fax: 304-357-4965
E-mail: aparkman@uchaswv.edu
Web: www.uchaswv.edu

Program Information:
Program begins: August
Duration of program: 48 months
Evening or weekend classes are available.

Application Information:
Enrollment of program: 22
Transfer students are accepted.

Financial Information:
Average cost of books: $350
% of students receiving aid: 85

Employment Profile:
% of students who pass the boards on their first try: 99
% employed within the first 6 months following graduation: 90
Average starting salary: $27,600

West Virginia Northern Community College

College Square
Wheeling, WV 26003

Contact Information:
Telephone: 304-233-5900
E-mail: rlucki@northern.wvnet.edu
Web: www.northern.wvnet.edu

Program Information:
Program begins: August
Duration of program: 21 months

Application Information:
Enrollment of program: 34
Transfer students are accepted.

Financial Information:
Tuition, resident: $1,416
Tuition, non-resident: $3,864
Average cost of books: $600

Employment Profile:
% of students who pass the boards on their first try: 90
% employed within the first 6 months following graduation: 95
Average starting salary: $30,880

Wisconsin

Madison Area Technical College

3550 Anderson Street
Madison, WI 53704

Contact Information:
Telephone: 608-246-6686
Fax: 608-246-6013
E-mail: ghojem@madison.tec.wi.us
Web: www.madison.cc.wi.us

Program Information:
Program begins: August
Degrees offered: Associate's, 24 months

Application Information:
Enrollment of program: 50
Transfer students are accepted.

Financial Information:
Tuition, resident: $3,202
Tuition, non-resident: $15,356
Average cost of books: $280
% of students receiving aid: 20

Employment Profile:
% of students who pass the boards on their first try: 100
% employed within the first 6 months following graduation: 100
Average starting salary: $28,000

Mid-State Technical College

2600 West Fifth Street
Marshfield, WI 54449

Contact Information:
Telephone: 715-389-7033
Fax: 715-389-2864
E-mail: sosborne@wctc.net
Web: www.midstate.tec.wi.us

Program Information:
Program begins: August
Duration of program: 22 months
Evening or weekend classes are available.

Application Information:
Enrollment of program: 24
Transfer students are accepted.

Financial Information:
Tuition, resident: $2,092
Tuition, non-resident: $12,495
Average cost of books: $372
% of students receiving aid: 33

Employment Profile:
% of students who pass the boards on their first try: 95
% employed within the first 6 months following graduation: 80
Average starting salary: $30,000

Northeast Wisconsin Technical College

2740 West Mason Street
PO Box 19042
Green Bay, WI 54307

Contact Information:
Telephone: 920-498-5533
Fax: 920-498-5673
Web: www.nwtc.tec.wi.us

Program Information:
Program begins: August
Duration of program: 20 months

Application Information:
Enrollment of program: 20

Financial Information:
Tuition, resident: $2,380
Tuition, non-resident: $16,554

Employment Profile:
% of students who pass the boards on their first try: 75
% employed within the first 6 months following graduation: 95
Average starting salary: $26,000

Western Wisconsin Technical College

304 North Sixth Street
PO Box 908
La Crosse, WI 54602-0908

Contact Information:
Telephone: 608-785-9244
Fax: 608-785-9194
E-mail: milischr@email.western.tec.wi.us
Web: www.western.tec.wi.us

Program Information:
Program begins: August
Duration of program: 19 months
Evening or weekend classes are available.

Application Information:
Enrollment of program: 22

Financial Information:
Tuition, resident: $2,664

Wyoming

Western Wyoming Community College

2500 College Drive
PO Box 428
Rock Springs, WY 82902-0428

Contact Information:
Telephone: 307-382-1799
Fax: 307-382-7665
E-mail: klizzi@wwcc.cc.wy.us

Program Information:
Program begins: September
Degrees offered: Certificate program, 10 months

Application Information:
Enrollment of program: 6
Transfer students are accepted.

Financial Information:
Tuition, resident: $1,098
Tuition, non-resident: $1,443
Average cost of books: $400
% of students receiving aid: 70

Employment Profile:
% of students who pass the boards on their first try: 66
% employed within the first 6 months following graduation: 100

Surgical Technologist

Jane M. Verpent, RN, BA
Director of Surgical Technology
University of Medicine & Dentistry
School of Health Related Professions
Scotch Plains, New Jersey

Job Description

What Do They Do?

Surgical technologists are health professionals who serve as important members of operating room teams. They work directly with surgeons, anesthesiologists, registered nurses, and other surgical personnel. It is their job to ensure that the operating room environment is safe, that equipment functions properly, and that the operative procedure is conducted under conditions that maximize patient safety. Surgical technologists prepare the operating room by selecting and opening sterile supplies. They must anticipate the needs of the surgeon so that they can pass instruments and provide sterile items in an efficient manner. Along with the registered nurse, the surgical technologist accounts for sponges, needles and instruments before, during and after surgery. During surgery they may hold retractors, sponge or suction the operative site, or cut sutures under the direction of the surgeon. After surgery, the surgical technologist prepares the operating room for the next patient.

Type of Person

A surgical technologist has expertise in the theory and application of sterile technique. He or she combines knowledge of human anatomy, surgical procedures and technology to facilitate the surgeon's performance in any surgical procedure. Surgical technologists must be able to perform under stressful conditions and in emergency situations. A surgical technologist must be able to adapt to changes, have a stable temperament, considerable patience and the ability to communicate effectively. A good surgical technologist should possess a strong sense of responsibility, excellent manual dexterity and strong physical stamina. He or she must be able to work quickly and accurately and be detail-oriented.

With Whom Do They Work?

Surgical technologists work with surgeons, anesthesiologist, registered nurses and other operating room personnel.

Employment

Places of Employment

Although most surgical technologists are employed in the operating room, either within a hospital or an outpatient surgical center, they may also work in labor and delivery by assisting in cesareans or in central supply services where they prepare instruments for surgery. They may also be employed privately by a surgeon. Other areas of employment may include central service management, materials management, organ and tissue procurement and medical sales.

Employment Outlook

The U.S. Bureau of Labor Statistics has projected rapid growth in the field of surgical technology. The profession is ranked as the seventh fastest growing health-related field.[1] Due to constant changes in healthcare and the need for cost containment, the demand for surgical technologists is overwhelming. Since this need is expected to continue to grow, the outlook for employment in the field of surgical technology appears to be excellent.

Salary

Salaries for surgical technologists range from $10.00 per hour in the more rural areas to $16.00 per hour in the more urban areas. The average salary is approximately $14.00 per hour. This translates to $20,800 to $29,120 yearly.[2]

Educational Programs

Length

Accredited surgical technology programs are offered at post-secondary institutions such as colleges, vocational and technical schools, the military, and structured hospital programs. The length of these programs ranges from 9 to 15 months for a diploma/certificate program, to two years for an Associate's degree program. The Associate's degree is the terminal degree in surgical technology.

Prerequisites

Prerequisites vary among programs. Some may require several college-level courses before entry. All programs require a high school diploma.

Curriculum

Surgical technology programs include both didactic and clinical components. The didactic portion of the program includes courses in anatomy and physiology, microbiology, pharmacology, medical terminology and surgical technology. The clinical surgical technology courses include studies in preparation for surgery, fundamentals of surgical care and surgical procedures.

Accrediting Body

Surgical technology programs are accredited according to essential standards set forth by the Accreditation Review Committee on Education in Surgical Technology (ARC-ST). Accreditation is granted by the Commission on Accreditation of Allied Health Programs (CAAHEP).

Accreditation Review Committee on Education in
Surgical Technology
7108-C South Alton Way, Suite 150
Englewood, CO 80112-2106
Telephone: 303-694-9262
Web address: www.arcst.org

Certification Board

The Liaison Council on Certification for the Surgical Technologist (LCC-ST) is responsible for creating and administering the national certification examination to any graduate of an accredited surgical technology program. To renew the six-year certificate, the certified surgical technologist (CST) must earn continuing education credits or re-take the certifying examination.

A student must be a graduate of one of the programs listed in this book that is accredited by CAAHEP to be eligible to take the certifying exam.

Liaison Council on Certification for the Surgical Technologist
7790 East Arapahoe Road, Suite 240
Englewood, CO 80112-1274
Telephone: 303-694-9264
Web address: www.lcc-st.org

Advice For Potential Students

Consider attending one of the programs that has been accredited through CAAHEP. Attending an accredited program will assure you that the program maintains and promotes appropriate standards of quality education. You should review the curriculum to confirm that it includes instruction in all surgical specialties and all aspects of the surgical environment. The program should incorporate both classroom and clinical education. Visit the school you are considering to evaluate the facilities. Ask how many of their graduates find jobs and ask where they are working.

For Additional Information

Organizations

Association of Surgical Technologists
7108-C South Alton Way, Suite 100
Englewood, CO 80112-2106
Telephone: 303-694-9130
Web address: www.ast.org

Publications

Surgical Technology: A Growing Career. Englewood, CO: Association of Surgical Technologists, 1995.
A brochure available free of charge from the Association of Surgical Technologists.

Internet Resources

Association of Surgical Technologists: www.ast.org
Accreditation Review Committee on Education in Surgical Technology: www.arc-st.org
Liaison Council on Certification for the Surgical Technologist: www.lcc-st.org

Arkansas

Westark Community College

PO Box 3649
Ft. Smith, AR 72913

Contact Information:
Telephone: 501-788-7855
Fax: 501-788-7869
E-mail: sfulbrig@systema.westark.edu
Web: www.westark.edu

Program Information:
Program begins: August
Duration of program: 9 months

Application Information:
Enrollment of program: 18
Transfer students are accepted.

Financial Information:
Tuition, resident: $1,190
Tuition, non-resident: $2,900
Average cost of books: $300
% of students receiving aid: 58

Employment Profile:
% of students who pass the boards on their first try: 70
% employed within the first 6 months following graduation: 92
Average starting salary: $18,000

California

Loyola Marymount University

7900 Loyola Boulevard
Los Angeles, CA 900458217

Contact Information:
Telephone: 310-338-4562
Fax: 310-338-4518
E-mail: dlinesch@lmumail.lmu.edu
Web: www.lmu.edu/acad/gd/mftintro.htm

Program Information:
Program begins: January, September
Duration of program: 24 months

Application Information:
Enrollment of program: 40

Financial Information:
Average cost of books: $800
% of students receiving aid: 50

Employment Profile:
% employed within the first 6 months following graduation: 100
Average starting salary: $35,000

ConCorde Career Institute

12412 Victory Boulevard
North Hollywood, CA 91606

Contact Information:
Telephone: 818-766-8151 ext. 251
Fax: 818-766-1587
Web: www.concordecareercolleges.com

Program Information:
Program begins: August
Duration of program: 11 months

Application Information:
Enrollment of program: 100

Hospital Consortium of San Mateo County

1600 Trousdale Drive
Burlingame, CA 94010

Contact Information:
Telephone: 650-696-7872
Fax: 650-696-7864

Program Information:
Program begins: August
Duration of program: 10 months

Application Information:
Enrollment of program: 17

Financial Information:
Tuition, resident: $3,750
Average cost of books: $195

Employment Profile:
% of students who pass the boards on their first try: 100
% employed within the first 6 months following graduation: 88
Average starting salary: $30,000

Loma Linda University
Nichol Hall Room 1926
Loma Linda, CA 92350

Contact Information:
Telephone: 909-824-4932
Fax: 909-824-4701
E-mail: dorothy-donesky@sahp.llu.edu
Web: www.llu.edu

Program Information:
Program begins: September
Duration of program: 11 months

Application Information:
Enrollment of program: 15
Transfer students are accepted.

Financial Information:
Tuition, resident: $12,109
Tuition, non-resident: $11,000
Average cost of books: $350
% of students receiving aid: 90

Employment Profile:
% employed within the first 6 months following graduation: 60
Average starting salary: $22,460

Naval School of Health Sciences—San Diego
PO Box 85122
San Diego, CA 92134-5291

Contact Information:
Telephone: 619-532-7821
Fax: 619-532-7796
E-mail: dmccain@hsd10.med.navy.mil

Program Information:
Program begins: August
Duration of program: 6 months

Employment Profile:
% employed within the first 6 months following graduation: 100
Additional information: Only active duty or service Navy enlisted personnel can attend.

Southwestern Community College
900 Otay Lakes Road
Chula Vista, CA 91910

Contact Information:
Telephone: 619-421-6700
Fax: 619-482-6439
Web: www.southwest.cc.nc.us

Program Information:
Program begins: June
Degrees offered: Associate's, 24 months

Application Information:
Enrollment of program: 20
Transfer students are accepted.

Financial Information:
Tuition, resident: $340
Average cost of books: $250
% of students receiving aid: 70

Employment Profile:
% of students who pass the boards on their first try: 85
Average starting salary: $30,000

Colorado

Pueblo Community College
900 West Orman Avenue
Pueblo, CO 81004

Contact Information:
Telephone: 719-543-8582
Fax: 719-543-8586
E-mail: kevin.frey@pcc.cccoes.edu
Web: www.pcc.cccoes.edu

Program Information:
Program begins: August
Degrees offered: Certificate program, 11 months

Application Information:
Transfer students are accepted.

Financial Information:
Tuition, resident: $2,635
Tuition, non-resident: $11,008

Employment Profile:
% of students who pass the boards on their first try: 86
% employed within the first 6 months following graduation: 90
Average starting salary: $20,000

Connecticut

Manchester Community-Technical College
MS 29, PO Box 1046
Manchester, CT 06045

Contact Information:
Telephone: 860-647-6186
Fax: 860-647-6370
E-mail: ma_parmelee@commnet.edu
Web: www.mctc.commnet.edu

Program Information:
Program begins: August
Duration of program: 21 months

Application Information:
Enrollment of program: 23
Transfer students are accepted.

Financial Information:
Tuition, resident: $3,945
Tuition, non-resident: $11,195
Average cost of books: $250

Employment Profile:
% of students who pass the boards on their first try: 100
% employed within the first 6 months following graduation: 85
Average starting salary: $29,000

Florida

Central Florida Community College
PO Box 1388
3001 Southwest College Road
Ocala, FL 34478-1388

Contact Information:
Telephone: 352-854-2322 ext. 1271
Fax: 352-873-5864
E-mail: frazierb@cfcc.cc.fl.us
Web: www.cfcc.cc.fl.us

Program Information:
Program begins: August
Degrees offered: Certificate program, 11 months
Evening or weekend classes are available.

Application Information:
Enrollment of program: 20

Financial Information:
Tuition, resident: $2,946
Tuition, non-resident: $8,453
Average cost of books: $500
% of students receiving aid: 61

Employment Profile:
% of students who pass the boards on their first try: 100
% employed within the first 6 months following graduation: 100
Average starting salary: $20,800

David G. Erwin Technical Center
2010 East Hillsborough Avenue
Tampa, FL 33610-8299

Contact Information:
Telephone: 813-231-1800
Fax: 813-231-1820
Web: www.erwin.org

Program Information:
Program begins: August
Duration of program: 14 months
Evening or weekend classes are available.

Application Information:
Enrollment of program: 39
Transfer students are accepted.

Financial Information:
Tuition, resident: $1,782
Average cost of books: $200
% of students receiving aid: 30

Employment Profile:
% of students who pass the boards on their first try: 90
% employed within the first 6 months following graduation: 100
Average starting salary: $19,780

Daytona Beach Community College
1200 West International Speedway Boulevard
PO Box 2811
Daytona Beach, FL 32120

Contact Information:
Telephone: 904-255-8131
Fax: 904-254-4491
E-mail: hunterm@dbcc.cc.fl.us
Web: www.dbcc.cc.fl.us

Program Information:
Program begins: June
Degrees offered: Certificate program, 10 months

Application Information:
Enrollment of program: 15

Financial Information:
Tuition, resident: $1,500
Tuition, non-resident: $6,378
Average cost of books: $450
% of students receiving aid: 30

Employment Profile:
% of students who pass the boards on their first try: 95
% employed within the first 6 months following graduation: 95
Average starting salary: $18,000

Lee County High Technical Center—North

360 Juanita Boulevard
Cape Coral, FL 33993

Contact Information:
Telephone: 941-574-4440 ext. 227
Fax: 941-458-3721
E-mail: donah@lee.k12.fl.us

Program Information:
Program begins: August
Duration of program: 11 months

Financial Information:
Tuition, resident: $1,300
Tuition, non-resident: $7,280

Lindsey Hopkins Technical Education Center

750 Northwest 20th Street
Miami, FL 33127

Contact Information:
Telephone: 305-324-6070 ext. 8015
Fax: 305-326-1408

Program Information:
Duration of program: 12 months

Application Information:
Enrollment of program: 16

Financial Information:
Tuition, resident: $1,936
Tuition, non-resident: $6,000
Average cost of books: $200
% of students receiving aid: 90

Employment Profile:
% employed within the first 6 months following graduation: 50
Average starting salary: $20,000

Sarasota County Technical Institute

4748 Beneva Road
Sarasota, FL 34233

Contact Information:
Telephone: 941-924-1365 ext. 372
Fax: 941-361-6886
E-mail: linda_swisher@scti.srgit.sarasota.k12.fl.us
Web: www.careerscape.org

Program Information:
Program begins: August
Duration of program: 12 months

Application Information:
Enrollment of program: 30

Financial Information:
Tuition, resident: $2,168
Tuition, non-resident: $5,974

Traviss Technical Center

3225 Winter Lake Road
Lakeland, FL 33803

Contact Information:
Telephone: 941-499-2700
Fax: 941-413-2067

Program Information:
Program begins: January, May, September
Duration of program: 10 months

Application Information:
Enrollment of program: 12
Transfer students are accepted.

Financial Information:
Tuition, resident: $1,138
Tuition, non-resident: $4,945
Average cost of books: $291
% of students receiving aid: 42

Employment Profile:
% of students who pass the boards on their first try: 92
% employed within the first 6 months following graduation: 100
Average starting salary: $22,000

Georgia

Athens Area Technical Institute

800 US Highway 29 North
Athens, GA 30601-1500

Contact Information:
Telephone: 706-355-5072
Fax: 706-369-5753
E-mail: jackson-streb@aati.edu
Web: www.athens.tec.ga.us

Program Information:
Program begins: September
Duration of program: 15 months

Application Information:
Enrollment of program: 15
Transfer students are accepted.

Financial Information:
Tuition, resident: $1,132
Tuition, non-resident: $2,264
Average cost of books: $550
% of students receiving aid: 95

Employment Profile:
% of students who pass the boards on their first try: 100
% employed within the first 6 months following graduation: 95
Average starting salary: $22,000

Augusta Technical Institute

3116 Deans Bridge Road/900 Building
Augusta, GA 30906

Contact Information:
Telephone: 706-771-4191
Fax: 706-771-4181
E-mail: hthomas@adminl.augusta.tec.ga.us
Web: www.augusta.tec.ga.us

Program Information:
Program begins: September
Duration of program: 15 months

Application Information:
Transfer students are accepted.

Financial Information:
Tuition, resident: $274
Tuition, non-resident: $526
Average cost of books: $250
% of students receiving aid: 100

Employment Profile:
% employed within the first 6 months following graduation: 100
Average starting salary: $20,000

DeKalb Technical Institute

495 North Indian Creek Drive
Clarkston, GA 30021

Contact Information:
Telephone: 404-297-9522
Fax: 404-294-0673
E-mail: pauls@admin2.dekalb.tec.ga.us
Web: www.dekalb.tec.ga.us

Program Information:
Program begins: September
Duration of program: 15 months
Evening or weekend classes are available.

Application Information:
Enrollment of program: 87
Transfer students are accepted.

Financial Information:
Tuition, resident: $1,000
Tuition, non-resident: $1,656
Average cost of books: $200
% of students receiving aid: 65

Employment Profile:
% of students who pass the boards on their first try: 100
% employed within the first 6 months following graduation: 96
Average starting salary: $20,000

Thomas Technical Institute

15689 US Highway 19 North
Thomasville, GA 31792

Contact Information:
Telephone: 912-225-5205
Fax: 912-225-5289
E-mail: shollima@ttin1.thomastec.ga.us

Program Information:
Program begins: August
Duration of program: 15 months
Evening or weekend classes are available.

Financial Information:
Tuition, resident: $1,104
Tuition, non-resident: $2,208

Illinois

Elgin Community College

1700 Spartan Drive
Elgin, IL 60123

Contact Information:
Telephone: 874-214-7303 ext. 7303
Fax: 847-622-0395
E-mail: mlange@mail.elgin.cc.il.us
Web: www.elgin.cc.il.us

Program Information:
Program begins: September
Duration of program: 12 months

Application Information:
Enrollment of program: 24
Transfer students are accepted.

Employment Profile:
% of students who pass the boards on their first try: 95
Average starting salary: $24,000

Illinois Central College

Peoria Campus Division
Peoria, IL 61635-0001

Contact Information:
Telephone: 309-999-4673
Fax: 309-673-9626
E-mail: rbriggs@icc.cc.il.us
Web: www.icc.cc.il.us

Program Information:
Program begins: August
Duration of program: 12 months

Financial Information:
Tuition, resident: $1,715
Average cost of books: $300

Employment Profile:
% employed within the first 6 months following graduation: 85
Average starting salary: $19,000

Parkland College

2400 West Bradley Avenue
Champaign, IL 61821

Contact Information:
Telephone: 217-351-2375
Fax: 217-373-3830
E-mail: jorandolph@parkland.cc.il.us
Web: www.parkland.cc.il.us

Program Information:
Degrees offered: Certificate program, 11 months

Application Information:
Enrollment of program: 24
Transfer students are accepted.

Financial Information:
Tuition, resident: $1,530
Tuition, non-resident: $5,614
Average cost of books: $300
% of students receiving aid: 50

Employment Profile:
% of students who pass the boards on their first try: 98
% employed within the first 6 months following graduation: 100

Trinity Medical Center

555 6th Street
Moline, IL 61265-1216

Contact Information:
Telephone: 309-757-3450
Fax: 309-757-2194

Program Information:
Program begins: July
Duration of program: 11 months

Application Information:
Enrollment of program: 10

Financial Information:
Average cost of books: $400
% of students receiving aid: 50

Employment Profile:
% of students who pass the boards on their first try: 75
% employed within the first 6 months following graduation: 90
Average starting salary: $19,000

Indiana

Bloomington Hospital

PO Box 1149
Bloomington, IN 47402

Contact Information:
Telephone: 812-353-5571
Fax: 812-353-5453
E-mail: lbarttett@bloomhealth.org

Program Information:
Program begins: February, August
Duration of program: 11 months

Financial Information:
Average cost of books: $420

Employment Profile:
% of students who pass the boards on their first try: 95
% employed within the first 6 months following graduation: 90
Average starting salary: $22,000

Ivy Tech State College—Indianapolis

Central Indiana Region
One West 26th Street, PO Box 1763
Indianapolis, IN 46206-1763

Contact Information:
Telephone: 317-921-4404
Fax: 317-921-4753
E-mail: whaver@ivy.tech.in.us
Web: www.ivy.tech.in.us

Program Information:
Program begins: March, September
Duration of program: 24 months
Evening or weekend classes are available.

Application Information:
Transfer students are accepted.

Financial Information:
Tuition, resident: $1,817
Tuition, non-resident: $3,309

Employment Profile:
% of students who pass the boards on their first try: 600
% employed within the first 6 months following graduation: 100
Average starting salary: $24,000

Ivy Tech State College—Lafayette

3101 South Creasy Lane
PO Box 6299
Lafayette, IN 47903

Contact Information:
Telephone: 765-772-9208
Fax: 765-772-9248
E-mail: dhall@ivy.tec.in.us
Web: www.ivy.tec.in.us

Program Information:
Duration of program: 24 months
Evening or weekend classes are available.

Application Information:
Transfer students are accepted.

Financial Information:
Tuition, resident: $4,450
Tuition, non-resident: $8,275
Average cost of books: $1,000
% of students receiving aid: 80

Employment Profile:
% employed within the first 6 months following graduation: 85
Average starting salary: $20,000

Ivy Tech State College—Michigan City

3714 Franklin Street
Michigan City, IN 46360

Contact Information:
Telephone: 219-879-9137
Fax: 219-879-9157
E-mail: ivy.tec.in.us
Web: www.ivy.tec.in.us

Program Information:
Program begins: July
Duration of program: 24 months
Evening or weekend classes are available.

Application Information:
Enrollment of program: 122

Financial Information:
Tuition, resident: $4,435
Tuition, non-resident: $8,275
Average cost of books: $800
% of students receiving aid: 30

Employment Profile:
% of students who pass the boards on their first try: 80
% employed within the first 6 months following graduation: 70
Average starting salary: $24,000

Ivy Tech State College Southwest—Evansville

3501 First Avenue
Evansville, IN 47710

Contact Information:
Telephone: 812-429-1490
Fax: 812-429-1483
E-mail: rleach@ivy.tec.in.us
Web: www.ivy.tec.in.us

Program Information:
Program begins: August
Duration of program: 24 months
Evening or weekend classes are available.

Application Information:
Enrollment of program: 16
Transfer students are accepted.

Financial Information:
Tuition, resident: $1,816
Tuition, non-resident: $3,309

University of Saint Francis

2701 Spring Street
Fort Wayne, IN 46807-1697

Contact Information:
Telephone: 219-434-7673
Fax: 219-434-7601
E-mail: eslagle@sf.edu
Web: www.sf.edu

Program Information:
Program begins: February
Duration of program: 18 months
Evening or weekend classes are available.

Application Information:
Enrollment of program: 40
Transfer students are accepted.

Financial Information:
Average cost of books: $350

Employment Profile:
% of students who pass the boards on their first try: 100
% employed within the first 6 months following graduation: 100
Average starting salary: $22,000

Vincennes University

1002 North First Street, HO-14
Vincennes, IN 47591

Contact Information:
Telephone: 812-888-5893
Fax: 812-888-4550
E-mail: ckeegan@indian.vinu.edu
Web: www.vinu.edu

Program Information:
Program begins: June, September
Duration of program: 18 months

Application Information:
Enrollment of program: 20
Transfer students are accepted.

Financial Information:
Tuition, resident: $3,334
Tuition, non-resident: $8,000
Average cost of books: $300

Employment Profile:
% employed within the first 6 months following graduation: 80
Average starting salary: $22,000

Kansas

Wichita Area Technical College

324 North Emporia
PO Box 3340
Wichita, KS 67202

Contact Information:
Telephone: 316-973-4370 ext. 4367
Fax: 316-973-4332
E-mail: mattinglyc@watc.tec.ks.us
Web: www.watc.tec.ks.us

Program Information:
Program begins: February, August
Duration of program: 10 months

Application Information:
Enrollment of program: 40
Transfer students are accepted.

Financial Information:
Tuition, resident: $1,200
Average cost of books: $600
% of students receiving aid: 75

Employment Profile:
% of students who pass the boards on their first try: 95
% employed within the first 6 months following graduation: 98
Average starting salary: $24,000

Kentucky

Central Kentucky Technical College

308 Vocational -Technical Road
Lexington, KY 40511-2626

Contact Information:
Telephone: 606-246-2400 ext. 272
Fax: 606-246-2504
E-mail: al.smith@kctcs.net
Web: www.ktcc.state.ky.us

Program Information:
Program begins: August
Duration of program: 23 months

Application Information:
Transfer students are accepted.

Financial Information:
Tuition, resident: $1,800
Tuition, non-resident: $3,000
Average cost of books: $345
% of students receiving aid: 24

Employment Profile:
% employed within the first 6 months following graduation: 80
Average starting salary: $26,000

Cumberland Valley Health Technology Center

US 25E South
PO Box 188
Pineville, KY 40977

Contact Information:
Telephone: 606-337-3106
Fax: 606-337-5662
Web: www.state.ky.us

Program Information:
Program begins: September
Duration of program: 11 months
Evening or weekend classes are available.

Application Information:
Enrollment of program: 15
Transfer students are accepted.

Financial Information:
Tuition, resident: $660
Tuition, non-resident: $1,320
Average cost of books: $460
% of students receiving aid: 87

Employment Profile:
% of students who pass the boards on their first try: 56
% employed within the first 6 months following graduation: 80
Average starting salary: $19,000

Kentucky Community Technical College

1501 Frederica Street
Owensboro, KY 42303

Contact Information:
Telephone: 502-687-7255 ext. 143
Fax: 502-687-7273

Program Information:
Program begins: August
Degrees offered: Certificate program, 11 months

Application Information:
Enrollment of program: 18
Transfer students are accepted.

Financial Information:
Tuition, resident: $620
Tuition, non-resident: $1,240
Average cost of books: $225

Employment Profile:
% of students who pass the boards on their first try: 95
% employed within the first 6 months following graduation: 90

Kentucky Technical—Madisonville Health Technical Center

750 Laffoon Street
Madisonville, KY 42431

Contact Information:
Telephone: 270-824-7552
Fax: 270-824-7069
Web: www.madtechcollege.com

Program Information:
Program begins: August
Duration of program: 11 months

Application Information:
Transfer students are accepted.

Financial Information:
Tuition, resident: $1,010
Tuition, non-resident: $1,920
Average cost of books: $750
% of students receiving aid: 50

Employment Profile:
% of students who pass the boards on their first try: 86
% employed within the first 6 months following graduation: 100
Average starting salary: $20,000

Louisiana

Bossier Parish Community College

2719 Airline Drive
Bossier City, LA 71111

Contact Information:
Telephone: 318-746-7754
Web: www.bpcc.cc.la.us

Program Information:
Program begins: August
Duration of program: 18 months

Application Information:
Enrollment of program: 13
Transfer students are accepted.

Financial Information:
Tuition, resident: $2,172
Tuition, non-resident: $6,252
Average cost of books: $644

Employment Profile:
% employed within the first 6 months following graduation: 80
Average starting salary: $21,000

Maine

Maine Medical Center

School of Surgical Technology
SMTC Fort Road
Portland, ME 04106

Contact Information:
Telephone: 207-767-9589
Fax: 207-767-9690
E-mail: mbien@smtc.net
Web: www.smtc.net

Program Information:
Program begins: March, September
Degrees offered: Diploma, 12 months

Application Information:
Enrollment of program: 36

Financial Information:
Average cost of books: $400

Employment Profile:
% of students who pass the boards on their first try: 97
% employed within the first 6 months following graduation: 99
Average starting salary: $24,900

Massachusetts

Charles H. McCann Technical School

70 Hodges Cross Road
North Adams, MA 01247

Contact Information:
Telephone: 413-663-5383 ext. 40
Fax: 413-664-9424
Web: www.mccanntech.org

Program Information:
Program begins: August
Duration of program: 9 months

Application Information:
Enrollment of program: 5

Financial Information:
Average cost of books: $350
% of students receiving aid: 75

Employment Profile:
% of students who pass the boards on their first try: 100
% employed within the first 6 months following graduation: 50
Average starting salary: $22,000

Michigan

Henry Ford Community College

5101 Evergreen Road
Dearborn, MI 48128

Contact Information:
Telephone: 313-317-6598
Fax: 313-317-6569
E-mail: drothger@hfcc.net
Web: www.hfcc.net

Program Information:
Program begins: April, August, December
Duration of program: 21 months

Financial Information:
Tuition, resident: $1,886
Tuition, non-resident: $2,964

Washtenaw Community College

OE 102 X
4800 East Huron River Drive, PO Box D-1
Ann Arbor, MI 48106-0978

Contact Information:
Telephone: 734-973-3457
Fax: 734-677-5078
E-mail: vmurphy@wccnet.org

Program Information:
Program begins: August
Duration of program: 12 months

Application Information:
Enrollment of program: 20
Transfer students are accepted.

Financial Information:
Tuition, resident: $2,229
Tuition, non-resident: $3,126
Average cost of books: $250
% of students receiving aid: 25

Employment Profile:
% employed within the first 6 months following graduation: 75
Average starting salary: $23,000

Minnesota

Northwest Technical College—East Grand Forks

2022 Central Avenue Northeast
East Grand Forks, MN 56721

Contact Information:
Telephone: 218-773-4623
Fax: 218-773-4502
E-mail: ruth.letexier@mail.ntc.mnscu.edu
Web: www.ntc-online.com

Program Information:
Program begins: August
Degrees offered: Associate's, 18 months
Evening or weekend classes are available.

Application Information:
Enrollment of program: 33
Transfer students are accepted.

Financial Information:
Tuition, resident: $4,579
Tuition, non-resident: $9,159
Average cost of books: $805
% of students receiving aid: 100

Employment Profile:
% of students who pass the boards on their first try: 95
% employed within the first 6 months following graduation: 97
Average starting salary: $25,000

Rochester Community and Technical College
851 30th Avenue Southeast
Rochester, MN 55904

Contact Information:
Telephone: 507-280-3118
Fax: 507-280-3180
E-mail: kathy.jacobson@roch.edu
Web: www.roch.edu

Program Information:
Degrees offered: Associate's, 18 months
Evening or weekend classes are available.

Application Information:
Transfer students are accepted.

Financial Information:
Tuition, resident: $2,250
Tuition, non-resident: $4,250
Average cost of books: $800

Employment Profile:
% of students who pass the boards on their first try: 95
Average starting salary: $25,000

St. Cloud Technical College
1540 Northway Drive
St. Cloud, MN 56301

Contact Information:
Telephone: 320-654-5921
Fax: 320-654-5981
E-mail: tlo@cloud.tec.mn.us
Web: www.sctcweb.tec.mn.us

Program Information:
Program begins: August
Degrees offered: Diploma, 12 months; Associate's, 18 months
Evening or weekend classes are available.

Application Information:
Enrollment of program: 17
Transfer students are accepted.

Financial Information:
Tuition, resident: $3,626
Tuition, non-resident: $7,252
Average cost of books: $500
% of students receiving aid: 32

Employment Profile:
% employed within the first 6 months following graduation: 100
Average starting salary: $24,000

Mississippi

Hinds Community College
1750 Chadwick Drive
Jackson, MS 39204

Contact Information:
Telephone: 601-372-6507
Fax: 601-371-3529
Web: www.hinds.cc.ms.us

Program Information:
Program begins: January
Duration of program: 12 months

Financial Information:
Tuition, resident: $1,640

Pearl River Community College—Poplarville
5448 US Highway 49 South
Hattiesburg, MS 39401

Contact Information:
Telephone: 601-554-9142
Fax: 601-554-9148
E-mail: ahinton@prcc.cc.ms.us
Web: www.prcc.ms.us

Program Information:
Program begins: August
Duration of program: 24 months

Application Information:
Enrollment of program: 20

Financial Information:
Tuition, resident: $2,025
Tuition, non-resident: $2,292
Average cost of books: $200
% of students receiving aid: 95

Employment Profile:
Average starting salary: $17,000

Missouri

Ozarks Technical Community College
1417 North Jefferson Avenue
Springfield, MO 65802

Contact Information:
Telephone: 417-895-7154
Fax: 417-895-7753
E-mail: tray@emh1.otc.cc.mo.us
Web: www.otc.cc.mo.us

Program Information:
Program begins: August
Duration of program: 9 months

Application Information:
Enrollment of program: 18
Transfer students are accepted.

Financial Information:
Tuition, resident: $1,470
Tuition, non-resident: $2,604
Average cost of books: $350
% of students receiving aid: 45

Employment Profile:
% of students who pass the boards on their first try: 95
% employed within the first 6 months following graduation: 90
Average starting salary: $24,000

St. Louis Community College at Forest Park
5600 Oakland Avenue
St. Louis, MO 63110

Contact Information:
Telephone: 314-644-9340
Fax: 314-644-9752
E-mail: dgerardot@fpmail.stlcc.mo.us
Web: www.stlcc.mu.us

Program Information:
Program begins: August
Duration of program: 12 months

Application Information:
Enrollment of program: 25
Transfer students are accepted.

Financial Information:
Tuition, resident: $2,206
Tuition, non-resident: $3,018

Employment Profile:
% employed within the first 6 months following graduation: 50
Average starting salary: $20,000

Three Rivers Community College
2080 Three Rivers Boulevard
Poplar Bluff, MO 63901-2393

Contact Information:
Telephone: 573-840-9685
Fax: 573-840-9184
E-mail: sdykes@trcc.cc.mo.us
Web: www.trcc.cc.mo.us

Program Information:
Program begins: August
Duration of program: 11 months
Evening or weekend classes are available.

Application Information:
Enrollment of program: 18
Transfer students are accepted.

Financial Information:
Tuition, resident: $1,599
Tuition, non-resident: $2,542
Average cost of books: $550
% of students receiving aid: 50

Employment Profile:
% of students who pass the boards on their first try: 70
% employed within the first 6 months following graduation: 90
Average starting salary: $16,000

Nebraska

Southeast Community College
8800 O Street
Lincoln, NE 68520

Contact Information:
Telephone: 402-437-2785
Fax: 402-437-2404
E-mail: kjuribe@sccm.cc.ne.us
Web: www.sccm.cc.ne.us

Program Information:
Program begins: August
Duration of program: 18 months

Application Information:
Enrollment of program: 44
Transfer students are accepted.

Financial Information:
Average cost of books: $220
% of students receiving aid: 50

Employment Profile:
% of students who pass the boards on their first try: 100
% employed within the first 6 months following graduation: 100
Average starting salary: $26,000

New Jersey

Bergen Community College
400 Paramus Road
Paramus, NJ 07652

Contact Information:
Telephone: 201-447-7944
Web: www.bergen.cc.nj.us

Program Information:
Program begins: September
Duration of program: 10 months

Application Information:
Enrollment of program: 31
Transfer students are accepted.

Financial Information:
Tuition, resident: $2,336
Tuition, non-resident: $4,672
Average cost of books: $450

Employment Profile:
% of students who pass the boards on their first try: 73
% employed within the first 6 months following graduation: 100

New York

New York University Medical Center
Surgical Technology Program
483 First Avenue
New York, NY 10016

Contact Information:
Telephone: 212-263-6644
Fax: 212-779-1493
E-mail: sheehmo1@popmail.med.nyu.edu
Web: www.surgtech.com

Program Information:
Program begins: March, September
Degrees offered: Certificate program, 12 months

Application Information:
Enrollment of program: 28

Financial Information:
Average cost of books: $400

Employment Profile:
% employed within the first 6 months following graduation: 100
Average starting salary: $31,000

Onondaga Community College
4941 Onondaga Road
Syracuse, NY 13215

Contact Information:
Telephone: 315-469-7741 ext. 2463
Fax: 315-469-2593
Web: www.sunyocc.edu

Program Information:
Program begins: August
Duration of program: 10 months

Financial Information:
Tuition, resident: $3,014
Tuition, non-resident: $6,028

Trocaire College
360 Choate Avenue
Buffalo, NY 14220-2094

Contact Information:
Telephone: 716-827-2454
Fax: 716-828-6107
E-mail: awill@altavista.net
Web: www.trocaire.edu

Program Information:
Program begins: August
Degrees offered: Associate's, 18 months
Evening or weekend classes are available.

Application Information:
Enrollment of program: 35
Transfer students are accepted.

Financial Information:
% of students receiving aid: 88

Employment Profile:
% of students who pass the boards on their first try: 90
% employed within the first 6 months following graduation: 97
Average starting salary: $21,400

North Carolina

Coastal Carolina Community College
444 Western Boulevard
Jacksonville, NC 28546-6877

Contact Information:
Telephone: 910-938-6274
Fax: 910-455-7027
Web: www.coastal.cc.nc.us

Program Information:
Program begins: September
Degrees offered: Diploma, 12 months; Associate's

Application Information:
Enrollment of program: 26
Transfer students are accepted.

Financial Information:
Tuition, resident: $720
Tuition, non-resident: $5,868
Average cost of books: $100
% of students receiving aid: 33

Employment Profile:
% of students who pass the boards on their first try: 95
% employed within the first 6 months following graduation: 93
Average starting salary: $18,720

Fayetteville Technical Community College
PO Box 35236
Fayetteville, NC 28303

Contact Information:
Telephone: 910-678-8492
Fax: 910-678-8500
E-mail: beddardk@ftccmail.faytech.cc.nc.us
Web: www.faytech.cc.nc.us

Program Information:
Program begins: September
Duration of program: 24 months

Financial Information:
Tuition, resident: $729
Tuition, non-resident: $5,912

Lenoir Community College
PO Box 188
Kinston, NC 28502-0188

Contact Information:
Telephone: 252-527-6223 ext. 802
Fax: 252-527-2712
E-mail: jes802@email.lenoir.cc.nc.us
Web: www.lenoir.cc.nc.us

Program Information:
Program begins: May
Duration of program: 12 months

Application Information:
Enrollment of program: 20
Transfer students are accepted.

Financial Information:
Tuition, resident: $777
Tuition, non-resident: $6,168
Average cost of books: $600
% of students receiving aid: 75

Employment Profile:
% of students who pass the boards on their first try: 80
% employed within the first 6 months following graduation: 35
Average starting salary: $21,000

Sandhills Community College
3395 Airport Road
Pinehurst, NC 28374

Contact Information:
Telephone: 910-695-3838
Fax: 910-692-2756
E-mail: mcculloughb@email.sandhills.cc.nc.us
Web: www.sandhills.cc.nc.us

Program Information:
Program begins: January, July
Duration of program: 12 months

Application Information:
Transfer students are accepted.

Financial Information:
Tuition, resident: $740
Tuition, non-resident: $6,281
Average cost of books: $450
% of students receiving aid: 70

Employment Profile:
% of students who pass the boards on their first try: 100
% employed within the first 6 months following graduation: 98
Average starting salary: $21,900

Ohio

Cincinnati State Technical and Community College
3520 Central Parkway
Cincinnati, OH 45223

Contact Information:
Telephone: 513-569-1673
Fax: 513-569-1659
E-mail: dantzlerw@cinstate.cc.oh.us
Web: www.cinstate.cc.oh.us

Program Information:
Program begins: February, July, September, December
Duration of program: 20 months
Evening or weekend classes are available.

Application Information:
Enrollment of program: 56

Financial Information:
Tuition, resident: $3,435
Tuition, non-resident: $6,870

Lorain County Community College
1005 North Abbe Road
Elyria, OH 44035

Contact Information:
Telephone: 800-995-5222
Fax: 440-366-4116
E-mail: psedlak@lorain.ccc.edu
Web: www.lorain.ccc.edu

Program Information:
Program begins: August
Degrees offered: Associate's, 20 months

Application Information:
Enrollment of program: 50
Transfer students are accepted.

Financial Information:
Tuition, resident: $3,105
Tuition, non-resident: $3,745
Average cost of books: $200

Employment Profile:
% of students who pass the boards on their first try: 95
% employed within the first 6 months following graduation: 99
Average starting salary: $26,000

Owens Community College
PO Box 10,000
Oregon Road
Toledo, OH 43699

Contact Information:
Telephone: 419-661-7338
Fax: 419-661-7287
E-mail: dwetmore@owens.cc.oh.us
Web: www.owens.cc.oh.us

Program Information:
Program begins: August
Duration of program: 24 months

Application Information:
Enrollment of program: 33
Transfer students are accepted.

Financial Information:
Tuition, resident: $2,280
Tuition, non-resident: $4,350
Average cost of books: $500
% of students receiving aid: 70

Employment Profile:
% of students who pass the boards on their first try: 100
% employed within the first 6 months following graduation: 100
Average starting salary: $22,000

Sinclair Community College
444 West Third Street
Dayton, OH 45402-1460

Contact Information:
Telephone: 937-512-2850
Fax: 937-512-5175
E-mail: jujohnso@sinclair.edu
Web: www.sinclair.edu

Program Information:
Program begins: September
Degrees offered: Associate's, 20 months

Application Information:
Enrollment of program: 37
Transfer students are accepted.

Financial Information:
Tuition, resident: $5,002
Tuition, non-resident: $10,309
Average cost of books: $500
% of students receiving aid: 60

Employment Profile:
% of students who pass the boards on their first try: 100
% employed within the first 6 months following graduation: 100
Average starting salary: $23,900

Youngstown Public School
Choffin Career Center
200 East Wood Street
Youngstown, OH 44503

Contact Information:
Telephone: 330-744-8763
Fax: 330-744-8705
E-mail: youn_odj@access-k12.org

Program Information:
Program begins: July
Duration of program: 10 months

Application Information:
Enrollment of program: 25

Financial Information:
Average cost of books: $350

Employment Profile:
% of students who pass the boards on their first try: 85
% employed within the first 6 months following graduation: 88
Average starting salary: $22,000

Oklahoma

Autry Technology Center
1201 West Willow
Enid, OK 73703

Contact Information:
Telephone: 405-242-2750 ext. 127
Fax: 405-233-8262

Program Information:
Program begins: September
Duration of program: 12 months

Application Information:
Enrollment of program: 10
Transfer students are accepted.

Financial Information:
Tuition, resident: $1,481
Tuition, non-resident: $5,080
Average cost of books: $600
% of students receiving aid: 45

Employment Profile:
% of students who pass the boards on their first try: 95
% employed within the first 6 months following graduation: 80
Average starting salary: $24,000

Canadian Valley Area Vocational Technical School
1401 Michigan
Chickasha, OK 73018

Contact Information:
Telephone: 405-224-7220

Fax: 405-222-3839
E-mail: followwilla@chick-ok.org

Program Information:
Program begins: March, September
Duration of program: 10 months

Application Information:
Transfer students are accepted.

Financial Information:
Tuition, resident: $525
Tuition, non-resident: $3,280
Average cost of books: $400

Employment Profile:
% employed within the first 6 months following graduation: 80
Average starting salary: $20,000

Metro Area Vocational-Technical School

Health Careers Center
1720 Springlake Drive
Oklahoma City, OK 73111

Contact Information:
Telephone: 405-424-8324 ext. 620
Fax: 405-424-9403
E-mail: vbushey@metrotech.org
Web: www.metrotech.org

Program Information:
Duration of program: 10 months
Evening or weekend classes are available.

Application Information:
Enrollment of program: 15

Employment Profile:
% employed within the first 6 months following graduation: 100
Average starting salary: $18,000

Northeastern Oklahoma A & M College

PO Box 3907
Miami, OK 74354-6497

Contact Information:
Telephone: 918-540-6314
Fax: 918-540-6471
E-mail: kmherrington@neoam.cc.ok.us

Program Information:
Program begins: August
Duration of program: 12 months

Application Information:
Enrollment of program: 12

Tulsa Technology Center

3420 South Memorial Drive
Tulsa, OK 74145-1390

Contact Information:
Telephone: 918-828-1036
Fax: 918-828-1039
E-mail: cdollar@tulsatec.org
Web: www.tulsatech.org

Program Information:
Program begins: August
Duration of program: 9 months
Evening or weekend classes are available.

Application Information:
Enrollment of program: 18
Transfer students are accepted.

Financial Information:
Average cost of books: $435
% of students receiving aid: 76

Employment Profile:
% of students who pass the boards on their first try: 95
% employed within the first 6 months following graduation: 99
Average starting salary: $18,000

Oregon

Mt. Hood Community College

26000 Southeast Stark Street
Gresham, OR 97030

Contact Information:
Telephone: 503-491-7179
Fax: 503-491-6047
E-mail: morfitt@mhcc.cc.or.us
Web: www.mhcc.cc.or.us

Program Information:
Program begins: September
Duration of program: 18 months

Financial Information:
Tuition, resident: $1,485
Tuition, non-resident: $4,995

Pennsylvania

Conemaugh Valley Memorial Hospital

1086 Franklin Street
Johnstown, PA 15905

Contact Information:
Telephone: 814-534-9772
Fax: 814-534-3244
E-mail: ppavlik@conemaugh.org
Web: www.conemaugh.org

Program Information:
Program begins: August
Duration of program: 12 months

Application Information:
Enrollment of program: 5
Transfer students are accepted.

Financial Information:
Tuition, resident: $5,884
Tuition, non-resident: $12,918
Average cost of books: $350

Employment Profile:
% of students who pass the boards on their first try: 90
% employed within the first 6 months following graduation: 82
Average starting salary: $20,000

Delaware County Community College

901 South Media Line Road
Media, PA 19063-1094

Contact Information:
Telephone: 610-359-5286
Fax: 610-359-7350
E-mail: jrothroc@dcccnet.dccc.edu
Web: www.dccc.edu

Program Information:
Program begins: May
Duration of program: 9 months

Financial Information:
Tuition, resident: $3,690
Tuition, non-resident: $7,440

Lancaster Institute for Health Education

143 East Lemon Street
Lancaster, PA 17602

Contact Information:
Telephone: 717-290-5511 ext. 7391
Fax: 717-290-5970
E-mail: equinus_tr@yahoo.com
Web: www.lha.org

Program Information:
Program begins: September
Duration of program: 12 months

Financial Information:
Average cost of books: $300

Employment Profile:
% of students who pass the boards on their first try: 90
% employed within the first 6 months following graduation: 90
Average starting salary: $20,700

Mt. Aloysius College

7373 Admiral Peary Highway
Cresson, PA 16630-1999

Contact Information:
Telephone: 814-886-6340
Fax: 814-886-2978
E-mail: csmith@mtaloy.edu
Web: www.mtaloy.edu

Program Information:
Program begins: January
Duration of program: 11 months

Application Information:
Enrollment of program: 29
Transfer students are accepted.

Financial Information:
Tuition, resident: $14,540
Tuition, non-resident: $9,000
Average cost of books: $300
% of students receiving aid: 88

Employment Profile:
% of students who pass the boards on their first try: 60

% employed within the first 6 months following graduation: 30
Average starting salary: $25,000

Reading Hospital and Medical Center

PO Box 16052
Reading, PA 19612

Contact Information:
Telephone: 610-988-8546
Fax: 610-988-5965

Program Information:
Program begins: January, August
Duration of program: 10 months

Financial Information:
Average cost of books: $165

Employment Profile:
% employed within the first 6 months following graduation: 100
Average starting salary: $22,500

Rhode Island

New England Institute of Technology

2500 Post Road
Warwick, RI 02886-2266

Contact Information:
Telephone: 401-739-5000 ext. 3318
Fax: 401-739-7738
E-mail: jfielding@neit.edu
Web: www.neit.edu

Program Information:
Program begins: April, October
Degrees offered: Associate's, 18 months
Evening or weekend classes are available.

Application Information:
Enrollment of program: 100
Transfer students are accepted.

Financial Information:
Average cost of books: $250

Employment Profile:
% of students who pass the boards on their first try: 95

South Carolina

Greenville Technical College

PO Box 5616
Greenville, SC 29606-8616

Contact Information:
Telephone: 864-250-8298
Fax: 864-250-8549
E-mail: burdinodb@gvltec.edu
Web: www.greenvilletech.com

Program Information:
Program begins: August
Duration of program: 28 months
Evening or weekend classes are available.

Application Information:
Enrollment of program: 30
Transfer students are accepted.

Financial Information:
Tuition, resident: $4,375
Tuition, non-resident: $11,200
Average cost of books: $1,000
% of students receiving aid: 50

Employment Profile:
% of students who pass the boards on their first try: 100
% employed within the first 6 months following graduation: 100
Average starting salary: $23,920

Midlands Technical College

PO Box 2408
Columbia, SC 29202

Contact Information:
Telephone: 803-822-3438
Fax: 803-822-3079
E-mail: oliverl@mtc.mid.tec.sc.us
Web: www.mid.tec.sc.us

Program Information:
Program begins: August
Degrees offered: Diploma, 12 months
Evening or weekend classes are available.

Application Information:
Enrollment of program: 18
Transfer students are accepted.

Financial Information:
Tuition, resident: $1,650
Tuition, non-resident: $4,968
Average cost of books: $500

Employment Profile:
% employed within the first 6 months following graduation: 100
Average starting salary: $20,000

Spartanburg Technical College

PO Drawer 4386
Spartanburg, SC 29305

Contact Information:
Telephone: 864-591-3870
Fax: 864-591-3708
E-mail: rogerse@spt.tec.sc.us
Web: www.spt.tec.sc.us

Program Information:
Program begins: June
Duration of program: 12 months

Application Information:
Enrollment of program: 23
Transfer students are accepted.

Financial Information:
Tuition, resident: $1,950
Tuition, non-resident: $2,445
Average cost of books: $400
% of students receiving aid: 53

Employment Profile:
% of students who pass the boards on their first try: 100
% employed within the first 6 months following graduation: 100
Average starting salary: $23,000

Tri-County Technical College

PO Box 587
Pendleton, SC 29670-0587

Contact Information:
Telephone: 864-646-8361 ext. 2225
Fax: 864-646-8256
E-mail: mthomas@tricty.tricounty.tec.sc.us
Web: www.tricounty.tec.sc.us

Program Information:
Program begins: August
Duration of program: 12 months

Application Information:
Enrollment of program: 20
Transfer students are accepted.

Financial Information:
Tuition, resident: $1,650
Tuition, non-resident: $5,268
Average cost of books: $500
% of students receiving aid: 30

Employment Profile:
% of students who pass the boards on their first try: 95
% employed within the first 6 months following graduation: 95
Average starting salary: $20,000

South Dakota

Presentation College

1500 North Main Street
Aberdeen, SD 57401

Contact Information:
Telephone: 605-229-8415
Fax: 605-229-8518
E-mail: snyderk@presentation.edu
Web: www.presentation.edu

Program Information:
Program begins: August
Duration of program: 18 months

Application Information:
Enrollment of program: 25
Transfer students are accepted.

Financial Information:
% of students receiving aid: 94

Employment Profile:
% of students who pass the boards on their first try: 80
% employed within the first 6 months following graduation: 100

Tennessee

Chattanooga State Technical Community College

4501 Amnicola Highway
Chattanooga, TN 37406-1097

Contact Information:
Telephone: 423-697-4491
Fax: 423-697-2413
E-mail: roddy@chattanooga.tec.tn.us
Web: www.cstcc.cc.tn.us

Program Information:
Program begins: September
Duration of program: 12 months

Application Information:
Enrollment of program: 18

Employment Profile:
% of students who pass the boards on their first try: 97
% employed within the first 6 months following graduation: 100
Average starting salary: $22,000

Ft. Sanders Regional Medical Center—Parkwest Medical Center

1901 Clinch Avenue
Knoxville, TN 37916

Contact Information:
Telephone: 423-693-5151 ext. 5236
Fax: 423-694-5804
E-mail: jagd34@aol.com

Program Information:
Program begins: August
Duration of program: 10 months

Application Information:
Enrollment of program: 7

Financial Information:
Average cost of books: $250

Employment Profile:
% of students who pass the boards on their first try: 95
% employed within the first 6 months following graduation: 100
Average starting salary: $18,800

Tennessee Technology Center—Memphis

550 Alabama Avenue
Memphis, TN 38105-3799

Contact Information:
Telephone: 901-543-6164
Fax: 901-543-6197
E-mail: cfarley@memphis.tec.tn.us
Web: www.memphis.tec.tn.us

Program Information:
Program begins: August
Duration of program: 12 months

Application Information:
Enrollment of program: 75
Transfer students are accepted.

Financial Information:
Tuition, resident: $1,500
Average cost of books: $169
% of students receiving aid: 50

Employment Profile:
% of students who pass the boards on their first try: 70
% employed within the first 6 months following graduation: 95
Average starting salary: $21,300

Texas

Austin Community College

1020 Grove Boulevard Building D
Austin, TX 78741

Contact Information:
Telephone: 512-223-6185
Fax: 512-223-6700
E-mail: kbaumbac@austin.cc.tx.us
Web: www.austin.cc.tx.us

Program Information:
Program begins: August
Duration of program: 12 months
Evening or weekend classes are available.

Application Information:
Enrollment of program: 21
Transfer students are accepted.

Financial Information:
Tuition, resident: $491
Tuition, non-resident: $785

Employment Profile:
% of students who pass the boards on their first try: 100
% employed within the first 6 months following graduation: 100
Average starting salary: $20,000

Baptist Health System

111 Dallas Street
San Antonio, TX 78205-1230

Contact Information:
Telephone: 210-297-9166
Fax: 210-297-0940
E-mail: cstarks@baptisthealthsystem.org
Web: www.baptisthealthsystem.org

Program Information:
Program begins: August
Degrees offered: Certificate program, 9 months

Application Information:
Enrollment of program: 12

Financial Information:
Average cost of books: $200

Employment Profile:
% of students who pass the boards on their first try: 100
% employed within the first 6 months following graduation: 100
Average starting salary: $18,000

Del Mar College

101 Baldwin and Ayers Streets
Corpus Christi, TX 78404

Contact Information:
Telephone: 512-886-1105
Fax: 512-886-1598
Web: www.delmar.edu

Program Information:
Program begins: June
Duration of program: 12 months

Application Information:
Enrollment of program: 24
Transfer students are accepted.

Financial Information:
Tuition, resident: $1,016
Tuition, non-resident: $1,304
Average cost of books: $900
% of students receiving aid: 50

Employment Profile:
% of students who pass the boards on their first try: 85
% employed within the first 6 months following graduation: 100
Average starting salary: $20,000

El Centro College

Main and Lamar Streets
Dallas, TX 75202-3604

Contact Information:
Telephone: 214-860-2242
Fax: 214-860-2268
E-mail: pfj5310@dcccd.edu
Web: www.ecc.dcccd.edu

Program Information:
Program begins: August
Degrees offered: Certificate program, 11 months
Evening or weekend classes are available.

Application Information:
Enrollment of program: 30
Transfer students are accepted.

Financial Information:
Tuition, resident: $737
Tuition, non-resident: $1,712
Average cost of books: $800
% of students receiving aid: 50

Employment Profile:
% of students who pass the boards on their first try: 90
% employed within the first 6 months following graduation: 100
Average starting salary: $23,000

Houston Community College

1900 Galen Drive
Houston, TX 77030

Contact Information:
Telephone: 713-718-7362
Fax: 713-718-7401
E-mail: sainz-c@hcc.cc.tx.us
Web: www.hcc.cc.tx.us

Program Information:
Program begins: August
Duration of program: 12 months

Financial Information:
Tuition, resident: $980
Tuition, non-resident: $3,570

Employment Profile:
% of students who pass the boards on their first try: 75
% employed within the first 6 months following graduation: 90
Average starting salary: $22,000

Kilgore College
1100 Broadway
Kilgore, TX 75662

Contact Information:
Telephone: 903-983-8163
Fax: 903-983-8600
E-mail: barnettl@kilgore.cc.tx.us
Web: www.kilgore.cc.tx.us

Program Information:
Program begins: August
Degrees offered: Certificate program, 12 months

Application Information:
Enrollment of program: 13

Financial Information:
Tuition, resident: $2,254
Tuition, non-resident: $2,990

South Plains College
1302 Main Street
Lubbock, TX 79401

Contact Information:
Telephone: 806-747-0576 ext. 4642
Fax: 806-765-2775
E-mail: acroft@spc.cc.tx.us
Web: www.spc.cc.tx.us

Program Information:
Program begins: September
Degrees offered: Certificate program, 12 months

Application Information:
Enrollment of program: 30

Financial Information:
Tuition, resident: $1,877
Tuition, non-resident: $3,754

Employment Profile:
% of students who pass the boards on their first try: 95
% employed within the first 6 months following graduation: 95
Average starting salary: $15,900

Tarrant County College—Northeast
828 Harwood Road
Hurst, TX 76054

Contact Information:
Telephone: 817-515-6568
Fax: 817-515-6700
E-mail: rthacker@tcjc.cc.tx.us
Web: www.tccd.net

Program Information:
Program begins: January, August
Duration of program: 11 months

Application Information:
Enrollment of program: 32
Transfer students are accepted.

Financial Information:
Tuition, resident: $2,500
Tuition, non-resident: $5,500
Average cost of books: $650
% of students receiving aid: 15

Employment Profile:
% of students who pass the boards on their first try: 100
% employed within the first 6 months following graduation: 100
Average starting salary: $22,000

Temple College
2600 South First Street
Temple, TX 76504

Contact Information:
Telephone: 254-298-8652
Fax: 254-771-3726
E-mail: carol.reinking@templejc.edu
Web: www.templejc.edu

Program Information:
Program begins: August
Duration of program: 12 months

Application Information:
Enrollment of program: 36
Transfer students are accepted.

Financial Information:
Tuition, resident: $1,404
Tuition, non-resident: $2,080

Employment Profile:
% of students who pass the boards on their first try: 80
% employed within the first 6 months following graduation: 50
Average starting salary: $18,720

Virginia

Sentara Norfolk General Hospital
600 Gresham Drive
Norfolk, VA 23507

Contact Information:
Telephone: 757-668-4240
Fax: 757-668-2905
E-mail: dbsandlo@sentara.com
Web: www.sentara.com

Program Information:
Program begins: January
Duration of program: 12 months

Application Information:
Enrollment of program: 18

Financial Information:
Average cost of books: $347
% of students receiving aid: 87

Employment Profile:
% of students who pass the boards on their first try: 86
% employed within the first 6 months following graduation: 100

Winchester Medical Center
1840 Amherst Street
Winchester, VA 22601

Contact Information:
Telephone: 540-722-8722
Fax: 540-722-8973
E-mail: sball@valleyhealthlink.com

Program Information:
Program begins: January, August
Duration of program: 12 months

Financial Information:
Average cost of books: $500

Employment Profile:
% of students who pass the boards on their first try: 95
% employed within the first 6 months following graduation: 100
Average starting salary: $22,000

Washington

Renton Technical College
3000 Northeast Fourth Street
Renton, WA 98056

Contact Information:
Telephone: 206-235-7812
Fax: 206-235-7832
E-mail: rthurston@rtc.ctc.edu
Web: www.renton-tc.ctc.edu

Program Information:
Program begins: January, September
Duration of program: 11 months

Application Information:
Enrollment of program: 33

West Virginia

West Virginia Northern Community College
15th and Jacob Streets
Wheeling, WV 26003

Contact Information:
Telephone: 304-233-5900 ext. 4456
Fax: 304-233-5837
Web: wvnet.northern.edu

Program Information:
Program begins: May
Duration of program: 10 months

Application Information:
Enrollment of program: 20

Financial Information:
Tuition, resident: $780
Tuition, non-resident: $2,244
Average cost of books: $500

Employment Profile:
% of students who pass the boards on their first try: 75
% employed within the first 6 months following graduation: 86
Average starting salary: $18,000

Wisconsin

Gateway Technical College

3520 30th Avenue
Kenosha, WI 53142-1690

Contact Information:
Telephone: 414-656-6956
Fax: 414-656-8966
E-mail: frazeen@mis.gateway.tech.wi.us
Web: www.gateway.tec.wi.us

Program Information:
Program begins: August
Duration of program: 24 months
Evening or weekend classes are available.

Application Information:
Enrollment of program: 20

Financial Information:
Tuition, resident: $2,820
Tuition, non-resident: $14,380
Average cost of books: $500
% of students receiving aid: 50

Employment Profile:
% of students who pass the boards on their first try: 50
% employed within the first 6 months following graduation: 75
Average starting salary: $25,500

Mid-State Technical College

2600 West Fifth Street
Marshfield, WI 54449

Contact Information:
Telephone: 715-387-2538 ext. 7030
Fax: 715-389-2864
E-mail: kaltmann@midstate.tec.wi.us

Program Information:
Program begins: August
Duration of program: 9 months
Evening or weekend classes are available.

Financial Information:
Tuition, resident: $1,938
Tuition, non-resident: $14,940

Employment Profile:
% employed within the first 6 months following graduation: 90
Average starting salary: $22,000

Milwaukee Area Technical College

700 West State Street
Milwaukee, WI 53233

Contact Information:
Telephone: 414-297-7153
Fax: 414-297-7851
E-mail: millerjr@milwaukee.tec.wi.us
Web: www.matc.edu

Program Information:
Program begins: August
Duration of program: 18 months

Application Information:
Enrollment of program: 52
Transfer students are accepted.

Financial Information:
Tuition, resident: $1,981
Tuition, non-resident: $13,917
Average cost of books: $300

Employment Profile:
% employed within the first 6 months following graduation: 100

Northcentral Technical College

1000 Campus Drive
Wausau, WI 54401

Contact Information:
Telephone: 715-675-3331 ext. 4497
Fax: 715-675-9776
E-mail: osness@northcentral.tec.wi.us
Web: www.northcentral.tec.wi.us

Program Information:
Program begins: January
Duration of program: 12 months
Evening or weekend classes are available.

Application Information:
Enrollment of program: 12
Transfer students are accepted.

Financial Information:
Tuition, resident: $2,252
Tuition, non-resident: $17,260

Employment Profile:
% of students who pass the boards on their first try: 100
% employed within the first 6 months following graduation: 76
Average starting salary: $21,000

Waukesha County Technical College

800 Main Street
Pewaukee, WI 53072

Contact Information:
Telephone: 414-691-5563
Fax: 414-691-5451
E-mail: kbraaten@waukesha.tec.wi.us
Web: www.waukesha.tec.wi.us

Program Information:
Program begins: August
Degrees offered: Associate's, 24 months
Evening or weekend classes are available.

Application Information:
Enrollment of program: 24
Transfer students are accepted.

Financial Information:
Tuition, resident: $2,400
Tuition, non-resident: $14,000

Employment Profile:
% employed within the first 6 months following graduation: 100
Average starting salary: $20,000

Western Wisconsin Technical College

304 North Sixth Street
PO Box 908
La Crosse, WI 54601

Contact Information:
Telephone: 608-785-9193
Fax: 608-785-9194
E-mail: willsr@al.western.tec.wi.us
Web: www.western.tec.wi.us

Program Information:
Program begins: August
Duration of program: 11 months

Application Information:
Enrollment of program: 10

Financial Information:
Tuition, resident: $2,006
Tuition, non-resident: $13,085
Average cost of books: $790
% of students receiving aid: 53

Employment Profile:
Average starting salary: $18,540

References

Introduction

1. "BLS Releases New 1998–2008 Employment Projections." Employment Projections Page. Bureau of Labor Statistics. 25 January 2000. stats.bls.gov/news.release/ecopro.nws.htm.
2. "BLS Releases New 1998–2008 Employment Projections." Employment Projections Page. Bureau of Labor Statistics. 25 January 2000. stats.bls.gov/news.release/ecopro.t06.htm.
3. www.hcfa.gov/init/bba/bbaintro.htm, 21 November 1999.
4. www.hcfa.gov/pubforms/transmit/b984160.htm, 21 November 1999.
5. "AOTA Celebrates Victory in Balanced Budget Refinement Act," *OT Practice*. (American Occupational Therapy Association, December 20, 1999) 4.

Art Therapist

1. *American Art Therapy Association Newsletter*, vol. XXXII, no. 4, Mundelein, IL: American Art Therapy Association, (Fall 1999): 3.
2. T. Rauch and D. Elkins, "Membership Survey Report 1996–1997," *Art Therapy Journal of the American Art Therapy Association*, vol.15, no.3 (1998): 191-202.

Athletic Trainer

1. National Athletic Trainers' Association Page, 21 November 1999, www.nata.org.
2. National Athletic Trainers' Association Page, 21 November 1999, www.nata.org.
3. National Athletic Trainers' Association Page, 21 November 1999, www.nata.org.
4. National Athletic Trainers' Association Page, 21 November 1999, www.nata.org.
5. National Athletic Trainers' Association Page, 21 November 1999, www.nata.org.

Cardiovascular Technologist

1. *Society of Vascular Technology Page*, 21 January 2000, www.svtnet.org/members/career.htm

Clinical Laboratory Technician and Scientist

1. D. Kellar and K. Gryniewski, "MLO's National Salary Survey," *Medical Laboratory Observer. Clinical Laboratory Reference 1999-2000*, (MLO Supplement, July 1999): 17-20.
2. L. Pallatroni, "MLO's National Salary Survey," *Medical Laboratory Observer. Clinical Laboratory Reference 1998-1999*, (MLO Supplement, July 1998): 23-29.
3. D. Falcone, "Continuing Education Resources for Laboratorians," *Medical Laboratory Observer. Clinical Laboratory Reference 1999-2000*, (MLO Supplement, July 1999): 5.

Dental Hygienist, Dental Assistant and Dental Laboratory Technician

1. P.R. Weiger, "Hot Careers and Getting Hotter," *Community College Week*, (May 18, 1998).

Dietitian/Nutritionist

1. The American Dietetic Association Page, 10 January 2000, www.eatright.org
2. The American Dietetic Association Page, 10 January 2000, www.eatright.org
3. The American Dietetic Association Page, 10 January 2000, www.eatright.org
4. The American Dietetic Association Page, 10 January 2000, www.eatright.org
5. The American Dietetic Association Page, 10 January 2000, www.eatright.org

6. The American Dietetic Association Page, 10 January 2000, www.eatright.org

7. The American Dietetic Association Page, 10 January 2000, www.eatright.org

Dietetic Technician

1. The American Dietetic Association Page, 10 January 2000, www.eatright.org

2. The American Dietetic Association Page, 10 January 2000, www.eatright.org

3. The American Dietetic Association Page, 10 January 2000, www.eatright.org

Emergency Medical Technician-Paramedic

1. Ty Mayfield, "JEMS' 1997 Provider Income Survey," *Journal of Emergency Medical Services*, (September 1998): 36-40.

Health Information Management Professional

1. American Health Information Management Association Page, 21 November 1999, www.ahima.org

2. American Health Information Management Association Page, 21 November 1999, www.ahima.org

Medical Assistant

1. *AAMA Role Delineation Study, Occupational Analysis of the Medical Assisting Profession.* (Chicago: American Association of Medical Assistants, 1996).

2. American Association of Medical Assistants Page, 21 January 2000, www.aama-ntl.org/what.html.

Occupational Therapist and Occupational Therapy Assistant

1. *Manual of the Official Documents of the American Occupational Therapy Association, 6th ed.* (Bethesda, MD: American Occupational Therapy Association, 1996), 206-210.

2. *Manual of the Official Documents of the American Occupational Therapy Association, 6th ed.* (Bethesda, MD: American Occupational Therapy Association, 1996), 123-125.

3. B. Sabonis-Chaffe, & S.M. Hussey, *Introduction to Occupational Therapy, 2nd ed.* (St. Louis: Mosby, 1998), 3.

4. 1998-99 Occupational Outlook Handbook: Occupational Therapy Assistants and Aides Page, Bureau of Labor Statistics, 27 November 1999. www.stats.bls.gov/oco/ocos166.htm.

5. 1998-99 Occupational Outlook Handbook: Occupational Therapists Occupational Therapy Assistants and Aides Page, Bureau of Labor Statistics, 27 November 1999. www.stats.bls.gov/oco/ocos078.htm.

6. 1998-99 Occupational Outlook Handbook: Occupational Therapy Assistants and Aides Page. Bureau of Labor Statistics, 27 November 1999, stats.bls.gov/oco/ocos166.htm.

7. "ACOTE Sets Timeline for Post Baccalaureate Degree Programs." *OT Week*, (August 26, 1999): 1-3.

8. "Guidelines for the Use of Aides in Occupational Therapy Practice." *American Journal of Occupational Therapy*, 53: 6, (November/December 1999): 595-597.

9. "ACOTE Sets Timeline for Post Baccalaureate Degree Programs." *OT Week*, (August 26, 1999): 1-3.

Ophthalmic Dispensing Optician

1. L. Krentz, *The Jobs Rated Almanac*, (New York: St. Martins Press, 1999), 102.

2. *Eyecare Business Magazine*, (Norwalk, CT: Boucher Communications, April 1997), 54.

Physical Therapist

1. American Physical Therapy Association Page, 4 January 2000, www.apta.org.
2. American Physical Therapy Association Page, 4 January 2000, www.apta.org.
3. American Physical Therapy Association Page, 4 January 2000, www.apta.org.

Physical Therapist Assistant

1. American Physical Therapy Association Page, 4 January 2000, www.apta.org

Physician Assistant

1. American Academy of Physician Assistants Page, 10 January 2000, www.aapa.org
2. American Academy of Physician Assistants Annual Census, (Alexandria: American Academy of Physicians Assistants, November 1999).

Radiation Therapist

1. *Radiologic Technologist Wage and Salary Survey 1997.* (Albuquerque: American Society of Radiologic Technologists, 1998), 29.

Radiographer, Diagnostic Medical Sonographer, and Nuclear Medicine Technologist

1. Bureau of Labor Statistics Page, 10 December 1999, lbcbls.gov/oco/ocos105.htm.
2. Bureau of Labor Statistics Page, 10 December 1999, lbcbls.gov/oco/ocos105.htm.

Respiratory Care Practitioner

1. Bureau of Labor Statistics Page, 10 January 2000, bls.gov/ocohome.htm
2. American Association for Respiratory Care Page, 10 January 2000, www.aarc.org.

Surgical Technologist

1. Association of Surgical Technology Page, 21 November 1999, www.ast.org.
2. *Surgical Technologist Survey*. (Englewood, CO: Association of Surgical Technology, 1998).

Index

A

C

D

F

H

I

J

M

Q

R

S

T

V

NOTES

NOTES

NOTES

NOTES

NOTES

NOTES

NOTES

NOTES

Make the Grade with Study Guides for the AP and SAT II Exams

AP Exams

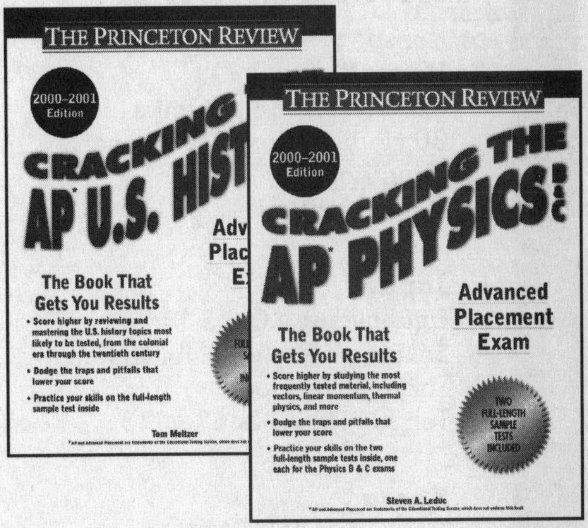

Cracking the AP Biology
2000-2001 Edition
0-375-75495-4 • $17.00

Cracking the AP Calculus AB & BC
2000-2001 Edition
0-375-75499-7 • $18.00

Cracking the AP Chemistry
2000-2001 Edition
0-375-75497-0 • $17.00

Cracking the AP Economics (Macro & Micro)
2000-2001 Edition
0-375-75507-1 • $17.00

Cracking the AP English Literature
2000-2001 Edition
0-375-75493-8 • $17.00

Cracking the AP European History
2000-2001 Edition
0-375-75498-9 • $17.00

Cracking the AP Physics
2000-2001 Edition
0-375-75492-X • $19.00

Cracking the AP Psychology
2000-2001 Edition
0-375-75480-6 • $17.00

Cracking the AP Spanish
2000-2001 Edition
0-375-75481-4 • $17.00

Cracking the AP U.S. Government and Politics
2000-2001 Edition
0-375-75496-2 • $17.00

Cracking the AP U.S. History
2000-2001 Edition
0-375-75494-6 • $17.00

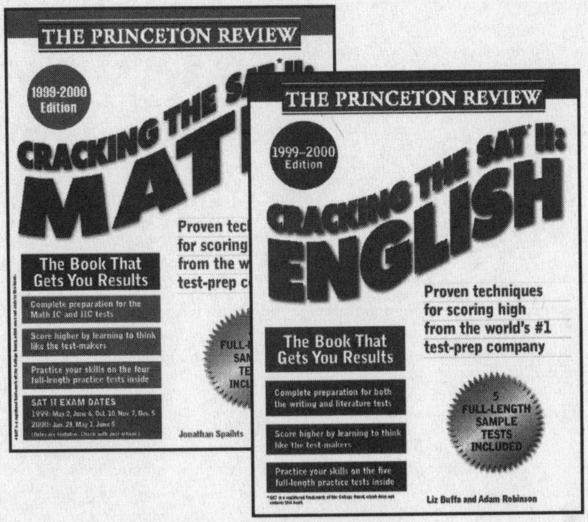

SAT II Exams

Cracking the SAT II: Biology
1999-2000 Edition
0-375-75297-8 • $17.00

Cracking the SAT II: Chemistry
1999-2000 Edition
0-375-75298-6 • $17.00

Cracking the SAT II: English
1999-2000 Edition
0-375-75295-1 • $17.00

Cracking the SAT II: French
1999-2000 Edition
0-375-75299-4 • $17.00

Cracking the SAT II: History
1999-2000 Edition
0-375-75300-1 • $17.00

Cracking the SAT II: Math
1999-2000 Edition
0-375-75296-X • $18.00

Cracking the SAT II: Physics
1999-2000 Edition
0-375-75302-8 • $17.00

Cracking the SAT II: Spanish
1999-2000 Edition
0-375-75301-X • $17.00

FIND US...

International

Hong Kong
4/F Sun Hung Kai Centre
30 Harbour Road, Wan Chai,
Hong Kong
Tel: (011)85-2-517-3016

Japan
Fuji Building 40, 15-14
Sakuragaokacho, Shibuya Ku,
Tokyo 150, Japan
Tel: (011)81-3-3463-1343

Korea
Tae Young Bldg, 944-24,
Daechi- Dong, Kangnam-Ku
The Princeton Review—ANC
Seoul, Korea 135-280,
South Korea
Tel: (011)82-2-554-7763

Mexico City
PR Mex S De RL De Cv
Guanajuato 228 Col. Roma
06700 Mexico D.F., Mexico
Tel: 525-564-9468

Montreal
666 Sherbrooke St.
West, Suite 202
Montreal, QC H3A 1E7 Canada
Tel: 514-499-0870

Pakistan
1 Bawa Park - 90 Upper Mall
Lahore, Pakistan
Tel: (011)92-42-571-2315

Spain
Pza. Castilla, 3 - 5º A, 28046
Madrid, Spain
Tel: (011)341-323-4212

Taiwan
155 Chung Hsiao East Road
Section 4 - 4th Floor,
Taipei R.O.C., Taiwan
Tel: (011)886-2-751-1243

Thailand
Building One, 99 Wireless Road
Bangkok, Thailand 10330
Tel: 662-256-7080

Toronto
1240 Bay Street, Suite 300
Toronto M5R 2A7 Canada
Tel: 800-495-7737
Tel: 716-839-4391

locations

Vancouver
4215 University Way NE
Seattle, WA 98105
Tel: 206-548-1100

National (U.S.)

We have more than 60 offices around the U.S. and run courses at over 400 sites. For courses and locations within the U.S. call 1-800-2-Review and you will be routed to the nearest office.